NO HAMLETS

C000048700

Andreas Höfele is emeritus Professor of English at Munich University. He is the author of *Stage, Stake, and Scaffold: Humans and Animals in Shakespeare's Theatre* (OUP, 2011) which won the 2012 Roland H. Bainton Prize for Literature. His publications in German include books on Shakespeare's stagecraft, late nineteenth-century parody, and Malcolm Lowry, as well as six novels. He served as President of the German Shakespeare Society from 2002 to 2011.

Praise for *No Hamlets*

'In taking this long view, Höfele rectifies any misconceptions we might have that 'right-wing Shakespeare' is purely a phenomenon of the Second World War, and in doing so he sheds fascinating light on less familiar aspects of German history in relation to right-wing politics and ideals and Shakespeare's role within these... Höfele's work has all the potential to become an instant classic, a standard work for academics and teachers alike.'

Alessandra Bassey, *Modern Language Review*

'I cannot remember reading so compelling, important, and revelatory a Shakespeare book as this one... This is a wonderfully, indeed movingly well-written book but the quality which particularly singles out *No Hamlets* is its intellectual and moral honesty.'

Ewan Fernie, *Shakespeare Jahrbuch*

'Höfele tells a remarkable story about the way Shakespeare provides imaginative resources for some of the most challenging and troubling thought of the modern era... also very much engaged with current conversations in early modern studies.'

Kevin Curran, *Studies in English Literature 1500–1900*

'An important addition to German twentieth-century cultural histories, the book also makes a significant contribution to Shakespeare studies... The introduction alone provides the most comprehensive yet concise account to date of German intellectual 'Hamletism'... eminently readable and incisive, aptly summarizing and clarifying key issues in twentieth-century German history and philosophy.'

Emily Oliver, *Journal of European Studies*

'*No Hamlets* is a remarkably informative and original interpretation of appropriations of Shakespeare by German intellectuals, poets, and politicians of the political right from the 1870s to the 1950s... a veritable treasure trove as well as a highly enjoyable and enthralling read... unique in the way in which it fuses reception and performance history with biography and political history.'

Anne Enderwitz, *The Germanic Review*

No Hamlets

*German Shakespeare from Nietzsche
to Carl Schmitt*

ANDREAS HÖFELE

OXFORD
UNIVERSITY PRESS

OXFORD
UNIVERSITY PRESS

Great Clarendon Street, Oxford, OX2 6DP,
United Kingdom

Oxford University Press is a department of the University of Oxford.
It furthers the University's objective of excellence in research, scholarship,
and education by publishing worldwide. Oxford is a registered trade mark of
Oxford University Press in the UK and in certain other countries

© Andreas Höfele 2016

First published in 2016
First published in paperback in 2021

Published in the United States of America by Oxford University Press
198 Madison Avenue, New York, NY 10016, United States of America

British Library Cataloguing in Publication Data
Data available

Library of Congress Cataloging in Publication Data
Data available

ISBN 978–0–19–871854–3 (Hbk.)
ISBN 978–0–19–285743–9 (Pbk.)

For Gabriele

Preface

As a German Shakespeare scholar, I never felt much drawn to the subject of Shakespeare in Germany. Apart from a few occasional papers I stayed clear of it.

What changed my mind—apart from a brief but intense encounter with a Nietzschean passage on Shakespeare while working on a previous book—was the resurrection of Carl Schmitt's all but forgotten *Hamlet* essay from the 1950s in English translation in 2009. Schmitt's *Hamlet or Hecuba: The Intrusion of the Time into the Play*, though remarkable enough in itself, was made even more remarkable to me by its modern Anglo-American readers' inclination to detach—or 'reclaim'— it from its author's political history, notably his involvement in the Third Reich. This struck me as a problematic effort to occlude 'the intrusion of the time', the very thing which Schmitt makes the *sine qua non* of tragedy itself and *Hamlet* in particular. There was, I felt, a need to supply what was being occluded: the 'form and pressure' of the time (*Ham.* 3.2.22) which had shaped Schmitt's essay and mindset.

From this grew the larger project of this book, the plan to explore the role of Shakespeare in the writings and thought of anti-liberal, rightist intellectuals from the founding of the German Empire in 1871 to the 'Bonn Republic' of the Cold War era. Despite its obvious relevance to Germany's calamitous twentieth-century history, this strand of German Shakespeare reception had not been treated in a sustained book-length study before.

Beginning with Friedrich Nietzsche, the chapters that follow trace the trajectory of the rightist engagement with Shakespeare to the poet Stefan George and his circle (which included such critic-scholars as Friedrich Gundolf and Ernst Kantorowicz), to the literary efforts of the young Goebbels during the Weimar Republic, to the Shakespeare debate in the Third Reich and its aftermath in the controversy over 'inner emigration'. I proceed from there to Carl Schmitt's *Hamlet* book of 1956, and finally to the end of the post-war period and its Shakespearean epilogue: Heiner Müller's grand-scale production of *Hamlet/Machine* at the Deutsches Theater in East Berlin in 1989.[1]

But can we, in this day of postmodern diffusion, still usefully employ the blunt old distinction of 'left' and 'right'? More specifically, can we apply the label 'right' to a figure as elusively multifaceted as Nietzsche, or to Carl Schmitt, whose largest support group in recent years would no doubt define its own position as 'left' (or at least 'leftish')? I would argue that indeed we can, so long as we do not overcharge the term with essentializing assumptions.

As I use the term here, 'right' serves for orientation and is not meant to reduce a variety of individualities to a single essence. Across their very pronounced

---

[1] Müller clearly does not, in any sense, belong to an intellectual tradition of the Right. For his inclusion in this book see Introduction, section IV, and Chapter 9.

differences, the authors discussed here do share a common set of views and attitudes that is recognizably rightist, i.e. anti-egalitarian, anti-democratic, and anti-liberal. Without exception, they condemn Western modernity and mechanized mass *civilization*, upholding in its stead an ideal of organic *culture*. The roots of the latter lie in an idealized past associated with the notion of *Abendland* (the Occident), the 'old European' heritage rooted in classical antiquity. Hostile to the rationalist Enlightenment and its universal humanism, these authors endorse hierarchical, authoritarian models of state and society and strong, charismatic leaders. They are elitist, although theirs is not an elitism that fawns on the aristocracy, which they often despise almost as much as the philistine bourgeoisie. In this sense they are not 'conservative'; they do not seek to bolster or restore the old upper classes.[2] Rather, they tend to see themselves as radicals—radically opposed to the status quo but often harking back to a lost past for their vision of the future. When they speak positively of 'the people' (*das Volk*), they generally mean the supposedly homogeneous ethnic group that constitutes 'the nation', although the degree of their national fervour varies considerably.

As late as 1981 it was still possible to maintain that the study of German Shakespeare reception continued to be dominated by Friedrich Gundolf's *Shakespeare and the German Spirit* (1911), a teleological narrative that saw the Bard's inspirational power culminate in the twin peaks of Goethe and the Romantic Schlegel–Tieck translation.[3] The rest of the nineteenth century was dismissed as a period of decline. As Rudolf Sühnel noted: '[T]he eighteenth century continues to be ploughed' while German Shakespeare reception in the nineteenth century 'remains terra incognita'.[4] Although this assessment no longer holds today, it is still true that for the late nineteenth and early twentieth century no narrative has emerged of similar consistency to that of Gundolf. His influence remains palpable even where (and precisely because) it is rejected.

I do not propose to offer an alternative *grand récit* here. Such narratives—more performance-focused or dedicated to the study of political appropriations of the left, for example—are not only possible, but do in fact exist.[5] The interest of the one unfolded here is to probe Shakespeare's cooptation into the siren songs of ideas and ideologies that proved disastrously attractive in German history. '[T]he sheer extent and pervasiveness of Shakespeare's influence in Germany', writes

---

[2] Political scientists have therefore objected to the term 'conservative revolution' as applied to radical right-wing intellectuals in the Weimar Republic. For a summary of the discussion: Stefan Breuer, *Anatomie der Konservativen Revolution* (Darmstadt: Wissenschaftliche Buchgesellschaft, 1993), 1–7. In everyday usage, of course, 'conservative' is often used in a looser sense, as a synonym of 'right-wing'.

[3] See Werner Habicht, *Shakespeare and the German Imagination* (Hertford: International Shakespeare Association, 1994); Roger Paulin, *The Critical Reception of Shakespeare in Germany, 1682–1914: Native Literature and Foreign Genius* (Hildesheim: Olms, 2003), 488–95.

[4] Rudolf Sühnel, 'Gundolfs Shakespeare. Rezeption—Übertragung—Deutung', *Euphorion* 75 (1981), 245–74 at 255.

[5] Wilhelm Hortmann, *Shakespeare on the German Stage*, vol. 2: *The Twentieth Century* (Cambridge: Cambridge University Press, 1998). Cf. also Simon Williams, *Shakespeare on the German Stage*, vol. 1: *1586–1914* (Cambridge: Cambridge University Press, 1990).

Roger Paulin, allows us to speak of, 'in Harold Bloom's terms, a "Shakespeare-haunted" culture'.[6] I do not map this haunting in all its ramifications and heterogeneity. My specific, narrower focus is on the extent to which a 'Shakespeare-haunted culture' informs the right-wing German intellect.

Central to my inquiry is the identification of Germany, the German national character, or more specifically the German intellectual, with Hamlet. It is in this recurring motif, born from the frustrations of the liberal-nationalist opposition of the 1840s, that the supposed special relationship of Germans with Shakespeare, their proprietary claim to 'our Shakespeare', found its most personal and at the same time highly political expression. Identification with Hamlet by no means waned in the decades after the revolution of 1848 but maintained a cultural and political force well beyond the turn of the century. Yet there are others beside Hamlet—Julius Caesar, for example, and Brutus. And there is also, quite unexpectedly, Othello.

Othello is something of a gatecrasher in this book. Originally uninvited, he now takes up a whole chapter. This is due to the help I received from Gerd Giesler, the editor of Carl Schmitt's diaries from the 1920s. He not only alerted me to the fact that the diaries contained dozens of references to Othello; he also most generously furnished me with the complete unpublished transcripts of Schmitt's journals, thus enabling me to present here, for the first time, Carl Schmitt's obsessive engagement with the Moor of Venice. Chapters 5 and 8 have greatly profited from Gerd Giesler's expert advice.

Invaluable advice also came from Dieter Schulz, who read the whole book in manuscript, and from Werner Habicht, Robert Weimann, and Ina Schabert, who read and commented on several chapters. Before her much-lamented death, Ruth von Ledebur accompanied the early stages of my work in progress with critical support. I will always be grateful to her.

I am greatly indebted to Bastian Kuhl for his bibliographical research and his untiring commitment in preparing the text for publication. My particular thanks go to Kay Henn and Tom Minnes for their excellent language advice.

The time for this book to materialize was provided by an 'Opus magnum' Grant from the Volkswagen Foundation and sabbatical leave from the University of Munich. I am deeply grateful for both.

I received helpful advice and support from Ruth Morse and Peter Holland, Maik Hamburger, Wilhelm Hortmann, Andreas Kablitz, Peter Marx, Heinrich Meier, Oliver Primavesi, Peter Strohschneider, Friedrich Vollhardt, and Wolfgang Weiss. Bettina Boecker provided a highly conducive working environment at the Munich Shakespeare Library. For opportunities to present work in progress I am grateful to Brian Cummings, Paul Franssen, Dominique Goy Blanquet, Ton Hoenselaars, Nathalie Vienne-Guerrin, and Richard Wilson. Three draft chapters benefited from the scrutiny of the '*Kränzchen*', a circle of my Munich colleagues and friends.

---

[6] Paulin, *The Critical Reception of Shakespeare in Germany*, 1.

Jacqueline Baker and Ellie Collins of Oxford University Press gave me their fullest support throughout. My thanks also go to Matthias Meusch and his staff at the Landesarchiv Nordrhein-Westfalen, Abteilung Rheinland, Düsseldorf, for facilitating my research in the Carl Schmitt papers, and to Jürgen Becker, trustee of the Schmitt estate, for kindly granting me permission to quote from the unpublished materials in the Düsseldorf archive. I am also grateful for the help I received from the Bundesarchiv Koblenz in my research on the Goebbels papers.

An earlier version of Chapter 8 appeared under the title 'Hamlet in Plettenberg: Carl Schmitt's Shakespeare', in Peter Holland, ed., *Shakespeare Survey* 65 (2012), 378–97, © Cambridge University Press, reproduced with permission.

Part of Chapter 7 draws on my 'Reeducating Germany: BBC Shakespeare 1945', in *Shakespeare and European Politics*, ed. Dirk Delabastita, Jozef De Vos, and Paul Franssen (Newark: University of Delaware Press, 2008), 255–77. An earlier version of the final section of Chapter 4 appeared as 'The Rebirth of Tragedy, or No Time for Shakespeare (Germany, 1940)', *Renaissance Drama* 38 (2010), 251–68.

I am indebted to Rebecca Faber and Anna Katharina Lauber for assistance in preparing the text for publication.

Above all, I thank my wife to whom I dedicate this book.

Contents

List of Illustrations

A Note on Texts and Translations

All Shakespeare quotations, unless otherwise stated, are from *The Norton Shakespeare*, 3rd edn, ed. Stephen Greenblatt et al. (New York: Norton, 2016).

Whenever possible, I have used published English translations of German texts. Where no published translation is referenced, the translations are mine.

Introduction

I NO HAMLETS!

This book takes its title from a decisive moment in German history, the moment when Germany ceased to be Hamlet. The moment is commemorated in the dedication which Horace Howard Furness wrote for the two *Hamlet* volumes of his *New Variorum Edition of Shakespeare* in 1877:

> To the
> 'German Shakespeare Society'
> of Weimar
> Representative of a people
> whose recent history
> has proved
> once for all
> that
> 'Germany is *not* Hamlet'
> these volumes are dedicated
> with great respect
> by the editor.

Furness, an American well-versed in things German,[1] was responding to the famous opening line of a poem by Ferdinand Freiligrath, published thirty-three years earlier: 'Deutschland ist Hamlet!'[2] The line, which quickly became a political slogan,[3] turned Shakespeare's hesitant prince into the tortured self-portrait of a nation that, in the words of Freiligrath's poem, 'broods and dreams and knows not what to do' instead of actively striving for freedom and national unity. But since their victory over France and the subsequent foundation of the German Empire in 1871, the Germans were Hamlets no more. Under Prussian leadership, a nation of self-doubters had risen to major power status and the identification with Shakespeare's pensive procrastinator had lost its foundation—'once for all'.

---

[1] See James M. Gibson, *The Philadelphia Shakespeare Story: Horace Howard Furness and the New Variorum Shakespeare* (New York: AMS Press, 1990), 8.

[2] Ferdinand Freiligrath, 'Hamlet', in his *Ein Glaubensbekenntniß* (Mainz: Zabern, 1844), 253–7.

[3] See Walter Muschg, 'Deutschland ist Hamlet', *Die Zeit*, No. 17, 24 April 1964, and No. 18, 1 May 1964. <http://www.zeit.de/1964/17/deutschland-ist-heimat> [*sic*] and <http://www.zeit.de/1964/18/deutschland-ist-hamlet-ii>, accessed 10 August 2015; Manfred Pfister, 'Germany is Hamlet: The History of a Political Interpretation', *New Comparison* 2 (1986), 106–26; Heiner O. Zimmermann, 'Is Hamlet Germany? On the Political Reception of *Hamlet*', in *New Essays on Hamlet*, ed. Mark Thornton Burnett and John Manning (New York: AMS Press, 1994), 293–318.

My interest is in what this happy closure leaves unclosed: the continuing impact of a political Shakespeare in Germany's history of ideas and ideologies, an influence whose scope, though centred on Hamlet, extends far beyond the gloomy Dane. Germany may have ceased 'to be Hamlet' for those who thought the nation to have reached its historical telos in the Wilhelmine Empire—among them Freiligrath himself, whose former republican sympathies, not untypically, gave way to a clamorous patriotism in poems like 'Hurra, Germania!' which celebrated the victory over France.[4] But those repelled by this new national self-aggrandizement could find in Hamlet, the brooding outsider at the raucous court of Denmark, a mirror for their disaffection. If Germany was 'officially' no longer Hamlet, discontent with the official Germany could still vent itself in a spirit of Hamlet-like loathing.

This split between the official Germany and its discontents is already implied in Freiligrath's poem. His simple equation 'Germany is Hamlet' actually marks a division, not one but two Germanies: the Germany of the reactionary rulers and the Germany suppressed by their rule. What the poem identifies as Hamlet is only the latter, the 'true' but suppressed Germany, whose opposition to the status quo makes it the nucleus of an *other* Germany. This other Germany recurs, time and again, in the writings and thought that will be discussed in this book, most prominently in the 'Secret Germany' of the poet Stefan George and his followers (Chapters 2 and 3). For Freiligrath in 1844, this other Germany was the liberal, democratic nation state, the state that was born and died in the failed (or 'incomplete') revolution of 1848. For the writers that will concern us here the 'true' Germany was different: certainly not liberal, certainly not a democracy, though perhaps even more Hamlet-like for that very reason. Mourners all, they sought the lost realm of a 'noble father in the dust' (*Ham.* 1.2.71). The ghost that stalks the battlements of their dreams is a messenger from a past that promises salvation for the future. This ghost speaks not of a liberty that goes with brotherliness and equality, but of one that bristles with claims of distinction, superiority, and the right of the stronger. In 1935, a century after Freiligrath, when the nightmare version of this dream was reaching its apogee, the dramatist Gerhart Hauptmann returned to the old Hamlet equation, at once denying and confirming it:

> Germany, thank God, is not Hamlet the inactive figure as he was formerly misunderstood, but Hamlet the problematic, richly emotional man of action. In youth, suffering, growth, defeat and victory, Hamlet has a much more universal Germanness than Faust and is inseparable from Germany's great spiritual destiny.[5]

My title, *No Hamlets*, tries to capture both the denial and the negation of that denial. It signals a continuing identification that is no less powerful when hidden or disavowed. A case in point is the squabble over Shakespeare that arose during the First World War. Addressing the German Shakespeare Society in 1915, Gerhart

---

[4] Ferdinand Freiligrath, 'Hurra, Germania!' (1870), in *Freiligraths Werke*, 2 vols, ed. Paul Zaunert (Leipzig and Vienna: Bibliographisches Institut, 1912), vol. 2, 146–8.
[5] Gerhart Hauptmann, Letter to Wulf Leisner, 9 December1935; quoted in Peter Sprengel, *Der Dichter stand auf hoher Küste: Gerhart Hauptmann im Dritten Reich* (Berlin: Ullstein, 2009), 100.

Hauptmann said that, even if England was where Shakespeare was born, Germany was where he was truly alive.[6] The English counter-thrust, in time for the 1916 Shakespeare tercentenary and shortly before the battle of the Somme, was delivered by the playwright Henry Arthur Jones. He refuted Hauptmann's proprietary claim to Shakespeare, and especially to Hamlet, by associating Germany with Macbeth instead: 'What evil angel of their destiny tempted the Germans to choose Macbeth for their anniversary offering to Shakespeare, in this year of all others? It is the very picture of their own character marching to its ruin.'[7] The identification of the Germans with Macbeth was made all the more forceful by the implied message that they were certainly no Hamlets.

But how did Germany come to be Hamlet in the first place? Before entering into my subject proper, it will be necessary to offer a brief account of its prehistory: first, an outline of Shakespeare reception in Germany up to Freiligrath's poem; second, a résumé of Germany's political history from the end of the 'Old Reich', the 'Holy Roman Empire of the German Nation' in 1806, to the founding of a new one in 1871, the opening moment of this study.

II GERMAN SHAKESPEARE

By 1916, when Henry Arthur Jones wrested the Bard from the clutches of the Hun, Shakespeare had long ceased to be a foreigner in Germany. The story of his appropriation (or 'nostrification', as one of the founders of the German Shakespeare Society called it[8]) has often been told. Its most popular version begins with an 'inflammation': 'For a genius', wrote Gotthold Ephraim Lessing in 1759, 'can only be inflamed [*entzündet*, also ignited or kindled] by another genius.'[9] The genius who was to do the inflaming was the English Shakespeare, of whom Lessing knew precious little at the time, the genius to be inflamed as yet nowhere in sight. The ten-year-old Goethe had just survived the smallpox; Schiller had eight months to wait before being born. German literature had, of course, the acknowledged genius of Klopstock, but his forte was the religious epic à la Milton. Lessing's sights were trained on drama. To be good, plays in the mid-eighteenth century had to observe

---

[6] Gerhart Hauptmann, 'Deutschland und Shakespeare', *Shakespeare-Jahrbuch* 51 (1915), vii–xii. On Shakespeare and the First World War: Balz Engler, 'Shakespeare in the Trenches', *Shakespeare Survey* 44 (1992), 105–11; Nicolas Detering, 'Shakespeare im Ersten Weltkrieg', in *Shakespeare unter den Deutschen*, ed. Christa Jansohn (Stuttgart: Franz Steiner, 2015), 175–96.

[7] Henry Arthur Jones, *Shakespeare and Germany* (London: Wittingham, 1916), 22. Jones's stridency is far in excess of Hauptmann's provocation. The dominant tenor of Hauptmann's speech is not proprietorially nationalistic, but pacifist and cosmopolitan: Shakespeare is a common 'treasure of humanity' (Hauptmann, 'Deutschland und Shakespeare', viii).

[8] 'Nostrifizierung': Franz von Dingelstedt, *Studien und Copien nach Shakespeare* (Pest, Vienna, and Leipzig: Hartleben, 1858), 5. A magisterial *History of Shakespearean Drama in Germany* appeared as early as 1870. Rudolph Genée, *Geschichte der Shakespeareschen Dramen in Deutschland* (Leipzig: Engelmann, 1870). The most recent study of the subject is Jansohn, ed., *Shakespeare unter den Deutschen*.

[9] 'Denn ein Genie kann nur von einem Genie entzündet werden'. Gotthold Ephraim Lessing, '17. Literaturbrief', in Lessing, *Werke und Briefe in zwölf Bänden*, ed. Wilfried Barner, vol. 4: *Werke, 1758–1759*, ed. Gunter E. Grimm (Frankfurt: Deutscher Klassiker-Verlag, 1997), 499–501 at 500.

the French neo-classical rules laid down for German emulation by the influential Leipzig professor of poetics Johann Christoph Gottsched. 'No one', Lessing wrote, 'would deny that the German theatre owes a great deal of its improvement to Herr Professor Gottsched.' And he continued with palpable relish: 'I am that no-one. I deny it outright.'[10]

When the ten-year-old Goethe, the as yet unborn Schiller, and other literary hopefuls of the *Sturm und Drang* (Storm and Stress) generation reached their twenties, the inflammation predicted by Lessing did indeed take place. Discarding French regularity in favour of English 'Nature', the young hotspurs of the 1770s and '80s made Shakespeare their idol. And although Goethe and Schiller in their riper years returned to a more 'regular', neo-classical agenda, the Shakespearean inflammation was crucial in releasing the creative energies that propelled German letters from parochial obscurity to European fame within a mere generation. Shakespeare, the catalyst of Germany's classical canon, was in time annexed to that canon as 'our third classic'.

In the German Shakespeare story, or Shakespeare myth,[11] the seventeenth of Lessing's *Letters on the Most Recent Literature* (1759–65), from which the quotations in the previous paragraph are taken, assumes 'a kind of status akin to Luther's ninety-five theses'.[12] Lessing's polemic is less than fair to Gottsched, and much of what he said about Shakespeare was derived from Voltaire and other French sources and 'told the world nothing about Shakespeare it did not already know'.[13] This may be so, but it hardly matters. Whatever its shortcomings, Lessing's '17th Letter on Literature' marks a new departure: the decisive inaugural push for Shakespeare's German canonization.[14]

The single most important individual inflammation with the Shakespeare virus is recorded on six handwritten pages and was not published until 1854. This was the speech which the 22-year-old Goethe delivered on Shakespeare's (German) name-day, the name-day for Wilhelm, on 14 October 1771. Its critical substance is slight. But as the expression of an enthusiasm that was to shape the course of German literature it can hardly be overrated:

> We honour today the memory of the greatest of wanderers and thus honour ourselves. We bear the seeds within us of the merits that we cherish. Do not expect me to write much and tidily; tranquillity of soul is no garment for a feast day; and as yet I have thought too little about Shakespeare; only sensed and felt at most, this was the best that I could do. The first page of his that I read made me his own for life, and when I was finished with the first play I stood like someone born blind whom a magical hand had suddenly given sight. I realized, I felt most vividly my existence expanded by

---

[10] Lessing, '17. Literaturbrief', 499.

[11] Cf. Habicht, *Shakespeare and the German Imagination*, 1. The German enthusiasm for Shakespeare, it should be noted, was not entirely uncontested. The chorus of approval was recurrently challenged by the dissonant voices of anti-Bardolators. See Chapter 6, section IV.

[12] Paulin, *The Critical Reception of Shakespeare in Germany*, 87.

[13] Paulin, *The Critical Reception of Shakespeare in Germany*, 90.

[14] Paulin concedes as much when he states that Lessing's 'Letter' 'effectively silenced the last authoritative anti-Shakespearean voice [in Germany]'. *The Critical Reception of Shakespeare in Germany*, 90.

an infinity; everything was new, unknown to me, and the unaccustomed light hurt my eyes. [...] I jumped high in the air and felt at last that I had hands and feet.[15]

The young Goethe's encounter with Shakespeare was an awakening, and thus much less about Shakespeare than about Goethe himself: *his* way forward, *his* new sense of empowerment, *his* rebellion against the literary establishment. Like Keats 'on first looking into Chapman's Homer', Goethe feels 'like some watcher of the skies / When a new planet swims into his ken'.[16] But unlike Keats, the epiphany does not arrest him in awestruck wonder; instead it makes him burst with restless energy.[17] His sense of liberation is boundless. Instead of Keats's self-effacing 'negative capability', Goethe is unstoppable in his assertion of the self and its power to achieve: the 'egotistical sublime' at the peak of its youthful dynamism.

For the young Goethe and his *Sturm und Drang* contemporaries, Shakespeare was the exemplary 'genius of pure subjectivity and individuality',[18] most fully expressed in Hamlet. While Shakespeare's dramaturgy became the model for Goethe's unrestrainedly 'irregular' history play *Götz von Berlichingen* (1773), Hamlet was the model for Werther, the hero of 'pure subjectivity' who propelled Goethe to European fame. *The Sorrows of Young Werther* (1774), which churchmen condemned as a lure to suicide and Napoleon confessed to have read no less than seven times, turned Shakespeare's melancholy prince into a contemporary man of feeling. Straining against the whips and scorns of a time too narrowly conventional to accommodate his ideals and aspirations, he finds all that life is otherwise lacking when he meets Lotte, a young woman who is unfortunately engaged to, and then marries, another man. After many heart-rending encounters with her, Werther sees the hopelessness of his passion and ends his agony by putting a bullet through his head. Both his trademark outfit—a dark blue tailcoat over a yellow waistcoat, yellow breeches and top boots—and his suicidal end found imitators. A veritable Werther-fever took hold of Goethe's impressionable readership.[19]

Werther was a crucial step in the integration of Hamlet into German culture. 'Hamlet-fever', writes Walter Muschg, could only catch on in Germany 'because there already was a Werther fever':

> One intensifying the other, the two maladies were basically one and the same. The shattered Hamlet was seen as a brother of the suicidal Werther, and even Goethe

[15] Johann Wolfgang von Goethe, 'Zum Schäkespears Tag' (1771), first printed in *Allgemeine Monatsschrift für Wissenschaft und Literatur*, April 1854. For part of the translation I draw on Williams, *Shakespeare on the German Stage*, vol. 1, 18.

[16] John Keats, 'On First Looking into Chapman's *Homer*', in *Major Works*, ed. Elizabeth Cook (Oxford: Oxford University Press, 2001), 32, ll. 9–10.

[17] See Williams, *Shakespeare on the German Stage*, 18: 'The most striking aspect of Shakespeare's impact is the limitless energy Goethe considered he gave him.'

[18] Jochen Schmidt, *Die Geschichte des Genie-Gedankens in der deutschen Literatur, Philosophie und Politik 1750–1945*, 2 vols (Darmstadt: Wissenschaftliche Buchgesellschaft, 1988), vol. 1, 167.

[19] On the reception of Goethe's Werther: Klaus R. Scherpe, *Werther und Wertherwirkung: Zum Syndrom bürgerlicher Gesellschaftsordnung im 18. Jahrhundert* (Bad Homburg: Gehlen, 1970). The Werther craze provoked many sardonic comments, a particularly succinct one from the aphorist Georg Lichtenberg: 'Werther—a heart with testicles'; quoted in David E. Wellbery, '1774, January–March: Pathologies of Literature', in *A New History of German Literature*, ed. David E. Wellbery, Judith Ryan, and Hans Ulrich Gumbrecht (Cambridge, MA: Harvard University Press, 2004), 386–92 at 389.

himself succumbed to this misunderstanding. From early on, *Hamlet* must have eclipsed all other works of Shakespeare for him. [...] In the year following the Hamburg performance [of *Hamlet* by the famous actor manager Friedrich Ludwig Schröder] Goethe began writing *Wilhelm Meister's Theatrical Mission* (1796) in which he meant to show his calling as the German Shakespeare and to make the engagement with Hamlet the turning point in Wilhelm's career. [...] That Wilhelm himself plays the lead character and the staging of Hamlet changes his life [...] underscores the fateful significance for his own development which Goethe ascribed to the play.[20]

For T. S. Eliot, Goethe's intensely personal investment in the play, or rather in the prince, makes him a prime example of 'that most dangerous type of critic, the critic with a mind which is naturally of the creative order, but which through some weakness in creative power exercises itself in criticism instead'.

Such a mind had Goethe, who made of Hamlet a Werther; and such had Coleridge, who made of Hamlet a Coleridge [...]. The kind of criticism that Goethe and Coleridge produced, in writing of Hamlet, is the most misleading kind possible. For they both [...] make their critical aberrations the more plausible by the substitution— of their own Hamlet for Shakespeare's—which their creative gift effects.[21]

For Goethe's contemporaries in Germany, Wilhelm Meister's reading of Hamlet was a revelation, the 'authorized version' which later readings could either follow, modify, or reject—but never ignore. The key passage reads like this:

[I]t is clear to me what Shakespeare set out to portray: a heavy deed placed on a soul which is not adequate to cope with it. And it is in this sense that I find the whole play constructed. An oak tree planted in a precious pot which should only have held delicate flowers. The roots spread out, the vessel is shattered. A fine, pure, noble and highly moral person, but devoid of that emotional strength that characterizes a hero, goes to pieces beneath a burden that it can neither support nor cast off.[22]

---

[20] Muschg, 'Deutschland ist Hamlet'.

[21] T. S. Eliot, 'Hamlet and His Problems', *The Athenaeum*, 26 September 1919, 940–1 at 940. Eliot's initial underestimation of Goethe is most baldly apparent in his statement: 'Of Goethe it is perhaps truer to say that he dabbled in both philosophy and poetry and made no great success of either; his true role was that of the man of the world and sage—a La Rochefoucauld, a La Bruyère, a Vauvenargues' ('Hamlet and His Problems', 940). Twenty years later, Eliot said this: 'It is an interesting sentence; interesting because it enunciates so many errors in so few words together with one truth: that Goethe is a sage.' In the same essay he writes: 'The wisdom of a great poet is concealed in his work; but in becoming aware of it we become ourselves more wise. That Goethe was one of the wisest of men I have long admitted; that he was a great lyric poet I have long since come to recognize; but that the wisdom and the poetry are inseparable, in poets of the highest rank, is something I have only come to perceive in becoming a little wiser myself.' 'Goethe as Sage', in Eliot, *On Poetry and Poets* (New York: Farrar, Straus and Cudahy, 1957), 256 and 264.

[22] Johann Wolfgang von Goethe, *The Collected Works*, vol. 9: *Wilhelm Meister's Apprenticeship* (1795/6), trans. and ed. Eric A. Blackall (Princeton, NJ: Princeton University Press, 1995), 146 (Book IV, Chap. 13). For a well-informed account of Goethe's evolving views on Hamlet, see Stephen Fennell, 'Johann Wolfgang Goethe', in *Great Shakespeareans*, ed. Adrian Poole and Peter Holland, vol. 3: *Voltaire, Goethe, Schlegel, Coleridge*, ed. Roger Paulin (London and New York: Continuum, 2011), 44–91 at 61–72.

The Romantic August Wilhelm Schlegel was enthusiastic: with the Hamlet theme in *Wilhelm Meister* Shakespeare had 'risen from the dead and walks among the living'.[23] Goethe had made Hamlet a contemporary.

He remained a contemporary throughout the next century.[24] The nineteenth century's 'speculative genius', Ralph Waldo Emerson wrote, 'is a sort of living Hamlet'.[25] Little wonder that in Germany, where this speculative bent flourished most unrestrainedly, Shakespeare's pensive Dane should prove an irresistible figure of identification. A nation of Hamlets, the Germans, in the words of Madame de Staël, 'abandon themselves, each separately, to all the impulses of an unrestrained imagination'; their 'eminent faculty of thought [...] rises and loses itself in vacuum, [...] penetrates and vanishes in obscurity [...] [and] confounds itself by the force of analysis'.[26] De Staël quotes the idiosyncratic Romantic humorist Jean Paul who 'said that the empire of the seas belonged to the English, that of the land to the French, and that of the air to the Germans' (35).

The satire in Jean Paul's remark and the critical edge in Madame de Staël's are unmistakable. But the Hamlet of Wilhelm Meister was first and foremost a positive figure: '[a] fine, pure, noble and highly moral person'. In this view, he was absolved of any blame for his inaction. Indeed his failure to act, far from being morally reprehensible, was the very proof of his 'highly moral' nature. Hamlet's virtue was inseparable from the scrupulous hesitancy that isolated him in a world of his own thoughts and disabled him for the world of action.

This reading of Hamlet was particularly accommodating to the mentality of the *Bildungsbürgertum*, Germany's bourgeois intelligentsia of the nineteenth century.[27] The social habitat of this class was emphatically private, its grasp on public affairs at best tentative in a country predominantly still governed by absolutist rulers. The emergence of a public sphere deserving of that name was effectively prevented by the fragmentation of the country. 'This division of Germany, fatal to her political force, was nevertheless very favorable to all the efforts of genius and imagination',

[23] August Wilhelm Schlegel, 'Etwas über William Shakespeare bei Gelegenheit Wilhelm Meisters' [Something on William Shakespeare on the Occasion of Wilhelm Meister], *Die Horen* 4 (1796), 57–112 at 58.

[24] This is particularly true not only of Germany, but also of Russia. When Russian intellectuals of the 1880s found in Hamlet the mirror image of their own inner strife, their 'predominant interpretation' was still 'shaped by Goethe's view': Ekaterina Sukhanova, *Voicing the Distant: Shakespeare and Russian Modernist Poetry* (Cranbury, NJ: Associated University Presses, 2004), 52. On Hamlet in Russia, see Eleanor Row, *Hamlet: A Window on Russia* (New York: New York University Press, 1976); also Boika Sokolova, 'Between Religion and Ideology: Some Russian Hamlets of the Twentieth Century', *Shakespeare Survey* 54 (2001), 140–51, and Mikhail P. Alekseev, ed., *Shekspir i russkaya kultura* [Shakespeare and Russian Culture] (Leningrad: Nauka, 1965). At the height of Russian Hamletism William Morris made the much-quoted remark: 'Hamlet [...] should have been a Russian, not a Dane.' Letter to Georgiana Burne-Jones, 17 March 1888, in *The Collected Letters of William Morris*, ed. Norman Kelvin, vol. 2, part B: *1885–1888* (Princeton, NJ: Princeton University Press, 1987), 755.

[25] Ralph Waldo Emerson, 'Shakespeare; or, the Poet', in *Representative Men*, in Emerson, *Essays and Lectures*, ed. Joel Porte (New York: Library of America, 1983), 710–26 at 718.

[26] Anne Louise Germaine de Staël, *Germany, by Madame the Baroness de Staël-Holstein*, ed. O. W. Wight (Boston, MA: Houghton Mifflin, 1859), 33 and 35. References to this edition are given in brackets in the text.

[27] This point is persuasively argued in Pfister, 'Germany is Hamlet'.

de Staël wrote in 1810 (32). But however favourable it may have been, the situation also entailed very real disadvantages:

> As there is no capital city in which all the good company of Germany finds itself united, the spirit of society exerts but little power; and the empire of taste and the arms of ridicule are equally without influence. Most writers and reasoners sit down to work in solitude, or surrounded only by a little circle over which they reign. (32)

Germany lacked what France and, of course, England too, so abundantly and conspicuously possessed: 'Society', a metropolitan sphere of communication where issues of the political, moral, and aesthetic *Zeitgeist* were defined and negotiated by an articulate public. The lack of 'society' made Germany's intellectual elite so quixotically unworldly. Intellectuals simply had no access to the world of affairs in the German states and statelets: 'The nobles', de Staël notes, 'have too few ideas, the men of letters too little practice in business' (34). 'Understanding is a combination of the knowledge of men and things'; society the only place where such knowledge can be acquired and exercised. But such a place was not to be found in Germany, and thus '[i]t is imagination more than understanding that characterizes the Germans' (34–5).

Madame de Staël's generalizations may be somewhat broad-brushed and Goethe, a busy minister to the Duke of Saxe-Weimar as well as Germany's undisputed 'poet-prince', posed an obvious exception to her rule. But she is right in marking as characteristically German a profound alienation between the intellectual and political spheres, an alienation that the bourgeois intelligentsia turned into a matter of principle: a fundamental gap between *Geist* and *Politik*, between a 'higher' sphere of the mind, a sphere governed by 'the true, the beautiful and the good' and a 'lower', 'corrupting' sphere of politics. The Hamlet of Wilhelm Meister has his place in this setting. Those who acquiesced in the situation could find their acquiescence ennobled by his nobleness.

But this positive view of Hamlet is, of course, open to question, if only because Hamlet so insistently questions himself. For Hegel, this was the defining trait of Hamlet, the trait that made him at once paradigmatically modern—meaning, for Hegel, 'romantic'—and deeply irritating. In his *Lectures on Aesthetics* (given between 1817 and 1829, published posthumously 1835–8), Shakespeare's *Hamlet* epitomizes Hegel's essential distinction between ancient and modern or 'romantic' tragedy, and he makes no bones about his preference for the former. The heroes of classical tragedy are single-mindedly dedicated to the one aim that defines them: 'Throughout they are what they can and must be in accordance with their essential nature.'[28] In modern tragedy, by contrast, 'the principle of subjectivity' gains sway: 'Therefore it takes for its proper subject-matter [...] the subjective inner life of the character' (1223). Hamlet exemplifies the specific qualities, but also the pitfalls, of this modern bent. '[I]n the portrayal of concretely human individuals', Hegel

---

[28] Georg Wilhelm Friedrich Hegel, *Hegel's Aesthetics: Lectures on Fine Art*, 2 vols, trans. and ed. T. M. Knox (Oxford: Clarendon Press, 1975), vol. 2, 1194. References to this edition are given in brackets in the text.

writes, 'Shakespeare stands at an almost unapproachable height' (1227). Yet there is no mistaking that Hegel regards *Hamlet*, for all its greatness, as an altogether harmful example, one to be held accountable for what he finds most objectionable in modern tragedy, 'this personal tragedy of inner discord', about which 'there is […] something now painful and sad, now aggravating':

> But what is worst of all is to exhibit such indecision and vacillation of character, and of the whole man, as a sort of perverse and sophistical[!] dialectic and then to make it the main theme of the entire drama […]. (1229)

Hegel's indignation is less directed at *Hamlet* the play than at Hamlet the prince as the prototype, or role model, of a specifically modern 'character'. This character, it seems, is not confined to drama, but symptomatic of a much wider problem in the contemporary psyche: a failure of will, a general weakening of energy and moral fibre caused by what Coleridge termed an 'overbalance in the contemplative faculty'.[29] Hamlet's malady becomes identified with the *mal du siècle*.

The general diagnosis acquires a specific and specifically bitter twist when applied to Germany. 'If a German had made Hamlet, I would not be a bit surprised. All a German needs is nice clear handwriting. He copies himself and out comes Hamlet', the critic Ludwig Börne wrote in 1828.[30] This is a compliment neither to Germany nor to Hamlet:

> A nightwatchman, he keeps watch and tells the time when others are sleeping and not interested, and sleeps when others are awake and busy. Like a follower of Fichte, he thinks nothing but 'I am me' and does nothing but posit his self. […] To compound his undoing, Hamlet knows himself very well, and his weakness is accompanied by his consciousness of it, which discourages him even more. Hamlet is a death philosopher, a night scholar.[31]

The contrast to Wilhelm Meister's Hamlet could not be more pronounced. Börne's Hamlet-bashing was at least partly motivated by the urge to bash the almighty Goethe. Goethe's Hamlet was weak but noble, while Börne's Hamlet is simply weak. Goethe's Hamlet was of tragic stature; Börne's is just a sorry figure and more than a little ridiculous. Returning from Wittenberg to Denmark, he

> instantly catches cold and has the sniffles from which tender souls so often suffer. Taken from the greenhouse of school, he is put out into the open air and withers. The son of a king, bred for war and the hunt, he spent his time in Wittenberg fighting over wild theses and chasing after lily-livered sophisms. The only useful thing for common life that he brought back from the university, the fencing skill which he is so proud of, spells his ruin. He is far-sighted, sees quite clearly the danger that threatens from far-away England; but he does not see the sharply honed sword point that glints only a finger's breadth away from his eyes.[32]

---

[29] Samuel Taylor Coleridge, 'Hamlet' (1818), in his *Lectures and Notes on Shakspere and Other English Poets* (London: Bell, 1904), 342–68 at 344.

[30] Ludwig Börne, 'Hamlet. Von Shakespeare' (1828), in Börne, *Sämtliche Schriften*, 3 vols, ed. Inge Rippmann and Peter Rippmann (Düsseldorf: Melzer, 1964), vol. 1, 482–98 at 498.

[31] Börne, 'Hamlet. Von Shakespeare', 489–90.   [32] Börne, 'Hamlet. Von Shakespeare', 489.

Börne was one of the most outspoken critics of the reactionary regime in the German states after the fall of Napoleon. His writings were censored, and his *Letters from Paris*, where he took up residence in 1830, argued for a revolution. Börne's Hamlet is a caricature of the German intellectual, a silly prig in the pirouettes of useless speculations. The faults that make this Hamlet so typically German were harmless, even amiable foibles to Madame de Staël; to Börne, they are an indefensible liability.

From here it is only a small step to Ferdinand Freiligrath's 'Deutschland ist Hamlet!' poem. The revolution advocated by Börne had still not happened in 1844; political conditions were, if anything, even more oppressive than in 1830; and those in opposition to them were still lost in feckless rumination. This is the situation that motivated Freiligrath's poetic wake-up call:

> Hamlet[33]
> Deutschland is Hamlet! Solemn, slow,
> Within its gates walks every night,
> Pale, buried Freedom to and fro,
> And fills the watchers with affright.
> There stands the lofty shape, white-clad,
> And bids the shrinker in his fear—
> 'Be mine avenger, draw thy blade,—
> They've pourëd poison in my ear!'
>
> With quaking bones still list'neth he,
> Till the dread truth stands wholly kenned,
> And vows he will the avenger be—
> But will he dare it in the end?
> He thinks—and dreams on dreams succeed—
> No means to steel his breast can start—
> Still for the high and daring deed
> There fails the high and daring heart.
>
> That comes of studying all too hard;
> He lay and read too much in bed;
> His blood grew sluggish, scarcely stirred—
> His breathing short—he was o'erfed!
> He span the learned yarn too well;
> His best of deeds was but his thinking;
> Too long in Wittenberg did dwell
> In college hall, or hall of drinking.

Though not exactly a masterpiece, the poem reads better in German than in this English version, authorized by the poet's daughter. Its message, broadcast in nine stanzas, comes across clearly and effectively. Germany's condition is serious but not hopeless. The tragedy has—'Thanks God!'—as yet only reached Act 4. The catastrophe can, if Hamlet 'seize the moment', be averted. But the closing

---

[33] Ferdinand Freiligrath, 'Hamlet', trans. William Howitt, in *Poems from the German of Ferdinand Freiligrath* (Leipzig: Tauchnitz, 1871).

lines underscore the precariousness of that 'if' by turning the focus on the poem's speaker himself:

> But one resolve!—the way stands clear—
> Think on the oath that thou hast sworn,
> Rush to the lists, and, void of fear
> Avenge thy father's ghost forlorn!
> Why all this pondering? Let it be—
> Yet—can I chide, myself a dreamer?
> Myself, in troth, a part of thee—
> Thou ever-wavering, lingering schemer?

Where Börne distanced himself from the German Hamlet malaise, Freiligrath diagnosed himself as having all the symptoms. In order to see what brought on the condition and cured it—at least according to Horace Howard Furness—within two decades of Freiligrath's self-diagnosis, we have to take a look at the broader cultural and political context.

III TWO EMPIRES AND A NATION

Xenia, or 'host gifts', a collection of 400 distichs co-written by Goethe and Schiller in 1795/6, contains one entitled 'The German Empire':

> Germany? But where is it? I know not how to find the country.
> Where the learned begins, the political comes to an end.

This is followed by 'German National Character':

> Any hope of forming yourselves into a nation, Germans, is in vain;
> Develop yourselves rather—you can do it—more freely as human beings![34]

A nowhere empire and a never nation: the verses confirm Jean Paul's *bon mot* that the Germans ruled but a realm of air. Kings of 'infinite space', they were 'bounded in a nutshell' and, like Hamlet, were haunted by dreams: not necessarily 'bad dreams', but pipe dreams (*Ham.* 2.2.231.15–17).

Goethe for one had no time for the national aspirations of the younger, Romantic generation. 'Germany? But where is it?' is not so much (as is often assumed) a sigh for what is lacking as a rebuff of the sighers.[35] In the later 1700s there was a growing wish for national unification but nothing like a unanimous desire for it. Much less

---

[34] Friedrich Schiller, *Sämtliche Werke*, 5 vols, ed. Peter-André Alt et al., vol. 1: *Gedichte/Dramen 1*, ed. Jörg Robert and Albert Meier (Munich and Vienna: Carl Hanser, 2004), 267. The two distichs are used as a starting point in Mary Fulbrook, *A Concise History of Germany*, 2nd edn (Cambridge: Cambridge University Press, 2004), 1, from which I take the quoted English translation. The first distich also features as the opening lines of Neil McGregor, *Germany: Memories of a Nation* (London: Allen Lane, 2014), 1.

[35] *Ungastliche Gaben* [Inhospitable Gifts], the title of a recent study on the subject, indicates the acerbic tenor of the *Xenien*. They offer a tour of the fads and foibles of the contemporary literary scene in Germany. Cf. Frieder von Ammon, *Ungastliche Gaben: Die 'Xenien' Goethes und Schillers und ihre literarische Rezeption von 1796 bis in die Gegenwart* (Tübingen: Niemeyer, 2005).

was there any party, political grouping, movement, or government actually working towards this goal in any practical way. National unity was as yet indeed nothing but a vision, one that entailed liberating the German people as well as uniting them. There was no consensus as to what liberation was supposed to mean and how far it was meant to go. In Schiller's view, expressed in his *Letters Upon the Aesthetic Education of Man* (1794), political reform had to be preceded by a spiritual and intellectual liberation initiated by the educated classes of society. 'German Empire and German nation', he wrote in 1797,

> are two different things. Segregated from the political, the German has created his own worth, and even if the empire perished, German dignity would remain uncontested. It is a moral quality, it lives in the culture and character of the nation, which is independent of its political fortunes. This realm flourishes in Germany, it is in full growth [...] and as the political realm shakes, the realm of the mind has become ever firmer and more consummate.[36]

The passage helps to clarify the tenor of the line: 'Where the learned [Germany] begins, the political comes to an end.' If this were from Freiligrath's 'Hamlet', it would be a critique of the learnedness that stifles political activity. Coming from Schiller (and Goethe), it says the opposite: politics does and should end once we enter the higher realm of the mind.

For many writers of the time, this idea of improving society through the shaping of minds (*Bildung*) made them seek reform within the existing monarchical order of the various German territories, especially after the Jacobin 'rule of terror' had quelled the initially widespread enthusiasm for the French Revolution. But the revolution did give momentum to the notion of a German republic. This idea had been entertained by more radical 'patriots' and 'democrats' since the mid-eighteenth century. The 'people's community' (*Volksgemeinschaft*), later notorious as a Nazi term, had its origin in the more radical strata of the Enlightenment. It went hand in hand with the idea of a 'constitution for all' (*Gemeinverfassung*), the idea of equal rights for all free German citizens. This nascent nationalism, Jost Hermand explains, emphasized 'Germanness' more in opposition to the Francophile court culture of the German rulers than in hostility towards the French people. Its ultimate goal grew from the Enlightenment ideal of universal humanity: a German republic as part of 'a united family of nations encircling the globe in a free, equal, and brotherly confederation of states'.[37]

But where or, actually, what was this Germany? The map of eighteenth-century central Europe shows a patchwork of some 300 sovereign political entities: kingdoms,

---

[36] Friedrich Schiller, 'Deutsche Größe' [German Greatness] (1797), in *Sämtliche Werke*, vol. 1, 473–8 at 474. The translation of the passage is quoted from Jost Hermand, *Old Dreams of a New Reich: Volkish Utopias and National Socialism* (1988), trans. Paul Levesque (Bloomington and Indianapolis: Indiana University Press, 1992), 5.

[37] Hermand, *Old Dreams of a New Reich*, 7. The Jacobin 'Republic of Mainz', founded under French patronage in 1792, was the first attempt to establish a democratic state on German territory. It ended the following year, when the city was recaptured by Austrian and Prussian troops. One of the leaders of the Mainz Jacobins was Georg Forster, the university librarian, who had accompanied James Cook on his second voyage to the Pacific. His *A Voyage Round the World* (1777) became a landmark in travel writing.

principalities, bishoprics, and free cities, with territories ranging from large to medium to small to minuscule. What held them together were the zigzag borders of the Holy Roman Empire, or, to give its full title, the Holy Roman Empire of the German Nation. These borders included territories we would never think of as even remotely German today, such as the 'Austrian Netherlands' (roughly today's Belgium), Bohemia and Moravia (today's Czech Republic and Slovakia). They excluded not only the German-speaking Swiss Confederation, but also considerable parts of the Empire's two largest and most powerful member states: Austria and Prussia. The Austrian Habsburgs had held the elective title of Holy Roman Emperor almost uninterruptedly since the fifteenth century. But the Habsburg dominions also encompassed the Kingdom of Hungary, Galicia (straddling parts of Poland and Ukraine), and other eastern European territories. The eastern part of the Kingdom of Prussia, in fact the entire province of that name, lay outside the Empire too.[38]

The Holy Roman Empire was nothing like a modern nation state or even a state at all. Although its name suggested that its elected emperors held their supreme power in direct succession from the mighty rulers of ancient Rome, in reality that power was narrowly circumscribed, subject to the consent of the electors and other regional princes and maintainable only through negotiation and concession. In the famous words of Voltaire, '[t]his agglomeration which was called and still calls itself the Holy Roman Empire was neither holy, nor Roman, nor an empire.'[39]

The German Empire and the German nation were indeed, as Schiller wrote, two different things. But 'German nation' could be two different things too. As Schiller (and Goethe) conceived it, it was the *geistige Nation*, a nation of the mind (or spirit), a unity of higher culture whose objective was not the establishment of a unified nation state but the progress of humanity. Schiller was all the more in favour of this spiritual Germany because, in 1797, the political prospects for Germany were dire. The Empire was tottering under the onslaught of the people's armies of revolutionary France. It broke down only a few years later when Napoleon successively vanquished the armies of Austria and Prussia. The new Empire of France swept the old Empire of Germany off the map. The last Holy Roman Emperor, Francis II from the House of Habsburg, abdicated in 1806. After over 800 years,[40] the Holy Roman Empire had ceased to exist.

Recent research has revised the once prevalent view that the dissolution of the old Empire caused little stir and less regret. On the contrary, sources suggest

---

[38] It was the possession of the province of Prussia which lay outside the Empire that enabled the Duke-Elector of Brandenburg, Frederick III from the House of Hohenzollern, to crown himself king—King of Prussia, that is—in 1701. Only the Habsburg Emperor would have been entitled to crown him King of Brandenburg, and, given the rivalry between the two powers, that was not a likely prospect.

[39] 'Ce corps qui s'appelait et qui s'appelle encore le saint empire romain n'était en aucune manière ni saint, ni romain, ni empire.' Voltaire, *Complete Works*, vols 22–26C: *Essai sur les mœurs et l'esprit des nations* (1756), ed. Bruno Bernard et al., vol. 24: *Chapitres 68–102* (Oxford: Voltaire Foundation, 2011), 41.

[40] The first holder of the title was Charlemagne, who was crowned Emperor by Pope Leo III in 800. But the title was contested in the ninth and tenth centuries and fell into abeyance until it was revived by Otto I in 962.

that contemporaries reacted 'not at all with indifference', but 'with horror', as an established, seemingly perennial 'worldview lost its world'.[41] The governmental authority of the *Altes Reich* (Old Empire) may have been quite limited (although that authority has often been underrated too[42]), but it held considerable power as an institution that embodied the idea of a collective identity across the fragmented German lands. Its demise enhanced rather than diminished this power. The phantom pain of the lost Empire grew in the course of the nineteenth century and did not disappear when a new German Empire was established under Prussian leadership in 1871. As the byzantine bureaucratic procedures of the old Reich faded into oblivion, its sacred glory could shine all the more brightly.

Napoleonic conquest of central Europe brought into being what had not existed before: a militant German nationalism contending for a German nation state. Its notion of what was truly *deutsch*, or, in the preferred old spelling, *teutsch*, harked back to the *Germania* of the Roman historian Tacitus. The virtues he extolled in the rough but honest, brave, and frugal Germanic tribes were eagerly claimed by the German patriots of the early 1800s, while the decadence which Tacitus deplored in his fellow Romans was just as readily projected onto the 'Romanic' French. The so-called Wars of Liberation (1813–15) which ended the French occupation were experienced as a great national awakening. The frustration was all the more keenly felt when this achievement failed to bring any advance towards German unification. The Congress of Vienna redrew many European boundaries in the interest of a lasting peace for the war-riven continent. But its conservative agenda, masterminded by the Austrian foreign minister Prince Metternich, crushed any nationalist, liberal, or republican aspirations. The new order was to restore what the French Revolution had shattered: the old monarchic regimes. In order to achieve a stable balance of power in central Europe, the major German states, notably Austria and Prussia, were substantially enlarged. While the old Reich had comprised over 300 independent territories, the German Confederation that was created at Vienna in 1815 consisted of thirty-nine. Prussia arguably benefited most from the redistribution, even though the Austrian emperor ostensibly retained his pre-eminence by becoming president of the German Confederation.[43]

The militantly conservative spirit of the new system installed in 1815 manifested itself most clearly in the Carlsbad Decrees (1819), a catalogue of penal measures intended to quell any liberal and nationalist stirrings.[44] The Metternich Restoration

---

[41] Wolfgang Burgdorf, *Ein Weltbild verliert seine Welt: Der Untergang des Alten Reiches und die Generation 1806*, 2nd edn (Munich: Oldenbourg, 2009), ix and title.

[42] See, for example, Jason Phillip Coy, Benjamin Marschke, and David Warren Sabean, eds, *The Holy Roman Empire, Reconsidered* (Oxford: Berghahn Books, 2010); Peter H. Wilson, *The Holy Roman Empire 1495–1806* (Oxford and New York: Oxford University Press, 2011); Joachim Whaley, *Germany and the Holy Roman Empire*, 2 vols (Oxford and New York: Oxford University Press, 2012).

[43] As had been the case with the Holy Roman Empire, substantial portions of both Austria and Prussia lay outside the German Confederation.

[44] The decrees were introduced in reaction to the murder of August Wilhelm Kotzebue, a popular writer and a well-known scorner of the patriotic democrats, by the fraternity (*Burschenschaft*) student Karl Ludwig Sand. In Freiligrath's 'Hamlet', the stabbing of Kotzebue doubles for the murder of Polonius: 'And then Polonius-Kotzebue / Is stabbed instead—of just the right one!'

launched Germany into a phase of repression, censorship, and pervasive police-spying, but also one of peaceful prosperity for the rising middle class. Two terms coined retrospectively characterize this dichotomy: *Biedermeier* refers to the life-style of the bourgeoisie, a lifestyle centred on domesticity and strict abstinence from politics.[45] *Vormärz* (literally 'pre-March') refers to the oppositional forces prior to the March Revolution of 1848. It is this opposition, smarting under its own ineffectuality, that finds expression in the Hamlets of Börne and Freiligrath. In Freiligrath's poem Hamlet, the overweight slacker, is sicklied o'er with more than a little *Biedermeier* inertia.

When the revolution eventually did take place, 'German history', according to A. J. P. Taylor, 'reached its turning-point and failed to turn'. '1848 was the decisive year of German, and so of European, history': after 'the failure of the revolution discredited liberal ideas [...], nothing remained but the idea of Force, and this idea stood at the helm of German history from then on'.[46] Published in 1945, soon after the liberation of the death camps had revealed the full extent of the Nazi horrors, Taylor's *The Course of German History* vividly registers the urge to explain 'at what point German history "went wrong"',[47] when and how it embarked on that 'special path' (*Sonderweg*) which ended in 'The German Catastrophe' of 1933–45.[48] Historians today would state the case less dramatically than Taylor, but 1848 certainly was a turning point. What happened afterwards, the course that eventually led to the unification of 'the delayed nation',[49] was not determined by a citizens' movement, but by monarchical power politics, a 'revolution from above', as some historians describe it.[50] The largely autocratic constitution established in 1871 granted only a fraction of the civil and parliamentary rights envisaged by the liberal revolutionaries in 1848.

The 'March Revolution' of 1848 was sparked by the 'February Revolution' in France and quickly spread across Baden, Prussia, Austria, and other German states. Liberal governments were established in a number of states, Metternich fled into exile, the Austrian emperor abdicated in favour of his nephew, and the Prussian

---

[45] Nowadays, the term *Biedermeier* most frequently applies to the furniture of the period.

[46] A. J. P. Taylor, *The Course of German History: A Survey of the Development of German History since 1815* (London: Hamish Hamilton, 1945), 68. Described as a mix of 'the profound [...] with the wise-crack' (Sigmund Neumann in *American Historical Review* 52.4 [1947], 730–3 at 731), Taylor's book remains a point of reference, even though its harsh criticism of bona fide democrats of the Weimar Republic is less than fair and some of its broader generalizations have not stood the test of more recent research.

[47] Barbara Eichner, *History in Mighty Sounds: Musical Constructions of German National Identity, 1848–1914* (Martlesham: Boydell & Brewer, 2012), 11.

[48] The term derives from Friedrich Meinecke, *Die deutsche Katastrophe: Betrachtungen und Erinnerungen* (Wiesbaden: Brockhaus, 1946). The debate over Germany's *Sonderweg*—what exactly defines it and if the concept is tenable at all—has generated a huge amount of writing which cannot be documented here. For an informed assessment of the debate, see Helmut Walser Smith, 'When the *Sonderweg* Debate Left Us', *German Studies Review* 31.2 (2008), 225–40.

[49] The term was coined by Helmut Plessner, *Die verspätete Nation: Über die politische Verführbarkeit bürgerlichen Geistes* (Stuttgart: Kohlhammer, 1959); first published under the title *Das Schicksal deutschen Geistes im Ausgang seiner bürgerlichen Epoche* (Zurich: Niehans, 1935).

[50] Cf., for example, Lothar Gall, *Bismarck: Der weiße Revolutionär* (Frankfurt am Main: Propyläen, 1980).

king, Frederick William IV, adapting to the spirit of the times, was seen riding through Berlin wearing a sash in the revolutionary tricolour of black, red, and gold, declaring his dedication to 'Germany's freedom, Germany's unity'.

In May 1848 Germany's first National Assembly convened in Frankfurt's St Paul's Church with the aim of drawing up a national constitution. But it was hampered by conflicting interests and factional disputes and also overtaxed by its monumental task. Unlike France, where the revolution of 1848 converted an existing nation state from monarchy to republic, the Frankfurt delegates were expected to produce not just a constitution, but also the state in which it was to apply. The shape of this state was controversial. While the moderate, middle-class majority aimed for a liberal parliamentary system in some form of constitutional monarchy, there was also a substantial minority pushing for a more radical republican model.[51]

By mid-1848, a counter-revolutionary backlash had set in. Renewed revolutionary pushes in various regions alternated with counter-pushes by the regular armed forces. By the end of 1848 state power in Prussia was firmly back in the hands of the monarch, and when the St Paul's Church assembly finally passed its long-debated constitution in March 1849, the revolutionary cause was all but lost. As a last resort, the assembly sent a delegation to the King of Prussia offering him the hereditary title of German Emperor. But Frederick William declined the offer. Although polite to the delegation, he was outspoken in a letter in which he vented his outrage at being offered a 'filthy' crown, debased by the 'stench of revolution'.[52]

The Frankfurt Assembly was dissolved in May, and after a final flare-up of insurrection in some areas, the revolution was over and the monarchic order fully re-established by the end of July 1849.[53] The revolutionaries had failed to achieve the 'Unity, justice, and freedom' which the 'pre-March' poet Heinrich Hoffmann von Fallersleben had demanded for the 'German fatherland' in his *Deutschlandlied* ('Song of the Germans') of 1841. Some form of parliamentary representation survived, most notably in Prussia, where the staunchly counter-revolutionary landowner Otto von Bismarck embarked on his political career as a member of the new Prussian *Landtag* (House of Representatives) in 1849.

In the two decades that followed, unity was achieved while freedom, as envisaged in 1848, fell by the wayside. But unity could mean two different things: a

[51] The *Communist Manifesto*, also a product of the revolutionary year 1848, did not begin to attract wider attention until the 1870s. The German revolution prompted Marx to return from his Belgian exile to Cologne, from whence he was expelled again in 1849.
[52] Frederick William IV in a letter to Christian von Bunsen, Prussian ambassador to the Court of St James's, 1842–54. Quoted in Hagen Schulze, *Germany: A New History* (1996), trans. Deborah Lucas Schneider (Cambridge, MA and London: Harvard University Press, 1998), 129. The letter can be found in Leopold von Ranke, ed., *Aus dem Briefwechsel Friedrich Wilhelms IV. mit Bunsen* (Leipzig: Duncker & Humblot, 1873), quotation at 235.
[53] Whether the revolution failed altogether or only remained 'incomplete' (Michael Stürmer, '1848 in der deutschen Geschichte', in *Sozialgeschichte heute: Festschrift für Hans Rosenberg zum 70. Geburtstag*, ed. Hans-Ulrich Wehler [Göttingen: Vandenhoeck & Ruprecht, 1974], 228–42) is a matter of debate among historians. If Germany's 'special path' is seen to have its disastrous telos in the Holocaust, the revolution of 1848 was a failure, repeated in the failure of Germany's second attempt at a liberal democracy with the collapse of the Weimar Republic in 1933. Recent accounts tend to take a more sanguine view. Looking beyond the Holocaust, they see the goals of 1848 eventually brought to a happy conclusion in the peaceful revolution of 1989.

lesser (*kleindeutsch*) or a larger (*großdeutsch*) solution. This arose from the rivalry between Prussia and Austria. The Vienna Congress had given Austria the presidency of the German Confederation, but Prussia was increasingly challenging that dominance. The conflict had come to a head at the Frankfurt National Assembly. Delegates from the southern, Catholic regions sided with Austria, those from the Protestant North with Prussia. It was clear that when the assembly, on a very narrow vote, decided to offer the imperial crown to the King of Prussia, Austria under its Habsburg emperor would not have been part of this Prussian-led German Empire. Excluding Austria, it would have been a *kleindeutsch* (literally: 'small-German') empire.

The Empire that eventually did emerge in 1871 was this 'small-German' Empire, a product not of patriotic idealism, but of Bismarck's *Realpolitik*, in which imperial aspirations played second fiddle to Prussian hegemony. As Minister President answerable only to his King, Bismarck accomplished unification through a skilful mix of diplomatic manoeuvring—including an alliance of convenience with the bourgeois German Progress Party and the National Liberals—and military force. In 1864, a conflict with Denmark over the duchies of Schleswig and Holstein saw Prussia and Austria fight victoriously side by side. Two years later, Bismarck escalated the tension with Prussia's rival by creating a situation in which Austria was more or less forced to declare war. Most German states and the liberal bourgeoisie objected to Prussian strong-arm politics, but failed to support Austria against the technologically superior Prussian army. One battle, fought on 3 July 1866 at Königgrätz (or Sadowa) in Bohemia, decided the war for Prussia and ended the prospect for a Greater Germany solution. The whole of Northern Germany was now under Prussian sway. All that remained was to bring the hesitant Southern German states into the fold. This required an external enemy, and none was better suited for the part than France. A coincidental dynastic issue[54] furnished Bismarck with the opportunity to, once again, push the opponent into the role of the aggressor. Now all of Germany could join in a truly national struggle against the 'hereditary enemy' from the Wars of Liberation. Within ten months, France's Second Napoleonic Empire was defeated and Germany's Second Empire, under the Prussian King Wilhelm III, now Kaiser Wilhelm I, triumphantly proclaimed, in the Hall of Mirrors at Versailles Palace, on 18 January 1871.

Three quickly victorious wars and the accomplishment of the long-delayed national unification—this is 'the recent history' referred to by H. H. Furness in the congratulatory dedication of his Hamlet volumes, the recent history which had proved once and for all that 'Germany is not Hamlet'. United at last, a nation and

---

[54] This was the claim to the Spanish throne of Leopold of Hohenzollern-Sigmaringen, a Prussian prince. Already pressurized by Prussia's uncomfortably potent 'North German Confederation', France now saw itself under threat of being encircled by a dynastic alliance between Prussia and Spain. French diplomatic pressure led to the withdrawal of the Hohenzollern claim. But when the French ambassador, approaching Wilhelm III during his stay at the resort spa of Bad Ems, asked him to guarantee that such a claim would never again be made, the King politely refused. A version of the encounter, much sharpened by Bismarck, was released to the press. It gave the French the impression—fully intended by Bismarck—that their ambassador had been treated with disrespect. Known as the 'Ems Dispatch', the report caused a public outcry in France and provoked Napoleon III into declaring war.

an empire that could proudly claim equality among the sovereign states of Europe, the new Germany might well have been expected to be the fulfilment of every national dream. And so it no doubt was, for most Germans, in the immediate aftermath of 1871.[55] But not for all.

For some, the new Germany, though disquietingly big in the eyes of its neighbours, was not big enough. Conservative traditionalists regarded the new Reich as a poor ersatz version of the true and holy old one. In their view, Bismarck's small-German Empire with its newly fledged Hohenzollern Kaiser was not the fulfilment but a sad travesty of the imperial dream. The authentic incarnation of that dream lay in a past that was still unrecovered, yet always waiting to be revived. This past was associated with the greater-German Habsburg Empire, which had foundered first in 1806 and then again, and conclusively, in 1866. But it also reached back to the remoter and, of course, largely imaginary glory of the medieval Hohenstaufen emperors, the venerated 'Redbeard' (Barbarossa) Frederick I and his maverick grandson Frederick II, whose dominions, though never anything like a stable political entity, stretched from the Baltic to the Mediterranean Sea. This conservative yearning for the old empire would never quite vanish. It was to gain renewed force in the 1920s when it associated itself with some of the most militantly nationalist tendencies.

Another variety of greater-Germany aspirations regarded Bismarck's empire as only the first step in Germany's progress to even greater imperial dominion. Now that the nation had won its rightful place among the leading powers of Europe, it deserved a share of the rest of the world. Bismarck, always careful not to upset the European balance of powers, was strictly opposed to such expansionism. Germany, he never tired of saying, was fully 'saturated' within its territory. An advocate of German colonialism received his famous rebuff: 'Your map of Africa is very nice. But my map of Africa lies in Europe. Here is Russia and here is France, and we are in the middle. That is my map of Africa.'[56]

But whatever Bismarck deemed advisable, the Reich under its new Kaiser Wilhelm II (who took less than two years to discharge the old chancellor) eagerly joined the competition for colonial empire. Even Max Weber, who is not particularly known for his nationalism, declared in 1895: 'We must understand that the unification of Germany was a youthful escapade which the nation committed in its old age and, because of its high costs, should have been left undone if it was meant to be the conclusion and not the starting point of Germany's imperialistic politics.'[57]

In its more militant varieties, Wilhelmine expansionism entailed a notion of national superiority which radicalized earlier ideas of Germanness and paved the way for the *völkisch* ideology of the Nazis. '*Deutschland, Deutschland über alles*', the

---

[55] Regional and confessional tensions did, of course, not simply disappear with the official founding of the Empire. Some of them, most notably the Protestant–Catholic conflict, intensified. Historians describe German unification as a protracted process in which 1871 marks an important stage, but not the end point.

[56] Quoted in Volker Ullrich, *Otto von Bismarck* (Reinbek bei Hamburg: Rowohlt, 1998), 101.

[57] Max Weber, *Der Nationalstaat und die Volkswirtschaftspolitik: akademische Antrittsrede* (Freiburg: Mohr, 1895), 32.

opening line of Hoffmann von Fallersleben's 'Song of the Germans', was originally intended to express the feeling that the unity and common good of the nation should rank above the particular interests of states and factions within the German nation. Now it became a battle cry to raise Germany above all other nations. The Reich of Bismarck's making was to be only the stepping stone towards the greater Reich to come.

Discontent with the Wilhelmine Empire could also arise for a reason that will seem incongruous with what has thus far been said: the reason that it was too liberal, rather than that it was not liberal enough. This is the view we find in Nietzsche and, to varying degrees, in all of his followers. It makes little sense in the light of the failure of 1848 and the sternly authoritarian nature of the Prussian-born Empire. But en route to unification the flexible Bismarck took much on board that was at odds with his initially ultra-conservative views. The liberal *Bürgertum* (bourgeoisie) was an increasingly dominant factor in the rapid social and industrial modernization of Germany. And even if the bourgeoisie did not, as Marx and Engels had hoped in 1848 and continued hoping, bring about the revolution, its economic power made it a crucial political force in the new Empire. Germany was turning at breakneck speed from a backward, predominantly rural country into a modern industrial nation. It had a parliament (the *Reichstag*) and parties, among them such inconveniently recalcitrant ones as the Social Democrats and the Catholic *Zentrum* (Centre). It had an ever-growing army of industrial labourers who worked under conditions of mechanized mass production. It had an extensive railway network and a modern banking system, trade unions and a liberal press. In other words, it had all the blessings or, as Nietzsche would see it, blights of modernity, not only in material but also in intellectual and ideological terms. The spirit that Nietzsche and those affiliated with his ideas saw as the driving force of this modernity was the spirit of liberalism: a general razing of distinctions and the higher aspirations of the few in favour of happiness for the many, a drive towards mediocrity and trivial bourgeois comfort, a dominance of petty self-interest and economic calculation. It is this view of liberal humanity that inspired Nietzsche's caricature of the tribe of 'the last men' in *Zarathustra*: 'They have left the regions where it was hard to live, for one needs warmth. [...] "We have invented happiness", say the last men, and they blink.'[58]

IV FROM NIETZSCHE TO SCHMITT: A SHAKESPEARE TRADITION OF THE RIGHT

'The "event" in German philosophy with the most profound impact on the whole of twentieth-century culture is, of course, Friedrich Nietzsche', writes Thomas Nipperdey in his magisterial *German History*.[59] Nietzsche's centrality in the intellectual landscape

[58] Friedrich Nietzsche, *Thus Spoke Zarathustra*, in *The Portable Nietzsche* (1954), trans. and ed. Walter Kaufmann (London: Penguin, 1976), 103–439 at 129–30.
[59] Thomas Nipperdey, *Deutsche Geschichte 1866–1918*, vol. 1: *Arbeitswelt und Bürgergeist* (Munich: Beck, 1990), 686.

of the *fin de siècle* makes him the obvious point of departure for this study. The reverberations of his explosive power register virtually everywhere. '[T]he challenge and significance of the Nietzschean impulse', writes Steven Aschheim, 'resides precisely in its pervasiveness, in its manifold and often contradictory penetration of crucial political and cultural arenas.'[60] Nietzsche's influence is by no means limited to what is called here an intellectual tradition of the Right.[61] But there can be no doubt that it was this tradition which he most strongly affected. When one reads some of Nietzsche's modern interpreters, this rightist slant—culminating in his appropriation by the Nazis—was largely, if not wholly, the product of wilful distortion: quotation out of context and falsifications by Nietzsche's ultra-rightist, anti-Semitic sister Elisabeth Förster-Nietzsche.[62]

But the counter-reading offered by Nietzsche's modern apologists is selective too. For the post-Second World War Nietzsche Renaissance, a degree of bowdlerization was necessary: objectionable passages had to be suppressed or toned down. Walter Kaufmann, Nietzsche's American interpreter and translator, was remarkably successful in making the prophet of 'aristocratic radicalism' (Georg Brandes's epithet for Nietzsche in 1889) compatible with notions of US democracy,[63] while French poststructuralists of the 1970s found a bona fide anti-fascist intercessor for Nietzsche's political innocuousness in Georges Bataille.[64] What can make these intercessions problematic is their blanking-out of a genuinely anti-democratic, anti-egalitarian thrust. Reclaiming Nietzsche for democracy requires the blurring of a crucial distinction: that between a left-leaning critique of liberalism and a right-wing critique of liberalism.[65] The authors that are the subject of this book[66] share with Nietzsche an anti-liberal bias which is emphatically anti-democratic, not just

---

[60] Steven E. Aschheim, *The Nietzsche Legacy in Germany, 1890–1990* (Berkeley, CA and London: University of California Press, 1992), 2.

[61] See, for example, Seth Taylor, *Left-Wing Nietzscheans: The Politics of German Expressionism 1910–1920* (Berlin: De Gruyter, 1990).

[62] See Carol Diethe, *Nietzsche's Sister and the Will to Power: A Biography of Elisabeth Förster-Nietzsche* (Urbana, IL: University of Illinois Press, 2003); Christian Niemeyer, '"die Schwester! die Schwester! 's klingt so fürchterlich!" Elisabeth Förster-Nietzsche als Verfälscherin der Briefe und Werke ihres Bruders—eine offenbar notwendige Rückerinnerung', *Nietzscheforschung* 16 (2009), 335–55. *The Will to Power*, published by Förster-Nietzsche one year after her brother's death (1901) was long believed to be his unfinished opus magnum, but is now generally recognized as Förster-Nietzsche's compilation of writings Nietzsche himself had never intended to publish. On Nazi misappropriations of Nietzsche, see, for example, Jacob Golomb and Robert S. Wistrich, eds, *Nietzsche, Godfather of Fascism? On the Uses and Abuses of a Philosophy* (Princeton, NJ: Princeton University Press, 2002).

[63] Walter A. Kaufmann, *Nietzsche: Philosopher, Psychologist, Antichrist* (Princeton, NJ: Princeton University Press, 1950); Nietzsche, *The Portable Nietzsche* (1954); Friedrich Nietzsche, *Basic Writings* (1967), trans. and ed. Walter A. Kaufmann (New York: Modern Library, 2000).

[64] In January 1937 Bataille dedicated an issue of *Acéphale* titled 'Reparations à Nietzsche' to the theme 'Nietzsche et les fascistes'.

[65] Such blurring seems to have become fashionable of late: witness the suggestion by the French economist Jacques Sapir that the radical Left should form an alliance against the euro with the right-wing Front National, which was promptly seconded by the philosopher Michel Onfray who regards himself as a libertarian socialist. See Alexandre Devecchio, 'Onfray, Sapir: le retour en force de la gauche du non', *Le Figaro*, 21 September 2015. <http://www.lefigaro.fr/vox/politique/2015/09/21/31001-20150921ARTFIG00338-onfray-sapir-le-retour-en-force-de-la-gauche-du-non.php>, accessed 24 September 2015.

[66] With the notable exception of Heiner Müller, who is discussed in the 'Epilogue'.

(as is sometimes averred in the case of Carl Schmitt) anti-parliamentarian. In the case of Nietzsche, the view, canonized by Walter Kaufmann, of him as an essentially apolitical philosopher jars not just with a few isolated aphorisms but with whole clusters of passages (e.g. *Twilight of the Idols*, 'Skirmishes of an Untimely Man', §§ 34–41). These make it difficult to claim Nietzsche for a politics that may pass as democratic in any sense, let alone 'Left', because their anti-egalitarian bias runs counter not only to liberal modernity itself but also to liberal modernity's left-leaning critics. These critics (whether feminist, postcolonial, or more generally postmodernist) all share the egalitarian premise of liberalism, contesting not the value of equality per se—quite the opposite!—but the failure of liberalism to live up to its egalitarian promise: its bolstering of existing inequalities under the cloak of a universalizing ideology of 'freedom'. Nietzsche's great appeal as a critic of the egalitarian pretence of liberal democracy makes him—and, *mutatis mutandis*, Schmitt[67]—a welcome resource for postmodern critiques of this ideology but must not obscure the fact that he attacks liberalism from a genuinely anti-egalitarian position. As Keith Ansell-Pearson points out, 'Nietzsche is committed to the enhancement of man and this enhancement does not consist in improving the conditions of existence for the majority of human beings, but in the generation of a few, striking and superlatively vital "highest exemplars" of the species.' This makes 'Nietzsche's political thinking [...] a source of difficulty, even embarrassment, because it fails to accord with the standard liberal ways of thinking about politics which have prevailed in the last 200 and more years.'[68] The embarrassment this might create for a left-oriented *critique* of liberalism has often gone unnoticed.[69]

The fascination of Nietzsche lies precisely in his resistance to any system or classifiable -ism. To reduce the literary brilliance and the sheer panache of his 'wild thinking' to narrowly 'right-wing' positions would be as misguided as to deny its sometimes troubling affinities to such positions. As with Nietzsche, admiration for Carl Schmitt's conservative iconoclasm is at least partly due to his stylistic panache, in particular his characteristically memorable axioms. 'Sovereign is he who decides on the state of exception':[70] in one bold stroke, this statement cuts the ground

[67] See, for example, the interesting adaptation of Schmittian positions in Chantal Mouffe, *On the Political* (London and New York: Routledge, 2005).

[68] Keith Ansell-Pearson, 'Introduction: On Nietzsche's Critique of Morality', in Friedrich Nietzsche, *On the Genealogy of Morality*, trans. Carol Diethe, ed. Keith Ansell-Pearson, revised edn (Cambridge and New York: Cambridge University Press, 2006), xiii–xxix at xxvii–xxviii.

[69] The tendency of deconstructing away the more disturbing aspects of Nietzsche's political thinking in French and Anglo-American criticism since the 1970s and 1980s came under attack in an important collection of French essays edited by Luc Ferry and Alain Renaut, *Why We Are Not Nietzscheans*, trans. Robert de Loaiza (Chicago, IL: University of Chicago Press, 1997), originally published in French in 1991. In a similar vein: Bruce Detwiler, *Nietzsche and the Politics of Aristocratic Radicalism* (Chicago, IL: University of Chicago Press, 1990); Frederick Appel, *Nietzsche Contra Democracy* (Ithaca, NY and London: Cornell University Press, 1999); and Domenico Losurdo, *Nietzsche, il ribelle aristocratico: Biografia intellettuale e bilancio critico* (Turin: Bollati Boringhieri, 2002). A particularly balanced view, neither demonizing nor idolizing, is offered by Henning Ottmann's magisterial *Philosophie und Politik bei Nietzsche*, 2nd edn (Berlin and New York: De Gruyter, 1999).

[70] Carl Schmitt, *Political Theology: Four Chapters on the Concept of Sovereignty* (1922), trans. George D. Schwab (Chicago, IL and London: University of Chicago Press, 2005), 5 (translation modified).

from under 'the entire tradition of juristic rationalism from John Locke to John Rawls' by placing the sovereign exception above and prior to the rule of law. According to Christopher Pye, '[t]he force and the promise of Schmitt's account consist in what it suggests about the irreducibly political character of the social and juridical domains'. 'For recent, Left-oriented political theorists', Pye observes, this 'has been as animating as it has been controversial'.[71] But in some discussions of Schmitt (not in Pye's) the attempt to 'rehabilitate Schmitt for democratic theory'[72] has tended to all but efface the controversial. My attempt in this book is not to discredit the legitimacy of making good use of Schmittian (or Nietzschean) thought 'for democratic theory'. My aim is, rather, to shed light on the large and powerful anti-democratic matrix in which this thinking is grounded and to which it adds intellectual momentum: a force in history which it is compelling to know about even, or indeed especially, if we do not like it.

To put Nietzsche at the beginning of a rightist intellectual tradition may well raise objections.[73] But the Nietzschean provenance of the strand of intellectual history to be discussed here can be in no doubt. A clearly anti-democratic attitude; an anti-bourgeois vitalism; the exclusivity of the untimely; contempt for modernity, liberalism, the masses, and the press; the worship of heroes, genius, 'higher men'—these Nietzschean elements recur in different variations throughout the authors in this book. Their 'family likeness' (Wittgenstein) constitutes a significant continuity, one that has not been recognized as a coherent strand within the history of German Shakespeare reception.

'German theory', especially in the area of political theology, has met with markedly increased interest in recent Shakespeare studies.[74] This interest has almost exclusively focused on just two of the authors to be discussed here: Nietzsche and Schmitt. A figure of such vast cultural influence as Stefan George has been largely ignored in Shakespeare studies or at best mentioned cursorily in connection with his internationally best-known disciple, Ernst Kantorowicz. Joseph Goebbels, on

---

[71] Christopher Pye, 'Against Schmitt: Law, Aesthetics, and Absolutism in Shakespeare's *Winter's Tale*', *South Atlantic Quarterly* 108.1 (2009), 197–217 at 198. Pye refers in particular to the political theorist Chantal Mouffe and her *The Return of the Political* (London and New York: Verso, 1993), esp. 117–33.

[72] David Pan, 'Afterword: Historical Event and Mythic Meaning in Carl Schmitt's *Hamlet or Hecuba*', in Carl Schmitt, *Hamlet or Hecuba: The Intrusion of the Time Into the Play* (1956), trans. and ed. David Pan and Jennifer R. Rust (New York: Telos Press, 2009), 69–119 at 87.

[73] The cautionary disclaimers with which Steven Aschheim prefixes his study *The Nietzsche Legacy in Germany, 1890–1990* illustrate how much such objections are to be reckoned with.

[74] See, for example, Victoria Kahn, *The Future of Illusion: Political Theology and Early Modern Texts* (Chicago, IL and London: University of Chicago Press, 2014); Jennifer Ann Bates and Richard Wilson, eds, *Shakespeare and Continental Philosophy* (Edinburgh: Edinburgh University Press, 2014), which contains chapters on Schopenhauer, Nietzsche, Heidegger, Schmitt, and Arendt; Julia Reinhard Lupton, *Citizen-Saints: Shakespeare and Political Theology* (Chicago, IL and London: University of Chicago Press, 2005) and *Thinking with Shakespeare: Essays on Politics and Life* (Chicago, IL and London: University of Chicago Press, 2011); Hugh Grady, *Shakespeare's Universal Wolf: Studies in Early Modern Reification* (Oxford: Clarendon Press, 1996) and *Shakespeare and Impure Aesthetics* (Cambridge and New York: Cambridge University Press, 2009); Ewan Fernie, *The Demonic: Literature and Experience* (London and New York: Routledge, 2013); Richard Wilson, 'Hamlet in Weimar: Gordon Craig and the Nietzsche Archive', *Shakespeare-Jahrbuch* 146 (2010), 26–48, and 'The Exception: Force of Argument in Terry Eagleton's *William Shakespeare*', *Shakespeare* 8.1 (2012), 1–12.

the other hand, though certainly the subject of much attention, has never been studied in a Shakespearean context as the third-rate young writer struggling for a literary career before embarking on a political one.

It is a truism that what ideas respond to and draw on for inspiration is not just other ideas, but a wider range of influences: political, social, cultural, and psychological. These influences will be given particular attention here: the constellations that shaped, and were in turn shaped by, specific appropriations of Shakespeare. My aim is to bring more topical, 'local' knowledge to an international discussion, to show the embeddedness both of individual engagements with Shakespeare, and of a whole strand of Shakespeare reception, in German history from the 1870s to the 1950s and eventually 1989, the year of German reunification. The case studies that follow will, I believe, furnish a larger picture, though hardly a simple or homogeneous one. Thinking with and about Shakespeare will be grounded in the life worlds of those who did the thinking, and their involvement in the cataclysmic history of Germany in the twentieth century.

Chapter 1 explores, for the first time, Nietzsche's relation to Shakespeare in its entire development from the juvenilia to his final utterances in the 'madness letters' (*Wahnbriefe*). Hamlet makes a brief but significant appearance in *The Birth of Tragedy*, where Nietzsche reverses the conventional 'romantic' interpretation of, in Hegel's words, 'a beautiful inner soul which cannot make itself actual'.[75] Nietzsche's Hamlet is anything but feeble, his revulsion a product not of straying into error but of true knowledge gained from his unflinching gaze into the terrible abyss of existence. In his 'pessimism of *strength*', he resembles the Dionysian Greeks and becomes a pivotal figure in Nietzsche's scheme of history as well as a life-long figure of identification.[76]

No less than Hamlet, Julius Caesar occupied Nietzsche throughout his life. The epitome of 'higher men', he is cited whenever Nietzsche needs an example of his aristocratic ethos of strength, the benchmark of the 'great politics' (*große Politik*) which he pits against the liberalist decadence of the present. What has remained hitherto unrecognized is the extent to which Nietzsche's image of Caesar is shaped by Shakespeare's Roman tragedy. His engagement with it is traced here from a school essay on the character of Cassius (1863) to his autobiographical résumé in *Ecce Homo*, where he declares: 'When I seek my ultimate formula for *Shakespeare*, I always find only this: he conceived of the type of Caesar.'[77]

Chapters 2 and 3 are devoted to Stefan George, the most important German poet between 1900 and 1930, whose influence extended well beyond poetry. Fashioning himself as a cultural and spiritual leader, George was the herald of an esoteric political theology centred on the idea of a 'Secret Germany' or 'New Reich'. The power which Nietzsche had dreamt of in his isolation became a reality for George in the circle of young, exclusively male devotees, the *George-Kreis*, over which he ruled with absolute authority as 'Master'.

[75] Hegel, *Aesthetics*, vol. 1, 583–4.
[76] Cf. Peter Holbrook, 'Nietzsche's *Hamlet*', *Shakespeare Survey* 50 (1997), 171–86.
[77] 'Why I Am So Clever', §4, in Friedrich Nietzsche, *Ecce Homo*, in *Basic Writings*, 655–791 at 702.

Chapter 2 examines the role Shakespeare played in this highly charged world and how he was absorbed into its cultural and political ideas. Neither George's translations of the sonnets nor his disciple Gundolf's *Shakespeare and the German Spirit* (or Gundolf's two-volume study of Shakespeare's plays published in 1928) are overtly concerned with politics. But in their cultural opposition to the modern bourgeois world they are also manifestos of what could be described as a radical anti-politics of untimeliness. Chapter 3 traces the idea of the 'New Reich' in the early work of George's disciple Ernst Kantorowicz, and re-examines his later landmark study of *The King's Two Bodies* (1957) in its Georgean context.

Chapters 4 and 5 focus on the decade following Germany's defeat in 1918, when the 'shame peace' of Versailles and the despised parliamentary system of the new republic deepened the chasm between Germany as it actually was and Germany as—according to the radical Right—it should be. The duality from which the formula 'Germany is Hamlet' drew its political edge is dramatized in Joseph Goebbels's confessional novel *Michael* (1924/1929) whose 'riven' hero, a thinly disguised portrait of Goebbels the would-be writer, is endowed with Hamletian as well as Werther-like characteristics. As a counterpoint to the novel and other literary efforts of the future minister of propaganda, this chapter also examines two 'democratic' Hamlets from the opposite side of the political spectrum: Asta Nielsen's film *Hamlet—Drama of Vengeance* (1920) and Leopold Jessner's theatre production of *Hamlet* featuring Fritz Kortner in the title role (1926). They obviously do not belong in a 'right-wing tradition' but run counter to it. They are included here because they epitomize the modernist culture of Weimar which, especially in the case of Jessner, became the object of countless attacks, the enemy to be annihilated.

Carl Schmitt's diaries of the 1920s, as yet only partially published, contain one reference to the 'Germany is Hamlet' topos, but they teem with references to *Othello*. In Chapter 5 these references are explored for the first time. Schmitt's obsession with Othello is intensely personal, but also revealingly political. Othello is the 'noble Moor' and a figure of identification for both Schmitt himself ('I must always be the betrayed one') and the betrayed Germany. But he is also a figure of abhorrence and abjection, a black growth in his own body which he must expel if he wants to survive.

With Hitler's takeover, which was greeted enthusiastically by many, though not all, rightist intellectuals, a triumphant Germany once again shed its Hamletian affiliations.[78] Chapter 6 discusses how Shakespeare was seamlessly incorporated into the cultural assets of the new regime;[79] he had, after all, been seen as the exemplary Germanic, or Nordic, dramatist since the days of Herder. But there was also opposition to this seemingly 'natural' alliance. As one Shakespeare sceptic declared: Shakespeare was the undisputed 'king of drama in [the] whole epoch [...] of tragic individualism'; but that epoch was over, and therefore Shakespeare had 'nothing of relevance to say to us anymore'.[80]

---

[78] Cf. Hermann Burte, *Sieben Reden* (Strasbourg: Hünenburg, 1943), 9.

[79] See Anselm Heinrich, '"It Is Germany Where He Truly Lives": Nazi Claims on Shakespearean Drama', *New Theatre Quarterly* 28.3 (2012), 230–42.

[80] Curt Langenbeck, *Die Wiedergeburt des Dramas aus dem Geist der Zeit* (Munich: Albert Langen and Georg Müller, 1941), 36.

Hamlet's perilous situation at the court of Claudius, summed up in his sigh: 'But break, my heart, for I must hold my tongue' (*Ham.* 1.2.159), readily lent itself to analogies with the predicament of non-Nazi Germans under Hitler. The most famous Third Reich stage Hamlet, played by Gustaf Gründgens, has been interpreted as a coded response to this predicament. Chapter 7 examines Gründgens's performance in this light and relates it to the post-war controversy over 'Inner Emigration', which renewed the association of Hamlet with Germany and her collective guilt.

Following its discovery by Anglo-American critics in the early 2000s, Carl Schmitt's *Hamlet or Hecuba* (1956) has been claimed as a major contribution to Shakespearean analysis and political and cultural thought. It has been discussed in connection with the work of such major twentieth-century thinkers as Benjamin, Arendt, and Adorno. My task in Chapter 8 is to give a fuller view of what Schmitt was aiming at and why, giving more attention than has hitherto been done to his predicament in post-war Germany. For Schmitt, I argue, Hamlet became a primal image of the condition of the post-war world and of his own place, or rather displacement, in it. If Hamlet, as Schmitt believes, is a portrayal of the 'torn', 'unhappy Stuart' James I, then he also stands for 'the schism that has determined the fate of Europe'.[81] That Hamletian schism extends to the 'torn' Germany of 1848, the war-devastated Europe of 1918, and 'the whole Western world', as Schmitt claimed in 1956. Hamlet is part and parcel of the larger eschatological scheme of Schmittian history and of Schmitt's personal role within it. In Schmitt's literary thinking (as also shown in Chapter 5), the political is inextricably bound up with the personal. Shakespeare's tragic hero serves as a double for Schmitt's own role in Germany's recent past—at least as he himself wished to present it—trying to prevent the worst but failing.

The Epilogue (Chapter 9) argues that the fall of the Berlin Wall in 1989 once more—and perhaps for the last time—gave credence to the identification linking Hamlet and Germany. This was evinced in Heiner Müller's eight-hour production of *Hamlet/Machine* at Berlin's Deutsches Theater in 1989/90. My intention is not, of course, to align Heiner Müller, the 'heir of Brecht', with the tradition of rightist cultural critique traced in the previous chapters. Müller's historical pessimism is the reverse image of Schmitt's: while Schmitt saw the West doomed to suffer the fate of Hamlet, Müller sees that fate as epitomizing the fall of the socialist East. In his production, it is Fortinbras, not Hamlet, who becomes the iconic representative of the West: a star warrior of global capitalism and the gravedigger of utopian hope.

When Horace Howard Furness claimed in 1877 that history had 'proved once for all that Germany is not Hamlet', his declaration was clearly premature. The ghost of Hamlet was to haunt German history for at least another century.

---

[81] Schmitt, *Hamlet or Hecuba*, 52.

1

Highest Formula
Nietzsche's Shakespeare

I UNDER THE WALLS OF METZ

In early August 1870, three weeks into the Franco-Prussian war, Friedrich Nietzsche and his sister Elisabeth were taking a vacation in the Swiss mountain valley of Maderan. Her brother was writing 'a dissertation on the "*Dionysian Viewpoint*"', she recalls, and 'while he was reading this aloud to me one day, we were interrupted by several charges from an old cannon'.[1] As it turned out, a telegram had arrived announcing the German victories at Weissenburg and Wörth, and their landlord, a Swiss doctor with German sympathies, had fired a salute to celebrate the news.

> But there was also news of 'heavy losses' and my brother turned as white as a sheet. For a long time he walked up and down on the terrace with Mosengel, a Hamburg painter, and finally approached me with a solemn mien. I felt what was coming and tears sprang to my eyes: 'Lisbeth, what would you do if you were a man?' 'Why, I should go to war, of course; it would make no difference about me but you, Fritz!' and I broke off into an uncontrollable fit of weeping.[2]

Nietzsche,[3] who had been appointed professor at Basle University the previous year, applied for leave at once. That he had to give 'the little that lay within [his] capacity to the alms box of the fatherland', he wrote, no one would 'find as natural and commendable as a Swiss Board of Education'.[4] Leave was duly granted to the young patriot, but—on account of Swiss neutrality—only to serve as a medical orderly. '[H]e would have much preferred', Elisabeth writes, 'to go as a combatant.'[5]

---

[1] Elisabeth Förster-Nietzsche, ed., *The Nietzsche–Wagner Correspondence*, trans. Caroline V. Kerr (London: Duckworth, 1922), 60–1.

[2] Förster-Nietzsche, ed., *The Nietzsche–Wagner Correspondence*, 61.

[3] The German reference edition of Nietzsche's works, posthumous fragments, and correspondence is cited under the following abbreviations:

KGW = *Werke. Kritische Gesamtausgabe*, 47 vols, ed. Giorgio Colli and Mazzino Montinari (Berlin and New York: De Gruyter, 1967–);

KSA = *Sämtliche Werke. Kritische Studienausgabe*, 15 vols, ed. Giorgio Colli and Mazzino Montinari (Berlin and New York: De Gruyter, 1980);

KSB = *Sämtliche Briefe. Kritische Studienausgabe*, 8 vols, ed. Giorgio Colli and Mazzino Montinari (Munich: Deutscher Taschenbuch Verlag, 1986).

[4] Letter to Prof. Wilhelm Vischer, President of the Basle Education Board, 8 August 1870. KSB 3, no. 89, 133–4. Nietzsche had given up his Prussian citizenship when he took up his post in Basle.

[5] Elisabeth Förster-Nietzsche, *The Young Nietzsche*, trans. Anthony M. Ludovici (London: Heinemann, 1912), 233.

In high spirits, Nietzsche, his sister, and Mosengel set out by slow train to Erlangen near Nuremberg, where the two men planned to take part in a training course in nursing:

> Fritz was in splendid condition, radiant with health, and overflowing with life and the lust of action. [...] We even sang [...]. Finally we all grew so excited and exultant that we laughed until we cried. [...] Every time the train stopped, and this happened again and again, for we were travelling in the most erratic fashion, one of us would cry 'Order!' whereupon we would all sit as stiff and as solemn as idols; but as soon as the train started off again, the fun was renewed.[6]

The fun came to an end when carriages full of wounded soldiers were added to the train, and 'we felt quite crushed at the thought of having been led [...] to such childish frivolity'.[7]

After nine days of training at the 'Whalefish', a hotel-turned-military-hospital in Erlangen, Nietzsche moved on to the sites of the recently fought battles in Alsace. What he experienced there, and especially on a transport of wounded soldiers back to Germany, was harrowing. 'I had a ghastly cattle-truck', he wrote to Richard Wagner,

> in which there lay six severely wounded men, and I was the only person there to give them their food, to bandage their wounds, and to see to them generally. All of them had bones broken, many had four wounds, and in addition to that I observed that two had hospital gangrene. The fact that I was able to endure these pestilential vapours, and could even sleep and eat, now seems to me quite miraculous.[8]

No sooner had he delivered his charges to the hospital at Karlsruhe than he himself was taken ill. Diagnosed with severe dysentery and diphtheria, he was brought back to the Whalefish as a patient after only nine days in the field. A drastic regimen of 'opium and tannin enemas combined with mixtures of lunar caustic [silver nitrate]' restored him to a modicum of health, but his nerves remained frayed. His war experience, he wrote, enveloped him 'like a dismal fog', and

> for a while I kept hearing a never-ending noise of lament. My intention to return to the war has thus become impossible. I must be content to watch from a distance and suffer vicariously.[9]

'As to Germany's victories', he concludes his letter to Wagner, 'I would prefer not to speak of them; they are writings on the wall, to be understood by all nations.'[10] Nietzsche's patriotism, at any rate, appears to have survived his war experience undiminished.[11] 'When would one have ever walked more proudly than now', he

---

[6] Förster-Nietzsche, *The Young Nietzsche*, 233.

[7] Förster-Nietzsche, *The Young Nietzsche*, 234.

[8] Letter to Richard Wagner, 11 September 1870. Förster-Nietzsche, *The Young Nietzsche*, 236.

[9] Letter to Carl von Gersdorff, 20 October 1870. KSB 3, no. 103, 149.

[10] Letter to Wagner, 11 September 1870. Förster-Nietzsche, *The Young Nietzsche*, 237 (translation modified). 'Über die deutschen Siege möchte ich kein Wort sagen: das sind Feuerzeichen an der Wand, allen Völkern verständlich.' KSB 3, no. 100, 143–4.

[11] Neither did the suffering he had personally witnessed prevent him from celebrating war as the great purger. Cf., for example, the following passage from *Human, All Too Human*, entitled '*War*

wrote as German forces closed in on Paris, 'and what German, meeting another German, would not now [...] have cause [...] to smile?'[12] At the same time, the prospect of a triumphant nationalism under Prussian leadership caused him considerable disquiet. To Cosima Wagner he expressed his fears of an impending upsurge of 'militarism and pietism' that would 'weigh down on everything'.[13] In a letter to Carl von Gersdorff he was even more outspoken:

> As regards the conditions of culture in the immediate future I feel the deepest misgivings. If only we are not forced to pay too dearly for this huge national success in a quarter where I at least refuse to suffer any loss! Between ourselves: I regard the Prussia of today as a power full of the greatest danger for culture. [...] At times it is very hard, but we must be philosophical enough to keep our presence of mind in the midst of all this intoxication, so that no thief may come to rob or steal from us—what the greatest military feats or the highest national exaltation would in my opinion never replace.[14]

Back in Basle, the young professor resumed his academic work. 'I have sought refuge in my studies from all the terrible images my travelling has shown me',[15] he wrote to Wilhelm Vischer, Professor of Classics and President of the Basle Board of Education. Vischer was the man to whom Nietzsche owed his appointment, at the precocious age of twenty-four, to a professorship in Greek.[16] So it is perhaps not surprising that Nietzsche should have mentioned Greek metrics, an innocuous philological topic, as his main current interest rather than his larger and much bolder project, which might have caused his benefactor some alarm. This work in progress, interrupted by the clarion call of the fatherland, was of a kind undreamt of in Vischer's—or anyone else's—school philology, an undertaking that would

---

essential': 'It is vain rhapsodizing and sentimentality to continue to expect much [...] from mankind, once it has learned not to wage war. [...] [S]uch a highly cultivated, and therefore necessarily weary humanity as that of present-day Europe, needs not only wars but the greatest and most terrible wars (that is, occasional relapses into barbarism) in order not to forfeit to the means of culture its culture and its very existence.' Friedrich Nietzsche, *Human, All Too Human*, trans. Marion Faber and Stephen Lehmann, ed. Marion Faber (London: Penguin, 2004), 230–1 (§477). In a similar vein: '*War is the father of all good things*; war is also the father of good prose.' Nietzsche, *The Gay Science. With a Prelude in Rhymes and an Appendix of Songs*, trans. and ed. Walter A. Kaufmann (New York: Vintage, 1974), 145 (§92). Cf. also, for example: *On the Genealogy of Morals*, in *Basic Writings*, 437–599 at 532 (§2/24).

   12 KSB 3, no. 101, 145.
   13 Letter by Cosima Wagner, 24 October 1870. She also records her husband's response to Nietzsche's misgivings. *Friedrich Nietzsche. Chronik in Bildern und Texten*, ed. Raymond J. Benders and Stephan Oettermann (Munich and Vienna: Hanser, 2000), 231.
   14 Letter to Carl von Gersdorff, 7 November 1870. *Selected Letters of Friedrich Nietzsche*, trans. Anthony M. Ludovici, ed. Oscar Levy (Garden City, NY and Toronto: Doubleday, Page & Co., 1921), 71.
   15 Letter to Wilhelm Vischer, 19 October 1870. KSB 3, no. 102, 146.
   16 For a full documentation of Nietzsche's Basle professorship, see Johannes Stroux, *Nietzsches Professur in Basel* (Jena: Frommannsche Buchhandlung, 1925). At the time of his appointment Nietzsche had not yet completed his doctorate. Notwithstanding the young man's 'formal insufficiency' (34), Vischer appointed him on the glowing recommendation Nietzsche received from Friedrich Ritschl (1806–76), one of the foremost classicists of his age. Nietzsche, Ritschl wrote, 'is the idol and (without wanting to be) the leader of all the young philologists here in Leipzig' (33). Nietzsche was appointed *professor extraordinarius* in February 1869 and promoted to *professor ordinarius* (full professor) on 9 April 1870.

carry Nietzsche beyond the confines of his discipline and eventually beyond academia altogether.

Two preliminary airings of this project, his public lectures on 'Greek Music Drama' (18 January 1870) and 'Socrates and Tragedy' (1 February 1870), had already caused 'horror and misunderstandings'[17] among his Basle audience. They formed the nucleus of what was to become Nietzsche's first book, *The Birth of Tragedy* (1871), his exposition of the Dionysian and the Apollonian as the two opposing and complementary forces fundamental to Greek culture. Looking back at this work from the vantage point of his 'Attempt at a Self-Criticism', added as a preface to the second edition of 1886, Nietzsche calls it 'an impossible book [...] badly written, ponderous, embarrassing, image-mad and image-confused, sentimental, in places saccharine to the point of effeminacy, uneven in tempo, without the will to logical cleanliness [...]'.[18] Elsewhere he concedes that his 'firstborn' now 'smells offensively Hegelian'.[19]

Yet Nietzsche does not disclaim the continuing validity of its central question and core ideas, nor its crucial relevance to the development of its author:

> Whatever may be at the bottom of this questionable book, it must have been an exceptionally significant and fascinating question, and deeply personal at that: the time in which it was written, in *spite* of which it was written, bears witness to that—the exciting time of the Franco-Prussian War of 1870/71. As the thunder of the battle of Wörth was rolling over Europe, the muser and riddle-friend who was to be father of this book sat somewhere in an Alpine nook, very bemused and beriddled, hence very concerned and yet unconcerned, and wrote down his thoughts about the *Greeks*—the core of the strange and almost inaccessible book to which this belated preface (or postscript) shall now be added. A few weeks later—and he himself was to be found under the walls of Metz, still wedded to the question marks that he had placed after the alleged 'cheerfulness' of the Greeks and of Greek art. Eventually, in that month of profoundest suspense when the peace treaty was being debated at Versailles, he, too, attained peace with himself and, slowly convalescing from an illness contracted at the front, completed the final draft of *The Birth of Tragedy out of the Spirit of Music*.[20]

Nietzsche's account of how the book came into being not just during but 'in *spite* of' the turbulences of the Franco-Prussian War presents an intriguing blend of immersion in, and detachment from, those historical events. Whether brooding in Alpine seclusion or 'under the walls of Metz', the young author, as portrayed in retrospect, seems curiously self-absorbed amidst the cataclysmic changes engulfing him. The end of the war and the end of his intellectual struggle happily coincide, a kind of double victory for himself and his country. But the parallel is ambiguous: we cannot quite decide whether Nietzsche lays his youthful work on the altar of Germany's national triumph or whether he matches it against that triumph as a landmark of equal significance. The latter interpretation would look forward to the euphoric egotism of *Ecce Homo* (1888); the former would be perhaps more in keeping with

---

[17] KSB 3, no. 58, 95.
[18] *The Birth of Tragedy*, in *Basic Writings*, 1–144 at 19 ('Attempt at a Self-Criticism', §3).
[19] *Ecce Homo*, 726 ('The Birth of Tragedy', §1).
[20] *The Birth of Tragedy*, 17 ('Attempt at a Self-Criticism', §1).

how his younger self actually felt, despite his misgivings about Prussian philistinism, at the founding moment of Germany's 'belated nationhood'.[21]

II DIONYSIAN DANE

Whatever enthusiasm Nietzsche may have had for national unity soon evaporated: In 1888 he writes: '"German spirit": for the past eighteen years a contradiction in terms.'[22] This sentiment postdates the writing of *The Birth of Tragedy* but is arguably foreshadowed in it. The whole drift of the book sets it radically apart from Wilhelminian triumphalism. Just when his country is embarking on a course of self-congratulatory optimism, Nietzsche preaches the virtue of pessimism. Just when Germany proves, 'once for all', that it is no longer Hamlet, Nietzsche elects Hamlet as the only true modern equivalent of Dionysian man.

In their study of *The Birth of Tragedy*, M. S. Silk and J. P. Stern make some useful clarifications:[23]

> The young classical scholar writes a book about tragedy that looks outwards beyond the tragedies of his beloved Greeks. Its further target, however, is not later drama, but a philosophy of life. Though he makes a determined attempt to see tragic form as a criterion of the tragic outlook, the two are separable, and it is ultimately the outlook, not the form, that concerns him. This is not in the end a genre study; and it is a symptom of this fact, as much as a mark of his Hellenocentricity, that he should have devised a construct so inescapably Greek that detailed discussion of other drama in its terms seems, to say the least, unreal. (280)

Nietzsche's categories 'have no temporal [i.e. historical] connection with the world of Shakespeare or with any tragic world except the Greek', and thus '[h]is thoughts on other drama, all in all, are perfunctory' (280). Shakespeare, who is, as Silk and Stern note, 'invoked with the utmost respect', cannot really play a major part in Nietzsche's reflections. For if his work 'is any kind of model for Nietzsche, it presents [...] obvious and embarrassing differences from the Greek' in having 'no music, except incidentally, and certainly no musical origin [...], no chorus [...] and [...] no comparable mytho-religious basis' (280).

> It is a sign of the remoteness of Nietzsche's mythic apparatus from Shakespeare that only once are the two directly associated, and even then in a very restricted way: Nietzsche compares the Dionysiac state of knowledge and lethargy with Hamlet's own (§7), but offers no discussion of the play itself in these terms. (280–1)

Silk and Stern also point to the fact that in the preliminary writings and notes for his book Nietzsche was far from clear on which side of the great divide in his historical scheme to place Shakespeare. Was he sicklied o'er with the pale cast of

---

[21] See Introduction, section III.

[22] *Twilight of the Idols*, in *The Portable Nietzsche*, 463–563 at 469 ('Maxims and Arrows', §23).

[23] M. S. Silk and J. P. Stern, *Nietzsche on Tragedy* (Cambridge: Cambridge University Press, 1981). Page references in brackets are to this text.

Socratic reason, Nietzsche's prime culprit for the decline of tragedy and thus ultimately for the life-denying rationalism of modernity?[24] Given that the lecture on 'Greek Music Drama' classes Shakespeare as a descendant of New Comedy,[25] the decadent genre that arose when the ascent of Socratic questioning had ousted the tragic spirit, this seems the only possible conclusion. And yet the same lecture also claims that 'English tragedy' (which can only mean Shakespeare) is 'much more impetuous, more Dionysian' than the Greek.[26]

But does Nietzsche's thought on Shakespeare warrant being dismissed as 'perfunctory'? In regard to drama *qua* drama, drama as genre, arguably yes. But hardly in regard to what Silk and Stern call the 'further target' of Nietzsche's book, its 'philosophy of life', its 'tragic outlook'. Here, Shakespeare's most famous dramatic character plays a far from perfunctory role. His entry is preceded by Nietzsche's explanation of the Dionysian chorus of satyrs as the foundation on which tragedy grew, and a discussion of its effect on the Greek audience:

> I believe, the Greek man of culture felt himself nullified in the presence of the satyric chorus; [...] state and society and, quite generally, the gulfs between man and man give way to an overwhelming feeling of unity leading back to the very heart of nature. [...] With this chorus the profound Hellene, uniquely susceptible to the tenderest and deepest suffering, comforts himself, having looked boldly right into the terrible destructiveness of so-called world history as well as the cruelty of nature, and being in danger of longing for a Buddhistic negation of the will. Art saves him, and through art—life.[27]

The ecstasy of this Dionysian dissolution of boundaries 'contains [...] a *lethargic* element'. A 'chasm of oblivion separates' it from 'the worlds of everyday reality'.[28]

---

[24] Cf. *The Birth of Tragedy*, 93 (§15): '[...] the influence of Socrates, down to the present moment and even into all future time, has spread over posterity like a shadow that keeps growing in the evening sun [...].'

[25] '[A] Greek would recognize in our tragedy almost nothing corresponding to his tragedy; although he would certainly guess that the entire structure and fundamental character of Shakespeare's tragedy is borrowed from what he would call *New Comedy*. In fact, it is from *this* source, after incredible stretches of time, that the Romanic-Germanic mystery- or morality-play, and finally Shakespearian tragedy, arises: in a similar way that, in its external form, the genealogical relationship of Shakespeare's stage to that of the New Attic Comedy cannot be overlooked.' Nietzsche, *Das griechische Musikdrama/ The Greek Music Drama* (1870), trans. Paul Bishop (New York: Contra Mundum Press, 2013), 2. At *The Birth of Tragedy*, 92 (§14), Nietzsche speaks of 'the *destruction* of the chorus, whose phases follow one another with alarming rapidity in Euripides, Agathon, and the New Comedy. Optimistic [Socratic] dialectic drives *music* out of tragedy with the scourge of its syllogisms; that is, it destroys the essence of tragedy [...].'

[26] Nietzsche, *Das griechische Musikdrama/The Greek Music Drama*, 26. In a note from the same period, Shakespeare appears as the 'musical Socrates', elsewhere as the 'utterly Dionysiac' successor to Sophocles. *Nachgelassene Fragmente* [Posthumous Fragments] 1870 7[131], KGW III/3, 201; NF-1870 7[134], KGW III/3, 201; NF-1871 9[132], KGW III/3, 334. Roger Paulin suggests that Nietzsche, in a 'failed attempt to bridge the worlds of Greek and Wagnerian drama', had planned 'a middle section on Shakespeare' to be included in *The Birth of Tragedy* (*The Critical Reception of Shakespeare in Germany*, 457). Peter Holbrook cogently argues for a 'profound kinship' between Nietzsche and Shakespeare because Nietzsche 'was fundamentally a dramatic thinker, apprehending the world through notions of character and action'. Holbrook, 'Nietzsche's Shakespeare', in *Shakespeare and Continental Philosophy*, ed. Bates and Wilson, 76–93 at 76.

[27] *The Birth of Tragedy*, 59 (§7).   [28] *The Birth of Tragedy*, 59 (§7).

But only for as long as it lasts. When the Dionysian experience is over and reality returns, revulsion ensues:

> In this sense the Dionysian man resembles Hamlet: both have once looked truly into the essence of things, they have *gained knowledge*, and nausea inhibits action; for their action could not change anything in the eternal nature of things; they feel it to be ridiculous or humiliating that they should be asked to set right a world that is out of joint. Knowledge kills action; action requires the veils of illusion: that is the doctrine of Hamlet, not that cheap wisdom of Jack the Dreamer who reflects too much and, as it were, from an excess of possibilities does not get around to action. Not reflection, no—true knowledge, an insight into the horrible truth, outweighs any motive for action, both in Hamlet and in the Dionysian man. [...] Conscious of the truth he has once seen, man now sees everywhere only the horror or absurdity of existence; now he understands what is symbolic in Ophelia's fate; now he understands the wisdom of the sylvan god, Silenus; he is nauseated.[29]

In nineteenth-century theories of tragedy and the tragic character, *Hamlet* regularly epitomizes the modern or romantic type of the genre, just as *Antigone* or *Oedipus Rex* typify the tragedy of classical antiquity. For Hegel, the hallmark of romantic or Shakespearean tragedy is its representation of '[t]he subjective infinity of man in himself'.[30] Hegel's Hamlet 'is a beautiful and noble heart; not inwardly weak at all, but, without a powerful feeling for life, in the feebleness of his melancholy he strays distressed into error' (583). Nietzsche's Hamlet, by contrast, is anything but feeble, his revulsion a product of true knowledge, not of straying into error, and his feeling for life, life's terrible essence, could not be more powerful. Instead of a Werther-like softness and 'the inactivity of a beautiful inner soul which cannot make itself actual or engage in the relationships of his present world' (a 'Jack the Dreamer'; 584), Nietzsche's Hamlet directs his unflinching gaze into the terrible abyss of existence. His inaction bespeaks not his inability to come to a 'firm decision' (584), but his contempt for action, his 'pessimism of *strength*'.[31] Nietzsche's Hamlet is thus emphatically anti-romantic.

At the same time, he is also unmistakably romantic. As the eighteenth-century aphorist Christoph Georg Lichtenberg remarked, 'To do the opposite of something is also a form of imitation.'[32] Thus, precisely by flaunting his opposition to the received romantic image of Hamlet, Nietzsche inevitably perpetuates it. If Hamlet's predicament, his knowledge and his revulsion, links him to Nietzsche's 'profound Hellene' waking from 'the rapture of the Dionysian state',[33] it also makes him the representative modern man under the thumb of Socratic rationalism to whom this ecstasy is no longer available, but who—solitary among his

---

[29] *The Birth of Tragedy*, 60 (§7).

[30] Hegel, *Aesthetics*, vol. 1, 576. Cf. Introduction, section II. Page references in brackets in the text are to this edition.

[31] *The Birth of Tragedy*, 17 ('Attempt at a Self-Criticism', §1).

[32] Christoph Georg Lichtenberg, *Aphorisms*, trans. and ed. R. J. Hollingdale (London: Penguin, 1990), 64. Lichtenberg (1742–99) was one of the very few German writers Nietzsche held in great esteem and later became an inspiration for his own aphoristic style.

[33] *The Birth of Tragedy*, 59 (§7).

contemporaries—is privileged and cursed to feel the loss. Not only does he know 'the terrible truth'; he also, like the poet-prophet in Coleridge's 'Kubla Khan', has 'drunk the milk of Paradise',[34] or can at least, like the author of *The Birth of Tragedy*, envision such Dionysian drunkenness.

The sense of loss and concomitant yearning for the 'overwhelming feeling of unity leading back to the very heart of nature'[35] are essentially romantic. Nietzsche readily admits as much in his 1886 self-critique:

> But, my dear sir, what in the world is romantic if *your* book isn't? Can deep hatred against 'the Now', against 'reality' and 'modern ideas' be pushed further than in your artist's metaphysics [*Artisten-Metaphysik*]? believing sooner in the Nothing, sooner in the devil than in 'the Now'? Is it not a deep bass of wrath and the lust for destruction that we hear humming underneath all of your contrapuntal vocal art […], a furious resolve against everything that is 'now' […].[36]

Humming underneath, Nietzsche's disgust with the present recalls Hamlet's 'old mole', an unlayed, unlayable, ghost.[37] On the Nietzschean stage of history, set up not only to reveal the birth of tragedy but also to inaugurate its rebirth in the romantic music-drama of Richard Wagner, the ghost of an idealized past is conjured up to shake the complacency of the present.

However brief the appearance of Hamlet in the book, it is nothing short of pivotal. The two states of history Nietzsche plays off against each other converge and collide in Hamlet. Hamlet embodies the link, but also the gap and the extreme tension between modern and ancient, the Socratic and the Dionysian, rationality and 'life'. In projecting these tensions at the heart of his philosophy onto Hamlet, Nietzsche turns Shakespeare's melancholy prince into something like an *alter ego*.[38] Hamlet shares, and serves to define, the philosopher's decentred position as the modern thinker looking through and beyond the calamities of modernity.

The romantic anti-romanticism of his portrayal also reflects the conflicted nature of the book itself—part antidote to, part symptom of, the decadence it

---

[34] Samuel Taylor Coleridge, 'Kubla Khan', in *The Major Works*, ed. H. J. Jackson (Oxford and New York: Oxford University Press, 1985), 102–4 at ll. 51–5:

> Weave a circle round him thrice,
> And close your eyes with holy dread,
> For he on honey-dew hath fed,
> And drunk the milk of Paradise.

[35] *The Birth of Tragedy*, 59 (§7).

[36] *The Birth of Tragedy*, 25 ('Attempt at a Self-Criticism', §7).

[37] 'Well said, old mole: canst work i'th' earth so fast?' (*Ham.* 1.5.164). The mole-motif is very familiar to Nietzsche. In a postcard he sent to his sister Elisabeth from Nice (11 November 1885) he calls himself 'the Hamletian mole' ('der hamletische Maulwurf', KSB 7, no. 644, 106). Only hinted at in the preface of 1886, the image occurs, fully fledged, two years previously in *Beyond Good and Evil* (1884) where Nietzsche mocks the tame skeptics and their alarm at a radical nihilism 'that does not merely say No […], but […] *does* No': '[A]nd even *Hamlet* is now prescribed by the doctors of the day against the "spirit" and its underground rumblings. "Aren't our ears filled with wicked noises as it is?" asks the skeptic as a friend of quiet, and almost as a kind of security police; "this subterranean No is terrible! Be still at last, you pessimistic moles!"' *Beyond Good and Evil. Prelude to a Philosophy of the Future*, in *Basic Writings*, 179–435 at 318–19 (§208).

[38] See Holbrook, 'Nietzsche's *Hamlet*'.

castigates. Although overtly unconcerned with politics, Nietzsche's cultural critique in *The Birth of Tragedy* is by no means apolitical. Where Hegel saw the spirit of world history (*Weltgeist*) reaching its telos in the Prussian state, Nietzsche sees hope for spiritual rebirth only in radical detachment from that state and its self-important philistinism. Although he 'does not speak for a broad movement [but] walks in ever greater isolation', Nietzsche thus 'becomes one of the leading spokesmen of the intellectual opposition against the new Reich'. Nietzsche 'terminated the union of thought and political action which conditioned German history at the time of the nationalistic unification movement: Art and philosophy turned away from the young nation-state to build their own domain.'[39] In Hamlet, the disaffected outsider at the boisterous court of Denmark, this turning away finds its iconic embodiment.

III BEGINNINGS

Nietzsche's earliest mention of 'Sheagspeare'—just the name, uncommented—occurs in a list of authors and essay topics he compiled as a fourteen-year-old schoolboy in a notebook in 1858.[40] Three years later 'Sheakspeare 9 volumes' heads the list of books that make up his 'library'.[41] Yet another list, another three years later, cites 'Gervinus, Shakesp<eare>' after Emerson and 'Bernhardy's literary history'[42] among his 'most read' books of 1863.[43] Given Shakespeare's prominent place in his canon,[44] it is not surprising that the young Nietzsche should have greeted the Bard's tercentenary with a celebratory poem of his own. Unusual for a birthday tribute, but all the more typical for the German brand of Bardolatry, this takes the death, not the birth, of Shakespeare as its starting point, only to stage, all the more spectacularly, his rebirth.[45] In ten stanzas of *ottava rima* (the form of Byron's *Don Juan*[46]), the poem recounts Shakespeare's afterlife, beginning with his burial in an obscure, mossy grave. His fame faded away, his theatre closed down and his plays denounced as the devil's work, he can only be performed at night and

---

[39] Theodor Schieder, 'Nietzsche and Bismarck', trans. Alexandra Hendee, *The Historian* 29.4 (1967), 584–604 at 586.

[40] Friedrich Nietzsche, *Jugendschriften, 1854–1861* (1933), ed. Hans Joachim Mette (Munich: dtv, 1994), 47.

[41] Nietzsche, *Jugendschriften, 1854–1861*, 250.

[42] Gottfried Bernhardy (1800–75), professor of classics at Halle, was the author of a much-reprinted history of Greek literature (1836).

[43] In later years, Gervinus comes in for quite a bashing ('Der platte und dumme Gervinus', 1869, 1[37], KGW III/3, 16). As early as 1867/8 Nietzsche takes a dim view of secondary literature: '[L]iterary studies are overdone. One should read Shakespeare rather than about him.' *Schriften der Studenten- und Militärzeit, 1864–1868* (1935), ed. Hans Joachim Mette and Karl Schlechta (Munich: dtv, 1994), 338.

[44] Such prominence is by no means unusual at the time. Reading Shakespeare (in the canonized Schlegel–Tieck translation) was part and parcel of an educated upbringing.

[45] The poem, dated April 1864, is untitled. Nietzsche, *Jugendschriften, 1861–64* (1934), ed. Hans Joachim Mette (Munich: dtv, 1994), 412–14.

[46] In *Ecce Homo* (701, 'Why I Am So Clever', §4) Nietzsche declares his early affinity to Byron: 'I must be profoundly related to *Byron's* Manfred: all these abysses I found in myself; at the age of thirteen I was ripe for this work.'

display his 'long-missed beautiful dream'[47] in secret. The Puritans with their 'stern souls' and 'self-inflicted hardships' would rather kill a king than watch one on stage. 'These people are too serious. So art takes flight / To France where it turns hollow, opulent and light'. The restoration of Charles II restores the stage but imbues it with a foreign taste. The periwigged hero, daintily footing it, 'Ne'er raging, always self-possessed / In verses stiff his heart expressed'. So Shakespeare continues to lie 'encoffined' and forgotten until Garrick comes along and, 'gloriously crushing his countrymen's apathy', initiates his revival. Like mountain-peaks struck by the rays of the morning sun while fog still encloses the valleys, 'the highest spirits' are the first to absorb this new light, which travels far as well as fast: the peak spirits are not to be found in England but, unsurprisingly, in Germany—in Lessing and Herder. Emulating Herder's *Sturm und Drang* style,[48] Nietzsche stages his Shakespearean sunrise as a mighty clash of elemental forces ('The nightly fogs more wildly surging / Shot through by flashing light wave after wave . . .'). Topping all this, the last stanza turns Shakespeare into a veritable Christ, his revival becoming a resurrection. The tomb, long sealed up by the rock of prejudice, is now open. He who was dead is living, 'walking miraculously among us'. And to this no longer dead, but living Shakespeare the young congratulator dedicates his poem.

Nietzsche's poetic effusion rehearses a conventional narrative: although it differs favourably from more chauvinistic versions of the German Shakespeare myth in unstintingly acknowledging the pioneering role of Garrick. It is a romantic tribute to Shakespeare, both in style and imagery and in its obligatory refutation of stilted French neo-classicism.[49] And it is located in a romantic context. Immediately preceding and immediately following it in the manuscripts are two more exercises in romantic sensibility. One is a kind of prose poem in which the speaker, somewhat as in Shelley's 'Ode to the West Wind', begs the thunderstorm to lift him out of his despondency ('And a voice sounded: "Be renewed!"');[50] the other a poem entitled 'Night Thought' in which the solitary speaker, musing on a lost love in his moonlit study, finds consolation in his books ('you thick tomes / You bellies full of wisdom'), especially in his Shakespeare: 'Friendly, I take you in my hand— / You gave me comfort, gave me wine and bread, / My Shakespeare, when pain cast me down [. . .] You remained true to me, deep vision!'[51]

---

[47] 'Dream' interestingly anticipates what would become the defining feature of Apollonian art, the art of representation (*Vorstellung*), in *The Birth of Tragedy*.

[48] 'If any man brings to mind that tremendous image of one "seated high atop some craggy eminence, whirlwinds, tempest, and the roaring sea at his feet, but with the flashing skies about his head," that man is Shakespeare!' Johann Gottfried Herder, *Shakespeare*, trans. and ed. Gregory Moore (Princeton, NJ: Princeton University Press, 2008), 1.

[49] After his rejection of Richard Wagner and his 'incurable romanticism' (*Human, All Too Human*, 5, 'Preface', §1) Nietzsche does a complete about-face, favouring classicistic French restraint over Romantic excess.

[50] *Jugendschriften, 1861–64*, 415–16. This text is a poetic variation on the theme of 'moods' ('*Über Stimmungen*') which Nietzsche treats essayistically in another text of the same month (April 1864): 'Be welcome, dear moods, wonderful changes of a stormy soul, manifold as nature herself, only more magnificent than nature because you [. . .] always strive upwards; [. . .] I am this moment in a different mood than when I began writing this.' *Jugendschriften, 1861–64*, 406–8 at 408.

[51] *Jugendschriften, 1861–64*, 409–11 at 410.

This is the Shakespeare of Romantic interiority, the Shakespeare who, like no other author, makes the reader feel 'understood' by what he reads. This understanding inevitably culminates in Hamlet, whose 'nighted colour' has encloaked the night thoughts of generations of aspiring poets since the 1770s. The Hamlet of this tradition, most influentially portrayed in Goethe's *Wilhelm Meister*,[52] harbours the sensitive soul of a poet; and consequently every sensitive poetic soul finds in himself a Hamlet. We have seen that Nietzsche came to reject this standard Romantic version of Hamlet in *The Birth of Tragedy*. We will also see, however, that he remained susceptible to the identificatory potential of Shakespeare's tragic prince. But first we must turn to another play and another player, or rather, set of players.

IV NOBLEST ROMAN

Nietzsche's attention to Shakespeare, though highly selective, is not focused on *Hamlet* alone. 'When I seek my ultimate formula for *Shakespeare*', he writes in *Ecce Homo*, 'I always find only this: he conceived of the type of Caesar.'[53] In *The Gay Science*, he calls *Julius Caesar* Shakespeare's 'best tragedy'.[54] *Hamlet*, by contrast, in a fragment from around the same time, is declared 'a failed play. I daresay its author would laughingly admit as much if I told him to his face.'[55] This verdict is not final (what Nietzschean verdict, one could ask, ever is?) and perhaps not even all that serious—more like a gleeful slap at a particularly sacred cow of bourgeois culture. When it comes to the final stock-taking of his favourite reading,[56] *Hamlet* is firmly back in Nietzsche's pantheon. But *Julius Caesar* seems never to have been banished from it. Of all of Shakespeare's plays it is the one that has the most enduring presence in Nietzsche's writings, first to last.

'Read Shakespeare', he writes in a letter to his sister, 'he is full of such strong men—rough, hard, powerful, men of granite. It is in men like these that our age is so poor.'[57] Hardly evocative of Hamlet, these characters are much closer to 'the Caesar type', or indeed to his Renaissance namesake, Cesare Borgia, whom Nietzsche came to extol, almost to the point of apotheosis, in the final years of his life.[58] Shakespeare's Rome becomes for Nietzsche the site where two exemplary antitheses to the modern age—Antiquity and the Renaissance—converge. The letter to his sister reflects the contemporary view of Shakespeare as a man of the Renaissance and

---

[52] See Introduction, section II.   [53] *Ecce Homo*, 702 ('Why I Am So Clever', §4).
[54] *The Gay Science*, 150 (§98).
[55] NF-1883 7[68], KGW VII/1, 273. The fragment begins: 'Taking Hamlet for a peak of the human spirit—I call that having a modest opinion of both spirit and peaks.' Nietzsche is anticipating T. S. Eliot's famous dictum: 'So far from being Shakespeare's masterpiece, the play is most certainly an artistic failure.' Eliot, 'Hamlet and His Problems', 940.
[56] *Ecce Homo*, 696–703 ('Why I Am So Clever', §§3–4).
[57] Letter to Elisabeth Nietzsche, November 1883, KSB 6, 452.
[58] Aldo Venturelli, 'Nietzsches Renaissance-Bild zwischen Erasmus und Cesare Borgia', Chapter 4 of his *Kunst, Wissenschaft und Geschichte bei Nietzsche. Quellenkritische Untersuchungen* (Berlin and New York: De Gruyter, 2003), 127–35 at 127.

creator of strong, even ruthless Renaissance characters (*Gewaltmenschen*). Nietzsche acclaims these strengths in order to disparage the weakness and life-negating morality of the present. 'The morality of the stage', by contrast, is life-affirming and thus, by conventional standards, not morality at all. It is most fully embodied in the Renaissance dramatist Shakespeare:

> Whoever thinks that Shakespeare's theatre has a moral effect, and that the sight of Macbeth irresistibly repels one from the evil of ambition, is in error: and he is again in error if he thinks Shakespeare himself felt as he feels. He who is really possessed by raging ambition beholds this its image with *joy*; and if the hero perishes by his passion this is precisely the sharpest spice in the hot draught of this joy. Can the poet have felt otherwise? How royally, and not at all like a rogue, does his ambitious man pursue his course from the moment of his great crime! [...] Do you suppose that Tristan and Isolde are preaching *against* adultery when they both perish by it? This would be to stand the poets on their head: they, and especially Shakespeare, are enamoured of the passions as such and not least of their death-welcoming moods [...] The tragic poet [...] cries [out]: 'it is the stimulant of stimulants, this exciting, changing, dangerous, gloomy and often sun-drenched existence. It is an *adventure* to live [...]'—He speaks thus out of a restless, vigorous age which is half-drunk and stupefied by its excess of blood and energy—out of a wickeder age than ours is [...][59]

In its general drift, the passage chimes with a *Zeitgeist* of cultural discontent that fuelled the contemporary strength-cults of 'Caesarism' and 'Renaissancism'.[60] What gives Nietzsche's admiration for Shakespeare's *Julius Caesar* a personal slant is his early focus on the conspirators, Brutus and, notably, Cassius. A school essay written in May 1863 offers 'A Character Description of Cassius from Julius Caesar'.[61] It undertakes a first foray into the psychology of *ressentiment*.[62] Cassius 'seems always to be wavering over what he hates more: tyranny or the tyrant. Surely he hates both, but the oppressive feeling of being up against a higher, more magnificent personality [...] incites his choleric temper to implacable resentment'

---

[59] Friedrich Nietzsche, *Daybreak: Thoughts on the Prejudices of Morality* (1881), trans. R. J. Hollingdale, ed. Maudemarie Clark and Brian Leiter (Cambridge: Cambridge University Press, 1997), 243–4. A precursor of this passage occurs, three years earlier under the title 'Shakespeare the Moralist': 'Shakespeare reflected a great deal on passions, and by temperament probably had very easy access to many of them (dramatists in general are rather wicked people).' Needless to say, 'wicked' is a compliment here. *Human, All Too Human*, 118 (§176).

[60] On Caesarism see, for example, Peter Baehr and Melvin Richter, eds, *Dictatorship in History and Theory: Bonapartism, Caesarism, and Totalitarianism* (Cambridge and New York: Cambridge University Press, 2004). The foundational text for the late nineteenth-century cult of the Renaissance is Jacob Burckhardt, *The Civilization of the Renaissance in Italy* (1860), trans. S. G. C. Middlemore, ed. Peter Murray, with an introduction by Peter Burke (London: Penguin, 2004). Nietzsche admired and became acquainted with Burckhardt, who held a professorship at Basle from 1858 to 1893. The two conversed and maintained an extensive correspondence though Burckhardt remained distanced from Nietzsche's developing philosophy. In a letter to another correspondent (Ludwig Pastor, 13 January 1896) Burckhardt declares: 'I have never conversed with him [Nietzsche] about the "*Gewaltmensch*".' Jacob Burckhardt, *Briefe*, vol. 10, ed. Max Burckhardt (Basle and Stuttgart: Schwabe, 1986), 263–4 at 264.

[61] *Jugendschriften, 1861–64*, 193–200. Page references in brackets are to this text.

[62] A related school essay written in September 1863 tackles the question: 'Can the Envious Man Ever Be Truly Happy?' *Jugendschriften, 1861–64*, 269–72.

(193). But the one 'redeeming trait of his nature' is his 'deep and sublime love for his friend' Brutus (194). Shakespeare's 'deep insight into the law of elective affinity' (193) stands out in the creation of these two complementary characters. Not the murder of Caesar, not the forum scene, but the crisis of their friendship in Act 4 is the culminating scene of the play (197). With a psychological acumen premonitory of his later work, Nietzsche fixes on Cassius, not Brutus, as the consummate embodiment of friendship, a friendship so absolute as to make this hard-boiled caustic soft and vulnerable:

> [H]e breaks down, this strong character, when the only sweetness in his life, his friend, seems lost to him [in the quarrel scene, 4.3] [...] He offers his heart, 'richer than Pluto's mine, richer than gold', to his erstwhile friend. And this is no exaggeration of the moment; the truly humane element in his character is a deeply buried but richly fertile root. His love for his only friend is tantamount to his love of the world, as Solanio says of Antonio in *The Merchant of Venice*. (197–8)

The reconciliation of the friends, Nietzsche's school essay continues, is followed by 'one of those masterstrokes' which Shakespeare seems to have 'overheard directly from nature':

> A poet enters who wants to reconcile the generals, a seemingly useless, superfluous, random figure. I could never understand his appearance and even now I am not sure that I have properly grasped it.
>
> Just as friends after a serious quarrel seek to outdo each other in mutual complaisances, so here the two, as it were, change their nature, each speaking in the spirit of the other. The art-loving Brutus sends the poet packing, while Cassius, the rough, stern soldier, apologizes and pleads for him. This is a poignant touch, and [...] [t]he following scenes in which the two souls, as it were, immerge in each other [...] appear to me like the last part of a symphony in which the same sounds that stormed and flashed in the Allegro are sounded again—now like a sad sigh of remembrance, now transfigured into the calmer tones of a heart come to rest. (198–9)

How deeply Shakespeare's fated pair captured the imagination of Nietzsche and his small circle of friends emerges in a letter he received in March 1866 from Carl von Gersdorff on the eve of the Austro-Prussian War. Gersdorff ends with Brutus's parting words before the battle of Philippi: 'If we do meet again, why, we shall smile; / If not, why then this parting was well made' (*JC* 5.1.121–2).[63] Nietzsche's reply on 7 April 1866 concludes: '[I]t is agreed, when we meet again, we shall smile—and rightly so.'[64]

Friendship is again the cue when, more than a decade later, Brutus makes a re-entry in one of Nietzsche's most telling comments on Shakespeare (*The Gay Science*, 1882). This time, however, the friendship is not between Brutus and Cassius but between Brutus and Caesar; and, lofty as it is, it is introduced only to

---

[63] 'Sehn wir uns wieder, lächeln wir gewiß, / Wo nicht, ist wahrlich wohlgetan dieß Scheiden (Shakes<peare> Jul. Caesar).' KGW I/3, 88.

[64] *Selected Letters of Friedrich Nietzsche*, trans. and ed. Christopher Middleton (Indianapolis: Hackett, 1996), 13.

be surpassed by the still loftier virtue that chooses freedom over friendship even at the price of murder:

> *In honour of Shakespeare.*—I could not say anything more beautiful in praise of Shakespeare, *the man*, than this: he believed in Brutus and did not cast one speck of suspicion upon this type of virtue. It was to him that he devoted his best tragedy—it is still called by the wrong name—to him and to the most awesome quintessence of a lofty morality. Independence of the soul!—that is at stake here. No sacrifice can be too great for that: one must be capable of sacrificing one's dearest friend for it, even if he should also be the most glorious human being, an ornament of the world, a genius without peer—if one loves freedom as the freedom of great souls and he threatens this kind of freedom. That is what Shakespeare must have felt. The height at which he places Caesar is the finest honor that he could bestow on Brutus: that is how he raises beyond measure Brutus's inner problem as well as the spiritual strength that was able to cut *this knot.*[65]

Nineteenth-century critics were not blind to the ironies of Shakespeare's portrayal of Caesar, the all too human weaknesses apparent in his susceptibility to Decius's adulation, his grandiloquence and colossally false sense of invulnerability. Nietzsche seems to have totally ignored these defects; not 'one speck of suspicion' ever taints his image of 'the most glorious human being'. One of the trinity of Paul Ricoeur's 'masters of suspicion',[66] Nietzsche never suspects Caesar.[67] His references to him are legion, and by far the majority of them are to the historical figure, not the dramatic character. But it is safe to assume that the dramatic character definitively shaped Nietzsche's view of the historical Caesar and that 'Shakespeare's best tragedy' exemplified for him not so much the gap between art and life, the epistemological pitfalls of representation, as art's capacity to reveal life in its essential truth. Nietzsche's 'ultimate formula for *Shakespeare*' ('he conceived of the type of Caesar')[68] asserts precisely that.

Nietzsche presents Brutus as a paragon of self-overcoming, the embodiment of what ranks highest in his ethical canon. Shakespeare's Brutus 'know[s] no personal cause to spurn at' Caesar, '[b]ut for the general' (*JC* 2.1.11–12). Nietzsche's Brutus is indifferent to 'the general'; his cause is entirely personal yet all the nobler for that: 'Independence of the soul!' This 'quintessence of a lofty morality' breathes the thin air of stratospherically 'higher men', the small circle of individuals in whom Nietzsche places his hope for humanity. Reversing Georg Brandes's epithet,[69] one

---

[65] *The Gay Science*, 150 (§98) (translation modified). Page references in brackets are to this text.

[66] Paul Ricoeur, *Freud and Philosophy: An Essay on Interpretation* (1965), trans. Denis Savage (New Haven, CT: Yale University Press, 1970), 32: 'Three masters, seemingly mutually exclusive, dominate the school of suspicion: Marx, Nietzsche, and Freud.'

[67] This is remarkable in view of contemporary opinions on Shakespeare's portrayal of Caesar. According to Gervinus (whose *Shakespeare*, as we have seen, was part of Nietzsche's early reading, though he later came to scorn its moralizing), Caesar 'speaks so much of having no fear, that by this very thing he betrays his fear'. *Shakespeare Commentaries*, trans. Fanny E. Bunnett, 2 vols (London: Smith, Elder, 1863), II, 720.

[68] *Ecce Homo*, 702 ('Why I Am So Clever', §4).

[69] Georg Brandes, 'An Essay on Aristocratic Radicalism' (1889), in his *Friedrich Nietzsche* (1990), trans. A. G. Chater (London: Heinemann, 1914), 1–56.

could speak of a 'radical aristocratism' when the pivotal crisis of the Roman state dwindles into insignificance before the vastness of the hero's inner problem: when Brutus kills not for the 'common good to all' (*JC* 5.5.72), but for the highly select 'freedom of great souls'.

Historical tragedy does, of course, tend to foreground the hero's personal dilemma, however firmly embedded in the larger political currents of the time it may be. Thus a stronger focus on the individual character is often adduced to distinguish Shakespeare's Roman tragedies from his more panoramic English histories. But Nietzsche sharpens this focus to the point of excluding all else. The political drama evoked by the mere name of Caesar becomes no more than a backdrop as Brutus's political motives give way to an ethics of 'higher men'. And as if to emphasize this move, politics does get a mention—only to be demoted to irrelevance by a sequence of rhetorical questions:

> Could it really have been political freedom that led this poet to sympathize with Brutus—and turned him into Brutus's accomplice? Or was political freedom only a symbol for something inexpressible? Could it be that we confront some unknown dark event and adventure in the poet's own soul of which he wants to speak only in signs? What is all of Hamlet's melancholy compared to that of Brutus? And perhaps Shakespeare knew both from firsthand experience. Perhaps he, too, had his gloomy hour and his evil angel, like Brutus. (150–1)

We can only speculate where these speculations might have been headed, whether or not Nietzsche had an inkling—perhaps even a specific hypothesis—as to what inexpressible something might lie behind the screen motivation of political freedom.[70] What is clear, though, is his endorsement of what M. H. Abrams termed the 'expressive theory of art',[71] the belief, spawned by the rise of Romanticism, that the authentic work must be rooted in its author's personal experience. Under this persuasion, the critic's task ultimately becomes less to look at than to see through the text, and what this exercise aims to reveal is not the nature of the created object but the mind or 'soul' of the artist who created it.[72] For all his dissent from the commonplace wisdom of his day, Nietzsche shared what might be called the 'biographical consensus' of nineteenth-century criticism. Where he strains beyond

---

[70] The most obvious instance of an 'evil angel' in Shakespeare (besides Brutus's dark hour in *JC* 4.3) is Sonnet 144: 'Two loves I have, of comfort and despair, / Which like two spirits do suggest me still.' The sonnets have always been a 'happy hunting ground' for biographical interpretation. Cf. Buck Mulligan's quip in James Joyce, *Ulysses*, ed. Jeri Johnson (Oxford: Oxford University Press, 1993), 239: 'Shakespeare is the happy hunting ground of all minds that have lost their balance.' The friend as 'angel' also occurs in Mark Antony's forum speech: 'For Brutus, as you know, was Caesar's angel' (*JC* 3.2.179).

[71] M. H. Abrams, *The Mirror and the Lamp: Romantic Theory and the Critical Tradition* (New York: Oxford University Press, 1953), 70.

[72] For a lucid critique of biography-as-criticism see Catherine Belsey, *A Future for Criticism* (Chichester: Wiley-Blackwell, 2011), 37–53. Nietzsche takes a notoriously dim view of female authorship; see, for example, his snide remarks on George Sand and George Eliot in *Twilight of the Idols*: 'They [the English] are rid of the Christian God and now believe all the more firmly that they must cling to Christian morality. That is an English consistency; we do not wish to hold it against little moralistic females à la Eliot.' Apropos George Sand: 'She wound herself like a clock—and wrote. [...] And how self-satisfied she may have lain there all the while, this fertile writing-cow who had in her something German in the bad sense.' *Twilight of the Idols*, 515–16 ('Skirmishes of an Untimely Man', §§5–6).

the conventional is in the passionate intensity of his biographical speculation. The passage from *The Gay Science* continues:

> But whatever similarities and secret relationships there may have been: before the whole figure and virtue of Brutus, Shakespeare prostrated himself, feeling unworthy and remote. His witness of this is written into the tragedy. Twice he brings in a poet, and twice he pours such an impatient and ultimate contempt over him that it sounds like a cry—the cry of self-contempt. Brutus, even Brutus, loses patience as the poet enters—conceited, pompous, obtrusive, as poets often are—apparently overflowing with possibilities of greatness, including moral greatness, although in the philosophy of his deeds and his life he rarely attains even ordinary integrity. 'I'll know his humor when he knows his time. / What should the wars do with these jigging fools? / Companion, hence!' shouts Brutus. This should be translated back into the soul of the poet who wrote it. (151)

Here it is again, the scene that impressed the young Nietzsche beyond any other. And here, again, is the jarring entry of the poet, its meaning now no longer in doubt. Howsoever unfathomable the rapport between Shakespeare and Brutus, that between Shakespeare and the intrusive poet is painfully clear. In Brutus's rejection of the vile rhymester (*JC* 4.3.134–6) Shakespeare castigates himself with Hamlet-like self-contempt. The end of the passage confirms what the italics in its opening sentence indicate: that it is 'Shakespeare, *the man*', with whom Nietzsche is concerned.

But why is it so clear to Nietzsche that this man should denigrate himself and his *métier* so abysmally before a Brutus with whom, after all, as the previous paragraph hints, he must feel intimately attuned? Throughout Nietzsche's writings, exhibitions of proud superiority, even self-aggrandizement, are interspersed with moments of self-abjection, where the critic of modernity feels himself inescapably tangled up in the condition he abhors. More specifically, *The Gay Science*—its title derived from Provençal *gai saber*, a troubadour term for poetry—is a reckoning not only of the strengths of writers and artists but emphatically also of their failings. Thus the section immediately preceding *In honour of Shakespeare* treats of *The loquacity of authors*, faulting luminaries such as Luther, Kant, Montaigne, and even the usually faultless Goethe for their lack of verbal restraint.[73] This critique of writers, in which stylistic and moral shortcomings are often difficult to tell apart, carries over into the section on Shakespeare. The moral inferiority ascribed to poets, 'who rarely attain even to ordinary uprightness', is the rule against which Shakespeare stands out as the shining exception. It is Shakespeare's honour to have honoured the murderer of Caesar with the loftiest possible motive; and, having conceived this sublimely 'honourable man', it is Shakespeare's honour to have recognized his infinite superiority over any mere producer of 'words, words, words'— including Shakespeare himself. This is why 'all of Hamlet's melancholy' fades before 'that of Brutus': he is the man of action. And although—or perhaps precisely because—the struggle of his 'dark hour' results in his committing what Nietzsche

---

[73] The parting shot of Section 97 is at Carlyle, the exemplary Victorian sage: 'A garrulousness due to an inner pleasure in noise and confused emotions.' *The Gay Science*, 150.

never failed to regard as a disastrous mistake, Brutus's 'inner problem' is incomparably more momentous than that of Hamlet, who scruples over the killing of a mere Claudius.

V CAESARIAN LEGACY

Hamlet's melancholy, moreover, is the malaise of the nineteenth century. Regardless of how *The Birth of Tragedy* ennobles it by association with the Dionysian Hellenes, it is the thought-sickness of the modern intellectual.[74] As Nietzsche's admired Emerson put it: the nineteenth century's 'speculative genius is a sort of living Hamlet'.[75] Hamlet may be the inescapable figure of identification, but for Nietzsche he is not Shakespeare's greatest achievement: 'When I seek my ultimate formula for *Shakespeare*, I always find only this: he conceived of the type of Caesar.'[76]

This statement, which appears in Chapter 2 ('Why I Am So Clever') of *Ecce Homo* (1888) and opens Nietzsche's last and most intricately layered reflection on Shakespeare, may seem baffling at first sight. The actual part of Caesar in Shakespeare's tragedy is, after all, relatively small. Many Shakespearean characters have more lines and are accorded far greater opportunity for the display of psychological depth. Julius Caesar is arguably not even the protagonist of the play (mis) named after him: 'It was to [Brutus]', we read in *The Gay Science*, 'that [Shakespeare] devoted his best tragedy—it is still called by the wrong name.'[77] The 'type of Caesar' can thus hardly refer to a particular mastery of character portrayal unless it be the shorthand mastery of the aphorist, the kind Nietzsche himself excelled in. But conceiving 'the *type* of Caesar' requires more than the art of psychologizing, much as Nietzsche praises this art and exults in his own attainments in it:[78] it takes a sense of the historical moment embodied by the brief actual lifespan of Julius Caesar and its unending reverberations down the centuries. This Caesarian moment, its exemplary singularity and continuing momentum, plays a crucial role in Nietzsche's cultural and political critique.

The political dimension of Nietzsche's thought becomes more pronounced between *The Gay Science* and the final phase of his writing.[79] To ignore or play down this dimension just because it fails to crystallize into a theoretical system or consistent programme of government is to miss the point.[80] What makes Nietzsche's

---

[74] Peter Holbrook, 'Nietzsche's *Hamlet*', has convincingly shown how a Nietzschean reading of *Hamlet* can help us make sense of the tranquillity and acceptance that Hamlet attains in Act 5. But while it is certainly possible to bring this perspective to bear on the play and its central character, there is no indication that Nietzsche himself ever entertained such a view.

[75] Emerson, 'Shakespeare; or, the Poet', 718.

[76] *Ecce Homo*, 702 ('Why I Am So Clever', §4).   [77] *The Birth of Tragedy*, 150 (§98).

[78] 'That a psychologist without equal speaks from my writings, is perhaps the first insight reached by a good reader' (*Ecce Homo*, 722, 'Why I Write Such Good Books', §5). 'Who among philosophers was a *psychologist* at all before me, and not rather the opposite, a "higher swindler" and "idealist"?' (*Ecce Homo*, 787, 'Why I Am a Destiny', §6).

[79] Cf. Ottmann, *Philosophie und Politik bei Nietzsche*, 239–92.

[80] Nietzsche may lack, as Brian Leiter argues, anything amounting to a *systematic* political philosophy (see 'Nietzsche's Moral and Political Philosophy', in *The Stanford Encyclopedia of Philosophy* [Summer

thinking political is precisely his questioning of politics itself. Indeed, his very 'unpoliticalness',[81] the Italian philosopher Massimo Cacciari argues, 'is the most radical criticism of politics'[82]—especially of what passed for 'large-scale' or 'great politics' (*große Politik*) in Nietzsche's contemporary Europe: 'the long-drawn-out comedy of its many splinter states as well as its dynastic and democratic splinter wills'.[83] This state of affairs, however,

> would come to an end. The time for petty politics is over: the very next century will bring the fight for the dominion of the earth—the *compulsion* to great politics.[84]

This passage from *Beyond Good and Evil* (1886), the first instance of Nietzsche claiming for himself the term 'great politics' in a non-ironic, non-pejorative sense,[85] strikes a note of apocalyptic utopianism that will recur, much amplified, in the final section of *Ecce Homo* ('Why I Am a Destiny'):

> For when truth enters into a fight with the lies of millennia, we shall have upheavals, a convulsion of earthquakes, a moving of mountains and valleys, the like of which has never been dreamed of. The concept of politics will have merged entirely with a war of spirits; all power structures of the old society will have been exploded—all of them are based on lies: there will be wars the like which have never yet be seen on earth. It is only beginning with me that the earth knows *great politics*.[86]

Its hyperbolic rhetoric notwithstanding, Nietzsche's prophesy has proved remarkably accurate about subsequent history: the overthrow of the old order in the first of two world wars, the global ideological conflicts that followed.[87] In his mission to blast the underpinnings of 'the old society' ('I am no man, I am dynamite'[88]) he heaps his contempt on the besotted chauvinism of the German Reich,[89] on 'England's

2011 edn], ed. Edward N. Zalta, <http://plato.stanford.edu/archives/sum2011/entries/nietzsche-moral-political/>, accessed 25 November 2012), but that does not make his philosophy 'unpolitical'. Besides, one may ask, does anything else in Nietzsche's philosophy amount to 'a system'? The view of Nietzsche as essentially non-political perpetuates the defensive reflex of Walter Kaufmann's influential post-war rescue mission aiming to disentangle Nietzsche from his Nazi-appropriators (Kaufmann, *Nietzsche: Philosopher, Psychologist, Antichrist*). Frederick Appel writes that '[b]y highlighting Nietzsche's contempt for conventional anti-Semitism, for nineteenth-century racism, and for German chauvinism, Kaufmann provided us with a valuable corrective', but that Kaufmann's 'essentially benign, emancipatory Nietzsche [...] turned out to be scarcely more accurate a description than the Nazis' Aryan version (albeit from a much more palatable perspective)'. Appel, *Nietzsche Contra Democracy*, 8–9.

  [81] 'I, the last *anti-political* German.' *Ecce Homo*, 681 ('Why I Am So Wise', §3).
  [82] Massimo Cacciari, *The Unpolitical: On the Radical Critique of Political Reason*, trans. Massimo Verdicchio (New York: Fordham University Press, 2009), 22; see also 97: 'Unpolitical does not mean [...] suprapolitical: its concept moves across the entire space of the political, the critique of its ideology and of its determination.' The problem with Cacciari's claim is that if Nietzsche is construed as repudiating *all politics*, Nietzsche's own anti-egalitarian politics can be deconstructed away as a mere exercise in a 'proto-postmodernist' perspectivism. For a treatment of Nietzsche's politics in this vein, see David Owen, *Nietzsche, Politics, and Modernity* (London: Sage, 1995).
  [83] *Beyond Good and Evil*, 321 (§208).
  [84] *Beyond Good and Evil*, 321 (§208) (translation modified).
  [85] Cf. Schieder, 'Nietzsche and Bismarck', 594.
  [86] *Ecce Homo*, 783 ('Why I Am a Destiny', §1).
  [87] Nietzsche's vision also anticipates Carl Schmitt's notion of 'global civil war'.
  [88] *Ecce Homo*, 782 ('Why I Am a Destiny', §1).
  [89] In a letter to Reinhart von Seydlitz (24 February 1887): 'German politics [...] are simply another kind of permanent winter and bad weather. Germany seems to me to have become, during the past

small-mindedness' and on 'the English principle of the people's right of representation'.[90] He dismisses representative democracy as 'the form of decline of the state'
and its institutions as 'no good any more'.[91] He condemns liberalism as a 'herd-an-
imalization' that makes men 'small, cowardly, and hedonistic',[92] but he is no less
stringent about its alternatives, socialism and anarchism:

> Whom do I hate most among the rabble of today? The socialist rabble, the chandala
> apostles, who undermine the instinct, the pleasure, the worker's sense of satisfaction
> with his small existence—who make him envious, who teach him revenge. The source
> of wrong is never unequal rights but the claim of 'equal' rights. What is *bad*? But
> I have said this already: all that is born of weakness, of envy, of *revenge*. The anarchist
> and the Christian have the same origin.[93]

The great modern exceptions to this scenario of general decline are Goethe—'not
a German event but a European one: a magnificent attempt to overcome the eighteenth century [...] by an *ascent* to the naturalness of the Renaissance'[94]—and
Napoleon, 'this synthesis of the *inhuman* and *superhuman*',[95] 'one of the greatest
continuators of the Renaissance [...] for what he wanted was one unified Europe
[...] as *mistress of the earth*'.[96]

The Renaissance is a significant marker here. Halfway between ancient and
modern, it connects Nietzsche's latter-day heroes to classical antiquity and its
Italian revival—the bold attempt, thwarted by the 'vengeful' German monk
Luther, of 'overcoming [...] Christianity in its very seat'.[97] What Nietzsche admires
in Goethe, and especially in Napoleon, ties in with a counter-image of decadent
modernity that finds political expression in the grand edifice of 'the *imperium
Romanum*, the most magnificent form of organization under difficult circumstances
which has yet been achieved, in comparison with which all before and all afterward
are mere botch, patchwork, and dilettantism'.[98]

---

fifteen years, a real school of stultification. Water, mess, and filth everywhere [...]; —that is how it
looks from the distance. Forgive me, as I ask you a thousand times, if it hurts your finer feelings,
but for this present-day Germany, bristling stiff with weapons though it may be, I no longer have
any respect. It represents the most stupid, broken-down, bogus form of the German *Geist* that there
ever has been—and this *Geist* has in its time certainly expected of itself all sorts of *Geist*-lessness.
I forgive nobody who compromises with it, even if his name is Richard Wagner [...].' Or, one might
say, especially if his name is Richard Wagner. *Selected Letters of Friedrich Nietzsche*, trans. Middleton,
262–3.

[90] 'Englands Klein-Geisterei' (NF-1884 26[335], KGWVII/2, 236); 'Bruch mit dem englischen
Princip der Volks-Vertretung' (NF-1884 26[336]).
[91] *Twilight of the Idols*, 543 ('Skirmishes of an Untimely Man', §39).
[92] *Twilight of the Idols*, 541 ('Skirmishes of an Untimely Man', §38).
[93] *The Antichrist*, in *The Portable Nietzsche*, 565–656 at 647 (§57).
[94] *Twilight of the Idols*, 553 ('Skirmishes of an Untimely Man', §49).
[95] *On the Genealogy of Morals*, 490 (§1/16).   [96] *The Gay Science*, 318 (§362).
[97] i.e. in Rome, the seat of the papacy. *The Antichrist*, 654 (§61). Nietzsche blames Christianity for
having 'found its mission in putting an end to precisely such an organization *because life prospered in
it*', for having destroyed the 'most admirable work of art in the grand style' which should have 'stood
there *aere perennius* [i.e. forever]' (*The Antichrist*, 647–8 [§58]).
[98] *The Antichrist*, 648 (§58).

At the heart of this ideal Rome stands the emblematic figure of Caesar, the embodiment of its very essence, the paragon of an unabashedly aristocratic, anti-liberal ethics of freedom:

> The human being who has *become free*—and how much more the *spirit* who has become free—spits on the contemptible type of well-being dreamed of by shop-keepers, Christians, cows, females, Englishmen, and other democrats. The free man is a *warrior*. How is freedom measured in individuals and peoples? According to the resistance which must be overcome, according to the exertion required, to remain on top. The highest type of free men should be sought where the highest resistance is constantly overcome: five steps from tyranny, close to the threshold of the danger of servitude. This is true psychologically if by 'tyrants' are meant inexorable and fearful instincts that provoke the maximum of authority and discipline against themselves; most beautiful type: Julius Caesar. This is true politically, too; one need only go through history. The peoples who had some value, *attained* some value, never attained it under liberal institutions: it was great danger that made something of them that merits respect. Danger alone acquaints us with our own resources, our virtues, our armor and weapons, our *spirit*, and *forces* us to be strong. *First* principle: one must need to be strong—otherwise one will never become strong. Those large hothouses for the strong—for the strongest kind of human being that has so far been known—the aristocratic commonwealths of the type of Rome or Venice, understood freedom exactly in the sense in which I understand it: as something one has or does *not* have, something one *wants*, something one *conquers*.[99]

It is passages like this (which defenders of Nietzsche's politics tend to either ignore or belittle)[100] that explain why it is Caesar, not Hamlet, who figures in Nietzsche's 'highest formula for *Shakespeare*'. Praise of Caesar is a constant throughout Nietzsche's writings, his greatness never even minimally in doubt, his name cited almost formulaically when a self-evident example of 'the highest men',[101] 'the highest type of free men',[102] or simply the 'genius'[103] is needed. In the increasingly sharp cultural-political polemics of Nietzsche's last phase, Caesar becomes the emblematic antagonist of the herd, the great singular figure towering above the levelling morality of the many, the counter-type of liberal modernity and its 'thickly padded humanity', which, as Nietzsche avers, would earn nothing but derision from earlier and 'healthier' epochs.[104]

But Caesar and Hamlet are also parallel in that they both represent opposition to Wilhelminian Germany: Hamlet is the disenchanted intellectual at the raucous feast of Germany's new self-declared greatness, and Caesar the luminous antithesis

---

[99] *Twilight of the Idols*, 542–3 ('Skirmishes of an Untimely Man', §38).

[100] Jarring with the view of Nietzsche as an essentially apolitical philosopher, passages like the one just quoted are by no means isolated but add up to extensive clusters: for example, *Twilight of the Idols*, 'Skirmishes of an Untimely Man', §§34–41 clearly hang together and provide the foundation for the concluding §§42–51.

[101] NF-1885 40[5], KGW VII/3, 362.

[102] *Twilight of the Idols*, 542 ('Skirmishes of an Untimely Man', §38).

[103] *Twilight of the Idols*, 533 ('Skirmishes of an Untimely Man', §31).

[104] *Twilight of the Idols*, 539 ('Skirmishes of an Untimely Man', §37): '[L]et us not doubt that we moderns, with our thickly padded humanity, which at all costs wants to avoid bumping into a stone, would have provided Cesare Borgia's contemporaries with a comedy at which they could have laughed themselves to death.'

('Hyperion to a satyr'; *Ham.* 1.2.140) to an upstart Prussian posing under the borrowed Caesarian title of *Kaiser*. The new-fangled German Reich, for all its imperial pretensions, is but a sorry parody of Nietzsche's *Imperium Romanum*, 'this most admirable of all works of art in the grand style';[105] it is a sorry parody, too, of the imperial vision of a Napoleon and the European scope of a Goethe.

Parody, however, when consciously embraced, is not necessarily a bad thing. Its very taint of the inferior, the secondary, and the belated may harbour the means to a precarious form of overcoming. In a thoroughly derivative, inauthentic culture, a culture posing in a 'style masquerade' for lack of a genuine style of its own, parody may prove the one way of rising to authenticity:

> [W]e are the first age that has truly studied 'costumes'—I mean those of moralities, articles of faith, tastes in the arts, and religions—prepared like no previous age for a carnival in the grand style, for the laughter and high spirits of the most spiritual revelry, for the transcendental heights of the highest nonsense and Aristophanean derision of the world. Perhaps this is where we shall still discover the realm of our *invention*, that realm in which we, too, can still be original, say, as parodists of world history and God's buffoons—perhaps, even if nothing else today has any future, our *laughter* may yet have a future.[106]

Ecce Homo presents itself as a 'meta-autobiography', as much 'about' its own process of being written as it is 'about' its writer's life. One way of attaining the reflexive level of the 'meta-'[107]—the way most readily associated with postmodernism but arguably no less germane to the *fin de siècle*[108]—is parody, a game which, according to Vladimir Nabokov,[109] can be used as a springboard 'for leaping into the highest region of serious emotion'.[110] Nietzsche the meta-autobiographer is consummately

---

[105] *The Antichrist*, 648 (§58).

[106] *Beyond Good and Evil*, 340 (§223). In the section immediately following (§224), Nietzsche includes the nineteenth century's love of Shakespeare among the symptoms of cultural decadence. Shakespeare, he claims, 'that amazing Spanish-moorish-Saxon synthesis of tastes that would have all but killed an ancient Athenian [...] with laughter or irritation', can only be enjoyed in an age of 'costumes', an age that is over-endowed with a 'historical sense': '[W]e—accept precisely this wild abundance of colors, this medley of what is most delicate, coarsest, and most artificial, with a secret familiarity and cordiality; we enjoy him as a superb subtlety of art saved up especially for us; and the disgusting odors and the proximity of the English rabble in which Shakespeare's art and taste live we do not allow to disturb us [...]' (342).

[107] Cf. Werner Wolf, 'Metareference across Media: The Concept, its Transmedial Potentials and Problems, Main Forms and Functions', in *Metareference across Media: Theory and Case Studies. Dedicated to Walter Bernhart on the Occasion of his Retirement*, ed. Werner Wolf (Amsterdam and New York: Rodopi, 2009), 1–85 at 3, where 'metaization' is defined as 'the movement from a first cognitive or communicative level to a higher one on which first-level utterances and above all the means and media used for such utterances self-reflexively become objects of reflection and communication in their own right'.

[108] I have discussed this in Andreas Höfele, 'Oscar Wilde, or, The Prehistory of Postmodern Parody', *European Journal of English Studies (EJES)*, Special Issue: *Postmodern Parody* (1999), 138–66.

[109] 'Satire is a lesson, parody is a game.' 'An Interview with Vladimir Nabokov, conducted by Alfred Appel, Jr.', in *Nabokov: The Man and his Work*, ed. L. S. Dembo (Madison, WI: University of Wisconsin Press, 1967), 19–44 at 30.

[110] Vladimir Nabokov, *The Real Life of Sebastian Knight* (Norfolk, CT: New Directions, 1959), 91. Cf. also Sander L. Gilman, *Nietzschean Parody: An Introduction to Reading Nietzsche* (Bonn: Bouvier, 1976).

adept at this game. When he sets out to 'tell his life to himself'[111] he dons the 'antic disposition' of Hamlet, a mode of masking and buffoonery. And it is in this mode that he presents his 'ultimate formula for *Shakespeare*'.

VI ECCE BACO(N)

> When I seek my ultimate formula for *Shakespeare*, I always find only this: he conceived of the type of Caesar. That sort of thing cannot be guessed: one either is it, or one is not. The great poet draws *only* from his own reality—up to the point where afterward he cannot endure his work any longer. When I have looked into my *Zarathustra*, I walk up and down in my room for half an hour, unable to master an unbearable fit of sobbing. I know no more heart-rending reading than Shakespeare: what must a man have suffered to have such a need of being a buffoon! Is Hamlet *understood*? Not doubt, *certainty* is what drives one insane—But one must be profound, an abyss, a philosopher to feel that way. —We are all *afraid* of truth. And let me confess it: I feel instinctively sure and certain that Lord Bacon was the originator, the self-tormentor of this uncanniest kind of literature: what is the pitiable chatter of American flat-and and muddle-heads to *me*? But the strength required for the vision of the most powerful reality is not only compatible with the most powerful strength for action, for monstrous action, for crime—it even presupposes it. We are very far from knowing enough about Lord Bacon, the first realist in every great sense of that word, to know everything he did, wanted, and experienced in himself. And damn it, my dear critics! Suppose I had published my *Zarathustra* under another name—for example, that of Richard Wagner—the acuteness of two thousand years would not have been sufficient for anyone to guess that the author of *Human, All-Too-Human* is the visionary of *Zarathustra*.[112]

This passage creates a veritable hall of mirrors, a tangle of identifications.[113] It takes up where the observations on Shakespeare's Brutus left off. While the Roman man of action (Caesar, not Brutus this time) and the contemplative Hamlet still appear as two distinct types, the aim now is not to play them off against each other— Brutus melancholy versus Hamlet melancholy—but to make them complementary aspects of a compound whole. If the Shakespeare of *The Gay Science* found a Brutus in himself, the Shakespeare of *Ecce Homo* much more assertively *is* a Caesar. And this assertion at once becomes the rule governing all subsequent identifications ('One cannot [...] one is [...] one is not'): first, the rule that transforms Shakespeare into the double of the creator of Zarathustra, who, by the same rule, *is* Zarathustra; then the rule that makes Zarathustra/Nietzsche the double of

---

[111] *Ecce Homo*, 677: '[A]nd so I tell my life to myself.'

[112] *Ecce Homo*, 702–3 ('Why I Am So Clever', §4), translation modified.

[113] The best study of these identifications is Christian Benne, 'Ecce Hanswurst—Ecce Hamlet: Rollenspiele in *Ecce Homo*', *Nietzscheforschung. Jahrbuch der Nietzsche-Gesellschaft* 12 (2005), 219–28. I am substantially indebted to Benne's reading. For another take on the passage see Scott Wilson, 'Reading Shakespeare with Intensity: A Commentary on Some Lines from Nietzsche's *Ecco Homo*', in *Philosophical Shakespeares*, ed. John J. Joughin (London: Routledge, 2000), 86–104.

Shakespeare/Hamlet. 'Is Hamlet understood?' Nietzsche asks rhetorically. He 'is understood', much in line with *The Birth of Tragedy*, if it is recognized that 'certainty', rather than uncertainty, is at the heart of his dilemma. But a new emphasis is now laid on Hamlet's buffoonery: he is the sufferer playing the fool, the *Hanswurst*[114] in German. *Hanswurst* becomes a key term in Nietzsche's late writings.[115] 'I have a terrible fear that one day I will be pronounced *holy*', he declares in the final chapter of *Ecce Homo*, 'I do not want to be a holy man; sooner even a buffoon [*Hanswurst*]. —Perhaps I am a buffoon.'[116] As 'a disciple of the philosopher Dionysus', the preface announces, 'I should prefer to be even a satyr to being a saint.'[117] The overt inconsistencies and volte-faces, the bragging and boastfulness of *Ecce Homo*—so blatantly at odds with Nietzsche's declaration that there is not a trace of presumptuousness in him[118]—can thus be accounted for by the *Hanswurst* role in which he cloaks his authorial performance.[119] For Nietzsche as well as for Hamlet, and for Nietzsche *as* Hamlet, this role—jesting, seeming-mad— is a mask to cover suffering: 'There are free, impudent spirits', he writes, at about the same time as *Ecce Homo*, in *Nietzsche Contra Wagner* (1888),

> who would like to conceal and deny that they are broken, incurable hearts—the case of Hamlet: and then even foolishness can be the mask for an unblessed all-too certain certainty.[120]

The convergence of suffering and buffoonery in Shakespeare/Hamlet as in Nietzsche/ Zarathustra also brings us back to the quarrel scene in *Julius Caesar* and the poet who unseasonably stumbles into it (4.3.123–37). Brutus calls him a 'cynic', and Nietzsche not only makes his dismissal harsher by shortening it[121] but also changes Schlegel's rendering of 'jigging fool' from *Schellennarr* to *Schellen-Hanswurst*.[122] Christian Benne points out that the *Hanswurst* and the cynic are closely affiliated in Nietzsche's late writings: in his letter to Georg Brandes (20 November 1888) he styles *Ecce Homo* a (kind of) 'cynicism that will make history'.[123] Thus 'the cynic is

---

[114] Literally 'John Sausage'; Jack Pudding would be a near-equivalent in English.

[115] See Benne, 'Ecce Hanswurst—Ecce Hamlet', esp. 220–1. 'God's buffoons' [*Hanswurste Gottes*] occurs, as we have seen, in the passage on parody (*Beyond Good and Evil*, §223) quoted earlier.

[116] *Ecce Homo*, 782 ('Why I Am a Destiny', §1).

[117] *Ecce Homo*, 673 ('Preface', §2). These statements are corroborated by letters from the same period (cf. Benne, 'Ecce Hanswurst—Ecce Hamlet', 220 n. 5), for example to Cosima Wagner (3 January 1889): 'I am told that a certain divine *Hanswurst* has finished his Dionysos-Dithyrambs these last few days.'

[118] Cf. *Ecce Homo*, 683 ('Why I Am So Wise', §4).

[119] Benne, 'Ecce Hanswurst—Ecce Hamlet', 220, speaks of a 'self-praise unprecedented in [all of] world literature'.

[120] *Nietzsche Contra Wagner*, in *The Portable Nietzsche*, 661–83 at 680.

[121] 'I'll know his humour when he knows his time. / What should the wars do with these jigging fools? / Companion, hence!' Nietzsche (*The Gay Science*, §98) has the German equivalent of 'He may know the times, but I know his temper,—away with the jigging fool [*Schellen-Hanswurst*]!' Kaufmann ignores this contraction, giving the original Shakespearean wording (cf. *The Gay Science*, 151).

[122] *Schellen* are the bells on the fool's cap.

[123] *Selected Letters of Friedrich Nietzsche*, trans. Middleton, 326. KSB 8, 482: 'Cynismus, der wel-thistorisch werden wird'. From his early writings onwards Nietzsche regards Cynic philosophy as a phenomenon of belatedness associated with 'humour, satire and parody as counterparts of tragedy'. Benne, 'Ecce Hanswurst—Ecce Hamlet', 224 n.12.

contained in the *Hanswurst,* and the *Hanswurst* is [...] contained in Hamlet, who in turn is contained in Shakespeare. And the virtuoso master behind all this role-playing bears the name—Francis Bacon.'[124] 'Philosopher' is the cue for this leap, which takes the game of identifications to the next level. In Benne's reading Bacon figures as the 'poet-philosopher' behind the 'author persona' of Shakespeare; just as Nietzsche himself, the 'real Nietzsche' as it were, speaks through 'Nietzsche' the extravagant author persona of *Ecce Homo.*

But Bacon is also emphatically the man of action, living proof that 'the power for the mightiest reality of vision is not only compatible with the mightiest power for action, for the monstrous in action, for crime—it even presupposes it ...'. It is the identification with Lord Bacon that raises Shakespeare from the abject position of the cynic poet in *Julius Caesar* 4.2. Benne argues that the 'personal "heart-rending" tragedy' of Nietzsche's Shakespeare lies in a personality split between the 'theoretical conception of the man of power [i.e. Caesar] on the one hand and the mundane *Hanswurst*-existence [of Shakespeare the actor, the doppelganger of the vile rhymester of *JC* 4.3] on the other'.[125] But if Shakespeare is Bacon, his conception of the man of power is anything but theoretical. It is drawn or created from[126] his own reality: not just 'guessed at' but known because he actually 'is it'. Nietzsche is 'instinctively certain' of this, having nothing but contempt for the 'American shallow-pates and muddle-heads' who seek to prove Bacon's authorship by dubious means of detection.[127] The mastermind of *Ecce Homo* is not only Hamlet/Shakespeare but also Caesar/Bacon: 'He is all in all', one might say, as does Stephen Dedalus constructing a similar web of identifications in *Ulysses.*[128]

The passage, then, construes a double concatenation of doubles converging in the autobiographical subject of *Ecce Homo*: Hamlet is Shakespeare is Nietzsche; Caesar is Shakespeare is Nietzsche.[129] For this double identification to work, Shakespeare must become Bacon, in whom reality of vision, the certainty that drives one insane, and the abyss that can only be endured by playing the fool conjoin with the mightiest force of action, the monstrous, the criminal. The very enigma of Bacon, about whom 'we do not know nearly enough', makes this 'first great realist' an ideal *alter ego* for the radically realistic anti-messiah of *Ecce Homo* whose exposure of Christianity will 'break [...] the history of mankind in two'.[130] Deriding the Baconians, Nietzsche appropriates their biographical phantasm for

---

[124] Benne, 'Ecce Hanswurst—Ecce Hamlet', 224.

[125] Benne, 'Ecce Hanswurst—Ecce Hamlet', 222.

[126] Nietzsche uses the German verb *schöpfen,* which comprises both meanings.

[127] Americans such as Delia Bacon and Ignatius Donelly were leading proponents of the Baconian hypothesis. Donelly's *The Shakespeare Myth* appeared the year before *Ecce Homo,* his *The Great Cryptogram: Francis Bacon's Cipher in Shakespeare's Plays* in the same year.

[128] 'He [Shakespeare] is the ghost and the prince. He is all in all.—He is, Stephen said. The boy of act one is the mature man of act five. All in all. In *Cymbeline,* in *Othello* he is bawd and cuckold. He acts and is acted on. Lover of an ideal or a perversion, like José he kills the real Carmen. His unremitting intellect is the hornmad Iago ceaselessly willing that the moor in him shall suffer.' Joyce, *Ulysses,* 204.

[129] In this and the two following paragraphs I am drawing on my discussion of the same passage in Andreas Höfele, *Stage, Stake, and Scaffold: Humans and Animals in Shakespeare's Theatre* (Oxford and New York: Oxford University Press, 2011), 263–6.

[130] *Ecce Homo,* 789 ('Why I Am a Destiny', §8).

his own phantasmal self-image as a historical *force majeure*.[131] The poet-philosopher must be able to conjure in himself the mindset, the drives, and the energy of the conquering man of action. But this would still be just 'guessing', imagining oneself as Caesar rather than *being* him. The bolder, less 'reasonable' reading transfers the poet-philosopher from the role of a reflector or recorder to that of an agent of history.[132] This ambition is much closer in spirit to the euphoric bravado of the opening announcement of *Ecce Homo*: 'Seeing that before long I must confront humanity with the most difficult demand ever made of it, it seems indispensable to me to say *who I am*.'[133]

What is that 'most difficult demand' with which the ill and isolated, largely unread author proposes to shake the world? There is no telling. 'I will do such things—' exclaims the powerless Lear on the brink of madness, 'What they are, yet I know not, but they shall be / The terrors of the earth!' (*Lr.* 2.2.462–3). The beginning of *Ecce Homo* suggests that the writer means his imminent feat to be more than just another piece of writing.[134] This would explain both the crucial role attributed to Caesar in 'my ultimate formula for *Shakespeare*' and the apparition of Lord Bacon as the true begetter, behind the mask of 'Shakespeare', of both Caesar and the heart-rending buffoonery of Hamlet.[135]

At issue for Nietzsche is the type, the perpetual idea, phantasm, or, as Shakespeare's play puts it, the ghost of Caesar that set in motion not just a dynasty but a whole history of Western rulership down to the investiture of the Prussian king Wilhelm as the first Kaiser, or Caesar, of Germany's 'Second Reich' in 1871. But world history, the history of an assassinated Roman general who spawned empires, does not happen out there; it is acted out as the personal psychodrama of the autobiographical author-subject of *Ecce Homo*. And thus the passage cannot end without tangling Richard Wagner in its web of masked identities, the man whom Nietzsche regards, despite their rift, as the most important and beneficial force in his life:

> Speaking of the recreations of my life, I must say a word to express my gratitude for what has been by far the most profound and cordial recreation of my life. Beyond a doubt, that was my intimate relationship with Richard Wagner.[136]

---

[131] Cf. the title of the last chapter of *Ecce Homo*: 'Why I Am a Destiny'; 'The uncovering of Christian morality is an event without parallel, a real catastrophe. He that is enlightened about that is a *force majeure*, a destiny—' (789, §8).

[132] What is important here, too, is Bacon's association with crime as a mark of greatness and heroic action, his reputation of having been '[t]he wisest, brightest, meanest of Mankind'. Alexander Pope, *An Essay on Man. In Epistles to a Friend*. Epistle IV (London: J. Wilford, 1734), 13, l. 277. Cf. also Nietzsche's remark on Catiline: 'Almost every genius knows, as one stage of his development, the "Catilinian existence"—a feeling of hatred, revenge, and rebellion against everything which already *is*, which no longer *becomes*. Catiline—the form of pre-existence of *every* Caesar.' *Twilight of the Idols*, 550–1 ('Skirmishes of an Untimely Man', §45).

[133] *Ecce Homo*, 673 ('Preface', §1).

[134] To be sure, the concluding section of *Ecce Homo* suggests that the world-shaking task has already been accomplished in his writings, which the autobiography recapitulates one by one. R. J. Hollingdale, in a note to his translation of the passage, suggests that '[t]he forthcoming *Revaluation of all Values*—together with the effect it may be expected to produce—is presumably what is meant here.' Friedrich Nietzsche, *Ecce Homo. How One Becomes What One Is*, trans. and ed. R. J. Hollingdale (London: Penguin, 2004), 105.

[135] Cf. Holbrook, 'Nietzsche's *Hamlet*'.   [136] *Ecce Homo*, 703 ('Why I Am So Clever', §5).

This acknowledgement immediately follows the antic parting-shot of the Shakespeare section. By '[s]uppos[ing] I had published my Zarathustra under [the] name [...] of Richard Wagner', Nietzsche renews and remodels the long-severed association to the point where the former intimates become indistinguishable. Not coequal, though: in serving as 'Shakespeare' to Nietzsche's 'Bacon', Wagner is clearly placed in the subordinate role, that of the Stratford actor whom the poet-philosopher-statesman used as a front. This role tallies with how Nietzsche judges his former idol in *The Wagner Case* (1888): more of an actor than a composer, his music a mere means to enhance theatrical posing. But Wagner's fall from grace exceeds the purely aesthetic:

> What did I never forgive Wagner? That he *condescended* to the Germans—that he became *reichsdeutsch*.[137]

Wagner's politics had become at least as offensive as his art.[138] Nietzsche's verdict on him sets him up as a negative example of what the Shakespearean reflection in *Ecce Homo* seeks to define in positive terms: a synthesis of art and politics through an intricate meshing of iconic identities. Only such a synthesis can aspire to the status of 'great politics'. Thus Caesar defines the 'highest formula' for Shakespeare, while Hamlet, the truest expression of Shakespeare's self, is his Zarathustra. Thus also Shakespeare must be Bacon, the poet not only a philosopher but a man of political action. Nietzsche's identification with Shakespeare, or rather his identification of Shakespeare as Nietzsche, could hardly be more total. As poet, philosopher, statesman, and criminal, the Shakespeare of *Ecce Homo* becomes the herald of Nietzsche's evangel of 'great politics'.

What Nietzsche envisions in Bacon/Shakespeare is a merger, as it were, of Napoleon and Goethe—'the *two great tentatives*',[139] unmentioned in this passage, but featured prominently in, for example, *Twilight of the Idols*.[140] Only a conjunction of their respective strengths can bring about the cultural and political renewal Nietzsche envisions.[141] Taking this up, Nietzsche's later follower Oswald Spengler declared: 'We Germans will not produce another Goethe, but a Caesar we will.'[142] Henning Ottmann comments:

> These may have been prophetic words when Spengler wrote them down in 1921. But they do not show what Nietzsche meant. Pure power politics was unjustifiable to him. Power had to have a suprapolitical, cultural and moral purpose or else Nietzsche rejected it. Contemporary power politics was 'small politics' [...] Bismarck's social Bonapartism was not even worthy of mention. He had no contemporary politician in

---

[137] *Ecce Homo*, 704 ('Why I Am So Clever', §5).

[138] Richard Wagner's politics had undergone a complete (but by no means atypical) change. At the time of the first Bayreuth festival, whose opening in 1876 was graced by the presence of the Kaiser himself, the revolutionary of 1848/9 had become a thoroughly establishment figure.

[139] 'Die *beiden großen Tentativen*'. NF-1888 15[68], KSA 13, 451.

[140] Cf. *Twilight of the Idols*, 552–4 ('Skirmishes of an Untimely Man', §§48–9).

[141] Cf. Ottmann, *Philosophie und Politik bei Nietzsche*, 275; see NF-1888 15[68], KSA 13, 451.

[142] Oswald Spengler, 'Pessimismus?', in *Reden und Aufsätze* (Munich: Beck, 1937), 79.

mind when he set his hope on a Caesar [...] Spengler, the late prophet of Caesarism, was an intellectual in a spiked helmet. Nietzsche was not.[143]

The spiked helmet, a symbol of Prussian militarism and thus of everything Nietzsche hated about Germany, found its iconic wearer in Wilhelm II, enthroned in June 1888. 'Have the young Kaiser shot by a firing squad' reads one of the dozens of frantic messages Nietzsche wrote in the days before his final breakdown in sobbing embrace of a cart-horse that he witnessed being cruelly whipped by its driver in Turin's Piazza Carlo Alberto. By this time great politics, always a utopian vision and not a programme for practical application, had crossed the Rubicon into the phantasms of omnipotence:

> I have just taken possession of my realm, will throw the Pope into prison, and have Wilhelm, Bismarck and Stöcker[144] shot.
> The Crucified One[145]

In another letter from the same day, 3 January 1889 ('To the Princess Ariadne, my Beloved', i.e. Cosima Wagner), Shakespeare, or rather Shakespeare's poetic begetter Bacon, takes up his place in the pantheon as the maze of identifications from *Ecce Homo* blooms into apotheosis:

> It is a prejudice that I am a man. But I have often enough lived among men and know all that men can experience, from the lowest to the highest. I have been Buddha among the Indians, Dionysus in Greece—Alexander and Caesar are my incarnations, as well as the poet of Shakespeare, Lord Bacon. Most recently I was also Voltaire and Napoleon, perhaps also Richard Wagner [...] This time, however, I come as the victorious Dionysus, who will make the earth a festival [...][146]

* * *

Thomas Mann chose Nietzsche as the model for the composer Adrian Leverkühn, the protagonist of his novel *Doctor Faustus* (1947), in which the narrative of the artist's pact with the devil, his rise to success and decline into madness, is complexly interwoven with the political history of Germany in the first half of the twentieth century. Mann's long essay 'Nietzsche's Philosophy in the Light of Contemporary Events', which was one of his addresses at the Library of Congress, offers a postscript to the novel. Taking Ophelia's lamentation 'O, what a noble mind is here o'erthrown!' as his starting point, Mann observes that many 'of the characterizations contained in the following verses [...] fit Nietzsche exactly'.[147]

---

[143] Ottmann, *Philosophie und Politik bei Nietzsche*, 275.

[144] Adolf Stoecker (1835–1909) was a prominent Lutheran clergyman, pastor to the imperial court in Berlin and Christian-social politician notable for his nationalism and anti-Semitism.

[145] Letter to Meta von Salis, 3 January 1889, KSB 8, 572.

[146] Letter to von Salis, 3 January 1889, KSB 8, 572–3.

[147] Thomas Mann, 'Nietzsche's Philosophy in the Light of Contemporary Events', in *Thomas Mann's Addresses Delivered at the Library of Congress*, ed. Don Heinrich Tolzmann (Berne: Peter Lang, 2003), 67–103 at 69. Page references in brackets are to this text. The essay has been variously read as a critique and an apotheosis of Nietzsche. It is actually both. See Eckhard Heftrich, 'Nietzsche als Hamlet der Zeitenwende', in his *Zauberbergmusik: Über Thomas Mann* (Frankfurt: Klostermann, 1975), 281–316; Thomas Körber, *Nietzsche nach 1945: zu Werk und Biographie Friedrich Nietzsches in der deutschsprachigen*

The fascination of Nietzsche, Mann suggests, is 'closely related to the one emanating through the centuries from that great character created by Shakespeare, the melancholy prince of Denmark' (69). 'We are face to face with a Hamlet-like fate, [...] one that inspires reverence and compassion' (93).[148] We are also face to face with the fate of Germany; for who, Mann asks, 'was more German than he, who was it that [...] exemplarily demonstrated to the Germans everything by which they have become a terror and a scourge for the world and have ruined themselves?' (101).

In Mann's reading, Germany and Hamlet converge in the tragedy of Nietzsche.[149]

Nachkriegsliteratur (Würzburg: Königshausen und Neumann, 2006), 68; Hermann Kurzke, *Thomas Mann: Epoche—Werk—Wirkung* (Munich: Beck, 2010), 283–4.

[148] Mann concedes that 'our reverence finds itself in something like a tight spot when that "socialism of the subjugated caste" which Nietzsche [...] scorned and branded as a poisonous hater of higher life, proves to us that his superman is nothing but the idealization of the fascist Fuehrer', but says he is inclined 'not to believe that Nietzsche created fascism, but rather that fascism created him—that is to say: [...] he functioned as an infinitely sensitive instrument of expression and registration [...] he presaged the dawning imperialism and as a quivering floatstick indicated the fascist era of the West [...]' ('Nietzsche's Philosophy in the Light of Contemporary Events', 93).

[149] For searching analyses of Mann's relation to Shakespeare, see Tobias Döring and Ewan Fernie, eds, *Thomas Mann and Shakespeare: Something Rich and Strange* (New York and London: Bloomsbury, 2015).

2

Shakespeare in the Master's Circle
Stefan George and the 'Secret Germany'

I PASSING THE TORCH

If Nietzsche was the tragic prophet of the *fin de siècle*, there were those who saw in him only the harbinger of an even greater figure. This is the role allotted to him in the final paragraph of Friedrich Gundolf's study *Caesar in the Nineteenth Century* (1926). Nietzsche, Gundolf writes, had reclaimed Caesar for the present

> with a visionary zeal that takes the forces of the past along into the future. [...] For Nietzsche, Caesar is Zarathustra recovered, the mature sovereign-sage. Nietzsche conceived this dream from the marriage of his desire with his vision. The command of the clairvoyant soul accompanies the times [...] until it becomes real once more in a living man. As yet, no sovereign has appeared who is also a sage; but already there is a sage among us with a sovereign will, knowing and loving, endowed with the Caesarian awe which Nietzsche prophesied.[1]

The sage with the sovereign will is not mentioned by name, but few of Gundolf's readers would have been in any doubt as to who was meant: the man whose most prominent disciple Gundolf was known to be—Stefan George (Figure 2.1).[2]

After decades of neglect, George (1868–1933) has met with an astonishing revival of interest. 'The sudden return of Stefan George is among the great surprises' of his academic life, writes Ernst Osterkamp, a George scholar of long standing—understandably so, because for the generation whose first steps in academia coincided with the student movement of the late 1960s, George 'represented [...] everything they opposed'.[3] In his own day 'as much an institution as a poet', George 'began as an admiring pupil of Mallarmé and ended as a national prophet'.[4] An alleged trailblazer of the Third Reich, he was anathema, with interest in his poetry being deemed a sure sign of rightist leanings. 'During the quarter century following 1968',

---

[1] Friedrich Gundolf, *Caesar im neunzehnten Jahrhundert* (Berlin: Georg Bondi, 1926), 88. This expands the last chapter of Gundolf's previous study, *Caesar, Geschichte seines Ruhms* (Berlin: Georg Bondi, 1924; Engl. *The Mantle of Caesar*, trans. Jacob Wittmer Hartmann [London: Cayme Press, 1929]).

[2] For the unlikely reader in need of clarification, the name index facing the last page of Gundolf's text has a single laconic entry 'George' referring to the quoted passage.

[3] Ernst Osterkamp, *Poesie der leeren Mitte: Stefan Georges Neues Reich* (Munich: Carl Hanser, 2010), 12–13.

[4] C. M. Bowra, *The Heritage of Symbolism* (London: Macmillan, 1943), 98.

Figure 2.1. Stefan George. Reproduced by permission of ullstein bild—Friedrich Mueller.

Osterkamp concludes, 'George was a figure of remotest literary history, his impact not even that of cobwebbed classic.'[5]

'Remote' in Germany, Stefan George was virtually unknown elsewhere. Even now, mention of him in English is typically accompanied by explanatory comparisons. 'His work, in its originality and impact, easily ranks with that of Goethe, Holderlin [*sic*!] or Rilke', claims a US university press website;[6] and a Canadian commentator blogging from Berlin helpfully submits that the poet's deceptively English-looking surname is pronounced tri-syllabically, 'gay-org-uh'.[7] George's younger contemporary Rilke is readily accessible in translation, but George's complete poems in English, often sadly enfeebled outside his native idiom, have long been out of print.[8] All the more remarkably, the first fully fledged critical biography

[5] Osterkamp, *Poesie der leeren Mitte*, 13.

[6] In the advertisement for Robert E. Norton, *Secret Germany: Stefan George and His Circle* (Ithaca, NY and London: Cornell University Press, 2002) on the Cornell University Press website: <http://www.cornellpress.cornell.edu/book/?GCOI=80140100070880>, accessed 4 September 2013.

[7] Stan Persky, 'Letter from Berlin: Secret Germany', 18 February 2010: <http://stanpersky.de/index.php/articles/letter-from-berlin-secret-germany>, accessed 4 September 2013. Not infrequently, one finds the poet's name misspelled 'Georg'.

[8] Together with Olga Marx (= Carol North Valhope), Ernst Morwitz, a Jewish emigré to America and one of George's closest followers, translated all of George's poems into English: *The Works of Stefan*

of George in any language was published by the American scholar Robert E. Norton in 2002.[9] While this pioneering effort attracted little attention in George's home country,[10] two subsequent publications hit the German bestseller lists for non-fiction. Thomas Karlauf's biography of George ran to four printings in its year of publication (2007), and Ulrich Raulff's *Circle without Master: Stefan George's Afterlife*, a reconstruction of Georgean networks from the poet's death up to almost the present day, won the prestigious Leipzig Book Fair Award in 2010.[11] The stir caused by these publications brought George back into the public arena where, despite or rather because of his reclusiveness and secrecy, he had once occupied a prominent place.

This all has little to do with the poetry per se. Rather, these recent books undertake a long overdue reconsideration of the nature of George's position and impact as an intellectual leader.[12] What held back this reconsideration for so long was an alliance between George's detractors and his partisans, an alliance that was no less effectual for being unintended. For the detractors, it was pointless to wrest this convicted reactionary from well-deserved oblivion. For the partisans—ageing survivors of the poet's original entourage and their acolytes—it was a sacred duty to protect the intimacies of the Master and his circle from invasive scrutiny. The published output of these guardians of the flame typically took the form of personal memoirs.[13] What they sought to record was an encounter with a uniquely charismatic personality which profoundly shaped their lives.

George. Rendered into English by Olga Marx and Ernst Morwitz (Chapel Hill, NC: University of North Carolina Press, 1949; repr. New York: AMS Press, 1966). Norton, *Secret Germany*, xvi, is categorical in his assessment that 'George has rarely been translated into English, and never well.' Early reviewers of the Marx/Morwitz translation were generally more approving, not least because they were aware of the enormous difficulty of the task. Cf. Ulrich K. Goldsmith in *Books Abroad* 24.3 (1950), 302; Edwin H. Zeydel in *The German Quarterly* 24.3 (1951), 205; Hans Jaeger in *Monatshefte* 45.6 (1953), 391–3. Morwitz and Valhope published their translation of part of George's œuvre in 1943. See Ernst Feise in *Modern Language Notes* 58.7 (1943), 568–9; Edwin H. Zeydel in *The Modern Language Journal* 27.4 (1943), 294–5; F. K. Richter in *The German Quarterly* 17.1 (1944), 52–3; Hermann J. Weigand in *The Journal of English and Germanic Philology* 43.1 (1944), 141–9. English audiences are more likely to encounter George's poetry in musical guise. Arnold Schönberg's song cycle opus 15 (1908/9), for example, a setting of fifteen poems from *Das Buch der Hängenden Gärten* (*The Book of the Hanging Gardens*) for mezzo-soprano and piano marks the beginning of the composer's atonal phase.

[9] Norton, *Secret Germany*. Prior to Norton's monograph, there is the pithy chapter on George by Peter Gay, 'The Secret Germany: Poetry as Power', in his *Weimar Culture: The Outsider as Insider* (1968) (New York and London: Norton, 2001), 46–69. Strangely, this receives no mention by Norton, Karlauf, or Raulff.

[10] It received a vitriolic review from one of the leading proponents of the George revival in Germany, Ulrich Raulff, 'Ihr wisst nicht, wer ich bin', *Süddeutsche Zeitung*, 11 June 2002, 18.

[11] Thomas Karlauf, *Stefan George. Die Entdeckung des Charisma* (Munich: Blessing, 2007); Ulrich Raulff, *Kreis ohne Meister: Stefan Georges Nachleben* (Munich: Beck, 2010).

[12] This is clearly indicated by the title of an important recent collection of essays by American, British, and German scholars: Melissa S. Lane and Martin A. Ruehl, eds, *A Poet's Reich: Politics and Culture in the George Circle* (Rochester, NY: Camden House, 2011).

[13] For example: Robert Boehringer, *Mein Bild von Stefan George*, 2 vols (Düsseldorf and Munich: Küpper, 1951); Edgar Salin, *Um Stefan George*, 2nd edn (Düsseldorf and Munich: Küpper, 1954); Edith Landmann, *Gespräche mit Stefan George* (Düsseldorf and Munich: Küpper, 1963). It is no accident that these books were all published by Helmut Küpper, successor to Georg Bondi, George's publisher. Another Georgean enclave and publisher of Georgeana was Castrum Peregrini at Amsterdam. See, for example, Berthold Vallentin, *Gespräche mit Stefan George* (Amsterdam: Castrum Peregrini, 1960); Kurt Breysig, *Stefan George. Gespräche, Dokumente* (Amsterdam: Castrum Peregrini, 1960).

The recent revival of George studies has made this charisma one of its prime objects of inquiry. Karlauf strikes the keynote in the title of his biography: *Stefan George: The Discovery of Charisma*. It was, he argues, George's sway over his followers on which the sociologist Max Weber modelled 'charismatic authority' in his typology of rule.[14] According to Weber, this type of authority is based 'on devotion to the exceptional sanctity, heroism or exemplary character of an individual person, and of the normative patterns or order revealed or ordained by him'.[15] Weber, the liberal humanist, knew and esteemed George but was critical of the cult of personality enveloping him.[16] Other, especially younger, men were simply overwhelmed. Here is the account of an acolyte:

> No one who has ever felt the glowing breath of living poetry for the first time will ever forget the moment when his heart beat faster in the throes of new fevers, when a tempest raged within him, undreamed-of vistas opened up before him and he was struck in awe by the sacred until finally a gush of tears restored him to his senses, back to his new self. [...]
>
> On a hot spring noon in 1913, a young student was walking along the high street of Heidelberg. He had just crossed Brunngässlein and was observing the stream of pedestrians [...] creeping languidly, exhausted by the unaccustomed heat, over the hot pavement. But suddenly the weary walkers seemed to rally: light-footed, with springy tread, a lone figure approached—everyone stepped out of his path lest his course be impeded. Almost floating on air, as if winged, he turned the corner towards Wredeplatz and was gone.
>
> The observer stood transfixed. The air of a higher sphere had touched him. He did not know what had happened and hardly where he was. Was this a man who had passed through the crowd? But he was distinguished from all other men [...] by an unconscious majesty and an effortless power. Next to him all others seemed pale, like soulless spectres. Was it a god who had parted the crowd and light-footedly sped on to other shores? But he had worn human garb [...] And the face? The observer remembered its features only indistinctly. They were chiselled, and their pallor added to the impression of the strange, the statuesque, the godlike. And the eyes? Suddenly the observer knew: it was the beam of those eyes that had enthralled him. Quickly, like a stroke of lightening, their glance had strayed over and penetrated him to the quick before the man wandered on with the trace of a smile. And now the knowledge dawned on him: if this had been a man, it could only have been Stefan George.[17]

Writing over three decades later, this is how Edgar Salin, professor of political economics at Basle,[18] described his first encounter with George: a veritable epiphany,

---

[14] Karlauf's argument gains corroboration from Weber's biographer; see Joachim Radkau, *Max Weber: A Biography*, trans.Patrick Camiller (in German: *Max Weber. Die Leidenschaft des Denkens*, 2005) (Cambridge: Polity Press, 2009), xv, 295, 394.

[15] Max Weber, *Economy and Society: An Outline of Interpretive Sociology* (1922), trans. Ephraim Fischoff et al., ed. Günther Roth and Claus Wittich (Berkeley, Los Angeles, and London: University of California Press, 1978), 215.

[16] George and Weber maintained informal social relations in the 1910s when Heidelberg, where Weber held a university chair, was something like the headquarters of George's entourage. See Marianne Weber, *Max Weber. Ein Lebensbild* (Tübingen: Mohr Siebeck, 1926).

[17] Salin, *Um Stefan George*, 11–12. The passage is also quoted (in a different translation) by Gay, *Weimar Culture*, 46–7.

[18] Edgar Salin (1892–1974), son of a German Jewish entrepreneur, volunteered in the German army in the First World War and was severely wounded on the Eastern Front. After serving as a diplomat

for Salin a captivation as life-changing as a religious awakening or falling in love at first sight. Becoming George's disciple actually combined elements of both. Salin recounts how he underwent a series of tests and interrogations to prove his worthiness—tests, for example, of his ability to read poetry aloud—and how he anticipated these trials with trepidation and dread of failure. But George could also be suddenly amiable and affectionate. Shifting between favours and rebuffs was part of the initiation process, the seductive mystique of the Master being heightened by his sphinx-like unpredictability.

Those who found acceptance had to submit unconditionally to George's rule. Young, impressionable, and, more often than not, in the throes of a crisis of orientation, they were desperately ready for what George had to offer: guidance towards an exacting way of life which held the promise of a spiritual regeneration, a 'new self'. Being taken under George's wing could also be a harrowing experience, as another acolyte, Ernst Glöckner, imparts in a letter to his companion and lover Ernst Bertram (4 April 1913):

> George [...] saw and recognized me, greeted me and invited himself in [to Glöckner's Munich flat]. And now my only wish is that I had never met this man. What I did that evening was beyond my control, I acted as in a dream, under the power of his will, having no will of my own, tractable, oh so tractable, like a child. It was a dreadful, unutterable, blissful, heinous and exalted experience with many shivers of happiness and as many gazes into an infinite abyss. I was a toy in his hands, I loved and hated at once [...].[19]

Glöckner's account shades into the Gothic when he describes the moment of surrender:

> Tall, eerily tall, [George] stood there, leaning against the wardrobe, and his eyes were those of a frightening dream. His voice was hard and full of metal, his forehead threatening and his mouth full of bitterness: 'Do you know why you didn't come to me? I know. Because you were afraid of the chasm that lies between me and you [...] And yet you feel that part of you belongs to me.' His face became that of a devil. I never knew that a man could look like that. Dusk had settled in the room, it was almost dark. His eyes were still aglow. He seized my hand. And what happened then was beyond my control. It happened and had to happen. I hated and loved the man from the bottom of my soul. I was trembling all over. I knew: This man is doing me violence—but I was no longer strong enough. I kissed the hand he offered and with choking voice uttered: 'Master, what shall I do?' He pulled me up to his chest, embraced me and kissed me on the forehead. He clutched me tightly as I clutched him. Softly he kept saying: 'My boy, my dear boy. My dear.' How I could bear this

---

in the German embassy at Berne, he began his academic career in Heidelberg, where he wrote his postdoctoral habilitation thesis on *Plato and Greek Utopia* (1921). As a professor at Heidelberg, he was the dissertation adviser of the American sociologist Talcott Parsons. In 1927 he took up the chair in political economics at Basle, where he spent the rest of his academic life, serving as Rector of the university before retiring in 1962. His publications include a *History of Political Economics* (1923), *Jakob Burckhardt and Nietzsche* (1938), and translations of several Platonic dialogues.

[19] Ernst Glöckner, *Begegnung mit Stefan George. Auszüge aus Briefen und Tagebüchern 1913–1934* (Heidelberg: Lothar Stiehm, 1972), 23.

I don't know. It felt good and sweet, and yet, at that moment, I despised myself as I have never despised myself before. I was grateful and hated him at the same time. It was dreadful.[20]

Glöckner was twenty-eight at the time, much older than most other novices, and for all his self-confessed weakness and emotional turmoil, he was capable of reflection. 'There is no excuse', George rebuked him, that Glöckner had not tried harder to meet him; that in fact he had not tried at all, but left everything to chance:

> I tried once more to defend myself. But he said: 'There is no excuse. You really should have come. Now you see what you would have been missing if fate had not been kind to you.' I thought to myself: 'What presumption!' I wanted to find him ridiculous but couldn't [...] There are men who are allowed any presumption and still do not become ridiculous.[21]

Oscillating between the benign and the demonic, George's charisma, as these accounts testify, had its basis in the direct personal contact between master and disciple. But its effect was felt in ever widening circles of influence. Walter Benjamin records how, during a stay in Heidelberg in 1921, he spent hours on the street just to catch a glimpse of the poet walking by. 'But this was at a time when the impact of his work had long since left a decisive impression on me.'[22] A single brief encounter in 1916 was enough to convince the political economist Kurt Singer, as he wrote to Martin Buber, that 'no man today embodies the divine more purely and creatively than George—but that is not enough: in George the present time has its hub and centre of renewal.'[23] Even Thomas Mann, although aware that George regarded him as a second-rate author, noted in his diary on 1 August 1921 that '"*die Wahrheit und das Leben*" [truth and life] could only be found in the sphere of George and his followers.'[24]

Radiating out beyond his immediate circle of admirers, George's auratic persona came to be perceived as a powerful cultural and, by extension, political force in

---

[20] Glöckner, *Begegnung mit Stefan George*, 26. Norton, *Secret Germany*, 505–11, discusses the passage at length.

[21] Glöckner, *Begegnung mit Stefan George*, 27. Ernst Glöckner (1885–1934) was the life-long partner of Ernst Bertram (1884–1957), whom he met in 1906. Bertram's influential book on Nietzsche (*Nietzsche: Attempt at a Mythology*, trans. Robert E. Norton [Urbana, IL: University of Illinois Press, 2009]) appeared in 1918 with George's publisher Georg Bondi. Bertram was both fascinated by and sceptical of George. He also maintained close relations with Thomas Mann, who was always *persona non grata* in the George Circle. Mann wrote more than 250 letters to Bertram, but their relations cooled when Bertram publicly supported the Nazi regime in 1933. See *Thomas Mann an Ernst Bertram—Briefe aus den Jahren 1910–1955*, ed. Inge Jens (Pfullingen: Günther Neske, 1960).

[22] Walter Benjamin, 'Über Stefan George', *Die Literarische Welt* 28 (13 July 1928), 3; reprinted in Benjamin, *Gesammelte Schriften*, vol. II, pt. 2: *Aufsätze, Essays, Voträge*, ed. Rolf Tiedemann and Hermann Schweppenhäuser (Frankfurt: Suhrkamp, 1977), 622–4 at 622. This was Benjamin's response to the question as to what George had meant for his personal development. The journal *Literarische Welt* had polled writers on the occasion of George's sixtieth birthday. Benjamin's statement is by far the most personal one.

[23] Quoted in Melissa S. Lane and Martin A. Ruehl, 'Introduction', in *A Poet's Reich*, ed. Lane and Ruehl, 1–22 at 1.

[24] Lane and Ruehl, 'Introduction', 3.

the 1910s and even more so in the 1920s. It was this political dimension of his charisma that qualified him to appear, in the quoted final paragraph of Gundolf's book, not as another Mommsen[25] but as another Caesar; not in other words, as a mere interpreter of Caesar's greatness, but a reincarnation of his spirit.

This spirit was perceived, just as it is in Nietzsche, as the very antithesis to the evils of contemporary mass culture. To his followers George embodied the same union of poet and ruler, a union which combined the 'vision of the most powerful reality [...] with the most powerful strength for action' that Nietzsche envisages in the Shakespeare passage of *Ecce Homo*.[26] But where Nietzsche proclaimed this idea in a wilderness of neglect, George willed it into existence. He became absolute ruler over an exclusive 'empire' of his own making, a 'Secret Germany'[27] pitted against the official Germany of the Wilhelmine Empire and its successor, the ill-fated Weimar Republic.

II 'THE MARRIAGE OF TRUE MINDS'

The early stages of George's career gave little indication that his influence was to extend well beyond the sphere of poetry; it was to this sphere, and to this sphere alone, that he was initially committed. George's poetic beginnings were closely linked with French Symbolism. Born in provincial Bingen on the west bank of the Rhine, he was the son of a wine merchant with family roots in Lorraine. He was introduced to Stéphane Mallarmé, grand master of Symbolism, during a stay in Paris in his early twenties and became a regular at Mallarmé's famous Tuesday soirées. Accordingly, *l'art pour l'art* was the doctrine flaunted in the opening editorial of the literary magazine George founded in 1892, *Blätter für die Kunst* ('Pages for the Arts'), a declaration of intent 'to serve art—especially poetry and the written word, and to exclude everything pertaining to the state and society [...] SPIRITUAL ART on the basis of a new way of feeling and making—an art for art's sake—[...] in opposition to the stale and inferior school sprung from a false notion of reality.'[28] What later became known as the *George-Kreis* ('George Circle') thus 'began as an association [*Zusammenschluss*]' of like-minded artists 'with limited [i.e. aesthetic] goals'.[29]

---

[25] Theodor Mommsen's monumental *History of Rome*, first published in three volumes in 1854–6 and winning its author the Nobel Prize for literature in 1902, more than any other work of historiography propagated a glowingly positive image of Caesar across nineteenth-century Europe.

[26] See Chapter 1 section VI.

[27] The term 'Secret Germany' was coined by George's friend the poet Karl Wolfskehl in 1910. Cf. Karlauf, *Stefan George*, 409. It is worth noting that the adjective *geheim* (secret) etymologically derives, like *unheimlich*, from *Heim* (home). In its original late medieval usage, *geheim* meant 'familiar', 'intimate'. This meaning survived in the title of *Geheimrat*, the 'trusted adviser' of a ruler, a privy councillor.

[28] *Blätter für die Kunst* 1.1 (1892), reprinted in Georg Peter Landmann, ed., *Der George-Kreis. Eine Auswahl seiner Schriften* (Cologne and Berlin: Kiepenheuer & Witsch, 1965), 15.

[29] Ute Oelmann, 'The George Circle: From *Künstlergesellschaft* to *Lebensgemeinschaft*', in *A Poet's Reich*, ed. Lane and Ruehl, 25–36 at 25.

After 1900 the goals expanded and the group became more tightly knit, changing from an association of kindred spirits to a circle of followers in which George became 'the Master' and his word, law. That George's dominance could assert itself increasingly unchecked was facilitated by the fact that his entourage was becoming younger and younger. While his earlier associates had been roughly his own age, Maximilian Kronberger ('Maximin') was only fifteen when he met the poet in 1903.[30] The juvenescence of his following was decisive for the expansion of George's mission: his aim to shape not just lyrics but lives—and thus ultimately the life of the nation, as Friedrich Gundolf explained in 1918: '[W]hat matters for George and his followers is not aesthetic play, not narcissistic and esoteric enjoyment of language; what we are talking about is a serious mission: the moulding of a man and a people.'[31]

Gundolf was the exemplary case. The first of George's young acolytes, he became something of a prototype for all later recruits, the favourite and first-in-rank among the disciples until his irrevocable fall from grace in 1922. 'Before [George] met Gundolf there was no "Circle", just a loose association of like-minded people.'[32] Born Friedrich Gundelfinger, the son of a Jewish professor of mathematics, he was renamed 'Gundolf' by George on their first meeting: a sovereign act of possessive knowing. Gundolf is who he became once and for all, the name under which he lies buried in Heidelberg's sylvan 'mountain cemetery'. Although his professional field was German, not English literature, Gundolf became the chief Shakespearean of the George Circle.

They met in the spring of 1899. George was thirty, Gundolf eighteen (Figure 2.2). Their introduction was arranged by George's friend and fellow poet, Karl Wolfskehl, who had met the young Friedrich half a year earlier in their mutual hometown of Darmstadt.[33] Tall and slender, 'his shoulders crowned with a captivatingly handsome boy's head',[34] the young man was also a budding poet. When Wolfskehl enthusiastically suggested that he be introduced to the greatest living poet, the boy's father intervened: not before Friedrich had completed his *Abitur*![35] Once this

---

[30] Born in 1888, Kronberger first attracted George's attention in 1902 when he was still only thirteen. He died in April 1904.

[31] Friedrich Gundolf, *Stefan George in unserer Zeit* (Heidelberg: Weiss, 1918), 12–13. The translation (modified) is taken from Alexander Mikhailovsky, *Three Principles of 'Political Theology' in the Stefan George Circle* (Moscow: National Research University, Higher School of Economics, Basic Research Program, Working Papers, Series: Humanities WP BRP 26/HUM/2013), <http://www.hse.ru/data/2013/05/08/1299213257/26HUM2013.pdf>, accessed 3 September 2014.

[32] Claude David, 'Gundolf und George', in *Euphorion. Zeitschrift für Literaturgeschichte* 75 (1981), 159–77 at 161: 'Gundolf is not just the First, he is the true founder.'

[33] Karl Wolfskehl (1869–1948), the son of a Jewish banker with family roots allegedly going back to the tenth century, went to the same Darmstadt grammar school as George and came under the spell of his poetry as a student at Gießen University, but did not meet George until 1893. Unique among George's associates, Wolfskehl insisted that it was the poetry, not the personal charisma of the poet that changed his life (Karlauf, *Stefan George*, 176). He remained a loyal friend and supporter to the end. Forced to leave Germany in 1933, he emigrated to Switzerland, then Italy, and eventually to New Zealand. The Munich home of Wolfskehl and his wife served George for many years as a regular lodging.

[34] Friedrich Wolters, *Stefan George und die Blätter für die Kunst. Deutsche Geistesgeschichte seit 1890* (Berlin: Georg Bondi, 1930), 168.

[35] Karlauf, *Stefan George*, 271–3.

Figure 2.2. Friedrich Gundolf in 1899. Reproduced by permission of Stefan George Archiv, Württembergische Landesbibliothek.

hurdle was cleared, the meeting took place. It proved decisive for them both: George found the perfect disciple, and Gundolf the master who would dominate the rest of his life.[36]

George's previous attachments to young men had been, at best, mixed successes. His attempt to befriend Hugo von Hofmannsthal came close to disaster; the attractive young music student Cyril Scott rejected all amorous advances. The one affair that did materialize left George with a feeling of having disclosed too much of himself to an unworthy companion.[37] With Gundolf, at last, everything turned out right. But warned by previous experience, George approached the young man cautiously. According to his biographer, 'he must have quickly realized that his beloved had no homoerotic proclivities.'[38] Yet eventually, by spring

[36] David, 'Gundolf und George', 163: 'In the relation between master and disciple George finally found the relationship which satisfied his will to power and also protected his shy, solitary and tormented nature.'

[37] Karlauf, *Stefan George*, 9–27, 265–6, 150–3. Cyril Scott (1879–1970), who later became known as a composer, gives a rather chatty account of his encounter with George in *Die Tragödie Stefan Georges: ein Erinnerungsbild und ein Gang durch sein Werk* (Eltville: Hempe, 1952).

[38] Karlauf, *Stefan George*, 279.

1900, a love affair did ensue. In 'Looking Back' (*Umschau*) George celebrates its consummation:

> You yielded wondering, and willingly sank down,
>   And moaned beneath the overflow of bliss,
> You rose: Around your limbs a stainless glory shone,
>   You were bewildered by a breathless kiss.
>
> And then the hour came—they rested in embrace,
>   Their lips still burning from a wilder hold,
> And to the room, through which the stars serenely gazed,
>   A dawn had come, suffused with rose and gold.[39]

Gundolf's admiration for his mentor's genius was boundless from the start. He unconditionally surrendered to George's guidance, as seen in one of his earliest letters, from 21 June 1899:

> Esteemed Master!
>
> The high task you set before my eyes has spurred me on: in the last few days I have translated, as well as I was able, some sixty sonnets, the first fifty in continuous sequence. Allow me to send you, esteemed Master, to whom alone I owe Everything, some of these exercises and trials.
>
> In deep and grateful reverence,
>
> Yours, Friedrich Gundolf[40]

The sonnets in question are Shakespeare's. The 'high task' George set had spurred the disciple to an astonishing feat in a time span far short of what one would think necessary to translate a third of Shakespeare's sonnets. Even though thirty-three of the translated sonnets lack the final couplet, the accomplishment remains extraordinary. It is proof of Gundolf's unlimited capacity for enthusiasm and a first example of his abundant, at times almost eruptive productivity. As George would acknowledge even after their final break-up, '[h]e was the most gifted of you all. He had thoughts, so many, from here to the sea. No sooner had he woken up than they began coming. No sooner had he put on his socks than he was sitting at the table writing.'[41]

Gundolf had enclosed translations of four Shakespeare sonnets (and two by Rossetti) with his first letter to George earlier in June 1899. These translations, George wrote back, were 'good in tone'; but rendering 'the immortal CLIV' into German, he warned, was an 'undertaking only for the darlings of the gods'[42]—to which the young translator modestly responded: 'Among the darlings of the gods [...] I dare not rate myself.'[43] Obviously this did not prevent him from trying all

---

[39] *The Works of Stefan George*, 184–5. Stefan George, *Sämtliche Werke*, 18 vols, ed. the Stefan George Society (Stuttgart: Klett-Cotta, 1982–2013), vol. 6/7: *Der siebente Ring*, ed. Ute Oelmann (1986), 70. 'Looking Back' (*'Umschau'*), of which the last two stanzas are quoted here, is one of twelve poems in which George reflects upon his relationship with Gundolf. Written between 1899 and 1902, they form part of *The Seventh Ring* (*Der Siebente Ring*), published in 1907.

[40] Gundolf to George, 21 June 1899. *Stefan George/Friedrich Gundolf. Briefwechsel*, ed. Robert Boehringer with Georg Peter Landmann (Düsseldorf and Munich: Küpper, 1962), 30.

[41] Robert Boehringer, *Ewiger Augenblick* (Düsseldorf and Munich: Küpper, 1965), 29.

[42] George to Gundolf, 11 June 1899, *Stefan George/Friedrich Gundolf. Briefwechsel*, 29.

[43] Gundolf to George, 15 June 1899, *Stefan George/Friedrich Gundolf. Briefwechsel*, 29.

the same, although the gods proved to be sparing with their favour. Before the month was over, Gundolf was complaining of the 'Sisyphean labour' of translation and his dwindling satisfaction with the results.[44] The project came to a halt and was not taken up again until seven years later, when the Master himself decided to take on 'the office of darling of the gods'[45] and 're-create' Shakespeare's sonnets in German. One might well speculate that the relationship between the poet-speaker and the fair youth as depicted in Shakespeare's sonnets 1–126 would have appealed to George as a compendium of the emotional amplitudes he himself had experienced in the halcyon days of his intimacy with Gundolf.[46] But a mirroring of merely private emotions was clearly not enough to draw Shakespeare and the sonnets to the centre of his attention.

For this to happen, Ernst Osterkamp suggests, another fair youth had to enter the Master's orbit.[47] This was Maximilian Kronberger ('Maximin'), a grammar school boy of poetical talent and captivating charm, whose sudden death of meningitis, a day after his sixteenth birthday in 1904 was glorified by George into an apotheosis. Death made Maximin immortal, furnishing George's adoration of youth with an imperishable icon. The cycle of twenty-two poems dedicated to Maximin in George's 1907 volume *The Seventh Ring* is a poetical theogony. It forms the centre not only of this volume but, according to Ute Oelmann, of George's whole œuvre.[48] Construing a typological analogy with the life and death of Jesus Christ, the Maximin cycle also evokes other, specifically poetic, deifications undertaken through the medium of sonnets: Dante's glorification of Beatrice, that of Laura by Petrarch (138). It was in this context, Osterkamp argues, that Mr W. H., 'the onlie begetter' of Shakespeare's sonnets, could become the 'prefiguration of M. K.' whom George, the only begetter of 'Maximin', turned into 'the god of his work and his state' (138). The centrality of Shakespeare's tribute to the fair youth for George's Maximin experience and its cultic idealization is signalled by their juxtaposition in a 'best of' special issue of *Pages for Art* in 1909. Fifteen of George's 're-created' Shakespeare sonnets immediately precede the Preface to Maximin 'who had been elevated to another star before his divinity became earthly like ourselves' (138). 'To some you are a child', 'Advent I', the first of the Maximin poems, begins,

> To some a friend, to me
> The god whom I divined
> And tremblingly adore.[49]

---

[44] Gundolf to Wolfskehl, 29 July 1899, quoted in *Stefan George/Friedrich Gundolf. Briefwechsel*, 30.

[45] Jürgen Gutsch, 'Einleitung', in *Friedrich Gundolfs Shakespeare-Sonetten-Fragmente*, ed. Jürgen Gutsch (Dozwil: EDITION SIGNAThUR, 2011), 7–19 at 9.

[46] The twelve poems in which George records the experience of these days run the gamut from happiness to estrangement and dejection, oscillating between a longing for closeness and the reluctance to allow it. See note 39 in this chapter.

[47] Ernst Osterkamp, 'Shakespeare und der Georgekreis', in *Shakespeare unter den Deutschen*, ed. Jansohn (Stuttgart: Franz Steiner, 2015), 131–42 at 137–8. References are given in brackets in the text.

[48] George, *Sämtliche Werke*, vol. 6/7, 191. On the cult of Maximin as a surrogate religion: Claus-Artur Scheier, 'Maximins Lichtung: Philosophische Bemerkungen zu Georges Gott', *George-Jahrbuch* 1 (1996/7), 80–106; Karlauf, *Stefan George*, 342–53.

[49] *The Works of Stefan George*, 194.

The Maximin experience promoted Shakespeare to George's exclusive pantheon of original spirits.[50] An earlier poem had referred to Shakespeare as '[t]he fog-islands' sombre lord of the spirit':[51] a more peripheral figure than Dante, for example, who always played a very tangible role in George's self-fashioning. In him George 'found the sublime simile of his vocation'[52] and prided himself on his Dantesque facial profile.[53] Shakespeare, his life and character as fog-bound as his native isles, hardly lent himself to such self-enhancement. But this very lack of biographical data made his sonnets an all the more suitable vessel for the gospel of divine youth.

When George took on the sonnets, it was resolved that Gundolf would go to work on Shakespeare's plays—an even more daunting challenge, one would think. But on George's scale, drama took second place to the lyric poem as the highest, most undiluted form of poetic expression. Drama, moreover, was intrinsically compromised by its association with the theatre, which George held in haughty contempt.[54] Gundolf, in any case, would not start from scratch but submit the canonical Schlegel/Tieck translation to a thorough revision—guided and aided by George himself.[55] The first volume, containing Gundolf's favourite Roman plays, *Coriolanus*, *Julius Caesar*, and *Antony and Cleopatra*, appeared in 1908 in the characteristically lavish Art Nouveau style of George's book designer Melchior Lechter.[56] The joint struggle for the optimal German Shakespeare was completed in 1918. It engendered the most intimate working relationship between the two men. 'Our joint work on Shakespeare has again, and more powerfully than ever, revealed George to me [...] in a way that can be sensed but not fully comprehended from his work', Gundolf wrote to Wolfskehl:

> He is the only genius of our time and a typical genius at that; and if we read in books about Goethe or Napoleon of all the things they knew and did [...] this doesn't give us a tenth of the knowledge gained through living participation in the work of such a man. I feel entitled to say that there are not three people in the world who know him

[50] On the distinction between 'original spirits' (*Urgeister*) and 'derivative beings' (*abgeleitete Wesen*) in the thought of the George Circle, see Gunilla Eschenbach, *Imitatio im George-Kreis* (Berlin and New York: De Gruyter, 2011), 1–7 and *passim*.

[51] *The Works of Stefan George*, 126. Originally in Stefan George, *Der Teppich des Lebens und die Lieder von Traum und Tod mit einem Vorspiel* (1900) (*Sämtliche Werke*, vol. 5, ed. Ute Oelmann [1984], 27).

[52] Friedrich Gundolf, *George* (Berlin: Georg Bondi, 1920), 53.

[53] A number of portrait photographs show George cultivating his Dante look. In a photograph taken at the Munich Artists' Carnival in 1904, he appears costumed as Dante. See Figure 3.2. Raulff, wickedly trenchant, calls George 'the evil aunt with the Dante profile'. Raulff, 'Ihr wisst nicht, wer ich bin', 18.

[54] George's estrangement from Hofmannsthal was aggravated when Hofmannsthal increasingly turned to writing for the stage. In the eyes of George and his circle, Hofmannsthal ceased to be a poet when he became a successful playwright and the librettist for Richard Strauss's operas.

[55] Gundolf revised the translations carried out by August Wilhelm Schlegel himself, whom he greatly admired, and re-translated the plays done by Schlegel's collaborators Dorothea Tieck and Wolf Graf Baudissin.

[56] *Shakespeare in deutscher Sprache. Herausgegeben und zum Teil neu übersetzt* [edited and in part newly translated] *von Friedrich Gundolf* (Berlin: Georg Bondi, 1908). Melchior Lechter (1865–1937) created the signature look of the publications of George and his Circle. By 1910, Lechter's opulent *Jugendstil* book decorations harking back to William Morris and the Kelmscott Press were beginning to look dated and later publications of the George Circle appeared in spare *Neue Sachlichkeit* designs.

[George] as I know him now, and it seems to me as if I did not really know him before the work on Shakespeare. And it often makes me sad that the wonderful essence of the man is never fully appreciated, not even by the most ardent admirers of his verses. [...] [B]ut no one can do justice to living beings who are GREAT— this is one of the tragic secrets from which the world draws its dark magic. Let us count ourselves lucky that we are witnesses.[57]

The aim of this collaborative effort was not to make Shakespeare more palatable to a modern German readership, let alone a theatre audience. Rather, it was to uncompromisingly uphold the poetic power of the original, reinforcing rather than levelling out its difficulties, its demanding, even forbidding unfamiliarity.

Gundolf's aim was to recast Shakespeare 'from the fullness of the German language', past and present. The archaic speech-forms thus reintroduced, because recognizably deliberate, were not seen as simply old-fashioned but as part of a poetic programme. It included going back to the roots and, in idiomatic phrases, staying so close to the original as to jolt the readers into a new awareness—at the price of being thought rarefied or even stilted.[58] In the words of the poet Rudolf Borchardt (1877–1945), one of George's most strident critics: 'Gundolf translates Shakespeare from German into "the language-body [*Sprachleib*] of the spirit to come" and from English into something he takes to be German.'[59]

Unperturbed by such detraction, the great work continued. 'I am living here completely dedicated to Shakespeare', Gundolf reported from the Swiss village of Wolfenschiessen, where he and the Master had gone into retreat, 'but soon it will be accomplished, and a splendid work it will be thanks to the Master's hand, which has kneaded the somewhat sloppy Gundel-tone into true marmoreal form.'[60]

III 'THE MASTER MISTRESS OF MY PASSION'

Most 'marmoreal' of all, Shakespeare's sonnets were exemplary: in George's hands they became self-contained artefacts, chiselled to stern, crystalline perfection. George completed the translation or, as he termed it, the re-creation (*Umdichtung*), in 1909. In his brief introduction he explains why Shakespeare's sonnets had hitherto met with little acclaim in Germany.[61] '[W]e are used to seeing all poetry as

[57] Gundolf to Wolfskehl, August 1908, Karl and Hanna Wolfskehl, *Briefwechsel mit Friedrich Gundolf 1899–1931*, ed. Karlhans Kluncker (Amsterdam: Castrum Peregrini, 1977), 66–8 at 67–8.
[58] Hortmann, *Shakespeare on the German Stage*, vol. 2, 87; cf. also Hanspeter Schelp, 'Friedrich Gundolf als Shakespeare-Übersetzer', *Shakespeare-Jahrbuch West* (1971), 97–117 at 97.
[59] Rudolf Borchardt, 'Intermezzo', in *Gesammelte Werke in Einzelbänden*, vol. 6: *Prosa I*, ed. Gerhard Schuster (Stuttgart: Klett-Cotta, 2002), 105–38 at 110.
[60] Letter to Wiesi de Haan, 5 July 1908, quoted in Boehringer, 'Einleitung', 17. 'Gundel', a diminutive form of Gundolf, was George's pet name for him.
[61] *Shakespeare Sonnette. Umdichtung von Stefan George* (Berlin: Georg Bondi, 1909), 5. The German spelling of sonnet is *Sonett*, one n, two t's. George always spelt the word with two n's and two t's. For a succinct account of George's 're-creation' of the sonnets: Ute Oelmann, 'Shakespeare Sonnette. Umdichtung', in *Stefan George und sein Kreis. Ein Handbuch*, ed. Achim Aurnhammer, Wolfgang Braungart, Stefan Breuer, and Ute Oelmann (Berlin and New York: De Gruyter, 2012), 238–54.

"romantic"', but these poems, 'despite being supreme poetry, are utterly "unromantic"'. Their subject matter, however, poses an even greater obstacle:

> Editors and explicators have fruitlessly argued over this for centuries: what was play, what was genuine feeling; who was the blond youth, who the black lady of the last section. They have guessed, racked and erred over this, completely misapprehending the soul tone. [...] [T]he duller minds saw but style exercises, the baser ones the image of their own loathing. But hardly anyone realised their true content: the adoration of beauty and the burning desire for eternity. In our own day, [...] poets have spoken frankly: at the centre of the sonnet sequence [...] stands the passionate devotion of the poet to his friend. One must accept this even if one cannot understand it and it would be foolish to defile with blame or apology what one of the greatest mortals found good. Materialistic and intellectualistic eras in particular have no right to make words about this subject since they have not even the slightest notion of the world-creating power of supersexual love.[62]

This declaration makes it clear that Shakespeare's sonnets are not just of private significance for George. His passionate plea for love over and above the sexual defines the bonding principle of the Circle, the erotic foundations of George's spiritual Reich in the face of an uncomprehending if not downright hostile environment. In showing 'what one of the greatest mortals found good' the sonnets provided an authoritative precedent for George's public championing of homoeroticism. If the poet's adoration for the 'master mistress of [his] passion' (Sonnet 20) attests to the world-creating power of male-to-male love, it also draws the all-important line at genital sex. The 'thing' with which doting Nature 'prick'd out' the fair youth is for women's use only:

> And for a woman wert thou first created,
> Till nature as she wrought thee fell a-doting,
> And by addition me of thee defeated,
> By adding one thing to my purpose nothing.
> But since she pricked thee out for women's pleasure,
> Mine be thy love and thy love's use their treasure. (9–14)

In Wilhelmine Germany, the distinction between 'love' and 'love's use' marked the difference between legal (if not exactly respectable) and criminal behaviour. Paragraph 175 of the penal code made homosexual intercourse a punishable offence, carrying monetary fines or prison sentences.

In 1909, the topic was very much in the public eye. The so-called Eulenburg affair had scandalized the nation for over three years and compromised leading members of the Kaiser's inner circle, the 'Camarilla', with allegations of homosexual conduct. The scandal was set off by the Jewish journalist Maximilian Harden, one of the most colourful and volatile intellectual figures of the period.[63] Harden

---

[62] The last two sentences are quoted in Robert E. Norton's translation: Norton, *Secret Germany*, 338.

[63] H. F. Young, *Maximilian Harden, Censor Germaniae: The Critic in Opposition from Bismarck to the Rise of Nazism* (The Hague: Nijhoff, 1959); Helga Neumann and Manfred Neumann, *Maximilian Harden (1861–1927): ein unerschrockener deutsch-jüdischer Kritiker und Publizist* (Würzburg: Königshausen & Neumann, 2003).

was not an anti-homosexual zealot; he had in fact previously campaigned for the abolishment of Paragraph 175. But when it came to fighting what he saw as the pernicious influence of the 'Camarilla' on the Emperor's politics, he did not hesitate to sling any available mud. Harden's chief target was Philipp, Prince of Eulenburg-Hertefeld, a close—perhaps the closest—personal friend of Wilhelm II. Eulenburg's affair with General Kuno, Count von Moltke was only the first in a series of revelations making the Kaiser appear to be enmeshed in a network of practising homosexuals. Harden's smear campaign resulted in a spate of trials, counter-trials, and court-martials. The horror of public disgrace it brought may well have prompted the suicides of six military officers in 1906/7 following blackmail.

Arguably the most damaging political scandal of Germany's Second Empire,[64] the Eulenburg affair, much like the Oscar Wilde trials in England a decade earlier, brought homosexuality to unprecedented public attention, mobilizing not only outraged conservatives, but also advocates of sexual reform. Dr Magnus Hirschfeld, pioneering sexologist and campaigner for homosexual rights, testified in the libel suit that Count von Moltke had filed against Harden—much, as it turned out, to the benefit of the defendant. Based on the deposition of Moltke's former wife and on his courtroom observation of Moltke, Hirschfeld declared that the Count clearly had a feminine side and was homosexually inclined even if he had never practised same-sex intercourse.[65]

The Eulenburg affair certainly did not make life easier for sexual dissidents. 'In view of recent events caution seems more imperative than ever', records the small but dedicated 'Scientific-humanitarian Committee of Munich' in its minutes of February 1908.[66] An earlier memorandum (December 1906) vividly captures the pitfalls of the 'scientific' approach to homosexuality—even when pursued with the best intentions. Hirschfeld, the memorandum complains, had 'unduly emphasized the pathological nature of homosexuality':

> His extensive description of the Berlin transvestite scene and of street prostitution have been equally detrimental to our cause.[67] [...] There is no good reason for harping on

---

[64] As Eulenburg's wife remarked to Hirschfeld, '[t]hey are striking at my husband, but their target is the Kaiser.' Magnus Hirschfeld, 'Vor fünfundzwanzig Jahren', *Die Freundschaft* 15.2 (1933), 2. Cf. James D. Steakley, 'Iconography of a Scandal: Political Cartoons and the Eulenburg Affair', in *History of Homosexuality in Europe and America*, ed. Wayne R. Dynes and Stephen Donaldson (New York: Garland, 1992), 323–85 at 330.

[65] Alois Brand, another activist for the cause of sexual minority rights and founder of the world's first homosexual periodical, *Der Eigene* (*One's Own*), was induced by the Eulenburg affair to make a similarly unfortunate intervention. Alleging that Imperial Chancellor Prince Bernhard von Bülow had been blackmailed for engaging in homosexual activities, he claimed that this put von Bülow under the moral obligation to work towards the abolition of Paragraph 175. Bülow sued for libel. Brand was found guilty and sentenced to eighteen months in prison.

[66] Wissenschaftlich-humanitäres Komitee München, Friday, 7 February 1908: Marita Keilson-Lauritz and Friedemann Pfäfflin, eds, *100 Jahre Schwulenbewegung an der Isar I: Die Sitzungsberichte des Wissenschaftlich-humanitären Komitees München 1902–1908* (Munich: forum homosexualität und geschichte münchen e.v., 2003), 60. Three months later the committee decided to disband due to continuing hostility to its cause.

[67] The allusion is probably to Magnus Hirschfeld, *Berlins Drittes Geschlecht* [Berlin's Third Sex] (Berlin and Leipzig: Seemann, 1904).

about venal and depraved love. On the contrary, it is highly damaging for the reputation and the best interest of our cause.

The emphasis should be on the advantageous effect of the relationship between two homosexuals, especially on the frequently so beneficial influence of an older man on a younger one. We should show how the friendship of an experienced, worldly-wise man can guide the youth through the thicket of adolescent temptations, cautioning and admonishing, approachable even where youthful sensitivity would naturally shy from asking the advice of a father or teacher.[68]

Both in what it deplores and in what it seeks to promote, the memorandum presents a pedestrian version of the Georgean position. George too rejected the medical, pathologizing view of homosexuality, but unlike the members of the Scientific-Humanitarian Committee he rejected the very term 'homosexuality' itself.[69] George was not propounding tolerance for a minority; he was making a haughty assertion of superiority. *Super*sexual (*übergeschlechtlich*) served not only as a sanitizing barrier against notions of sexual perversion but also, as in Nietzsche's *Übermensch*, as an index of pre-eminence. What George's pedagogic eros sought to engender was a nobler breed of men.

Three years after the publication of *Shakespeare Sonnette*, George saw fit to reconfirm his position on the friendship cult as part of a general clarification of his position. This took the form of an editorial in the 1912 *Yearbook for the Spiritual Movement* (*Jahrbuch für die geistige Bewegung*), jointly authored by Gundolf and his co-editor Friedrich Wolters. Inaugurated in 1910 and discontinued after only three volumes, the *Yearbook* was intended to complement the *Pages for the Arts* as the official bulletin of Circle policy, reflecting the evolution of George's mission from self-sufficient art to wider issues of cultural critique and life reform.

The 1912 editorial begins with a sweeping condemnation of the present: '[E]veryone from the Emperor to the lowest worker feels that it cannot possibly go on like this [...] No one can still honestly believe in the foundations of the present state of the world.'[70] What follows is a list of symptoms itemizing the ills of modernity: from science gone rampant to the neglect of greatness and great men, from the decay of humanism to the rise of the masses and of 'modern woman', who is to blame for 'some of the worst' modern heresies, such as 'theosophy and the peace movement':

That the Germans are turning, as the French already have and the Americans will, into a feminized people is a greater social danger than the thousand particular ills described by the newspapers. [...] Never again can a great man go forth from such desubstanced, uprooted, reflected stock.[71]

---

[68] Keilson-Lauritz and Pfäfflin, eds, *Sitzungsberichte des Wissenschaftlich-humanitären Komitees München*, 58.

[69] 'Scientific' and 'humanitarian' (as opposed to 'humanist'), too, ranked high on George's list of hate words.

[70] [Friedrich Gundolf and Friedrich Wolters,] 'Einleitung der Herausgeber', in *Jahrbuch für die geistige Bewegung* 3 (Berlin: Verlag der Blätter für die Kunst, 1912), v–viii at v.

[71] [Gundolf and Wolters,] 'Einleitung der Herausgeber', vi.

After this paroxysm of misogynist loathing, the vindication of friendship comes as a positive counterweight. 'Progressive man', that Georgean *bête noire*, is alarmed by genuine friendship because it is not immediately convertible into usefulness. In the eyes of certain people it is, moreover, objectionable because of its alleged proneness to certain 'excesses'. 'We', however,

> do not ask whether the devotion of Schiller's Don Carlos to [his friend] Posa, or of Goethe's Ferdinand to Egmont [...] have anything to do with a witch-hunting paragraph in the code of law or a ridiculous medical category. Instead we have always found in these relationships an essential constituent of German culture. Without this eros, we find education merely a business or just prattle [...] It is not morality that even now prejudices people against such friendship. They are equally opposed to, indeed repulsed by, the love of Dante for Beatrice as they are by that of Shakespeare for his friend: theirs is the aversion of the American-type man who, lacking all sense of pathos, is against any form of heroic love. That we have nothing to do with the rather obnoxious people who whine for the abolition of certain penal laws should be clear from the fact that the most unsavoury attacks on us have been mounted from those quarters.[72]

What George had briefly but emphatically proclaimed in his preface to the sonnets is taken up and elaborated by his heralds, Gundolf and Wolters. The position they carve out bristles on two fronts with contempt for philistine prejudice and just as scathingly for homosexual rights activists and medical reformers of the Hirschfeld type.[73] The Circle was pitted against the conservative morality but equally, if not more so, enraged by liberal progressivism. 'Progress' was one of the dirtiest words in the George Circle's vocabulary, closely tied up with the blights of the modern world and, notably, that horror of horrors, 'feminization'.[74] When Sabine Lepsius, one of George's few long-standing female friends,[75] took offence at the *Yearbook*'s denigration of women and praise of homoerotic *Jünglingsliebe*, she received a highhanded reprimand from Gundolf: what she imagined boy love to be was a 'chimera created by females who can think only in sexual terms and are afraid of competition [...] If you really want to know what we are talking about, I recommend that you read Plato instead of the Harden trials.' If she could not appreciate the fact that *Jünglingsliebe* was a matter of 'world forces, not of medicinal problems', she forfeited her right to count herself among George's faithful.

---

[72] [Gundolf and Wolters,] 'Einleitung der Herausgeber', vi–vii.

[73] Hirschfeld's pioneering yearbook *Jahrbuch für sexuelle Zwischenstufen* (1899–1923) published a highly acclamatory article on male eros in the work of Stefan George in its 1914 issue: Peter Hamecher, 'Der männliche Eros im Werke Stefan Georges', *Jahrbuch für sexuelle Zwischenstufen* 14 (1914), 10–23. There is no indication that George or any of his followers took notice of this.

[74] 'We are no enemies to woman, only to "modern woman", fragmented, progressive, godless woman' [Gundolf and Wolters], 'Einleitung', v–vi.

[75] The home of the portrait painter Sabine Lepsius (1864–1942) and her husband Reinhold, also a painter, was a meeting point for Berlin's intellectual elite. George, a regular guest since 1897, frequently gave readings there. Lepsius recounted her friendship with the poet in Sabine Lepsius, *Stefan George: Geschichte einer Freundschaft* (Berlin: Verlag Die Runde, 1935). On the women among George's devotees: Ute Oelmann and Ulrich Raulff, eds, *Frauen um Stefan George* (Göttingen: Wallstein, 2010).

Whatever the Master's actual love life,[76] the official policy of the Circle, both in the 1909 preface and the 1912 editorial, was to promote eros and deny physical sex: not only physical sex, but also, and perhaps more importantly, the use of 'sex' as a label for categorizing identity. 'The sodomite', writes Michel Foucault, 'was a temporary aberration, the homosexual was now [around 1900] a species.' Marked by 'a kind of interior androgyny, a hermaphrodism of the soul', this 'species' was neither quite male nor quite female.[77] George, by contrast, preached an unequivocally masculine eros of friendship. This was the precondition of his success. Shunning anything that smacked of unmanliness, George ensured his appeal not only with those in his Circle who were not gay but also with an ever-widening following beyond the Circle. Proclaiming a love that dare not *quite* speak its name made it possible for his Circle to become a model for the sodalities of the German youth movement and for all-male groups on the far right of the political spectrum.[78] A demonstratively manly eros blended easily with hero-worship and a cult of leadership, while the idea of a shared secret heightened the charismatic appeal of the Master's exclusive entourage in the eyes of many of his admirers, especially the younger ones. Among the arcana of empire, secret love constituted one of the strongest ties of George's secret Reich.

The intimacy between George and Gundolf which had begun under the aegis of Shakespeare's sonnets long survived their love affair. As the Circle grew and its mission expanded into a philosophy of life and 'the moulding of [...] a people',[79] the more intimate Shakespearean constellation of poet and fair youth gave way to a more communal Platonic eros as the dominant erotic paradigm of the Circle, which its members now often referred to as 'the state'.[80] George found his own

[76] In a number of cases, George ordered his letters to be destroyed by the recipients, who seem to have done so without exception. There is only one letter extant that explicitly refers to sexual intercourse—in which Ernst Glöckner describes himself as having 'moaned under the weight of your [George's] body'; quoted in Norton, *Secret Germany*, 510, and more fully in Wolfgang Braungart, *Ästhetischer Katholizismus. Stefan Georges Rituale der Literatur* (Tübingen: Niemeyer, 1997), 250 n. 122. An explicit account of the sexual initiation rite which George allegedly administered personally to his novices is quoted in Raulff, *Kreis ohne Meister*, 514–15. This is based on the (rather questionable) testimony of Robert von Steiger, one of George's young friends in the late 1920s, and recorded in a letter by someone who made Steiger's acquaintance in Marrakesh in 1971.

[77] Michel Foucault, *The History of Sexuality*, vol. 1: *The Will to Knowledge* (1976), trans. Robert Hurley (London: Penguin, 1998), 43.

[78] Rudolf Borchardt accused the George cult and the 'pederastic youth movement' in general as trailblazers of National Socialism. Borchardt, *Aufzeichnung Stefan George betreffend*, ed. Ernst Osterkamp (Munich: Rudolf Borchardt-Gesellschaft, 1998), 94.

[79] Gundolf, as quoted earlier, see n. 31 in this chapter.

[80] Apparently it was Friedrich Wolters (1876–1930) who first used the term 'state' in relation to the Circle (see David, 'Gundolf und George', 166). Introduced to George in 1904, Wolters became a central figure of the Circle, in later years something like its chief ideologist. Together with Berthold Vallentin he initiated the *Yearbook* and was thus a major force in the turn towards the more outward-directed political course which the Circle adopted in the 1910s and 1920s. Wolters's overblown pathos and strident zeal were something of an embarrassment to more subtle-minded fellow Georgeans. But his energetic loyalty was much appreciated by the Master and earned him the honourable task of writing *Stefan George und die Blätter für die Kunst*. Gundolf dismissed it as the official 'church-history' of the 'George-orthodoxy' and a 'hopelessly bad, utterly dishonest book' (Letter to Julius Landmann, 16 November 1930, in *Stefan George/Friedrich Gundolf. Briefwechsel*, 390).

vision anticipated in Plato's state and its philosopher-king, the vision of a new 'spiritual Reich' under a poet-ruler sustained by the erotic force extolled in the *Symposium* and the *Phaedrus*.[81]

IV SHAKESPEARE AND THE GERMAN SPIRIT

On 12 August 1899, Gundolf proudly reported to Karl Wolfskehl the receipt of a letter from George:

> Today I must joyously tell you that yesterday I received my third letter from the Master [...] [a]nd with it the following glorious and exhilarating original verses:
>
> > Why probe so much in men who are remote, why read the legends through,
> > If you yourself can find the words to tell a later age:
> > You, for a time, were this to me, and I was that to you!
> > Is that not light and truth beyond what zeal can gauge?
>
> More happiness than I could expect.[82]

What made Gundolf happy was in fact a rebuke, the first of many on the same account: George wanted Gundolf to become a poet. In reply to Gundolf's first letter George had addressed him as 'my dear poet'.[83] Gundolf's scholarly vein seemed to him a distraction from this goal. Rather than immerse himself in the study of history and legend, he should immortalize the fleeting moment of their love in verse. Much as Gundolf deferred to George's authority, in this case he stood his ground. The great men of the past were anything but 'remote' to him; history was and remained his passionate interest. At their first meeting he importuned George with the question of who was greater, Alexander or Caesar,[84] a point that cannot have mattered much to George. For George, the poet or the 'maker'[85] must not stoop to anything inferior to original poetic 'making'. Gundolf insisted that culture could not thrive in creative making alone but depended on those who talked about it: 'Culture depends, I believe, not so much on the existence of great spirits as on their being recognized.'[86] For greatness to survive, it needed the herald as well as the maker. And this is what Gundolf essentially became, 'the herald of

---

[81] For a discussion of the 'amalgam between Plato and George', see Mikhailovsky, *Three Principles of 'Political Theology' in the Stefan George Circle*, 9, and M. A. Maiatsky, *Spor o Platone. Krug Stefana George i nemetskiy universitet* (Moscow: Izdatel'skiĭ dom Vyssheĭ shkoly ėkonomiki, 2012).

[82] Gundolf to Wolfskehl, 12 August 1899, Karl and Hanna Wolfskehl, *Briefwechsel mit Friedrich Gundolf 1899–1931*, 46. The translation is by Marx and Morwitz, *The Works of Stefan George*, 229. The original is in *Stefan George/Friedrich Gundolf. Briefwechsel*, 33 (George to Gundolf, 10 August 1899); a minimally altered version of it became part of *The Seventh Ring* (*Der Siebente Ring*, 1907).

[83] George to Gundolf, 11 June 1899, in *Stefan George/Friedrich Gundolf. Briefwechsel*, 29.

[84] See *Stefan George/Friedrich Gundolf. Briefwechsel*, 27.

[85] See Sir Philip Sidney's classic remark: 'The Greeks called him "a poet," which name hath, as the most excellent, gone through other languages. It cometh of this word *poiein*, which is "to make": wherein I know not whether by luck or wisdom, we Englishmen have met with the Greeks in calling him "a maker".' Sidney, *An Apology for Poetry (or The Defence of Poesy)*, 3rd edn, ed. Geoffrey Shepherd and R. W. Maslen (Manchester and New York: Manchester University Press, 2002), 84.

[86] The 19-year-old Gundolf in a letter to Wolfskehl, 22 September 1899. Karl and Hanna Wolfskehl, *Briefwechsel mit Friedrich Gundolf 1899–1931*, 63.

greatness', as Wolfskehl captioned his tribute on Gundolf's fiftieth birthday.[87] 'Let me have another ten years of health', he wrote to George, 'and I will be the man to make all your ur-thoughts and ur-experiences the common property of German culture.'[88]

Julius Caesar, Goethe, and, of course, George himself became subjects of Gundolf's enthusiastic heralding but, as a Heidelberg colleague said in his memorial address, 'all lines in Gundolf's work converged on Shakespeare'.[89] And it is with *Shakespeare und der deutsche Geist* that he made the greatest impact. This was an extended version of his postdoctoral *habilitation* thesis completed in an incredible three months of well-nigh manic productivity in 1910.[90] 'Now that it is finished', he triumphantly wrote to George,

> I see that I have written it as one possessed and that it is the product [...] of a will that far transcends what little knowledge and ability I have: it has become the living [...] compendium of the Spiritual Movement, just as your books are its Bible. No part of it is dead, [...] everything is pervaded by the life that you have breathed into us. As for myself, I am and remain your silliest one [*Dein Dümmstes*], but I take the fact that I have been able to write this book as proof that there are holy marriages in which heavenly children are begot by parents less than divine. But I also know that in these two months I have acquired a new meaning and rendered the 'State' the greatest possible service. I owe this, like everything else, to you, and you shall hear me rejoice without seemly modesty. For it is your child that I am praising—not yours alone, but it derives its finest strengths from you.[91]

George categorically denied having any truck with academic *Wissenschaft*: 'No road leads from me to scholarship', he famously declared.[92] But in fact the most talented of his disciples excelled in scholarship, not poetry. The Circle spawned only imitative versifiers,[93] but several remarkably original academics. For all of George's protesting, their brand of *Wissenschaft* drew its inspiration directly from the Master.[94] But was it actually *Wissenschaft* at all? Some people doubted that

---

[87] Karl Wolfskehl, 'Künder der Größe. Friedrich Gundolf zu seinem heutigen fünfzigsten Geburtstag', *Münchner Neuste Nachrichten*, 20 June 1930, 1.

[88] Gundolf to George, *c.* 10 November 1910, *Stefan George/Friedrich Gundolf. Briefwechsel*, 211.

[89] 'Auf Shakespeare laufen alle Grundlinien von Gundolfs Schaffen zu—und in ihm laufen sie alle zusammen'. Otto Regenbogen, 'Friedrich Gundolf zum Gedächtnis' (1931), in *Kleine Schriften*, ed. Franz Dirlmeier (Munich: Beck, 1961), 555–70 at 565.

[90] Gundolf submitted the first part—one third—of the final book version for his *habilitation*. Its title was *Shakespeare and the German Spirit before [the Appearance of] Lessing*. He completed his habilitation on 26 April 1911; the book appeared in May.

[91] Gundolf to George, *c.* 12 October 1910, *Stefan George/Friedrich Gundolf. Briefwechsel*, 206–7.

[92] Salin, *Um Stefan George*, 49. The German term *Wissenschaft* comprises scholarship in the humanities (*Geisteswissenschaft*) as well as natural science research (*Naturwissenschaft*). The most influential distinction of the two branches of *Wissenschaft* was undertaken by Wilhelm Dilthey, who held Hegel's chair in philosophy at the University of Berlin from 1882 to 1908. Dilthey sought to emancipate the humanities by assigning them a methodology of their own independent from the dominant natural science paradigm. See Wilhelm Dilthey, *Selected Works*, vol. 1: *Introduction to the Human Sciences*, ed. Rudolf A. Makkreel and Frithjof Rodi (Princeton, NJ: Princeton University Press, 1991).

[93] On poetic imitation as a deliberately adopted practice of the Circle, see Eschenbach, *Imitatio im George-Kreis*.

[94] The type of *Wissenschaft* inspired by George and practised by his academic followers has engendered much discussion and research. The earliest monograph on the subject, Hans Rößner, *Georgekreis*

Gundolf's *Shakespeare and the German Spirit* properly belonged in this category—doubts that were raised again, a decade later, about Ernst Kantorowicz's *Frederick the Second*. Gundolf's book defied scholarly precedent, so much so that it was sometimes classed as a hybrid of scholarship and art, *Wissenschaftskunst*, a tribute to its singularity but also a kiss of death.[95] But the success of the book spoke for itself: with over 90,000 copies sold, it was the bestselling of all Circle publications.

The highest accolade came from the philosopher Wilhelm Dilthey (1833–1911). Reading *Shakespeare and the German Spirit* made him feel, he said, like Moses being granted a view of the Promised Land.[96] Dilthey found his pioneering concept of *Geisteswissenschaft* ideally realized in Gundolf's study; a *Wissenschaft* freed from the constraints of positivism dedicated to the exploration of *Geist*, the intellectual and artistic spirit of a period as embodied in its cultural manifestations and their continuing power to generate inspirational experience (*Erlebnis*).

In a programmatic preface Gundolf boldly dismisses all previous work on the history of Shakespeare in Germany. Past scholarship, he asserts without specifying titles or authors,[97] had confined itself to sifting the documents—'assessments, translations, adaptations, borrowings and imitations'—but failed to ask 'what particular forces are operative in and expressed by them'. It is Gundolf's aim to identify these forces, 'the forces that determined Shakespeare's entrance into German culture' as well as 'the forces that his entrance awakened and brought to fruition'.[98]

> All individual testimony, manifestations and persons as well, is a bearer and product of living movements; the history of motifs, ideas and persons is in effect a history of forces [...] This does not mean that persons are unimportant in history—they are in fact all-important: for it is only in the individual symbol that the universal reveals itself [...]. (vii)

Thus the particulars of German Shakespeare reception merge in a single overarching trajectory:

> The history of Shakespeare in Germany is [...] the most important symbol of the process by which creative reality was first delivered up to and then wrested away from

---

und Literaturwissenschaft (Frankfurt: Moritz Diesterweg, 1938), is a Third Reich work seeking 'to overcome the spiritual movement of the George circle as a late form of humanism from the vantage point of the national socialist worldview' (Preface, without page number). Recent studies include Carola Groppe, *Die Macht der Bildung. Das deutsche Bürgertum und der George-Kreis 1890–1933* (Cologne, Weimar, and Vienna: Böhlau, 1997); Barbara Schlieben, Olaf Schneider, and Kerstin Schulmeyer, eds, *Geschichtsbilder im George-Kreis. Wege zur Wissenschaft* (Göttingen: Wallstein, 2004); Bernhard Böschenstein, Jürgen Egyptien, Bertram Schefold, and Wolfgang Vitzthum, eds, *Wissenschaftler im George-Kreis. Die Welt des Dichters und der Beruf der Wissenschaft* (Berlin and New York: De Gruyter, 2005).

[95] Ernst Osterkamp, 'Friedrich Gundolf zwischen Kunst und Wissenschaft. Zur Problematik eines Germanisten aus dem George-Kreis', in *Literaturwissenschaft und Geistesgeschichte 1910–1925*, ed. Christoph König and Eberhard Lämmert (Frankfurt: Fischer, 1993), 177–98.

[96] Cf. Sühnel, 'Gundolfs Shakespeare', 245.

[97] In highly unorthodox manner—especially in the German academic context—Gundolf dispenses with footnotes and largely with bibliographical references as well.

[98] Friedrich Gundolf, *Shakespeare und der deutsche Geist* (Berlin: Georg Bondi, 1911), vii. Page references to this edition are given in brackets in the text.

rationalism and thus again made fruitful for German poetry. Like no one else, Shakespeare is the creativity of life incarnate. Using his example to show that process as a *unified* becoming is the task, new in both method and intent, that we have set ourselves. (vii)

Knowledge of historical particulars was necessary only as a background and an archive from which to select what is essentially 'a living movement' and gives 'the stream of history' a new direction: 'a new influx' altering the 'the colour of the stream' (viii).

Gundolf's notion of history is unmistakably Nietzschean. In making 'life' the ultimate criterion of relevance and usefulness in the study of history, he is drawing on the second of Nietzsche's *Untimely Meditations: Of the Advantages and Disadvantages of History for Life* (1874).[99] Nietzsche's diagnosis of his century's *malaise*, its excessive burden of historical knowledge, is echoed in Gundolf's dismissal of the hunter-gatherer approach to historical research, which Nietzsche classes as 'antiquarian'. Gundolf's own work comes closest to what Nietzsche calls 'monumental' history: a celebration of greatness in the past for the sake of greatness in the future. Shakespeare is Gundolf's supreme standard of such greatness, and just as his book on Caesar in the nineteenth century ends with the prospect of a revival of Caesarian greatness, *Shakespeare and the German Spirit* ends by extolling the Bard as the model whose 'power of reality' offers a unique challenge and a unique promise for the future:

> All of the nineteenth century's efforts have perhaps only this in common: that they strove for reality. That in this search things more chimerical than the wildest fantasies of Romanticism were taken for real—money for example—and that reality was sought in things rather than in people, in clothes rather than in bodies, does not diminish the fact of that will for reality. What most of us lack is the strength for reality. And if we seek a master who will give us all of reality and the strength to bear it, this is Shakespeare. Gaining and shaping his reality to our sense of life is a task of the new German spirit. (360)

For Gundolf, as for Nietzsche, the greatness of Shakespeare and the greatness of Caesar are not so much distinct as they are manifestations of a common principle or force, a force to be pitted against the chaos of modernity. Combating the levelling drift of contemporary civilization, a rigorously selective historiography, Gundolf argued in an essay published a year after his Shakespeare book, must recreate these 'heroes' as 'cultural saviours' (*Kulturheilande*), models for the return to a lost cultural unity: 'More than anyone else, Shakespeare has recovered the unity of man and the world for us in lived experience.'[100] *Shakespeare and the German Spirit* is embarked on a mission of cultural salvation which is at the heart of Georgean *Kreispolitik* (circle politics).

---

[99] Friedrich Nietzsche, *On the Uses and Disadvantages of History for Life* (1874), in Nietzsche, *Untimely Meditations*, 2nd edn, trans. R. J. Hollingdale, ed. Daniel Breazeale (Cambridge: Cambridge University Press, 1997), 57–123.

[100] Friedrich Gundolf, 'Vorbilder' [Models, or, Exemplary Men], *Jahrbuch für die geistige Bewegung* 3 (1912), 1–19 at 16.

Gundolf's history proceeds in three stages which correspond to the three parts, or 'books', of his study. The first, 'Shakespeare as Matter', covers the two centuries prior to Lessing, the second, 'Shakespeare as Form', deals with Lessing and Wieland,[101] while the third, 'Shakespeare as Substance', continues from Herder via the Storm and Stress period to the Weimar classics Goethe and Schiller and their Romantic counterparts Schlegel and Tieck. This last stage is the decisive one: 'creative reality' was 'wrested away from rationalism and thus again made fruitful for German poetry'.[102] In this period German literature, in just a few decades, rose from parochial obscurity to European eminence thanks to the inspirational power of Shakespeare.

The outline of the story was not new, but the force of Gundolf's argument and his rhetorical panache made it irresistible. His account is boldly synthetic; his polemics, dedicated to separating what is dead from what is living, no less boldly antithetic. Gundolf's powers of synthesis are manifest not only in the overall architecture of his book but also in individual passages. 'In Herder', for example, 'the three major directions the German spirit had hitherto taken towards Shakespeare coalesce [...]: Lessing's rationality, mainly as a sense of history, the sensuality of Wieland and Gerstenberg as a taste for colour and atmosphere, and Hamann's acclamation of creative power' (213). Gundolf's antitheses tend to epigrammatic terseness: 'Lessing vindicates Shakespeare *vis à vis* the Greeks by saying: Shakespeare is art too; Herder by saying: the Greeks are nature too' (203). Or, 'Faust suffers because he doesn't have enough life, Hamlet because he has too much' (249). This last one concludes a full page of compact and densely argued comparison between Goethe's *Faust* and Shakespeare's *Hamlet*. It illustrates both the compelling strength and the weakness of Gundolf's approach, more noticeable now than to his original readership. He is not content until he has hammered his subtle perceptions into essentializing distinctions. He wants each historical current, each poet or critic neatly summed up in a single descriptive term or phrase and pinned in a grid of binary distinctions.

Such essentializing also informs the most important of Gundolf's syntheses, the one in which his narrative reaches its climactic telos: the union of the antithetical forces of the Classic and the Romantic, Goethe and August Wilhelm Schlegel, the genius poet and the genius translator. Emphasizing over and over the disparity between them, a disparity in kind as well as in stature, Gundolf sharply distinguishes between 'language creator' and 'language master'. The former—'Dante is the purest example'—is 'the true poet':

> In order to create language, to shape it for the future, it takes someone capable of new experience arising directly from what is yet unformed; one who does not merely re-live what is already formed. This distinguishes the language creator from the language master. (353)

---

[101] Christoph Martin Wieland (1733–1813), a leading writer of the German Enlightenment, rendered twenty-two Shakespeare plays into German prose (1762–6). Although Wieland was disparaged by younger poets as a representative of the stuffy older generation, it was mostly his translations that gave them Shakespeare, their paragon of liberated naturalness.

[102] As Gundolf puts it in his preface (vii).

Needless to say, Goethe is a 'creator', Schlegel a mere 'master'. But only the conjunction of their very different capacities could accomplish the absorption of Shakespeare into German culture and, through it, the entelechy or 'coming-to-itself' of the German spirit. This was the achievement of Schlegel's translation 'in which the German spirit and the soul of Shakespeare found expression in a common medium' (353):

> The language with which [Schlegel] translated seventeen Shakespeare plays is the application to Shakespeare of the possibilities of expression which Goethe had opened up [...] A mere language master, he was nevertheless able to accomplish the task because Goethe through his *ur*-experience [*Urerlebnis*] [...] had paved the way for him. (354)

Gundolf no doubt was, as Oskar Walzel noted in his review for *Shakespeare-Jahrbuch*, a 'word artist';[103] perhaps, the compliment implied, a little too much of the artist. Gundolf's scholarship was not above rebuke: Walzel detects instances of sloppy terminology and some rather serious errors of judgement, especially with regard to German Romanticism, Walzel's field of specialization. These errors evince the flaw in Gundolf's method: 'Soaring too high above things', whereby he 'fails to do them justice'.[104] But the review concludes on a peaceable note:

> I hope that the objectionable aspects will fade from my memory as the details of the book recede and only the overall impression will remain. This mountain, whose ascent also had agonizing moments for me, will, I hope, become entirely dear to me when I see it from a distance towering high above its neighbours.[105]

A 'mountain' towering over its neighbours, Gundolf's account became the founding charter of what later critics have described as not the history, but 'the myth' of the German Shakespeare. 'This myth', Werner Habicht writes,

> can be briefly described as follows: In eighteenth-century Germany, between the ages of rationalism and romanticism, young intellectuals began to 'discover' Shakespeare, and in doing so, they miraculously discovered themselves, a national identity, the German spirit and the potential for a national literature of the future. As a consequence, Shakespeare legitimately achieved the status of a timeless German classic.[106]

Gundolf's account canonized not only the peak of German Shakespeare reception but also the notion of its subsequent decline. After Goethe—'what a flattening, what a narrowing not only of the persons but of the Zeitgeist!' (357). With Nietzschean stridency, Gundolf condemns the second half of the nineteenth century as 'a time of artistic barbarism and spiritual exhaustion' (321). How unfortunate

---

[103] Oskar Walzel, Review of Gundolf, *Shakespeare und der deutsche Geist*, in *Shakespeare-Jahrbuch* 48 (1912), 259–74 at 259. Walzel (1864–1944) was an innovator in his own right. The title of his lecture on *The Mutual Illumination of the Arts* (*Die wechselseitige Erhellung der Künste* [Berlin: Reuther & Reichard, 1917]) became something of a catchphrase and a programme for a comparative interdisciplinary approach to art and literature. Cf. Ulrich Weisstein, *Comparative Literature and Literary Theory: Survey and Introduction* (1968), trans. William Riggan (Bloomington, IN: Indiana University Press, 1973), esp. 150–66.

[104] Walzel, Review, 272.   [105] Walzel, Review, 274.

[106] Habicht, *Shakespeare and the German Imagination*, 1.

that Schiller, not Goethe, had come to dominate the popular perception of Shakespeare—Schiller who had totally misconstrued Shakespeare as a moralist:

> For a century all aesthetic and moral thinking was dominated by Schiller's perspective, and only since Nietzsche has a point of view outside of morality been attained which is needed to cleanse the real Shakespeare of the one currently prevailing. (290)

'Gundolf's apotheosis and his verdict' dominated the study of German Shakespeare reception well into the 1980s: scholars 'kept ploughing' the eighteenth century, while the nineteenth century largely 'remained *terra incognita*'.[107] Moreover, far beyond the field of Shakespeare studies, Gundolf's bestseller was perceived as the spectacular debut of a new paradigm in literary studies, namely *Geistesgeschichte*.[108] To be sure, Gundolf's work by no means met with general approval, and even among its admirers only a few became converts to its method. But to quote T. S. Eliot, its arrival noticeably altered 'the existing order' of things, requiring a readjustment of the field of literary history as a whole.[109] Gundolf's new approach and the small but distinct body of George-inspired scholarship that followed in its footsteps posed a fundamental challenge to the prevalent 'causalistic-psychological conception of *Wissenschaft* in general'.[110]

In fact, according to Ernst Troeltsch it entailed a veritable revolution. Troeltsch (1865–1923), a Protestant theologian, cultural philosopher, and liberal politician, offers the most incisive contemporary analysis of the George Circle's academic profile. In his 1921 review of two recent publications by followers of George,[111] he still refers to Gundolf's 1911 Shakespeare book as the exemplary achievement of what in the meantime had become a school. Troeltsch credits Gundolf's 'brilliant early work' (535) on Shakespeare with a distinctively individual quality of its own. He calls it 'an achievement of the truest and best and at the same time most philosophical historicism' (535–6), but also finds in it the more questionable hallmarks of the George school: its contempt for conventional philology, for anything even remotely tending towards popularization and general education; its Nietzschean aristocratism and neo-Hellenic cult of the body as the indispensable safeguard against the deadly grip of rationalism. The crusade against reason in particular

---

[107] Sühnel, 'Gundolfs Shakespeare', 255.

[108] This 'can be translated either as "intellectual history" or "spiritual history"'. Andrew L. Yarrow, 'Humanism and Deutschtum: The Origins, Development, and Consequences of the Politics of Poetry in the George-Kreis', *The Germanic Review* 58 (2001), 1–11 at 1.

[109] T. S. Eliot, 'Tradition and the Individual Talent' (1919), in *Selected Prose of T. S. Eliot*, ed. Frank Kermode (London: Faber and Faber, 1973), 37–44 at 38–9: 'The existing order is complete before the new work arrives; for order to persist after the supervention of novelty, the whole existing order must be, if ever so slightly, altered; and so the relations, proportions, values of each work of art toward the whole are readjusted.'

[110] Ernst Troeltsch, 'Die Revolution in der Wissenschaft' (1921), in Troeltsch, *Kritische Gesamtausgabe*, 19 vols, ed. Friedrich Wilhelm Graf et al., vol. 13: *Rezensionen und Kritiken (1915–1923)*, ed. Friedrich Wilhelm Graf (Berlin and New York: De Gruyter, 2010), 519–63. Page references to this essay are given in brackets in the text.

[111] These were: Erich von Kahler, *Der Beruf der Wissenschaft* (Berlin: Bondi, 1920); Arthur Salz, 'Für die Wissenschaft gegen die Gebildeten unter ihren Verächtern', *Jahrbuch für Gesetzgebung, Verwaltung und Volkswirtschaft im Deutschen Reich (Schmollers Jahrbuch)* 45 (1921), 65–94. Kahler and Salz were followers of George, but not members of his inner circle.

causes Troeltsch profound misgivings. And while he admits that there is 'much that is dead and conventional in our academic life' (561), his plea is for a return to rationality in the humanities.

The most interesting part of Troeltsch's review comes at the end, when he probes the political dimension of the revolution in the humanities, its curiously contradictory relation to the revolution at large:

> Essentially there is the most paradoxical contradiction. The 'revolution in the humanities' is in fact the beginning of the great world reaction against the democratic and socialist enlightenment, against the autocracy of organised reason and its concomitant belief in the equal rationality and good sense of all human beings. It is just like when Novalis said of Edmund Burke that he had written a highly revolutionary book against the revolution. These books too [by George's followers] are revolutionary books against the revolution. This is a new Romanticism, and for all its differences from the old one it is deeply and truly connected to it. (562)

On the face of it, Gundolf's *Shakespeare and the German Spirit* pays little regard to anything outside the sphere where 'spirit' reigns supreme. And when Gundolf speaks, as he sometimes does, of 'Shakespeare's realm', that realm is as removed from the politics of real life as Prospero's isle. Those who contemplate the enormous social and political forces changing the world in the aftermath of the Great War will only see 'the powerlessness of such Romanticism. But those', Troeltsch concludes, 'who are aware of the importance of doctrines and ideals will not regard this intellectual turn as [...] a thing of no consequence' (563).

V BELOVED ENEMY

The world had fundamentally changed between the publication of *Shakespeare and the German Spirit* (1911) and Troeltsch's 1921 comment. A realm no longer existed where 'spirit' could be thought to thrive in splendid self-sufficiency. And with the transformation of the world the George Circle underwent a transformation too, its doctrines and ideals becoming increasingly involved in the ideological struggles of the time.

When the Great War broke out in 1914, Gundolf, like most of George's acolytes, was carried away on the general wave of enthusiasm. Peacetime differences no longer seemed to matter when the Kaiser declared in parliament: 'I know no parties anymore, only Germans!'[112] In this spirit of patriotic concord surely even the schism between the secret and the official Germany would evaporate. Or so the disciples thought.[113] But the Master remained strangely aloof from the general excitement. Vacationing in Switzerland, he chose to prolong rather than cut short

---

[112] Verhandlungen des Reichstags, *Stenographische Berichte*, 1914–16, vol. 306, 1.

[113] Gundolf in a letter to George (*c.* 30 July 1914): 'I feel that (however one may have stood toward the Prussians up to now) it is now a matter of our Germany...and I am happy that the momentous decision will now become visible for us as well, the secret Germany too.' *Stefan George/Friedrich Gundolf. Briefwechsel*, 254. Trans. Norton, *Secret Germany*, 517.

his stay despite his followers' urgent pleas that his presence was never more needed than at this hour.[114] When he finally announced his return to Germany, he ended on a cautionary note: 'I call to you all: whether it ends well or badly: —the most difficult part will not come UNTIL AFTERWARDS!!'[115]

George's reserve towards the national war effort did not spring from pacifist leanings. As had Nietzsche and indeed like countless other intellectuals and artists at the time, he regarded peace as morbid stagnation, war as the great and necessary purge. A prophet of doom, George revelled in visions of global conflagration: before the new order could emerge, the old one had to be destroyed, root and branch. No surprise, then, that George's followers should think their enthusiasm for war fully sanctioned by the Master's own, particularly as it had issued from his most recent volume of poetry, *Star of the Covenant* (*Stern des Bundes*, 1913). 'God's war has been ignited for us', declares its 'Closing Chorus', 'God's wrath is upon our brows'.[116] So full of intimations of war is the volume that George saw fit to add a note of rectification to the second edition:

> This book was courted by misunderstandings which, though it is easy to see how they arose, were utterly unfounded. It was said that the poet had dealt with actualities of the present rather than with distance and dream, and that he had set out to write a breviary for the people and more especially for the younger generation fighting at the front. But the order of events was this: THE STAR OF THE COVENANT was originally intended for a circle of intimate friends. [...] The torrent of events which followed immediately upon publication made wider strata emotionally receptive for a volume which might have remained a sealed book for years to come.[117]

The wish to align war as George extolled it with war as it actually was bore some rather unsavoury fruit. When the German First Army devastated Louvain, the 'Belgian Oxford', in late August 1914, burning the famous old library and killing some 250 citizens, Romain Rolland castigated the atrocities in a widely publicized protest letter addressed to Gerhart Hauptmann, Nobel laureate for literature of 1912: 'Are you a descendant of Goethe', he asked, 'or of Attila?'[118] First Wolfskehl, then Gundolf took it upon themselves to set the Frenchman right. Ignoring the cause for Rolland's protest, Wolfskehl incongruously burst into a rant:

> [T]here is another Germany, behind the exterior [...]. This Germany says to you in Europe's difficult hour: this unwanted war, which was forced upon us, is essential nonetheless, it had to strike for the sake of Germany and of the world of European humanity [...]. We did not want it, but it comes from *God*. Our poet knew of it. He saw and presaged this war and its necessity and its virtues long before [...] any papers

---

[114] Pointedly unimpressed by the general war commotion, George lectured Gundolf that 'what's hot in the kitchen cools at the table' and that for the time being he saw no reason to hurry to leave Switzerland. George to Gundolf, 13 August 1914, *Stefan George/Friedrich Gundolf. Briefwechsel*, 256.

[115] George to Gundolf, 26 August, 1914, *Stefan George/Friedrich Gundolf. Briefwechsel*, 258.

[116] George, *Sämtliche Werke*, vol. 8: *Der Stern des Bundes*, ed. Ute Oelmann (1993), 114. For the Marx/Morwitz translation of the poem, see *The Works of Stefan George*, 278.

[117] *The Works of Stefan George*, 348 (translation modified).

[118] Quoted in Norton, *Secret Germany*, 522. The letter, together with Hauptmann's coolly unapologetic response, appeared in *Frankfurter Zeitung*, 12 September 1914.

began to rustle. The *Star of the Covenant* is that book of prophecy, that book of necessity and conquest. [...] Thus we stand in the midst of death and ruins under the star, one *covenant* and one *unity*. [...] From now on our *deeds* will be our words.[119]

Gundolf did at least address Rolland's point but fell to lecturing on the true nature of culture:

Thus the whining and tantrums about destroyed artistic treasures is (as far as it is honest) tired Romanticism and comes out of a shallow, false conception of culture, as if it consisted in collecting and the piety of observers. Culture is not a possession [...], it is creating, destroying, changing—and Attila has more to do with culture than all the Shaws, Maeterlincks, d'Annunzios, and so on combined. [...] Whoever is strong enough to create is also permitted to destroy, and if our future were not able to create anymore, then it would have no right to enjoy the past.[120]

In the heady days of August 1914 Gundolf had envied his Heidelberg friends for marching off to the front.[121] But when Germany's heavy losses in the Battle of the Somme resulted in an extension of the draft and he was called up himself, his fervour quickly gave way to a desperate urge to escape the hardships of soldiering.[122] After several failed attempts[123] to obtain a dispensation, it was the influential industrialist Walter Rathenau who effected Gundolf's transfer to the War Ministry's press office in Berlin. George made no bones about his disapproval. Disconsolate as he had been when Gundolf was called up, and shaken by the deaths of so many of his young men, he was still adamant that it was one's duty to stay where one had been placed and endure whatever that entailed.[124] For Gundolf to have sought help from one of the leading representatives of odious bourgeois liberalism was a betrayal of principles, 'in glaring contrast to the life we have lived so far'. At a time like this there were 'difficult situations—in which it is more dignified to stay— than to accept ANY help offered'.[125]

Greater strain on the relationship between Master and disciple, however, threatened from another quarter. George tolerated his acolytes having affairs with

---

[119] Quoted in Norton, *Secret Germany*, 522–3. For the following paragraphs I am indebted to Norton's detailed discussion.

[120] Friedrich Gundolf, 'Tat und Wort im Krieg', *Frankfurter Zeitung*, 11 October 1914, quoted in Norton, *Secret Germany*, 523–4. Norton points out that the only subsequent reproduction of Gundolf's text (Landmann, ed., *Der George-Kreis. Eine Auswahl aus seinen Schriften*) tactfully omits this passage.

[121] Letter to George, 14 August 1914, *Stefan George/Friedrich Gundolf. Briefwechsel*, 256.

[122] Gundolf was a 'shoveller', a non-combatant soldier charged with the maintenance of fortifications behind the front line.

[123] One of these attempts involved Paul Clemen, Professor of Art History at the University of Bonn, a man with excellent connections at the imperial court, and father of Wolfgang Clemen, the Shakespeare scholar.

[124] The most harrowing of these losses was the double suicide of Bernhard Graf Uxkull Gyllenbrand and his friend Adalbert Cohrs in July 1918. The two young officers were arrested as deserters in the attempt to cross the Dutch border and shot themselves while in military police custody. When George received the news, he felt 'as if he had had both his legs shot off' (Landmann, *Gespräche mit Stefan George*, 187). Mention of their desertion was carefully omitted in the Circle's official commemoration of the suicides.

[125] George to Gundolf, 23 February 1917, quoted in Norton, *Secret Germany*, 539.

women—as long as they were casual and did not interfere with 'State matters';
even marriage was acceptable as long as the bride was considered suitable and the
groom not too close to the Master's heart.[126] In Gundolf's case there were quite a
few women to tolerate. His 'spiritually aimless and irresponsible bedding of that
sex', George warned, might do more than mere physical harm.[127] When, in 1917,
one of Gundolf's relationships resulted in pregnancy, George vetoed Gundolf's
plan to marry the mother.[128] Gundolf acquiesced. But by this time he was already
drawn to the charms of another woman, Elisabeth ('Elli') Salomon. His attachment to her quickly exceeded the tolerable level of superficiality. A student of
national economy, she had entered the George orbit two or three years before the
war, turning the head of more than one of his followers. She was reputed a flirt,
'half child half cat',[129] and by 1919 there was a *roman à clef*—the revenge of a
spurned admirer—detailing her escapades.[130] Not only the Master himself thought
it highly objectionable when Gundolf, the first and foremost pillar of the 'State',
fell into Elli's tender trap.[131] But Gundolf would not be dissuaded. Elli, he pro-
tested, was being unfairly maligned. Especially after she had nursed Gundolf
through a life-threatening bout of pneumonia during the icy winter of 1918/19,
there was no question of his parting from her. At age thirty-nine, Gundolf refused
to obey the Master's command in a painful bid for independence. At a time when
George was regrouping his forces after the casualties of war, his second-in-command
was drifting towards an inevitable rift.

The tension is captured in Gundolf's dialogue poem 'Caesar and Brutus' of
1919. Set after the battle of Pharsalus, it confronts Brutus, who has fought on the
side of the defeated Pompey, with the victorious Caesar. But the historical situation
is not even mentioned. All that matters is the contradictory personal relationship
expressed in Caesar's opening salutation: 'Saved! Are you hale, beloved enemy?'[132]
There is no hate on either's part, but there is an obstacle to friendship that Caesar's
magnanimous peace offer cannot remove: justice, or rather, as Brutus sees it, the
lack of it:

> Hate you I don't. But grieve for us
> That I can't love you as I would:
> For the sake of justice.

---

[126] Claus von Stauffenberg's marriage, for example, was no problem at all; but it was understood
that his brother Berthold—for George much the more extraordinary figure—had to stay single.

[127] George to Gundolf, 29 February 1916, *Stefan George/Friedrich Gundolf. Briefwechsel*, 280.

[128] The abandoned mother, Agathe Mallachow, almost too aptly named her daughter Cordelia.
'I have become a father', Gundolf wrote to Wolfskehl (20 December 1917); 'this is part of the tribulations of war.' Quoted in Karlauf, *Stefan George*, 515.

[129] Lothar Helbing, 'Gundolf und Elli', in *Stefan George. Zwei Vorträge mit einem Vorwort von
Lothar Helbing*, ed. Elisabeth Gundolf (Amsterdam: Castrum Peregrini, 1965), 25. See note 140.

[130] Albrecht Schaeffer, *Elli oder Sieben Treppen. Beschreibung eines weiblichen Lebens* (Leipzig: Insel,
1919).

[131] George went so far as to say that Gundolf's infatuation with Elli was proof of 'a sick spot in his
brain'. Landmann, *Gespräche mit George*, 157.

[132] Friedrich Gundolf, 'Caesar und Brutus', in *Gedichte von Friedrich Gundolf* (Berlin: Georg Bondi,
1930), 41–5 at 41.

'Then love me as you can', Caesar replies, 'for the sake of blood'. Justice, he declares, is just a word, a weightless abstraction when measured against the living bond of 'two beings / breathing one another through open senses [...] feeling and grasping one another and filled to the brim with manly trust'. How can justice, he asks, 'this homeless nothing', come between them? But Caesar's nothing becomes a something, or even a someone, in Brutus's reply. And justice being a feminine noun in German (*die Gerechtigkeit*), Brutus seems suddenly to be pleading for a woman:

> O could you see her
> As truly as you see yourself and me! Caesar, she lives
> And I for her [...]

The poem ends at an impasse, the tension in the opening oxymoron 'beloved enemy' unresolved:

BRUTUS:
I do not hate, I do not defy...I suffer.
Give me your hand.
CAESAR:
Be as you must and trust.

The crisis that had inspired the poem remained equally unresolved. As if to force a return to their old closeness by publicly demonstrating his loyalty, Gundolf's book on George, completed in the same year, struck levels of hero worship that even some of George's followers found extravagant.[133] The crisis escalated when Gundolf announced his intent to marry Elli. 'I cannot have such a one as a daughter-in-law', George is reported to have said.[134]

The last straw was the publication, in 1922, of Gundolf's study of Heinrich von Kleist, which in George's view was yet another work of superfluous *Wissenschaft*.[135] Like Gundolf's previous books, it appeared with George's publisher Bondi under the official imprint of the Circle. But its flyleaf bore the author's dedication 'To Elisabeth Salomon', supposedly inserted without George's knowledge. This was unforgivable, a breach of faith that terminated all relations. And although George may have suffered nearly or, as some said, equally as much from the separation as Gundolf, he never relented. When, three years later, a chance encounter occurred on Heidelberg's castle hill, George refused to acknowledge Gundolf's greeting and afterwards remarked on how ridiculous it had been when Gundolf 'sheepishly doffed his little hat'.[136]

Gundolf, for his part, never gave up his faith in the Master. When he eventually married Elisabeth in November 1926, already afflicted by the cancer that would kill him less than five years later, he once more pleaded his case to the man who still ruled his life:

---

[133] Gundolf, *George*.
[134] Boehringer, 'Einleitung', *Stefan George/Friedrich Gundolf. Briefwechsel*, 23.
[135] Karlauf, *Stefan George*, 524.   [136] Landmann, *Gespräche mit Stefan George*, 143.

I have decided to marry Elisabeth Salomon this year as my heart and my conscience command me, convinced that I am thus violating your wish but not your law, since this creature deserves your mercy more than I do. Since I was unable to convince you, I therefore prefer to go to hell with her than to heaven without her. I know the consequences: the sorrow through you and for you, and I shall bear them. I am not deserting you even if you reject me.

Your Gundolf[137]

Earlier that year, Gundolf had delivered a lecture on *Antony and Cleopatra* to the German Shakespeare Society in Weimar. For those who knew him it was clear that Gundolf 'was weaving his own fate into this reading'[138] and projecting the forces that were tearing his life apart onto the doomed Antony.

The play had always been Gundolf's favourite. The first one he translated, it was also the inspiration for an earlier dialogue poem, 'Caesar and Cleopatra' (1904). George had accepted it for *Pages for the Arts* but faulted it as falling short of its lofty subject. It was presumptuous, he wrote, 'to recreate this powerful, this dazzling and definitive queen!'[139] Gundolf conceded the smaller scale of his poem: 'A recreation of the divine Cleopatra she certainly isn't, more half child, half cat à la Wiesi. But perhaps the vast shadow of the former looms too much over her.'[140]

In the 1926 lecture, Gundolf extols *Antony and Cleopatra* as one of the two summits of Shakespeare's tragic art, the unsurpassable peak of tragic sorrow being *King Lear*. 'The most glorious celebration of plenitude is *Antony and Cleopatra*.'[141] It is an exemplary testimonial to the artist's maturity, the work of a man who has reached a state of calm, unbiased knowledge and 'a freedom of spirit that even the most brilliant young genius cannot attain' (307):

---

[137] *Stefan George/Friedrich Gundolf. Briefwechsel*, 371–2; I am quoting Norton's translation, *Secret Germany*, 617. Lothar Helbing (= Wolfgang Frommel), 'Gundolf und Elli. Vorwort', in Elisabeth Gundolf, *Stefan George. Zwei Vorträge mit einem Vorwort von Lothar Helbing* (Amsterdam: Castrum Peregrini, 1965), 5–33 at 26, patronizingly reprimands Gundolf for using the hackneyed phrase 'rather to hell with her than to heaven without her' which belongs to the stock in trade of 'pubescent love lyrics'.

[138] Boehringer, 'Einleitung', *Stefan George/Friedrich Gundolf. Briefwechsel*, 23.

[139] George to Gundolf, 2 January 1904, *Stefan George/Friedrich Gundolf. Briefwechsel*, 143. Cf. Boehringer, 'Einleitung', 20.

[140] Wiesi de Haan, the sister of Wolfskehl's wife Anna. Awed though he was by Shakespeare's queen of 'infinite variety', the young Gundolf apparently felt no inhibitions in identifying real-life Cleopatras among his acquaintance. The formulation 'half child half cat' recurs in a rather unfavourable portrayal of Elli by the editor of her—surprisingly favourable—reminiscences of Stefan George (Helbing 'Gundolf und Elli', 25). Helbing/Frommel's preface is an exercise in hagiographic piety by one of the poet's greatest admirers. He defends George's judgement, deplores Gundolf's infatuation, and questions the purity of Elli's motives. This forms a strange prelude to her two essays: one recollecting her encounters with George and Rilke, the other defending George against allegations of ideological affinities to Nazism. Frommel described his first encounter with George as the turning point in his life, but it is not clear whether such an encounter actually ever took place. Thomas Karlauf, 'Meister mit eigenem Kreis. Wolfgang Frommels George-Nachfolge', *Sinn und Form* 2 (2011), 211–19.

[141] Gundolf's Weimar lecture became the chapter on *Antony and Cleopatra* in his two-volume study *Shakespeare. Sein Wesen und Werk*, 2 vols (Berlin: Georg Bondi, 1928), vol. 2, 306–32 at 310. Page references to this edition are given in brackets in the text.

A youth can be a rebel and an enthusiast but he is caught up in his fervour or his hate [...]—his No depends on the Yes of others, his Yes on a master or leader or a band of like-minded companions. (307)

The dependencies described here sound more like Gundolf's than those of Shakespeare, and if he thought he had overcome them his reading of the play's central triangle tells otherwise. The struggle between Octavius and Cleopatra takes place 'within Antony' (319). 'Open on all sides', he is 'infiltrated and then flooded by her' (320).

One should not imagine her as a wanton who calculates weaknesses and exploits them. Her cunning is nature not calculation. It is her Dionysian mimic gift to enter into each moment, to become what she wants to have, to stir up what she wants to attract. Only the impenetrable Octavius allows her no access. (320)

The Queen of Egypt and the future Emperor are pitted against one other, not as mere characters but as opposing principles: Cleopatra as 'the realm of nature incarnate', Octavius as 'the personified spirit of the state' (323).

A lesser charm than Cleopatra's would not have corroded Antony. A lesser man than Antony would not have unleashed all her charms. A stronger mind than his would have tamed them as Julius Caesar did. They both endanger the realm and confront the One who must protect it. [...] He [Octavius] is the state. (323)

Only when Antony lets himself be lured back to Egypt does Octavius' 'sober disapproval turn into personal wrath' (324). '[T]enacious, relentless, coldly calculating as well as deeply smouldering' (324), this wrath is not dictated by personal rage but by reasons of state and hence 'unalterable law' (324). And it is directed less at the seductress, who is merely acting according to her nature, than at the seduced Antony: '[F]orswearing his Romanness', he has become 'a traitor to his own good parts, his country, his friendship, in short all Roman and masculine values' (324).

Was the world, as Dryden subtitles his version of *Antony and Cleopatra*, 'well lost' for the man who had given all for love?[142] A poem 'To my Master', written shortly after his cancer operation in 1927, renewed Gundolf's plea for forgiveness: 'I am your child, feel what I was / Even in the night scream of separation.' Although he continued to suffer from 'his One wound', he never questioned the choice that had caused it, as one of his last poems affirms:

> More truly I stride as one orphaned
> Without staff, or track or cord
> Knowing only God and Love
> Through the jolting throng,
> Death's marked out walk.

Gundolf died, only 51, on George's sixty-third birthday, 12 July 1931. The medical cause was cancer, but none of his friends was in any doubt that what had killed him was banishment from the Master's Circle.

---

[142] John Dryden, *All for Love, or, The World Well Lost* (1677).

VI ESSENTIAL SHAKESPEARE

> The Shakespeare philologists—whatever their merits as investigators of facts—
> stopped before the real secret of Shakespeare, the entrance of which was closed
> to them, because of their insufficient methodical instruments. Gundolf is
> cognizant of all the facts they are likely to have, but takes them for granted.
> His work begins where that of the philologists has ended: he interprets what
> they have merely put in order.

This statement by Elisabeth Gundolf, written in English,[143] was most likely part of
her attempt to find a British publisher for her late husband's work, a project that
never materialized. The particular work in question is *Shakespeare. Sein Wesen und
Werk*, first published in 1928. Its two densely printed volumes run to over 900
pages;[144] it is the *summa* of Gundolf's life-long engagement with Shakespeare.
Omitting three, *Henry VI*, *Henry VIII*, and *Pericles*, Gundolf devotes a chapter to
each of the remaining thirty-four plays of the canon plus the sonnets. But unlike,
for example, Granville-Barker's *Prefaces to Shakespeare*, which began to appear two
years later, Gundolf offers something other than a series of readings of individual
plays.[145] This is indicated by the key term of his title: *Wesen* (essence, innermost
being). The conventional duo would be *Leben und Werk* ('life and work'). *Wesen*
aims much deeper. If 'life and work' links artistic creation to the circumstances that
condition it, *Wesen* is the core that remains when all contingencies have been
stripped away. It is the thing itself or, more precisely, the soul or spirit of the thing
itself. In Shakespeare's case, as in the case of every *Urgeist*, every truly original poet,
this essential thing defies conditioning.

It is one of the fundamental tenets of George and his circle that the truly great
men owe nothing to their time, at least nothing of importance, nothing that
defines their greatness. All hunting for sources, influences, or mundane biographical facts is therefore futile. Shakespeare's only relevant relation to his age is that he
transcends it.[146] Gundolf's sovereign contempt of philological research stems from

---

[143] The unpublished text—either a lecture or a report for a British publisher—is held by the
Gundolf Archive at the University of London's Institute of Modern Languages Research and quoted
in Eudo C. Mason, 'Gundolf und Shakespeare', *Shakespeare-Jahrbuch* (1962), 110–77 at 112. Mason's
long essay is the most thorough and incisive analysis of Gundolf's *Shakespeare. Sein Wesen und Werk*.
I am much indebted to it in what follows.

[144] In the second edition (Düsseldorf: Küpper, 1949) the text amounts to almost 1,300 pages. Page references given in brackets in the text are to the two volumes of the first edition (Berlin: Georg Bondi, 1928).

[145] Nevertheless the greatest merits of Gundolf's study, Mason says, are his insightful comments on
the particularities of individual plays. This is a paradox: Gundolf excels in what he emphatically
rejects: '[H]e who so high-handedly disparages all that is intellectual, analytical and derived in other
critics and wants to demonstrate the inadequacy of a rational approach to Shakespeare proves [...]
a master of intellectual criticism, an acute observer, describer, comparer and dissector' ('Gundolf und
Shakespeare', 115–16). Gundolf's 'true strength as an interpreter of Shakespeare' may well 'consist in
this impressive perspicacity of an intellectual malgré lui [...]' ('Gundolf und Shakespeare', 115–16).
Mason concludes that Gundolf's study may not differ so fundamentally in principle or method from
the Shakespeare philologists as he (and his widow) would have us believe. His distinctiveness, Mason
argues, lies in the sheer intelligence of his analysis, not least in an area Gundolf never tires of dispar-
aging: the psychological analysis of Shakespeare's characters.

[146] As, indeed, he transcends all other early modern English dramatists, with whose work, Mason
notes, Gundolf is largely unfamiliar (Mason, 'Gundolf und Shakespeare', 158–9).

this creed, which is faithfully echoed by his widow: the philologists have nothing to tell that Gundolf does not know. They know nothing of what he has to tell: 'the real secret of Shakespeare'.

This secret is Shakespeare's *Wesen* as encrypted in his *Werk*. The scanty documentary evidence of Shakespeare's life from baptism to second-best bed reveals nothing of importance; only his work does. In its (presumed) chronological sequence, the work affords the only true insight into Shakespeare's inner life. This is so not because Shakespeare made it the channel of personal confession, but because the creatures of his imagination 'give testimony of their personal creator' (I 288), because his heroes are the 'embodied forces of his personal soul' (I 199). To fathom this 'unfathomable soul' (II 301) is the true aim of Gundolf's study. It can be achieved because Shakespeare 'is mystically present in his creatures' (I 316), his 'mood immediately perceivable' (II 403) through his characters, especially in the late plays. Thus the dialogue between Florizel and Perdita in *The Winter's Tale* 4.4 (after Polixenes has discovered and forbidden their love) is fraught with intimations of death, Gundolf writes, 'as the bitter limit of the beautiful moment':

> But this is not *their* sentiment; it is that of their poet. In Florizel, the manly youth, the knowledge of his creator manifests itself as fortified courage, freely and chastely armed against any obstacle [...]. (II 556)[147]

A contemporary reviewer praised Gundolf's *Shakespeare* as 'one of the most magnificent documents of intuitive scholarship',[148] and it is indeed on intuition alone that Gundolf's claims depend: not only those like the one just quoted, but also his larger claims about Shakespeare's life and *Wesen*. As early as 1904, Gundolf's intuitive perception of the essential Shakespeare had been sparked by a face-to-face encounter with the Bard. This moment of epiphany or *Wesensschau*[149] took place when he was shown Shakespeare's purported death mask, the cherished property of a resident of Gundolf's hometown Darmstadt. 'It is the most sublime and noble

---

[147] FLORIZEL [to PERDITA] Why look you so upon me?

> I am but sorry, not afeard; delayed,
> But nothing altered. What I was, I am,
> More straining on for plucking back, not following
> My leash unwillingly. (*WT* 4.4.453–7)

Throughout his study, Gundolf quotes, and interprets, Shakespeare in his own German translation. This leads to some errors (among them, as Mason, 'Gundolf und Shakespeare', 129, points out, the belief that the title *Winter's Tale* refers in any significant way to winter). It is also worth noting that in the passage quoted Gundolf omits the speeches by Camillo and Old Shepherd (*WT* 441–53), so that Florizel's answer follows immediately after Perdita ('I'll queen it no inch farther / But milk my ewes and weep', *WT* 440–1). Clearly, what the 'low' characters have to say seems dispensable to Gundolf.

[148] Karl Heinrich Ruppel, *Kölnische Zeitung* (1928), quoted in the publisher's blurb on the back cover of the second edition of Gundolf's *Shakespeare*.

[149] *Wesensschau*, this key term of Husserl's phenomenology, denotes the immediate, intuitive recognition of the essence (*Wesen*) of a given phenomenon. See the entry on 'Eidetic insight (*Wesensschau*, *Wesenserschauung*)' in Dermot Moran and Joseph Cohen, *The Husserl Dictionary* (London and New York: Continuum, 2012), 91–2.

head I know', Gundolf wrote to George, 'only shopkeepers can doubt its authenticity ...'.[150] Gundolf captured what the mask revealed to him in a poem:

> Was this the god who calmly moulded earths
> The man who had to suffer through all hells?
> [...]
> The whole world as torment and dream and knowing
> Flows mutely from these cold darknesses
> Afterglow of deepest blaze and brightest light.

In the 1928 *Shakespeare*, Gundolf intuits as the decisive juncture in Shakespeare's life the sonnets. In the adoration of the fair youth they register the poet's 'erotic breakthrough', the crucial event in the poet's life which lays the ground for the profound erotic crisis, again connected with the young man (not a word is wasted on Anne Hathaway), that initiates the dark phase of Shakespeare's middle years. Such speculation, and the phases it deduces from the changing tone or mood of Shakespeare's œuvre, is hardly unusual. It belongs to the standard repertoire of the kind of psychologizing biography that reads the work as a code for the life. Where Gundolf differs from other portrayals is in the key role he allots to homoerotic desire and a George-like youth cult: 'For the poet of the Renaissance the young man is [...] recompense for the lost deity' (I 465–6).[151]

This mention of the Renaissance would seem to suggest a historicist orientation. But Gundolf's Renaissance is very much a construct—Jacob Burckhardt radicalized by Nietzsche—and a code word for the neo-pagan antithesis to modern materialism and restrictive Christianity, particularly Protestantism. In this, as in much else, George's elitist 'untimeliness' derives from Nietzsche, even though the Master came to distance himself from Nietzsche with increasing stridency.[152] Gundolf did not follow suit. His 1920 monograph tribute to George repeatedly names the two as kindred spirits, with George having to share at least some of his uniqueness with Nietzsche.

In Gundolf's *Shakespeare*, the Nietzschean element arguably even outweighs the Georgean. The fact that the dramatist earned his living in the most sociable of all art forms does not prevent Gundolf from finding him a man single-mindedly

---

[150] Gundolf to George, 27 April 1904, *Stefan George/Friedrich Gundolf. Briefwechsel*, 153. Ludwig Becker, a court painter for the ducal family of Hesse-Darmstadt, had acquired the mask in the late 1840s. According to Robert Boehringer ('Einleitung', 18), Gundolf wrote his Shakespeare translations 'under the patronage' of, or 'sheltered' (*beschirmt*) by it. Gundolf's brother argued somewhat more guardedly for the authenticity of the mask: Ernst Gundolf, 'Zur Beurteilung der Darmstädter Shakespeare-Maske', *Shakespeare-Jahrbuch* 64 (1928), 132–40. The mask is now in the reading room of the Darmstadt university library.

[151] Mason, 'Gundolf und Shakespeare', 126, notes the unmistakable proximity to George's deification of 'Maximin'.

[152] Heinz Raschel, *Das Nietzsche-Bild im George-Kreis, ein Beitrag zur Geschichte der deutschen Mythologeme* (Berlin and New York: De Gruyter, 1984). George's poem 'Nietzsche' in *The Seventh Ring* (1907) ends with the much-quoted, and much-derided, dictum: 'It should have sung, / This first new soul, it never should have spoken.' Rudolf Borchardt acerbically noted: 'One would have liked to hear Nietzsche's stentorian burst of laughter.' Borchardt, 'Stefan Georges *Siebenter Ring*', in *Prosa I*, 68–104 at 78.

dedicated to his inner vision, deeply contemptuous of society in general and theatre audiences in particular. This concurs with George's scorn of the masses and of the stage as the medium that panders to their vulgar tastes. But George shared this attitude with and relayed it to a band of followers, whereas Gundolf's Shakespeare, like Nietzsche, is an essentially solitary figure. Indeed solitariness becomes the defining quality of his sublime singularity. All that is truly great in him is not owing to his age but 'belongs solely to his solitary self' or to what Gundolf calls 'trans-social nature'. In the interplay between solitary self and trans-social nature, Shakespeare overcomes the conditioning fetters of social, religious, and moral convention. The most liberated of men, he is beyond good and evil, 'as free from morality as creation itself' (I 97). A 'once-human *Übermensch*' (II 419), Shakespeare has overcome the merely human and attained the condition of the Nietzschean superman.

The reviewer for *Nouvelles Littéraires* praised Gundolf for having achieved a 'rebirth of his subject', a rebirth, we might add, out of the spirit of Nietzsche. In Gundolf's account, the author of *Antony and Cleopatra* sounds like the Dionysian Hamlet of *The Birth of Tragedy*, his wisdom born of his 'undisguised insight into the terrible essence of the world and humanity without the comforting belief in a redeeming beyond, without any illusory hopes for personal happiness or common welfare' (II 330). This tragic clear-sightedness results not in fainthearted despondency but in an affirmation of life in its tragic essence. 'By realizing his terrible visions [Shakespeare] acclaims them' (II 5). '[H]is destruction is not negation but celebration … his downfalls are not punishments but sacrifices' (II 310).

In his effort to penetrate to the essence of his subject, Gundolf goes into linguistic gymnastics, stalking Shakespeare's incommensurability in ever more rarefied neologisms. 'All-' becomes a favourite prefix in compounds such as 'all-pervasiveness' (*Alldurchdringung*) or the virtually untranslatable *Allentfremdung* ('all-disengagement', 'all-alienation') (II 348) and *Allsehertum* ('all-seer-dom', 'omni-visionariness'). What these terms strain to convey is an emphatic comprehensiveness, the immeasurable expanse of the Shakespearean universe and the measureless capacity of its creator's solitary (all-)soul whence this universe has its being. It is through Shakespeare's all-comprehending vision (his *Allsehertum*) that his 'human figures' 'reveal the world forces' (I 249). Staged in the tragedies are not conflicts between individuals, let alone social conflicts, but 'forces', 'powers', in which life itself releases its demonic energies. Shakespeare is 'the dramatist of the life forces' (I 208). 'Life' has the highly charged sense of Nietzschean and post-Nietzschean vitalism (*Lebensphilosophie*). Shakespeare's tragic heroes are either bearers of life forces or engaged in tragic struggles to overcome them. In this, they are all embodiments of their maker's *Wesen*. Shakespeare could not have created his great heroes and villains if he were not their equal: 'Not fantasy, much less scholarship can credibly revive the heroes, only a soul their equal' (II 306). We have found the same view in the Shakespeare passage in Nietzsche's *Ecce Homo*: 'one cannot invent it, either one is it or one is not.' If the Shakespeare of *Ecce Homo* is Caesar as well as Bacon as well as Nietzsche, and his Hamlet a self-portrait of the artist-philosopher as king and clown,[153] Gundolf's Shakespeare is 'a kingly soul in fool's

---

[153] See Chapter 1, section VI.

motley' (I 450), a born aristocrat, but not in any way related to Bacon, who is too much on the side of rationalism to qualify for Gundolf's approval. The Bard's true compeer can be glimpsed in the character of 'the secret ruler' (I 293) ascribed to Shakespeare in Gundolf's discussion of Prince Hal in *1 Henry IV*. 'It is not as if Shakespeare had made Hal his masked fate [...] as he did with Prospero, the banished magus.' But 'the serene calm and taut strength of the secret ruler who awaits his hour [...] unperturbed by the taunts and sneers of the ignorant' (I 293) can only be imagined by someone who knows from his own experience 'this dangerous and enticing state of the unacknowledged genius' (I 293). Again the idea is, as in Nietzsche, that one cannot invent these things, only draw them from one's own self. This self and its permanent expectancy are unmistakably modelled on George, ruler of a secret realm always waiting for its moment of emergence.

At the end of his earlier book, *Shakespeare and the German Spirit*, Gundolf had co-opted Shakespeare into this emergence. Shakespeare, he wrote, supremely possessed what the present so deplorably lacked: the strength to truly see and bear reality. Emulating this Shakespearean strength, Gundolf concluded, was a crucial task for 'the *new* German spirit' (360). In the *Shakespeare* of 1928, little is left of this missionary drive. The narrative, quite apart from being embedded in a wealth of detailed dramatic analysis, plays out on the inner stage of 'the solitary self'. The momentary glimpse of the 'secret ruler' evokes no entourage of secret followers. The telos of this *Shakespeare* is not the emergence of a realm but the disappearance of a poet. In the farewell gesture of *The Tempest*, 'Shakespeare himself truly vanishes, absorbed into the world he first embodied, then execrated, then enchanted' (II 437).

By 1928, whatever fantasies of rule and power were entertained by George's followers had passed from Gundolf and his Shakespeare to other heralds and *their* heroes.

3

In the Master's Circle (II)

Ernst Kantorowicz

I HERALD OF THE HIDDEN KAISER

When the Kingdom of Italy, in May 1924, celebrated the seven-hundredth anniversary of the University of Naples, a foundation of the Hohenstaufen Frederick II, a wreath might have been seen on the Emperor's sarcophagus in the Cathedral of Palermo with this inscription:

> SEINEN KAISERN UND HELDEN
> DAS GEHEIME DEUTSCHLAND

This is not to imply that the present Life of Frederick II was begotten of that episode ... but that the wreath may fairly be taken as a symbol that—not alone in learned circles—enthusiasm is astir for the great German Rulers of the past: in a day when Kaisers are no more.[1]

This prefatory note opens another scholarly bestseller by one of George's disciples. Equally ground-breaking and equally controversial as Gundolf's 1911 *Shakespeare and the German Spirit*, Ernst Kantorowicz's *Frederick II* (1927) made its author famous overnight.[2] Gundolf had been thirty-one; Kantorowicz was thirty-two at the time of publication and obviously just as committed to the German spirit as his predecessor. Like Gundolf's book, Kantorowicz's *Frederick II* presented itself as a piece of Nietzschean monumental history celebrating the greatness of its historical subject as an inspirational model for a present badly in need of such models.

Born in 1194, Frederick II became King of Sicily at the age of four, King of Germany at eighteen, and Holy Roman Emperor at twenty-six. He retained that

---

[1] Ernst Kantorowicz, *Frederick the Second 1194–1250*, trans. E. O. Lorimer (London: Constable, 1931), 'Prefatory Note'. Page references to this text are given in brackets in the text. The inscription in English translation reads: 'To its Emperors and Heroes | The Secret Germany'.

[2] The most thoroughly researched account of Kantorowicz's biography prior to his emigration is Eckhart Grünewald, *Ernst Kantorowicz und Stefan George. Beiträge zur Biographie des Historikers bis zum Jahre 1938 und zu seinem Jugendwerk 'Kaiser Friedrich der Zweite'* (Wiesbaden: Steiner, 1982). Shorter accounts in English are Robert E. Lerner, 'Ernst H. Kantorowicz (1895–1963)', in *Medieval Scholarship: Biographical Studies on the Formation of a Discipline*, ed. Helen Damico and Joseph B. Zavadil, vol. 1: *History* (New York and London: Garland, 1995), 263–76, and, by the same author, 'Ernst Kantorowicz and Theodor E. Mommsen', in *An Interrupted Past: German-Speaking Refugee Historians in the United States after 1933*, ed. Hartmut Lehmann and James Sheehan (Cambridge: Cambridge University Press, 1991), 188–205. For a freer, more reflective treatment of the subject, see Alain Boureau, *Kantorowicz: Stories of a Historian* (1990), trans. Stephen G. Nichols and Gabrielle M. Spiegel (Baltimore, MD and London: Johns Hopkins University Press, 2001).

title, against papal opposition, for three decades up to his death in 1250. Excommunicated twice, he was alternately praised as 'the wonder of the world' (*stupor mundi*), the 'greatest of the rulers of the earth', and condemned as 'the son and disciple of Satan' or the *preambulus Antichristi* (predecessor of the Antichrist). Jacob Burckhardt called him 'the first modern man on the throne'.[3] Nietzsche praised him as 'that great free spirit, the genius among German emperors'.[4] For Kantorowicz he was the supreme artist of statecraft,[5] a figure in whom history and myth, *Realpolitik* and dream, cultured refinement and unflinching cruelty were inseparably entwined. He was, writes Kantorowicz, 'in fact probably the most intolerant Emperor that ever the West begot', but then '[a] tolerant judge is like luke-warm fire' (270).

> The Germans recognized Frederick II as fate incarnate and as doom; they yearned for him, they shrank from him. With him the Empire fell; but more than a century of safety were the few hours during which a German Emperor was privileged to tread such dangerous heights. […] For this stranger, this Roman of Swabian race, embodied that European-German personage whom men had dreamt of, who combined the triple culture of Europe: the cultures of the Church, the East, the Ancients. The Church was to Frederick II something […] which lay behind him. Nietzsche called Frederick 'to my mind the FIRST EUROPEAN' […] (387)

All that the Secret Germany worshipped in its emperors and heroes was united in this singular figure and celebrated in Kantorowicz's book.[6] The author, writes Peter Gay, 'did more than report medieval legends; his language, in its hyperbole, its shimmering vagueness, its ecstatic approval, conveys a highly tendentious—I am tempted to say erotic—engagement with its subject, and implies belief in these legends as deep truths, relevant to a suffering Germany. It was history as political poetry.'[7]

But 'political poetry' was hardly the order of the day in a discipline still largely committed to an ideal of scientific objectivity epitomized by Leopold von Ranke's much-quoted maxim to 'just say how it really was'.[8] Like Gundolf before him, Kantorowicz's tendentious enthusiasm triggered a heated debate about historical methodology, which even made it into the national press. 'Academy versus Mythical Vision', titled *Vossische Zeitung* (9 June 1929).[9] Yet even the book's opponents

---

[3] '[D]er erste moderne Mensch auf dem Throne'. Jacob Burckhardt, *Die Kultur der Renaissance in Italien. Ein Versuch* (1860), ed. Walther Rehm (Herrsching: Pawlak, 1981), 29. Middlemore's translation renders Burckhardt's words freely and inaccurately as 'the first ruler of the modern type'. *The Civilization of the Renaissance in Italy*, 20.

[4] Nietzsche, *The Antichrist*, 653 (§60).   [5] Boureau, *Kantorowicz*, 16.

[6] For sample quotations and a critique of the totalitarian tendencies of Kantorowicz's *Frederick II* see David Norbrook, 'The Emperor's New Body? *Richard II*, Ernst Kantorowicz, and the Politics of Shakespeare Criticism', *Textual Practice* 10.2 (1996), 329–57, especially at 331–2.

[7] Gay, *Weimar Culture*, 51.

[8] '[B]loß sagen, wie es eigentlich gewesen.' Leopold von Ranke, *Geschichte der romanischen und germanischen Völker von 1494 bis 1535* (Leipzig: Reimer, 1824), vi. Fritz Stern, *The Varieties of History from Voltaire to the Present* (New York: Vintage, 1973), 57, translates the whole paragraph in which the famous phrase occurs: 'To history has been assigned the office of judging the past, of instructing the present for the benefit of future ages. To such high offices this work does not aspire: It wants only to show what actually happened.'

[9] Grünewald, *Ernst Kantorowicz und Stefan George*, 86. For documentation of the whole debate: Grünewald, *Ernst Kantorowicz und Stefan George*, 81–101, and Lerner, 'Ernst H. Kantorowicz (1895–1963)', 268–9.

could not simply dismiss it. And so the young author, as exceptional in his unpro-fessorially elegant appearance as he was in his method, was given the opportunity to defend his approach before Germany's historical professoriat at the 1930 convention of the profession, the *Historikertag*.

History, he claimed, comprised two distinct activities, research and historiographic representation (*Darstellung*). 'Positivist historical *research* is guilty of an encroachment upon the domain of art if it tries to force the *writing* of history under its work rules.'[10] This encroachment, Kantorowicz insisted, was not just an issue of historical method, it infringed upon 'the humanity of the historiographer' (91) and made him a creature of bloodless indifference, the scholarly analogue of the equally indifferent, 'highly suspect' belletristic author of popular history books for the general public, who can adapt 'any theme to the viewpoint of any party, nationality or *Weltanschauung*' (92). Both types of historical author lacked the 'spiritual commitment to history' (94) which was the hallmark of the true historian. This commitment had to be rooted in, and was indeed indistinguishable from, a commitment to the nation. 'National feeling and feeling for the truth', Kantorowicz insisted, belonged together. 'For historiography essentially belongs to the national literature. It is conceived and understood from the standpoint of Germanness, regardless of whether it concerns the history of the fatherland or not. Its addressees are those few who are truly cultured and the intellectual leaders of the nation' (94–5). What then, Kantorowicz rhetorically asked, was the 'scholarly value' of the historical writings of the George school? Their 'scholarly value', he answered, consisted in 'serving the nation'.

A fiery plea for a nationally committed art of history-writing, the lecture had undoubtedly been vetted by the Master himself. Its rhetoric impressed, even if it did not convince, the majority of the audience. Kantorowicz, who was 'self-educated as a medieval historian',[11] obtained a professorial chair at Frankfurt only two years later, though this had probably less to do with winning converts to his creed than with improving his credentials as a properly 'scientific' historian. *Frederick II* conspicuously flouted academic convention in that it contained no source references at all. In 1931, it was followed by a 300-page supplementary volume (*Ergänzungsband*) that contained nothing else. If the original volume was eccentric in its omission, the supplement was almost as eccentric in plethora.[12] Overwhelmingly learned, it pointed the way to Kantorowicz's later work, which, at least at first sight, seems to belong to an altogether different author:

> The great distance between Kantorowicz' mythologizing biography of Frederick II and the demythologizing study of legal theology in *The King's Two Bodies*, published thirty years later on a different continent [may suggest] that there were two Kantorowiczes, that Ernst Kantorowicz, his own early enthusiasm purged by the extremity of National

[10] Ernst Kantorowicz, 'Grenzen, Möglichkeiten und Aufgaben der Darstellung mittelalterlicher Geschichte', quoted in Grünewald, *Ernst Kantorowicz und Stefan George*, 91.

[11] Lerner, 'Ernst Kantorowicz and Theodor E. Mommsen', 188.

[12] Ernst Kantorowicz, *Kaiser Friedrich der Zweite. Ergänzungsband* (Berlin: Georg Bondi, 1931). This volume was as carefully read and edited by George on its way into print as the Friedrich-book itself; quite surprising in view of George's low regard of scholarship.

Socialism, became the Ernst Kantorowicz who refused to sign the loyalty oath required of all the instructors at the University of California. But just as the two bodies of the king was a medieval legal fiction, so too the 'two Kantorowiczes' is a modern fiction, for there were not so much two Kantorowiczes as one man who may have gone through a political odyssey but who nevertheless maintained many of the attachments and values of his past.[13]

Born in Posen (now Poznań), then capital of the Prussian province of the same name, Ernst Hartwig Kantorowicz (1895–1963) was the son of a wealthy distillery owner who, like the rest of the town's Jewish elite, staunchly sided with imperial Prussian Germany in politics and culture. Having served and distinguished himself in the German army during the First World War Kantorowicz fought, 'with rifle and gun',[14] in several rightist 'free corps' units afterwards: first against the surrender of his native province to the newly-founded Polish Republic, then against the Spartacist revolutionists in Berlin and finally in Munich where he helped to put paid to the short-lived Munich Soviet Republic in May 1919.[15] These activities did not prevent him from matriculating in political economy, first in Berlin, then in Munich, and finally in Heidelberg where he moved for the winter semester of 1919.[16] It was in Heidelberg that he met Stefan George.[17]

Kantorowicz quickly gained the Master's respect and a sobriquet expressing it: 'the Chevalier'.[18] Whether George's poem on 'The Graves in Speyer' with its tribute to 'the greatest of the Fredericks'[19] had been the original inspiration of Kantorowicz's *Frederick II* cannot be said with any certainty. What is clear, though, is that George strongly supported the book and ensured that it would be published under the sign of the swastika, the stamp of his approval, by the publisher of his own works.[20] *Frederick II* drew on a complex of mythical ideas revolving around

---

[13] Carl Landauer, 'Ernst Kantorowicz and the Sacralization of the Past', *Central European History* 27 (1994), 1–25 at 3.

[14] Quoted in Lerner, 'Ernst H. Kantorowicz (1895–1963)', 268.

[15] Karlauf, *Stefan George*, 547–8.

[16] He completed his PhD thesis, *Das Wesen der muslimischen Handwerkerverbände* ('The Nature of Muslim Craftsmen's Guilds') in 1921. His supervisor was Eberhard Gothein, professor of political economy and the father of Percy Gothein (1896–1944), one of George's most enthusiastic followers. Percy's avid recruiting of handsome ephebes became something of an embarrassment to the Master. See Karlauf, *Stefan George*, 540–6.

[17] It was in Heidelberg also that he met Woldemar ('Woldi') Count Uxkull-Gyllenband (1898–1939), a student of ancient history who became his 'dining companion and bedmate', to whom he dedicated *Frederick II*. Like Kantorowicz, Uxkull had been a soldier during the Great War and an anti-Spartacist fighter afterwards. His politics were staunchly nationalist and, even during his relationship with Kantorowicz, at least latently anti-Semitic. Together with his younger brother Bernhard, he had made Stefan George's acquaintance as early as 1907 and was one of the novices admitted to the Inner Circle at its first post-war meeting in Heidelberg in 1919.

[18] 'George said of him that he was what the French called a chevalier and that he was so completely a chevalier as one rarely found nowadays. Lithe and yet masculinely firm, suave, elegant in his dress, gestures and language, Kantorowicz had something of a foilsman.' Boehringer, *Mein Bild von Stefan George*, vol. 1, 180.

[19] *The Works of Stefan George*, 164. 'Die Gräber von Speyer' was originally published in *Der Siebente Ring* (1907). The poem was occasioned by the opening of medieval emperors' graves in Speyer Cathedral in 1900, followed by their public exhibition in 1906.

[20] In his dealings with the publisher Georg Bondi, George did not reveal Kantorowicz's name until shortly before publication.

Figure 3.1. Stefan George and the Stauffenberg brothers, Claus (left) and Berthold (right), in 1924. Photo by permission of Stefan George Archiv, Württembergische Landesbibliothek.

'Secret Germany', 'the New Reich', and 'the hidden Kaiser'; ideas that became central concerns to George and his acolytes during the Weimar years and attest to the Circle's increasing politicization.

Not long after Kantorowicz, three younger novices were admitted to the Master's orbit: the 19-year-old Berthold von Stauffenberg, his twin brother Alexander and their younger brother Claus, the future would-be Hitler assassin (Figure 3.1). Gifted, good-looking and full of enthusiasm, the young counts were also prized for their family name, which seemed to link them directly to the Kaisers and heroes of the Secret Germany:

> The arrival of the Stauffenberg brothers caused an unbelievable excitement in the George Circle. Their suggestive name coinciding with the Staufer studies of the historian Ernst Kantorowicz and George's secret claim to the spiritual leadership of Germany, steeped everything in a luminous mythical haze. Those caught up in it took it for a vision of great clarity.[21]

The years following Germany's defeat and the tumultuous beginnings of the Weimar Republic were seething with 'apocalyptic expectations',[22] hopes for a

---

[21] Peter Hoffmann, *Claus Schenk Graf von Stauffenberg und seine Brüder* (Stuttgart: Deutsche Verlags-Anstalt, 1991), 61.

[22] Klaus Vondung, 'Apokalyptische Erwartung. Zur Jugendrevolte zwischen 1910 und 1930', in *'Mit uns zieht die neue Zeit': der Mythos Jugend*, ed. Thomas Koebner, Rolf-Peter Janz, and Frank Trommler (Frankfurt: Suhrkamp, 1985), 519–45.

messianic rebirth from the ruins of the old order. George and his Circle were prime suppliers of such hopes, especially among the various ramifications of the German youth movement.[23] The suggestive darkness of George's vision was precisely what heightened its appeal. Where politics and politicians, in particular the representatives of the Republic and its parliamentary system, were held in contempt, the ostensibly 'unpolitical' stance of the poet cast an alluring spell on those seeking orientation in times of confusion. In the flicker of their forest campfires the idealistic youths of the *Wandervogel* and other groups did indeed take the 'luminous mythical haze' of George's poetry for a vision of great clarity, a beacon of hope and a prophecy of national rebirth: the dawning of a New Reich.

While poetry remained the Master's almost exclusive medium of expression (though his production dwindled and some critics thought him already dated by 1920),[24] spiritual leadership was the goal to which all energies were now directed. With Gundolf's fall from grace the role of opinion leader fell to the energetic Friedrich Wolters.[25] Always cruder in his exegetic broadcasting of the Master's voice than Gundolf, he did not scruple to translate poetry into propaganda. The Secret Germany moved closer to the arena of public debate, almost, but never quite crossing the line into real politics. Maintaining his pre-war positions, George clearly interfaced with the post-war *Zeitgeist*[26] and gained a wide following among those 'disinherited conservatives' who, according to Fritz Stern, 'had nothing to conserve'. Confirmed enemies of the Republic, they 'sought to destroy the despised present in order to recapture an idealized past in an imaginary future'.[27]

---

[23] Walter Laqueur, *Young Germany: A History of the German Youth Movement* (Piscataway, NJ: Transaction Publishers, 1984); Peter D. Stachura, *The German Youth Movement, 1900–1945: An Interpretive and Documentary History* (London: Macmillan, 1981).

[24] Karlauf, *Stefan George*, 735.

[25] After a doctorate in history, Friedrich Wolters (1876–1930) became the private tutor of Prince August Wilhelm of Prussia, the fourth son of the Kaiser, and in that capacity ghost-wrote the PhD dissertation of his academically untalented pupil. Wolters became a follower of George in 1909/10 and the co-editor, with Friedrich Gundolf, of the *Yearbook for the Spiritual Movement*. His essay entitled 'Rule and Service' (*Herrschaft und Dienst*, 1909) became an important programmatic statement of the aims of the George Circle. A professor of history at Marburg, later at Kiel, Wolters wrote the official history of the Circle—*Stefan George und die Blätter für die Kunst. Deutsche Geistesgeschichte seit 1890* (1930). George authorized the book, but many followers found it bigoted and doctrinaire (Gundolf called it sanctimonious—*pfäffisch*).

[26] Karlauf, *Stefan George*, 510.

[27] Fritz Stern, *The Politics of Cultural Despair: A Study in the Rise of the Germanic Ideology* (Berkeley and Los Angeles: University of California Press, 1961), xvi; quoted in Karlauf, *Stefan George*, 510. Stern is writing here about the 'Conservative Revolution'; both the label itself and George's relation to the writers and opinions subsumed under it are disputed. Yet Stern's description clearly applies to the mindset which gave rise to George's idea of the New Reich and from which it drew such avid approval. Stern's conclusion, again not referring to George in particular, seems equally pertinent: 'I believe that this particular reaction to modernity was deeply embedded in German thought and society, and that this curiously idealistic, unpolitical discontent constitutes the main link between all that is venerable and great in the German past and the triumph of national socialism.' Stern, *Politics of Cultural Despair*, xxiii. The term 'Conservative Revolution' was given currency by Armin Mohler, *Die konservative Revolution in Deutschland 1918–1932. Grundriss ihrer Weltanschauungen* (Stuttgart: Friedrich Vorwerk, 1950).

Kantorowicz's *Frederick II* appealed strongly to such sentiments. Ever since the Wars of Liberation against Napoleon, the Staufer or Hohenstaufen dynasty held a special place in the German nationalist imagination. This manifested itself in the popular legend of the sleeping Kaiser enclosed in the Kyffhäuser mountain. During his long slumber his beard was supposed to have grown through the stone table in front of him and in his country's hour of need he would step forth and restore his realm to its former glory. The sleeping Kaiser was generally thought to be Frederick I, known as Frederick Barbarossa (Redbeard). His sturdy soldiership and solid Swabian pedigree made him a much more satisfactory national father figure than his successor Frederick, the maverick *Übermensch* from Italy. The paternal Hohenstaufen was construed as a prefiguration of the paternal Hohenzollern, Wilhelm I, 'Barbablanca', as the popular novelist Felix Dahn ludicrously dubbed him.[28] But Whitebeard, this conveniently normalized version of the fabled emperor, drew on a transmogrification of the myth:

> Frederick II [Kantorowicz writes] is gradually metamorphosed into the bearded Barbarossa, the immortal boy into the aged man. Germany's dream was changed, and change of myth reflects the changing life and longings of a people. The snow-white sleeper whose beard has grown through the table on which his elbow rests has no message for the German of to-day: he has his fulfilment, in the greatest vassal of the Empire, the aged Bismarck. The weary Lord of the Last Day has naught to say to the fiery Lord of the Beginning, the seducer, the deceiver, the radiant, the merry, the ever-young, the stern and mighty judge, the scholar, the sage who leads his armed warriors to the Muses' dance and song, he who slumbers not nor sleeps but ponders how he can renew the 'Empire'. The mountain would to-day stand empty were it not for the son of Barbarossa's son. The greatest Frederick is not yet redeemed, him his people knew not and sufficed not. 'Lives and lives not,' the Sibyl's word is not for the Emperor, but for the German People.[29]

Concluding Kantorowicz's over 600-page tribute to the last of the Hohenstaufen, this passage evinces a division we have encountered before, notably in the equation of Germany with Hamlet.[30] There are, again, two Germanies, not one: the official Germany—in the quoted passage nothing but a dull afterglow of Bismarck's fallen empire—and the other, true or 'secret' Germany labouring to emerge with new urgency. Although Hamlet does not figure here, we find the same dual structure for which he had served as a powerful symbol since the thwarted revolution of 1848. In Freiligrath's poem, Germany-Hamlet is warned to beware of a Laertes with his poisoned *French* rapier, in danger of losing his inheritance to an invading army.[31] The role of France, Germany's putative 'hereditary' enemy (*Erbfeind*), in enforcing the 'shame peace' of Versailles and the 'black shame' of the occupation of

---

[28] The Kyffhäuser monument, a textbook example of Wilhelminian (II) bombast completed in 1896, shows both emperors, Wilhelm I on horseback and Frederick I sitting on a stone bench. The message is obvious: Wilhelm is rightful heir to the Staufer's Holy Roman Empire; in him the Kyffhäuser prophecy has been fulfilled.

[29] Kantorowicz, *Frederick II*, 688–9.   [30] See Introduction, section II.

[31] Freiligrath's poem admonishes Hamlet to 'seize the moment': 'Ere rushing comes a Northern route / To seize thine heritage and home / Oh take thou heed—though much I doubt / That this time it from *Norway* come.' Freiligrath, 'Hamlet', trans. Howitt.

the Rhineland by French colonial troops[32] made this threat seem a reality. What Hegel said of Hamlet—'his deeds consist in his longing' ('Sein Thun ist das Sehnen')[33]—could well be applied to the adherents of the anti-bourgeois right who 'sought a breakthrough to the past, and [...] longed for a new community in which old ideas and institutions would once again command universal allegiance'.[34] Kantorowicz's siren song of imperial glory furnished these diffuse longings with an eminently 'usable past'.[35]

How closely Kantorowicz's *Frederick II* tied in with the Master's own mythologizing is shown by George's last volume of poetry, *Das neue Reich* (*The New Realm*), which appeared in 1928.[36] Coming fifteen years after *Star of the Covenant* (1913), it contained much that had been written, and published, earlier. 'The Poet in Times of Confusion', from whose last words the volume took its title, had first appeared in 1921.[37] In it, George programmatically stakes his claim to spiritual leadership:

> But in a mournful age it is the poet
> Who keeps the marrow sound, the germ alive.
> He stirs the holy flame that leaps across
> And shapes the flesh in which to burn, discovers
> The truth of tidings which our fathers gave:
> That those elected to the highest goal
> Begin by passing through the waste, that once
> The heart of Europe shall redeem the earth.
> And when the final hope has almost perished
> In sternest grief, his eyes already see
> A coming light.[38]

The miseries of the present will be overcome by a return to the chiliastic prophecies of the past, and Germany, the heart of Europe, will redeem the earth. En route to

[32] 'The black shame' or 'the black disgrace' were terms of outrage at France's use of African troops in the occupation of the Rhineland. Posters, caricatures, newspaper articles, and parliamentary petitions imputed the rape of German women by black African soldiers. See Iris Wigger, '"Die schwarze Schmach". Afrikaner in der Propaganda der 1920er Jahre', in *Das Jahrhundert der Bilder 1900–1949*, ed. Gerhard Paul (Göttingen: Vandenhoeck & Ruprecht, 2009), 268–75.

[33] Georg Wilhelm Friedrich Hegel, *The Phenomenology of Spirit* (1807), trans. A. V. Miller, ed. J. N. Findlay (Oxford: Clarendon Press, 1977), 201. Quoted in Anselm Haverkamp, 'Stranger Than Paradise. Dantes irdisches Paradies als Antidot politischer Theologie', in *Geschichtskörper. Zur Aktualität von Ernst H. Kantorowicz*, ed. Wolfgang Ernst and Cornelia Vismann (Munich: Fink, 1998), 93–103 at 100.

[34] Stern, *Politics of Cultural Despair*, xvi.

[35] Van Wyck Brooks, 'On Creating a Usable Past', *The Dial* 64.7 (11 April 1918), 337–41.

[36] Stefan George, *Das neue Reich* (Berlin: Georg Bondi, 1928). 'Holy Saint Francis how new this all is!' wrote the philosopher Elisabeth Landmann, one of George's female friends, after receiving the volume, adding politely, since most of the poems were not new at all, 'and a good thing, too, that not *everything* is new because who could have digested that'. Quoted in George, *Sämtliche Werke*, vol. 9: *Das Neue Reich*, ed. Ute Oelmann (2001), 114.

[37] 'Der Dichter in Zeiten der Wirren', *Sämtliche Werke*, vol. 9, 27–30. The poem is dedicated to Bernhard Count Uxkull Gyllenband, who had killed himself in summer 1918 after being arrested trying to desert from the army. See Chapter 2, note 124.

[38] *The Works of Stefan George*, 296.

this redemption, Kantorowicz's *Frederick II* obviously had a part to play in recovering 'the truth of tidings which our fathers gave'.

One of the few poems in *Das neue Reich* that were actually new is the one in which George himself finally adopts the term that had long been associated with him and his circle: 'Secret Germany'.[39] It follows the familiar chiliastic pattern. From a present '[d]oomed to perdition and death' springs the promise of ultimate redemption:

> Only what consecrate earth
> Cradles in sheltering sleep
> Long in the innermost grooves,
> Far from acquisitive hands,
> Marvels this day cannot grasp
> Are rife with the fate of tomorrow.[40]

The affinity with Kantorowicz and the Hohenstaufen myth is clear. The fate of tomorrow is cradled, like the sleeping Kaiser, in consecrated earth. Nothing could convey a more total isolation from current politics than this image of a Secret Germany enshrined in its subterranean cave. But the shrine became all too hospitable to myth-mongers with very real political power.[41] Frederick II had become 'the bearer of a Fascist dream', Kantorowicz enthusiastically reported from Palermo in 1924.[42] Little could he suspect that his as yet unwritten book on Frederick would eventually find its way into the hands of the Duce himself—a gift from Hermann Göring.[43]

II 'I HAVE BEEN SENT WITH TORCH AND STEEL': GEORGE AND THE NEW MASTERS

To what extent did George's prophecies anticipate, or even promote, the fate of Germany's actual National Socialist tomorrow? In her comment to Volume 9 of the *Complete Works* edition Ute Oelmann explains that George's idea of a New

---

[39] Karl Wolfskehl introduced the term in the first issue of the *Yearbook for the Spiritual Movement* where he recounts the history of *Pages for the Arts*; Norton, *Secret Germany*, 434–5. For the nineteenth-century pre-history of the idea of a 'Secret Germany', see Grünewald, *Ernst Kantorowicz und Stefan George*, 74–80.

[40] *The Works of Stefan George*, 307. 'Geheimes Deutschland', *Sämtliche Werke*, vol. 9, 45–9.

[41] In his rallying call before the fascist 'March on Rome' Mussolini declared: 'We have created a myth, this myth is a belief, a noble enthusiasm; it does not need to be a reality, it is a striving and a hope, belief and courage. Our myth is the nation, the great nation which we want to make into a concrete reality for ourselves.' Quoted in Carl Schmitt, *The Crisis of Parliamentary Democracy*, trans. Ellen Kennedy (Cambridge, MA: MIT Press, 1988), 76.

[42] Quoted in Karlauf, *Stefan George*, 557.

[43] Kantorowicz mentions this in a letter to the publisher Ursula Küpper (24 May 1963), who tried to persuade him to agree to a re-edition of *Frederick II*: 'A book which Himmler had on his bedside table and which Göring gave to Mussolini with a personal dedication should better be left to fall into oblivion.' Quoted in Grünewald, *Ernst Kantorowicz und Stefan George*, 165. However, Kantorowicz did eventually consent to a new printing, which appeared without the original prefatory note in 1963.

Reich had little in common with the 'Third Reich' as envisioned and promoted as a nationalistic catchphrase by Arthur Moeller van den Bruck, one of the writers now grouped under the rubric of 'Conservative Revolution'.[44] Instead, she suggests, there is a 'structural similarity' between George's New Reich and the 'Third Reich' of the twelfth-century mystic Joachim of Fiore. Following the realm of the Father and the realm of the Son, this third Reich, the realm of the Spirit, constitutes the highest stage of earthly life, leading up to the Last Judgement.[45] Advocates of George tend to favour such safely remote points of reference. But the Master's realm-to-come spoke powerfully to the nationalist sentiments of the present. This appears in the quotation with which Oelmann concludes her comment. It is from the letter of thanks by the Jewish philosopher Edith Landmann, one of the few women who managed to sustain a long friendship with George. On receiving a copy of *Das neue Reich* she enthused that, in this volume, 'it was not an individual speaking but as if the New Reich itself had raised its thundering voice [...] He who began in solitude now sounds forth the soul of a whole people.'[46] It is this overblown sense of importance, a hubris that 'proclaimed the master of a sect the lord of the epoch',[47] which inevitably kindled a sense of political mission, and political influence, within the Circle itself. Though George (quoting Landmann again) 'preferred to be Kaiser of the Secret Germany to being President of the secret-less one',[48] he occasionally flirted with the idea of getting actively involved in politics[49] and was always flattered to be told of his impact on the nation at large.

George and his Circle kept a wary distance from Hitler and the rising Nazi party. Like other ultra-conservative intellectuals they shrank in disgust from the sheer vulgarity of the movement.[50] Yet at the same time, and again like many other

---

[44] Arthur Moeller van den Bruck, *Germany's Third Empire*, trans. E. O. Lorimer (London: George Allen & Unwin, 1934); orig.: *Das dritte Reich* (Hamburg: Hanseatische Verlagsanstalt, 1923). Breuer, *Anatomie der Konservativen Revolution*; Roger Woods, *The Conservative Revolution in the Weimar Republic* (New York: St. Martin's Press, 1996); on Moeller van den Bruck: Stern, *Politics of Cultural Despair*, 183–266.

[45] Ute Oelmann, 'Anhang', in *Sämtliche Werke*, vol. 9, 114–75 at 120–1. Oelmann fails to note, however, that Joachim was invoked by Nazi ideologists too, as is shown in Matthias Ried, *Joachim von Fiore—Denker der vollendeten Menschheit* (Würzburg: Königshausen & Neumann, 2004). But it is true that the 'Dream of the Third Reich' was dreamt by writers of diverse political persuasions. See, for example, Waldemar Gurian, 'Ein Traum vom Dritten Reich', *Hochland* 22 (1924/5), 237–42. Gurian, a student of Carl Schmitt, offered a clear-sighted analysis of such dreaming as a symptom of political despair in a book he published shortly before the Nazi takeover: Walter Gerhart (=Waldemar Gurian), *Um des Reiches Zukunft. Nationale Wiedergeburt oder politische Reaktion?* (Freiburg: Herder, 1932). See Friedrich Vollhardt, 'Hochland-Konstellationen: Programme, Konturen und Aporien des Kulturkatholizismus am Beginn des 20. Jahrhunderts', in *Moderne und Antimoderne. Renouveau Catholique und die deutsche Literatur des 20. Jahrhunderts*, ed. Wilhelm Kühlmann and Roman Luckscheiter (Freiburg: Rombach 2008), 67–100.

[46] Edith Landmann, Letter to George, 3 November 1928, quoted in Oelmann, 'Anhang', 121.

[47] Hans Egon Holthusen, *Das Schöne und das Wahre. Neue Studien zur modernen Literatur* (Munich: Piper, 1958), 57.

[48] Landmann, *Gespräche mit Stefan George* 138.

[49] Breysig, *Stefan George*, 27: in conversation with Breysig (3 November 1916) George declared that '[i]f everything [...] went wrong and no better man were available to take over the lead (i.e. the office of Imperial Chancellor), he would do it.'

[50] Even George's Jewish publisher Georg Bondi disclaimed any link between the Nazi symbol and the swastika or 'sun wheel' displayed on publications of the Circle. The Circle, he insisted, had a prior

right-wing intellectuals, George revelled in the vision of a ruthless barbaric leader uprooting a hopelessly decadent civilization. Just such a barbarian appears in his poem 'The Burning of the Temple': 'I have been sent with torch and steel', he explains his mission to the fearful priests, so 'that you / Grow hard and not that I grow soft.' The poem ends with the temple burning, 'and half a thousand years must come / And go before it can arise again.'[51]

When the actual New Reich was launched on 30 January 1933, and masses of Germans hailed Adolf Hitler as the *Führer* who would 'break [...] the chains and sweep [...] aside the rubble',[52] reactions among George's followers were divided. Some became Nazis, others didn't. Some, like the Stauffenberg brothers, were enthusiastic at first and became disenchanted later.[53] Showing his characteristic sphinx-like inscrutability, the Master himself withdrew into silence. 'We hope that his silence means resistance', Klaus Mann wrote in October 1933, and 'if he wants to end his life as he has lived it [...] may he preserve towards this new Germany the same gesture that the old one compelled: his head averted from a race that daily entraps itself more deeply into the shame of which he wanted to purge it.'[54] Much in the same vein is Walter Benjamin's often-quoted remark in a letter to Gershom Scholem that 'if ever God has punished a prophet by fulfilling his prophecy, then that is the case with George.'[55]

Courted by the new masters of Germany, George declined offers of academy membership and an honorary pension, but in a tortuous correspondence with the Prussian Ministry of Culture he did not deny his 'progenitorship' of the new regime. The official Germany celebrated his sixty-fifth birthday on 12 July 1933 with the accolades due to a man whom the new regime would have liked to co-opt as poet laureate. George spent the day in Berlin but made sure that only a handful

claim to it and would therefore go on using it. Anyone with but the slightest knowledge of these books, he declared, would 'know that they have nothing to do with politics'. Quoted in Karlauf, *Stefan George*, 578. There is a good deal of naivety in this. But there is also an element of what one might describe as 'competitive adaptation'. As with the swastika, so with their use of the terms *Reich* and *Führer*, George's acolytes could always claim that they were only upholding their ownership claim against vulgar appropriations of what by right belonged to them. But by the late 1920s both the terms and the symbol had taken on quite specific political meanings. The haughty refusal to acknowledge this was, intentionally or not, a disingenuous way to profit from their dangerous appeal. Walter Benjamin is particularly clear-sighted about this. He concludes his review of *The Poet as Leader in Germany's Classical Period* (1928) by George's then current favourite, the precociously gifted Max Kommerell, with the ominous remark that 'the "secret Germany" [...] ultimately is nothing but the arsenal of the official Germany, in which the magic hood of invisibility [*Tarnkappe*] hangs next to the helmet of steel.' 'Against a Masterpiece', in Walter Benjamin, *Selected Writings*, vol. 2, pt. 1: *1927–1939*, ed. Michael W. Jennings (Cambridge, MA and London: Harvard University Press, 2005), 378–85 at 384.

[51] *The Works of Stefan George*, 319 and 321. 'Der Brand des Tempels', *Sämtliche Werke*, vol. 9, 61–9.

[52] 'The Poet in Times of Confusion', in *The Works of Stefan George*, 295–7 at 297. 'Der Dichter in Zeiten der Wirren', *Sämtliche Werke*, vol. 9, 27–30.

[53] See Chapter 6, section I.

[54] Klaus Mann, 'Das Schweigen Stefan Georges', *Die Sammlung* 1.2 (October 1933), 98–103 at 103.

[55] Quoted in Norton, *Secret Germany*, 742. Norton seems to assume that Benjamin wrote this in condemnation of George. It is more likely that Benjamin meant that George's fears—not his hopes— had come true. On this question Karlauf, *Stefan George*, 765–6 nn. 57 and 59.

of friends knew his whereabouts.[56] He left for Switzerland soon after, never to return. But to speak of 'voluntary exile'[57] unduly clarifies what was in fact anything but clear. Since October 1931 he had spent most of his time in Minusio on Lago Maggiore, the village quiet and warm climate suiting his declining health.[58]

Some of George's most talented and most intimate friends were Jews. When Edith Landmann asked him what he thought of the anti-Semitism of the new regime he brushed her off saying: 'When I think of what lies ahead for Germany in the next fifty years, that Jew thing [*Judensach*] is not so important.'[59] Kantorowicz, obviously unsure of where the Master stood, gingerly took a similar line in his birthday letter to George (10 July 1933):

> May Germany become as the Master dreamt it would be! And if the events of today are not just a grimace of that wished-for ideal but indeed the right path to its fulfilment, then may all this be well. And then it is immaterial whether one man can—or rather: may—walk along on this path or must step aside rather than rejoice. 'Imperium transcendat hominem' [the Empire shall prevail over the individual man], declares Frederick II, and I would be the last to contradict that.[60]

III PROFESSING THE SECRET GERMANY

Five months later George was dead. His burial in Minusio was arranged so discreetly that the Secret Germany could bid farewell to its leader before the representative of the official Germany, Ernst von Weizsäcker, the German envoy to Switzerland, arrived on the scene. As the faithful were dispersing at the train station, Ernst Kantorowicz was appalled to note that several of the younger ones exchanged a Nazi salute.[61]

His was a rather special situation. A decorated Great War veteran and free corps fighter, the author of a book which Hitler himself confessed having read twice, he had all the credentials for success under the new regime—except that he was a Jew.[62] His 'front-fighter' status exempted him from the first wave of university purges, though it would not have protected him from the later ones. He requested, and was granted, leave for the 1933 summer semester, but decided to resume his teaching in the winter term following. On 14 November he gave what he introduced as 'a kind of inaugural lecture'. In view of 'the tremendous events of the last

---

[56] Karlauf, *Stefan George*, 624.

[57] As, for example, Gay does in *Weimar Culture*, 47.

[58] Clotilde Schlayer, *Minusio: Chronik aus den letzten Lebensjahren Stefan Georges*, ed. Maik Bozza and Ute Oelmann (Göttingen: Wallstein/Castrum Peregrini, 2010).

[59] Landmann, *Gespräche mit Stefan George*, 209.

[60] Quoted in Grünewald, *Ernst Kantorowicz und Stefan George*, 122.

[61] E[dgar] S[alin], 'Ernst Kantorowicz, 1895–1963' (n.p.: privately printed, 1963), 7.

[62] This is the gist of Norman F. Cantor's polemic against Kantorowicz in the chapter 'The Nazi Twins: Percy Ernst Schramm and Ernst Hartwig Kantorowicz' in his *Inventing the Middle Ages: The Lives, Works, and Ideas of the Great Medievalists of the Twentieth Century* (New York: William Morrow, 1991), 79–117 at 95: '[E]xcept for the misfortune of being a Jew [...] he was the ideal Nazi scholar and intellectual.' Cantor was not aware of—or chose to ignore—Kantorowicz's 're-inaugural lecture' of November 1933.

months', he explained, it seemed appropriate 'to seize the opportunity of a mere resumption of teaching to introduce oneself once more to one's listeners'.[63] This reintroduction would take the form of a confession or profession of faith because 'why would one hold the title of professor if one did not have the courage to be a "professor" at such a decisive hour'. The title of the lecture was 'The Secret Germany', its aim to clarify that the Germany of the Nazis was not the Germany George and his followers had envisioned. The lecture makes no direct reference to the new rulers but that in itself is a statement: Kantorowicz has not a single word of praise for their recent triumph. Instead he emphasizes the esoteric nature of the Secret Germany, its spirituality and transcendence of a chauvinist, narrowly parochial Germanness. Nietzsche is quoted—'in order to become more German one has to de-Germanize oneself'—and Goethe: '[T]he perfect German always has to be more than German' (87). Hence the supreme rulers of the 'Secret Germany' were never the popular favourites of the nation (84). Not even Barbarossa, that universal favourite, was as popular imagination would have had him: more spiritual, more driven by the idea of Roman greatness than by provincial power politics (85). And when it came to 'the greatest Frederick', the last of the Hohenstaufen, the history books were missing the point when they complained: 'But he was not German' (86).

Kantorowicz's lecture displays all the politico-theological myth-making, all the ardent rhapsodizing over the hidden kings and poet-leaders of the nation that made *Frederick II* such an intoxicating read to the nationalist right. Kantorowicz the 'professor' is not a bit more democratic or less elitist than before. But it took considerable courage to profess this particular kind of elitism when rampant populism ruled the state as well as the streets. In the boldest part of his lecture Kantorowicz came perilously close to openly challenging the regime. What 'the heroes of the secret Reich' have to teach, he told his student audience, extended beyond spirit and intellect even to 'bodily gesture' (*leibliche Gebärde*):

> Only from the rulers of the 'Secret Germany' can you learn the genuine German gesture, the eternal German way. Every gesture, to be sure, can be performed in a hundred different ways; but only *one* way is right among ninety-nine wrong ones. A look at a Greek grave relief will tell you that—for as long as men have existed— only *one* way to shake hands is the right way. (90)

In November 1933, Kantorowicz's reference to the genuine German greeting gesture inevitably evoked the new greeting gesture introduced by the Nazis, the right arm extended into the air known as the *Hitlergruss* or the *deutscher Gruss* which appalled Kantorowicz a month later when he saw it used after the Master's funeral at Minusio. What the 'professor' of the Secret Germany was telling his students,

---

[63] Ernst Kantorowicz, 'Das Geheime Deutschland. Vorlesung, gehalten bei Wiederaufnahme der Lehrtätigkeit am 14. November 1933', ed. Eckhart Grünewald, in *Ernst Kantorowicz. Erträge der Doppeltagung Institute for Advanced Study, Princeton, Johann Wolfgang Goethe-Universität, Frankfurt*, ed. Robert L. Benson and Johannes Fried (Stuttgart: Steiner, 1997), 77–93 at 77. Page references in brackets are to this text.

then, in almost so many words, was to avoid the 'Hitler greeting', the public sign of allegiance to the new Germany. Not counting those who, like Wolfskehl, had already been forced into exile, Kantorowicz was alone among George's followers in publicly distancing himself from the new regime. Whatever reservations other Circle members may have had, they kept quiet about them. And not a few hailed the coming of Hitler as the fulfilment of the Master's dream.[64]

Intended as re-inaugural, the lecture came to be Kantorowicz's swan song as a German professor. Threats of a boycott by the Nazi student organization made a continuation of his teaching impossible. Unwilling to take the loyalty oath to the Führer, which became obligatory for civil servants in 1934, he applied for and was granted emeritus status. After two terms as an unpaid visiting fellow at Oxford, where he met and became intimate with the Master of Wadham College, Maurice Bowra,[65] he returned to Berlin where he lived under increasingly difficult conditions until November 1938. He narrowly avoided the pogroms of the 'Crystal Night' and escaped, with Bowra's help, to England. After two months in Oxford he embarked to New York and eventually found temporary employment at Berkeley.[66] California, he wrote to his Heidelberg acquaintance Edgar Salin, was at least 'human' and the best of all places on 'this strange and basically uninteresting continent', but still, he carped to Bowra, there was 'no enchantment except ice-cream for which I do not fall'.[67]

But Kantorowicz soon became reconciled to his American environment, fulfilling the prediction expressed by another émigré historian from Germany, Theodor Ernst Mommsen. 'I think in the long run you will get along fine and be comfortable here', Mommsen had written from New Haven in 1938: '—better than many Germans who come here with a dreadful academic arrogance (stuffed shirts!) determined to show people what German "Wissenschaft" is.'[68] After a string of temporary contracts, Kantorowicz was finally appointed full professor in 1945, the happy conclusion to his years in precarious transit.

Or so it seemed until, in 1949, the Regents of the University of California demanded all faculty members to swear loyalty to the United States government

[64] Woldemar von Uxkull, Kantorowicz's old flatmate, in the meantime professor of ancient history at Tübingen, did just that in a lecture entitled 'The Revolutionary Ethos of Stefan George', much to Kantorowicz's horror. Uxkull died in a road accident in 1939, a victim of his passion for fast cars. See Robert E. Lerner, 'Letters by Ernst Kantorowicz Concerning Woldemar Uxkull and Stefan George', *George-Jahrbuch* 8 (2010), 157–74 at 170.

[65] C. M. Bowra, *Memories 1899–1939* (Cambridge, MA: Harvard University Press, 1967), 286–91. On the relationship between Kantorowicz and Bowra, see also Lerner, 'Letters by Ernst Kantorowicz'.

[66] Norman F. Cantor's claim that '[t]he Nazi big shots worked to protect [Kantorowicz] into the summer of 1938' ('The Nazi Twins', 95) lacks any foundation whatsoever. For Kantorowicz's life in Germany prior to his emigration: Grünewald, *Ernst Kantorowicz und Stefan George*, 136–48; for his narrow escape: Bowra, *Memories*, 303–5; for the circumstances of his immigration into the US: Peter Th. Walter and Wolfgang Ernst, 'Ernst H. Kantorowicz. Eine archäo-biographische Skizze', in *Geschichtskörper*, ed. Ernst and Vismann, 207–31.

[67] Letter to Edgar Salin, 22 September 1939; letter to Bowra, 19 November 1939; both quoted in Lerner, 'Letters by Ernst Kantorowicz', 168 and 171.

[68] Theodor E. Mommsen, Letter to Kantorowicz, 8 May 1938, quoted in Walter and Ernst, 'Ernst H. Kantorowicz. Eine archäo-biographische Skizze', 224.

and that they were not Communists. Kantorowicz, who had refused to swear loyalty to Hitler, refused to comply and became a leading voice in the resistance to the oath. 'Perhaps I have been sensitive', he explained,

> because both my professional experience as an historian and my personal experience in Nazi Germany have conditioned me to be alert when I hear again certain familiar tones sounded. Rather than renounce this experience, which is indeed synonymous with my 'life,' I shall place it, for what it is worth, at the disposal of my colleagues who are fighting the battle for the dignity of their profession and their university.[69]

Kantorowicz elaborated further in a letter to the president of the University of California, flourishing his anti-Communist credentials and contritely regretting the way in which he acquired them:

> My political record will stand the test of every investigation. I have twice volunteered to fight actively, with rifle and gun, the left-wing radicals in Germany; but I know that by joining the white battalions I have prepared, if indirectly and against my intention, the road leading to National Socialism and its rise to power. I shall be ready at any moment to produce sworn evidence before the Federal Bureau of Investigation, which has admitted me to citizenship during the war. But my respect for the University of California is such that I cannot allow myself to believe that the base field of political inquisition, which paralyzes scholarly production, should be within the range of its activities.[70]

Keeping up his resistance to the loyalty oath to the end, Kantorowicz was one of the 'thirty-one last-ditch "nonsigners"'[71] who were dismissed by the Regents in August 1950 and only reinstated after a collective lawsuit against their dismissal in April 1951. But by this time he had already moved to the Institute for Advanced Study at Princeton, and it was here that he completed the book that, against all odds,[72] brought him worldwide fame.

IV 'GLIST'RING PHAETHON': RICHARD II, OR, THE POET'S FALL

The King's Two Bodies: A Study in Medieval Political Theology[73] reflects both the contrast and the continuity in its author's 'two lives'.[74] What had always been at

---

[69] Ernst H. Kantorowicz, *The Fundamental Issue. Documents and Marginal Notes on the University of California Loyalty Oath* (Berkeley, CA: privately printed, 1950), 1. The text is available online: <http://sunsite.berkeley.edu/uchistory/archives_exhibits/loyaltyoath/symposium/kantorowicz.html>.

[70] Letter to President Robert G. Sproul, 4 October 1949, in Kantorowicz, *The Fundamental Issue*, 7.

[71] Lerner, 'Ernst H. Kantorowicz (1895–1963)', 268.

[72] Herbert S. Bailey, Jr, the director of Princeton University Press, wrote to Robert J. Oppenheimer in 1955 that he thought it 'reasonable to suppose that fifteen hundred copies [...] can be sold over a period of perhaps ten years'. Quoted in Lerner, 'Ernst Kantorowicz and Theodor E. Mommsen', 197.

[73] Ernst H. Kantorowicz, *The King's Two Bodies: A Study in Medieval Political Theology* (Princeton, NJ: Princeton University Press, 1957). Page references in brackets in the text are to this edition.

[74] Raulff, *Kreis ohne Meister*, 274, calls Kantorowicz's transition from one life to another an 'Argonauts' achievement' (*Argonautenleistung*), transacting 'rebuildings and adaptations [while] on the move'. Neither seamless continuity ('once a Georgean, always a Georgean') nor before-and-after dichotomy, Raulff argues, do justice to the complex realities of this process of 'translation'.

the centre of Kantorowicz's research, the transference between the spiritual and secular spheres in the authorization of medieval kingship, is for the first time explicitly termed a 'political theology'. And in exploring the politico-theological legal fiction of twin-bodied kingship, Kantorowicz again drew on sources that positivist detractors of his early work would have deemed inappropriate. In *Frederick II* he had begun 'his account [...] by adducing poetry, continued it with frequent reference to manifesto and rumour, and ended it by citing prophecy'.[75] In *The King's Two Bodies*, 'he lavished two entire chapters on the imagery and ideas of two major works of literature':[76] Shakespeare's *Richard II* and Dante's *Divine Comedy*. The continuum of theme and approach becomes even more obvious if Kantorowicz's third monograph, *Laudes Regiae*, is taken into account; a study of the changes in 'theocratic concepts of secular and spiritual rulership'[77] as indicated by the forms and formulae of liturgical acclamation. Begun in Germany as early as 1934, *Laudes Regiae* was eventually published in the United States in 1946.[78]

Yet the contrast is just as striking. In his speech at the historians' convention in 1930, Kantorowicz had fervently refuted the view of his main opponent, Albert Brackmann, that a historian should not write 'either as a George disciple, or as a Catholic, Protestant, or Marxist, but only as a truth-seeking human being'.[79] This ideal of detached truth-seeking, Kantorowicz had objected, turned the historian into a creature of bloodless indifference, lacking what was essential, the commitment to 'the worthy future and honour of the nation'.[80] In *The King's Two Bodies* he was apparently speaking with the voice of just such a creature, declaring in his preface that

> [t]he fascination emanating as usual from the historical material itself prevailed over any desire of practical or moral application [...]. This study deals with certain cyphers of the sovereign state and its perpetuity [...] *exclusively from the point of view of presenting political creeds such as they were understood in their initial stage* and at a time when they served as a vehicle for putting the early modern commonwealths on their own feet. (viii–ix; my italics)

The disavowal of his former commitment could not be more plain. His aim is to analyse not to advocate, let alone convert his readers to the political theology his book expounds. It is the historical material itself that determines the agenda. Truth-seeking attention to the historical material, and the historical material only, precedes and indeed precludes any ideological bias. The commitment of the historian, Kantorowicz seems to be saying, is to explore the past, not to influence the

---

[75] Lerner, 'Ernst H. Kantorowicz (1895–1963)', 269.

[76] Lerner, 'Ernst H. Kantorowicz (1895–1963)', 273.

[77] Ernst H. Kantorowicz, *Laudes Regiae: A Study in Liturgical Acclamations and Medieval Ruler Worship* (Berkeley, CA: University of California Press, 1946), ix.

[78] Robert Lerner ('Ernst H. Kantorowicz [1895–1963]', 274), writing from a historian's point of view, rates *Laudes Regiae* as Kantorowicz's most enduring achievement, a view that would hardly find adherents among literary scholars.

[79] This was the closing sentence of Brackmann's review of Kantorowicz's *Frederick II*: Albert Brackmann, 'Kaiser Friedrich II in "mythischer Schau" ', *Historische Zeitschrift* 140 (1929), 534–49 at 549. Quoted in Grünewald, *Ernst Kantorowicz und Stefan George*, 91.

[80] Lerner, 'Ernst H. Kantorowicz (1895–1963)', 270.

present or the future. Robert Lerner sums up the contrast: '*Frederick II* is a rousing narrative about a German emperor, published without documentation and replete with ideological judgements; *The King's Two Bodies* (1957) is an obtrusively learned study, addressed to elucidating a peculiarity of English law and lacking apparent ideological agenda.'[81] Along with this change, Lerner writes, went 'a new tone of distancing irony': '[H]e altered his style; its magniloquence and bardic qualities became lapidary and aloof. Even [his] lavish displays of technical erudition had a rhetorical aspect: apparently he now meant to subvert "devotions", "dogmas", and "idols" by dissecting them clinically.'[82]

In his preface Kantorowicz acknowledges the modern ramifications of his subject yet disclaims their relevance for his enquiry. His study is

> an attempt to understand and, if possible, demonstrate how [...] certain axioms of a political theology which *mutatis mutandis* was to remain valid until the twentieth century, began to be developed during the later Middle Ages. It would go much too far, however, to assume that the author felt tempted to investigate the emergence of some of the idols of modern political religions merely on account of the horrifying experience of our own time in which whole nations, the largest and smallest, fell prey to the weirdest dogmas and in which political theologisms became genuine obsessions defying in many cases the rudiments of human and political reason. Admittedly the author was not unaware of the later aberrations; in fact, he became the more conscious of certain ideological gossamers the more he expanded and deepened his knowledge of the early development. It seems necessary, however, to stress the fact that considerations of that kind belonged to afterthoughts, resulting from the present investigation and not causing it or determining its course. (viii)

Recent commentators have found the 'rhetorical [...] convolution'[83] of this 'coy denial'[84] less than persuasive. That he was 'admittedly not unaware' of the 'later aberrations' of his theme sounds all too transparently understated from the author of *Frederick II*, the reformed right-wing militant who blamed himself for having inadvertently helped to advance the Nazi cause. If he really wanted to contain his inquiry in the safe seclusion of antiquarian scholarship, *Political Theology* was hardly the right flag to sail it under.

Kantorowicz must, of course, have been aware of the term's chequered political record. His choice can be at least partly explained as an attempt to reclaim it from the political ends it had been made to serve in the recent past, including the ends of his own myth-making in *Frederick II*, a political theology if not in name then clearly in substance. The subtitle, then, is as ambivalently perched between a self-contained past and its uncontainable reverberations as the preface's declaration—or, more precisely, denial—of purpose. Like that denial—the announcement of what the book

---

[81] Lerner, 'Ernst H. Kantorowicz (1895–1963)', 270. 'Granted such a contrast', Lerner asks rhetorically, 'how else can one explain it than by a spectacular change of heart caused by repentance for having contributed to the rise of Nazism and a consequent retreat into esoteric superspecialization?' (270).

[82] Lerner, 'Ernst H. Kantorowicz (1895–1963)', 271.

[83] Richard Halpern, 'The King's Two Buckets: Kantorowicz, *Richard II*, and Fiscal *Trauerspiel*', *Representations* 106 (2009), 67–76 at 67.

[84] Victoria Kahn, 'Political Theology and Fiction in *The King's Two Bodies*', *Representations* 106 (2009), 77–101 at 79.

does *not* intend to go into—the subtitle conjures up the harsh background noise of the twentieth century at the same time as it ostensibly shuts it out from a study focused on a phenomenon that is clearly designated as *medieval*. But why, one may well ask, evoke the noise in the first place if not to ensure our awareness of its being shut out?

Along with the denial of topical relevance, the book also seems to deny the reader a coherent argument. But the apparent lack of an overarching thesis[85] has not prevented critics such as Victoria Kahn and Richard Halpern from detecting forceful intervention in a very contemporary debate in the plethora of medieval and early modern sources. Concentrating on the book's two 'literary' chapters, they suggest that *The King's Two Bodies* should be read as a critical response to Carl Schmitt's autocratic version of political theology and particularly, as Kahn argues, to Schmitt's anti-liberal depreciation of the aesthetic.[86] The term 'political theology' alone—though Schmitt had no monopoly on it—lends plausibility to the idea. What seems less clear, though, is that Kantorowicz aimed to refute Schmitt's depreciation of the aesthetic. This depreciation can be traced back to Schmitt's polemics against *Political Romanticism* (1919)[87] where he denounces not the aesthetic per se, but an aesthetic (i.e. 'impressionistic', noncommittal) attitude in politics. Schmitt's depreciation of the 'merely' aesthetic in art was not formulated until his 1956 essay on Hamlet, which Kantorowicz most certainly had not read.[88] While it makes eminent sense—and especially in Kahn's essay renders highly illuminating results—to *compare* Kantorowicz's views with those of Schmitt and to analyse their 'striking [...] similarities and differences',[89] there is little justification for casting this comparative analysis as a drama of two 'strong thinkers'[90] in a cut-and-thrust over the power of political myth-making. For one thing, in all of his

---

[85] Lerner mentions that '[i]n the publicity form for *The King's Two Bodies* [Kantorowicz] left blank the space asking for "the author's own version of the thesis of his book"'. Lerner, 'Ernst H. Kantorowicz (1895–1963)', 273.

[86] Halpern, 'The King's Two Buckets', 67, says that Kantorowicz 'engages in a critical dialogue' with Schmitt that is 'sharply polemical'. According to Kahn ('Political Theology and Fiction'), 'Kantorowicz's argument should be seen as a response to the work of Carl Schmitt on the one hand and Ernst Cassirer on the other' (77) and his chapter on Dante as 'an aggressive rewriting of Schmitt' notably 'in the pride of place [Kantorowicz] gives to literature' (88). Other readings relating Kantorowicz to Schmitt include Alain Boureau, *Kantorowicz*, and Haverkamp, 'Stranger Than Paradise'. While Haverkamp compellingly analyses Dante's earthly paradise, and Kantorowicz's reading of it, as an 'antidote' to political theology of the Schmittian kind, he wisely refrains from ascribing this antidotal function to any anti-Schmittian *intention* on the part of Kantorowicz.

[87] Carl Schmitt, *Political Romanticism*, trans. Guy Oakes, with a new introduction by Graham McAleer (New Brunswick, NJ and London: Transaction, 2011).

[88] Schmitt's anti-aestheticism has been lucidly analysed by Kahn herself in 'Hamlet or Hecuba: Carl Schmitt's Decision', *Representations* 83 (2003), 67–96. The prominence of Schmitt and his Hamlet essay in academic discourse today, especially in the US, should not obscure the fact that Schmitt had virtually dropped off the radar in 1957: his visibility was at an all-time low. *Hamlet or Hecuba* had a small print run from a small press and, even in Germany, received very little attention. In America it was totally unknown at the time.

[89] Kahn, 'Political Theology and Fiction', 83.

[90] See the notion of 'strong poets' developed in Harold Bloom, *The Anxiety of Influence* (Oxford: Oxford University Press, 1973).

bulging apparatus of footnotes, which leaves nothing and virtually no one unmentioned, Kantorowicz never once mentions Schmitt.[91]

If the spectre of Schmitt inhabits *The King's Two Bodies* at all, he shares that part with another, to Kantorowicz much more familiar, ghost. This ghost appears, like the ghost of the father in *Hamlet*, right at the outset:

> Mysticism, when transposed from the warm twilight of myth and fiction to the cold searchlight of fact and reason, has usually little left to recommend itself. Its language, unless resounding within its own magic or mystic circle, will often appear poor or even slightly foolish, and its most baffling metaphors and highflown images, when deprived of their iridescent wings, may easily resemble the pathetic and pitiful sight of Baudelaire's Albatross. Political mysticism in particular is exposed to the danger of losing its spell or becoming quite meaningless when taken out of its native surroundings, its time and its space. (3)

Striking a wistfully ironic note—almost reminiscent of Thomas Mann's late style— the opening of Kantorowicz's introduction appeals to the reader's benevolence by admitting the shortcomings of the ensuing topic from a rational point of view. At the same time he refuses to accept that view unconditionally. His sympathy is clearly with the warm twilight and the beautiful mysteries which reason coldly dispels. If Kantorowicz in his preface goes out of his way to deny any 'kind of personal pressure behind [his] book',[92] in the introduction he strikes a highly personal note. This will not be apparent to every reader, but it is all the more transparent to the initiated. When Kantorowicz says of the language of mysticism that it is understood only 'within its own magic or mystic circle' the keyword of course is 'circle'. From the observation on 'magic or mystic' circles in general a very specific instance of such a circle emerges. This is corroborated by the poetic associations of 'baffling metaphors and highflown images' and clinched by the reference to Baudelaire's albatross:

> The Albatross
>
> Often, to amuse themselves, the men of a crew
> Catch albatrosses, those vast sea birds
> That indolently follow a ship
> As it glides over the deep, briny sea.

[91] The very fact that Schmitt is *not* mentioned may, in some quarters, count as strong evidence that he *must* indeed be meant. But why, one may well ask, should Kantorowicz suppress (or repress) the name? It can be argued that the term 'political theology' alone suffices to establish a deliberate connection to Schmitt and his central tenet that 'all significant concepts of the modern theory of the state are secularized theological concepts'. But the interplay between secular and religious ideas and practices in the world of medieval politics had been Kantorowicz's principal theme from the beginning; it is the thematic strand that runs through virtually all of his work from *Frederick II* to *Laudes Regiae* and *The King's Two Bodies*. Nowhere in this work is there any reference to Schmitt's writings or opinions, and the same goes for Kantorowicz's intellectual environment. As far as I can see, Schmitt is entirely absent from the writings of the George Circle as a whole, despite the fact that several members of that Circle were jurists. He simply did not figure—much as one might think he would have, or should have, particularly during the 1920s—as a fellow anti-liberal with strongly 'old European' sympathies. This doesn't invalidate Kahn's finely calibrated comparative analysis of Kantorowicz's position in relation to Schmitt (and Cassirer, who actually *is* mentioned in *The King's Two Bodies*). But it does her view of authorial intent as a deliberate 'response' to Schmitt.

[92] Norbrook, 'The Emperor's New Body?', 331.

Scarcely have they placed them on the deck
Than these kings of the sky, clumsy, ashamed,
Pathetically let their great white wings
Drag beside them like oars.

That winged voyager, how weak and gauche he is,
So beautiful before, now comic and ugly!
One man worries his beak with a stubby clay pipe;
Another limps, mimics the cripple who once flew!

The poet resembles this prince of cloud and sky
Who frequents the tempest and laughs at the bowman;
When exiled on the earth, the butt of hoots and jeers,
His giant wings prevent him from walking.[93]

Baudelaire's famous allegory of the high-soaring poet grounded among the philistines was one of the 109 poems of *Les Fleurs du Mal* that Stefan George translated, or 're-created', between 1891 and 1900. 'More than any other poet, more even than Mallarmé, was Baudelaire George's teacher.'[94] Kantorowicz could not have alluded more directly to the Master short of citing George himself. And no poem by the Master would have suited the purpose quite as well as Baudelaire's. There are poems in which George fashions the poet (i.e. himself) as suffering, shunned, the eternal outcast. But there is none in which he allows the poet to look as pitifully awkward (*gauche et veule*) and as pathetically out of place as Baudelaire's grounded albatross. For George's poet, and George-as-Poet, any present ordeal is fraught with future promise, if only the promise of doom. Such teleology, however, is entirely missing from the image of the Albatross. His flight is definitely over; he has been, as Kantorowicz puts it, 'deprived of [his] iridescent wings' once and for all. Kantorowicz had to turn to George's French teacher for a poem that offered him a vantage point from which to look back at Stefan George and his magic circle.

George has more than a cameo part in *The King's Two Bodies*. Looking back at him and looking back at medieval kingship complement and illuminate each other. Historicizing George, 'the *homme fatal* in whom the German destiny is uniquely epitomised',[95] is a way of bringing the political theology of the King's two bodies into the present. Recent criticism has noted the blending of legal and literary fiction in Kantorowicz's account.[96] This blending begins with the oblique but powerful invocation of George in the opening paragraph which associates mysticism, myth, and fiction with the working of poetry. Immediately following Baudelaire's albatross-poet the focus shifts to *political* mysticism. With George in mind, this does not so much shift away from poetry as highlight another side of it. Kantorowicz points up this two-sidedness of George's poetry in a letter to Maurice

---

[93] Charles Baudelaire, 'The Albatross' (L'Albatros), in *The Flowers of Evil*, trans. William Aggeler (Fresno, CA: Academy Library Guild, 1954), 18.

[94] Georg Peter Landmann, 'Anhang', in George, *Sämtliche Werke*, vol. 13/14: *Die Blumen des Bösen. Umdichtungen*, ed. Georg Peter Landmann (1983), 163–84 at 164.

[95] Raulff, *Kreis ohne Meister*, 303.

[96] Kahn, 'Political Theology and Fiction'; Halpern, 'The King's Two Buckets'; Lorna Hutson, 'Imagining Justice: Kantorowicz and Shakespeare', *Representations* 106 (2009), 118–42.

Bowra (19 November 1943) responding to Bowra's recently published book on *The Heritage of Symbolism*.[97] The book's 'architecture', he writes, is excellently balanced:

> To begin with Valéry, who is nearest to the tradition, and to end with Yeats, who is farthest, is absolutely convincing, and so is George as the central axis and pivot. For in his work the two trends of symbolism—let us call them the 'aesthetic' and the 'political' urges—overlap and coincide for reasons which are difficult to explain but which are in full agreement with the strange transcendency of German political reality.[98]

The letter makes no attempt to explain 'the strange transcendency', perhaps because earlier efforts to do so had failed. In his recollection of their early days together in Oxford, Bowra writes that Kantorowicz 'was liable to talk about a thing called "secret Germany", which, though meaningful enough in German, lacked substance in English'.[99]

George and the political mysticism of the 'Secret Germany' are substantially present in *The King's Two Bodies*. Though duly noted by practically every commentator, the fact that Shakespeare and Dante were deities in the George pantheon has not been given much attention. Their treatment in the book entails more than a filial tribute to Kantorowicz's former mentor, let alone a bland endorsement of George's aesthetic canon. Rather, it is a way of engaging with the problematic nature of the George Circle, the illusion of his sovereign rule.

Richard II's rule, to be sure, is real enough, at least for the first two acts of the play. But they do not register in Kantorowicz's reading. Neither the king's trespass on Bolingbroke's patrimony which, in the logic of feudal obligation, is actually a trespass on his own right to be king[100] nor Gaunt's philippic against the leasing out of 'this sceptered isle' (*R2* 2.1.40) are allowed to distract from the central idea that '*The Tragedy of King Richard II* is the tragedy of the King's Two Bodies' (26). This idea and 'the varieties of royal "duplications" which Shakespeare has unfolded' is examined in 'the three bewildering central scenes of *Richard II*' (26–7). Each is dominated by one of three variants of royal duplication or, as Kantorowicz puts it, 'three prototypes of "twin-birth" ' (27): the 'King', who dominates in the scene on the Coast of Wales (3.2), the 'Fool' who does so in the scene at Flint Castle (3.3), and the 'God' in the abdication scene at Westminster (4.1). The triadic neatness of the arrangement is taken even further by the observation that in each of the three scenes the same triadic 'cascading' takes place: 'from divine kingship to kingship's "Name", and from the name to the naked misery of man' (27).

[97] Bowra, *The Heritage of Symbolism*. The book is dedicated 'To L. v. W.', Lucy von Wangenheim, Woldemar von Uxkull's half-sister with whom both Kantorowicz and Bowra had love affairs. Lerner, 'Letters by Ernst Kantorowicz', 162.

[98] Lerner, 'Letters by Ernst Kantorowicz', 170.

[99] Bowra, *Memories*, 290.

[100] As York reminds Richard in *R2* 2.1.195–9:

> Take Hereford's rights away, and take from Time
> His charters and his customary rights;
> Let not tomorrow then ensue today;
> Be not thyself, for how art thou a king
> But by fair sequence and succession?

Kantorowicz's reading takes up at a point when Richard's regiment is already gone, making him, in the words of Marlowe's equally luckless king Edward, but a 'perfect shadow [...] in a sunshine day'.[101] Yet it is still the type, or aspect, of the 'King' that dominates in this scene. However, much as Richard's demonstratively tactile salute to his 'dear earth' (*R2* 3.2.7)[102] aims to suggest otherwise, his realm has no more material reality than the realm dreamt up under the Master's tutelage in a magic circle that called itself 'the State'. And Richard's appeal to the angelic hosts at the beck of the Lord's Anointed is drunk with the same auto-suggestive hope that conjured up hosts of high-spirited youths spearheading towards George's New Reich.

Richard, Kantorowicz writes,

> is still sure of himself, of his dignity, and even of the help of the celestial hosts, which are at his disposal:
>   For every man that Bolingbroke hath press'd...,
>   God for his Richard hath in heavenly pay
>   A glorious angel. (29)

But in this scene Kantorowicz already sees the 'cascading' from kingship as substance to kingship as a mere name, 'as it were, a metamorphosis from "Realism" to "Nominalism"' (29):

> The Universal called 'Kingship' begins to disintegrate; its transcendental 'Reality', its god-like existence, so brilliant shortly before, pales into a nothing, a *nomen*. (29)

George's 'State', one might say, was permanently, indeed systemically, beset with such a realism–nominalism problem. Its existence required the constant assertion of its reality; its reality was founded on nothing but the assertion of its existence. This comes to the fore in some of the more extravagant claims made by or about George, notably in the years following Germany's military defeat, the years when Kantorowicz had joined the Circle and Wolters enunciated its political agenda. 'This', George is recorded to have triumphantly exclaimed on a winter evening in 1920/1, holding up the last edition of *Pages for the Arts*, 'This is Germany's victory over France!'[103] And Wolters, lecturing on 'Goethe as a Teacher of Patriotic Thinking', blustered: 'Let [Germany's enemies] search for our buried weapons! The place of the spirit will not be found; and stronger, now as ever, than any buried

---

[101] 'But what are kings, when regiment is gone, / But perfect shadows in a sunshine day? / My nobles rule, I bear the name of king'. Christopher Marlowe, *Edward II*, in *Doctor Faustus and Other Plays*, ed. David Bevington and Eric Rasmussen (Oxford and New York: Oxford University Press, 1995), 323–402; 5.1.26–8.

[102] KING RICHARD [...] I weep for joy

> To stand upon my kingdom once again.
> Dear earth, I do salute thee with my hand,
> Though rebels wound thee with their horses' hooves.
> As a long-parted mother with her child
> Plays fondly with her tears and smiles in meeting,
> So weeping, smiling, greet I thee, my earth,
> And do thee favor with my royal hands. (*R2* 3.2.4–11)

[103] Karlauf, *Stefan George*, 530.

weapons are the weapons which the poet forges. [...] Greater than the forbidden general staff is the circle of leaders that *he* fosters, more dangerous than all the secret paramilitary units is the heroic youth that *he* spawns.'[104]

Kantorowicz seems never to have thought very highly of Wolters,[105] yet he no doubt shared the self-intoxicating belief in those imaginary hosts the German spirit could and eventually would mobilize; his *Frederick II* is full of it. And this belief—in retrospect no more than a quirky delusion—was taken seriously enough, like Richard's belief in his heavenly support army, by at least part of the public at large. How else could George have been included with political leaders such as Woodrow Wilson, Clemenceau, Hindenburg, Gandhi, and Lenin in a 1929 newspaper front-page pictorial of 'contemporary figures who have become legends'?[106]

'Legend' is perhaps more aptly applied to George than to any of the other figures on that page. Its suggestion of myth and fiction, of something more, but also less, than real, captures the elusive quality of the power George commanded. By the time he was writing *The King's Two Bodies*, Kantorowicz must have been acutely aware of precisely this quality. His early enthusiasm having been shattered by harsh realities, he did not discard it as worthless, but seems to have viewed it with a mixture of disenchantment and nostalgic regret. His reading of *Richard II*, so concentrated on the political dilemma of the King that the politics of England virtually disappears, has something of a swan song of the elusive Kingdom of his poet-mentor.

What Kantorowicz has to say about the tragic division of two-bodied kingship, and later on in the book about the fictionalizing of 'the Crown' as a political concept, not only opens up the road towards constitutionalism[107] but also reflects upon the fictionalizing powers of George's 'State', the poetic *fiat* in its constitution. Having been part of this 'State', Kantorowicz had first-hand experience of myth-making at work. As a believer he would have taken a 'realist' position towards the George myth. As the demystifying scholar of *The King's Two Bodies* he could not but recognize it as a 'nominalist' fiction. George's mythical elevation of art was the very opposite to demystification; it was a belated essentializing of the myth's unquestionable reality. And it was this use of myth that George shared with its fascist abusers.[108]

Kantorowicz's unravelling of the fiction of the king's two bodies is a demystifying not only of divine kingship but also of its twentieth-century *imitatio* in George's 'State' and its manufactured pagan quasi-divinity. Bolingbroke, in this reading, would not be Hitler but the representative of the power of cold reason, the very modernity against which George shored up the power of his poetry and personal charisma.

[104] Quoted in Karlauf, *Stefan George*, 529.

[105] In a letter to the publisher Ursula Küpper (13 December 1962) Kantorowicz speaks of 'Wolters' bigotry [*Pfafferei*] with which I don't want to have anything to do'. Quoted in Grünewald, *Ernst Kantorowicz und Stefan George*, 163.

[106] Norton, *Secret Germany*, ix. The paper was *Das Illustrierte Blatt*, a pictorial weekly issued by the publishers of the country's leading quality paper, *Frankfurter Zeitung*.

[107] Kahn, 'Political Theology and Fiction', 85 and 93.

[108] See n. 41 in the present chapter.

Shakespeare's Richard II, Gundolf had written, 'is a poet, [...] a poet in the wrong place, at the wrong time'.[109] The connection between King and poet and, by extension, between Shakespeare's poet-king and the poet George is most palpably manifest in the middle section of Kantorowicz's triptych, which stands under the sign of the Fool, the figure that dominates the scene at Flint Castle (3.3). The neat consistency of Kantorowicz's triadic pattern—three scenes, three figures, three 'cascading' steps—makes it easy to swallow the Fool along with the King and the God without noticing the peculiarity of the middle figure. While King and God are, one might say, the natural, self-evident terms, the Fool is not. This is not to question the aptness of Kantorowicz's choice. On the contrary, the choice seems particularly, even brilliantly apt. But I suggest it should be noticed *as* a choice, one that rings with a subtle echo of the opening of the Introduction, where he says that mysticism will appear 'poor or even slightly foolish' outside its own time and place.

This, as we have seen, is followed by the mention of 'baffling metaphors and highflown images', of being 'deprived of iridescent wings', and it leads up to 'the pathetic and pitiful sight of Baudelaire's Albatross' (3). This string of images strikingly connects to the scene at Flint Castle, notably to its central action and the speech that couches its performance in 'baffling metaphor'. The Albatross is the *prince des nuées*, the 'monarch of the clouds' in Roy Campbell's translation. Richard, 'whose personal badge', Kantorowicz reminds us, 'was the "Sun emerging from a cloud"' (32), enters the scene still high up on the walls of the castle, his sun-like appearance set off against 'envious clouds' (*R2* 3.3.65). His descent and the speech embellishing it ensue from Northumberland's demand

> that the king come down into the base court of the castle to meet Bolinbroke, [to which] Richard [...] retorts in a language of confusing brightness and terrifying puns:
>
> > Down, down I come like glist'ring Phaethon:
> > Wanting the manage of unruly jades....
> > In the base court? Base court, where kings grow base,
> > To come at traitors' calls, and do them grace.
> > In the base court? Come down? Down court! down king!
> > For night-owls shriek where mounting larks should sing.
>
> (III.iii.178ff.) (32)

Like Baudelaire's poet-albatross, the King, grounded and grown base in the base court, becomes a figure of fun, the now useless accoutrements of his elevation, a mockery.

Coming down to the base court like glist'ring Phaethon, he also evokes the other emblematic high-flyer of antiquity whose fall was caused, not by unruly jades, but by a failing of wings. 'The Sun imagery', writes Kantorowicz, 'reflects the "splendour of the catastrophe" in a manner remindful of Brueghel's *Icarus* and Lucifer's fall from the empyrean, reflecting also those "shreds of glow... That round the limbs of fallen angels hover"' (32–3). With this quotation, the source of which remains unnamed, the poet who had so far been invoked only by proxy, under the

---

[109] Gundolf, *Shakespeare. Sein Wesen und Werk*, vol. 1, 265.

guise of his French predecessor, is made to speak in his own voice. The poem most readily evoked by Brueghel's *Icarus* would be Auden's 'Musée des Beaux Arts',[110] and Kantorowicz may well have thought of it, too. But his quotation, which merges the fall of Icarus with that of Lucifer (from a Miltonian 'empyrean') in a more universal panorama of brightness hovering over ruin, is from Stefan George's four-line poem 'Northern Painter' (*Nordischer Meister*), and the painter in question is not Brueghel but Rembrandt:

> We brooded through the night to find the clue
> To both your secret and your flaw. You rimmed
> Your painted heavens with the residue
> Of light around a fallen angel's limb.[111]

George's poem, in turn, has its roots in Baudelaire's 'Les phares' ('The Beacons'), which George translated as well. Here, Rembrandt, his 'gloomy hospital [...] Lit for a moment by a wintry sun',[112] figures in the succession of painters from Leonardo to Delacroix whom Baudelaire celebrates as 'the beacons' whose 'impassioned sobs that through the ages roll' are 'the clearest proofs / That we can give of our nobility'.

The dense allusive web Kantorowicz weaves around Richard's descent from solar height to 'night-owl' doom suggests a more than just scholarly, or antiquarian, fascination. A clue to the more personal stakes involved is hidden in a remark cloaked in Kantorowicz's most demonstratively scholarly manner. The prominence of the sun imagery in the play, he writes, has been 'noticed at different times'; 'and occasionally a passage reads like the description of a Roman *Oriens Augusti* [Sunrise of Augustus] coin (III.ii.36–53)' (32). The observation is annotated by a long footnote referring to the sun motif in Richard's heraldic badges and banners and to other discussions of the play's sun imagery. Most notably it refers to a footnote in another critic's discussion of *Richard II*. This is John Dover Wilson's 'Introduction' to his Cambridge edition of the play, published in 1939, to which Kantorowicz declares himself indebted. What is of interest here, however, is not Wilson's footnote itself, but the sentence to which it is affixed:

> As for symbolism [Wilson writes], three writers have lately independently drawn attention to the sun-image, which dominates the play as the swastika dominates a Nazi gathering.[113]

---

[110] W. H. Auden, 'Musée des Beaux Arts', in *Another Time* (London: Faber and Faber, 1940), 34.

[111] *The Works of Stefan George*, 235. 'Die Leuchttürme', *Sämtliche Werke*, vol. 13/14, 17–18.

[112] The original stanza reads:

> Rembrandt, triste hôpital tout rempli de murmures,
> Et d'un grand crucifix décoré seulement,
> Où la prière en pleurs s'exhale des ordures,
> Et d'un rayon d'hiver traversé brusquement;

Charles Baudelaire, 'Les phares', in *Les fleurs du mal*, ed. Jacques Dupont (Paris: Flammarion, 2012), 64.

[113] John Dover Wilson, 'Introduction', in Shakespeare, *King Richard II* (Cambridge: Cambridge University Press, 1939), ix–lxxxvi at xii. The three writers referred to by Wilson are Paul Reyher, Caroline Spurgeon, and Wolfgang Clemen.

The swastika and the Nazis pop up as if in passing and disappear again equally casually. To the reader of today it sounds almost callously nonchalant. To Wilson it obviously didn't. He had recently witnessed just such a swastika-dominated gathering in Germany where he had lectured from his *Richard II* introduction at the seventy-fifth anniversary of the German Shakespeare Society in Weimar[114] and attended the military parade on Hitler's fiftieth birthday in Berlin. On this latter occasion the British Embassy had secured him a place 'within an easy lobbing distance' from the Führer. If only, Wilson mused airily in his memoirs, he had had a 'Mills bomb' (hand grenade), he could have ended the show and 'saved the world in a way more effective than Chamberlain ever thought of'.[115]

Thus a much more sinister sun rises from Kantorowicz's learned allusion to Rome's first emperor, the symbol of two fatefully entangled empires. The sun-wheel of Stefan George's secret realm was also the swastika of Hitler's 'Thousand-Year Reich', the same emblem that adorned Kantorowicz's monument to the Holy Roman Emperor Frederick II with its prophecy of a rebirth of imperial glory in the spirit of Stefan George.

But it is the setting, not the rising sun that makes the fall of Richard II the perfect image of the poet's dream-realm toppling, Phaethon-like, into the nightmare reality of the Third Reich. 'Wanting the manage of unruly jades', Richard powerfully evokes the idea of forces getting out of hand, a hubristic fantasy of control giving way to the shock of an uncontrollable plunge.

In his letters Kantorowicz repeatedly referred to the Nazis, and the Germans under Nazi rule, as 'sorcerer's apprentices'.[116] Like the eponymous protagonist of Goethe's ballad '*Der Zauberlehrling*' who conjures up spirits in his master's absence, the Germans were unable to control 'the spirits that they summoned'.[117] The political application of the poem and its famous line was (and is) commonplace in the German-speaking world. But for Kantorowicz the parable clearly implicated the sorcerer as well. 'The spirits that *they* summoned' were, after all, the spirits originally summoned by *him*, the great enchanter of youth and collector of 'apprentices', Stefan George.[118] Analogously, the fall of Phaethon re-enacted by Shakespeare's Richard II implicates not only the wayward son but also the sun-father whose power he borrows. Thus the Georgean subtext of Kantorowicz's chapter on *Richard II* is tribute and farewell to a dream that failed, the wistful, elegiac regret for a vanished illusion.

---

[114] The lecture, given in April 1939, appeared under the title 'The Political Background of Shakespeare's Richard II and Henry IV', *Shakespeare-Jahrbuch* 75 (1939), 36–51.

[115] John Dover Wilson, *Milestones on the Dover Road* (London: Faber and Faber, 1969), 219. In 1936 Neville Chamberlain struck up a correspondence with Wilson, whose writings on Shakespeare he admired. The correspondence lasted until the beginning of the Second World War.

[116] Lerner, 'Letters by Ernst Kantorowicz', 166.

[117] The story of the sorcerer's apprentice—with Mickey Mouse in the title role—forms a famous sequence of Walt Disney's *Fantasia* (1940).

[118] Gay, *Weimar Culture*, 47, refers to George's disciples as '[s]orcerer's apprentices' who 'could not exorcise the spirits they had helped call up'.

V DANTE, OR, THE CORPORATE
BODY OF HUMANITY

The crowning moment of *The King's Two Bodies*, arguably the telos towards which the whole book has been moving, occurs in Chapter 8, the chapter on Dante. After having guided Dante through Hell and Purgatory, Virgil dismisses his pupil '[l]apidarily, as a Roman would', with 'six all-embracing words':

TE SOPRA TE *corono e mitrio*.[119]
Dante crowned and mitred over Dante himself: there is no need to emphasize that this verse is pregnant with implications and allusions, and that its fulness, radiating into so many directions, is as inexhaustible as that of any work of art charged with life. (494)

Pregnant indeed, this crucial scene clearly implies and alludes to Stefan George. It is inconceivable that Kantorowicz, commenting on it, would not have thought of the poet who saw himself, and was seen by his followers, as Dante's legitimate modern heir. A photo taken during the 1904 Munich carnival season shows George dressed as Dante (Figure 3.2); in jest perhaps, but there is little indication that he or his solemn fellow-mummers took the identification less than seriously.[120]

Figure 3.2. Stefan George as Dante, Munich Artists' Carnival, 1904. Photo by permission of Stefan George Archiv, Württembergische Landesbibliothek.

---

[119] *Purgatorio*, XXVII.142.
[120] Gay, *Weimar Culture*, 48, notes that 'the hundreds of photographs of the George circle show not a smile among them'.

It was not only his poetic genius that earned Dante the highest place of honour in the George Circle. It was also Dante's claim to the poet's equality of rank with a Caesar, 'the equiparation', as Kantorowicz calls it elsewhere, of their offices symbolized 'by means of a *tertium*, the crown of laurel'.[121] On a par with the sovereign ruler, the sovereign poet as conceived by Dante was the antecedent of George's own aspiration to rule, 'crowned and mitred over himself', as the sovereign of his own 'State'. The prominence Kantorowicz allots to the coronation of Dante in the overall scheme of his book clearly points to the importance of this Georgean background.[122]

But the drift of Kantorowicz's argument just as clearly points away from George. The Dante chapter may, as Victoria Kahn observes, be 'in line with Stefan George's elevation of literature to the highest form of culture', but its constitutionalist, 'even protoliberal ideal of human autonomy' runs counter to Georgean tenets of sovereignty.[123] Like Schmitt's idea of sovereignty, to which it is neither connected nor indebted, George's idea of sovereignty as authoritatively embodied by himself is essentially tied to the person of the monarch, the singular, exceptional figure, in George's case the charismatic leader who makes himself the object of a cult of personality. Kantorowicz's Dante is no such figure. He is not one of Gundolf's poet-heroes. 'The great man', Gundolf had written in 1921, 'is the highest form in which we experience the divine'.[124] The author of *Frederick II* would no doubt have agreed with this (he might have added the demonic to the divine). But in *The King's Two Bodies* the accent falls differently.[125] Dante is 'invested with man's body corporate and politic':

[121] Ernst H. Kantorowicz, 'The Sovereignty of the Artist: A Note on Legal Maxims and Renaissance Theories of Art', in *Selected Studies* (Locust Valley, NY: J. J. Augustin, 1965), 352–65 at 362. Dante's idea was taken up and performed by Petrarch, who 'received the crown of laurel on the Roman Capitol and thereby demonstrated to the world of learning and art universally to what extent indeed king and poet moved *pari passu*' (Kantorowicz, 'The Sovereignty of the Artist, 262). And, later in the same essay: 'Again, we notice, that a legal prerogative due to the sovereign *ex officio* has been passed on to the true Renaissance sovereigns, the artists and poets, who ruled *ex ingenio*' (364).

[122] Landmann, *Gespräche mit Stefan George*, 45, recalls George defending Wolters's tract 'Rule and Service' ('Herrschaft und Dienst', 1909) on account of its central Georgean idea: 'that creating poetry is a ruling' (*'dass Dichten ein Herrschen ist'*).

[123] Kahn, 'Political Theology and Fiction', 93. Kantorowicz's 'proto-liberal' reading of the passage is rejected as anachronistic by Anna Maria Chiavacci Leonardi in her critical edition of Dante's *Purgatorio*: Dante Alighieri, *Commedia*, vol. 2 (Milan: Mondadori, 1994), 817. My thanks to Gerhard Regn for bringing this to my attention.

[124] Friedrich Gundolf, *Dichter und Helden* (Heidelberg: Weiss'sche Universitätsbuchhandlung, 1921), 25.

[125] Where the accent does not fall differently is in the esteem for the secular. In *Frederick II*, Kantorowicz, following Nietzsche, extols the secular absolutism of Frederick's rule, his challenge to papal prerogative and its theological underpinnings. This line continues in *The King's Two Bodies*. In both books Kantorowicz offers a diagnostics—though no theory—of secularization. 'Dante', he writes in *The King's Two Bodies*, 'did not turn *humanitas* against *Christianitas*, but thoroughly separated the one from the other; he took the "human" out of the Christian compound and isolated it as a value in its own right—perhaps Dante's most original accomplishment in the field of political theology' (465). Like Carl Schmitt, Kantorowicz posits the theological provenance of secular concepts of rule and political order, but for him this does not diminish the validity of the latter: the secular is not conceived in terms of a lapse from the religious but as 'equal in rank, though different in kind' (469). Kantorowicz's archaeology of secularization, like that of Hans Blumenberg, can thus be seen as supporting *The Legitimacy of the Modern Age* (Blumenberg, *Die Legitimität der Neuzeit* [Frankfurt: Suhrkamp, 1966]; Engl. trans. Robert Wallace [Cambridge, MA: MIT Press, 1983]). Unlike Kantorowicz, who is simply un-Schmittian, Blumenberg is intentionally anti-Schmittian.

Hence, he was entitled to receive the insignia of his universal and sovereign status, crown and mitre, which conferred on him not so much the dignity of emperor and pope [...] but conferred that almost objectified 'Dignity of Man' which 'never dies' [...] (493)

What stands out, in other words, is not his singularity but his representativeness. This is a direction in which George would not have wanted his divinities to be moved. He would have sensed, with disapproval, what recent commentators have detected too: an undercurrent that is tentatively democratic, not striving towards the rebirth of lost empires but endorsing the institutions and political culture of Kantorowicz's new homeland, that epitome of modernity most abhorred by George: the United States of America. Instead of heroic exceptionalism, Kantorowicz throws in with the dignity of *humanum genus*—a prefiguration of the body corporate of the modern Everyman.

If the chapter on *Richard II* casts Kantorowicz's commemoration of George as a tragic epitaph, the Dante chapter strikes a more positive note. Something like a Hegelian sublation (*Aufhebung*) is achieved. George's reactionary politics, his fundamentalist opposition to modernity,[126] is blanked out while his aesthetic values remain. They come to the fore when Kantorowicz speaks, palpably in excess of what his argument requires at this point, of the aesthetic power of Dante's verse, 'its fulness, radiating into so many directions, [...] as inexhaustible as that of any work of art charged with life' (494).

No less susceptible than Kantorowicz to the aesthetic power of George's poetry but even more acutely aware of its pitfalls, Theodor W. Adorno culminates his oration 'On Lyric Poetry and Society',[127] published in the same year as *The King's Two Bodies*, with reflections on one of the songs from *The Seventh Ring* 'whose eccentric boldness', he writes, 'was rescued from the frightful cultural conservatism of the George circle only when the great composer Anton von Webern set them to music' (50).[128] George's poetry, he argues, 'the poetry of an imperious individual' (51), rejects the bourgeois framework that is the condition of its very existence. The poetry must therefore 'simulate [...] a feudal condition'; 'it has no other locus from which to speak than that of a past seigneurial society' (51). Common experience is allowed into the hermetic domain of its language 'only at the price of mythologization' (52). Adorno astutely notes 'the quixotism of this enterprise' (52) but concedes that despite its failings, or indeed precisely because of them, George's

---

[126] Cf. Stefan Breuer, *Ästhetischer Fundamentalismus: Stefan George und der deutsche Antimodernismus* (Darmstadt: Primus, 1996), esp. 226–40.

[127] Theodor W. Adorno, 'On Lyric Poetry and Society' (1957), in *Notes on Literature I*, trans. Shierry Weber Nicholsen (New York: Columbia University Press, 1991), 37–54. Page references are given in brackets in the text.

[128] Elsewhere, Adorno asserts that some aspects of George, especially his cult of leadership, are beyond redemption: 'Where George descends to praise of Führerdom, he shares in the guilt [of having promoted Nazi ideology] and cannot be rescued.' Adorno, 'Stefan George', in *Notes on Literature II*, trans. Shierry Weber Nicholsen (New York: Columbia University Press, 1992), 178–92 at 179 (translation modified). Adorno studiously avoids mentioning that Webern, who rescued George's poetry from 'frightful cultural conservatism', was a man of ultra-conservative politics and, at least temporarily, sympathized with the Nazis. See also Gert Mattenklott, 'Benjamin und Adorno über George', in *Wissenschaftler im George-Kreis*, ed. Böschenstein et al., 277–90.

poetry offers authentic opposition to the pressures of alienated modernity and even the hint of a utopian promise. Detached from 'the realm of ends', its language 'represents the idea of a free humankind, even if the George School concealed this idea from itself through a base cult of the heights'. Even so, Adorno concludes, George's 'lyric speech becomes the voice of human beings between whom the barriers have fallen' (53–4).

Simulating the feudal conditions of 'a past seigneurial society', Kantorowicz's Georgean sobriquet, the Chevalier, may be cited in support of Adorno's critique. What Adorno calls the 'quixotism' of the Georgean enterprise is captured in Kantorowicz's reading of *Richard II*. But clearly Kantorowicz also experienced, with the poet as well as his poetry, what Adorno describes as the liberating force of 'the voice of human beings between whom the barriers have fallen'.

Kantorowicz never renounced the Master. To his dying day he kept a photograph of Stefan George on his desk, 'a *quasi*-substitute of that topical skull which Kantorowicz described [...], with reference to pictorial representations of *Saint Jerome in his Study*, as "more a scholarly prop than a memento mori"'.[129] A sign of continuing loyalty to George and his vision, the dead Master's portrait may have also served as a continuing memento of how much of that vision had proved untenable, illusory, even pernicious. But perhaps the exiled professor from Germany, safe in his American study, attained to the art of Falstaff, who could see through Shallow's deluded reminiscences of youthful exploits and still find the words that have made them immortal:

We have heard the chimes at midnight.

---

[129] Walter and Ernst, 'Ernst H. Kantorowicz. Eine archäo-biographische Skizze', 217–18. The quotation within the quotation is from Kantorowicz, 'Die Wiederkehr gelehrter Anachorese im Mittelalter', in *Selected Studies*, 339–51 at 351.

4

Millions of Ghosts

Weimar Hamlets and the Sorrows of Young Goebbels

I ELSINORE-BERLIN: PICKING UP SKULLS

On 11 April 1919, five months to the day after the Armistice was signed at Compiègne, readers of *The Athenaeum* found a revenant Hamlet surveying the spiritual aftermath of the Great War:

> From an immense terrace of Elsinore which extends from Basle to Cologne, and touches the sands of Nieuport, the marshes of the Somme, the chalk of Champagne, and the granite of Alsace, the Hamlet of Europe now looks upon millions of ghosts. [...]
>
> If he picks up a skull, it is a famous skull. Whose was this? This was Leonardo. He invented the flying man; but the flying man has not exactly served the intentions of the inventor. [...] And this second skull is Leibniz, who dreamed of universal peace. And this was Kant, who begat Hegel, who begat Marx, who begat...
>
> Hamlet hardly knows what to do with all these skulls. But if he leaves them!...Will he cease to be himself? His terribly clairvoyant mind contemplates the transition from war to peace. This transition is more obscure, more dangerous, than the transition from peace to war. All the peoples are troubled by it. And I, he says, I, the European intellect, what shall I become? And what is peace? Peace is perhaps the condition of things in which the natural hostility of man to man is expressed in creations instead of in the destructions that war engenders. It is the period of creative competition, and the struggle of productions. But I, am I not tired of producing? [...]
>
> Farewell ghosts! The world needs you no longer, nor me. The world, which calls by the name of 'progress' its tendency towards a fatal precision, marches on from Taylorization to Taylorization. Still a certain confusion reigns, but it will soon be cleared away, and we shall see appear a miracle of animal society, a perfect and final antheap.[1]

This passage concludes the first of two 'Letters from France' which John Middleton Murry, *The Athenaeum*'s editor, had commissioned from Paul Valéry. The war is over but the times are clearly out of joint. Peace, Valéry suggests, may prove the more problematic condition, especially after this war. Valéry's Hamlet, representing the European intellectual, is not merely unable to cope with an

---

[1] Paul Valéry, 'Letters from France. I. The Spiritual Crisis', *The Athenaeum*, 11 April 1919, 182–4 at 184. The French version of Valéry's two Letters was subsequently published under the title 'La crise de l'esprit' in *La Nouvelle Revue Française* (1919).

overwhelming task, he no longer knows what the task might be or even if there is a task at all.

Valéry's 'Letter' opens with: 'We civilizations now know that we are mortal.' Mortal like the long-gone civilizations of Elam, Niniveh, and Babylon, whose 'total ruin [...] meant as little to us as their existence'. But the ruin of modern Europe conflates those ancient disasters with the present catastrophe:

> Thus the spiritual Persepolis is ravaged equally with the material Susa. All is not lost, but everything has felt itself perish.[2]

Two years later another contributor to *The Athenaeum* drew the same long-distance parallel in what was to become the most famous twentieth-century poem in English:

> What is the city over the mountains
> Cracks and reforms and bursts in the violet air
> Falling towers
> Jerusalem Athens Alexandria
> Vienna London
> Unreal[3]

T. S. Eliot no doubt had read and approved of Valéry's *Athenaeum* article; just as Valéry, in making Hamlet the incarnation of the European intellect, was no doubt aware of the long-standing highly fraught identification of Hamlet with the intellect—or the mind, or the spirit—of one European country in particular, Germany.[4]

Valéry's conceit supplants and incorporates this identification. As he picks up the skulls of German thinkers, Valéry's European Hamlet ponders the transience of an intellectual tradition in which he, Hamlet, had figured as an identificatory icon. But in pondering his own obsolescence and the obsolescence of the culture that sustained him, Hamlet is also attesting to his undiminished timely relevance. With his trademark skull, he is, after all, the most readily identifiable memento of mortality in the European imaginary and thus never more relevant than now, with millions of ghosts and a civilization in ruins. In 1919, Hamlet's 'embassy of death',

---

[2] Valéry, 'Letters from France', 182.
[3] T. S. Eliot, 'The Waste Land', ll. 371–6, in Eliot, *Collected Poems 1909–1962* (London: Faber and Faber, 1963), 61–86. Eliot's *Athenaeum* pieces include 'Hamlet and His Problems', review of *The Problem of Hamlet* by J. M. Robertson, in *The Athenaeum*, 26 September 1919, 940–1; 'A Romantic Patrician', review of *Essays in Romantic Literature* by George Wyndham, ed. Charles Whibley, in *The Athenaeum*, 2 May 1919, 265–7; 'Criticism in England', review of *Old and New Masters* by Robert Lynd, in *The Athenaeum*, 13 June 1919, 456–7. For a discussion of Eliot's *Athenaeum* reviews, see Mark Jeffreys, 'The Rhetoric of Authority in T. S. Eliot's Athenaeum Reviews', *South Atlantic Review* 57.4 (1992), 93–108.
[4] This identification had percolated into popular consciousness. Caricatures on both sides of the front made ample use of it—either harping on or denying Germany's alleged Hamlet-likeness. See Ton Hoenselaars, 'Great War Shakespeare: Somewhere in France, 1914–1919', in *Actes des congrès de la Société française Shakespeare* 32 (2015), <http://shakespeare.revues.org/2960>, accessed 26 August 2015. On other forms of nationalist Shakespeare appropriation during the First World War: Engler, 'Shakespeare in the Trenches', and Werner Habicht, 'Shakespeare Celebrations in Times of War', *Shakespeare Quarterly* 52.4 (2001), 441–55.

to quote Wilson Knight's famous 1930 essay,[5] was far from over. It was just going into a new phase.

The Great War had revoked Germany's entitlement to the role of Hamlet and recast her, as Henry Arthur Jones wrote in 1916, as a bloodthirsty Macbeth.[6] But Shakespeare's melancholy prince continued to haunt troubled minds in the troubled republic that followed on the demise of the Wilhelminian Empire. For the political right wing, Germany's defeat in 1918, the 'shame peace' of Versailles, and the despised parliamentary system of the Weimar Republic had widened the chasm between Germany as it actually was and Germany as the rightists thought it should be. The slogan 'Germany is Hamlet' had originally drawn its political edge from just such a disparity between the actual and the ideal state of the nation. Even with Germans basking in the glory of victory over France and revelling in newly founded empire in 1871, it retained its hold over those who, like Nietzsche, looked on the new state with Hamletian disaffection. After the lost world war the disparity acquired increased topical urgency.

Berlin held a rather special place among the Babylons and Ninivehs of post-war Europe. During Germany's short-lived first democracy, Berlin epitomized the crisis of modernity, but also the unparalleled upsurge of cultural energies set free by that crisis. The Republic was incongruously named after provincial Weimar, but its centre of gravity, culturally no less than politically, was of course Berlin. Weimar stood for the hope of a new beginning in the spirit of Goethe rather than Bismarck. But the prime reason for holding the constituent national assembly in the theatre at Weimar was, as noted by Philipp Scheidemann, the first minister-president of the new state, that Berlin simply was not safe.[7]

Berlin never did become quite safe for the Republic. Even in the relatively prosperous middle years of the decade, when even in Germany the 1920s were starting to be called 'golden', the metropolis remained a hotbed of violent political controversy. Not long before the Wall Street Crash of 1929, when the liberal foreign secretary Gustav Stresemann said that Germany was 'dancing on a volcano', he was referring to the economy; but the metaphor was soon seen to epitomize the sensibility, lifestyle, and mood of a whole generation.[8]

Valéry's Hamlet or the Tiresias of Eliot's *Waste Land* could not have found a more suitable stage for their cultural pessimism than 1920s Berlin. Nowhere was tradition more recklessly challenged, the disruptive force of modernity more keenly felt and more eagerly fuelled than here. Berlin afforded an exemplary instance of what Eliot described as 'the immense panorama of futility and anarchy which is contemporary history'.[9] But widespread as it was, especially among the German bourgeoisie, cultural pessimism was, of course, not the only possible

---

[5] G. Wilson Knight, 'The Embassy of Death: An Essay on *Hamlet*', in his *The Wheel of Fire: Interpretations of Shakespearean Tragedy* (London: Methuen, 1930), 15–50.

[6] Jones, *Shakespeare and Germany*, 22. See Introduction, section I.

[7] Cf. Gay, *Weimar Culture*, 1.

[8] It is reflected in publications such as Thomas W. Kniesche, *Dancing on the Volcano: Essays on the Culture of the Weimar Republic* (Rochester, NY: Camden House, 1994).

[9] T. S. Eliot, 'Ulysses, Order and Myth' (1923), in *Selected Prose of T. S. Eliot*, ed. Kermode, 175–8 at 177.

response to the post-war condition. 'Progress', that favourite hate-word of the intellectual right, held out genuine hope for those who felt the past was anything but a paradise lost.

Hamlet, it would seem, was more naturally aligned with a backward-looking rhetoric of loss, of yearning for an unrecoverable past, a past that never really existed except as the ghost of a heroic fantasy. Believers in the popular stab-in-the-back legend could read a Hamletian pattern into the recent course of events, seeing Germany's defeat and the abdication of the Kaiser as due not to Allied military victory but to the November 1918 revolt of the German armed forces and its leftist instigators. Murder most foul, in other words, and crying out for revenge. The legitimate old order had been treacherously overturned by the so-called 'November criminals', the father-monarch replaced by a breed of latter-day Claudiuses, 'cut-purses of empire and rule', mock-kings 'of shreds and patches' (*Ham*. 3.4.102).

The deficiency of the new democratic leadership was lampooned in countless caricatures. By far the most damaging image was a holiday snapshot which Friedrich Ebert, the Social Democratic provisional president designate of the Republic, had incautiously allowed to be taken of himself and his cabinet minister for the armed forces after a swim in the Baltic. Exposing the new leadership in their soggy swimming trunks and all-too-average humanity, the photo was leaked to the press and featured on the title page of *Berliner Illustrierte* on the very day of Ebert's election. The most widely circulated illustration of anti-Republican animus, it was cited in countless unfavourable comparisons between then and now which, like Hamlet in the Closet Scene, exhort the viewer to '[l]ook here upon this picture, and on this' and berate the 'judgment' that '[w]ould step from this to this' (*Ham*. 3.4.53 and 70–1), from the impeccable dignity of the Empire to the shameful nakedness of the Republic:[10]

> [F]or madness would not err
> Nor sense to ecstasy was ne'er so thralled
> But it reserved some quantity of choice
> To serve in such a difference. (*Ham*. 3.4.73–6)

But yearning for lost Wilhelmine glory was not the only sentiment that could attach itself to Hamlet. The post-war decade saw not one but many Hamlets emerge from the debris of the old order, each with his own message and with agendas as various and conflicted as the decade itself. And if the times were glaringly out of joint, the leaders of the old regime were as much to blame as the new ones. All across the political spectrum, Hamlet could be adopted as the champion of the young against the old, a natural ally of youth movements both left and right for whom salvation from present ills demanded a radical break with the legacy of the fathers.[11] Hamlet's alternating between despair and exhilaration, brooding inertia

[10] For a concise discussion of the 'swimming trunks photo', its political reverberations, and further literature about the scandal: Walter Mühlhausen, 'Die Weimarer Republik enblößt: Das Badehosen-Foto von Friedrich Ebert und Gustav Noske', in *Das Jahrhundert der Bilder, 1900–1949*, ed. Gerhard Paul (Göttingen: Vandenhoeck & Ruprecht, 2009), 236–43.

[11] On the German youth movement (*Jugendbewegung*), a variety of groups and attitudes all dedicated to the 'myth of youth', see Howard Paul Becker, *German Youth: Bond or Free* (New York: Oxford

and sudden bouts of energy hit the nerve of a generation. His *Weltschmerz* was spacious enough to accommodate malcontents of all persuasions, to make him a 'figure of universal empathy', the 'best friend'[12] of leftists and rightists alike. The lines of divergence between left and right were in any case not always as clearly drawn as one might expect. In the cultural and political ferment of Weimar, Hamlet was a signifier floating in a sea of troubles as various as the doctrines of salvation which promised to end them.

Railing at outrageous fortune, forever yearning but forever unable to achieve, Hamlet epitomizes the unresolved tensions and deeply felt provisionality of a time drifting towards cataclysmic upheaval. We have encountered this mood in the millennialism of George's New Reich. Hamlet is clearly not the figure on whom 'the fate of tomorrow'[13] can be built, not 'the one who [...] breaks the chains and sweeps aside the rubble'.[14] But he spoke to, and was made to speak for, the fears and frustrations from which such millennial hopes arose and drew their dangerous attraction.

To illustrate the cultural and political ferment of the Weimar period I begin with two Hamlets that resist the reactionary, backward-yearning slant of Wilhelminian nostalgia. Nor do they indulge in visions of millennial overcoming. Instead they both align the play with modernity, albeit in widely different ways. Both draw a good deal of their power from their infraction of the German Hamlet tradition and its latently anti-modern drift in which 'the very age and body of the time', could so plausibly find 'his form and pressure' (*Ham.* 3.2.22) during the post-war decade. The first example is the 1920/1 film *Hamlet: Drama of Vengeance*, directed by Svend Gade and Heinz Schall with the Danish actress Asta Nielsen in the title role. The other is Leopold Jessner's 1926 production of *Hamlet* at the Prussian State Theatre, in which Fritz Kortner played the prince.

The Gade–Nielsen film and the Jessner–Kortner theatre production are the two most unorthodox *Hamlets* of the Weimar period. They are also by far the two most important ones. They clearly do not belong in the rightist intellectual tradition which this book explores. What motivates their inclusion here, apart from their intrinsic interest, is the way in which they challenge and indeed run counter to that tradition. Especially in Jessner's case, this incurred intense animosity from right-wing commentators. To conservative and Nazi critics his *Hamlet* epitomized the cultural decadence of the Republic, the decadence assailed in the rantings of Michael, the hero of a novel by another would-be Hamlet, the young Joseph Goebbels.

University Press, 1946; repr. London: Routledge, 1998); Stachura, *The German Youth Movement*; Walter Laqueur, *Young Germany: A History of the German Youth Movement* (New York: Basic Books, 1962); Koebner et al., eds, *'Mit uns zieht die neue Zeit'. Der Mythos Jugend.*

[12] Franz Richard Behrens (Erwin Gepard), 'Meinem besten Freunde—Hamlet' (1920), in Behrens, *Werkausgabe*, vol. 4: *Mein bester Freund—Hamlet. Drehbücher, Kinotexte, Filmkritiken*, ed. Gerhard Rühm and Monika Lichtenfels (Munich: edition text+kritik, 2012), 286–9 at 286.

[13] George, 'The Poet in Times of Confusion', in *Works of Stefan George*, 297.

[14] George, 'Secret Germany', in *Works of Stefan George*, 307.

II 'IN VERY DEED A WOMAN': ASTA NIELSEN'S HAMLET

Hamlet: Drama of Vengeance was Asta Nielsen's fifty-second film since beginning her movie career in 1910 but the first produced by her own company, Art-Film.[15] Nielsen was thirty-nine when the film was shot in Berlin in the summer of 1920 and an international—or rather, *the* international—film star. Worshipped by the men in the trenches on both sides, she was anything but conventionally 'beautiful': 'Her enormous dark eyes, thin lips, masklike face, and slender, boyish figure contrast[ed] starkly with prevailing female body norms',[16] especially those prevailing in the American film business (Figure 4.1). The *Variety* commentator sourly remarked after seeing the American première of Nielsen's *Hamlet*:

> Miss Neilson's [*sic*!] abilities are exceptional, but they are not the type to enrapture the American public. Almost emaciated, she has command and distinction of movement. Her facial pantomime is of considerable range, but dead whites and blacks have to be used to overcome her physical deficiencies.[17]

Other commentators on both sides of the Atlantic saw the very opposite of 'deficiencies': She is 'the drunkard's vision and the lonely man's dream', Guillaume Apollinaire is said to have written[18] in a tribute that sounds a bit like Walter Pater's famous eulogy on the *Mona Lisa*, whose beauty '[a]ll the thoughts and experience of the world have etched and moulded'.[19]

Rather than conforming to existing styles, Nielsen created her own. Her androgynous appearance, which prior to Hamlet had been foregrounded in several comic breeches parts and was emphasized by her trend-setting *Bubikopf* gamine hairstyle, made her an iconic embodiment of the independent working New Woman.[20] She was as much a role model for women as an object of male fantasies.

---

[15] The film exists in several different versions. I have used the restored colour print version prepared by the Deutsches Filminstitut Frankfurt: *Asta Nielsen. Hamlet & Die Filmprimadonna*, Edition filmmuseum 37, 2007. Discussions of the film include: Lawrence Danson, 'Gazing at Hamlet, or the Danish Cabaret', *Shakespeare Survey* 45 (1992), 37–51; Ann Thompson, 'Asta Nielsen and the Mystery of Hamlet', in *Shakespeare the Movie: Popularizing the Plays on Film, TV and Video*, ed, Lynda E. Boose and Richard Burt (London: Routledge, 1997), 215–24; Tony Howard, *Women as Hamlet: Performance and Interpretation in Theatre, Film and Fiction* (Cambridge: Cambridge University Press, 2007), 137–59; Judith Buchanan, *Shakespeare on Silent Film: An Excellent Dumb Discourse* (Cambridge and New York: Cambridge University Press, 2009), 217–40; Simon Ryle, *Shakespeare, Cinema and Desire: Adaptation and Other Futures of Shakespeare's Language* (Basingstoke: Palgrave Macmillan, 2010), 129–74.

[16] Gary Morris, 'Asta Nielsen', *Bright Lights* 16 (1996), <http://brightlightsfilm.com/16/asta.php>, accessed 23 March 2014.

[17] Leed, 'Hamlet', *Variety*, 11 November 1921. To put this verdict in perspective it helps to read the slating Rudolph Valentino's *The Sheik* receives on the same page. For this and many other, mostly German, press clippings I owe thanks to Christof Schöbel of the Deutsches Filminstitut—Deutsches Filmmuseum, Frankfurt.

[18] I have been unable to trace the original quotation: Howard, *Women as Hamlet*, 144, quotes Apollinaire as quoted in Pablo Diaz, *Asta Nielsen* (Berlin: publ. unknown, 1920), 69.

[19] Walter Pater, *The Renaissance* (1893) (Berkeley and Los Angeles: University of California Press, 1980), 98–9; Danson, 'Gazing at Hamlet', 44, suggests the parallel.

[20] For a discussion of this social context: Katharina von Ankum, ed., *Women in the Metropolis: Gender and Modernity in Weimar Culture* (Berkeley, Los Angeles, and London: University of California Press, 1997).

Figure 4.1. Asta Nielsen as Hamlet. Photo by permission of ullstein bild—ArenaPAL / Ronald Grant Archive.

When this Mona Lisa of the silent screen took on the Mona Lisa of literature, her version of Hamlet boldly supplied what T. S. Eliot found so regrettably missing in Shakespeare's play: an appropriate 'objective correlative' for Hamlet's bottomless grief.[21] In the Nielsen film,

> Hamlet is [...] a woman passed off by her mother as a boy in order to secure the succession. All conflicts arise from this. Hamlet must play a false game throughout, hiding his deepest heart's desire for his friend [Horatio].[22]

Being trapped in the wrong sex and thus forever denied the love of one's life—what indeed could be more tragic!

The idea for this quirky take on the Hamlet story came from the crackpot labour of love of an American amateur Shakespearean, Edward P. Vining. *The Mystery of Hamlet* (1881) is one of those wonderfully wacky attempts at a once-for-all solution where centuries of learned precursors have stumbled clueless in the dark. Why does Hamlet talk so much rather than act, why is he so impulsive, prone to tears and dissimulation, why so prissily nauseated by Yorick's skull and so afraid of

---

[21] Eliot, 'Hamlet and His Problems', 941.
[22] H. L., Review of *Hamlet*, *Deutsche Lichtspiel-Zeitung*, 26 February 1921.

death, why so ungallantly harsh towards Ophelia but loving towards Horatio? These and a host of other traits, Vining decides, 'are far more in keeping with a feminine than with a masculine nature'.[23] The prince, in other words, must be a princess in disguise, not just a 'womanly man' but 'in very deed a woman, desperately striving to fill a place for which she was by nature unfitted'.[24]

Firmly grounded in the gender stereotypes of his day and convinced that a man in love with another man *can* only be a woman,[25] Vining's theory ironically enabled Nielsen to subvert the very foundations on which this theory was built. Nielsen's Hamlet mercurially crosses and re-crosses gender boundaries, 'destabiliz[ing] the polarized opposition between masculine and feminine identities'.[26] The Vining-based script, for all its 'melodramatic absurdity',[27] thus becomes an ideal vehicle for Nielsen's performance of gender-as-performance, as she 'adopts self-consciously manly poses to delude her on-screen (and entertain her off-screen) public'.[28] Unlike all her female predecessors in the part, from Sarah Siddons to Sarah Bernhardt, Nielsen does not impersonate a man. She plays a woman impersonating a man. This adds a complexity to the part that owes little to Shakespeare but speaks strongly to the concerns of the time. As Tony Howard points out, Nielsen's 'Hamlet was a study of young people reinventing gender roles in the aftermath of war and its explosion of patriarchal tradition. [...] [H]er film condemns everyone, female or male, who collaborates with reactionary structures of gender and power.'[29]

But this does not mean that the forces of the young, vibrantly centred in Nielsen's Hamlet, are allowed to prevail. The film alternates (again quoting Howard) 'between scenes of Hamlet *performing*, where she is all-powerful, and sequences where she is trapped alone by shadows and stones'.[30] Thus Hamlet, as in Saxo Grammaticus, resolutely traps and kills Claudius in a fire but still ends up trapped herself by the machinations of an unprecedentedly evil Gertrude, who is entirely of the script-writer's own invention. The film closes 'over her dead body' after Horatio finally discovers his friend's secret by accidentally touching her breast: 'Only death reveals your secret to me. Your golden heart was that of a woman. Too late—beloved—too late.'

This is certainly not Shakespeare, but neither was it meant to be. 'The film *Hamlet*', Erwin Gepard declared, 'has only parts of the subject matter and a few

---

[23] Edward P. Vining, *The Mystery of Hamlet: An Attempt to Solve an Old Problem* (Philadelphia: J. P. Lippincott & Co., 1881), 48. That the film actually plucks out the heart of the Hamlet mystery by making us share in her secret is noted by Ryle, *Shakespeare, Cinema and Desire*, 140.

[24] Vining, *The Mystery of Hamlet*, 59. Vining made it not only into the footnotes of Ernest Jones's *Hamlet* study but also into Stephen Dedalus's 'dissertation on Shakespeare' in Chapter 6 of *Ulysses*, where we find not only that 'Vining held that the prince was a woman' but also the observation that 'Shakespeare is the happy hunting-ground of minds that have lost their balance.'Joyce, *Ulysses*, 190 and 239.

[25] Danson, 'Gazing at Hamlet', 42.

[26] Patrice Petro, *Joyless Streets: Women and Melodramatic Representation in Weimar Germany* (Princeton, NJ: Princeton University Press, 1989), 153.

[27] Howard, *Women as Hamlet*, 140.   [28] Buchanan, *Shakespeare on Silent Film*, 227.

[29] Howard, *Women as Hamlet*, 146 and 152.   [30] Howard, *Women as Hamlet*, 150.

characters in common with Shakespeare. In no way is it a reworking of the Shakespearean drama.'[31] Gepard should know: he wrote the screenplay. His authorial hand has heretofore been either ignored or belittled.[32] Erwin Gepard was the pseudonym 'behind which', as a contemporary film journal confided to its readers, 'one of the most controversial Expressionist poets is hiding'.[33] This was Franz Richard Behrens, author of *Blood Blossom* (*Blutblüte*), a volume of radically experimental war poems published in 1917 while the author was a soldier on the Western Front.[34] After the war, Behrens worked as a journalist and screen-writer. His last poem appeared in 1925, and he was subsequently so entirely forgotten that people thought him long dead when his poetry was rediscovered in the 1970s. There is now a four-volume edition of his works, the last volume containing his film criticism and his screenplays, including *Hamlet*.[35]

Gepard's disclaimer defined Nielsen's PR strategy throughout. The news that she was planning to make a *Hamlet* movie had caused some negative advance publicity. There had been talk of a 'Shakespeare forgery'. The way to deflect this was to declare that her *Hamlet* was *not* Shakespeare's but a 'Drama [...] after motifs of the Hamlet Saga discovered by Professor Vining'. Vining did eventually become a professor—though not of English literature—but he had certainly not discovered the saga, recorded by Saxo Grammaticus, on which Gepard draws for the death of Claudius.

With his unorthodox treatment of *Hamlet* under the protective cloak of one professor, Vining, Gepard took the liberty of railing at all others. In a prologue which did not make it into the film he has a 'big crowd of grave professors with beards and glasses' demonstrating their disapproval in front of a cinema, then engaging in a lecture-hall battle over the true meaning of Hamlet. Their turbulent dispute is cut short by the appearance of Shakespeare himself. The script has him turning in his grave, then rising from it and presenting himself at the lectern:

> He yawns, stretches, knocks over all the books. The professors scatter in all directions. Shakespeare stands smiling in all his vigour. He fades out. Hamlet's dreamy head emerges from the fading Shakespeare.[36]

Then Hamlet breaks into soliloquy, borrowing Macbeth's: 'Life's but a walking shadow' (*Mac.* 5.5.23–8). All that survives of this prologue in the film are the eight opening title cards citing Voltaire, Herder, Goethe, and, of course, Vining with the

---

[31] Behrens (Erwin Gepard), 'Meinem besten Freunde—Hamlet', 288.

[32] Cf., for example, Howard, *Women as Hamlet*, 142: 'Though Gepard researched *Hamlet's* sources, Nielsen's inspiration was Vining [...].' This is misleading: Gepard did indeed do the research and, according to Nielsen, hit upon the 'old saga according to which Hamlet was a woman'. This enabled him 'to present the theme in a new version'. Nielsen quoted in Renate Seydel and Allan Hagedorff, *Asta Nielsen. Ihr Leben in Fotodokumenten, Selbstzeugnissen und zeitgenössischen Betrachtungen* (Munich: Universitas, 1981), 158.

[33] Unattributed item 'Aus dem Glashaus', in *Film Kurier*, 24 June 1920.

[34] Franz Richard Behrens, *Blutblüte* (Berlin: Verlag Der Sturm, 1917).

[35] Behrens, 'Hamlet', in *Mein bester Freund—Hamlet*, 7–69.

[36] Behrens, 'Hamlet', 11.

final verdict: '*Hamlet war in Wirklichkeit ein Weib!*'—'Hamlet was in reality a woman!'

Gepard's professor-bashing may seem no more than a schoolboy joke, a mere diversion from the film's more serious concerns. But it is perhaps symptomatic of the film's and its makers' general attitude towards established authority.[37] Silly as it may seem, the scuffle in the lecture hall makes a claim of entitlement, raising—and answering—the question as to who owns Hamlet. Certainly not those who have always owned him or thought they did. This message is even more emphatically delivered in Gepard's essay 'To my best friend—Hamlet':

> People ask me every day: 'How can you presume to rewrite Hamlet for film?' Because I love Hamlet! Because he is my best friend! [...] I want to show Hamlet, this figure of universal empathy [...] to people of all nations [...] Today there is only one medium that can make everyone on earth feel touched by Hamlet: film!—And because there is only one person today who can represent Hamlet, that person is a woman and her name is: *Asta Nielsen*!
>
> Storms of outrage broke out among the philistine guardians of art and culture when this idea first surfaced. Hamlet—the immortal masterpiece [...] not only reworked but [...] played by a woman?[38]

Gepard surely overdramatizes the advance hostility to Nielsen's project. But his claim for a universally popular Shakespeare with Asta as its iconic embodiment is authentic. He emphatically reiterates it in his 'Asta-Ode' (1923), a 600-line Nielsen-filmography in verse:

> On the stages Hamlet struggles with the barrage of forty
> > regular and irregular syllables
> Asta stands as Hamlet and doesn't even have to act
> She's just there.
>
> [...]
>
> Only grafters in patent leather shoes people the stages now

---

[37] Willy Haas, perhaps the most astute reviewer of Nielsen's film, thought that Gepard had not gone far enough. Instead of blasting professorial authority, he argued, Gepard had succumbed to it: 'But Herr Erwin Gépard has been—too modest. All too modest, he has not taken on the part of Caesar [who burnt the library of Alexandria] or Herostratus [who burnt the temple of Artemis] but the part of the whining university professor. He has not set fire to an Alexandrian library but sat down in one and—studied. For hours, for days, for weeks. And there he read something about an old manuscript that another university professor had discovered somewhere. That makes two university professors already. In the manuscript it says—well: Hamlet was not a man but a girl. Okay. Fine by me. Quite amusing. But now: let's go! *Du Courage, Molière*! Gritty, irreverent, incorruptible, cynical writer of comedies! The new Hamlet! Hamlet as a female transvestite—let's have it! Great!

But Herr Erwin Gépard is simply too modest. The whole Hamlet thing has obviously been an embarrassment to him. Out of modesty he chose to simply divide up the old chronicle plus Shakespeare into scenes and scenelets, to play up the pomp and circumstance, to suppress the psychological dimension and thus—hot-headed Expressionist that he is—to produce a grand historical costume drama entitled *Hamlet* whose author one might well think to have been Wildenbruch oder Josef von Lauff [two representatives of conventional nineteenth-century historical drama]. This is the sad drama of the modest Erwin Gépard.' Willy Haas, 'Hamlet', *Film-Kurier* 31.5 (5 February 1921).

[38] Behrens, 'Meinem besten Freunde—Hamlet', 286.

> So the poor are spared the dumbest farces
> The poor are with Asta at the movies
> There *is* such a thing as justice on earth[39]

Nielsen's *Hamlet*, it has been remarked, is very much a post-First World War film. Its interiors were shot in a converted aircraft factory and, as one critic somewhat wistfully remarked, the drapings of the great hall at Elsinore were made from the wing coverings of German Albatros fighter planes. The opening battle between Denmark and Norway recalls images of modern trench warfare rather than chivalric heroism. Old Hamlet is not a towering paternal ghost but a faltering war invalid. And when Hamlet meets Fortinbras at Wittenberg, their decision to forget their fathers' enmity resonates with the founding spirit of the League of Nations. All this gains additional depth when we consider that the script was written by a man whose first published poem, under the title 'Expressionist Artillerist', appeared during the battle of Verdun. He was one of those for whom the downfall of the old order did not spell the death of civilization but the hope of a new beginning.

III REPUBLICAN SHAKESPEARE: JESSNER'S *HAMLET* AT THE PRUSSIAN STATE THEATRE

The same is true of Leopold Jessner.[40] And he is also an exemplary case of how fragile that hope was. Jessner's appointment as head of the Prussian State Theatre in 1919 marked a radical break with tradition. He was a Jew and a Social Democrat. The always latently and often openly anti-Semitic conservative press noted that, with his appointment, the 'Jewification' of Berlin theatres was complete. The former Imperial Court Theatre, now Prussian State Theatre had been the last one headed by a gentile '*Intendant*'.[41] It had been the representative theatre of the old order, its repertoire and production style reflecting the rigidly conventional taste of the Kaiser's court.[42] Jessner converted this stronghold of Wilhelminian culture into the representative stage of the new republic. For a short while—no more than four or five years—his work defined the cutting edge of modernity in theatre.

---

[39] Franz Richard Behrens, 'Asta-Ode', in Behrens, *Werkausgabe*, vol. 1: *Blutblüte. Die gesammelten Gedichte*, 2nd edn, ed. Gerhard Rühm (Munich: edition text+kritik, 1995), 259–83 at 280–1.

[40] The most comprehensive study of Jessner is Matthias Heilmann, *Leopold Jessner—Intendant der Republik. Der Weg eines deutsch-jüdischen Regisseurs aus Ostpreußen* (Tübingen: Niemeyer, 2005); see also: Andreas Höfele, 'Leopold Jessner's Shakespeare Productions 1920–1930', *Theatre History Studies* 12 (1992), 139–55; Hortmann, *Shakespeare on the German Stage*, 340–1; Anat Feinberg, 'Leopold Jessner: German Theatre and Jewish Identity', *Leo Baeck Institute Year Book* 48 (2003), 111–33; Peter W. Marx, 'Stufen der Abstraktion: Leopold Jessners Shakespeare-Inszenierungen 1919–1932', *Shakespeare-Jahrbuch* 146 (2010), 60–77.

[41] This was Botho von Hülsen, an aristocrat of typically Prussian military background and rather limited artistic talent. He resigned, not long after the Kaiser himself, in 1918. The Weimar Republic, in name still the German Empire, was a federal republic, with Prussia as the largest constituent democratic-parliamentary free state in the federation.

[42] While the transition from Naturalism and Symbolism to the new Expressionist drama was in full swing on the more progressive stages, the Imperial Court Theatre had still not got as far as Ibsen.

When Jessner chose Schiller's *Wilhelm Tell* for his opening production, this seemed to signal a continuation of the old Court Theatre tradition. But even as the curtain rose, revealing an abstract sculptural set instead of the customary cardboard Swiss Alps, the new direction became clear. Unprecedented tumult broke loose in the audience when Fritz Kortner stormed on stage in the role of Tell's antagonist Gessler. Dressed in a black uniform bedecked with military medals, he slapped his polished knee boots impatiently with a riding crop, an obvious caricature of Wilhelminian militarism or, as Kortner writes in his autobiography, a premonition of Hitler's vain Reich Marshal Göring.[43]

Such direct satirical jabs, however, were the exception rather than the rule in Jessner's style. His landmark *Richard III*, which ran almost simultaneously with Asta Nielsen's *Hamlet*, emphasized Shakespeare's modernity by placing the rise and fall of the villain on an abstract, 'timeless' stage dominated by a monumental flight of stairs. This is reminiscent, or rather 'preminiscent', of Jan Kott's 'great staircase' of history.[44] Jessner also anticipated Kott in approaching Shakespeare as a contemporary.[45] '*Zeitausdruck*' is the term he used to define his aims: combining elements of timeless simplicity with an unmistakably modern consciousness. Instead of the escapist theatre magic of a Max Reinhardt, Jessner offered 'the abstracts and brief chronicles of the time'. Audiences were overwhelmed by the driving pace of Jessner's productions, a dynamism strikingly embodied in his most important lead actor, Fritz Kortner.

Their collaboration was never without tension. The *Hamlet* of 1926 marked their reunion after an interval of several years. But quite contrary to expectations, Kortner did not dominate this production in the way he had *Richard III*. Jessner was simply not interested in the psychology of Hamlet. That, he said, had been treated exhaustively in so many scholarly studies and by so many excellent actors that 'the gramophone record of "To be or not to be" has become worn. The prince's melancholy has become proverbial and thus a cliché.'[46] Neither was he interested in just another trendy modern-dress 'Hamlet in tails'. Two of those were being staged at the time, one in Hamburg and one in Vienna, a German version of H. K. Ayliff's Birmingham Repertory production featuring Reinhardt's star actor Alexander Moissi.[47]

---

[43] See Fritz Kortner, *Aller Tage Abend* (1959), 3rd edn (Munich: dtv, 1971), 226. Cf. Richard D. Critchfield, *From Shakespeare to Frisch: The Provocative Fritz Kortner* (Heidelberg: Synchron, 2008), 35–40.

[44] Jan Kott, *Shakespeare Our Contemporary*, trans. Boleslaw Taborski (London: Methuen, 1964), 8.

[45] For the theatre, Jessner once said, there is no such thing as a classic: 'There are only hundred-year-old, fifty-year-old, and twenty-year-old poets of today.' Leopold Jessner, 'Das Theater. Ein Vortrag', *Die Scene* 18.3 (March 1928), 66–74; reprinted in Jessner, *Schriften: Theater der zwanziger Jahre*, ed. Hugo Fetting (Berlin: Henschel, 1979), 97–110 at 103.

[46] Jessner, 'Das Theater', 106.

[47] *Hamlet*, Thalia Theater, Hamburg, 22 April 1926, directed by Hermann Röbbeling, Hamlet: Ernst Deutsch. The playbill announces that the play will be performed in twentieth-century costumes with the participation of a jazz band. The programme features a blank verse dialogue between the director and Shakespeare in which the Bard approves of the director's modern production style.

Hamlet, Deutsches Volkstheater, Vienna, 10 April 1926, directed by H. K. Ayliff, Hamlet: Alexander Moissi. My thanks to Claudia Blank, Director of the Deutsches Theatermuseum, Munich, for pointing me to these two contemporary productions.

Figure 4.3. Fritz Kortner as Hamlet. Photo by permission of ullstein bild—Zander & Labisch.

This was written in 1930, shortly after Jessner—worn down by constant attacks— had handed in his resignation.

***

Both Nielsen's *Hamlet* film and Jessner's *Hamlet* production challenged the prevailing interpretive tradition. Their approach differed crucially from Paul Valéry's. He had invoked the familiar traditional image of Hamlet in order to look at a world that had become radically unfamiliar. Nielsen and Jessner defamiliarized Hamlet and immersed him in the currents of accelerating modernity, changing him to enable his participation in changing the world rather than just watching it change. Valéry's Hamlet is a prophet of loss. Theirs, each in his (or indeed her) own way, is a bearer of promise, albeit a promise tragically thwarted.

But the differences between Nielsen's film and Jessner's theatre production are at least as significant. Most striking of all was the difference in contemporary responses. Nielsen's Hamlet challenged traditional gender norms. But this challenge apparently gave no offence to anyone. A Jewish Hamlet donning the blond wig derived from Goethe had an infinitely greater scandal potential than a Danish actress's gender-bending androgyny. Friend and foe alike, the reviews of Jessner's *Hamlet* were either openly political or bristling with the tension of political undercurrents. Such tension is entirely absent from the reviews of Nielsen's film. If the guardians of culture were, as Gepard/Behrens alleges, up in arms over the female Hamlet, they grumbled silently.[53]

IV *MICHAEL*, OR, THE SORROWS OF YOUNG GOEBBELS

The Republican modernity which the *Hamlets* of Nielsen and, more politically explicitly, Jessner epitomized was summarily rejected after the Nazi takeover in 1933. In a speech to the heads of German theatres in May 1933, Joseph Goebbels, appointed to the newly created post of Minister of Propaganda, laid down the rules for the future course of German theatre.[54] It was crucial to recognize, he told his audience, that 'the movement which has now victoriously marched into the state' (29) had 'dethroned the individual' and was replacing 'the deification of the individual' with the 'deification of the *Volk*' (30). While the theatre of the Republic had heaved 'the suppressed complexes of some diseased person onto the stage, things that were of no interest to the *Volk*', '[w]e want to bring art back to the *Volk* and the *Volk* back to art' (37). He outlined how this was to be achieved in terms of an ultimatum:

> German art in the decades to come will be steely-romantic, unsentimental, it will be national with great pathos and communally binding—or it will not be. (36)

That such art could not be preached into existence soon became apparent. The drab mediocrity of Nazi drama and the solemn stiltedness of the *Thingspiel*, a type of *völkisch* outdoor theatre harking back to primeval Germanic rites,[55] signally failed to live up to the minister's ambition.

More to our purpose than the failed future, however, is a look at the condemned past. It will reveal Goebbels's own entanglement in what he so stridently rejected. If ever a writer heaved his suppressed, or indeed unsuppressed, complexes onto the stage or page, it was Goebbels, smarting under the double handicap, physical and social, that life had dealt him. If Hitler was a failed artist, his most devoted disciple was a failed writer. Determined to become great in the world, young Goebbels counted on literature as a means to this end.

The intensity of the resentment that the future propaganda minister felt towards the Weimar literary scene was palpably fuelled by his failure to become

---

[53] A likely explanation for this is the vast difference in institutional status between theatre and cinema. Film was just beginning to be accepted as a legitimate art form and had nothing like the cultural prestige of the theatre, especially *this* theatre.

[54] Joseph Goebbels, 'Rede des Reichspropagandaministers Dr. Joseph Goebbels vor den deutschen Theaterleitern am 8. Mai 1933', *Das deutsche Drama* 5 (1933), 28–40. Page references in brackets refer to this text.

[55] *Thingspiele* were originally to be performed nationwide in four hundred purpose-built arenas but the plan was abandoned after only forty had been completed. See William Niven, 'The Birth of Nazi Drama? *Thing* Plays', in *Theatre under the Nazis*, ed. John London (Manchester and New York: Manchester University Press, 2000), 45–95; Gerwin Strobl, *The Swastika and the Stage: German Theatre and Society, 1933–1945* (Cambridge and New York: Cambridge University Press, 2007), 65–79.

part of it. The nationwide burning of the books of some of the most highly acclaimed contemporary authors on 10 May 1933 must have been deeply satisfying to the man who could now triumphantly obliterate those whom he had struggled in vain to emulate.[56] Of his literary output—a novel, five plays, several novellas, and stacks of poems[57]—only his novel made it into print, and that not until Goebbels had graduated from literature to politics and was able to avail himself of the party-owned Franz-Eher-Verlag, publisher of *Mein Kampf*, the party newspaper *Völkischer Beobachter*, and Goebbels's own 'fighting-paper', *Der Angriff* (Attack).

Goebbels's novel, *Michael, A German Fate on Diary Pages*, appeared in 1929. Its initial success was minimal but its author's Third Reich eminence pushed the shelf-warmer to its seventeenth edition and a total of over 80,000 copies by 1942. In the form of a fictional diary, it is clearly modelled on Goethe's early novel in letters, *The Sorrows of Young Werther* (1774). On 150 sparsely printed pages it relates the story, but mostly the musings and rantings, of Michael Voormann, a soldier returned from the Great War. Studying at Freiburg, Munich, and Heidelberg, Michael devotes little thought to his academic subject (what that subject might actually be is never made quite clear) but all the more to his own misery and that of his downtrodden nation, the one inseparably entwined with the other. He writes a play and falls in love with a 'brown-blond' fellow student called Hertha Holk. The relationship is troubled but, unlike Werther, Michael does not kill himself for love. Instead he is killed in a mining accident, having abandoned both Hertha and the academy for the harsh but authentic life of a worker. The universities in the novel are those where Goebbels himself studied, and the affair with Hertha Holk is based on his difficult relationship with Anka Stalherm, whose well-to-do parents had disapproved of the penniless suitor with a limp.[58]

---

[56] Planned and staged by the Nazi German Student Organization, the book-burning campaign received official sanction through an address given by Goebbels two days after his speech to theatre managers at the book burning at Berlin's Opera Square. See Helmut Heiber, ed., *Goebbels-Reden*, vol. 1: *1932–1939* (Düsseldorf: Droste, 1971), 108–12.

[57] The plays, as listed in Ralf Georg Reuth, *Goebbels*, trans. Krishna Winston (San Diego, CA: Harvest, 1994), 440, are: *'Judas Iscariot: Eine biblische Tragödie in fünf Akten'* (1918); *'Heinrich Kämpfert. Ein Drama in drei Aufzügen'* (1919); *'Kampf der Arbeiterklasse'* (The Struggle of the Working Class) (1919/20); *'Die Saat: Ein Geschehen in drei Akten'* (The Seed) (1920); *'Der Wanderer: Ein Spiel in einem Prolog, elf Bildern und einem Epilog'* (1923, unfinished). This last play was completed in 1927; Goebbels had it staged at a Nazi theatre in Berlin in November 1928. On Goebbels the writer: Marianne Bonwit, *'Michael*, ein Roman von Joseph Goebbels, im Licht der deutschen literarischen Tradition', *Monatshefte* 49.4 (1957), 193–200; Hans-Jürgen Singer, 'Michael oder der leere Glaube', *1999. Zeitschrift für Sozialgeschichte des 20. und 21. Jahrhunderts* 2.4 (1987), 68–79; Lovis Maxim Wambach, *'Es ist gleichgültig, woran wir glauben, nur dass wir glauben': Bemerkungen zu Joseph Goebbels' Drama 'Judas Iscariot' und zu seinen 'Michael-Romanen'* (Bremen: Schriftenreihe des Raphael-Lemkin-Institutes für Xenophobie- und Antisemitismusforschung, 1996); Kai Michel, *Vom Poeten zum Demagogen: Die schriftstellerischen Versuche Joseph Goebbels* (Cologne, Weimar, and Vienna: Böhlau, 1999); David Barnett, 'Joseph Goebbels: Expressionist Dramatist as Nazi Minister of Culture', *New Theatre Quarterly* 17.2 (2001), 161–9.

[58] Cf. Reuth, *Goebbels*, 22–39; see also Toby Thacker, *Joseph Goebbels: Life and Death* (Basingstoke: Palgrave Macmillan, 2009), 17–19, and Peter Longerich, *Joseph Goebbels. Biographie* (Munich: Siedler, 2010), 29–37.

Even more closely autobiographical in an earlier version,[59] Michael is a composite portrait of the 'artist' himself and his friend Richard Flisges, to whose memory the novel is dedicated: 'a brave soldier of labour who died a hard death in a mine near Schliersee on 19 July 1923'.[60] Goebbels had admired Flisges for doing what his handicap had prevented him from doing: fighting and distinguishing himself in the war. Flisges's decision to abandon his university course and work as a miner further enhanced his hero-status, as did his death, which the novel elevates to an act of quasi-religious self-sacrifice for the future of the nation. Weaving Flisges's biography into his own, Goebbels creates an ideal version of himself and declares it to be representative of the burdens and hopes of a whole generation. *Michael* is offered as a 'modest, silent mirror [that] reflects all the forces that are shaping us young people into a thought today and a power tomorrow'. The Preface declares that 'youth is always right in any conflict with old age' and: 'We look towards the day that will bring the storm wind' (3). Such sentiments are familiar from the poetry of Stefan George. Darkly intimated in George's New Reich, they acquire a much more specific direction in Goebbels's novel. Here is the protagonist meeting the coming saviour in a Munich beer hall:

Revelation! Revelation!

[...]

Amid the ruins, someone is standing and raising the flag high. (82)

[...]

All at once, the people around me are not strangers. They are all my brothers.

[...]

He is no speaker. He is a prophet!

[...]

I no longer know what I am doing.
I am beside myself.
I shout, 'Hurray!' No one is surprised.
The man on the podium gazes at me for a moment. Those blue eyes strike me like flaming rays. This is a command!

[...]

I am reborn as of this moment. (83)

Needless to say, writing of this calibre cut no ice in the literary world of the Weimar Republic. Only once before the fall of the Republic did Goebbels have the pleasure of basking in the admiration of Berlin's literary in-crowd. This was how Heinz Pol,

---

[59] Of the earliest nucleus of the novel, a three-part manuscript entitled '*Michael Voormann's Jugendjahre*' written in 1919, only the first and third parts survive. Bundesarchiv Koblenz, NL 118/126 and NL 118/115/116. For a detailed account of the evolution of *Michael* see Michel, *Vom Poeten zum Demagogen*.

[60] Joseph Goebbels, *Michael, ein deutsches Schicksal in Tagebuchblättern*, 17th edn (Munich: Franz Eher Nachfolger, Zentralverlag der NSDAP, 1942), 5. English translation: Joseph Goebbels, *Michael*, trans. Joachim Neugroschel (New York: Amok Press, 1987). Page references in brackets refer to this text.

the commentator of the left-leaning satire magazine *Weltbühne* ('World Stage'), saw it: There had been a literary social event

> three weeks ago on the premises of Berlin's [...] Blau-Weiss tennis club where Arnolt Bronnen, the poet of the Third National, celebrated his wedding to the primordial mother of the white mice. In the hubbub of the well-mixed crowd were to be seen the publisher Ernst Rowohlt and the Berlin labour leader Doctor Joseph Goebbels. 'Prost', said Rowohlt, downed his champagne and ate the glass. 'Prost, my dear Goebbels, I hope I will have the pleasure of publishing your next book.' The labour leader smiled his famously bewitching smile and said darkly: 'That depends on the percentage, Herr Rowohlt.' Some of the guests, not much versed in contemporary German literature, intervened and asked with astonished face: 'But is it true that Doctor Goebbels has actually written a book? We had no idea!' The labour leader dismissed this with a casual wave of his fist, while Rowohlt answered in his usual candid manner: 'Is it possible you don't know the great confessional novel by the party comrade titled 'Michael', published by Eher-Verlag of Munich? In hardcover, it costs 5 marks, a price which I couldn't have done it for.' Everyone clapped, and Goebbels was much celebrated that evening.
>
> Ever since his fame as a poet has been spreading like wildfire in the fashionable salons of Berlin's Westend [...] It is now de rigueur not only to have attended one of his rallies (and have a small bruise to show for it) but also to realize that the dictator of Nollendorf Platz is a heavyweight epic poet and a tender lyrical talent.[61]

Unfortunately Goebbels's take-off into literary fame never happened, although the wedding party did take place and Goebbels actually attended it.[62] The wedding party is the overture to Pol's slating of Goebbels's novel in *Die Weltbühne*.[63] Pol has a field day. Taking his cue from Goebbels's prefatory remark that *Michael* is a 'modest, silent mirror' of social forces shaping the young, Pol mercilessly exposes the glaring immodesty and foaming bombast of the novel. The story need only be

---

[61] Heinz Pol, 'Goebbels als Dichter', *Die Weltbühne* 27.1 (1931), 129–33 at 129–30. Page references given in brackets in the text. One of the eccentricities ascribed to the publisher Ernst Rowohlt (1887–1960) was his habit of eating glasses.

[62] Friedbert Aspetsberger, *Arnolt Bronnen. Biographie* (Vienna, Cologne, and Weimar: Böhlau, 1995), 573–4. Arnolt Bronnen (1895–1959) is called 'the poet of the Third National' because of his veering from ultra-left to ultra-right. A Communist and early associate of Brecht, he became a supporter of the nascent Nazi movement and a personal acquaintance of Goebbels. Dropped by the Nazis because of his Jewish father, he drifted to the left again, spending the last years of his life in East Berlin. His bride was Olga Förster-Prowe (1909–35), a Russian-born actress who was also Goebbels's mistress. She was a Soviet agent from 1932 to 1935, giving rise to doubt about the official cause of her early death, suicide. At the second showing of the film based on Remarque's *All Quiet on the Western Front* at Berlin's Nollendorf-Film Theatre on 6 December 1930, she released a horde of white mice in the packed theatre. This as well as other disturbances by Nazis in the audience led to the interruption of the show, with Förster-Prowe being carried out of the cinema in triumph by the Nazi provocateurs. The film was banned shortly afterwards for 'jeopardizing Germany's repute'. Goebbels celebrated this as a 'victory of the street' or *Filmsieg* (film victory).

[63] *Die Weltbühne* was banned by the Nazis in 1933. Its editor, Carl von Ossietzky (1889–1938), was imprisoned in a concentration camp. In 1936, he was retroactively awarded the 1935 Nobel Peace Prize. He was released but died soon afterwards as a consequence of the treatment he had suffered. Heinz Pol [=Heinz Pollack] managed to escape from Germany and eventually settled in the US, where he continued to work as a journalist and writer.

retold to reveal its flatulent inanity. But for all its laughable inadequacy, it is 'a damned serious matter' (133):

> The case of Goebbels would be simple if we were living in a healthy country. The gigantic platitudes of this megalomaniac hysteric would then be of interest to medical science only. But as things stand, the author [...] is a political reality. The fact that the intellectual and political power of this reality is stripped to its marrowless bones in this book doesn't bother him [Goebbels], and millions of Germans, a large segment of our youth among them, don't notice even if we rubbed their noses in it. (133)

But not even Pol foresaw quite how serious the matter actually was. '[T]he pillars of the Third Reich', he wrote, were not real revolutionaries: 'they will not make heads roll'. Instead, 'like Herr Michael, they will fling Nietzsche quotations about like hand grenades' (133).[64]

V 'A MACBETH WHO SPOKE FOR HIMSELF'

The delusion in Pol's prophecy had become woefully clear by the time another reader made the acquaintance of Goebbels's novel. This was the poet Stephen Spender, who was travelling in devastated Germany in the summer of 1945 'on a mission to inquire into the lives and ideas of German intellectuals, with a particular view to discovering any surviving talent in German literature'.[65] Goebbels had not survived, nor did he have much literary talent, but Spender devotes a whole chapter to him, beginning with the astonishing statement that 'Goebbels is a magnetic writer for young people' and 'communicates the excitement of the Nazi movement luridly but effectively' (177). Spender cites from Goebbels's diary entry for 30 January 1933, the day Hitler was appointed Chancellor: 'It is all like a dream. The Wilhelmstrasse belongs to us. Already the Führer is working in the *Reichskanzlei*. [...] We all are dumb with emotion. Each of us shakes the Führer's hand, and it is as though our troth to each other were pledged again and renewed. Wonderful, how simple the Führer is in his greatness, how great in his simplicity.'[66] 'One opens a book', Spender comments, 'and reads a page like this in a public library in Germany [...] with somewhat the same emotion as one stumbles on a mass grave' (178).

Spender highlights what he sees as the key features in the writings of Hitler and Goebbels: a paradoxical combination of 'most extreme disingenuousness with

---

[64] An objection raised against the *Weltbühne*'s Nazi-bashing both at the time and in retrospect is that it tended to underestimate their lethal seriousness. See Friedhelm Greis and Stefanie Oswalt, eds, *Aus Teutschland Deutschland machen: Ein politisches Lesebuch zur 'Weltbühne'* (Berlin: Lukas, 2008), 441–8.

[65] Stephen Spender, *European Witness* (New York: Reynal & Hitchcock, 1946), ix. Page references are given in brackets in the text.

[66] The Chancellery was located in Wilhelmstrasse in Berlin from 1875 to 1945. Spender must have read this excerpt from Goebbels's diaries in: Joseph Goebbels, *Vom Kaiserhof zur Reichskanzlei: eine historische Darstellung in Tagebuchblättern (Vom 1. Januar 1932 bis zum 1. Mai 1933)* (Munich: Eher, 1934). Another selection from the diaries was published immediately after the war: [Joseph Goebbels,] *Wie konnte es geschehen? Auszüge aus den Tagebüchern und Bekenntnissen eines Kriegsverbrechers*, ed. Max Fechner (Berlin: Dietz, 1945).

most extreme frankness'[67] (178), a streak of 'hysterical tension' (179) boding calamity even in moments of triumph, a 'fairy tale' or boys' adventure element and a prevalent strain of 'baseness, vulgarity, *Gemeinheit*' (181). However,

> [t]he most appalling and also the most enthralling thing about Goebbels's writing is its note of an impersonal confidence which certainly does not come quite from Goebbels himself. It comes, rather, from a feeling that he is supplying the evil which hundreds and thousands of Germans want.
>
> The power of this evil is that it goes back to a very deep source and is completely genuine. All Goebbels's later works are so tainted with propaganda [...] that it is difficult to calculate what is genuine and what is the 'party line'. One has to go back to Goebbels's first work, a novel called *Michael*, published in 1929, to discover that the real Goebbels is essentially the Nazi Goebbels, from the days when he was a rebellious student at Heidelberg to his dramatic death in the Reichschancellory in 1945. (181–2)

The rest of the chapter, much the larger part, is given to a reading of the novel in search for 'what is genuine' about it and what this reveals about 'the real Goebbels'. 'As a novel', Spender writes, '*Michael* does not exist, and even within its limits as an expressionist document, it scarcely rises above schoolgirlish journalism' (182). There is no lack of evidence for this, nor for what Spender dismisses as

> crude propaganda and [...] ideas which it is difficult to take any more seriously than Friedrich *Gundolf*, the famous Heidelberg professor, was disposed to take the young Goebbels's atrocious verse drama on the subject of Jesus, the writing of which is described in *Michael*. (184)

The play Goebbels actually did write was on the subject of Judas Iscariot and certainly never shown to Gundolf.[68] But more to Spender's point is what he finds to

---

[67] This, Spender writes, is most strikingly borne out by 'Hitler's famous remark that in deceiving the people it is necessary to tell the biggest lie possible, because the greater the lie the more avid they are to believe it. At first, it seems amazing that he should expose his own method so flagrantly, until on reflection one sees that it is itself an example of the method he recommends. If people will believe any lie, however large, they will also not believe any truth, however evident, if they do not wish to do so. And Hitler realized that nothing flattered his "masses" so much as talk about the "masses": for sometimes they liked to think of themselves as the great, great-hearted masses, and sometimes they liked as it were to be treated confidentially and separately, and to take the side of Hitler in despising the "masses". Thus Hitler and Goebbels played a double game with their followers' (178–9).

[68] The rumour that Gundolf was Goebbels's doctoral supervisor dies hard. As late as 2009, it is perpetuated in Toby Thacker's otherwise well-informed biography (Thacker, *Goebbels*, 18). Goebbels's personal connection to Gundolf was tenuous. He attended Gundolf's lecture course on 'The Founders of the Romantic School' in the summer semester of 1920. In the following winter semester Gundolf did not teach at all, and prior to 1925 he did not take on a single doctoral student. Goebbels's PhD supervisor was Gundolf's (Jewish) colleague Max von Waldberg (1858–1938). Lacking Gundolf's charisma, Waldberg was a dedicated doctoral adviser. The famous Gundolf lectured to packed auditoriums, but he shirked the laborious task of supervising theses and seems to have routinely referred candidates to the uncomplaining Waldberg. 'You want a good pair of boots, don't you?' Gundolf is reported to have said to one applicant before passing him on to Waldberg, 'If I were you I'd go to a solid shoemaker and not to Hans Sachs.' Gerhard Sauder, 'Positivismus und Empfindsamkeit: Erinnerung an Max von Waldberg', *Euphorion* 65 (1971), 368–408 at 380. The influence of Gundolf's views and style, however, is all too obvious in Goebbels's thesis on the obscure dramatist Wilhelm von Schütz (1776–1847), a very minor Romantic: Paul Joseph Goebbels, '*Wilhelm v. Schütz als Dramatiker: Ein Beitrag zur Geschichte des Dramas der Romantischen Schule*', unpubl. doctoral dissertation, Heidelberg, 1922. On Goebbels the *Germanist* see Helmut Neuhaus, 'Der Germanist Dr. phil. Joseph

be more 'genuine': 'the sense of defeat, of reaction against post-war decadence, of national humiliation' (184). Even closer to the 'real Goebbels' is 'something less dramatic and perhaps profounder': a 'sense of boredom with modern civilization' (184), an existential *ennui* rooted in the nineteenth century, 'in Baudelaire, Carlyle, Wagner and many other European artists' (184).

Michael, Spender claims, is a rogue offshoot of this tradition. The ennui of cultural discontent led artists like Baudelaire to a glorification of Satan. Spender finds the same trait in Goebbels's novel. When Michael exclaims in one of his spasmodic outbursts, 'I am a hero, a God, a Saviour!' Spender asks: 'What kind of God is this, one is left wondering. That Michael feels affinities with Satan is evident' (189). And: 'There is little doubt that Goebbels, if he had read more, would have recognized himself in the demoniac aspect of Byron, and in the Satanism of Baudelaire' (191).

The devil, of course, is inevitably waiting in the wings whenever there is mention of Faust. And, to be sure, in his declamations about the German national character Goebbels predictably hits upon the cliché of the 'Faustian' nature of the German soul. More explicitly, the devil is conjured up in the shadowy character of the Russian Communist Ivan Wienurowsky. Initially drawn to him, Michael soon comes to recognize him as his deadly antagonist. Ivan represents Russia, just as Michael stands for Germany.[69] Seeing an eschatological battle between the two nations as inevitable, Michael anticipates it in a hallucinatory vision of a fight between himself and Wienurowsky on the outskirts of the mining town that is Michael's new place of work:

> I seek green. I find nothing.
>
> [...]
>
> I rush through the streets, into the city and out again.
> Out! Out! Into the fields.
> But everywhere towers, chimneys, masts, factories!
> Grey upon grey and sunshine above.
> White sunshine.
> Am I then mad? I dream?
> Has the world gone under?
> Do no human beings live any more? Only beasts still? Black beasts? devils, devils in mines?
> Am I myself a beast, a black beast, a devil, a devil of the mines?
> I am as though whipped on by demons.
> One of them sits inside me, observing me, another, a second one also.
> Inexorable. Sharp. Critical.
> Ivan Wienurowsky!
> Now I have you, damnable dog!

Goebbels. Bemerkungen zur Sprache des Joseph Goebbels in seiner Dissertation aus dem Jahre 1922', *Zeitschrift für deutsche Philologie* 93 (1974), 398–416.

[69] The name Michael or Michel has long been in use as a personification of Germany or Germans. In fact, Germany's last offensive on the Western Front in 1918 was dubbed the 'Michael Offensive'.

You beast! You devil! You Satan!
Come here, I'll cast you out. I'll cast you out by your throat.
You will never down me. Never! Never!
We shall see who is stronger.

[...]

I run farther.
Farther! Farther!
To the end of the earth!
I fight with Ivan Wienurowsky! He is nimble as a cat.
But I am stronger than he.
Now I have him by the throat.
I thrust him to the ground.
He lies there!
With the death rattle, with blood running from his eyes.
Die, you carrion!
I tread upon his skull.
And now I am free!
The last opponent thrust to the earth.
The poison is out.
I am free!
I remain! I remain!
I will free myself. Free myself with my own strength.
I will show a way, strike a breach, be an example.
I throw myself on the ground and kiss the earth.
Hard brown earth.
German earth! (Spender, 193–4)

'It is difficult to imagine', Spender writes, 'that anyone can have thought *Michael* to be other than a book by a criminal written for criminals, and I do not really believe that anyone with the least enlightenment ever did think so' (183). Spender's point is that the author-protagonist shares this awareness of evil and deliberately embraces it:

The message of *Michael* is 'Evil, be thou my good,' but there is also an attempt to prove that evil is good because the German evil is made virtuous by destroying other evils.[70] (184–5)

---

[70] The worst of these 'other evils', according to the novel, is 'the Jew'. Michael, Spender writes, 'identifies himself with Christ', and 'Christ is the great enemy of the Jews, whom he drove out of the Temple with whips' (186). That Jesus himself was a Jew is no obstacle because Michael decides that 'Christ cannot have been a Jew. I do not have to demonstrate this scientifically. It is a fact' (186). Spender quotes the book's most extended anti-Semitic tirade ('for me the Jew is simply a physical malady [...] He is the abscess on the body of our sick people [...] Can the lungs make peace with the tuberculous bacilli?', 187) but omits to mention the narrative setting that occasions it and makes it, if anything, even nastier. Michael has taken time off his studies and gone to a small North Sea island in order to work on his play about Jesus Christ:

I would like to be a pastor on this island. Explain the Sermon on the Mount to simple people and let the world be the world.
    I have not seen any Jews as of yet. That is a true delight. (Goebbels, *Michael*, 44)

For Spender, this is where the book's documentary and even literary interest lies:

> [I]t confirms the intuitions of poets. A Macbeth who spoke for himself, without hav-
> ing the aid of [the] genius of Shakespeare would express just such thoughts as: 'Now
> I am free! The poison is out!' In fact, the thoughts of Goebbels with regard to Russia,
> are identical with those of Macbeth with regard to Banquo and his sons. As long as
> Russia exists, he must feel:
>
> Then comes my fit again: I had else been perfect;
> Whole as the marble, founded as the rock;
> As broad and general as the casing air:
> But now I am cabin'd, cribb'd, confined bound in
> To saucy doubts and fears. (194)

Thirty years after Henry Arthur Jones had found Macbeth to be the perfect image of
Germany, the perpetrators of the Holocaust fitted the part even better, Goebbels in
particular. Suicidal murderers of their own children, Goebbels and his wife made the
perfect latter-day 'dead butcher and his fiend-like queen' (*Mac.* 5.7.99). Intimations
of *Macbeth's* teeming multitude of demons and beasts seem to hover over the hallucinatory battle between Michael and his Russian adversary. And equally well might
the fevered dialogue of Macbeth and his Lady before they kill Duncan invoke the
infanticidal Joseph and Magda Goebbels in the Reichskanzlei on 1 May 1945. The
association is made all the more eerily vivid for the reader of Goebbels's novel who
notes, as Spender does, its mushy sentimentalizing of mothers and children[71]:

> MACBETH
>   I dare do all that may become a man;
>   Who dares do more is none.
> LADY MACBETH   What beast was't, then,
> That made you break this enterprise to me?
> When you durst do it, then you were a man;
> And to be more than what you were, you would
> Be so much more the man. [...]
>   I have given suck, and know
> How tender 'tis to love the babe that milks me;
> I would, while it was smiling in my face,
> Have plucked my nipple from his boneless gums
> And dashed the brains out, had I so sworn as you
> Have done to this. (*Mac.* 1.7.46–59)

Macbeth is under no illusion as to his utter culpability for his crimes. But does the
same hold true for Goebbels? The problem with Spender's reading is that he makes
this assumption and that he applies it not only to the Goebbels of 1945[72] but also

---

[71] 'Mother-love and love of children are invoked to gild the pill of undiluted evil' (Spender, 185).

[72] To the very last Goebbels, like Hitler, professed his belief to have acted for the greater good of
the nation. The farewell letter to his wife's son Harald (from her first marriage to the industrialist
Günther Quandt), written on 28 April 1945, concludes: '[M]ay you always be proud of having
belonged to a family which, even in misfortune, remained loyal to the very end to the *Führer* and his
pure sacred cause.' Quoted in Thacker, *Goebbels*, 300.

to the author of *Michael*. Thinking of him 'as a serpent's egg' (*JC* 2.1.32), Spender finds the Nazi criminal prefigured in the book. With the Nazi horror barely a year past and the devastations it caused before his very eyes, Spender's assumption is understandable. But neither the words 'Evil, be thou my good' nor the sentiment they express are to be found in the text, though one might be tempted, like Spender, to think that they should be. Given the Nazi leaders' glorying in their manipulative sway over the 'masses',[73] how could they *not* be aware of their own evil? And would not a denial of any such awareness, the assumption of some scrap of 'good faith' relieve the greatest evil-doers in modern history of guilt at least in some small part?

Macbeth might be thought of as a literary forebear of the Nazi Joseph Goebbels, but Michael, as Goebbels conceived him, most definitely is not. What Goebbels, the lapsed Catholic, showed in his fictional *alter ego* has nothing to do with sin or a commitment to evil. Nor does it derive from those nineteenth-century glorifica-tions of Satan which Spender introduces as a bridge to span the gap between Macbeth and modernity. Spender's argument becomes somewhat strained:

> However, whereas Baudelaire knew that Satan was Satan, but preferred Satan to respectability, the Nazis called Satan, Christ. In justice to the Nazis it may be said, though, that perhaps it requires more courage to put Satanic philosophy into action than to make it a literary fashion, and that perhaps, in order to put it into action, it had to pretend to be Christian. (191)

There is, it is true, a lot of talk about Christ in the novel[74] and some talk, mostly figurative, of the Devil, or 'devils'. Much of this derives from Michael's (and Goebbels's) admiration for Dostoevsky. But Spender not only overestimates its importance as an ideological pretence for the Nazis in general, he also misjudges its tenor and provenance in the novel. The aesthetic diabolism of the Romantic tradition[75] depended on the *frisson* of sin extracted from the residues of a Christian framework of belief. With this framework dissolving, the Satanic glamour of evil goes out of fashion. Authentic transgression now sails under a new flag, no longer within Christian coordinates but beyond them, no longer as a choice of evil over good but proclaiming a freedom beyond good and evil. Overlooked by Spender, this source of inspiration was all too obvious to Goebbels's earlier critic Heinz Pol when he lampooned Goebbels as flinging 'Nietzsche quotations like hand grenades'. Nietzsche, in one form or another,

---

[73] See n. 67 in this chapter.

[74] Christ is conscripted into Michael's particular brand of anti-Semitic, anti-Marxist national 'socialism': 'Christ is the genius of love, as such the most diametrical opposite of Judaism, which is the incarnation of hate. [...] The Jew is the lie personified. When he crucified Christ, he crucified everlast-ing truth for the first time in history. [...] The idea of sacrifice first gained visible shape in Christ. Sacrifice is intrinsic to socialism. [...] Distribute your property to the poor: Christ. Property is theft— so long as it does not belong to me: Marx. [...] Christ: the principle of love. Marx: the principle of hate' (Goebbels, *Michael*, 65–6).

[75] Charted in Mario Praz's classic study *The Romantic Agony*, trans. Angus Davidson (London: Oxford University Press, 1933), this tradition has more recently been examined by, among others, Peter A. Schock, *Romantic Satanism: Myth and the Historical Moment in Blake, Shelley, and Byron* (Basingstoke and New York: Palgrave Macmillan, 2003); cf. also Fernie, *The Demonic*.

was the indispensable *sotto voce* of all contemporary rightist bluster with any intellectual pretension.[76]

Goebbels's Michael is no exception. He pledges himself, not to immorality under a Christian dispensation but to a new morality deriving from Nietzsche, a *Herrenmoral* fuelled by fanatic nationalism.[77] Unlike Dostoevsky's Raskolnikov Michael never actually commits a crime; his murder of Wienurowsky is purely imaginary. Nor are his beliefs and ideas exposed to be perniciously false, as Raskolnikov's certainly are. On the contrary, they are emphatically endorsed both by the narrative itself and by the authorial dedication and preface. *Michael* is offered not as the progress of a guilt-ridden evil-doer but as the sorrows of a noble soul bearing up against a sea of troubles. The Shakespearean character haunting the book is not Macbeth; it is Hamlet.

VI PRINCE NARCISSUS

Michael has been aptly described as a patchwork of quotations 'wilfully torn from context'.[78] The hero's inner life is assembled like Frankenstein's monster from the 'disjected members' of a jumble of dead masters, Goethe, Nietzsche, Dostoevsky, and a host of others. In this chamber of distorted echoes, there is only one explicit pointer to Hamlet:

> Old Europe is going down the drain.
> Yes, it's a mad world! Thrift, Horatio! (86)

It is significant that Michael does not mention Hamlet at all but puts himself in his place. Instead of speaking about Hamlet, he speaks as Hamlet. In assuming this position, or pose, he follows a long line of predecessors, with Goethe and Nietzsche, his two most frequently cited authorities, prominently among them. Hegel sternly disapproves of this tradition in his *Aesthetics*, holding *Hamlet* responsible for what he finds most objectionable in modern tragedy, 'this personal tragedy of inner discord' which makes 'indecision and vacillation of character, and of the whole man' perversely 'the main theme of the entire drama'.[79] What Hegel objects to is not so much the play as the prince, the objectionable role model of a specifically modern character type.

In Goebbels's *Michael* we encounter the last spasms of this character's progeny. An obvious link to his predecessors is his rampant narcissism.[80] Diagnoses of narcissism in Hamlet take their cue from Freud's seminal essay on 'Mourning and

---

[76] See Aschheim, *The Nietzsche Legacy in Germany, 1890–1990, passim.*

[77] 'A true German is a God-seeker all his life' (23). 'The modern man is intrinsically a seeker of God, perhaps a Christ-man' (65). Michael's God is a Nietzschean God of strength: 'God helps the bold and strikes down the craven' (32).

[78] Bonwit, 'Michael', 196. Bonwit lists the writers, artists, and composers mentioned or quoted in the novel but misses the quotation from *Hamlet.*

[79] Hegel, *Aesthetics*, vol. 2, 1229. Cf. Introduction, section II.

[80] Narcissism rarely fails to appear in analyses of Goebbels's personality. It figures prominently in Peter Longerich's recent biography.

Melancholia' (1917). Freud identifies a 'process of regression [...] to narcissism'[81] as a key feature of melancholia, and most of the symptoms which he adduces are easily recognizable in Shakespeare's melancholy prince.[82] Long before Freud—and also long before 'narcissism' came into use as a psychological term—a disapproving commentator diagnosed Hamlet's sensitive German soul-sibling Werther as a

> Narcissus to whom everything he lays his hand on, everything that catches his eye becomes a mirror and who, in lovingly ogling himself, must needs become either totally effeminate or perish [...and] is a bad example for our German youth.[83]

Modern psychoanalytical critics have diagnosed Werther as an 'infantile personality', a narcissist seeking to fill his inner void with work and his yearning for an unattainable love object, a married woman.[84] One critic makes him something like a walking encyclopaedia of narcissistic symptoms such as megalomania, melancholia, extreme vulnerability, existential angst, restlessness, lack of drive, violent mood swings and loss of reality, prone to idealization, with an unfulfillable urge for creativity and a euphoric suicidal drive.[85]

All of this—and then some—can be found in *Michael*. 'I am', he exclaims, 'no longer a human being. I am a titan. A god!' (104). The text is riddled with such fits of egomania which are not intended as funny or, as in James Hogg's *Confessions of a Justified Sinner*, the ravings of a fanatic sociopath. Rather, they offer what the preface claims is a 'modest, silent mirror' (3), 'mirror' being perhaps more aptly chosen than the author intended. The world as the novel presents it is indeed nothing but a mirror for Michael's careening mental states, a supply of settings in which to reflect his overblown ego. Ordinary mortals may go on holiday by the sea or in the Alps. In *Michael* these modest activities erupt into staccato existential outbursts:

> There it rises, in the distance. Blue—gray.
>
> Infinity! That is the sea!
>
> Thalatta! I would like to shout.

---

[81] Sigmund Freud, 'Mourning and Melancholia', in *The Standard Edition of the Complete Psychological Works of Sigmund Freud*, 24 vols, ed. James Strachey, vol. 14: *On the History of the Psycho-Analytic Movement, Papers on Metapsychology and Other Works* (London: Hogarth Press, 1953), 243–58 at 250.

[82] Thus, when we read that the occasions giving rise to melancholia 'extend for the most part beyond the clear case of a loss by death, and include all those situations of being slighted, neglected or disappointed' (Freud, 'Mourning and Melancholia', 251) it is difficult not to think of Hamlet. 'Narcissism' may be well said to 'bleed [...] through [Hamlet's] suicidal meditations'. Marvin W. Hunt, *Looking for Hamlet* (New York and London: Palgrave Macmillan, 2007), 137.

[83] Wolfgang Menzel, *Die deutsche Literatur*, 2nd edn (Stuttgart: Franckh, 1836), 46; quoted in Georg Jäger, 'Goethes Werther im gesellschaftlichen Kontext', *Goethezeitportal*, <http://www.goethezeitportal.de/digitale-bibliothek/forschungsbeitraege/autoren-kuenstler-denker/goethe-johann-wolfgang-von/georg-jaeger-goethes-werther-im-gesellschaftlichen-kontext.html>, accessed 28 October 2014.

[84] Reinhart Meyer-Kalkus, 'Werthers Krankheit zum Tode. Pathologie und Familie in der Empfindsamkeit', in *Urszenen. Literaturwissenschaft als Diskursanalyse und Diskurskritik*, ed. Friedrich A. Kittler and Horst Turk (Frankfurt: Suhrkamp, 1977), 76–138 at 92, speaks of Werther's 'self-deification in a narcissistic mirror-world'.

[85] Gerhard Oberlin, *Goethe, Schiller und das Unbewusste. Eine literaturpsychologische Studie* (Giessen: Psychosozial-Verlag, 2007), 69.

That was how the Greeks greeted the ocean.
Thalatta! Thalatta! (41–2)

After more such clamour the passage ends with yet another exclamation, this time borrowed from Nietzsche: '*Flamme bin ich sicherlich!*'[86] Only the very best will do to illumine the depths of the hero's soul. His flight into the mountains is a veritable Ride of the Valkyries:

15 February
To the mountains! To the gods!
I must find myself.
Abandon everything. Cities, people, the world.
See nothing more, hear nothing more!
Stay alone in my loneliness!

18 February
I want to seek here!
Snow and eternity!
Mountains, friends!
You giant, you are my god!
You loom in majestic isolation.
Light! Let there be light!
I softly drink peace into my shredded heart.
Now I wish to work. Perhaps it will comfort me. (75)

Readers do well to refrain from drawing inferences about Shakespeare's personality from Hamlet's narcissism; and although the autobiographical roots of *Werther* are well known, no one would read the hero of the novel as a self-portrait of its author. In the case of Goebbels and his protagonist such differentiation would be pointless. The diarist-hero of *Michael* speaks with much the same voice as Goebbels the author-hero of his own diaries. Even more than the novel in letters, the novel-as-diary offers its writer-protagonist a stage to strut and fret before his own eyes: 'One must become the focal point around which everything turns' (69), Michael muses, only a few lines after impersonating Hamlet with 'Thrift, Horatio!' (68).

Michael's egomania is all the more obtrusive for his creator's inability to invest the hero's physical environment with any degree of reality.[87] The novel's shadowy supporting cast serve as mere cue-givers, the defenceless audience of Michael's grandiose orating. When dialogue occurs—and quite a bit does—it invariably turns on the life and opinions of the protagonist. Thus a typical conversation, which Michael soon turns into a monologic harangue, opens with Hertha Holk observing: 'You are an idealist, Michael, even in your attitude towards women' (29).

Michael's 'idealism' regarding women turns out to be that '[a] woman's task is to be beautiful and to bring children into the world' (31), and even Hertha calls this reactionary. But Hertha, like everyone else in the book who disagrees with Michael,

---

[86] 'Flame I am assuredly.' Nietzsche, *The Gay Science*, 67 ('Joke, Cunning, and Revenge. Prelude in German Rhymes', §62).

[87] It is symptomatic of Goebbels's lack of clarity that readers (Spender for one) are easily confused as to Michael's place of study. Heidelberg is initially only a stopover *en route* to Freiburg. This does not become clear until there is mention of the famous Freiburg Minster (10) and the open gullies 'running

is wrong, and the relationship with her must come to an end. 'You did not understand me' (81), he says in his farewell letter. And she confesses: 'My faith began to falter. We women cannot live without faith in a man' (80). 'You believed', he responds, 'my *Sturm und Drang* was terrible. You did not realize that my ways were not only new [...] but also higher than the ways of the golden mean' (81).

Belief is crucial not only at this stage, but in the novel as a whole. Without it, life is not worth living: 'Someone shall come!', Michael exclaims, meaning a saviour of the German nation: 'If I did not have the faith, I would not know how to go on with living' (31).[88] And:

> In my best hours, I believe in myself.
> It does not much matter what we believe, so long as we believe. (23)

This echoes a thought Goethe expressed (in a letter to Betty Jacobi in December 1773):

> Whether they believe in Christ, or Götz, or Hamlet, it's all the same; just let them believe in something. He who believes in nothing, despairs of himself.[89]

Boldly pairing Götz von Berlichingen, the hero of his own 'Shakespearean' history play, with Hamlet and Christ, Goethe's statement registers the height of his early Shakespeare enthusiasm. With its cheery panache, it is vintage *Sturm und Drang* and characteristic of the young Goethe, much favoured by Michael over the Privy Councillor Goethe of later years and much imitated in Michael's own effusions. For Michael to call a phase in his own life his *Sturm und Drang* is more than a manner of speaking. *Sturm und Drang*, Storm and Stress, was the exemplary youth movement in German literature and thus, in a Gundolfian perspective, in the growth of the German spirit. It stands for the perfect match of generational mood and historical moment, and the young Goethe was its paragon. What Goebbels thought the times needed was a new *Sturm und Drang*, a storm to scatter all that was rotten and debased and a hindrance to life. 'We look towards the day that will bring the storm wind' (3), the Preface ominously declares, and invokes the uncorrupted energies of the young, their 'spirit of resurrection'.[90]

If an old man, according to Goethe, 'is always a King Lear',[91] a young man may be said to be a Hamlet—not perhaps every young man, but most definitely the young Michael. Much as the novel is indebted to *Werther*, its hero seems even closer to the Shakespearean character who continually occupied Goethe during his

---

beside the pavements' (11), a distinctive feature of Freiburg's old town. Michael's move to Heidelberg does not occur until page 105: 'I have come to Heidelberg to turn a new leaf.'

[88] 'We young people will not perish as long as we believe in our mission' (33).

[89] *Der junge Goethe*, 5 vols, ed. Hanna Fischer-Lamberg (Berlin and New York: De Gruyter, 1999), vol. 1, 59.

[90] The latter phrase is in the 1923 version of the novel: Joseph Goebbels, '*Michael Voormann. Ein Menschenschicksal in Tagebuchblättern*' (1923), unpublished typescript, BA Koblenz, NL 118/127, fols. 1–256.

[91] 'Ein alter Mann ist stets ein König Lear!' Johann Wolfgang von Goethe, 'Zahme Xenien I', in *Sämtliche Werke. Briefe, Tagebücher und Gespräche*, vol. I, 2: *Gedichte 1800–1832*, ed. Karl Eibl (Frankfurt: Deutscher Klassiker-Verlag, 1988), 623.

Werther phase.[92] More scathing in his critique of contemporary life than Werther, Michael is also more embittered in his recurrent Hamlet-like loathing: 'It disgusts me' (41). 'The city and the people disgust me; I am degenerating here' (75). Political pamphlets fill him with loathing: 'I am deeply disgusted at the thought of them' (88); and loathing is typically linked to a sense of failure and indecision:

> I am nauseated by every printed word. [...]
> 　Sometimes I sit around for hours, indolent and undecided, doing nothing, thinking nothing. Then again, I am haunted by a thousand devils, I forge plan upon plan.
> 　But I do not begin to carry out any of them. (91)

In a fit of Hamletian self-reproach he exclaims: 'Oh, you cowardly soul! I laugh at myself. Then I rage again, hatred, anger, fury! I bang on the walls, I punch myself. I curse life' (79).

Unlike Hamlet, though much like Werther, Michael waxes tearfully sentimental over children and especially mothers: 'Mother! Most beautiful word! / Mother! Good Mother! / I have nothing, only a mother!'[93] But unlike Werther,[94] Michael shares Hamlet's reverence for an idealized father figure. Although the old in general are useless and corrupt and Michael places all hope for redemption in the young, the redeemer is a figure of paternal authority. This is the Führer who puts in cameo appearances as the orator, the 'prophet'. Michael encounters him twice in the novel, and on both occasions, like Coleridge's ancient mariner, he 'holds him with his glittering eye'. The conversion is instantaneous: the disciple is enthralled at first sight.[95] Hertha Holk's mysterious grey-green eyes are eclipsed by the 'two blue stars' (124) of the prophet's eyes.[96]

The personal is political. To some extent this is, of course, true of Werther.[97] But it is more crucially true of *Michael*. While Werther agonizes first and foremost over

---

[92]　Muschg, 'Deutschland ist Hamlet', as cited in Introduction, section II: 'From early on, Hamlet must have eclipsed all other works of Shakespeare for [Goethe]. [...] In the year following the Hamburg performance [of Hamlet by the famous actor manager Friedrich Ludwig Schröder] Goethe began writing *Wilhelm Meister's Theatrical Mission* in which he meant to show his vocation as the German Shakespeare and to make the engagement with Hamlet the turning point in Wilhelm's career. [...] That Wilhelm himself plays the lead character and the staging of Hamlet changes his life [...] underscores the fateful significance for his own development which Goethe ascribed to this drama.'

[93]　Goebbels, '*Michael Voormann*', BA Koblenz, NL118/127, fols. 1–256.

[94]　M. D. Faber, 'The Suicide of Young Werther', *Psychoanalytical Review* 60 (1973), 239–76 at 258, psychoanalyses Werther's antagonism towards society as 'hostility toward the father'.

[95]　Cf. Chapter 2, section I, Edgar Salin's first encounter with Stefan George.

[96]　The translation fails to capture the—now obsolescent—compound *Augenstern* in the German original, which combines the notion of starlike eyes with 'the apple of one's eye'. A song known to every German at the time was '*Puppchen, du bist mein Augenstern*' (1913; 'Dolly, you are the star in my eye') by the operetta composer Jean Gilbert (pseudonym of Max Winterfeld, 1879–1942).

[97]　Georg Lukács's 1936 essay 'Die Leiden des jungen Werther' ('The Sorrows of Young Werther', in *Goethe and His Age*, trans. Robert Anchor [London: Merlin Press, 1968], 35–49) set the tone for subsequent Marxist readings of the novel, particularly in East Germany, which saw Werther as the 'representative of a "progressive bourgeoisie" in the "revolutionary phase" of its early ideological and economic development'. Jürgen Scharfschwerdt, 'Werther in der DDR. Bürgerliches Erbe zwischen sozialistischer Kulturpolitik und gesellschaftlicher Realität', *Jahrbuch der Deutschen Schillergesellschaft* 22 (1978), 235–76 at 240. Such readings find support in the controversy over *Werther* among Goethe's contemporaries. See Jäger, 'Goethes Werther im gesellschaftlichen Kontext', 1.1.

Durchbrechender Michael

Figure 4.4. Fidus, 'Durchbrechender Michael'. Reproduced by permission of Hessisches Hauptstaatsarchiv.

the unattainable married Lotte, and the stifling restraints of society as well, Michael's personal predicament is always directly linked, indeed identified with the predicament of the downtrodden nation. His fate, as the subtitle announces, is a German fate; it is the fate of Germany: 'I suffer for a poor, errant, lost nation' (87).

If Shakespeare's hero proclaims himself to be 'Hamlet the Dane' (*Ham.* 5.1.237) Goebbels's ersatz Hamlet is emphatically Michael the German.[98] This is corroborated by the, to my knowledge, only artistic offshoot of Goebbels's novel, a print by the artist Fidus (pseudonym of Hugo Reinhold Karl Johann Höppener, 1868–1948) which celebrates the Nazi takeover in 1933 in the image of a Michael heroically breaking his chains (Figure 4.4). A minor Symbolist and proponent of nudism and Germanic light-and-sun mysticism, Fidus had become an enthusiastic supporter of the Nazis after hearing a speech by Goebbels at the *Sportpalast* in 1930 and joined the Nazi Party in 1932.[99] His 'Durchbrechender Michael' (Michael breaking

---

[98] See n. 69 in this chapter.

[99] As an artist Fidus found little favour with the Nazi leadership. Fidus's portrait of the Führer was rejected by Hitler himself as disgusting. In 1937 his work was classified as 'degenerate'. See Janos Frecot, Johann Friedrich Geist, and Diethart Kerbs, *Fidus, 1868–1948* (Munich: Rogner & Bernhard, 1972), 202.

through) provides a happy sequel to the novel's tragic ending, somewhat like the Hamlet of the 1778 *Sturm und Drang* adaptation who manages to break the prison walls of Denmark and survive the play.[100]

We have seen that, contrary to prediction, the German Hamlet did survive into the Wilhelminian era, and Hamlet's disaffection with the boorishly festive court of Denmark became an emblematic embodiment of the intellectual alienated by the complacent philistinism of the newly-grand Reich founded in 1871. Under the altered circumstances of the Republic, Goebbels's Michael—as derivative of Nietzsche's anti-Wilhelminian Hamlet as he is of Goethe's *Sturm und Drang* hero Werther—has a mission of Nietzschean 'great politics'.[101] 'I am in the process of demolishing the old world of faith in me. I shall raze it totally. Then I shall build a new world' (23). Nothing less than an 'assault on all altars' (86) will do because '[t] his system is overripe for destruction' (91). A national revolution is called for, one that it would be wrong to call 'conservative' because it 'wants Germany's future, not the restoration of a shattered past' (92). Apocalyptic in tone as well as message, the words of the blue-eyed beer hall messiah 'boom like the Last Judgment' (83). And the millennial telos of Michael's yearnings is undiluted Stefan George:

> The ranks fill up, an army arises,
> A nation, a community.
> Thought binds us [...]
> And thus we shall give shape to the new Reich. (78)

With the times out of joint and the state rotten, Michael only wants to set things right and take revenge. The mono-drama of his quest for personal and national salvation is clearly also a drama of revenge: vengeance for the 'shame peace' of Versailles, vengeance for the 'stab in the back' dealt to Germany's unvanquished armed forces by serpent politicians who 'now wear[s] [the] crown' (*Ham.* 1.5.40).

VII COURTING DEATH

Stephen Spender found *Michael* to be proof of an unbroken continuity in Goebbels's mindset from his student days to his death (182). Heinz Pol, in his *Weltbühne* review, diagnosed the novel as pure Nazism. But while both are right in finding Nazi ideology in the published text of 1929, it is non-existent in its predecessor, the unpublished '*Michael Voormann. A Human Fate on Diary Pages*'. This was completed in 1923, the year when Goebbels met Hitler, the epiphanic encounter in the beer hall which the 1929 version depicts so glowingly. Goebbels revised the text in 1928 when the Nazi Party underwent a temporary downturn of fortune on its rise to power.[102] At that point fully embarked on his Party career, Goebbels subjected the novel to thoroughgoing ideological streamlining. The *Michael* of

---

[100] [Friedrich Ludwig Schröder,] *Hamlet, Prinz von Dänemark. Ein Trauerspiel in sechs Aufzügen. Zum Behufe des Hamburgischen Theaters* (Hamburg: Heroldsche Buchhandlung, 1778), 128.

[101] See Chapter 1, section VI.   [102] Michel, *Vom Poeten zum Demagogen*, 126.

1929 exudes Nazi dogma page after page, while its predecessor, though fervently patriotic, sounds a much more diffuse mix of anti-capitalism, millenarian hope and Nietzschean overcoming. A crucial difference is indicated by the shift from 'human fate' to 'German fate' in the subtitle. While the Michael character of 1929 wants to bring salvation to Germans, the 1923 Michael wants to save the whole human race, even—at least not expressly excluding—Jews.[103] 'When I redeem myself, I redeem humanity', he declares in 1923.[104] In 1929, this becomes: 'When I redeem myself, I redeem my people' (54). The emphasis shifts from *Mensch* (human being; 'man' as species) to 'German' and *Mann* ('man' as opposed to woman, but more emphatically opposed to 'weakling'). The revised text adds the adjective 'German' whenever possible, forty-nine times in all. In 1923 Michael goes to see a performance of Hebbel's Jewish tragedy, *Herod and Mariamne*. In 1929 the play is 'Aryanized', but everything else, including the set, remains the same: 'I saw Hebbel's *Die Nibelungen* in a theater, with red lights and a warm-blue background, measured gestures and restrained ardor in style and language' (67).[105]

The new humanity of the 1923 version, much in line with the Expressionist quest for a 'New Man',[106] even has room for transnational cooperation, especially with Russia, the nation Goebbels admires for being the least American, i.e. least liberal-capitalist-technified in Europe. In the 1929 version, the German Michael and the Russian Ivan 'stand as relentless opponents, facing one another' (122); in 1923 they 'stand facing one another/ each other as equal partners'. 1929 presages the Second World War; 1923, a utopia of world peace:

1929:	1923:
Armed to the teeth, for it is the ultimate struggle!	Both shall give and both shall take.
	In both lies the future.
Pan-Slavism! Pan-Germanism!	In me, too, Iwan Wienurowsky!
Who shall win the future?	You do not believe in me.
No, I am not an apostate. I believe in us, in Germany!	All the more firmly do I believe in myself.
	I live and will live!

---

[103] Michel, *Vom Poeten zum Demagogen*, 130, argues that in 1923 Goebbels still had to avoid alienating Jewish publishers as well as his 'half-Jewish' girlfriend Else Janke. In 1928 both considerations no longer applied. On Janke's objecting to Goebbels's anti-Semitism, see Longerich, *Joseph Goebbels*, 47. Wambach (*Es ist gleichgültig, woran wir glauben . . .*, 4) plausibly argues that Goebbels would hardly have made Judas the hero (!) of his play *Judas Iscariot* (1918) if he had been a full-blown anti-Semite at the time. And before his fateful encounter with Hitler, Goebbels was not above scatological Nazi baiting: '*If I but see a swastika, / I feel the urge to make caca*' (*Seh ich nur ein Hakenkreuz, krieg ich schon zum Kacken Reiz*), quoted in Reuth, *Goebbels*, 38.

[104] Goebbels, *Michael Voormann*, BA Koblenz, NL118/127, fols. 1–256.

[105] Both changes are noted by Michel, *Vom Poeten zum Demagogen*, 128–9.

[106] On the idea of the 'New Man', see Walter H. Sokel, *The Writer in Extremis: Expressionism in Twentieth-Century German Literature* (Stanford, CA: Stanford University Press, 1959), 141–91. On Goebbels's engagement with the Expressionist search for the 'New Man', see Ulrich Höver, *Joseph Goebbels: ein nationaler Sozialist* (Bonn and Berlin: Bouvier, 1992), 41–6. Michel, *Vom Poeten zum Demagogen*, 84–5, points out that the poems in *Michael* are far too conventional to qualify as Expressionism. But see Goebbels, *Michael*, 62: 'We people of today are all expressionists.'

1929:	1923:
The Reich will come amid pain and suffering!	Cross swords?
	Put up your sword, Iwan Wienurowsky!
The world today has good reasons to despise that which pretends to be Germany.	United we will go into the future!
	Into the coming millennium![107]
We believe in ourselves all the more powerfully. We are here! We young men live, and we shall cross swords with all enemies of our kind, fighting for the future.	
When we come to ourselves again, the world shall tremble before us.	
The globe belongs to he who takes it.	
(122–3)	

The published *Michael*, then, may still represent 'the real Goebbels' (Spender, 182), yet this is definitely not the 'rebellious student at Heidelberg' (Spender, 182) but to a great extent already the Nazi *Gauleiter* of Berlin or, as Pol calls him, 'the dictator of Nollendorfplatz'. The propaganda in the published novel virtually bursts its narrative seams. The 1923 text by and large manages to maintain the form of a fictional diary. The 1923 *Michael Voormann* is—preposterous as it sounds—a better book, or shall we say: a slightly less bad book.

In both versions, the economy (*die Wirtschaft*) is to blame for everything, more specifically the capitalist profiteers running it. They are the target of Michael's Hamletian 'Thrift, Horatio!' Schlegel's *Hamlet* translation renders this passage as '*Wirtschaft, Horatio!*', a phrase that became nearly proverbial in German, while the word *Wirtschaft* in the meaning of 'thrift' has virtually disappeared. Rendered back into English, Michael is thus saying: 'The economy, Horatio!' This connects with what precedes it:

> The people are out in the streets, rioting and demonstrating.
> The lords and masters are at the conference table, calmly finishing their game. (68)

The passage is identical in both versions but the identity of 'the fine gentlemen' and their gambling for money are given a stridently anti-Semitic slant in the revised version:

> Money is the standard of value used by liberalism. [...] Money makes the world go round! A dreadful statement when true. [...] Money—Jew. The thing and the person, they belong together.
> Money has no roots. It exists above the races. It gradually eats its way into the sound organisms of the nations, slowly poisoning their creative strength. (114)

Michael's outrage at the Claudiuses of the Republic, though just as vehement in the 1923 version, is much less ideologically focused than in the 1929 text, his

---

[107] Near the end of the book, learning that Ivan has been shot by corrupt fellow Communists in the Soviet Union, Michael acknowledges: 'I am infinitely indebted to you.' The sentence is missing in the 1929 text (152).

discontent much closer to the *Weltschmerz* of his literary forebears Werther and the German Hamlet. It is to them that the novel looks for its death drive.

Shakespeare's Hamlet of Act 5 Scene 2, most critics concur, differs from the agitated, tormented melancholic of the earlier acts in that he has acquired at least a modicum of equanimity or acceptance, expressed in his calm resolve to 'Let be.'[108] On the penultimate page of his diary, Goebbels's Michael attains a similar condition of calm composure. In a letter to his mother, Michael takes stock of his life. Echoing Hamlet's 'providence in the fall of a sparrow' (*Ham.* 5.2.191–2), he concludes that '[n]othing happens for nothing on this earth' (128). Having found his way, having 'overcome', he now knows that 'life is worth living' and that '[w]e are not put into this world in order to suffer and die' (128). Despite the seemingly upbeat message, the fates are all too audibly rustling their wings. Though not exactly a suicide note, this is a farewell letter. Lest the reader miss it, the last sentence spells it out: 'Everything is a beginning, a consequence, or an end' (128).

In February 1930, only a few months after *Michael* was published, the 22-year-old Horst Wessel died in a Berlin hospital after being shot in the face, allegedly by a Communist attacker, some four weeks earlier.[109] Wessel, the son of a Protestant minister, was the leader of a Berlin SA troop particularly notorious for its brutality and a protégé of Goebbels. 'A young martyr for the Third Reich', Goebbels wrote in his diary on 23 February 1930 after learning of Wessel's death. Immediately recognizing the propaganda potential, Goebbels went about making Wessel the exemplary martyr of the Nazi movement, the central icon of its elaborate cult of the dead. The 'Horst Wessel Song', with lyrics by the martyr himself, later became something like Germany's second national anthem. The crazy heights of his glorification can be gauged in a pronouncement such as the following: 'How high Horst Wessel towers over Jesus of Nazareth—the Jesus who pleaded that the bitter cup might pass him by. How unattainably high all Horst Wessels stand above Jesus!'[110]

This goes a good deal farther than Goebbels was prepared to go in puffing up the hero of his novel. The label Michael ultimately arrives at to locate his political position is 'Christ-Socialism' (82). But Michael clearly points the way towards Horst Wessel. University drop-outs and would-be poets both, they trade the effete sphere of the intellect and mere 'words, words, words' for the manly domain of hard manual labour—the one breaking coal in the mines, the other breaking Communist skulls in the streets. Death in both cases is sacrificial (though certainly not in the case of Wessel's actual death); both die for the greater good—Christ-like—so that others may live.

---

[108] In the Second Quarto, but not in the Folio text, it concludes Hamlet's reflection on the 'special providence in the fall of a sparrow' (*Ham.* 5.2.191–5).

[109] The exact circumstances and motives of the attack have never been fully clarified. For a recent account of the case, see Daniel Siemens, *The Making of a Nazi Hero: The Murder and Myth of Horst Wessel* (London and New York: I. B. Tauris, 2013).

[110] *Der Brunnen—Für deutsche Lebensart* (ed. Frithjof Fischer) in its issue of 2 January 1934. Quoted in F. L. Schumann, *Hitler and the Nazi Dictatorship: A Study in Social Pathology and the Politics of Fascism* (London: Hale, 1936), 368.

But where the Michael of the 1929 version is the brother of Horst Wessel, his 1923 predecessor still bears some resemblance to the brother of all humanity whom screen-writer Erwin Gepard celebrated in his homage to Hamlet, everyone's 'best friend', the 'figure of universal empathy', companion 'to people of all nations'.[111] The more 'literary' Michael of 1923 is also a more troubled figure, the exact mirror of its struggling author, torn between grandiose self-delusion and abysmal self-doubt.

Suicide, though not literally occurring in the book, is still very much part of its mental landscape, both in its indebtedness to the suicidal Werther and the suicidal musings of Hamlet and in the hero's courting of sacrificial death. Though ostensibly accidental, Michael's death is as inevitable as Hamlet's and, given the identificatory relation between hero and author, a kind of suicide in effigy. For the young Goebbels, killing his literary doubles was a way to, as it were, have his narcissistic cake and eat it too: savouring the grand finale, he could still witness its effect on a chosen audience. This is the case at the end of Goebbels's most clearly confessional opus, the play *Heinrich Kämpfert*, in which the author's doppelganger lengthily extemporizes before downing his deadly potion. Too noble to bear 'the proud man's contumely' and 'the pangs of despised love' (*Ham.* 3.1.70–1), he wallows in a Hamletian brew of *Weltschmerz*, self-pity and gallows sarcasm.

Kämpfert, as his name indicates, has had to fight all his life.[112] A penniless student, seriously ill from overexertion, he has found employment in the aristocratic von Hermstädt household as the private tutor of the youngest son. He falls in love with the boy's sister, Else. Loving him also, she asks her widowed mother, the head of the family, for money to pay for medical treatment. The mother agrees on the condition that the lovers renounce any joint future and that Kämpfert formally beg for the money. Naturally, he would rather die than bend to the will of dowager Frau von Hermstädt:

> What Else will say!—Will she understand her Kämpfert?—I don't think so!—Ha, it would never have worked out anyway—never!—She will marry one of the fine gentlemen—(bitter:) Ha, ha, ha, yes, yes, one of the fine gentlemen—damn it, even now a devil grabs me when I think how he will touch her pure, holy body with his sleazy paws!—Just as well you won't have to see that, Kämpfert, it might drive you to murder! (Long pause) I will have another cigarette—my last one. (Lights a cigarette) Life was beautiful after all, despite the poverty, the hunger and the thirst, damned beautiful!—Damn it, here comes temptation again,—Kämpfert be strong—(he takes the glass) here's to you, death, you are my friend—here's to you, old pal—[113]

Dedicated 'To my youth!', the play records Goebbels's troubled relationship with Anka Stalherm, the model also for Michael's Hertha Holk. The hero's suicide is

---

[111] Behrens, Meinem besten Freunde—Hamlet, 286.

[112] *Kämpfer* is German for 'fighter'. To fight without surrender is also one of the central tenets of Michael's creed.

[113] Joseph Goebbels, '*Heinrich Kämpfert. Ein Drama in drei Aufzügen*', handwritten MS, BA Koblenz, NL 1118/114, fol. 1.

something like a literary blackmail note to his well-to-do sweetheart, whose financial support Goebbels detested but could not refuse.

Anka Stalherm is also the dedicatee of another literary suicide committed by the young author. 'Judas Iscariot, A Biblical Tragedy in Five Acts' does not feature the arch-villain of the Christian tradition but an idealist fighting for radical social reform.[114] Jesus, instead of striving for the same goal, postpones salvation to an indefinite later beyond, whereupon Judas betrays him. Judas is not, of course, interested in the money; he wants to replace Jesus as the liberator of his people. The ultimate outsider, Judas is yet another fictional persona in which the author indulged his need for tragic self-dramatization. The emotional need of the author virtually erupts on a page that contains the draft of a soliloquy in which the protagonist racks his brains over his plan to betray Jesus. Torn between resolution and hesitancy, he ends on a note of Hamlet-like self-contempt. Goebbels himself seems to have lost confidence at this point. The soliloquy begins with whole sentences in high, if hackneyed, rhetorical style; it peters out in a few sketchy notes: 'derision of himself, the author of plans, without tackling the execution'. And where the notes end the page is cluttered with manic repetitions of Anka's family name: Stalherm Stalherm Stalherm Stalherm Stalherm [...] (Figure 4.5).[115]

***

The heroic posturing of these literary suicides found a gruesome replication in the death scene in the Reich Chancellery on 1 May 1945. In between lay Goebbels's glory years, recorded on more than six thousand pages of diary, his ascent to the heights of his youthful dream of becoming 'a great man'.

Basking in his newly-won magnificence, Goebbels records one particularly gratifying event in the spring of 1933, a tea at the Ministry of Propaganda: 'All the stars present. [...] They all make a good impression. Feel at ease with us. Hitler delighted. A splendid afternoon.'[116] An incident that must have been a little damper at this otherwise perfect social occasion left no trace in the diary. It occurred when the Führer urged his neighbour at table 'to resume her film career in the service of the Reich'. When she replied that she did not play political roles, he assured her that this was no problem, adding gallantly that he could give a two-hour speech '"without anyone understanding a word of it. But you make a single gesture—and hundreds of thousands see it and understand it." "Oh," Asta Nielsen replied, "you mean this one?" and lifted her arm in a Nazi salute', whereupon 'Hitler's face turned stiff.'[117]

The scene, if it actually happened that way, recalls the impish subversiveness of her Hamlet. Nielsen also declined the offer made by Goebbels that same afternoon to head up a production company of her own. But she stayed on in Germany until

[114] Goebbels's positive portrayal of Judas is not without precedent. Wambach, *Es ist gleichgültig, woran wir glauben...*, 4 and 9–10, outlines an alternative nineteenth-century literary tradition in which Judas appears as a freedom fighter.

[115] Joseph Goebbels, *Judas Iscariot*, BA Koblenz, NL 118/117, fol. 1, 1457.

[116] *Die Tagebücher von Joseph Goebbels*, 27 vols, ed. Elke Fröhlich et al., pt. 1, vol. 2/III, ed. Angela Hermann (Munich: K. G. Saur, 2006), 160.

[117] Julie Allen, 'Tea with Goebbels and Hitler: Asta Nielsen in Nazi Germany', *Journal of Scandinavian Cinema* 2.3 (November 2012), 333–41 at 335.

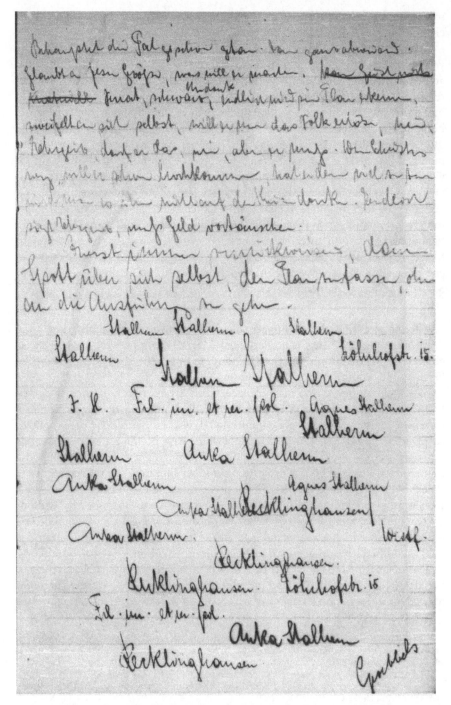

Figure 4.5. Manuscript page from Goebbels's *Judas Iscariot*. Reproduced by permission of Deutsches Bundesarchiv, Koblenz.

1937 and retained her German friendships throughout the war, which tainted her reputation in post-war Denmark.

Needless to say, the Hamlet of the Prussian State Theatre, Fritz Kortner, was not invited to tea with the new rulers. Nor was Jessner. He left Germany in 1933 and died in exile in Los Angeles in December 1945.[118] Kortner also went into exile and survived, though eleven members of his family did not. When he returned to Germany after the war, he shared the experience of other returnees: hostility from those who had stayed.

Goebbels's diary entry captures his thrill at having Germany's leading screen idols lined up under his roof. But what really made the afternoon so splendid was that Hitler was there to applaud it. Time and again in his diaries we find Goebbels craving the Führer's approval. In a passage of particularly frenetic filial devotion the diarist slips into Hamlet's words to Horatio; this time the words about his father (*Ham.* 1.2.187):

> He is a man, take him for all in all.
> (13 April 1926)[119]

The spell of this über-father would not be broken until another war had hatched still more millions and millions of ghosts.

---

[118] There apparently were thoughts among the US military administrators in Germany of giving Jessner a role in the rebuilding of the German theatre. Whether he would have been willing to take on such a role is not known.

[119] 'Er ist ein Mann, nehmt alles nur in allem.' *Die Tagebücher von Joseph Goebbels*, pt. 1, vol. 1/II, ed. Elke Fröhlich (2005), 73.

5

Little Otto

Carl Schmitt and the Moor of Venice

I GERMANY 1923

On or around 1 December 1923, Carl Schmitt, professor of public law at the University of Bonn, jotted this in his diary: '"Germany is Hamlet"—Oh, alas, not for a long time anymore.'[1] Three weeks after Hitler's only just barely foiled 'beer hall putsch' in Munich had once again demonstrated the fragility of the Weimar political system,[2] Carl Schmitt, the advocate of dictatorial decisionism, was invoking Shakespeare's notoriously indecisive prince as a figure of identification for his troubled country. Hyperinflation was at its peak, the price of a newspaper, as Schmitt notes on 9 December, a dizzying half trillion Reichsmark. Was this a time for Hamlet nostalgia? Clearly, it was strong decision-making, not melancholy brooding, that must save the tottering state. And strong decisions were at the heart of Schmitt's political creed. His 1922 treatise on the concept of sovereignty famously opens with: 'Sovereign is he who decides on the state of exception.'[3]

It is safe to assume, then, that Schmitt's sigh for a Hamlet-like Germany expressed no longing for Hamletian 'dithering' and 'blathering'.[4] Schmitt thought there was more than enough of that under the Weimar parliamentary system. Instead, quite contrary to the original, negative tenor of Freiligrath's 'Hamlet', his quoting of Freiligrath's famous opening line was to declare Germany's moral bankruptcy. It is Hamlet the noble soul, not Hamlet the procrastinator, whose passing

---

[1] Carl Schmitt, *Der Schatten Gottes. Introspektionen, Tagebücher und Briefe 1921–1924*, ed. Gerd Giesler, Ernst Hüsmert, and Wolfgang H. Spindler (Berlin: Duncker & Humblot, 2014), 499. Quotations from this edition are given (date; page number) in the text.

[2] The Munich putsch, known in Germany as the *Hitlerputsch*, was the first attempt by Adolf Hitler—along with Erich Ludendorff, the de facto commander in 1917/18 of the Imperial German Army, and other right-wing leaders—to seize power in Munich on 8 and 9 November 1923. The coup broke down in a shootout with police at Munich's Feldherrnhalle. Hitler was arrested and sentenced to a prison term. His harangues in court gained him nationwide publicity and his relatively commodious imprisonment gave him the leisure to write *Mein Kampf.*

[3] Schmitt, *Political Theology*, 5 (translation modified). The standard translation of German *Ausnahmezustand* would be 'state of emergency', which fails to capture Schmitt's distinction between 'normal/legal' and 'exceptional/extra-legal' states. Translator Schwab drops the *Zustand* ('state of') altogether rendering *Ausnahmezustand* as 'exception'. This seems somewhat too broad, extending the meaning well beyond the political.

[4] See Seamus Heaney's (self-)portrayal of Hamlet: Heaney, 'Viking Dublin: Trial Pieces', in his *North* (London: Faber and Faber, 1975), 23.

Schmitt laments. This becomes clear from the passage preceding the quotation, which is not about Hamlet at all. It is about Othello:

> Othello: the fate of man: he murders the civilization which adopted him out of mercy, out of loneliness; then he murders himself. A ridiculous fate in the eyes of a Romanic [person][5] as well as a Slav; the Romanic I don't understand because he thinks in institutions; the Slav I don't understand because he does not think in institutions. Man stands between the two. Ghastly situation. The consequence is jealousy. Black with jealousy; the constant homelessness. He marries an Italian girl. But that's not it; for Ludendorff's Germany had nothing noble such as Othello always retains; he went the way of suicide. (499)

Written in almost undecipherable shorthand,[6] Schmitt's diaries often display a kind of mental shorthand too. His associative leaps—the leap, for example, from Othello's Italian marriage to Ludendorff's Germany—are not always easy, or indeed possible, to follow. But the general drift is clear enough. Othello is noble, Ludendorff is not. The quartermaster general and, after Hindenburg, the most prominent representative of the Kaiser's army, Erich Ludendorff was also the most prominent figure in the militant ultra-right in the early 1920s, at a time when Adolf Hitler was only beginning to emerge from sectarian obscurity. Ludendorff is a contemptible relic of the *ancien régime*, as obsolete as the Kaiser himself. 'So Wilhelm II is still alive, […] Ludendorff is still alive', Schmitt notes in September 1923. 'Let's finally kill the dead.'[7] After the botched Munich putsch Ludendorff sank even lower in Schmitt's esteem. There is no trace of nobleness, nothing remotely tragic in this failure.[8] This, by contrast, evokes the tragic failure of Hamlet and begets the thought of a lost Hamlet Germany towering morally over Ludendorff Germany.

Hamlet, however, appears as just an afterthought; Schmitt is much more interested in Othello. From 1921 to 1924 his diaries contain just two references to Hamlet but over sixty to the Moor of Venice. Othello, not Hamlet, symbolizes 'the fate of man', more specifically the fate of one particular man: Carl Schmitt. 'Othello haunts me' (26 November 1921; 22), he writes to Kathleen Murray, his Irish-Australian paramour. Another letter to her reveals this in phantasmagoric detail:

> After my lecture […] I couldn't help but read Othello. Each word was still alive and I felt no difference between the English and the German text. I trembled as in the theatre that day and thought I was sitting next to you; I reached for your hand. Listen:

---

[5] Romanic: *der Romane*. The word is highly unusual in German and almost impossible to render in English. Schmitt uses it analogously with *der Slave*, the Slav, as a collective descriptor of the people (French, Italian, Spanish, Portuguese) that speak a Romance language, to whom he ascribes a common ethnic character.

[6] Schmitt practised a personal variant of 'Gabelsberger' shorthand. Reinhard Mehring dedicates his biography of Schmitt to 'Hans Gebhardt (1925–2013), the only reader of Schmitt's shorthand'. Reinhard Mehring, *Carl Schmitt: A Biography* (2009), trans. Daniel Steuer (Cambridge and Malden, MA: Polity Press, 2014).

[7] Schmitt, *Der Schatten Gottes*, 482.

[8] Although twenty people died in the shootout at the *Feldherrnhalle*, Ludendorff was later acquitted of all charges because of his merits in the war.

That handkerchief did an Egyptian to my mother give, She was a charmer. There's magic in the web of it etc. and the terrible line: *When I love thee not, Chaos is come again, where shall Othello go?* It is all still alive. What is time. Worse than you, I have no sense of time. Anyone who can be so lonely has no sense of time. Time is a social convention. I am lonely without you. Loneliness used to be my friend. She gave me intensity and acuity. Now she came to me draped like a black funeral horse, saying: Once, when I was your friend, you were not lonely, now you are dying of longing. Where is your new lady friend? I was always there when you called me. Your new friend comes and leaves again. Don't call me anymore, go to your new friend! I answered: You are a stern mistress, but I ask you not to speak badly of my new lady friend: I love her more than anything, even more than you; are you such an ordinary woman as to rail at the mere thought of another woman? My lady friend (not new friend, eternal friend, I cannot imagine a time when she was not my friend, neither in the past nor in the future. I have no sense of time anymore since I fell in love with her). My lady friend is beautiful and a lively child, but she knows you too and you are no stranger to her. She can become your friend too if you understand her. That calmed her, seemingly. She becomes friendlier. Many merry and gaudy people arrive, Twine the Tailor who tells her mother:[9] I have always had great success with women, but the greatest on Monday, the 2nd of January 1922, the year of our lucky number; a lovely Australian, and a pretty candidate to boot, did not want to go home because I was there, and was sad to death when everyone wanted her to leave: A Truffaldino laughed at him.[10] Leandro spun a highly romantic yarn saying: She loves you more than me because you are a tailor. She doesn't love me because I am a romantic and without irony.—Exam topic. Twine the Tailor bleats: This is the difference. Your royal highness is the topic for an exam; I am a topic for enthusiasm. Papageno laughs at Tamino and tells him: Prince, you are not even an exam topic and have made less of an impression than I have with my flute. Suddenly she is silent. Othello comes and everything disappears.—Blue haze before his great pain, his black tragedy.

Do you still hear me, *Countess?* Are you still there? Tell me that you love me.

I kiss your eyes and your heart. My heart throbs with love and longing for you as loudly as you have ever heard it throb. *God bless you, K., a thousand blessings on you, dear heart*—Carl. (19 January 1922; 31)[11]

II TROUBLED PROFESSOR

Carl Schmitt kept a diary—at times several diaries—throughout most of his life. Their publication—four volumes to date, more in the offing[12]—has revealed a deeply conflicted personality, subject to mood swings of almost bipolar intensity, a

---

[9] 'her mother': Kathleen Murray's mother.

[10] 'A Truffaldino laughed at him': 'him' = Twine the Tailor = Carl Schmitt.

[11] The italicized lines are in English in the original.

[12] Carl Schmitt, *Tagebücher Oktober 1912 bis Februar 1915*, ed. Ernst Hüsmert, 2nd edn (Berlin: Akademie-Verlag, 2005); *Die Militärzeit 1915–1919. Tagebuch Februar bis Dezember 1916. Aufsätze und Materialien*, ed. Ernst Hüsmert and Gerd Giesler (Berlin: Akademie-Verlag, 2005); *Tagebücher 1930 bis 1934*, ed. Wolfgang Schuller and Gerd Giesler (Berlin: Akademie-Verlag, 2010); *Der Schatten Gottes*, ed. Giesler et al. (2014).

man plagued by anxiety and self-doubt, veering between extremes of elation and despair.

The outward course of his life gives little indication of this. Awarded a *summa cum laude* law doctorate at barely twenty-two (1910), Schmitt weathered the Great War in the security of a military office job in Munich, where his duties included observing left-wing periodicals and other potentially subversive publications. Boringly undemanding, the job allowed him time off to write his habilitation thesis and lecture at the (then German) University of Strasbourg. He was transferred to the headquarters of the Munich military administration at the end of the war and experienced at close quarters some of the violent unrest during the short-lived Bavarian Soviet Republic.[13] He was discharged from military service in 1919 and taught at Munich's commercial college for the next two years. His first appointment to a regular university professorship took him to the small university at Greifswald, a former Hansa town on the Baltic coast. Within a year, an offer from Bonn delivered him from 'the arctic fields of Pomerania' (5 October 1921; 10) and, at only thirty-three, took him to the top of the academic ladder: a chair at one of Germany's most prestigious universities. Schmitt's swift ascent was owed to a steady output of high-profile publications that established his reputation as both a legal scholar and a political writer with strong, anti-parliamentarian views and a gift for polemics and brilliant abbreviation (Figure 5.1).

But while his professional fortunes were on the rise, his inner life, as recorded in the diaries, seems to have been in a permanent state of emergency. Like Dr Jekyll he is afflicted with the 'profound duplicity of life',[14] a morbid awareness of the demons lurking beneath the surface of everyday normality. Interrupting a string of thoughts on Othello, he bursts out: 'What am I: a veil embroidered with rationalist arabesques and condictions[15] over an irrational abyss' (March 1924; 527). Straining against the fetters of his middle-class existence, his nervous sensitivity constantly hovers on the edge of breakdown:

> At 8 o'clock I was ready to commit suicide, to sink into the world of night and into silence in calm superiority. Then I thought of nothing but pursuing a career in the world. A few hours later I did not care about anything and wanted to become a soldier. This inconstancy is driving me mad; what shall I do? In an hour, I will shoot myself out of fury over my own triviality. (6 September 1915)

There is an element of self-dramatization here, but nothing like the hollow posing we find in the diaries of Joseph Goebbels. Schmitt's lower-class Catholic background, not dissimilar to that of Goebbels, begot a comparable blend of ambition and self-doubt, resentment and grovelling. Schmitt's fluctuating anti-Semitism, incongruously paired with numerous Jewish friendships, seems to at least partly derive from his social inferiority complex. Schmitt, however, is at least aware of, and capable of analysing, his moral deformations:

---

[13] By his own account, this involved witnessing an officer being shot in immediate proximity.

[14] Robert Louis Stevenson, *Strange Case of Dr Jekyll and Mr Hyde*, ed. Richard Dury (Edinburgh: Edinburgh University Press, 2006), 58.

[15] Condiction (*Kondiktion*)—legal term: claim for the restitution of a thing or payment.

Figure 5.1. Carl Schmitt in 1930. Photo by permission of ullstein bild.

What a jumble of things I am! A money-grubbing, ambitious serveling; a lazy, resigned Schmitt, a solitary, proud Roman, a vain, anxious to please sensualist; all poise and dissolute; cruel and compassionate; hard and soft; believing and unbelieving.[16]

Incessantly 'brooding over his problematic character',[17] Schmitt labels himself as 'Proletarian' and even intends to write a character study of the type with opportunism as the essential trait. 'The Proletarian, or, the Plebeian', he notes, '[h]is instinct: to creep or to strut, as the situation demands. He is *ad alterum*',[18] i.e. he adapts to every other person he encounters.

As one of the editors of Schmitt's diaries remarks: 'I know of no contemporary of Schmitt—nor of anyone today—whose written records reveal the psychological state of their author so unsparingly as these diaries.'[19] The area of Schmitt's private life most unsparingly disclosed is his sexual obsessions, the tribulations of a man 'driven by erotomania'.[20] 'Often bursting with sexual craving' (27 February 1923; 164),

---

[16] This is from Schmitt's unpublished diaries 1925–29 (39ʳ). See n. 62 in this chapter.
[17] Mehring, *Carl Schmitt*, 67.
[18] Schmitt, *Die Militärzeit 1915–1919*, 124. See Mehring, *Carl Schmitt*, 67.
[19] Wolfgang Schuller, 'Nachwort', in Schmitt, *Tagebücher 1930–1934*, 457–67 at 464.
[20] Gerd Giesler and Wolfgang H. Spindler, 'Einführung', in Schmitt, *Der Schatten Gottes*, xi–xxii at xiii. The term 'erotomania' seems justified not so much by excessive sexual activity as by the anxious intensity with which Schmitt experienced and observed his sexual drives.

he guiltily notes his 'ejaculations'. 'I sneak from a conference so horny I have to bite my fingers', he records in November 1912.[21]

Earlier that year, he met the first love of his life, Carita, a Spanish cabaret dancer, who turned out to be the Serbian aristocrat Pabla von Dorotić but was, ultimately, no aristocrat at all. The daughter of a tinsmith,[22] Carita, or Pabla, was the classic femme fatale and the answer to the young jurist's dreams of Bohemian abandon. He fell for her head over heels, idolizing her in long passionate love letters whenever they were apart. Marriage had to be postponed when her passport mysteriously disappeared—and with it the evidence of her humble origins and real date of birth (1883, not 1888 as she pretended). But under wartime conditions an exceptional licence was granted and the marriage eventually went ahead in February 1915. Such was Schmitt's devotion to 'Cari' that he added her name to his on the title-page of his publications. His brilliant dressing-down of *Political Romanticism* (1919) appeared under the name Schmitt-Dorotić.

Yet even in the heyday of his infatuation Schmitt was obsessed with jealousy, and it is this obsession that cues Othello's first appearance in his diaries: 'What jealousy means: the other can be what oneself is not, that is, faithful. Othello was not faithful' (26 October 1912; 27). The remark occurs amidst drafts of gushing love letters to Cari and reflections on the unfathomable nature of desire:

> Why is a man in love anti-social when he faithfully clings to one woman and fears […] to lose her, whereas the normal healthy guy who tags along with everything, goes to war merrily and conducts his career by the book is always polygamous, enjoying paid whores *and without self-destructive jealousy at all?*' (26 October 1912; 27, italics original)

Schmitt must have found something of both types in himself, the vulnerably faithful lover and the robust philanderer being not so much separate characters as two sides of his own personality. The clinging single-mindedness of devotion is required for jealousy to reach its full self-destructive power, a single-mindedness that isolates the lover not only from his social environment but ultimately from the beloved as well and encloses him in the solitary confinement of his passion. But the mind of the philanderer is required for jealousy to arise in the first place. By proverbial logic 'it takes one to know one' and only the unfaithful can suspect unfaithfulness in others. This is why Othello must have been unfaithful. The seed of his towering jealousy is his knowledge of unfaithfulness in himself.

Not until November 1921 does Othello return to 'haunt' the diarist (26 November). But although he has been long absent and now becomes suddenly ubiquitous, the continuity in Schmitt's view of the character is striking. Under 'reflections on Othello' he notes: 'Psychologically the reflex of his own unfaithfulness' (March 1924; 527).[23] Despite the lack of written traces between 1912 and

---

[21] Quoted in Giesler and Spindler, 'Einführung', xiii.

[22] The church register of the Viennese suburb of Gumpendorf names as her parents Johann Dorotić, tinsmith from Agram (Zagreb), and his wife Johanna, née Schachner, from Regensburg (Gerd Giesler, personal communication).

[23] The same thought occurs in an entry of January 1923 (430): 'Betrayed betrayer. (There are no betrayers other than betrayed betrayers and no betrayers other than the betrayed; laws of reciprocity).' Recurring also is the idea that a man's desire to dominate a woman is rooted in his own inner void. Cf.

1921 Othello seems to have never been lost from Schmitt's mind, the gap of years attesting latency rather than absence. Schmitt was a regular writer but also a regular reader and re-reader of his diaries; and when Othello returns, Schmitt's original insight into the nature of his predicament is taken up and fans out in many directions.

By this time, the autumn of 1921, his great love for Cari had turned sour. Schmitt eventually saw what others had seen or at least suspected all along: that he had been duped by an impostor. Whether his wife was also unfaithful does not emerge from the diaries but is strongly suggested in Alice Berend's novel *The Lucky Fellow*, a *roman-à-clef* published in 1919. Schmitt figures as the unworldly, innocent scholar Professor Böckelmann, who is brazenly cuckolded by his young wife Marianne.[24] The Schmitts were by now living separately with Cari still occupying their Munich flat. He was trying to not just divorce her but have the marriage annulled by a Canon court. Under the Catholic dispensation, this would have been the only way for him to remarry.

For in the meantime a new star had entered his orbit: Kathleen Murray, whom he likes to address as 'Countess', a devoutly Catholic Australian student of Irish descent. Schmitt goes to church but also to bed with her and helps her write a doctoral dissertation in German on Taine and English Romanticism.[25] Her supervisor is Ernst Robert Curtius of the University of Marburg, a prominent scholar, later famous, with connections to the George Circle[26] and an acquaintance of Schmitt.[27] Again, Schmitt is head over heels in love, gushing in his adoration, consumed with desire, idolizing Kathleen's beauty but repelled by her vulgarity, extolling her goodness but suspicious of being exploited again, plagued by recurrent fits of jealousy.

Although marriage is made impossible because of Schmitt's failure to obtain the annulment of his marriage to Cari, the lovers pledge their troth to one another. But once her doctorate is completed, 'the Countess'—unlike her Yeatsian namesake unwilling to jeopardize her soul—sails for Australia, a trail of desperate love letters following her from port to port. The correspondence continues even after Schmitt

26 October 1912; 27: 'Whence the urge to enslave a girl, to dominate her completely [...]?' Most men, Schmitt asserts, would jump to the opportunity of having the woman they love hypnotized, and would reveal their 'destructive [...] lust for power' in the commands they would give their helpless beloved. 'But what is the deeper meaning of this preposterous desire? Perhaps [it is] only *an expression of their own emptiness*, their insecurity, [...] the need to compensate [for] their *inner void and hollowness* [...]' (italics added).

[24] Alice Berend, *Der Glückspilz* (Munich: Albert Langen, 1919).

[25] Kathleen Murray, *Taine und die englische Romantik* (Munich and Leipzig: Duncker & Humblot, 1924).

[26] Curtius's magisterial *European Literature and the Latin Middle Ages* (Princeton, NJ: Princeton University Press, 1953; original German publication 1948) was praised by T. S. Eliot as 'this magnificent book'. For Curtius's connections to the George Circle, see: Friedrich Gundolf, *Briefwechsel mit Herbert Steiner und Ernst Robert Curtius*, ed. Lothar Helbing and Claus Victor Bock (Amsterdam: Castrum Peregrini, 1963).

[27] Schmitt's attitude to Curtius was highly ambivalent. Whereas the letters display all due collegial esteem, the diary records less warmth: 'Curtius has thanked me for my "brilliant essay". To think of that cold, vain man sent cold shivers down my spine' (13 May 1923; 195). Curtius seems to have been aware of the relationship between Schmitt and Murray.

has entered into a new affair with a Munich doctor, Lola Sauer, which in turn overlaps with his growing attachment to a young Serbian student, Duška Todorović. Having enlisted her help as a translator for his enquiries into Cari's Serbian background, he is initially not much drawn to her. But by mid-1923, the diaries register all the previous symptoms of his unrest. Passionately in love again, he is as torn between faith and doubt as ever before. With Duška, trust—though always brittle—eventually prevails. They marry in 1926.

III GOD'S SHADOW

These personal entanglements set the stage for the drama of Othello in Schmitt's diaries. The plural, diaries, is called for because, from 1922 to 1924, Schmitt kept a second, more free-floating journal of notes, letters, and reflections parallel with his regular daybook. This bears the title *The Shadow of God*, and it is fitting that the majority of his thoughts on Othello are set down here, in the shadow of God. 'God casts a shadow', Schmitt writes,

> because He has substance, because He is not merely an iconostasis,[28] a functional concept or an empty fact, but something solid.
> The shadow is proof of a substance and a solidity. (March 1923; 456–7)[29]

Schmitt derives this idea from Psalm 121:5–6, which he quotes: 'The LORD is thy shade upon thy right hand. / The sun shall not smite thee by day, nor the moon by night' (October 1922; 405). But Schmitt omits the crucial half-line preceding his quotation: 'The Lord is thy keeper.' In the psalm, God's shadow offers shelter. For Schmitt it means the opposite: instead of shelter, a state of utter unprotectedness. God's shadow is 'even blacker' than the 'great darkening' diagnosed by contemporary observers of cultural decline.[30] 'Not light and darkness', he insists, 'but light and shadow' (March 1923; 456–7).

Othello is at the centre of this shadow, his skin colour the visible imprint of the shadow's 'even blacker' darkness and the opposite of light. Schmitt praises,[31] and draws on, Victor Hugo, who saw this dichotomy at the heart of the play:

> What is Othello? He is the night. A towering, fateful figure. Night falls in love with day. The dark loves the dawn, the African adores the white woman. Desdemona is both clarity and madness for Othello. That is why he succumbs to jealousy so quickly. [...] Jealousy abruptly turns the hero into a monster. The black man becomes the Negro. It is as if the night had given death a quick signal.[32]

---

[28] A wall of icons, separating the nave from the sanctuary in Eastern Orthodox churches.

[29] Cf. Gerd Giesler, Ernst Hüsmert, and Wolfgang H. Spindler, 'Vorwort', in Schmitt, *Der Schatten Gottes*, v–vii at vi.

[30] Schmitt specifically refers to an acquaintance of his, the Austrian Expressionist artist and writer Albert Paris Gütersloh (1887–1973).

[31] February 1924; 517.

[32] Victor Hugo, *William Shakespeare*, trans. Melville B. Anderson (Chicago, IL: McClurg, 1887), 242.

Echoing Hugo, Schmitt makes the play crackle with his own obsessions:

> Othello a man: night yearning for light. Why is light a woman. The man's darkness is yearning for the light of a woman. That is madness. Both things happen by physical law. It is unthinkable the other way round because woman's darkness is incapable of yearning for light. She hates the light. She would kill a man out of greed for possession, not out of passion: *If the chaos will come. [sic!]* (March 1923; 455)

Labouring under a permanent crisis of faith, Schmitt amalgamates the shadow of God with the shadow cast by a woman, or 'Woman'. Hence the betrayal of faith, leitmotif of his tortured ruminations, is always double-coded: erotic as well as religious. The string of associative leaps on the theme of shadows that begins with the quote from Psalm 121 ends with Villiers de l'Isle Adam quoting Byron: 'On eût dit que cette femme projetait son ombre sur le cœur de ce jeune homme' (March 1923; 455). In Byron this reads: '[S]he knew, / For quickly comes such knowledge, that his heart / Was darken'd with her shadow'.[33]

Sexual and spiritual desperation are inextricably entangled in *The Shadow of God*. It is this convergence that makes Othello's 'black tragedy' (19 January 1922; 31) the perfect mirror of Schmitt's own predicament. In a partly illegible entry from January 1923 he notes:

> I suddenly get no answer from anyone and am not seen by anyone any more. I feel a darkness spreading around me and it is as if my head were wrapped in a dark cloth. Meanwhile, I realise the meaning [of this]: just as the magic is gone and the miracles which can <......> will cloak in silence and darkness, so one is thrust into darkness and loneliness. I shall have to bear it. One day, the light will come. (436)

Schmitt's racist tendencies, always ignited by Jews,[34] are conspicuously absent when it comes to Othello. What matters more than his race[35] is that he is *déraciné*, the outsider uprooted from his, or indeed any, sustaining social cohesion:

> Othello: Marriage is a social institution, there is no marriage without social milieu, the man must supply the social milieu. A déraciné cannot marry; if he does, he kills the woman. Jealousy becomes the form of her execution; he drags the woman into his nothingness. (February 1923; 447)

---

[33] Lord Byron, 'The Dream', ll. 91–3, in *The Poetical Works of Lord Byron* (London, New York, and Toronto: Oxford University Press, 1966), 92.

[34] See, for example, his casual dig at Gundolf: 'How much nobler Georges Sorel [the anti-liberal French philosopher] [...] is than this Jew Gundelfinger, Heidelberg Professor <...>, enemy of unity, such a pantywaist' (September 1923, 483). Calling Gundolf by his original name is standard anti-Semitic practice. After 1933 Schmitt would do the same in his notorious attacks on the nineteenth-century legal thinker and politician Friedrich Julius Stahl (1802–61) whom he consistently refers to as Stahl-Jolson. See, for example, Carl Schmitt, 'Rechtsstaat', in *Nationalsozialistisches Handbuch für Recht und Gesetzgebung*, ed. Hans Frank (Munich: Zentralverlag der NSDAP, 1935), 6. William E. Scheuermann, *Carl Schmitt: The End of Law* (Lanham, MD: Rowman & Littlefield, 1999), 294, comments: 'Schmitt's anti-Semitic diatribes against Julius Stahl (originally Jolson) seem to have been his very own "contribution" to Nazi anti-Semitism. Stahl's name is dirtied in many of Schmitt's texts from this period.'

[35] Othello's race is mentioned in *The Shadow of God* but never in the sense of a racial slur.

Eight months later, he notes:

> Othello, the uprooted one, who has had an Emilia already, although she also lived in loneliness. One must view this in institutional terms, not psychologically. The black man—the lonely one (a function, not an institution).
>
> Lonely is he who has no Emilia. The black man who has no colour and so much colour. (22 October 1923; 492)

If Hamlet is 'too much in the sun' (*Ham.* 1.2.67), Othello is too much in the shade. He has so much colour that it isolates him in a white environment; no colour at all because blackness is a total absence of light. Schmitt's sense of his own 'black' solitude makes Othello—uprooted, betrayed, jealous—not a special minority case, but representative of the human condition. Under God's shadow, Othello's fate becomes 'the fate of man' (November/December 1923; 498; quoted at the beginning of this chapter).

The passage that makes this claim also makes two significant exclusions. Slavs and Romance peoples are excepted from the universal category: 'Humanity stands between the two' (November/December 1923; 498). Humanity, in other words, is German, the normative middle between the Slav and 'Romanic' mentalities. Sharing Othello's fate, Germany, especially in its abject post-Versailles condition, is 'ridiculous in the eyes' of its neighbours East and West; it is (or at least sees itself as) the nation permanently misunderstood. But there is much virtue, Schmitt suggests, in such misunderstanding: it is the qualification needed in order to understand Othello. Only someone who understands, as Schmitt declares he does, neither the Slav nor the Romance mind is capable of comprehending the fate of Othello and thus capable of recognizing Othello's fate as his own. Clearly such a mind has to be essentially German; and so it is only fitting for Schmitt to find that *Othello* 'is more beautiful in German than in English' and even to claim that 'Othello is a German play' (December 1923; 506). Not only a German play, but also one with a German protagonist. In a letter to Lo Sauer, Schmitt's Munich physician friend, he reports: 'Tonight I dreamt your name was Othella and I kissed you in my dream. When I awoke it occurred to me that Othello is the diminutive form of Otto' (January 1923; 437). It is hard to think of a name more fraught with Germanness than Otto. Otto as in Otto the Great (912–73), who begat the line of medieval kings and emperors known as the Ottonians,[36] or as in Otto von Bismarck, the 'Iron Chancellor' and 'Architect of Empire'. Schmitt's dream effects no mere 'naturalisation': rather than turning *into* a German, Othello turns out to *be* German, his core identity cloaked by an Italian diminutive. 'Othello', we read in another entry, 'the moor with the Germanic name and the Germanic fate; the willow song a wisp of Germanic fog in Venice' (July/August 1923; 472).

---

[36] Arnulf of Milan describes Otto the Great as 'the first of the Germans to be called the emperor of Italy'. Arnulf von Mailand, *Liber gestorum recentium*, ed. Claudia Zey (Hanover: Hahn, 1994), I.7; trans W. North, <http://www.acad.carleton.edu/curricular/MARS/Arnulf.pdf>, accessed 9 March 2015.

Even closer to the bone is another dream in which Othello appears rooted not just in the dreamer's own nationality, but literally in his 'own proper entrails' (*JC* 5.3.96):

> Dream in the night of December 29/30, 1923: A moor, a negro is growing out of my body. I hear a voice: Once you have been christened with this sauce nothing can save you. (Wonderful in Othello: no miracle will save you); I feel I must suppress the 'black' within me, else I shall be lost. (505–6)

'The black' (*der Schwarze*; i.e. the black man) is both an alien body and inalienably part of the body he inhabits. He can, at best, be suppressed, but not expelled. Like Lear in his strongly auto-aggressive curse on Goneril, Schmitt can no more expel 'the black' than Lear can the daughter whom he describes as part of his own flesh:

> Or rather a disease that's in my flesh
> Which I must needs call mine. Thou art a boil,
> A plague-sore, an embossèd carbuncle
> In my corrupted blood. (*Lr.* 2.2.402–5)

Schmitt's Othello is both the disease within his flesh and the noble sufferer by whose image he sees '[t]he portraiture of his [own]' (*Ham.* 5.2.67.11). On the one hand the 'frantic Othello-affect' causes him 'insane headache[s]' (9 April 1924; 335) and 'heart cramps' (5 February 1922). On the other hand, the 'noble moor Othello' (15 February 1924; 517) is the identificatory model whose tragic fate mirrors Schmitt's own afflictions. Usually *Hamlet* is regarded as the play that asks, rather than answers, questions, the play whose self-scrutinizing hero interminably throws our own questions back at us. For Schmitt, it is Othello who is both infinitely revelatory and infinitely baffling.

> Othello: He did not love, otherwise he would not have been jealous, jealousy has nothing to do with love? (Othello has nothing to do with jealousy). In any case: I see that I am capable of Othello's deed? What is Othello's deed: smash an idol. (15 February 1924; 517)

It is interesting to see how Schmitt's trademark rhetoric of certainty is derailed by the insertion of two question marks. Jealousy has nothing to do with love. Or has it? I am capable of Othello's deed. Or am I? The declarative mode of Schmitt's famous aphorisms runs up against a subject that defies certainty. This subject is not just a character in a play, but the troubled diarist himself. Much as he protests in another note on Othello that 'one must see all in institutional terms, not psychologically' (October 1923; 492), such analytical detachment will simply not hold up against the turmoil and contradictions of Schmitt's Othello experience.

At the core of this experience is the '[s]tarting point for everything about Othello: *If I don't love you, chaos will come.* The centre: the dark, chaos was the tail. The woman becomes ugly like his face' (March 1924; 526). The crucial phrase is also found in the letter to Kathleen Murray quoted earlier (19 January 1922; 31): 'When I love thee not, Chaos is come again, where should Othello go?' Schmitt combines lines from Act 3 (*Oth.* 3.3.91–2) with a line from Act 5 (5.2.278) as if they formed a single passage. This contracts the action of the whole play to its central peripety, its single catastrophic reversal. Time is suspended. The moment of decision coincides with its outcome. Othello, already infected with suspicion but still hesitating on the brink of jealousy, becomes simultaneous with the Othello to whom chaos has come, who has murdered Desdemona and who has nowhere to go. Compressed in this way, the tragedy freezes in a loop of interminable repetition.

This is how it plays out in Schmitt's diaries: '[a] nightmarish situation' (November/December 1923; 498–9) in which the desperate need for love and for faith in love is always attended by the nagging fear of betrayal. 'But you are being betrayed again, for she adores not you, but the world and life' (January 1922; 34). The 'she' is Kathleen Murray. Following almost instantly upon his declarations of love to her in the 'Othello letter' of 19 January, this entry comes in a string of reflections in which his love for her, or for any woman, is dismantled with relentless disillusionment. Drawing on Luke 4:9–11, Satan's third temptation of Christ ('And he brought him to Jerusalem, and set him on a pinnacle of the temple, and said unto him, If thou be the Son of God, cast thyself down from hence') Schmitt writes: 'Cast yourself down to the level of this woman. The woman will, if need be, accompany you to the ramparts of the temple, but there is no comfortable passage to be had on the ramparts of the temple' (January 1922; 34).

> Raise your fantasy to ever greater height, climb to the pinnacle of life and know that only you yourself are ascending to these peaks. Once you have climbed so high, you will suddenly see that you are alone; the woman has not followed you. You see her down below, with boredom on her face. (January 1922; 35)

What Schmitt seeks from Kathleen, as from Carita before her and Duška after her, is salvation. But even as he seeks it he realizes the futility of his 'blasphemous' quest for the woman whom he 'loves more than God'. Man 'calls a woman saviour. What is a woman supposed to save a man from! A woman can save him from another woman at best, until he has gone so far with her that he needs salvation again' (January 1922; 34).

The swings are extreme. Abruptly cutting from gushing love letter to self-disdain and bitter reproach, Schmitt, like Othello, knows no middle ground between total devotion and total disenchantment. But unlike Othello he swings back and forth, at times even trapped in both extremes at once. The pattern is still the same in February 1924, although the baton of Schmitt's redeeming angel has passed from Kathleen to Duška:

> Beloved woman, I kiss your hands, grateful for your beautiful letter, and do not want to be or remain anything other than your soul, always and in everything your soul.— (Posted on February 16)
>
> Wandered about aimlessly all day, close to madness. In the evening I thought of going to confession with Father Feldmann, but I couldn't; it would have been a betrayal of Duschka. Then I looked at Rembrandt's drawings, monstrous happenings, and found

that they have nothing to do with me and yet that I am very close to such things. Isn't it ridiculous to build one's happiness on a woman? On the secularized Madonna? (February 1924; 517–18)[37].

IV GREEN-EYED MONSTER

It is one thing to be Othello; quite another to identify with him. The latter necessarily includes the knowledge of the whole story and thus the knowledge of Desdemona's innocence. But certainty of that knowledge would make identifying with Othello pointless. So identifying with Othello entails—and certainly entailed for Schmitt—a kind of double vision: the torments of jealousy coexisting with the 'meta-torment' of suspecting this jealousy to be a delusion. Schmitt seems never to have quite persuaded himself of the innocence of his Desdemonas, having been hoodwinked by the first, Carita. But neither did he ever quite trust his own doubts. The prime mover of doubt in Shakespeare's play, however, is conspicuously absent from Schmitt's Othello. The position of 'honest Iago', the third corner in the fatal triangle, remains empty.[38] The issue of betrayal plays out strictly between Schmitt and the woman he loves (and questions) or indeed within his own troubled mind.

In the psycho-drama of Schmitt's *Othello*, props become fraught with fatality. 'Dear Countess', he croons in the bloom of their relationship 'remain mine, as I will remain yours, kiss the ring, K., and give my love to the green colour of your knitted jacket, there's magic in its web' (*Oth.* 3.4.66; January 1922; 32). Much more serious than this playful invocation of Desdemona's strawberry-spotted handkerchief was the discomfiture arising over a blanket that Schmitt wanted to give Duška as a present. So unsettling was the incident caused by this gift that Schmitt wrestled with it in both of his parallel diaries:

> Night from November 21 to 22 [1923]: I had to think again and again in agonizing uncertainty what it means that Duschka allowed me to give her the blanket, but then folded it up again and did not want to have it any more when I said I wished I had 'bought' her a better one. The word 'buy' offended her so much[;] she eventually allowed me to give her the blanket but shortly afterwards gave me back a dollar which she owed me—as if she were trying to liquidate everything.
>
> I see now that it is not passivity, as I had thought, which is at the centre of her being but a horrible negativity. She has the egoism of her illness.[39] I am horrified by her egoism. [...] I must always be the betrayed one, that's for sure. For I am capable of sacrifice, she is not. What a horrible situation.

---

[37] The Marian resonances in the character of Desdemona have often been noticed; see, e.g. Ruben Espinosa, *Masculinity and Marian Efficacy in Shakespeare's England* (Farnham and Burlington, VT: Ashgate, 2011), 91–148; Lisa Hopkins, ' "Black but beautiful": Othello and the Cult of the Black Madonna', in *Marian Moments in Early Modern British Drama*, ed. Regina Buccola and Lisa Hopkins (Farnham and Burlington, VT: Ashgate, 2013), 75–86; Greg Maillet, 'Desdemona and the Mariological Theology of the Will in *Othello*', in *Marian Moments*, ed. Buccola and Hopkins, 87–110.

[38] Iago occurs only once in *The Shadow of God* (March 1924; 527).

[39] Duška suffered from severe tuberculosis.

Then I wondered hundreds and thousands of times whether to bring her the blanket or not; I want to take it to her, calmly, as if nothing had happened. But that's no good, for the blanket has become a symbol like Othello's handkerchief.

She has been well now for a month, her illness is coming back: despair, fear, insecurity and turmoil; thoughts of suicide and mad worries over the love of a girl.

This is Romanticism, a condition which is anachronistic. One can no longer be romantic today; that time is past, the illusion of the individual. Women can still be [romantic]. A man nowadays must become a nihilist or a Communist or a Roman Catholic. Otherwise he is at best Othello. I see this and take refuge in the egoism of a woman because he (!) is incapable of egoism himself. (495–6)

A reader may find it hard to take Duška's hesitance about a present that is 'bought' as proof of her 'horrible negativity' and egoism. But the intensity of Schmitt's distress is all too obvious, his self-reproach and self-pity inextricably enmeshed with Othello, the eternal victim of betrayal who 'loved not wisely, but too well' (*Oth.* 5.2.337). Schmitt's midnight ruminations make his private sorrows blend seamlessly with the ideological perplexities of his time. His published views—anti-Romantic, pro-Roman Catholic[40]—clash with the experiential reality of his agonizing. Nihilist, Communist, Roman Catholic—if none of these three options of what a man 'must become today' is available, only Othello remains: 'most decent' (*anständig*) of sufferers in the anachronistic plight of Romantic passion. Slipping from first to third person pronoun, the grammar virtually amalgamates Schmitt with Othello in the last sentence: '*I* [...] resort to the egoism of the woman, because *he* is incapable of egoism'. 'I' and 'he' become one and the same.

Unlike Othello's handkerchief, the ominous blanket does not precipitate disaster. Tragedy is avoided, as Schmitt's parallel diary records:

Wednesday, 21/11/23

Slept very badly last night. Tortured agonising whether I should bring Duschka the blanket. Horrible fear of betrayal, horrendous; ejaculation. Got up tired at half eight, felt better with light of day. Two letters from McK which I did not open. Must finally shake off K. [...] I could not work because I was always waiting for Duschka, horrible fear, heart trouble. No work done. So the morning passed. At noon I bought papers, went home tired, ate tired, then suddenly the decision to take a walk to Venusberg. That did me good. Then to bed, 2 hours, nothing but waiting for 6 o'clock so that I could go see Duschka. Had a very nice coffee and ate Bosnian slatko, then took the blanket and 3 beautiful chrysanthemums to Duschka. She was wonderfully friendly [...] we kissed, read Hölderlin's *Heimat* [...] Wonderful child [...] Stayed until 9:15, then home in a veritable ecstasy. [...] Happily to bed. (275)

But Schmitt's faith remains fragile. New doubts assail him when Duška takes a trip to her hometown Agram (Zagreb) 'because of her glasses'. This, he suspects, is a pretext: 'I know that she is going because of the Russian actors. Startled that she concealed this from me. Suddenly a terrible thought' (15 February 1924; 315).

---

[40] See, for example, Carl Schmitt, *Roman Catholicism and Political Form* (1923), trans. and ed. G. L. Ulmen (Westport, CT: Greenwood Press, 1996).

'For an hour I walked up and down the room saying out loud: She is lying, she is lying, she is lying, oh God, she is lying' (515–16).[41]

In his agony, he writes (but apparently never sends) her a letter protesting that he does *not* mistrust her. But why did she not tell him that she was going home because of the Russian theatre? Was she afraid he would have mistrusted her if she had? Frantic swings reveal the depth of his confusion:

> Not for a moment was I mistrustful. I would have been ashamed if I had been. [...] I have overcome all mistrust. You must not push me into it. [...] My soul was free of mistrust. But [...] I warn you never to conceal anything from me. Oh how beautiful your letter is. You are my faithful woman. I do not want to be anything else but always and in everything your soul.
>
> (This letter I have burnt). (The glasses, lost in Hamburg on 21/3/1924)[42]
>
> --
>
> When I had written this I thought: Why is she lying to me? She is lying, perhaps she is lying like Desdemona, but it is dangerous. Am I not a duped fool? Of course.
>
> --
>
> A quarter of an hour later: I cannot understand my agitation; she means well; like Desdemona. (516)

V FAITHFUL GYPSY

The feeling that he is (of course) 'the duped fool' asserts itself again and again in Schmitt's diaries. A nagging ground note of his relations with the world at large,[43] it flares up most violently in his relations with women. 'Betrayed and lied to. Desperate yearning for help, love, goodness, trust. But I remain alone' (5 August 1922; 126). '[T]hought of K. Am I not a poor, betrayed dog after all' (29 May 1922; 91). Complaints like these could be cited *ad infinitum*. They are the ferment of Schmitt's fixation on Othello. But they also spark his own literary production.

In ancient Athens, the feasts of tragedy came with a comic dessert. Something like a satyr play, Schmitt's parable of 'The Faithful Gypsy' modulates the tragic betrayal of Othello in a caustic key. The story was never developed beyond a skeleton version of about half a dozen typewritten pages.[44] Even so, it was complete enough for Schmitt to read or recount it to his friends on various occasions. The

---

[41] Like the blanket incident, the incident of the glasses is recorded in both parallel diaries.

[42] This last remark in brackets was added later. Schmitt's diaries are full of such hindsight observations and comments.

[43] e.g. 'The feeling of being betrayed is the beginning of wisdom. Today we feel betrayed by democracy' (January 1922; 43).

[44] This was first published in *Schmittiana* 7 (2001), 19–27, and reprinted as an appendix to Schmitt, *Der Schatten Gottes*, 564–9 (references to this text are given in brackets). Schmitt completed the 'Faithful Gipsy' during his stay, with Kathleen Murray, in Marburg in April 1922. 'I am sending you The Faithful Gipsy as an Easter salute', he wrote to his friend, the writer and critic Franz Blei (1871–1942): 'Please do not change anything. I know it is clumsy. But it should stay as it is. A small [...] journal would print it. But I would prefer a nice little book' (Letter to Franz Blei, 12 April 1922, quoted in Schmitt, *Der Schatten Gottes*, 69, n. 202). Blei thought the story did indeed need to be

story is this: Once upon a time there lived, in the Carpathians, a gypsy who had a beautiful wife. She 'accuses herself of a grave sin' whose exact nature remains undisclosed. The local priest declares the matter to be beyond his authority. He advises the gypsy's wife to undertake a pilgrimage to Rome in order to obtain personal absolution from the Pope. Rome is a long way away and the journey toilsome. But the wife vows to spare no effort for the salvation of her soul. However, since her health is delicate and her beauty might suffer, she tells her husband that it would be best if he carried her. 'That way, she could fulfil her vow and let her husband share in the blessings of the pilgrimage. So the gypsy took his wife on his back and they set off on their journey to Rome' (564). At each turn of their picaresque progress across Europe the pampered wife sanctimoniously exploits and gulls her husband, collecting a string of admirers who venerate her for her goodness and piety. In Rome at last and enjoined by his wife to hurry for the papal audience, the faithful husband, tripping, 'uttered a dreadful curse, hit his head on a marble statue and dropped to the ground, dead' (566). His pious wife is a great success in Rome and when she dies not long afterwards she is instantly sanctified. But there are also detractors who dispute her saintliness. Violent altercations ensue and a great many people lose their lives in the fray.

Schmitt rounds off the story with an ironical, meta-narrative afterword in which he relates how each of the people to whom he told the story understood it differently. Some of these people are probably fictitious, others are certainly not, although the comments Schmitt attributes to them almost certainly are. A 'Miss Doris Abbott of Boston, USA', for example, 'called the gypsy a *nature's gentleman* and strongly recommended that the tale be included in story-books for boys so as to provide Germans, at long last, a worthy example for imitation. But, of course, the gypsy should not be allowed to curse' (569). A Latvian student, 'who was an ardent Bolshevik, called the gypsy a symbol of the proletarian carrying the burden of capitalist luxury', whereas 'an Irishwoman, Kathleen Murray', declared 'that she had never heard a more beautiful apology of Roman Catholicism' (569). From the 'cleverest woman I had met so far' comes the comment: 'This is the story of every marriage.' More specifically, it is the story of Schmitt's marriage and the cleverest woman, unmistakable because 'she hailed from the former Habsburg monarchy', is his first wife Carita (569).

'The Faithful Gypsy' coincided with what seems to have been the high-water mark in his relationship with Kathleen Murray. Schmitt visited her for a whole month in Marburg. Officially in separate lodgings, the two managed to spend quite a few nights in the same bed. This involved some involuntary comedy, as when the Herr Professor had to dive behind the wardrobe to escape notice by the cleaning woman, and, inevitably, the lovers were eventually discovered by Kathleen's formidable landlady, 'the correct Frau Finner' (11 April 1922; 69).[45] Schmitt is more than frank about their activities: 'Wonderful in bed, in love and enraptured

---

changed, and extended too. But Schmitt was not amenable to this; his plans for publication came to naught.

[45] 'Frau Finner had come into [Kathleen's] room, barred me from the house, told her to vacate the room by 1 o'clock Saturday etc. Disgusting' (15 April 1922; 70).

by K.'s beauty, her hairstyle, her black hair, her plenteous flesh, her gorgeous thighs, caressed her till she reached ecstasy, it did not take long. She [is] always quite wet, fell asleep tired, intoxicated, sexual frenzy' (5 April 1922; 66). But amidst all the rapturous excitement, Schmitt experienced sudden attacks of emptiness and loathing. Effusions like 'I love and admire her beyond words' and detailed records of his 'ejaculations' and her 'ecstasies' ('2 ecstasies by hand', 8 April 1922; 68) alternate with total disaffection: 'I really have nothing to do with K. What a mistake' (13 April 1922; 70). 'I want to run away, I could cry, so betrayed do I feel' (6 April 1922; 67).

The faithful gypsy reflects this mix of infatuation and disgust. As Schmitt's parodic self-portrait, he plays the quixotic counterpart to Shakespeare's tragic Moor: 'Othello and the faithful gypsy', Schmitt notes, '[t]he American woman is right; every man carries his wife' (March 1923; 455). Even closer than counterparts, the two figures merge into one, becoming '[t]he faithful gypsy Othello (a coloured man)' (September 1923; 489). The story of the faithful gypsy may read like an exercise in light-hearted sarcasm, yet there is nothing light or sprightly about the thoughts and sentiments it records and engenders. 'Never heard a story', Schmitt notes, 'which has prompted so much philosophizing. [...] It is a gratifying fact for a story to have such interpretability, and that despite its many flaws' (April 1923; 466–7).

Othello and the faithful gypsy are dwellers of the same darkness. Tellingly, Schmitt's gloss on God's shadow is nested between two reflections about the faithful gypsy:

> Let's start a great conspiracy of the Irish, the Jews, the illegal Germans, the [*several words overwritten and illegible*] uprooted, <...> the longing, of the guests among the natives, the lean among the fat? Of the faithful gypsies?
>
> ----------------------------------
>
> The shadow: God casts a shadow because He has substance, because He is not just an iconostasis, a functional concept or an empty fact, but something solid.
>
> The shadow is proof of a substance and a solidity.
>
> ----------------------------------
>
> The faithful gypsy: Why is he a gypsy, can one raise the question of his nationality? Why is he not a German? He is silent? What does his silence consist in? Should he not be a gypsy like Don Quixote? Isn't he a proletarian because he curses? (March 1923; 456–7)

God is all substance and firmness; the sentences about him are declarative. The gypsy, by contrast, is afloat with questioning and uncertainty. Endlessly interpretable, he is woven into a web of fluid relations. Disassociating him from more determinate identities has the paradoxical effect of linking him all the more forcibly to them. Why indeed isn't he German? Can we be sure he isn't? And if he *should* be a Don Quixote, perhaps he is more than half-way one already. In Schmitt's tentative roll-call for 'a great conspiracy' the faithful gypsies feature climactically at the end, subsuming all the motley crew that precedes them. Most remarkable for including the Jews, the line-up assembles those who are excluded, the outcasts, the abject.

Abjection plays a key role in Schmitt's self-fashioning throughout the diaries. Exemplary victims of betrayal, the faithful gypsy and the Moor Othello are also exemplary figures of abjection. This is why the man who carries his wife on his back across Europe is not a German; but it is also why 'the *illegal* Germans' can find a place in the companionship of the gypsies.

Illegal Germans, but nevertheless legitimate: what this key distinction in Schmitt's legal thought—one that would prove notoriously accommodating to the Nazis[46]—suggests here is the split we have encountered in various guises before: the split between the 'official' and the 'true' Germany, or, in Stefan George's term, the 'Secret Germany'. But Schmitt's would-be conspirators have little in common with the heroic youths of George's Graeco-Germanic idealism. They resemble more the radically displaced figures seeking shelter in the hovel in Act 3 of *King Lear*. Their state is stateless, utter unbelonging. They share the homeless condition of the gypsy, but also his other attribute: like him, they are faithful, even *the* faithful. A band of brothers in abjection, they cross the boundary that is fundamental to Schmitt's famous concept of the political: 'the specific political distinction', he claims, 'is that between friend and enemy'.[47] In a space where this distinction obtains, Jew and German could never rub shoulders. Their fellowship can only exist in an extra-political zone of un-distinction. It can only exist in the dark: the dark of God's shadow, and the belief that it is *God's* shadow demands an act of faith on the part of those labouring under it. Visibly centred between the two gypsy paragraphs on the diary page, the declarative statement on God's solid substance performs what it declares: it casts its shadow over the two adjoining entries.

Darkness is the great eraser of distinctions: 'When all candles bee out all cattes be gray.'[48] For Schmitt, the virtuoso of razor-sharp distinctions, darkness is 'Chaos [...] come again', the dissolution of all order, a state as threatening as it is tempting.[49] It encompasses the chaotic ambivalence of his erotic obsessions, his adoration and abhorrence of women, their flesh, their fluids and their smells that send him alternately into raptures of ecstasy and shudders of disgust. He recoils from '[t]he stench of a whore', he notes '[t]he womanish smell of the lasciviousness of a sinful woman' (January 1923; 426). During their Marburg romp, he records with relish how Kathleen 'is always quite wet' (5 April 1922; 66) when he caresses her, or,

---

[46] Carl Schmitt, *Legality und Legitimacy* (1932), trans. Jeffrey Seitzer (Durham, NC: Duke University Press, 2004). Written after the Nazis' success in the 1932 elections, the book can be read as a warning against a takeover of power which is legal but illegitimate—in fact, precisely the kind of takeover that took place on 30 January 1933. But the legal/legitimate distinction proved highly adaptable to the demands of the new regime, justifying as legitimate what was clearly illegal, as in Schmitt's defence of the murder of Ernst Röhm and other leaders of the paramilitary SA (the Brownshirts) in the Night of the Long Knives in 1934: 'The Führer Protects the Law' ('Der Führer schützt das Recht', *Deutsche Juristenzeitung* 39 [1934], cols 945–50).

[47] Carl Schmitt, *The Concept of the Political*, trans. George D. Schwab (Chicago, IL and London: University of Chicago Press, 2007), 26.

[48] John Heywood, *The Proverbs of John Heywood* (1546), ed. Julian Sharman (London: George Bell & Sons, 1874), 22.

[49] Schmitt felt a similar threat of dissolution emanating from the sea, 'the Neptunic, the dissolution, the mystery, consuming my consciousness, draining my soul; my fear by the Baltic Sea in Greifswald, my anxiety in Heligoland, the monstrous, snake-poisonous, Medusa-like of the swamp. How the world began: God separated land from sea' (December 1922; 424).

almost scientifically: 'very wet, large amount of liquid. How strange' (18 April 1922; 72). About Lola Sauer he writes: 'What I took to be the sweet dew of innate nobleness in her is probably just the salty residue of the sea' (November 1922; 413). Her surname—German for 'sour'—fills him with misgivings as their relationship—and with it, her 'sweet dew'—turns, quite literally, 'sour'. A dream triggers a graphic moment of anagnorisis:

> Night of Dec. 18/19, 1922: Half asleep I saw: the tower of which I spoke, the lonely tower is something else; it is the Sauer garage. Then I remembered: On December 1, 1922, after the meeting with my wife, the waiter at the *Parkhotel* where I had breakfast brought me an egg that was rotten and smelt disgusting; and the smell was the same as that of L's axillary secretions, with whom I had been the night before.
>
> -----------------------------------
>
> Tuesday, Dec. 19, 1922: She has long gone Sauer [sour].

Schmitt's abjection of the female objects of his sexual appetite and his sexual disgust goes hand in hand with his abjection of himself. This finds exemplary expression in the *alter ego* figures of the gypsy and the Moor. Nothing illustrates this more graphically than the dream in which Othello, 'the Negro', grows out of his body while a voice tells him that once he is 'christened with this sauce nothing can save [him]' (29/30 December 1923; 505–6). The touch of (or 'christening with') repulsive liquids ranks high on anyone's scale of disgust, arguably topped only by their ingestion. But surpassing even this is the horror that makes Schmitt's dream seem like a prequel of the 'Chestburster Scene' from the film *Alien* (1979), where the repulsively viscid foreign body erupts from the victim's own flesh.[50]

'Chaos and monster are the terms of Othello', Schmitt writes (April 1924; 529). His identification with Othello is what German identifications with Hamlet, for all their bitter self-reproach, never were: a defilement, a deeper blackening of the self than Shakespeare's black prince ever warranted. Unlike Hamlet, Othello cannot 'cast [his] nighted colour off' (*Ham.* 1.2.68), nor can he deny that this colour denotes him truly (cf. *Ham.* 1.2.83). The 'black man' must be, and perhaps can be contained, but he can only be contained within. There is no cutting the umbilical cord of this monstrous birth: the self can never wholly separate itself from what it abjects. The abject offers inroads to the enemy. Thus Schmitt's Othello-self is constantly forming symbiotic alliances, overlapping with inimical others:

> Sexualism is proletarian [...]
> Sexualism is anarchistic;
> Sexualism is Jewish;
> Proletarian-anarchistic sensualistic—Jewish (I am speaking here only of the godless Jews).
> Othello the proletarian: sensualistic, anarchistic. (April 1924; 529)

---

[50] The film, and especially this scene, has received considerable attention in discussions of the abject. See, e.g. Anette Kuhn, ed., *Alien Zone* (London: Verso, 1990), esp. the chapters by Barbara Creed and Judith Newton. The seminal study of abjection is Julia Kristeva, 'Approaching Abjection', in her *Powers of Horror* (New York: Columbia University Press, 1982), 1–31.

Othello is the code word for the 'thing[s] of darkness' that Schmitt must '[a]cknowledge mine' (*Tmp.* 5.1.278–9):[51] not only things to which he would readily admit—'sexualism' and the proletarian—but also that thing he would most sharply disown: Jewishness.[52] But the form in which these elements are itemized suggests a new approach. The things of darkness are brought to light, the light of taxonomical distinction. Slowly, and by no means surely, Schmitt's identification with Othello gives way to a more detached, analytical attitude. But relapses into the darkness of Othello do occur. In November 1923, just seeing 'Duschka cross the street with a foreigner' sets his jealous reflexes on full alert. When he confesses this to her, 'she said I was an Othello' (12 November 1923; 269).

But it is Duška who eventually makes it possible for him to exorcize his black doppelganger. Her trip to Zagreb ('because of her glasses') in February 1924 brings on the necessary crisis, plunging him into frenzies of jealous suspicion.[53] But all for the good, it seems: his agony effects a catharsis. A month later, 23 March, the diary records:

> Slept badly last night, only consolation: 'Your faithful Frau Duschka'.[54] She has saved me from the fate of Othello; she is my only support. Had breakfast in the morning, wanted to fetch the glasses (what a superstitious thing! the glasses!). But they were nowhere to be found. [...] Wrote to Duschka, [...] happy to have some quiet. [...] [T]hen to the Hansa Theater, Othello with Wegener,[55] a wild beast, Eisler[56] was there with Fräulein Basseches [...] We had supper at a restaurant, conversation about Othello. She understood nothing. I was tired. Fear of what is to come. (328)

[51] Notwithstanding his disapproval of Othello staged as a wild beast (see n. 55 in this chapter), Schmitt sees some overlap between Othello and Caliban: 'Instead of a guardian angel, the lower strata of humanity have a guardian gorilla. He carries them through barren valleys and over stony mountains, helping them like a Caliban. Women do not seek their angel but rather the gorilla. They love and adore him in his human shape, as ruler or feudal lord etc.' (January 1923; 436).

[52] See, for example, the rancidly clever remark: 'Rubber is the spleen of the mechanical within the organic, it is the traitor in its elasticity. It is the modern Jew among the organic substances' (January 1922; 43).

[53] Any mention of the word 'glasses', he notes on 27 February, is enough to make him jump: 'At 5 o'clock (I am expecting the postman; the word "glasses" startled me; she spoke of getting glasses in Agram [Zagreb]!)' (522).

[54] This is how Duška had signed a letter.

[55] The actor Paul Wegener (1874–1948) is remembered mostly for his leading parts in two landmark silent films: *The Student of Prague* (1913) and *The Golem* (1920). His stage performance of Othello as 'a wild beast' (at Breslau and on tour) caused heated controversy. Applauded for his expressive force, he was also sharply criticized for his alleged debasement of Shakespeare's noble Moor. See: Ludwika Gajek, *Das Breslauer Schauspiel im Spiegel der Tagespresse: das Lobetheater im ersten Jahrfünft der Weimarer Republik (1918–1923)* (Wiesbaden: Harrassowitz, 2008), 107–9. The parallel diary records that Schmitt left the theatre before the end: 'Wegener turned Othello into a wild beast: a great actor but raw and brutal; the great work of art was still recognisable despite his ludicrous tail and the growls he uttered in order to prove how "demonic" he was. It would have felt like a betrayal of Duschka, her beauty and purity, if I had watched it any longer. I left during Act 4. She would have left too. I felt it and went with her' (March 1924; 526).

[56] Bernhard Georg Eisler (1892–1983) was, after the death of his brother Fritz (1887–1914), one of Schmitt's closest friends. Eisler, who was Jewish, emigrated to England, then to the United States in 1934. He returned to Hamburg in 1963. After decades of alienation, there were two reconciliatory telephone conversations shortly before Eisler's death in 1983. Schmitt, *Der Schatten Gottes*, 4 n. 3.

No happy ending this, nor is there one in sight. Schmitt's emotional life continues to be turbulent. But a note of hope is struck in a draft letter to Duška:

Today I have bought the piano score of the opera Otello. The day after tomorrow the Shakespearean drama will be given here, with a famous actor from Berlin as Othello; I will probably go and see it. All this reminded me how much I owe you, dear Duschka: I feel quite free, I admire the greatness of the drama, I love Othello, the poor, noble Othello, but without the harrowing identifications that tormented me so terribly in the past. Dear woman, dear mother of this wonderful freedom that makes me so happy. With great love I kiss your hand.

On the 22nd: Do you not feel how my whole being has changed when I speak of Othello? I see him as an unfortunate brother whose fate I have been spared thanks to your love and goodness. (21/22 March 1924; 526)

The relief is palpable. Like a fever broken and sweated out, Schmitt's release from his tortured identification with the 'black man' (492, 506) engenders a surge of notes on Othello, a stock-taking and a leave-taking:

Othello: the homeless man seeking adventure (*an extravagant and wheeling stranger of here and every where*).
Iago: Ich bin nicht, der ich bin. *I am not what I am* (1.1).
(God says of himself: I am who I am; the Devil: I am not who I am)[57]
Actuality is negation
   The passivity of woman (a bad woman would have known how to answer Othello's accusations; Desdemona does not know what to say).

[...]

One can perhaps interpret Othello differently: he had to be a North African, a wild Berber who naturally punishes the adultery of his wife by killing her and the adulterer. How ridiculous; this may all be correct, but it does not interest me.

[...]

Reflections on Othello
Othello: psychologically an act of proletarian violence.
Psychologically a reflex of his own unfaithfulness.
Ethnologically the legal perception of a North African.
Jealousy: a phenomenon of competitiveness; hence the Russians do not understand it or they hate it.[58] (March 1924; 527)

After this point Schmitt's absorption with Othello seems to peter out. A note of finality is perceptible in a diary entry of February 1924 at the height of the 'glasses-crisis', when Schmitt is torn between jealous doubts and his desperate will to believe in Duška's 'goodness'. Marking, perhaps, the watershed moment when

---

[57] Schmitt attributes the same statement to the Leviathan: 'I heard in a dream: the Leviathan speaks / I am not I' (17 February 1924; 518).

[58] The Russians' inability to understand Othello (see also Schmitt, *Der Schatten Gottes*, 499) is also maintained a few weeks earlier: 'Othello: what psychology, exactly what Tolstoy could not understand. The futility of sagacious reasoning which occurs when someone is uprooted. Sagacity as surrogate <...> of the instincts. The hate of circumstantial evidence (like Dostoevsky, Karamazov as the principle of tragic sagacity)' (17 February 1924; 518).

he is beginning to see his way out of his Othello obsession, Schmitt sums up his view in something like a farewell tribute:

> Who really knows you, you noble moor Othello? A firm, strong rock, an Italian diminutive—in foreign dress and in essence diminished, for the bells, the jester's bells of jealous men are now mixed with the vain ring of your noble name.
>
> Noble Othello, you had the courage to do your deed; without hesitation and without psychology; in the forthright logic of your fate. You are so straightforward that few great poets have comprehended you as did Victor Hugo, who made you a terrifying symbol of night, so straightforward that professors don't pry into you as they do with your unhappy, problematic brother Hamlet. You good, honest moor. (February 1924; 517)

But the farewell is not final.

VI STRANGER AND ENEMY

Schmitt broke off *The Shadow of God* at the end of 1924. 'From Kathleen, via Lola', his biographer notes, 'Schmitt's path had found its destination: Duška'.[59] Even so, life remained troubled. Duška suffered from severe tuberculosis. After months in a sanatorium in Lugano, she eventually returned to Bonn in January 1925. Over Easter, Schmitt took her on a trip up the Moselle, the same route he had taken with Kathleen Murray three years before. He and Duška got engaged, but the obstacle that had prevented his marriage to Kathleen still prevailed: in June, the Church authorities ruled against the annulment of his first marriage. He filed an appeal but had little hope of success. He and Duška departed on an engagement trip to the coast of Illyria, as he calls it, and met the prospective bride's father in Podravska (Salina) near Zagreb. He was now determined to marry Duška regardless of the consequences. 'I am through with Christianity', he noted in January 1926. Friends did not hide their misgivings over his choice of bride: another Serbo-Croatian, and life-threateningly ill at that. The diary records a conversation with the theologian Erik Peterson in December 1925: 'We talked about marriage and about Othello; he thinks it strange that I want to get married [...]' (1 December 1925).[60] Schmitt was again mulling over Othello. 'The black man', it seems, was back with a vengeance:

Friday, 12 February 1926

Horrible dream in the morning: I am in Giessen on the Lahn River (and in recalling that this river runs by Marburg I think of Kathleen); I am to give a lecture on

---

[59] Mehring, *Carl Schmitt*, 170. The following account of Schmitt's engagement and the early years of his second marriage is based on Mehring, 170–9.

[60] This and the following quotations are from the unpublished transcripts of Schmitt's diaries, 1925 to 1929. Erik Peterson (1890–1960) was a Lutheran professor of church history and New Testament theology at Bonn. He was best man at Schmitt's wedding. His conversion to Catholicism in 1930 cost him his professorship, and his rejection of political theology in *Monotheism as Political Problem* (*Monotheismus als politisches Problem*, 1935) meant the end of his friendship with Schmitt. Peterson's studies in eschatology and the Judaic element in the early church are now recognized as major contributions to twentieth-century theology.

parliamentarism [...]. Duschka is sitting next to me with a dreadfully caricatured point-ed-flat Slavic nose. I stupidly say that I want to have money for my lecture. Later I am walking with Duschka by a pond [...]. Suddenly she says she wants to learn how to dance and go on the stage, a professor had told her she had talent. She laughs at me and says that she has lied to me again. I am horrified. I say: A day after our wedding!

The wedding went ahead on 8 February 1926, a low-key registry office ceremony with exactly three people present: the two obligatory witnesses (one of whom was Erik Peterson) and Schmitt's sister Anna, who happened to be in Bonn at the time. Schmitt's wedding present to himself was the collected works of Machiavelli—aptly enough for a man who had just stepped over to the wrong side of Church law. Once the ceremony was over, Schmitt spent the afternoon preparing a lecture which he was scheduled to deliver to a Catholic student fraternity that same evening. The next day, 9 February, the diary records that Duška was 'coughing blood again'. Hoping perhaps that she might benefit from a warmer climate, she left to visit in Croatia. But on 22 March Schmitt received a 'telegram from Duška that she has had a severe lung haemorrhage'. Barely recovered, she returned in May but was desperately ill again by late June, this time with pleurisy, and spent the next four months in hospital. Schmitt visited her daily.

But he also began seeing 'Fräulein Lizzi', a shop assistant whose name in the diary changes to Magda when the affair begins to heat up. Magda is 'loving and devoted, but often abrasive' (19 October 1926), the diary records. They have sex on the train and in 'a secluded lane' by the river (27 September 1926), and even meet in the newly rented house Schmitt moved into after Duška was admitted to hospital. Schmitt curses the 'horrendous stupidity of [his] 2nd marriage' (8 October 1926), muses over his 'disturbed sexuality' (14 September 1926), and continues to faithfully record his ejaculations. When Duška is eventually discharged from hospital it 'feels strange to have a woman in the house' (1 November 1926). Marital relations are resumed but the result is less than satisfactory. 'Ejaculation but no release', the diary notes. 'No release without conquest.' The affair with Magda continues. According to Schmitt's biographer, the triangle became 'a comparatively stable arrangement' thanks to a 'division of labour': Duška for loving care, Magda for sex.[61]

Othello returns to the core of Schmitt's personal and political concerns during this period. In the 'parallel diary' of late 1925[62] he presides over a meditation whose starting point is familiar: Othello's 'Germanic name is Italianised so that his race cannot be discerned' (fol. 4^r). Similarly, Schmitt notes, 'the names of Dalmatian cities have been covered with [an] Italian drapery' (fol. 4^r), Split becoming Spalato, Dubrovnik Ragusa. Duška's native country had deeply impressed him. It appealed to his passion for lost causes and the vanished splendours of old Europe. He pays

---

[61] Mehring, *Carl Schmitt*, 175.

[62] As was his habit earlier, Schmitt continued to keep '*Parallel-Tagebücher*' from 1925 to 1929, topical notebooks like 'The Shadow of God', in addition to his regular diary. I am grateful to Gerd Giesler for having given me access to the draft transcripts. The entries in the two 'parallel diaries' are rarely dated; the bracketed references refer to the pagination of Schmitt's manuscript (*Parallel-Tagebuch I*, Schmitt papers, RW 265-19604).

tribute to it in the essay 'Illyria—Notes on a Dalmatian Journey'.[63] 'The word Illyria', it begins, 'has vanished from today's politics' (483) and with the word all sense of its historical significance and cultural legacy. Napoleon's Kingdom of Illyria, which lasted only five years,[64] was the final tribute to the greatness of a country whose 'enormous conjunction of the most various races' and 'fantastic mix of languages and religions' (484) made it a microcosm of European diversity. The vicissitudes of its political history stand in contrast to the immutable beauty of a land which has been 'the object of politics for a millennium and a half' (484). Illyria's history of foreign occupation renders it deeply sympathetic to Schmitt, who smarted under the allied occupation of the Rhineland after the First World War.[65] The affinity between Illyria and downtrodden Germany seemed to culminate in recent history. Serbia's shattering military defeat in the Great War forms the background of a poem by Milutin Bojić (1892–1917) which Schmitt (presumably with Duška's help) translates into German at the end of his essay: 'Our fatherland is famed for misfortune. / We carry it in us as we go' (488).

Illyria was under Venetian rule for almost a millennium. Lucky for once, however, it has escaped the latter-day fate of its former mistress: the adoration of the Romantics, 'the vanguard of the bourgeois era, the spearhead of those masses of travellers who have become a veritable *Völkerwanderung* organised by hotel owners' (485). Schmitt's contempt for romanticized Venice is offset by his esteem for the Venetian city state at the height of its power: 'The great architecture of the Dalmatian cities is the sign of its rule' (484).

> But in its colourfulness [Venice] retains something Illyrian. The variety and splendour of its colours is, after all, so great that the hero of the greatest drama set in Venice had to be a moor because a white face would have appeared pale and feeble amidst so much colour. The fabulous figure of Othello, white Desdemona's black husband, 'the brown son of the yellow desert',[66] the warrior without home or social milieu, whose jealousy is merely the [...] veil in which the consequence of his homelessness is psychologically enveloped, who does not slay or stab, but strangles his wife so as not to defile her white purity with red blood, the dark hero of a brightly coloured play, the

---

[63] 'Illyrien—Notizen von einer dalmatinischen Reise' first appeared in the Catholic intellectual journal *Hochland* 23.3 (1925), 293–8. Schmitt notes the arrival of his offprints of the essay in the same diary entry (1 December 1925) in which he records his conversation about marriage and Othello with Erik Peterson (1 December 1925). The essay is reprinted in Carl Schmitt, *Staat, Großraum, Nomos: Arbeiten aus den Jahren 1916–1969*, ed. Günter Maschke (Berlin: Duncker & Humblot, 1995), 483–90. References to this text are given in brackets in the text.

[64] It is true that Napoleon revived the name Illyria when the region was incorporated into the French Empire from 1809 to 1813. But the 'Kingdom of Illyria' was actually revived later, after Napoleon's defeat at Waterloo, when the region came under Austrian rule (1816). In 1849 the 'Kingdom' disappeared for good.

[65] The Bonn area was not vacated by the French until 31 January 1926.

[66] Schmitt could be (mis)quoting the poem 'Algiers' by the now forgotten German poet Eduard Prutz (1816–72). Like his contemporary Ferdinand Freiligrath, Prutz was a supporter of the national liberation movement that led to the Revolution of 1848. The syrupy, sentimental 'Algiers' is about a blond, blue-eyed German Foreign Legionnaire who releases his Algerian prisoner ('the brown son of the desert, a slender moor') when he hears the story of his love for Fatme ('Oh Fatme, Fatme, you the crown of virgins!') and is reminded of his own sweetheart back home in Germany in a little house by the woods.

moor with the Germanic name Otto to which an Italian diminutive has been appended like a jester's bell, the noble general Othello, the poor, lonely Othello with his Germanic fate—he belongs symbolically, perhaps, to Illyria. But the Venetians are Italians, not Illyrians. (485)

Othello's trail of epithets bursts upon the reader like a subterranean stream suddenly breaking the surface. It is as if Schmitt were trying to condense all his thoughts on Othello into one paragraph. Now an honorary Illyrian as well as an honorary German, Othello seals the tragic affinity of the two nations.[67] His colour, the signature of a fundamental homelessness, is immersed in, and set off against, the bright colours of Venice as well as against the pure white of Desdemona. Jealousy is once more dismissed as just a psychological 'veil'. The fool's bell of the cuckold implied in the Italian diminutive inappropriately belittles the noble desert warrior. At the same time it deepens his tragedy: ridicule heaps insult on injury, thus compounding the fate of the outcast as the tragic fool.

The Othello passages of the 'parallel diary I' of 1925–6 not only connect with the historical and geopolitical reflections of the essay on Illyria; they also tie up with other issues in Schmitt's writings at the time. Almost all of Schmitt's topical interests seem to be drawn into the dark mirror of Othello, there to be shaped and reshaped, examined and re-examined in endless reflection. While the Illyria essay just states Othello's homelessness, the diary probes further, asking who is homeless and what it means to be homeless. In the *longue durée* of Schmitt's historical imagination, the Renaissance Othello doubles as a touchstone and avatar of the crises of modernity:

> The homelessness of Othello is not that of a Proletarian who has never had a home and does not want one; or rather: his home is the desert; but that is no home (his home is not the desert; he had a mother, of whom he speaks, and he is of royal lineage).
> He is not homeless, he is the stranger.
> Homelessness, rootlessness is the impossibility of trust:
> *I think my wife be honest and think she is not;*
> *I think that thou art just and think thou art not.*
> The obliteration of trust and of the possibility of truth.
> This is the obliteration of knowledge resulting from the obliteration of faith and trust.
>
> --
>
> Othello: his jealousy contains the feeling of competition, a dangerous, threatening competition. But who is he jealous of? Of Cassio, not just anyone. He is jealous, that is, of a well-educated man from a good family with good connections [...]
> The Proletarian has a feeling of being betrayed; not so much a feeling of competition (which entails some activity);
> the feeling of competition is an individual complex, hence not proletarian. Othello is the lonely one, the insolent individual, the stranger, not the proletarian, neither bourgeois competition with its specific, active anxiety, nor the proletarian sense of being systematically betrayed. (fol. 4ʳ)

[67] Duška was an Eastern Orthodox Serb but grew up in what is now Croatia. The national distinctions that sparked war in former Yugoslavia in the 1990s were of no concern to Schmitt writing in the 1920s.

The competitive liberalism of the bourgeoisie and the proletariat's all-encompassing sense of betrayal are the Scylla and Charybdis of the modern world against which Schmitt makes his case for authoritarian state power. They are also the blights that dominate his private life. The feeling that he 'must always be the one betrayed' (November 1923; 496) goes hand in hand with the needling competitiveness of academia, the arena of his bourgeois career.

> The concept of 'betrayal' is too complicated for me. When is someone betrayed? When error is planted in him and he is harmed. But isn't everything an error (isn't life the error) and what is harm? I know nothing any more. Is Iago a product of Othello? He is jealous of Cassio.[68] (fol. 4ᵛ)

> The feeling of being betrayed. What malice! What do people live on? One betrays the other. But I betray them all. What malice! Betraying and being betrayed are always the same; the greater the betrayal, the greater the superiority. The Prince of this World betrays us all. (And betrays himself). (fol. 5ʳ)

The general predicament of a world in which faith and trust have been obliterated repeats itself over and over again in the circular microcosm of Schmitt's personal quandaries. Othello, he notes, 'abuses the sacraments' (fol. 5ʳ) by swearing sacred oaths (*Oth.* 3.3.463–5) and making the murder of Desdemona appear as a sacrifice. The most important sacrament for Schmitt at the time was the sacrament of marriage. Marrying Duška is an infringement of this sacrament and means breaking with the Catholic Church, the institution that has always been a mainstay of his life and beliefs. It is the existential importance of his decision, the irrevocable contract he is about to enter (and the contract—with the Church—he is about to irrevocably sever) that directs his most extended reflection on Othello's jealousy:

December 1925:

> To speak of the jealousy of Othello is a stupid figure of speech. Especially when Stendhal says of Byron, or Byron says of himself, that he has committed 'the crime of Othello', that is, killed a woman out of jealousy. Othello's jealousy is clearly not just the jealousy of someone in love. The most important thing is that Othello is Desdemona's husband and that the unfaithfulness of his wife is not just a betrayal and a disgrace but makes his whole existence meaningless. How, then, does he love Desdemona? *She loved me for the dangers I had passed. And I loved her that she did pity them.*
> This is surely not a psychological foundation for jealousy in the usual sense. As a stranger, he has married a Florentine [*sic*!]; that is his position; now he has come to dread the consequences of the futility of such a union; and he is jealous; yet not of just anybody, but of Cassio, the Florentine from a good family.
> The jealousy of Othello could also be understood in terms of Strindbergian feelings. Strindberg's jealousy is that of a woman. And, by the way, although he draws on all of literature, Strindberg does not concern himself with Othello. He could have just made the stupid remark that Othello was instinctively right, that he had intuited the as yet uncommitted faithlessness of Desdemona and had, so to speak, anticipated it. This would be stupid in a Strindbergian and at the same time proletarian way. It has also

---

[68] Apropos Iago Schmitt also notes: 'Is Iago a Florentine (Machiavelli?) (III.1, beginning). Cassio says: "*I never knew / A Florentine more kind and honest.*" (splendid!)' (fol. 5ʳ).

been said that Othello is not jealous. Dostoevsky said he is the opposite, he is credulous. All of this is psychology. In the fog of psychology everyone is jealous and also credulous, psychology is 'the stick with two ends'. One could talk endlessly and never come to a conclusion. But what is more important is that Othello is based on clear concepts—concepts, decisions and instructions. (fols. 6ʳ–7ʳ)

We will encounter Schmitt's rejection of 'the fog of psychology' again in a later chapter, and it will again be accompanied by Schmitt's own psychologizing.[69] Clearly, it is psychological intuition—an intuition sharpened by his own dilemma—that prompts Schmitt to surmise Othello's misgivings about his mismatched marriage. The compatibility of the spouses is crucial—and crucially lacking in Othello and Desdemona, just as Schmitt fears it might be crucially lacking in his own marriage.[70] But as so often with Schmitt, the personal is political and, vice versa, the political is intensely personal. The mismatch between Othello and Desdemona is a mirror for reflecting his own anxieties but it also goes to the heart of marriage as an institution:

> Othello: marriage like every institution is founded on homogeneity; this is lacking in Othello; marriage is not founded on contract alone. A modicum of homogeneity. But at the same time also heterogeneity (the heterogeneity of man and woman within the homogeneity of race or nation! Similarly the state: the heterogeneity of a group within the same unit!) (fol. 16ʳ)

Homogeneity is crucial in Schmitt's essay *The Concept of the Political*. Published in 1927, it hinges on Schmitt's famous claim that the foundational criterion of the political—as opposed to the moral, economic, or aesthetic—is the distinction between friend and enemy.[71] The entity to which this distinction relevantly applies is the state. And conversely: only with regard to the state is the friend–enemy distinction political, because only the sovereign state can enact the ultimate consequence of it: war.[72] Essential for the coherence of the state is not, in Schmitt's view, its constitution but the homogeneity of its people. The same applies to democracy, the rule of the *demos* (the people), which Schmitt sharply differentiates from the liberal parliamentary system of representation:

> Every actual democracy rests on the principle that not only are equals equal but unequals will not be treated equally. Democracy requires, therefore, first homogeneity and second—if the need arises—elimination or eradication of heterogeneity.[73]

In this conception of the nation state as the substantive, not just formally legal or constitutional, union of a homogeneous people, heterogeneity is the mark of the political enemy. He 'need not be morally evil or aesthetically ugly [...]. But

---

[69] See Chapter 8.

[70] Cf. the 'horrendous stupidity of my 2nd marriage' (8 October 1926).

[71] Schmitt, *The Concept of the Political*, 26.

[72] 'The political entity presupposes the real existence of an enemy and therefore coexistence with another political entity. [...] The political world is a pluriverse, not a universe.' Schmitt, *The Concept of the Political*, 53. The League of Nations was thus bound to fail—a liberal illusion which Schmitt, like a latter-day Machiavelli, opposed with his hard-headed realism.

[73] Schmitt, *The Crisis of Parliamentary Democracy*, 9.

he is, nevertheless, the other, the stranger; and it is sufficient for his nature that he is, in a specially intense way, existentially something different and alien.'[74] Inherent in Schmitt's philosophical nationalism is thus 'a logic of xenophobia': 'Only when the other has been politically marked as a "stranger" can he be treated as "enemy".'[75]

Within this conceptual framework, the characterization of Othello as 'the stranger' is both plausible and somewhat baffling. It is plausible because Othello makes a perfect match with the category of the stranger as developed by early twentieth-century sociologists, most influentially by Georg Simmel.[76] Unlike the 'wanderer', who comes today and leaves tomorrow, the stranger, Simmel says, 'comes today and stays tomorrow'. Simmel's crucial insight is the intricate meshing of distance and closeness that places the stranger not simply outside the community but in a special position within it. Nearness makes distance all the more visible, a distance predicated on origins. The stranger, as Schmitt never tires of saying of Othello, is deracinated, rootless.[77]

The case for Othello as stranger-and-therefore-enemy is much less obvious, not only because of Schmitt's strong identificatory attachment to 'the noble moor' (February 1924; 517) but also from a political perspective, because Othello has 'done the state some service, and they know't' (*Oth.* 5.2.332). Even so, from the point of view of Schmitt's *Concept of the Political*, the equation of Othello the stranger with Othello the enemy would seem unavoidable. '[E]xistentially something different and alien',[78] he does after all meet the key criterion of the enemy. But Schmitt's image of Othello is too complex for such a simple equation. The positive and the negative side are inseparably entwined. Thus what we find is that the divide between friend and enemy runs right through Schmitt's Othello; just as it does in Shakespeare's tragedy where this comes to the fore in Othello's dying speech and action:

> Set you down this,
> And say, besides, that in Aleppo once,
> Where a malignant and a turbaned Turk

---

[74] Schmitt, *The Concept of the Political*, 27.

[75] Friedrich Balke, 'Die Figur des Fremden bei Carl Schmitt und Georg Simmel', *Sociologia Internationalis* 1 (1992), 35–59 at 42.

[76] Simmel's classic essay on the stranger originally appeared as an excursus to a chapter on the sociology of space in Georg Simmel, *Soziologie: Untersuchungen über die Formen der Vergesellschaftung* (Leipzig: Duncker & Humblot, 1908). An English version is 'The Stranger', in Simmel, *On Individuality and Social Forms*, ed. Donald Levine (Chicago, IL: University of Chicago Press, 1971), 143–50.

[77] The example that occurs most readily to Simmel and his contemporary sociologists is the Jew. He is near, a neighbour and a fellow citizen, but 'rootless', and 'essentially' (though by no means actually) a 'wanderer'. For Schmitt, the step from Jew-as-stranger to Jew-as-enemy would seem to be an obvious one, but the equally obvious Shakespearean example, Shylock, is oddly not mentioned in Schmitt's cogitations on the stranger in Shakespeare's Venice. For an analysis of the inherently racist stereotyping of 'the Jew' in early twentieth-century German sociology, see Karl-Siegbert Rehberg, 'Das Bild des Judentums in der frühen deutschen Soziologie. "Fremdheit" und "Rationalität" als Typusmerkmale bei Werner Sombart, Max Weber und Georg Simmel', in *Rassenmythos und Sozialwissenschaften in Deutschland*, ed. Carsten Klingemann (Opladen: Westdeutscher Verlag, 1987), 80–127.

[78] Schmitt, *The Concept of the Political*, 27.

> Beat a Venetian and traduced the state,
> I took by th' throat the circumcisèd dog
> And smote him thus.
> [*He stabs himself.*] (Oth. 5.2.344–9)

Critics have often observed that Othello divides himself here into two opposing parts: agent and patient, executioner and criminal, Venetian and Turk, or, in Schmitt's terms, friend and enemy. Othello's parting gesture as both representative and enemy of the state of Venice gives the stamp of finality to the irreconcilable opposites that rend his existence, the hopelessness of his unbelonging. This makes Othello representative of humanity in general and, as we have seen in the diary entry discussed at the beginning of this chapter, he also comes to stand for the specific plight of post-First World War Germany. The entry ('Othello: the fate of man') predates the *Concept of the Political* by about three years. But in making Othello the representative of humanity who '*stands between*' the two opposing principles of 'Romanic' institutionalism and 'Slavic' anti-institutionalism, or form and formlessness, Schmitt also names the two enemies threatening the human (i.e. German) middle ground from either side. They are, prima facie, only opposite principles—and ethnically stereotyped ones at that—and Schmitt's *Concept of the Political* leaves us in no doubt that when he speaks of war he means real war, not a mere contest of ideas. But the hostile principles or modes of thought from which Schmitt distances Othello as well as himself also stand for Germany's geopolitical enemies on the two fronts, East and West, of the Great War.

Schmitt's comment on Othello's suicide follows the direction of the protagonist's final speech: away from Desdemona and her suffering, towards Othello's own plight and its larger symbolic significance.[79] Othello's killings are construed as a self-revolving act of double murder: 'Out of his loneliness'—the 'eternal homelessness' of the stranger—'he murders the civilization which adopted him out of mercy, out of loneliness; then he murders himself' (November/December 1923; 498). Schmitt never doubts that this self-administered retaliatory justice is honourable. Unlike 'the Germany of Ludendorff', Schmitt's Othello preserves his nobility to the end.[80]

---

[79] The larger significance of Othello prompts the only mention of Stefan George in Schmitt's Shakespearean reflections. Schmitt copied into his diary a conversation with the Master recorded in Marianne Weber's memoir of her husband Max Weber: 'That I (Marianne Weber) found Othello so painful and terrible, almost the product of an utter coldness of heart, seemed to him [George] a purely psychological, false and effete view: "Child, child! You must see it cosmically, not as an individual fate"' (fol. 30ʳ). 'Rather like Vic. Hugo then', Schmitt wonders, 'the struggle between night and light?' In his last entry on Othello Schmitt takes up the black-and-white contrast again, (mis)quoting the lines: 'Her face [*recte*: name], that was as white [*recte*: fresh] / As Dian's visage, is now begrimed and black / As mine own face. The line stands up to a thousand examinations. An abyss of psychology without any effort at psychologizing' (fol. 39ʳ).

[80] Elsewhere in the diary, Schmitt notes apropos 'The ending of Othello: For naught I did in hate, but all in honour' (fol. 20ʳ). Othello's view of his motives has had few adherents in recent decades. See, for example, Stephen A. Shapiro, 'Othello's Desdemona', *Literature and Psychology* 14 (1964), 56–61 at 59: 'In the last scene of Othello, Desdemona says, "That death's unnatural that kills for loving" (V.ii. 42). She thus prepares us to reject Othello's estimation of himself as "one that lov'd not wisely but too well." And Othello's protest that "nought did I in hate, but all in honour" (V.ii.295) is nothing but an evasion of self-knowledge.'

VII CAPTIVE CAPTAIN

When Schmitt eventually returned to Shakespeare it was not to Othello,[81] but to his 'unhappy, problematic brother Hamlet' (February 1924; 517): first with the preface he wrote to Lilian Winstanley's *Hamlet and the Scottish Succession*, translated into German by his daughter Anima, then with the study that developed out of this preface, *Hamlet or Hecuba* (1956).[82] The interim had seen him progress to a professorship at Berlin's venerable Frederick William (now Humboldt) University and the position of legal adviser to the short-lived last chancellor of the Weimar Republic, Kurt von Schleicher. At the time of the Nazi takeover in January 1933, this latter assignment could well have got him into trouble, but it did not. Instead, Hitler's 'National Revolution' raised him to even greater heights: the chairmanship of the National Socialist German Association of Jurists (*Nationalsozialistischer Deutscher Juristen-Bund/NSDJB*) and the title of a Prussian state councillor. The most prominent lawyer and 'crown-jurist' of the Third Reich, he gave his learned approval to the dictatorial measures of the new regime. These included the Nuremberg Race Laws passed in September 1935, which classified sexual relations between Jews and 'Aryans' as miscegenation (*Rassenschande*: 'racial defilement'), a severely punishable offence.

Under the title 'The Constitution of Freedom',[83] Schmitt exulted that '[f]or the first time in many centuries, the concepts in our constitution are once again German' (324). The constitutions of the recent past had been derivative of 'Anglo-French law':

> Their citizen was an unsuccessful copy of the *citoyen*. [These] constitutions did not speak of German blood and German honor. The word 'German' appeared only in order to emphasize that 'all Germans are equal before the law'. But this sentence, which would have found its correct meaning in a concept of 'German' that aims at substance and recognizes the people [*Volk*], instead served to treat aliens in species and Germans equally and to view anyone who was equal before the law as German [...] Today the German people has [...] become the German people again. Under the law of 15 September, German blood and German honor are the main concepts of our law.

---

[81] There is some indication, however, that even when he stopped writing about Othello, Schmitt continued to talk about him. This is suggested by the appearance of some of Schmitt's most characteristic views on the Moor of Venice in an essay on *State and Drama* (Berlin: Junker und Dünnhaupt, 1932) written by an acquaintance of his, Gustav Steinbömer. Othello, Steinbömer writes, 'is no pariah and no outcast, but a great lord. [...] He is a noble and wise general [...] But he is a stranger without a home or a state. [...] Jealousy is only the medium through which the tragedy of the homeless man unfolds itself' (10).

[82] See Chapter 8.

[83] Carl Schmitt, 'The Constitution of Freedom', trans. Belinda Cooper, in *Weimar: A Jurisprudence of Crisis*, ed. Arthur J. Jacobson and Bernhard Schlink (Berkeley, Los Angeles, and London: University of California Press, 2000), 323–5. References to this edition are given in brackets in the text. The original appeared as Carl Schmitt, 'Die Verfassung der Freiheit', *Deutsche Juristen-Zeitung* 40 (1935), cols 1133–5. The title takes up the theme of the Nuremberg party rally, the *Reichsparteitag der Freiheit*, at which the notorious race law 'for the Protection of German Blood and German Honour' (*Gesetz zum Schutz des deutschen Blutes und der deutschen Ehre*) was proclaimed. The Reichstag, which had been especially convened in Nuremberg for the occasion, also passed the Statute on Reich Citizenship (*Reichsbürgergesetz*) redefining German citizenship and a law which replaced the Republic's black, red, and gold tricolour with the red swastika flag.

The state is now a tool of the people's strength and unity. The German Reich now has a single flag—the flag of the National Socialist movement—and this flag is not only composed of colors, but also has a large, true symbol: the symbol of the swastika that conjures up the people. (324–5)

What Schmitt calls here 'the constitution of freedom' was at first primarily directed at Jews, but later expressly stipulated 'Gypsies, Negroes or their bastard offspring'.[84]

Schmitt, it appears, had laid to rest the ghost of Othello, whose relations with Desdemona would have carried the death penalty under the new statutes. Neither the Moor nor the faithful gypsy were the kind of stranger it would have been safe to harbour under one's roof, let alone embrace as one's blood brothers. Schmitt had escaped from the chaos of Weimar into the arms of the new order. But while this order, with its uncompromising distinction between friend and enemy, may have seemed to endorse Schmitt's normative idea of the political, it also blunted the creativity that had enabled him to produce such ideas. Nothing Schmitt wrote during the phase of his greatest public success comes anywhere near the quality of his earlier writings.[85] What he had to say, it seems, found its enabling condition in the inner and outer chaos that Schmitt called The Shadow of God, that zone of un-distinction where he encountered himself in the black face of Othello.

* * *

There is a postscript to this: In early 1941 Schmitt read Herman Melville's novella *Benito Cereno* and was enthralled at once.[86] Closely based on a factual account,[87] it tells the story of Benito Cereno, the captain of a Spanish slave ship, the *Saint Dominick*. He loses command, and most of his crew are killed when the slaves revolt and take over the ship. Cereno is left alive and forced to navigate the *Saint Dominick*, now under the command of the slave leader Babo. But this is not revealed until the end of the story, which is told from the first-person perspective of Almasa Delano, the captain of an American merchant vessel that encounters the by now badly dilapidated *Saint Dominick* off the coast of Chile. Invited on board the Spanish ship, the American captain and his officers are treated to an elaborate charade. Cereno behaves oddly, but the unshakably naive Delano suspects nothing: as far as he is concerned, this is a slave ship and Cereno is its captain. Only when the Americans take their leave does the truth emerge. At the very last

---

[84] *Ministerialblatt für die Preußische innere Verwaltung*, 26 November 1935; quoted in Sybil H. Milton, '"Gypsies" as Social Outsiders in Nazi Germany', in *Social Outsiders in Nazi Germany*, ed. Robert Gellately and Nathan Stoltzfus (Princeton, NJ: Princeton University Press, 2001), 212–32 at 216.

[85] By the time Schmitt wrote his book on the *Leviathan* of Thomas Hobbes (1938), the days of his public success under the Nazi regime were over. Carl Schmitt, *The Leviathan in the State Theory of Thomas Hobbes*, trans. George D. Schwab and Erna Hilfstein (Santa Barbara, CA: Greenwood Press, 1996).

[86] Schmitt's fascination is documented in his correspondence with Ernst Jünger, with whom he engaged in an extended discussion of the comparative merits of Melville and Poe. See Ernst Jünger and Carl Schmitt, *Briefwechsel. Briefe 1930–1983*, ed. Helmuth Kiesel (Stuttgart: Klett-Cotta, 1999).

[87] Amasa Delano (1763–1823), *Narrative of Voyages and Travels in the Northern and Southern Hemispheres: Comprising Three Voyages Round the World; Together with a Voyage of Survey and Discovery, in the Pacific Ocean and Oriental Islands* (Boston: House, 1817).

moment, Cereno escapes his captors with a desperate leap into the departing American dinghy. The rebellious slaves are arrested, and Babo is tried and executed. But Benito Cereno does not long survive him. Broken by his ordeal, he dies soon after Babo's execution.

By the time Schmitt read Melville's story he had fallen out of favour with the regime. A campaign launched against him by rival Nazi lawyers in 1936 cost him his party offices and, if only for a short while, threatened graver repercussions. Powerful patrons intervened and saved his Berlin chair and even the title of State Councillor. But although he continued as a highly respected member of his profession, published widely, and lectured at home and abroad, his relation to the regime became one of wary detachment.

Benito Cereno spoke strongly to Schmitt's geopolitical interests at the time: the relationship between land and sea power, and the 'translation of empire' from the Old World to the New, the overthrow of European cultural traditions by modern mass civilization.[88] But more than anything else, Melville's novella became his personal myth, the perfect allegory of his situation under the Nazis as he would have the world understand it after 1945. Vindicating his behaviour as role-play enforced by Babo-Hitler and his 'brown' barbarians, Schmitt's identification with Melville's doomed hero went so far that he took to signing himself 'Benito Cereno'.[89] 'I am the last conscious representative of the *jus publicum Europaeum*', he wrote during his internment by the Americans, 'and I am experiencing its demise just as Benito Cereno experienced the journey of the pirate ship.'[90]

'The black man', it seems, had caught up with him again. Not in the shape of Shakespeare's noble Moor and certainly not as a friend and brother, but as a hostile other which is so symbiotically enmeshed with the self that the self cannot survive its amputation:

'You are saved,' cried Captain Delano, more and more astonished and pained; 'you are saved: what has cast such a shadow upon you?' 'The negro.'[91]

Schmitt never escaped the shadow either.

---

[88] 'Together with his friend Ernst Jünger, Schmitt read the American authors Herman Melville and Edgar Allan Poe as prophets of the global situation of World War II and of the post-war period, including [...] the waning of the epoch of national sovereignty.' Thomas O. Beebee, 'Carl Schmitt's Myth of Benito Cereno', *Seminar: A Journal of Germanic Studies* 42.2 (2006) 114–34 at 114. Non-Schmittian critics have often focused on the question of whether the novella is racist and pro-slavery or anti-racist and abolitionist. See Lea Bertani Vozar Newman, 'Benito Cereno', in her *Reader's Guide to the Short Stories of Herman Melville* (Boston, MA: G. K. Hall, 1986), 95–153 at 130–45.

[89] Beebee, 'Carl Schmitt's Myth of Benito Cereno', 120: 'Shortly after the end of the war, Schmitt asked that a *Waschzettel* [blurb] be printed with any future editions of his book *Leviathan*, first published in 1938. It warned against reading the book, and was signed at the bottom not by "Carl Schmitt," but by "Benito Cereno."' For Schmitt's use of Benito Cereno as an allegory of his plight under the Nazis: Ruth Groh, *Arbeit an der Heillosigkeit der Welt: Zur politisch-theologischen Mythologie und Anthropologie Carl Schmitts* (Frankfurt: Suhrkamp, 1998), 135–46.

[90] Carl Schmitt, *Ex Captivitate Salus: Erfahrungen der Zeit 1945–47* (Cologne: Greven, 1950), 75. Scheuermann, *Carl Schmitt: The End of Law*, 177–8, plausibly suggests that Schmitt found his situation in American captivity and, more generally, the situation of America's global ascendancy over the declining powers of Europe, allegorized in 'Benito Cereno', too.

[91] Herman Melville, 'Benito Cereno', in *The Writings of Herman Melville*, vol. 9: *The Piazza Tales and Other Prose Pieces 1839–1860*, ed. Harrison Hayford et al. (Evanston, IL: Northwestern University Press, 1987), 47–117 at 116.

6

Third Reich Shakespeare

I CONSPIRATORS' CHOICE

When the three Booth brothers, Edwin, Junius, and John Wilkes, performed Shakespeare's *Julius Caesar* at the Winter Garden Theatre in November 1864, this was acclaimed as 'the greatest theatrical event in New York history'.[1] But the event dwindled to the status of a footnote when John Wilkes Booth changed the course of American history with his performance a few months later at Ford's Theatre in Washington DC. That event, too, was given a Shakespearean touch when the actor exclaimed, after shooting Lincoln: 'Sic semper tyrannis' ('Thus always to tyrants'), the words attributed to Brutus at Caesar's assassination.[2]

Five and a half decades later, the same play, *Julius Caesar*, was again tackled by three brothers; this time not to high public acclaim, but in private. In a performance of the night scene before the battle of Philippi (*JC* 4.3) which the three Stauffenberg brothers gave at their family home in 1920, Berthold took the part of Caesar's ghost, his twin Alexander played Brutus, and the thirteen-year-old Claus played Brutus's servant Lucius. But it was Claus, the youngest, who took the leading role in the assassination attempt on Hitler on 20 July 1944, which, unlike that of Booth, unfortunately failed to change the course of history. After the event a copy of *Julius Caesar*, with Brutus's part marked out, was apparently discovered open on Claus von Stauffenberg's desk.[3]

Stefan George, who became the guiding influence on their lives, had been right in believing that the brothers were destined for greatness, although he could not possibly have foreseen the specific shape of that destiny. There is no telling whether he would have approved of his disciples' actions[4] but there can be no doubt that they felt sanctioned by his teachings. In the final weeks of Operation Valkyrie,

[1] Philip Kunhardt, Jr, *A New Birth of Freedom* (Boston: Little, Brown, 1983), 342–3. The proceeds were donated towards a Shakespeare statue for Central Park by John Quincy Adams Ward (1830–1910), which still stands today.

[2] Cf. David Herbert Donald, *Lincoln* (New York: Simon & Schuster, 1995), 585–99; see also Michael W. Kauffman, *American Brutus: John Wilkes Booth and the Lincoln Conspiracies* (New York: Random House, 2004). The words are also the state motto of Virginia.

[3] Bernhard Minetti, *Erinnerungen eines Schauspielers*, ed. Günther Rühle (Stuttgart: Deutsche Verlags-Anstalt, 1985), 108.

[4] The George biographer Robert E. Norton claims that George would have condemned the assassination attempt and regarded Stauffenberg as a traitor. Norton, 'Lyrik und Moral', *Die Zeit*, 20 July 2009, <http://www.zeit.de/2009/30/Dichter-George>, accessed 21 June 2015.

Claus von Stauffenberg drew up an 'Oath' to which he and his closest associates committed themselves. It is unmistakably inspired by the Master:

We believe in the future of the Germans.

We know that the German has powers which designate him to lead the community of the occidental nations towards a more beautiful life.

We acknowledge in spirit and in deed the great traditions of our nation which, through the amalgamation of Hellenic and Christian origins in the Germanic character, created western man.

We want a New Order which makes all Germans supporters of the state and guarantees them law and justice, but we scorn the lie of equality and we bow before the hierarchies established by nature.

We want a nation which will remain rooted in the soil of the homeland close to the powers of nature, which will find its happiness and its satisfaction in its given surroundings and, free and proud, will overcome the low passions of envy and jealous resentment.

[...]

We pledge to live blamelessly,
to serve in obedience,
to keep silent unswervingly,
and to stand for each other.[5]

The future Germany envisaged in this secret manifesto has obviously very little in common with the type of democracy on which the post-war Federal Republic was to be modelled. Reading more like an oath of loyalty to the Secret Germany of Stefan George, it represents the most high-minded form of the national idealism which helped bring the Nazis to power and which the Nazis incessantly invoked in maintaining that power. Whether the conspirators' 'cause or [their] performance / Did need an oath' (*JC* 2.1.134) is a moot point; just as it is debatable whether Brutus was well-advised to prevent such an oath ('No, not an oath.' *JC* 2.1.113) immediately before launching into a speech that puts his fellow conspirators under the even greater obligational power of their blood:

> [...] when every drop of blood
> That every Roman bears, and nobly bears,
> Is guilty of a several bastardy
> If he do break the smallest particle
> Of any promise that hath passed from him. (*JC* 2.1.135–9)

Both Stauffenberg's oath and Brutus's non-oath testify to their author-speakers' ethical norms and code of honour. In both cases these norms are pitted against a political reality that has effectively cut the ground from under them. Brutus's aristocratic republicanism is a lost cause in a Rome inexorably pushing towards the dictatorial rule of empire. The same holds for Stauffenberg. Even if the bomb in his briefcase had killed the tyrant, the ideals Stauffenberg sought to recover were so

---

[5] The document is quoted in Peter Hoffmann, *Stauffenberg: A Family History, 1905–1944*, 3rd edn (Montreal: McGill-Queen's University Press, 2008), 293–4.

tainted by the crimes committed in their name that no purgative deed, however courageous and noble, could have restored them to a state of innocence.[6] Stauffenberg's deed, as the 'Oath' proclaims it, is the Secret Germany's ultimate, most heroic attempt to win the future by recovering the past, an attempt to reclaim a national ideal from the Nazis, who had abused and perverted it. The term 'conservative revolution' is perhaps never more appropriately applied than to the ill-fated officers' putsch of 20 July 1944, in which members of a military elite steeped in aristocratic traditions of service and duty to the nation fought to salvage or 'conserve' their vision of a 'holy Germany'.[7]

When supporters of the Earl of Essex had the deposition of King Richard II performed for them at the Globe on the eve of their rebellion, they were attempting to persuade themselves that such a thing could actually be done. Stauffenberg's choice of *Julius Caesar* offered more ambivalent encouragement: such a thing, it shows, could be done and still be doomed to failure.

But the ambivalence of Shakespeare's *Julius Caesar* was not lost on the Nazi leadership either and occasionally drew their comment. Walter Thomas, dramaturge for the Second German Shakespeare Week (10–15 October 1937), recalls that Rudolf Hess applauded the performance but commented in private afterwards that the play might prove dangerous 'if it fell into the wrong hands'.[8]

The organizers of the Bochum event were obviously well aware of this danger and determined to avert it by firmly denying that it even existed. The festival week, a joint venture between the German Shakespeare Society and the Bochum theatre under the direction of Stefan George's cousin Saladin Schmitt, was dedicated to the Roman plays.[9] Werner Deetjen, the president of the society, made sure the audience got the right message. He wrote, in the booklet accompanying the event:

> In our time, which again firmly emphasises the heroic, we welcome with particular joy the plan to put before our eyes, through these performances of the Roman plays, several heroic figures who far transcend the level of average humanity. [...] Julius Caesar,

[6] The attempts of the conspirators to win support abroad came to naught. See Klemens von Klemperer, *German Resistance against Hitler: The Search for Allies 1938–1945* (Oxford: Oxford University Press, 1994). One of the members of the conspiracy, the diplomat Adam von Trott, failed to convince Maurice Bowra that there was such a thing as an opposition to Hitler. Bowra regarded Trott, who was executed within days of the failed plot in July 1944, as untrustworthy and communicated this view widely, thereby preventing the success of Trott's mission in both Britain and the US. Bowra later conceded that his 'main reason for suspicion was quite unfounded' and that 'my rejection of him remains one of my bitterest regrets'. Bowra, *Memories*, 306.

[7] According to George's biographer, Stauffenberg's last words in front of the firing squad were 'Long live the secret Germany!' (Karlauf, *Stefan George*, 638); but most witnesses claim they were 'Long live holy Germany!' Hoffmann, *Stauffenberg*, 277.

[8] W. Th. Andermann (=Werner Thomas), *Bis der Vorhang fiel* (Dortmund: Schwalvenberg, 1947), 324–7 and 337. See Werner Habicht, 'Shakespeare und der deutsche Shakespeare-Mythus im Dritten Reich', in *Anglistik: Research Paradigms and Institutional Policies, 1930–2000*, ed. Stephan Kohl (Trier: Wissenschaftlicher Verlag Trier, 2005), 79–111 at 106.

[9] The first 'German Shakespeare Week', held in Bochum in 1927, offered all ten of Shakespeare's English history plays directed by Schmitt, who had begun as a talented poet but found his real vocation in the theatre. See *Saladin Schmitt. Blätter der Erinnerung*, ed. City of Bochum (Bochum: Ferdinand Kamp, 1964); Ruth von Ledebur, *Der Mythos vom deutschen Shakespeare. Die Deutsche Shakespeare-Gesellschaft zwischen Politik und Wissenschaft 1918–1945* (Cologne: Böhlau, 2002), 20–9; and Hortmann, *Shakespeare on the German Stage*, vol. 2, 93–101.

the solitary figure with his self-sacrificing heroism, a figure who commanded all of the poet's love, completely dedicated himself to the service of the fatherland. He increased and strengthened the realm and falls before completing his great work, but his mighty spirit prevails even after his death. Caesar dominates the whole tragedy; he is the hero of this highly political drama, not Brutus, as they seem to think nowadays in France. To represent Caesar [...] as a weak-willed old man is completely wrong.[10]

Not only critics from France might well, and did, question the proposition that Caesar commanded Shakespeare's undivided love. Many nineteenth-century Shakespeareans who also happened to be admirers of Julius Caesar were puzzled if not downright indignant that the greatest of poets had, as they saw it, failed to do justice to the greatest of men. According to an American critic, Shakespeare's Caesar 'is indeed little better than a grand strutting piece of puff-paste [...], than which nothing could be further from the truth of the man'. After detailing this 'truth of the man' in a paean to his supreme qualities, the critic concluded: 'This [...] contradiction between Caesar as known and Caesar as rendered by [Shakespeare] is what, more than anything else in the drama, perplexes me.'[11]

If President Deetjen was determined not to acknowledge any of the perplexing features of Shakespeare's Caesar, his vice-president, Professor Wolfgang Keller of Münster, at least conceded some ambivalence. Unlike other dramatists, he explains, Shakespeare was interested not in the struggle between Caesar and Pompey but in the assassination of Caesar and its tragic consequences:

Therefore the life of Brutus fills his play—that of Caesar is over in Act three. Nevertheless, Caesar's gigantic imperatorial figure looms so large beside that of Brutus that the shadow of the dead man falls darkly over the second half of the play. Brutus is closest to Shakespeare's heart, Caesar dominates his imagination.[12]

A difference of opinion—or just a circumspect division of labour, sailing sympathy with Brutus the tyrannicide under the flag of extolling Caesar the tyrant? Closer study of the history of the German Shakespeare Society during the Third Reich makes such a balancing act quite plausible.[13] The case of *Julius Caesar* shows some of the complications involved in accommodating Shakespeare to the new order after 1933.[14] For all its massive efforts at thought-control, the regime acted much

---

[10] Werner Deetjen, 'Die Zweite Deutsche Shakespeare-Woche', in *Festschrift zur Zweiten Deutschen Shakespeare-Woche*, ed. City of Bochum and the German Shakespeare Society (Leipzig: Max Beck, 1937), 6–10 at 8–9.

[11] Henry N. Hudson, *Shakespeare: His Life, Art, and Characters*, 2 vols (Boston: Ginn, 1872), vol. 2, 224. H. H. Furness's variorum *Julius Caesar* gives a highly instructive selection of similar statements. I have discussed this in more detail in Andreas Höfele, 'Beware the Ides of March: Shakespeare and the 19th-Century Caesar Myth', *Cahiers Elisabéthains* 89 (Autumn 2016, forthcoming), Special Issue: *Shakespeare and Myth*, ed. Florence March, Jean-Christophe Mayer, and Nathalie Vienne-Guerin. As noted in Chapter 2, Nietzsche apparently had no problem to reconcile his unqualified admiration for Caesar with an equally unqualified admiration for Shakespeare's portrayal of Caesar.

[12] Wolfgang Keller, 'Shakespeares Römerdramen', in *Festschrift zur Zweiten Deutschen Shakespeare-Woche*, 11–14 at 13. After Deetjen's death in 1939 Keller succeeded him as president of the German Shakespeare Society.

[13] Von Ledebur, *Der Mythos vom deutschen Shakespeare*, 92–157 and 192–233.

[14] Shakespeare's reception in Nazi Germany has been the subject of numerous studies. See for example Werner Habicht, 'Shakespeare and Theatre Politics in the Third Reich', in *The Play out of*

less consistently than its rhetoric would suggest. Situational contingencies and fierce competition among the various agencies of cultural policy[15] resulted in a far from consistent response to the Bard.

II SHAKESPEARE AND THE GERMANIC SPIRIT

'Heroic', 'steely romantic', 'unsentimentally direct', 'national with great pathos', and 'communally binding': this is how Goebbels, in his inaugural address to directors of German theatres on 8 May 1933, envisaged the art of the next decade. Art would either be like this, he declared, or it would not be at all.[16] No one, he said, could stand aside at this moment of national renewal and pretend that art was above politics (31). But knowing how to sweeten threat with promise, he assured his listeners that as long as they did not persist in the errors of the past, as long as they opened their hearts to the vital forces of the time and the communal urge of the people (*Volksdrang*; 37), their artistic freedom would be respected. 'We are much too artistically inclined', Goebbels said, to infringe upon 'the laws of artistic form' (31). 'We', he suggested, were in fact colleagues. Politics, after all, was an art too, even 'the highest of all arts' (31). While the sculptor imposed form on 'dead stone', the statesman did the same to the living masses, 'breathing form and life into them so that they become a people' (31).[17] The unbounded liberal individualism of the past, manifesting itself in the self-centred experiments of the avant-garde, had severed the vital link between art and the people. The crucial mission now was to restore that link, 'to lead art back to the people in order to lead the people back to art' (37).

Goebbels ended his speech with the assurance that there would be 'no restrictions on artistic creativity' (37). 'We do not intend to limit or narrow your sovereign rule over your subject matter' (37). If art let itself be carried by 'the same eruptive values' as current politics, it would 'mobilise the masses […], and you [the theatre directors] will find the same enjoyment in your work as we do in our

---

Context: Transferring Plays from Culture to Culture, ed. Hanna Scolnicov and Peter Holland (Cambridge: Cambridge University Press, 1989), 110–20; Rodney Symington, *The Nazi Appropriation of Shakespeare: Cutural Politics in the Third Reich* (Lewiston, NY: Edwin Mellen Press, 2005); John London, 'Non-German Drama in the Third Reich', in *Theatre under the Nazis*, ed. John London (Manchester and New York: Manchester University Press, 2000), 222–61.

[15] See for example Reinhard Bollmus, *Das Amt Rosenberg und seine Gegner. Studien zum Machtkampf im nationalsozialistischen Herrschaftssystem* (Stuttgart: Deutsche Verlags-Anstalt, 1970).

[16] Goebbels, 'Rede des Reichspropagandaministers Dr. Joseph Goebbels vor den deutschen Theaterleitern am 8. Mai 1933', 36. Page references are given in brackets in the text. I have quoted the passage in Chapter 4. It is also discussed in Habicht, 'Shakespeare and Theatre Politics in the Third Reich', 110, and William Grange, 'Ordained Hands on the Altar of Art: Gründgens, Hilpert, and Fehling in Berlin', in *Theatre in the Third Reich: The Prewar Years*, ed. Glen W. Gadberry (Westport, CT and London: Greenwood Press, 1995), 75–89 at 78.

[17] Wolfram Pyta, *Hitler. Der Künstler als Politiker und Feldherr. Eine Herrschaftsanalyse* [Hitler: The Artist as Politician and Military Commander. An Analysis of Rule] (Munich: Siedler, 2015) argues that Hitler's sway over both his immediate subordinates and the population at large crucially depended on his projection of himself as an artistic genius.

political art [...] If you cooperate, our sympathy and support will not be lacking. We stand by you if you stand by us' (39).

Such wooing did not fail to impress. Yet the minister's call for that 'steel-throbbing [*stahldurchzittert*], iron Romanticism which you see in our symbols, hear in our marching steps' (35) failed to produce the dramatic masterpieces that would match up to the self-declared 'greatness' of the time. As it turned out—and as the blending of politics and art in Goebbels's speech indicates—the only form of theatre at which the Nazis excelled were the mass spectacles of the Nuremberg party rallies.[18] What happened in the actual playhouses of the Reich was by and large much more conventional, and purposely so. Although the theatres, like every other area of German culture, were subjected to *Gleichschaltung* (bringing in line), the repertoire was not dominated by Nazi propaganda plays. A more defining feature of Third Reich theatre politics was, in Werner Habicht's words, 'the official insistence on conservative, true-to-score performances of the classics, on the principle of *Werktreue*'.[19] As William Grange puts it: 'The imposition of the Nazi lexicon on the entirety of German theatre became secondary [...] to an old-fashioned reverence for theatre [which the Nazi leadership] had learned as schoolboys.'[20]

From the beginning, it was never in doubt that the classical repertoire of the German stage was to be a mainstay of Third Reich culture. Goebbels's call for a new spirit did not imply that this spirit could only manifest itself in new plays. Indicating the direction in which he wanted the theatre to move, he cited a production of Schiller's *Wilhelm Tell*, which premièred at the Deutsches Theater, Berlin, on 5 May 1933, 'an artistic feat' that he said was 'absolutely up to date':

[A]nyone in touch with the present moment had the feeling: this drama was written only yesterday. But it is well over a hundred years old. There were no storm troopers marching in it, only Swiss peasants. Yet it was so absolutely modern [...] and seized the spectators with such force that one simply could not resist its tremendous impact. (36)[21]

---

[18] The spectacle of the Nazi Party rallies was transferred to film in the two propaganda films by Leni Riefenstahl, *Victory of Belief* (1933) and *Triumph of the Will* (1935), the latter, according to Susan Sontag, 'the most successfully, most purely propagandistic film ever made'. Sontag, 'Fascinating Fascism', *The New York Review of Books*, 6 February 1975, <http://www.nybooks.com/articles/archives/1975/feb/06/fascinating-fascism>, accessed 14 May 2015.

[19] Habicht, 'Shakespeare and Theatre Politics in the Third Reich', 117.

[20] Grange, 'Ordained Hands on the Altar of Art', 79–80. Grange also shows that the fierce competition between Goebbels, who, as minister for theatre, was in charge of the Deutsches Theater, Berlin, and Hermann Göring, who, as prime minister of Prussia, was in charge of the Prussian State Theatre (formerly Jessner's stage), led to a race for the most star-studded casts and the highest artistic standards, not to a contest in ideological fervour and political correctness.

[21] The production was directed by Carl Ludwig Achaz-Duisberg, and the cast included Heinrich George, one of the stars of the period, as an impressive Gessler. The other production Goebbels praised was *Schlageter*, written by the Nazi dramatist Hanns Johst, a member of Alfred Rosenberg's *Kampfbund für deutsche Kultur* (Militant League for German Culture). Dedicated to Adolf Hitler, this play about a free corps fighter who was executed by the French occupying forces in 1923 premièred at the Preußisches Staatsschauspiel on Hitler's birthday, 20 April 1933. Like Horst Wessel (see Chapter 4, section VII), Albert Leo Schlageter, who was celebrated as 'the first soldier of the Third Reich', became a mythical figure in the Nazi cult of the 'martyrs' of their movement. Cf. Manfred Franke, *Albert Leo Schlageter. Der erste Soldat des Dritten Reiches. Die Entmythologisierung eines Helden* (Köln: Prometheus-Verlag, 1980).

Shakespeare's place in the classic German repertoire was undisputed. Like the rest of this repertoire, his plays were thought to have suffered at the hands of a decadent, predominantly Jewish, modernism.[22] Time and again the name Jessner served as a shibboleth for every desecration the theatre of the Republic had to answer for. After the 'degenerate art' of the Weimar stage, the masterpieces of the past were to be restored to their true form and meaning in a spirit of reverence. 'Wherever Shakespeare is brought to life on the stages of the Third Reich', we read in a popular introduction to Shakespeare in 1940, 'he is treated with that reverence for the greatness of his genius which was entirely lost in the years of decline', i.e. the years of the Weimar Republic.[23]

Hitler himself had defined this attitude in *Mein Kampf*, where he denounces 'the artistic aberrations' of modernity as 'morbid monstrosities [...] produced by insane and degenerate people':

> What would the great dramatists of other times have said [...]? How exasperated Schiller would have been, and how Goethe would have turned away in disgust! But what are Schiller, Goethe and Shakespeare when confronted with the heroes of our modern German literature? Old and frowsy and outmoded and finished. For it was typical of this epoch [the early twentieth century] that not only were its own products bad but that the authors of such products and their backers reviled everything that had really been great in the past. This is a phenomenon that is very characteristic of such epochs. The more vile and miserable are the men and products of an epoch, the more they will hate and denigrate the ideal achievements of former generations. [...] [This] was not a question of new, though wrong, cultural ideas but of a process which was undermining the very foundations of civilization. [...] If the creative spirit of the Periclean age be manifested in the Parthenon, then the Bolshevist era is manifested through its cubist grimace.[24]

This is Hitler the creator of vapid water-colours ranting at those who had dared to thwart his artistic ambitions.[25] Reactionary philistinism of this kind could count on broad approval from the conservative middle classes. To this mode of thinking, the status of the established 'classic' is never in question, but simply taken for granted, a cultural icon of established value eliciting a fixed set of 'proper' responses.

Shakespeare features in much the same way in Alfred Rosenberg's *Myth of the Twentieth Century*. Together with a dozen other all-time luminaries—Michelangelo, Rembrandt, Dante, Goethe, Beethoven, etc.—Shakespeare is not paid any particular attention, let alone explored in detail. He is cited as a cliché of greatness,

---

[22] Three groundbreaking innovators of the German-speaking stage between the 1890s and 1920s were Jewish: Otto Brahm (1856–1912), Max Reinhardt (1873–1943), and Leopold Jessner. Erwin Piscator (1893–1966) and Bertolt Brecht were condemned for their leftist politics.

[23] Paul Meißner, *Shakespeare* [Sammlung Göschen vol. 1142] (Berlin: De Gruyter, 1940), 111.

[24] Adolf Hitler, *Mein Kampf*, trans. James Murphy (London: Hurst and Blackett, 1939), 205–6.

[25] Hitler applied for admittance to Vienna's Academy of Fine Arts twice and was twice rejected (1907 and 1908), because 'the sketches which I had brought with me unquestionably showed that painting was not what I was suited for but that the same sketches gave clear indications of my aptitude for architectural designing'. *Mein Kampf*, 28.

ready to hand when an outstanding instance of breadth, height, or depth of vision is needed.[26]

The first thing to note about Shakespeare in the Third Reich, then, is not that his standing was remarkably high, but that his undisputedly high standing was quite unremarkable, a foregone conclusion. This is hardly surprising. The default position with regard to Shakespeare, after 1933 as much as before, was and always had been the certainty of his towering greatness. Much as they saw themselves as revolutionaries, the Nazis did not question this certainty. And when some of them did, they were clearly articulating a minority position, which itself followed the venerable precedent of a nineteenth-century minority of Shakespeare detractors. These detractors—the dramatist Christian Grabbe, for example—had not so much diminished the Bard as testified to his overwhelming presence, finding their own efforts at dramatic composition stunted by the shadow of a giant.[27] We will come back to Shakespeare's Nazi detractors, but take a look first at the dominant chorus of approval and the way in which it claimed a special affinity between Shakespeare and the Third Reich.

'Shakepeare and Us', a brief essay published in Alfred Rosenberg's *National Socialist Monthly* in 1934, did just that. Written by Rosenberg's personal secretary, Thilo von Trotha, it was clearly intended to settle the issue of Shakespeare's position in the new Germany. If indeed it was an issue: the very brevity of the piece (just over 500 words) suggests that there was no ground for contention at all. Von Trotha briskly refutes the view, recently stated by 'a personality from abroad',[28] that Shakespeare wrote only in order to entertain and fill his theatre: 'We believe that Shakespeare, like all great Nordic artists, created his work from inner necessity and that behind all of his creations there lies a clear, tangible world view [*Weltanschauung*]' (74). Trotha is equally dismissive of 'the so-called problematics' of Shakespeare, 'this nineteenth-century invention': 'For all their immense richness, the works of Shakespeare are really very simple, as plain and simple as Nordic art always is' (75). And, just as plainly and simply, Trotha declares: 'Shakespeare was the creator of Nordic character drama' (74). In Greek tragedy the fate of the hero is determined from without. The tragic fate of Shakespeare's heroes 'is determined from within'. 'For us the whole value of Shakespeare's world view is comprised in this finding' (75):

---

[26] For example: 'The Northlander [...] wishes for inwardly conditioned, organically creative rhythm. There are naturally only a few who are capable of carrying this Nordic rhythm throughout their entire life, through their entire works. But because of this they are the greatest of our spirit, our race. [...] This is revealed to us in the works of Michael Angelo, Shakespeare, and Beethoven.' Alfred Rosenberg, *The Myth of the Twentieth Century*, trans. James Whisker, <https://archive.org/details/TheMythOfThe20thCentury>, accessed 19 August 2015. Rosenberg, often called the chief ideologue of the NSDAP, was the 'Führer's deputy for the ideological education of the NSDAP' (*Beauftragter des Führers für die gesamte geistige und weltanschauliche Erziehung der NSDAP*) and head of the *Amt Rosenberg* (ARo, Rosenberg Office), one of the official bodies for cultural policy and surveillance within the Nazi Party. He was often at loggerheads with Goebbels's Reich Ministry of Propaganda. Cf. Bollmus, *Das Amt Rosenberg und seine Gegner*.

[27] Christian Dietrich Grabbe, 'Über die Shakspearo-Manie' (1827), in Grabbe, *Werke und Briefe. Historisch-kritische Gesamtausgabe*, ed. Alfred Bergmann, vol. 4 (Emsdetten: Lechte, 1966), 27–55.

[28] Thilo von Trotha, 'Shakespeare und wir', *Nationalsozialistische Monatshefte* 5 (1934), 74–5 at 74. Page references are given in brackets in the text.

'[I]n the face of destiny man's ultimate decision comes from within, from his character, not from without' (75). This is why Shakespeare 'should more than ever be known in Germany today'. His 'truly Germanic mixture of wisdom and inner passion, of relentless hardness and human kindness should meet with true understanding in our great and hard time' (75). This is no time for 'the aesthetic quibbling of oversubtle scholars': 'For us Shakespeare is red-blooded life itself' and, Trotha concludes, 'one of the great liberators of the Germanic spirit' (75).

The idea of Shakespeare as 'Nordic' long antedates the Nazi vogue. 'The alliance of the German spirit with the North', Ernst Bertram said in a lecture he delivered at the University of Copenhagen in 1925, even 'preceded the Romantics'. It was already apparent in 'our eighteenth century, which culminated in the battle of minds over the greatest of "Nordic" poets, Shakespeare'.[29]

It was Herder, arguing for the idea of folk poetry, who emphasized the Nordic or Germanic roots of English culture. The English Shakespeare, he suggested, was much better suited to the German mentality than French classicism was. But the drift of his argument was less an essentializing of national character than an acknowledgement of cultural variety: while Sophocles had 'presented, taught, moved and edified Greeks, Shakespeare teaches, moves and edifies Nordic people'.[30] His divergence from the norms of classical tragedy was to be explained historically. The 'new Athenians of Europe', as Herder mockingly calls the French, had not recognized the unbridgeable gap between antiquity and the present, making their efforts at tragedy but 'an effigy outwardly resembling Greek drama; but the effigy lacks spirit, life, nature, truth […]' (21–2). Greek tragedy—its unity and simplicity of form—grew naturally from the unity and simplicity of Greek life; it was the perfect expression of its time and place of origin. Hence the seeming 'artificiality of the rules of Greek drama was—not artifice at all!' (9). The conditions under which Shakespearean drama arose were entirely different. 'Shakespeare was confronted with nothing like the simplicity of national manners, deeds, inclinations, and historical traditions that formed the Greek drama' (28–9). And thus to demand that something like 'Greek drama arise then, and in England' and that it 'develop naturally […] is worse than asking a sheep to give birth to lion cubs' (26).

Herder's historical argument and his advocacy of cultural diversity were made to disappear in nationalist appropriations of his thought. The Nazis summarily co-opted him as the progenitor of the *völkisch* idea. Under these auspices, the long-established notion of Shakespeare's special affinity with Germany shifted in emphasis from *Geist* ('mind' or 'spirit') to 'blood' and 'race'. In a keynote address to the German Shakespeare Society in 1936, Heinz Kindermann, a particularly zealous Nazi supporter, made it clear that 'the relations between Shakespeare and the German nation […] are not just the relations between Shakespeare and the "German spirit", as Gundolf presented them', but 'relations of blood'. The crucial nexus is not one between Shakespeare and German literature but that existing

[29] Ernst Bertram, 'Norden und deutsche Romantik' [The North and German Romanticism], in his *Deutsche Gestalten. Fest- und Gedenkreden*, 2nd edn (Leipzig: Insel, 1935), 168–91 at 175.

[30] Herder, *Shakespeare* (1773), trans. and ed. Moore, 26. Page references in the text are to this edition.

'between Shakespeare and German "folkhood" [*Volkheit*]',[31] a term, he adds, that was coined by Goethe—though hardly intended in the sense suggested by Kindermann, whose 'biological anthropological history of literature' was much indebted to the 'research' of Hans F. K. Günther, the leading authority on eugenics and Nazi 'race science' (*Rassenkunde*).[32]

Reichsdramaturg Rainer Schlösser, head of theatre in Goebbels's ministry of propaganda, cited Günther in an essay entitled 'The Immortal Dialogue about the Tragic': Nordic art, Günther averred, always centred on the experience of inevitable tragic doom, 'the insight into a tremendous fate that elevates man as it crushes him'.[33] Touching on the 'deepest secrets of our race', this insight had found dramatic expression in Sophocles's *Oedipus Rex*, which according to Schlösser was 'still the greatest and most compelling example of Nordic spirituality'.[34] Sophocles— Nordic? Odd as it may seem, this is in keeping with the circular reasoning of the American lawyer Madison Grant, a world authority on racial theory. If the 'Nordic race' represented the pinnacle of humanity, then the greatest achievements of human civilization must be credited to that race even if they had emerged in the area inhabited by the inferior 'Mediterranean race'. Only 'when mixed and invigorated with Nordic elements', could it give 'us' (!) 'the most splendid of all civilizations, that of ancient Hellas, and the most enduring of political organizations, the Roman State. [...] [I]ts love of organization, of law and military efficiency, as well as the Roman ideals of family life, loyalty, and truth, point clearly to a Nordic rather than to a Mediterranean origin.'[35] No wonder Hitler loved Grant's bestselling *The Passing of the Great Race* and (in a letter to its author) called it 'my Bible'.[36]

The idea of an ethnically mixed people being 'nordicized'[37] and thereby upgraded on the scale of racial perfection appealed strongly to Nazi ideologists. After all, no stretch of the racist imagination could mistake the population of Germany for pure-bloodedly Germanic. Even Hans Günther, the race pundit, did not claim that. In his bestselling *Racial Science of the German People* (*Rassenkunde des deutschen*

---

[31] Heinz Kindermann, 'Shakespeare und das deutsche Volkstheater', *Shakespeare-Jahrbuch* 72 (1936), 9–41 at 9. Kindermann showed a remarkable degree of ideological flexibility after the war. He was reinstated to his chair at Vienna in 1954 and ended up as the most prominent German-speaking theatre historian of the post-war era. His ten-volume *Theatre History of Europe* (1957–74) became a standard reference work.

[32] Known as 'Race Günther' (*Rassegünther*) or 'Race Pope' (*Rassenpapst*), he held a newly created chair of racial theory at Jena from 1930. He joined the NSDAP in 1932. His work was translated into English and found much favour with eugenicists in the US. Hans F. K. Günther, *The Racial Elements of European History*, trans. G. C. Wheeler (London: Methuen, 1927).

[33] Günther quoted in Rainer Schlösser, 'Das unsterbliche Gespräch über das Tragische. Dramaturgie als Gesetzeswerk nordischer Kultur', *Wille und Macht*, 1 June 1937, 5–14 at 6.

[34] Schlösser, 'Das unsterbliche Gespräch über das Tragische', 6.

[35] Madison Grant, *The Passing of the Great Race; or, The Racial Basis of European History* (New York: Charles Scribner's Sons, 1916), 139. Grant (1865–1937), a friend of several US presidents, including Theodore Roosevelt and Herbert Hoover, was an influential supporter of the introduction of restrictive immigration and anti-miscegenation laws in the US in the 1920s. He was also an avid conservationist, campaigner for many endangered animal species, and co-founder of the Save the Redwoods League.

[36] Quoted in Stefan Kühl, *The Nazi Connection: Eugenics, American Racism, and German National Socialism* (New York: Oxford University Press, 1994), 85.

[37] A verb coined by Grant which the Nazis readily adopted into their vocabulary (*aufnorden*).

Volkes, 1922) he describes the Germans as a mix of Nordic, Mediterranean, Dinaric (Balkan), Alpine, and East Baltic features. So there was always room for improvement through eugenic measures. When Günther, shortly after being appointed to the board of the German Shakespeare Society,[38] addressed the 1937 annual meeting, he unsurprisingly found the Bard to be a supporter of that very idea. 'From fairest creatures we desire increase' (Sonnet 1, 1. 1): clearly the poet's plea to the young man to replicate his beauty ('breed another thee', Sonnet 6, 1. 7; 'print more, not let the copy die', Sonnet 11, 1. 10) attested to Shakespeare's eugenicist agenda. Under the title stolen from Heinrich Heine's famous essay, Günther argued that 'Shakespeare's Girls and Women' were the perfect embodiment of essential Germanic qualities. The most praiseworthy of these qualities was a healthy Germanic instinct that drew them to marriage partners best suited for the breeding of first-rate offspring. According to Günther, Shakespeare's exemplary female characters were intended to drive home 'the *völkisch* value of marriage and family [...] as a means of increasing the vitality of a people'.[39]

'Race science', however, could also jeopardize Shakespeare's Nordic credentials. This is what happened in Gustav Plessow's pamphlet *About Shakespeare's Nordicness*, a curious mix of zealotry and baffling flashes of heterodoxy. No wonder the Gestapo found this man somewhat 'intransparent' (*undurchsichtig*), though this probably had more to do with his contacts abroad than with his probing of Shakespeare.[40] Bent on 'laying bare the race traits of [Shakespeare's] soul',[41] Plessow begins with the Chandos portrait. No trace of the oriental, he asserts, 'no drooping fleshy nose, no folded eyelids that look like heavy curtains'; yet the brown eyes and dark brown hair are clearly more Mediterranean than Nordic, although even 'behind [...] brown eyes', Plessow reassures the reader, 'there may dwell a pure Nordic race-soul' (*Rassenseele*, 8). But the plays resist this happy conclusion. Love, as Shakespeare depicts it in *Romeo and Juliet* for example, is, again, more Mediterranean than Nordic. In the cranky terminology Plessow borrows from Ludwig Ferdinand Clauß's *The Nordic Soul*,[42] it is the love of the Mediterranean 'performer' or 'actor' (*Darstellungsmensch*) rather than that of the Nordic 'achiever' (*Leistungsmensch*). 'The love of the *Leistungsmensch*', we learn, 'shows its specific character in between copulations; that of the *Darstellungsmensch* culminates in them' (10). Cleopatra's

[38] Von Ledebur, *Der Mythos vom deutschen Shakespeare*, 140–1.
[39] Hans F. K. Günther, 'Shakespeares Mädchen und Frauen', *Shakespeare-Jahrbuch* 73 (1937), 85–106 at 98. Heinrich Heine, *Shakespeares Mädchen und Frauen* (Paris and Leipzig: Brockhaus & Avenarius, 1839).
[40] With a PhD in German literature, Plessow established a course for English and American culture at the Technical University of Aachen in 1936. When the Nazi *Rektor* of the university fled in May 1945, Plessow served as interim president for a few months. See Ulrich Kalkmann, *Die Technische Hochschule Aachen im Dritten Reich (1933–1945)* (Aachen: Wissenschaftsverlag Mainz, 2003), 285–9.
[41] Gustav L. Plessow, *Um Shakespeares Nordentum* (Aachen: J. A. Mayer'sche Verlagsbuchhandlung, 1937), 7. References to this text are given in brackets.
[42] Ludwig Ferdinand Clauß, *Die nordische Seele. Eine Einführung in die Rassenseelenkunde* (Munich: J. F. Lehmann, 1932).

love, like Juliet's, is of the consuming, all-absorbing—in a word: Mediterranean—type, the same Mediterranean type as that of the poet himself.[43]

But, Plessow asks rhetorically, can we deduce '[h]ow Shakespeare loved' (12) from the characters in his plays? Many of them, he admits, are mere figures in the plot. Others, however, 'contain [the dramatist] himself: Hamlet, Coriolanus, Angelo (from *Measure for Measure*)', for example. They are 'confessional characters' (12). Among them, only brave Talbot and Percy Hotspur, the 'northern youth', are immediately recognizable as Nordic. They represent a line of characters which Plessow somewhat tentatively extends to Richard III, Henry V, and Coriolanus. Such 'lines' of characters, he adds in a footnote, were extensively used by Gundolf. But rather than capping this with the customary denouncement of Gundolf's errors, Plessow adds a list of examples from Gundolf's *Shakespeare* of 1928 (24).

The yield of true-bred Nordic characters remains conspicuously sparse. Quite a number of plays, *Macbeth* and *King Lear* for example, that one would think might have increased the count are curiously ignored. And so is Prospero, the character most commonly taken for a self-portrait of his author. Astonishingly, Cleopatra of all people is conscripted to swell the muster of Shakespearean Nordics. Her sudden shift from eroticism to heroism in Act 4 is read as a change from Mediterranean flightiness to Germanic loyalty to the death. This 'leap from one race into another' not only accounts for 'the dichotomy in the character of Cleopatra' (28), it also suggests that there are 'at least two race-souls in the poet himself' (29). With Shylock a third one comes into play:

> Thinking of Shylock one might conclude that Shakespeare was a Jew. This thought must be shelved; for this study is concerned only with races. The Jews, however, are not a race in the scientific sense of the word. (29)

In racial terms, Plessow explains, the Jews predominantly fall into the category of the oriental *Erlösungsmensch* ('redemption man' or 'salvation man'). The most bizarre of Clauß's classifications, this term identifies Christianity and its central concept, redemption (*Erlösung*), as essentially 'oriental'. The need for redemption, the idea of man's corrupted flesh requiring salvation through the spirit, presupposes a sharp division of body and soul. 'The struggle between the spirit and the flesh' is an 'oriental race-trait'. 'This struggle does not exist in the Nordic person' (30). Nor does it trouble Shylock, who is therefore irrelevant for Plessow's argument (30). But it does trouble the corruptible Angelo. He is an epitome of the 'salvation man'. No wonder therefore, Plessow writes, that the most acute analysis of his character was written by a fellow 'oriental', the Jewish critic Gustav Landauer, whom Plessow quotes at length.[44] Angelo's 'oriental' nature may come as a surprise, but it is nothing like as unexpected as what follows: the assertion—in no

---

[43] Given the Nazi persecution of homosexuals, it is remarkable how casually Plessow mentions Shakespeare's devotion to the young man of the sonnets in his discussion of the dramatist's love life.

[44] Gustav Landauer, *Shakespeare in zwei Bänden. Dargestellt in Vorträgen*, 2 vols (Frankfurt: Rütten & Loening 1922), vol. 2, 23 and 25. The anarchist, or anarcho-pacifist Landauer, a leading member of the Bavarian Soviet Republic (*Münchner Räterepublik*), was murdered by the police in Munich's Stadelheim prison in May 1919. His Shakespeare lectures were posthumously edited by Martin Buber.

need of further demonstration because it has allegedly long been proven by Shakespeare scholars (33)—that 'Angelo and Shakespeare are one and the same, that Angelo is a confessor' (33), a character through whom Shakespeare unburdens himself. Shakespeare's composite 'race-soul', in other words, contains a strong dose of the 'oriental'!

Plessow extends this perilous line of thought to the character he has left until last: Hamlet (33–4). If anything, the rift between flesh and spirit is even deeper in him than it is in Angelo. His yearning for redemption, 'deliverance from existence' (33) could not be more poignantly voiced in passages like the famous 'To be or not to be'. 'Who would speak of achievement [*Leistung*] here? Who will regard Hamlet as purely Nordic after this?' (33).

The conclusion seems inevitable. If Angelo is 'oriental', then Hamlet must be too. It is almost as if 'race science' gave Fritz Kortner's Hamlet a belated nod of approval. But Plessow pulls back at the last moment. Christianity, that spawn of an alien eastern race, may be to blame for Hamlet's un-Nordic contempt of the flesh.[45] Religious indoctrination, 'nurture' rather than 'nature', may have caused this 'pseudo-morphosis' (34), a bending of Hamlet's character away from its genetic heritage, and the same may be true of Shakespeare himself. 'May', as Plessow insists, for there can as yet be 'no final verdict' (35). Evidence of all three racial types, the Mediterranean, the Nordic, and the Oriental, can be found in Shakespeare's works. 'Well over half of them are not Nordic' (35). Each of the plays contains 'traces of all three race-styles' (35) but the œuvre as a whole shows a preponderance of the Mediterranean in the early works and an increase of the Nordic element in the middle years. 'After that the Oriental comes to the fore. Finally (in the Romances) the Oriental and the Mediterranean enter into marriage' (!) (33).

Plessow's conclusions are not exactly propitious to the Nordic cause. And while he dutifully declares that 'everything human is determined by race' (38), he follows this with the equally categorical statement that 'racially pure humans do not exist any longer' (38). He also admits that he cannot claim mathematical proof for his findings. All he has been able to do is try to convince his readers, whose own racial make-up may lead them to draw different conclusions (36). In the end, 'race' seems to be almost entirely in the eye of the beholder. 'Therefore each generation [*Geschlecht*—also: lineage, race] will favour that translation [in the sense of inter-pretation] which best agrees with its own racial composition. Should this compos-ition one day be accomplished in a pure Nordic style, then only the Nordic will be discernible in Shakespeare' (38).

Plessow's study tips the normative rigour of 'race science' into a vortex of rela-tivism. Whether inadvertently or by intent, he must have cooled the enthusiasm for further inquiry into Shakespeare's 'race-soul'. Whatever the actual circulation and impact of his study, it clearly demonstrated the slipperiness of the subject.

---

[45] Plessow was an active supporter of the crackpot 'Ludendorffian' *Bund für Gotterkenntnis* (associ-ation for the knowledge of God), a Germanic, neo-pagan, strongly anti-Semitic sect founded by Mathilde Ludendorff, the wife of General Erich Ludendorff, Quartermaster General of the Kaiser's army in the First World War and Hitler's co-putschist in the Munich beer hall putsch of 1923.

Shakespeare continued to be routinely labelled 'Germanic' or 'Nordic' but by the end of the 1930s the 'race science' approach had run out of steam.[46]

World events forced a change of priority. When the German invasion of Poland sparked the outbreak of another world war, Shakespeare's standing in his adopted fatherland was again at issue. The question was no longer whether he was truly Nordic but whether he was still 'ours'. The answer was no less emphatically affirmative than it had been during the previous war. When a Bavarian party official took it upon himself to stop a production of *Hamlet* at Munich's *Kammerspiele* theatre in September 1939, the ban was promptly revoked by *Reichsdramaturg* Dr Schlösser.[47] Up until the closing of the theatres in 1944 most of Shakespeare's plays were permitted to be performed on the stages of the Third Reich.[48]

Bard support arose from various quarters, including the leadership of the Hitler Youth. Five months into the war, a special issue of its *Will and Power* journal appeared under the title *Shakespeare 1940*. Its editorial strikes a characteristic note of self-congratulation: 'It is a sign of the strong that they are able, indeed that they feel the urge to see what is good and what is truly accomplished even in the enemy.'[49] Demonstrative love of Shakespeare had served the Nazis before as proof of their open-mindedness and magnanimous appreciation of the merits of other nations. 'We Germans', declares Herbert Frenzel in the same special issue, 'have not only, through Goethe, created the concept of "world literature", we have also demonstrated to the world what proper cultivation of world literature means. [...] The Englishman Shakespeare has found a foster-nation in us.'[50] Britain, by contrast, can no longer claim him as her own, as the dramatist Hermann Burte declares in a particularly rabid diatribe:

> The unity of blood, will and character has been lost in the British people. Puritanism in the intellectual sphere has Hebrewised it, liberalism in the economic sphere has Jewified it. They no longer have poets like Marlowe who drew the Jew of Malta, or Shakespeare who drew the Jew of Venice severely but humanely and rejected him. [...]

---

[46] An essay by Karl Schümmer, 'Shakespeare. Nordischer Mythus und christliche Metaphysik' (Nordic Myth and Christian Metaphysics) appeared in *Hochland* 9 (1938/9), 191–205. In accordance with the journal's Catholic orientation, and diametrically contrary to Plessow/Clauß's racial Nordicism, Schümmer argues for a continuum between Nordic sagas and Christian belief in Shakespeare's drama. Shakespeare, he writes, 'makes us see into depths where myth and [Christian] revelation seem to merge' (193). *Macbeth* is 'a myth of Nordic winter' (192), but it is also an expression of the 'yearning for salvation' (194).

[47] Werner Habicht, 'German Shakespeare, the Third Reich, and the War', in *Shakespeare and the Second World War: Memory, Culture, Identity*, ed. Irena R. Makaryk and Marissa McHugh (Toronto, Buffalo, and London: University of Toronto Press, 2012), 22–34 at 22.

[48] Boguslaw Drewniak, *Das Theater im NS-Staat* (Düsseldorf: Droste, 1983), 249. On Shakespeare's prominence in the Third Reich theatre repertoire: Thomas Eicher, 'Teil II: Spielplanstrukturen 1929–1944', in *Theater im 'Dritten Reich'*, ed. Henning Rischbieter (Seelze-Velber: Kallmeyer, 2000), 279–486, esp. 297–316.

[49] 'Shakespeare 1940', unsigned editorial in *Wille und Macht* 8 (1 February 1940), 1.

[50] Herbert A. Frenzel, 'Ist Shakespeare ein Problem?' [Is Shakespeare a Problem?], *Wille und Macht* 8 (1 February 1940), 2–3 at 2. The chronological survey of German literature (*Daten deutscher Dichtung. Chronologischer Abriß der deutschen Literaturgeschichte*) Frenzel first published, with his wife Elisabeth Frenzel, in 1953 became a bestselling reference work in post-war Germany; it went into its 35th edition in 2007.

The day of the German has come. It is his vocation to give Europe meaning, to erect his realm at its centre and to give the people of the centre their rightful patrimony at last after pain, injustice and persecution.[51]

The dignitaries of the German Shakespeare Society were somewhat more moderate in tone, but not all that different in their drift. In his presidential address at the 1940 annual meeting Wolfgang Keller, too, combined condemnation of the British enemy with praise of Germany's undaunted loyalty to Shakespeare. 'Out there', he began dramatically,

> in and above the wild North Sea our brave troops attack, by ship or swift aeroplane, the British warships and their hiding places; the Britons who in alliance with our never-resting enemies in the West wage a mortal war of extermination against us.
>
> Yet we are celebrating Shakespeare, a son of the English earth. Is it permissible for us to do this?[52]

Keller's 'yes' is as emphatic as it is predictable: Shakespeare has nothing in common with 'the British politicians and speculators who are fighting our German Empire':

> Three hundred and fifty years ago, with holy pride and ardent love, he stood up for his country and his people—for a heroic England under the authoritarian rule of Queen Elizabeth, and he was happy with this form of rule: *Merry Old England*. This England is dead too. It resembled our Germany of today much more than it does the democratic, or rather plutocratic, trading power which dominates the British Empire today. The Elizabethan attitude to life was heroic, soldierly, youthful and aspiring, hungry for action and adventure. And it was William Shakespeare who gave the most beautiful expression to this truly Germanic attitude, keeping it alive for all time. (2)[53]

The present moment was particularly suited to celebrating Germany's rightful claim to Shakespeare: two hundred years previously, 'shortly after 1740' (2), the Prussian envoy to London, Caspar von Borck, had produced the first complete German translation of a Shakespeare play, *Julius Caesar*. 'With this deed, the Germans were the first among all the nations of Europe to claim their right of ownership to Shakespeare' (2). And it was exactly one hundred years previously,

---

[51] Hermann Burte, 'Der englische und der deutsche Tag', *Wille und Macht* 8 (1 February 1940), 3–9 at 8–9. Burte was included in the list of 'God-gifted artists' drawn up in 1944, which exempted him from being drafted into the *Volkssturm* (people's storm), the German national militia created during the last months of the war.

[52] Wolfgang Keller, 'Ansprache und Jahresbericht des Präsidenten Professor Wolfgang Keller', *Shakespeare-Jahrbuch* 76 (1940), 1–10 at 1. Page references are given in brackets in the text.

[53] Claims for the affinity between Shakespeare's England and Hitler's Germany were quite common. Published in the German Shakespeare Society's book series, Eduard Eckhardt's monograph on *Shakespeare's Views on Religion and Morality, the State and the People* (1940) quotes Ulysses' 'degree' speech from *Troilus and Cressida* (1.3) at length, following it with the rhetorical question: 'Is it not as if the poet wanted to pillory the heinous mismanagement of our Weimar government after 1918? [...] His closing words, too, suggest a comparison with the Germany of 1918. All of the enemy's encroachments and breaches of law were made possible only because at the crucial moment of the armistice the German people did not stand together but tore itself apart in unrest and discord.' Eduard Eckhardt, *Shakespeares Anschauungen über Religion und Sittlichkeit, Staat und Volk. Ein Versuch* (Weimar: Hermann Böhlaus Nachf., 1940), 121–2.

Keller reminds his audience, in 1840, that the last volume of the Schlegel–Tieck translation 'gave us Shakespeare as a German classic' (2).

III TRANSLATOR'S BATTLE

His listeners most likely knew, and therefore Keller does not mention, the part the German Shakespeare Society had recently played in cementing the official monopoly of Schlegel–Tieck against its modern competitor Hans Rothe.

Rothe's translations, which in some cases are actually adaptations, had enjoyed considerable success since the 1920s. Deliberately accessible and stage-oriented, they sought to replace what Rothe dismissed as the antiquated poeticism of Schlegel–Tieck with an idiom that aimed to be at once more modern and closer to Shakespeare, especially when it came to rendering Shakespeare's bawdy. Support for Rothe came mainly from theatre practitioners. They pleaded the merits of a rejuvenated Shakespeare, one that would be more palatable than Schlegel–Tieck for modern actors and audiences. Academic Bard lovers with a preservationist attitude—an overwhelming majority in the German Shakespeare Society—took umbrage at his liberties with the text.[54] Small wonder, then, that Rothe included the Society ('which meets annually for a dinner in honour of the deceased Grand Dukes of Saxe-Weimar-Eisenach'[55]) in a satirical attack on his conservative critics that was published after the breakthrough Berlin stage success of his version of *Troilus and Cressida* in 1927. Ironically entitled *Reasons that Speak Against a New Translation of Shakespeare*, the slender pamphlet lampoons the objections of his critics by parodically endorsing them:

> Modern expressions—it is sometimes claimed—are conducive to the actor's appeal and the audience's comprehension. This claim, born from sheer insolence, is easily rebutted, for the actor is not a modern person and the stage is the mouthpiece of the past. (5)

Being old, the translation of 'the Schlegel–Tieck brothers' must be good, and because 'the twins' 'have translated all of Shakespeare's œuvre, nothing remains to be done' (2).

Rothe's point was repeated by Joseph Goebbels in his keynote address at the Reich Theatre Week in Munich on 12 May 1936—though without any trace of irony. 'We have a well-defined idea of our classics,' he declared, 'and wish that this idea finds expression in the modern theatre. We do not want experiments in this

---

[54] Initially, though, Rothe had courted the Society's favour, apparently with some success. At the 1921 meeting he was given the opportunity to read from his translations, and during the 1924 conference his version of *Macbeth* was performed by the Weimar Theatre. An extensive review balancing strengths and weaknesses of his work appeared in *Shakespeare-Jahrbuch* 1924. Objecting to Rothe's cuts and structural rearrangements, the reviewer singled out *Troilus and Cressida* as the translator's prime achievement. In this lesser known play, he wrote, 'the reader does not have to wrestle with his memories of the familiar wording of previous translations.' Eugen Kilian, 'Shakespeare. *Macbeth. König Lear. Troilus und Cressida. Wie es euch gefällt. König Richard II. Was ihr wollt.* Übersetzt von Hans Rothe', *Shakespeare-Jahrbuch* 59/60 (1924), 205–17 at 212.

[55] Hans Rothe, *Gründe, die gegen eine Neuübersetzung Shakespeares sprechen* (Leipzig: Paul List, 1927), 2–3. Page references are given in brackets in the text.

field and must protect the classics from them.'[56] Goebbels's verdict, which was received with 'tumultuous applause', settled a controversy which had gone on, with increasing intensity, for the better part of two years. It amounted to a ban of Rothe's translations from the stages of the Reich. Henceforth, Shakespeare was to speak nothing but Schlegel–Tieck.

Government ministers usually have more pressing things to do than pass sentence in a dispute over the quality of a literary translation. But it is perhaps even more surprising that such a dispute could have arisen in the first place, let alone continue for the length of time that it did in a totalitarian state that dedicated itself to the forcible 'bringing in line' (*Gleichschaltung*) of all areas of life and the stifling of any dissent. Well over a hundred comments on the pros and cons of the Rothe translations did appear in newspapers and journals between 1934 and 1936, a public debate almost unparalleled in the Third Reich.[57]

Equally remarkable is an entry in Goebbels's diary which preceded his ban on Rothe by less than three months. On 27 February 1936 he noted:

> I met Hans Rothe, the Shakespeare translator. He made a good, modest impression and his arguments are intelligent and persuasive. But I will still not be able to help him.[58]

The Rothe case is a staple of all accounts of Shakespeare in the Third Reich. But Goebbels's curiously sympathetic note seems to have been overlooked. If Rothe's translations were, as a diatribe from the Rosenberg camp had it, a 'Crime Against Shakespeare',[59] how could the minister of propaganda even talk to this 'criminal', let alone be favourably impressed by him? Rothe's defence strategy takes us some way towards an answer. In early 1936, he entered the fray with a pamphlet against his detractors entitled *The Battle for Shakespeare. A Report.*[60] In it, he highlights the inadequacies of the Schlegel–Tieck translation and explains the principles of his own; he answers the linguistic objections of his critics and castigates their inconsistencies. But the grounds for objection against him had changed from language to ideology, and his fiercest attackers came from Rosenberg's 'NS Cultural Community' (*NS-Kulturgemeinde*). Their target was the 'spirit' of his translation, a spirit that must be exorcized because it reeked of decadent Weimar modernism. Rothe needed to gain ideological ground on his enemies. Obviously this could not be done by facing them directly, still less by defending what they condemned. So instead of countering their charges or indeed acknowledging them in any way, Rothe offers

---

[56] Excerpts from the speech appeared in *Hamburger Nachrichten*, 12 May 1936. Quoted in von Ledebur, *Der Mythos vom deutschen Shakespeare*, 229.

[57] As Ruth von Ledebur points out, 'there are hardly any other examples where such a controversy was carried out not only in scholarly circles but even in daily papers'. Von Ledebur, *Der Mythos vom deutschen Shakespeare*, 225. The German Shakespeare Society's involvement in the Rothe affair is most fully and instructively discussed in von Ledebur, *Der Mythos vom deutschen Shakespeare*, 214–33. I am much indebted to her study.

[58] *Die Tagebücher von Joseph Goebbels*, pt. 1, vol. 3/I, ed. Hermann (2005), 386.

[59] Werner Kurz, 'Verbrechen an Shakespeare', *Bausteine zum deutschen Nationaltheater* 4 (1936), 33–42.

[60] Hans Rothe, *Kampf um Shakespeare. Ein Bericht* (Leipzig: Paul List, 1935/6). The preface is dated November 1935, the copyright year given in the imprint is 1936. Contemporary responses show that the book must have been out in January 1936. Page references are given in brackets in the text.

his translation as a bona fide contribution to the cultural revolution initiated by the Third Reich. This line of argument—one he is likely to have pursued in his meeting with the minister of propaganda—may well have appealed to Goebbels, even if it cut no ice with the Rosenberg camp.

Opening his pamphlet with a section entitled 'Storm and Stress', Rothe evokes the familiar story of the rebirth of German literature under the aegis of Shakespeare. His tone is heavily ironic:

> Those young people must have lost their minds. Who gave them the right to spew out works in which one irregularity chased the next [...]? [...] The host of level-headed critics confronted these young rebels in desperation: did these immature youths not realize that everything a Gottsched had taught and fixed for all time was in danger of being overrun and forgotten? The critics were quite aware that a kind of mental fever must have befallen the pitiable authors of these shameful monstrosities [such as Goethe's *Götz von Berlichingen* and Schiller's *Robbers*] and that a stern and timely rebuke would lead them back to the columned halls of the French tragedians Racine and Corneille. This fever so sternly reprimanded by their elders was the Shakespeare fever. [...] The hope those critics harboured of a return to Gottsched and Racine has not been fulfilled. [...] Shakespeare, the consummation of the greatest epoch in English theatre history, has thus crucially influenced, nay, almost brought forth a second theatre culture: that of Germany. (7)

Rothe's opening move deftly construes a parallel between the reactionaries of the 1760s hankering after starched classicism with the modern-day defenders of the Schlegel–Tieck translation. Although not a word is directly said about what in Nazi parlance figured as the 'German Revolution' of 1933, the reference is unmistakable. It is more explicitly reiterated throughout the pamphlet whenever Rothe claims the appropriateness of his translation to 'the new time', a standard formula for the Nazi present. 'At a time of renewal', he asks rhetorically,

> can anyone in Germany demand that Shakespeare translation revert to its state in 1810? Shakespeare translation, too, must be submitted to the melting pot of the new time. (76)

Populism is a prime ingredient of the new time and Rothe's best hope, or so he must have thought, of currying favour with the regime. The Renaissance, he declares, was 'more or less alien to the people' (*volksfremd*), a foreign import. Shakespeare, by contrast, was a man of the native English theatre and thus a man of the people because 'the theatre was rooted in the spiritual ur-drives of the Volk' (11). In construing an opposition between the literati and the people, Rothe was tapping into Nazi resentments against 'intellectuals'. Fully in tune with the anti-intellectual *Zeitgeist*, he claimed that it was one of the prime advantages of Shakespeare's England that 'there was no criticism' (17). Before the year was over, the same would be true of Germany. On 26 November 1936 Goebbels decreed that instead of criticism of works of art there would henceforth be only descriptive 'reporting' or 'accounting' (*Kunstbericht* instead of *Kunstkritik*).[61]

---

[61] The ban was apparently motivated by Goebbels's frustration that, four years into the Third Reich, a genuinely National Socialist brand of criticism had failed to emerge. Criticism as actually practised still smacked of the liberal past. As one of the decree's approving contemporary commentators observes:

The men of the theatre, Rothe claims, were always suspect to 'the reactionary forces' (12). They were craftsmen (*Handwerker*) first and foremost, a class much courted by the Nazis and sentimentalized in Nazi propaganda. Playwriting, Rothe correctly avers, did not take place in an intellectual ivory tower. It was a trade, he suggests, much like that of the modern 'film author' (14)—an attempt, perhaps, to capitalize on Goebbels's known commitment to the new medium.[62] The individualist notion of intellectual property was therefore quite alien to Elizabethan playwriting; it was a 'narrow' and 'timid' idea (16). Against it stood the vital force (*Lebenskraft*) of the theatre and its communal creativity:

> In the Elizabethan age nothing of any vital force was ever lost. All of the thought of the Elizabethan stage was thrown into the great melting pot. Each dramatist worked on the shoulders of his predecessor. They all [...] devoted their whole intensity to their task [...] and the result was a communal work of eternal duration. (17)

It took the genius of Shakespeare, Rothe continues, to crown this communal achievement. But Shakespeare, like his colleagues and predecessors, was a man of the Elizabethan theatre, not a literary author as the Romantics would have us think of him. Few modern critics would dispute that. Nor would they fundamentally disagree with Rothe that the Shakespearean texts we have are fluid, imprecise, sometimes even a patchwork of Shakespearean and non-Shakespearean passages. Rothe's main authority for this is J. M. Robertson,[63] whose critical 'disintegration' of the Shakespeare canon appealed to T. S. Eliot's anti-Romantic reflexes, but drew heavy rebuke from E. K. Chambers.[64] Robertson's heterodoxy serves Rothe as a stepping stone to an even bolder proposition of his own. If Shakespeare's words are so ensconced in uncertainty, we must probe deeper. Words, Rothe boldly concludes, are the medium, but not the essence of Shakespeare's art. Essential Shakespeare, he claims, is 'based on the word, transmitted by the word—but not bound to the word' (27).

This is not exactly the view one would expect from a translator, but it is one that goes a long way towards defending the most controversial aspect of Rothe's

---

'With the death of the criticism of yesteryear, a system of the past has ceased to exist because it no longer fulfills the demands of our time. This criticism and its practitioners have failed just as their political liberalism has failed. The critical reviewer is replaced by the responsible personality who can demand the same freedom and recognition as the artist because, like the artist, he is sworn to that liberty whose highest law is the people, its blood and its race.' Wolf Braumülller, 'Schlagt die Rezensenten tot! Kritik, Kunstbetrachtung und Kulturpolitik', *Niedersächsische Hochschul-Zeitung*, December 1936, 41–2 at 42. Braumüller also wrote a refutation of Rothe's pamphlet; see n. 68 in this chapter.

[62] Goebbels noted in his diary (16 December 1941): 'It is my ultimate goal to establish the German film as a globally dominant cultural power.' *Die Tagebücher von Joseph Goebbels*, pt. 2, vol. 2, Fröhlich (1996), 519. Cf. Felix Moeller, *The Film Minister: Goebbels and the Cinema in the 'Third Reich'* (Stuttgart and London: Edition Axel Menges, 2000).

[63] J. M. Robertson, *The Shakespeare Canon*, 5 vols (London: Routledge; New York: E. P. Dutton, 1922–30).

[64] T. S. Eliot, *The Sacred Wood: Essays on Poetry and Criticism* (London: Faber and Faber, 1920), 95–103; E. K. Chambers, 'The Disintegration of Shakespeare', in *Aspects of Shakespeare: Being British Academy Lectures (1923–1931)*, ed. J. W. Mackail (Oxford: Clarendon Press, 1933), 23–48. For a recent discussion: Cary DiPietro, 'The Shakespeare Edition in Industrial Capitalism', *Shakespeare Survey* 59 (2006), 147–56.

work: his wilful encroachment (as his critics saw it) on the integrity of Shakespeare's plots, his bold cuts and additions. They drew their justification not from pedantic adherence to a text that was unreliable anyway, but from an intuitive perception of the true spirit of Shakespeare. Never unduly modest, Rothe was sure he recognized this spirit wherever it might be found and that his re-creations brought it to life in authentic modern form. Rothe's belief in his special vocation as Shakespeare's modern representative was further bolstered by the experiments in 'sound analysis' (*Schallanalyse*) he conducted under the guidance of the inventor of this arcane method, the medieval philologist Eduard Sievers.[65] These experiments, Rothe proudly asserts, incontrovertibly established that the 'sound curve' of his own verse almost uncannily matched that of Shakespeare's. Needless to say, Schlegel–Tieck were out of sync at every turn. On the strength of his unique attunedness to Shakespeare's verse-flow and spirit, it is Rothe's goal

> to attempt a solution in the spirit of the Elizabethan theatre that has the same effect in the theatre today that the play would have had then if Shakespeare himself had written it. This is how the 'new versions' [*Neufassungen*] within the complete edition came into being. They were meant to [...] recover these forgotten plays for our time. They have recovered them. The new version of *The Comedy of Errors* has ranked at the top of the performance statistics for two years, and *Two Gentlemen of Verona* promises to be equally successful. Both plays—what an expansion of the Shakespeare idea!—have already been translated back into English. (67)

Politics apart, such views were bound to collide with the ingrained literary conservatism of the great majority of Shakespeareans, both academic and amateur. Rothe's lack of respect for the Shakespearean original had been the main objection to his work well before the advent of the Third Reich. What he was now attempting was to gild his literary modus operandi with the pathos of the national revolution, thereby placing himself on the winning side of history. The battle for Shakespeare, Rothe claims, was always a struggle over crucial issues of German culture:

> One must recognize it as a spiritual phenomenon of the first order that this struggle has recently flared up anew, with a resolve and a passion which is no longer expended on Shakespeare anywhere else in the world. Again the Shakespearean world picture seems under threat; again has his enormous work given us occasion to clarify questions of German *Weltanschauung*.
> And again it is a battle of the past with the new. (31)

The notion of 'battle', 'struggle', or 'fight' (*Kampf*) is of obvious centrality in Nazi ideology. To be a 'fighter' is the German character trait par excellence, ubiquitously invoked in the gushings of Goebbels's *Michael*. Riding the trend, Rothe exploits the *Kampf* pathos in a passage equating the England of Elizabeth with the Germany of the author of *Mein Kampf*:

> Battles of the mind are generally not fought for their own sake. They are usually the manifestation of world-historical changes. It is certainly no accident that the battle

---

[65] Sievers (1850–1932) is mostly remembered for his groundbreaking work on Germanic (Old Saxon and Anglo-Saxon) verse structures. His sound analysis is considered more of an esoteric quirk.

over a Romantic versus an Elizabethan Shakespeare has now reached its climax. For the Germany of today has much in common with the England of the great Elizabeth. Just as in England, after the years of dark destructiveness under the reign of the Catholic Mary, a Protestant era set about building an empire that was to endure for centuries, so has the will to build anew prevailed in Germany after the destruction of the war years and the aimlessness of the post-war years. One could write an interesting essay about the kinship of the two epochs [...]. The great Elizabeth was no Romantic. She did not unite England, nor vanquish Spain under the sign of the 'blue flower' [*blaue Blume*, the symbol of German Romanticism]. (45)

Those who are still crusading for the old Shakespeare of the Romantics, Rothe suggests, have fundamentally misunderstood the times: the Elizabethan past and also the German present. Rothe published his translation under the label 'The Elizabethan Shakespeare'.[66] In *The Battle over Shakespeare* he was trying to convince the reader that it was also the authentic National Socialist version of Shakespeare.

But, unsurprisingly, to no avail. His opportunism fooled no one (except, perhaps, the minister of propaganda, but only briefly). It is a moot point whether he laid it on too thick or not thick enough, or perhaps actually both at the same time. His mimicry of Nazi attitudes went no further than extolling the national revolution. It glorified the life forces of the *Volk*, but had nothing to say about blood or race. Steering clear of 'the Nordic' and of anti-Semitic vituperation, it paraded a kind of 'diet Nazism' thinly coating Rothe's genuine, though rather cranky, Shakespearean agenda.[67]

His defence was relentlessly demolished in a special issue of the 'NS Cultural Community' journal *Building Blocks for a German National Theatre*. It should be clear, concludes one of Rothe's detractors, 'that [his] thinking derives from an outlook that has nothing to do with the sincere striving of our time for clarification'.[68] 'Not his opponents', gloats another, 'but [Rothe] himself is the reactionary [whom] time will pass over.'[69] A third reviles the theatrical quality of Rothe's translations: '[P]laying Shakespeare in Rothe's versions [...] is tantamount to the offence Jessner committed against the genius of Shakespeare with his modern-dress Hamlet.' And he concludes:

> If the quarrel about Rothe has been good for anything it is that it has enabled us to sort the wheat from the chaff and [...] recognize those who, despite their ostensibly

[66] Hans Rothe (trans.), *Der Elisabethanische Shakespeare*, 9 vols (Baden-Baden and Geneva: Holle, 1957).
[67] Rothe made a second attempt to win Goebbels over to his side. In a letter from London (dated November 1936) he made the sensible point that far from ensuring homogeneity, the monopoly of Schlegel–Tieck would actually lead to a 'fraying out' (*Zerfaserung*) of the canonical texts because they would inevitably have to be modified for modern stage production. What would be performed would not be Schlegel–Tieck, but an unlimited variety of versions 'after Schlegel–Tieck'. Performing such versions, which vary from production to production, is common practice today. Quoted in Habicht, 'Shakespeare und der deutsche Shakespeare-Mythus im Dritten Reich', 93.
[68] Wolf Braumüller, '"Der Kampf um Shakespeare": Eine Entgegnung auf Hans Rothes Bericht', *Bausteine zum deutschen Nationaltheater* 4 (1936), 51–62 at 62.
[69] Reinhold Zickel von Jan, 'Wir brauchen Shakespeare!', *Bausteine zum deutschen Nationaltheater* 4 (1936), 47–51 at 51.

national socialist views still advocate the kind of art for which there is no room in the Third Reich. [...] Anyone who, like Rothe, [...] lays hands on the intellectual property of the nation and of centuries deserves nothing but unconditional rejection by the German theatre because it is contaminated by him in its very foundations. To the superficial observer the Rothe bacillus may at first seem pleasant and wholesome; in a wider perspective it is vermin that eats at the very marrow and core of German theatre.[70]

This is the rhetoric that abetted the Holocaust, the kind of animal imagery that was luridly visualized in the 1940 propaganda 'documentary' *The Eternal Jew*.[71]

Such extreme character assassination, one would think, should have clinched the case. But Goebbels, deferring the inevitable, decided to consult the president of the German Shakespeare Society, Werner Deetjen.[72] Deetjen answered promptly, acknowledging, though not specifying, 'certain merits' of Rothe's work, but categorically dismissing it as a whole. Rothe's encroachments, he said, were 'insupportable'. 'If Herr Rothe is of the opinion that we live in an age of sober-mindedness [...] and that the translator is therefore obliged to choose a language corresponding to that of the average person today I can by no means agree with him' (274). Rather than seeking to conform to a lower level, the translator should strive to 'elevate his national comrade [*Volksgenosse*] to his own level'. If any modifications of the established text should prove necessary 'they must be carried out with discretion and reverence' (275), both of which he found missing in Rothe:

> The marvellous poetic language of the Schlegel–Tieck translation is trivialized by him for the sake of 'better understanding' through modern expressions and phrases, and he does not flinch at grossly violating good taste. (275)

Deetjen blamed Rothe for exposing some of Shakespeare's bawdy, which Schlegel–Tieck had tactfully glossed over. Other critics had already homed in on this as one particularly objectionable example of Rothe's 'naturalism', his overall tendency to lower the Bard rather than honour his sublimity. Rothe, Deetjen admits, shows some theatrical skill, but this does not exculpate him from 'sinning against Shakespeare the poet' (275). Lowering the tone in order to make Shakespeare more suitable for the actor of today is wrong because

> [f]rom this point of view the verses of our own classical poets would have to be altered too for the convenience of the actor. Where is the respect for the poet and his work!? The actor must see it as his noblest task to serve them and not to bend them to his

---

[70] Karl Künkler, 'Hans Rothe und das Theater', *Bausteine zum deutschen Nationaltheater* 4 (1936), 43–7 at 46–7.

[71] *Der ewige Jude. Ein Dokumentarfilm über das Weltjudentum.* Produced by Deutsche Filmherstellungs- und Verwertungs GmbH (DFG) for the *Reichspropagandaleitung* of the Nazi Party; directed by Fritz Hippler. Goebbels personally supervised the production. Cf. Saul Friedländer, *The Years of Extermination: Nazi Germany and the Jews 1939–1945* (London: Weidenfeld & Nicolson, 2007), 20–2.

[72] Goebbels's letter suggests that he consulted (or intended to consult) 'several scholars, critics and contemporary poets'. If he did, there is no record of it. Facsimile reproductions of Goebbels's letter (29 January 1936) and the responding letter by Werner Deetjen (8 February 1936) are in von Ledebur, *Der Mythos vom deutschen Shakespeare*, 273–5; page references in brackets in the text.

own will. The kind of musicality that has fascinated actors in the Schlegel–Tieck translation for over a century and inspired them to give their best is lacking in the naturalism of Rothe; his language is that of everyday life, above which the audience wants to be uplifted in the theatre, if they regard the stage, as Schiller and Richard Wagner have done, as not just a place of entertainment and diversion. Heil Hitler! (275)

Apart from this parting salute and the reference to the 'national comrade' (*Volksgenosse*), it is likely that Deetjen would have passed much the same judgement before 1933, or, had he lived, after 1945. Deetjen's verdict expresses not so much the spirit of Nazidom as the conservatism of the academic establishment and the membership and executives of the German Shakespeare Society. Ironically, it was Rothe who made use of Nazi rhetoric in order to defend himself, while Deetjen could refrain from political argument and still deliver exactly what was expected of him.[73] The letter—possibly in conjunction with other, similar letters—supplied Goebbels with the 'unbiased' scholarly expertise he could refer to in his public pronouncement against Rothe. Deetjen's statement is an instructive instance of the kind of behaviour which in post-war retrospect could be claimed to have reconciled the irreconcilable: service to the regime and a sense of 'having remained decent' (*anständig geblieben zu sein*).

IV THE REBIRTH OF TRAGEDY, OR NO TIME FOR SHAKESPEARE

If the question of the definitive German Shakespeare was settled at the Reich Theatre Week in May 1936, the question of what the definitive new German drama should look like, and what model it should emulate, remained unresolved. Was Shakespeare, Goethe's 'star of the fairest height',[74] the lodestar to follow on *The German Way to Tragedy*? A pamphlet by Werner Deubel published under this title in 1935 seems to suggest just that.[75] Its opening page proudly declares:

> It was not by accident that the Germans—and only the Germans—were the first to discover, translate, perform Shakespeare and adopted him so eagerly that the great tragedian who 'teaches, nourishes and edifies Nordic men' (Herder) has since appeared to belong in a deeper sense more to the Germans than to the English. (5)

But this is only the prelude to a disquisition not on tragedy as such, but tragedy as a vehicle for a tragic philosophy of life, 'biocentric'—as opposed to 'logocentric'

---

[73] Cf. von Ledebur, *Der Mythos vom deutschen Shakespeare*, 221–3.

[74] Johann Wolfgang von Goethe, 'Zwischen beyden Welten', in *West-östlicher Divan*, ed. Hendrik Birus (Frankfurt: Deutscher Klassiker-Verlag, 1994), 84.

[75] Werner Deubel, *Der deutsche Weg zur Tragödie* (Leipzig: Wolfgang Jessen, [1935]). Page references in brackets in the text. Deubel (1894–1949) was a minor dramatist and the author of the ultra-right-wing manifesto *Deutsche Kulturrevolution, Weltbild einer Jugend* [German Cultural Revolution, World View of the Young] (Berlin: Verlag für Zeitkritik, 1931).

(17)—and deeply embedded in the 'reawakened' German 'blood-feeling' (*Blutgefühl*) (6) which rebels against the debasement of the heroic:[76]

The German Revolution [meaning the Nazi takeover of 1933] is in a most profound sense a resurgence of the centuries-long struggle for a tragic culture. [...] Every tragedy is heroic. But the reverse is true also. True heroism is always a manifestation of the tragic. (6)

'Because its highest powers—fate and elementary reality—are life forces, tragedy is geared towards biocentric values and its religion is a religion of life' (54). Deubel's overheated vitalism is of unmistakably Nietzschean provenance, as is his rejection of Christianity. The 'logocentric' religions of Christianity and its Protestant derivative, German idealism, are incapable of tragedy. At the centre of Christianity stands the Saviour, the Redeemer. He presupposes a humanity that feels in need of redemption because of its sense of guilt, its sinfulness. 'At the centre of tragedy stands the hero. And the hero, whether he be good or bad, does not feel sinful and hence not in need of redemption' (54).

Deubel's dichotomy of the heroic and the Christian closely matches the distinctions used in Plessow's analysis of Shakespeare's 'Nordicness': the Nordic 'achiever' (*Leistungsmensch*) pitted against the 'oriental', Christian 'salvation man' (*Erlösungsmensch*). What we also find, however, are traces of Gundolf, a secret legislator still, although of course an unacknowledged one. In his 1928 Shakespeare study he too had resorted to Nietzschean 'powers' or 'forces' as the ultimate determinants and prime movers of Shakespearean drama.[77]

Deubel's *völkisch* glorification of heroic death certainly hit the mood of the moment. But *The German Way to Tragedy* did little to provide direction for the great new national drama that was still reluctant to be coaxed into existence.[78] The 'degenerate' modernist styles of Naturalism and Expressionism were clearly out of the question, making the adoption of a traditional template imperative. The most obvious choice was, of course, Germany's own classics, Goethe and—as the more prolific and more truly 'dramatic' dramatist—Schiller. Schiller's historical dramas had provided the formula for a host of minor playwrights throughout the nineteenth and early decades of the twentieth century. This derivative line of production continued and even received a boost in the 1930s, but the more astute

---

[76] In one of his notes Deubel polemicizes against the anti-heroism of naturalist drama in which 'the ruin of a drunken coachman or the labour pains of a cow are deemed as worthy of poetic representation as, if not worthier than, the shattering fate of a hero' (74).

[77] See Chapter 2, section VI.

[78] Another attempt at clarifying the parameters of a national drama, predating the Nazi takeover by a year, was Gustav Steinbömer's *Staat und Drama* (1932; see Chapter 5, n. 81). Steinbömer was a close acquaintance of Carl Schmitt and shared his rejection of liberalism. In *State and Drama* he celebrates Shakespearean drama as the highest form of political drama (which to him means quite simply the highest form of drama) and concludes his historical survey with the claim that 'the bourgeois drama' of the age of liberalism 'with its abolition of the public sphere has effectively annihilated itself' (46). Clearly 'the struggle for a new German drama [...] must therefore go hand in hand with the struggle for a new German state' (46). Like Deubel, he gives no indication as to what the new drama should actually look like. Instead he concludes his essay with a recommendation of Stefan George's dialogue poetry as a 'pre-stage' for a drama to come 'in a different artistic form but of equal human dignity' (50).

traditionalists realized that it had long since exhausted its creative potential. Turning to the Weimar classics, then, meant not imitating them but adopting the model which they themselves had adopted.

It might be expected that this was the point at which Shakespeare would have triumphantly entered upon the scene. But far from it. In developing towards their more austere 'classical' phase around 1800, both Goethe and Schiller had traded their youthful Shakespeare enthusiasm for a more reserved admiration. Not only did they increasingly disapprove of Shakespeare's indecorous mixing of high seriousness and low comedy; they also objected to his loose, multi-scenic dramaturgy, the very same structural feature which they had so zealously copied in their earlier plays. Goethe, now established as director of the Weimar court theatre, found Shakespeare's dramaturgy incompatible with contemporary stage conditions, and when Schiller adapted *Macbeth* for Goethe's stage, he replaced the porter scene with a pious morning song. In the decade of their close collaboration—the decade (1794–1805) that is generally considered the 'classical' apotheosis of German literature—Goethe and Schiller favoured the Greeks over Shakespeare in their thoughts on dramatic art, especially tragedy.

This reversal on the part of Weimar's twin divinities became the crucible of anti-Shakespeareanism, prefiguring the dispute over the true nature of the prospective National Socialist drama. What the dispute boiled down to was a simple alternative: Weimar (the classical Weimar of Goethe and Schiller) or Shakespeare. In the course of the 1930s, Weimar increasingly supplanted Shakespeare. In 1936, Eberhard Wolfgang Möller, a dramatist on the staff of Dr Rainer Schlösser's *Reichsdramaturgie*, condemned 'Shakespearomania'[79] as a curse on German drama and Shakespeare himself as a typically 'un-German', 'foreign' idol. But the case was by no means closed; the controversy continued. In the words of the *Reichsdramaturg*: 'The struggle for stylistic clarification among young German dramatists has not yet been decided.'[80] Even if some 'still' favoured the Shakespearean model, 'which requires a way of acting that is merely characteristic and individualistic', the greatest talents 'tend more and more towards the ideals of an austere form' resembling, he adds for clarification, the Führer's monumental architecture. But Schlösser himself was not prepared to commit fully to the Weimar model, as seen in his keynote address to the 1937 convention of the German Shakespeare Society. On that occasion he felt obliged to assure the members of the Society that Shakespeare (in Schlegel–Tieck's German) was indeed part of 'our very own' cultural heritage.

It was after this defence that Curt Langenbeck, one of the Third Reich's up-and-coming dramatic talents in the 1930s, launched the next attack on Shakespeare, taking up the task left unfinished by Werner Deubel. Langenbeck pointed the way German tragic drama was going to take—and which way definitely not. In his pamphlet *The Rebirth of Drama from the Spirit of the Times*,

---

[79] The term is used by Christian Dietrich Grabbe in his polemic 'Über die Shakspearo-Manie' (1827), and again, with greater resonance, by Roderich Benedix, *Die Shakespearomanie. Zur Abwehr* (Stuttgart: Cotta, 1873).

[80] Rainer Schlösser, 'Die Jugend als Erbe der deutschen Bühnenkunst', *Frankfurter Theater Almanach* 20 (1936/7), 21.

originally presented as a lecture for the KdF (*Kraft durch Freude*: 'Strength Through Joy') organization in November 1939, he proclaimed in no uncertain terms that whatever precedent the new drama would be modelled on, it would not be that of Shakespeare. Shakespeare, Langenbeck maintained, was obsolete: he was the undisputed

> king of drama in that whole epoch [...] of tragic individualism. But because we, the Germans of today, are about to ring out this epoch, Shakespeare, much though we may still admire his art, has nothing of relevance to say to us any more; he cannot help us advance on the new road that we know to be the right one.[81]

This does not mean, he continued, that Shakespeare should be struck from the repertoire at once. On the contrary, the staging of his plays should be permitted to go on because sooner or later, he said, the audience will realize

> that an aesthetic delight becomes empty once it is no longer in accord with the needs of our soul and the demands of our destiny in any way. (36)

Langenbeck presents himself as a seeker after truth, a young man (he was thirty-three) aware of his own limitations but full of hope and enthusiasm, eager to serve the great national cause as best he can.[82] By the age of thirty, he had become a dramaturge at the theatre in Kassel (1935) and, only two years later, head dramaturge at the Bavarian State Theatre in Munich. After debuting with a comedy in 1933, Langenbeck continued his career as a playwright in a vein of high seriousness. By 1940 he had had five more plays produced, all of them in solemn verse spouting noble sentiment, all of them centred on larger-than-life heroic protagonists doomed to a tragic fate. Schiller, Kleist, and the neo-classicism of Paul Ernst[83] are the easily detectable sources of his inspiration: Weimar, in a word, not Shakespeare.

The Nietzschean title of Langenbeck's pamphlet signals a strong sense of mission, a cultural critique in the name of a vitalistic dynamism. Each individual life, the text begins, is part of, and answerable to, Life as a whole, just as each individual person is part of the *Volk*. This truth may be lost in times of hollowness and superficial intellectualism. Needless to say, the times alluded to were those of the Weimar Republic. At this point, standard procedure would have been for the speaker to extol Germany's rise from its vale of sorrows (i.e. democracy) thanks to the

---

[81] Langenbeck, *Die Wiedergeburt des Dramas aus dem Geist der Zeit*. Page references are given in brackets in the text.

[82] Born, like Friedrich Engels, in what is now the city of Wuppertal, Langenbeck too was the son of a factory owner and spent his early years in Germany and abroad in his father's business before going to university and taking up literature as a profession.

[83] The writer Paul Ernst (1866–1933) developed a theory of tragedy in his *Der Weg zur Form. Ästhetische Abhandlungen vornehmlich zur Tragödie und Novelle* (Berlin: Julius Bard, 1906). Like Langenbeck after him, he regarded Shakespearean drama as the antithesis to his normative concept of tragedy, which was based on the classical Greek model. Ernst's ideas had fairly wide currency in the 1930s. They are discussed in Hans Neuhof, 'Moderne Shakespearekritik: Paul Ernst', *Shakespeare-Jahrbuch* 70 (1934), 65–88. On Paul Ernst, see also: Georg Lukács, 'The Metaphysics of Tragedy' (1910), in *Soul and Form*, trans. Anna Bostock (Cambridge, MA: MIT Press, 1974), 152–74.

'National Revolution' of 1933. But Langenbeck chooses a different, much more sombre tack:

[T]here are [...] times when men are forced to learn that historical events are like natural disasters. Reason fails [...] and suddenly the individual man finds himself exposed, even sacrificed to the incomprehensible force of events. Darkly he feels that he must settle an extraordinary accumulated debt—must, whether he wants to or not—because his ancestors have left too great a debt unpaid, too great a debt owed to Life and Fate. And this individual man, all these individual men, realize that they can only pay this debt with their manhood [*Mannheit*], because there is no longer the faith in them that would enable them to settle legitimately their enormous debt to the almighty creditors Life and Fate. No reckoning in this world is ever lost—even if it were five hundred years old and had been burnt or exterminated by the sword fifty times since. It must be repaid—and there is no God who will ask by whom. Since a man owes everything to the whole of the Volk and to Life, it is he who must answer for those of his forebears and lineage who have incurred the debt. Men are often reluctant to submit to this terrible justice because they lack understanding and see only themselves. And they feel entitled to be outraged because they feel they are treated so unjustly. But that is of no account at all. There is no more delusion, no more redemption. All they are free to decide is whether to withdraw from this final reckoning—if so, they admit their weakness, their depravity or, at best, their indifference to the impending ruin of their world and their Volk—or they can decide for themselves to be strong enough to persevere through a chaos of violence and darkness and to pay with their lives for all those who, beside them and before them, have missed life's ultimate purpose, its meaning and its truth. In so doing they profess to themselves and to all those shrouded in a cloud of unknowing that a truly new life can arise from those purified and firmly resolved hearts that endure the terrible truth and affirm it by their deeds.
Our time is such a time. (10–11)

Langenbeck's idea of 'the tragic' shares Deubel's rampant *völkisch* rhetoric, his heroic bathos, pseudo-Nietzschean vitalism, and neo-pagan contempt for Christian 'redemption'. Like Deubel, he mimics Nietzsche in his pathos of 'no delusion', a self-unsparing acceptance of the hard realities of Life and Fate. Clarification is not what he seeks to achieve. If we cannot put our finger on what exactly that 'extraordinary accumulated debt [...] owed to Life and Fate' might be, or exactly how it may have been incurred in the first place, this accords perfectly with the author's intent. It is one of the commonplaces of Nazi ideology (borrowed from turn-of-the-century *Lebensphilosophie*) that all the deepest things in life are beyond the reach of analytical reasoning. In such matters as this cosmic debt, '[r]eason fails', and the truth can only be 'felt darkly'. If anything, the millenarian bathos of the passage is even more blatant in the German original.

Langenbeck is ostensibly not speaking about drama at all; his subject is politics, not theatre. But as it turns out, the two are indistinguishable. Those who heed the call to take upon themselves their historical mission, to pay the debt accrued by their forebears, will perform in a tragic action. If all art, all cultural activities under Nazi rule had to be political, politics itself, as Walter Benjamin argued, became aestheticized.[84]

---

[84] Cf. Benjamin's often-quoted observation: 'The logical result of Fascism is the introduction of aesthetics into political life. The violation of the masses, whom Fascism, with its Führer cult, forces to

Speaking as he was on 29 November 1939, three months into the Second World War, Langenbeck exhorts his listeners to adopt the attitude of a tragic hero. Those, he says, who thought that once the 'National Revolution' had taken place they could settle comfortably into life under a new and better regime could not be more mistaken. The true ordeal was only just beginning. 'The practical objective of this war is clear: a curtailment of English influence and English arrogance in accordance with the natural strength of the German people and its existential demands sanctioned by both nature and history' (13).

But the ultimate goal is a spiritual rebirth: 'That we as human beings, as Germans, will emerge more pious, purified and, yes, more beautiful from this war' (14). The crucial lesson to be learned is that the individual must abandon any private interests he may harbour and commit himself fully and 'religiously' to the greater cause:

> Only those individuals harbour within themselves something of the origin of Life, and only those peoples can be sure of a future, who are ready to face up to their destiny piously, neither sceptically nor stoically. (15)

Those, on the other hand, who are not ready for destiny 'cannot grasp the meaning of tragedy, much less be capable of making one' (16).

The spirit from which tragedy is to be reborn, then, is the spirit that piously accepts destiny and does not ask whether it is happy or not. In the grand scheme determined by the forces of Life, destiny, and *Volk*, individual guilt is meaningless. There is no personal God who guarantees the observance of moral standards. Rather than taking arms against a sea of troubles and by opposing end them (cf. *Ham.* 3.1.58–9), the proper course for the tragic hero is pious compliance with the inescapable necessity to put an end to himself. The general drift of Langenbeck's concept of tragedy is towards depersonalization, a strongly anti-individualistic bias. Personal conflict or a 'tragic flaw' rooted in the passions of the individual are dismissed as essentially alien to tragedy proper. And so is, as the lengthy quotation just displayed shows, personal guilt.[85]

Two things follow from Langenbeck's views on tragedy. First, his own attempts in the genre must be numbingly undramatic if they are as drained of personal antagonism as his precepts demand. This suspicion is signally confirmed by Langenbeck's *Das Schwert* (The Sword, 1940) in which the hero, once he has realized the will of Fate, can only execute that will (which happens to mean executing

---

their knees, has its counterpart in the violation of an apparatus which is pressed into the production of ritual values. All efforts to render politics aesthetic culminate in one thing: war.' Walter Benjamin, 'The Work of Art in the Age of Mechanical Reproduction', in *Illuminations*, trans. Harry Zorn, ed. Hannah Arendt (New York: Schocken Books, 1969), 217–51 at 241.

[85] An important semantic feature of that quotation has been lost in my translation. The German word I have rendered as 'debt' is *Schuld*; and *Schuld* also means 'guilt'. Guilt rather than debt is what we would expect to find in a treatise on tragedy. Guilt was of central importance in Lessing's reflections on the nature of tragedy and in those of his many successors. But guilt can only maintain such central importance in a character-based concept of tragedy. And it is such a concept that Langenbeck rejects, advocating instead a 'guilt-free' tragedy. Langenbeck uses the word *Schuld*, but consistently collocates it with verbs that push its meaning in the direction of (amoral) debt to be paid rather than (moral) guilt to be expiated.

his brother). And second, Shakespeare stands for just about everything this concept of tragedy rejects. Inevitably, Langenbeck classes him as essentially non-tragic: all we see in Shakespeare is 'characters'—'heightened mirror-images of real individuals'—blindly crashing into each other in their obsessive passions:

> And when such a Shakespearean man eventually goes to his death, all we can say is that he has exhausted himself, that a dangerous excess of passion has spent itself [...] The ending of such a play almost always leaves us cold, somehow dejected; none of those Richmonds or Fortinbrasses that always appear in some form or other can alter that; because we rightly sense that a similarly terrible and meaningless spectacle may repeat itself on the next best occasion. [...] The end of all Shakespearean *Trauerspiele* is devastating. Demons have wreaked havoc with a man; the result is a corpse. Now nature will seek out her next victim [...] (35)

Such an ending impoverishes instead of enriching us. 'We are left without ethos or law.' With the Greeks, the hero is aware of his duty and by fulfilling that duty to the death satisfies the will of both fate and the gods, 'purifies life' and leaves the world a better place. 'Thus a subtraction—a man who has had to sacrifice himself and therefore has ceased to exist—accomplishes a gain: in vitality, in insight, in cosmic order' (35)

Even in Nazi Germany, one did not bash the Bard without letting oneself in for some bashing back. A champion for Shakespeare arose in Josef Magnus Wehner, the culture-page editor of the leading Munich newspaper, *Münchner Neueste Nachrichten*. A heated controversy ensued, beginning with three articles by Wehner, followed by two ripostes from Langenbeck and a two-part conclusion by Wehner.[86] In his first sally, Wehner attacks Langenbeck's view of Greek antiquity as too narrowly idealistic. He roundly dismisses Langenbeck's claim that the first precondition of proper, that is, Greek, tragedy is a worldview in which there is no belief in any kind of hereafter. This claim does indeed sit oddly with the pervasive religious tone of Langenbeck's homily, especially with his tenet that an authentically tragic worldview requires that 'man must have a belief, a belief in God', albeit a god or gods 'who are neither benevolent nor merciful or compassionate but violent, cruel, beautiful—not dissimilar to nature, her forces and laws' (25).

Wehner's second article disputes Langenbeck's assessment of Shakespeare as the creator of mere 'characters'. Pitting Shakespeare's cosmic range, his infinite vitality, depth, and wisdom against the 'Euclidian choreography of Greek drama', he takes particular issue with the Greeks' monopoly on doom and fate:

> 'Mere characters'?—my dear poet Curt Langenbeck, I too believe in doom and fate— but do the Greeks really have the advantage over Shakespeare in this? Is fate not simply

---

[86] The complete series of articles is as follows: Wehner, 'Der Dichter und der Hades' (16 February 1940); Wehner, 'Curt Langenbeck und Shakespeare' (18 February 1940); Wehner, 'Die Wiedergeburt des Dramas' (21 February 1940); Langenbeck, 'Christentum und Tragödie' (24 February 1940); Langenbeck, 'Shakespeare—ein Problem für unsere Zeit' (2/3 March 1940); Wehner, 'Der Streit um den Hades' (6 March 1940); Wehner, 'Götter, Sowohl-als-auch-Leute und Shakespeare' (9/10 March 1940). Wehner, who was no less outspoken in his support of Nazism than his opponent, reprinted these articles in a volume of his collected essays entitled *Vom Glanz und Leben deutscher Bühne: Eine Münchner Dramaturgie. Aufsätze und Kritiken 1933–1941* (Hamburg: Hanseatische Verlagsanstalt, 1944), where they appear under the chapter heading 'Battle for Shakespeare'.

This humanist plea almost certainly made no dent in Langenbeck's ideological armour. Nor would it have impressed him that Pfitzner retaliated to the Bard-bashing of the Nazi Hellenists with some rather silly Greek-bashing of his own. Langenbeck, at any rate, persisted in giving rebirth to tragedy and capturing the spirit of the time, although his next effort fell dismally wide of the mark. *Das Schwert* (The Sword), which premièred on 23 November 1940, was accused of 'dictatorial puritanism' by the official Nazi newspaper *Völkischer Beobachter*.[95] It also ran afoul of the authorities for ideological reasons. War, the play asserts, is noble and necessary, peace a cowardly evasion. This, one would think, should have gone down well enough. But Langenbeck erred in giving the pacifist Evruin far too much space to present his—albeit supposedly fallacious—argument before being sacrificed to necessity by his noble brother Gaiso. Nor did Gaiso's subsequent suicide provide an acceptable finale at a time when the war effort called for relentless optimism.

The play might have fared better later in the war, when the destruction Germany had wreaked on others rebounded on the Reich itself and the proclamation of total war deliberately embraced, even glorified, the possibility of self-destruction.

It was at this stage that Langenbeck attracted international attention. On 3 April 1944, two months before D-Day, *Time* magazine gave its readers this report on the enemy's cultural war effort:

> In Munich last month the Nazis and Japs were clasped in a tender esthetic embrace. Nazi Playwright Curt Langenbeck had adapted the most famed of Japanese dramas, *The 47 Ronin*, which was produced with considerable care and éclat. To the opening of *Treue* (Loyalty) went Gauleiter Giesler and other Nazi party officials to welcome the representatives of 'our great ally', Japanese ambassador Oshima, Japanese Minister Sakuma.

'*Treue*', the article goes on in vintage *Time*-ese, 'richly satisfies the Jappetite for bloodshed. It contains 49 successful murders and suicides, a few unsuccessful ones.'

The story of the forty-seven faithful samurai who avenge the death of their master, Count Enya, on the treacherous Prince Moronao is based on a mid-eighteenth-century Japanese play by Takeda Izumo. His is the best known of many dramatizations of a famous episode in Japanese history which took place in 1702/3 and is commemorated annually to this day on 14 December. In 1942 and 1943, the story had already been given two German stage versions: *Bushido* by Arthur Schneider and *Samurai* by Mirko Jelusich. With a revenge plot hinging on a hero who bides his time before striking and lulls his enemy into a false sense of security with a subterfuge of drunken debauchery, and with a villain (Moronao) who has engineered his victim's death out of lust for the latter's wife, we might well suspect that the play captured 'the Jappetite for bloodshed' by stirring in a good measure of Teutonic Hamletophilia. The reviewer of the *Münchner Neueste Nachrichten* suggests as much. The swearing of the conspirators' oath, language

---

[95] Richard Biedrzynski, 'Tragödie—mathematisch gelöst', *Völkischer Beobachter*, 25 November 1940.

rich in imagery, and especially the humorous touches in some of the most oppressive scenes, 'remind one more of Shakespeare than the Greeks'. He notes this as something of a surprise. And so, in view of Langenbeck's known disapproval of Shakespeare, it certainly was. But it would go too far to speak of a change of heart. Despite being written in blank verse, despite its intimations of *Hamlet* and its sporadic attempts at comic relief, the play's overall design, mood, and *Weltanschauung* are firmly grounded in Langenbeck's earlier doctrine. *Treue*— loyalty—was a cornerstone in the Nazi edifice. Every SS man wore the motto 'Loyalty is my honour' on his belt buckle. With the Wehrmacht retreating on all fronts and Allied bombers flattening German cities, *Treue* became even more the word of the moment. Loyalty to the death—this was what the propaganda machine clamoured for, and it is what Langenbeck's play dutifully offers in its five cumbersome acts.[96]

The play has one major 'character' in Langenbeck's own pejorative sense of the word. This is the villain, Prince Moronao, whose obsessive passion for Kaoyo, the wife of Count Enya, leads him to the murder of Enya and thus sets the revenge action in motion. The limitations Langenbeck sees in Shakespeare's characters find exemplary illustration in his own Moronao. When he 'eventually goes to his death, all we can say is [...] that a dangerous excess of passion has spent itself'. True to style, Moronao is given a seduction scene reminiscent of Richard Gloucester wooing Lady Anne. But Moronao is, of course, not the hero of the play. The hero is Yuranoske, the first knight of the murdered Enya, and he is what a hero, according to Langenbeck, should be: heroic. Much less individual as a character than Moronao, he is more like a literary version of the monumental statues of Arno Breker, a luminary on the 'God-gifted' list, whose allegorical figures of 'Comradeship', 'The Party', or 'Sacrifice' propagated Nazi ideals in sculptural form. Unlike the 'merely individual', passion-driven character of the Shakespearean type, Yuranoske is a man fully aware of his duty, a man whose every action is determined by that duty. His revenge is retarded by external forces, not by any hesitancy on his part. Duty once recognized is law to him, absolute necessity. The tragic knot is tightened and the hero ennobled even further through his knowledge that if he lives up to his duty and kills Moronao, he and his forty-six companions will face certain death. But the law of loyalty makes revenge an ethical necessity, even if the law of the state demands the death of the avengers. This comes close to the dilemma set forth in the Sophoclean *Antigone*, whose ethical symmetry (Antigone is right, but so is Kreon) has always enthralled theorists of classical tragedy.

The imperative to act demands unconditional acceptance of doom. Personal considerations such as his family's well-being cease to matter. He must live out his destiny:

[96] Curt Langenbeck, *Treue* (Munich: Albert Langen and Georg Müller, 1940). In 1944, Wilhelm von Scholz contributed *Ayatari*, another play of heroic Japanese bloodshed. See Günter Rühle, 'Rufe nach Treue', in his *Theater in Deutschland*, 962–3. See also Bill Maltarich, *Samurai and Supermen: National Socialist Views of Japan* (Oxford, Berne, and Berlin: Peter Lang, 2005).

Because I must do now what is decreed
And what I do is absolutely right,
I trust with fervid heart in loyalty
[...]
He only who in stony vale of sorrows
Proves loyal and preserves his trust and faith
Will see life's luminous heights one day again!
The holy government of our world—
Boldly I say it—must be very pleased
That now man's courage undergoes a test
Where all his worth's at stake [...][97]

The topicality of this speech, which is delivered by the hero in a central scene of the play, would have been only too obvious to an audience in March 1944. Six months before the mobilization of the *Volkssturm* committed a million boys and retirement-age men to prolonging a lost war, *Treue* is suffused with poetically refined versions of the rhetoric which the not so 'holy government' of Germany was using in order to exhort the population to hold out. 'He who overtaxes men courts disaster', one of Yuranoske's followers warns, but he is promptly rebuked: 'Only he who dares the utmost shall prevail.'[98] Fantasies of *Endsieg* (final victory) and glorifications of heroic self-destruction merge in a solemn ritual of death. This is Yuranoske's son Rikiya speaking to his beloved, Komitsu:

Rikiya: My future lies behind me. I just am.
Komitsu: O, you terrify me, Prince! What is a youth who can speak like a god?
Rikiya: I do not know. I know not what he is. I know but what he has.
Komitsu: Say it.
Rikiya: Shall I?
Komitsu: Yes, my Prince.
Rikiya: He has death.
Komitsu: And that is his triumph?
Rikiya: He has vanquished death.
Komitsu: That is his life.
(Silence)[99]

In the play's Munich première on 6 March 1944, Rikiya—an idealized role model for a Hitler Youth drafted into the *Volkssturm*—was played by the 25-year-old Austrian actor Bernhard Wicki, who became a film director after the war. His masterpiece, *Die Brücke* (*The Bridge*, 1959),[100] shows the disastrous influence of such role models and the perverted idealism propagated through them in the story of a group of adolescent boys who are recruited into the Wehrmacht in the spring

---

[97] Langenbeck, *Treue*, 59.   [98] Langenbeck, *Treue*, 58.
[99] Langenbeck, *Treue*, 58.
[100] *Die Brücke* was nominated for an Academy Award and won the Golden Globe Award as Best Foreign Film in 1960.

of 1945. All but one of them are killed in the attempt to defend a strategically meaningless local bridge against US tanks. The film powerfully demystifies the heroic death cult that was exalted in plays like Langenbeck's *Treue*. Rikiya's solemn platitudes bear out Benjamin's dictum that the fascist effort 'to render politics aesthetic' has its inevitable telos in war. The reality of war, however, in which the boys in Wicki's film find themselves trapped, defies any effort at aestheticization. Rather than heroism, the film's devastating battle scenes emphasize 'the boys' fear and disorientation'.[101]

Reading Langenbeck's *Treue* is instructive, not least because it suggests that those Third Reich ideologists who rejected Shakespeare may have actually understood him better than those who co-opted him as a kindred spirit. Langenbeck was right in distrusting the Bard. Shakespeare's multiperspectival dramaturgy, his multidimensional 'mixed' characters—prey to contradictory impulses, torn by doubts, wavering—are hardly suited to orchestrate the apotheosis of a collective death wish. If Macbeth, in the last act, could be said to act out such a wish, his frame of mind has nothing in common with the high-flown solemnity of Yuranoske. While *Treue* unreservedly glorifies its hero, *Macbeth*, far from glorifying its protagonist, relentlessly dismantles his delusions. As the cornered tyrant must recognize the futility of his ambitions ('Tomorrow and tomorrow and tomorrow', *Mac*. 5.5.19) and the deceptiveness of 'these juggling fiends' (5.7.49) whose equivocations he took as assurances of success, Shakespeare's play offers a ringside view of the final moments of a crumbling dictatorial regime—certainly a timely parable for the Nazi leaders in early 1945, but hardly one they would have chosen for edification. Instead, they opted for a dose of that *Durchhaltepropaganda* (*durchhalten*—to hold out) which was supposed to mobilize the population for a hopeless last-ditch effort. After his last radio address to the German people on 30 January 1945, Hitler and his staff at the *Reichskanzlei* watched a screening of *Kolberg*, the film that tells the story of the heroic—and ultimately successful—defence of the besieged Prussian fortress town of Kolberg against superior Napoleonic forces in 1807. Like *Kolberg*, Langenbeck's *Treue* serves the self-congratulatory delusions of a regime bent on a doomsday mission. *Macbeth* exposes these delusions for what they are: the last resort of desperate criminals.

---

[101] Anne-Marie Scholz, '*The Bridge on the River Kwai* (1957) Revisited: Combat Cinema, American Culture and the German Past', *German History* 26 (2008), 219–50 at 243. Scholz interestingly discusses *Die Brücke* as a response to *The Bridge on the River Kwai*.

7

'But break, my heart, for I must hold my tongue'
Hamlet in Inner Emigration

I 'A THOROUGHLY MANLY FIGURE'

In 1919, Paul Valéry imagined Hamlet picking up skulls from the battlefields of Europe for contemplation. In 1945, not even skulls remained of the victims whose ghosts most insistently called for remembrance. Gassed and burnt in the incinerators of the death camps, these victims had no burial in the ground. In Paul Celan's haunting 'Death Fugue',

death is a master from Germany
he calls out more darkly now stroke your strings then you will rise as smoke
you will rise into air
then a grave you will have in the clouds there one lies unconfined[1]

By no stretch of the imagination could Valéry's Hamlet of Europe have foreseen the industrial-scale murder committed by a people that once found its own image reflected in Shakespeare's hesitant prince. In a way even less foreseeable at the time of H. H. Furness's 1877 dedication '[t]o the "German Shakespeare Society" of Weimar', world history, in 1945, could not have proved more definitively 'that "Germany [was] not Hamlet"'.[2]

As we have seen, Furness's claim was premature. While the official Germany traded Hamlet's 'pale cast of thought' for those 'enterprises of great pitch and moment'(*Ham.* 3.1.84–5) that befitted its newly-gained great-power status in the 1870s, Hamlet's sardonic detachment continued to provide a model of intellectual resistance to the swelling tide of imperial self-importance. If this was so during Germany's Second Empire, it might well be expected to have appealed again under the Third Reich: the more the official Germany shed any semblance to Shakespeare's noble prince, the more readily he might have lent himself as a model of a better, more humane Germany suppressed by the Nazis. Hamlet's withdrawal into his

---

[1] Paul Celan, 'Todesfuge/Death Fugue', in *Poems of Paul Celan*, trans. Michael Hamburger (London: Anvil Press Poetry, 1995), 62–5 at 65.
[2] 'De-Hamletized Germany 1933/45', Carl Schmitt notes in his diary on 25 May 1958. Carl Schmitt, *Glossarium. Aufzeichnungen aus den Jahren 1947 bis 1948*, ed. Gerd Giesler and Martin Tielke (Berlin: Duncker & Humblot, 2015), 369.

own world of thoughts might well have been seen to offer a classic precedent of what became known as 'inner emigration'. But like the term, the phenomenon it describes is much more easily traceable in its retrospective, post-war formation than during the Nazi era itself.

The Hamlet who actually dominated on stage and page during the Third Reich was not a sensitive dreamer, not Wilhelm Meister's tender soul 'without the strength of nerve which forms a hero'.[3] Most definitely, he was not the 'weakling or nervous artist type'[4] that had—allegedly—run riot on the decadent Weimar stage. The Hamlet played in 1936 by Willy Birgel, for example, an actor on the brink of stardom in Goebbels's film industry, was approvingly described as 'steel-hard, a thoroughly manly figure'.[5] If the 'rotten state' opposed by the likes of this boldly resolute prince bore any relation to contemporary history, it inevitably pointed to the immediate past: both the actor's acting and the prince's action were targeting the rotten state of Weimar.

Active Hamlets had trodden the boards in Germany before. Friedrich Ludwig Schröder, in his landmark production of 1778, gave the part a dynamism that was a far cry from Wilhelm Meister.[6] More recent precedent was afforded by Gerhart Hauptmann, whose lifelong preoccupation with the play and the prince produced a spate of Hamletian offshoots: two adaptations of Shakespeare's play (1927, 1930), a dramatic prequel entitled *Hamlet in Wittenberg* (1935) and the semi-autobiographical novel *Im Wirbel der Berufung* (*In the Throes of Vocation*), which was begun in 1924 and finally published in 1936. Modelled on *Wilhelm Meister's Apprenticeship*, the novel is set in the escapist idyll of a late nineteenth-century miniature dukedom, where the young author Erasmus Gotter experiences a series of love entanglements while preparing a production of *Hamlet* at the local court theatre. Gotter's idea of Hamlet is the very opposite of Wilhelm Meister's, and the version of the play eventually performed in the novel borrows its main features from Hauptmann's previous adaptations. Like the novel's protagonist, Hauptmann justified his radical alterations by referring to the thoroughly corrupted nature of the surviving Shakespearean texts, making their transmission from author's pen to actor's stage to printed page sound like a veritable steeplechase of unavoidable mishaps caused by careless scribes, scattered papers, egotistical actors, and cloth-eared stenographers. The rewriting of *Hamlet* is thus an attempt to restore 'the immortal Hamlet torso' to its original wholeness through a mobilizing of 'poetic intuition', 'a summons of all the creative forces against the destructive ones'.[7] The extant texts are marred, on the one hand, by 'bone loss', but on the other by 'pathological swellings' (946); the restorer must therefore make bold cuts as well as prosthetic additions in the spirit of the original. The whole of the fourth act,

---

[3] Goethe, *Wilhelm Meister's Apprenticeship*, 146 (Book IV, Chap. 13).
[4] Werner Papsdorf, 'Theaterschau', *Shakespeare-Jahrbuch* 72 (1936), 248.
[5] Wolfgang Stroedel, *Shakespeare auf der deutschen Bühne vom Ende des Weltkriegs bis zur Gegenwart* (Weimar: Hermann Böhlaus Nachf., 1938) 47.
[6] See Williams, *Shakespeare on the German Stage*, vol. 1, 67–87.
[7] Gerhart Hauptmann, 'Hamlet. Einige Worte zu meinem Ergänzungsversuch' (1927), in Hauptmann, *Sämtliche Werke*, ed. Hans-Egon Hass, vol. 6: *Erzählungen, theoretische Prosa* (Frankfurt and Berlin: Propyläen, 1996), 943–61 at 947. References to this edition are given in brackets in the text.

Hauptmann says, is nothing but a 'field of rubble' where the action comes to almost 'complete stagnation' (952). It also contains the gravest flaw of all, which motivates Hauptmann's most radical alteration: his re-ascription of Laertes's rebellion to Hamlet. Never, he claims, would Laertes 'the correct courtier' (948) have instigated such a coup, nor would he, a man without the slightest entitlement to the crown of Denmark, have found followers to support him. The whole affair, Hauptmann argues, makes much better sense with Hamlet, who is 'loved by the multitude', '[t]h'expectation and rose of the fair state' (*Ham.* 3.1.149): 'Hamlet executes the rebellion: it lies in his nature, it lies in the plot, the natural dynamics of the play' (950).

Hauptmann stuck to his guns, unimpressed by the legions of critics and theatregoers who found nothing wrong with a rebellious Laertes, and unmoved by the rather mixed reception his 'corrected' *Hamlet* found on its première in 1927.[8] The point of interest for us here is that Hauptmann's adaptation implanted an active Hamlet into the very plot structure of the play: 'Hamlet wants to unmask his uncle. Tenacious and strong-willed, he doggedly pursues his goal. There are countless proofs of his strong will' (950).[9] Hauptmann was certainly no trailblazer for the Nazis, but he was not immune to a *Zeitgeist* so eminently favourable to his view of Hamlet. Having endorsed Germany's proprietary claim to Shakespeare during the First World War, Hauptmann renewed this claim in 1935:

> Germany, thank God, is not Hamlet the inactive figure as he was formerly misunderstood, but Hamlet the problematic, richly emotional man of action. In youth, suffering, growth, defeat and victory, Hamlet has a much more universal Germanness than Faust and is inseparable from Germany's great spiritual destiny.[10]

In April 1944, when Germany's fate was rather less than great, Hauptmann once again confirmed his view of Hamlet in a letter to the actor who played the part in Hauptmann's version of the play at Vienna's *Volkstheater*: the production, he declared, was 'an act of truth that disarms nonsense'.[11]

---

[8] Hauptmann was bitterly sarcastic about the critics' (especially the famous Alfred Kerr's) negative response to the Dresden première of his adaptation, which he directed himself; see Gerhart Hauptmann, *Diarium 1917 bis 1933*, ed. Martin Machatzke (Frankfurt and Berlin: Propyläen, 1980), 104–7. As if to bolster his bid for canonical status, he published a furtherly revised version in an expensive Art Nouveau-style edition adorned with woodcuts by Edward Gordon Craig in 1929. William Shakespeare, *Die tragische Gechichte von Hamlet Prinzen von Dænemark in deutscher Sprache. Neu übersetzt und eingerichtet von Gerhart Hauptmann* (Weimar: Cranach-Presse, 1929). Inspired by William Morris's Kelmscott Press, Cranach-Presse was founded and run by the diplomat, writer, and patron of modern art, Harry Graf (Count) Kessler. Between 1913 and 1931 it produced around seventy editions for bibliophiles, the Hauptmann/Craig *Hamlet* being considered one of its finest achievements and a prime example of twentieth-century printer's art. It was also published in an English version, edited by John Dover Wilson, in 1930.

[9] The fact that proofs of Hamlet's 'strong will' are more readily available in Shakespeare's sources than in his play does not concern Hauptmann. The sources have at least the same authority for him as the Quartos and the Folio. Hence the text in the Cranach Press edition is framed by extracts from Saxo Grammaticus and Belleforest.

[10] Hauptmann, Letter to Wulf Leisner, 9 December 1935; quoted in Peter Sprengel, *Der Dichter stand auf hoher Küste*, 100.

[11] Hauptmann, Letter to Andreas Wolf, 28 April 1944; quoted in Sprengel, *Der Dichter stand auf hoher Küste*, 99.

II THE CASE OF GUSTAF GRÜNDGENS

To what extent the most famous stage Hamlet of the Third Reich conformed to this heroically active model or subverted it is a matter of dispute. This *Hamlet*, directed by Lothar Müthel,[12] premièred at the Prussian State Theatre in January 1936. The title part was played by Gustaf Gründgens, the real-life model of the careerist star actor Hendrik Höfgen in Klaus Mann's novel *Mephisto*.[13] Appointed *Intendant* (director) of the Prussian State Theatre by Hermann Göring in 1934, Gründgens has been criticized for his Third Reich eminence but also given credit for using it to protect endangered colleagues. He brought all his technical brilliance and physical dynamism to the part. There was nothing wrong with the way this lithe, blond prince swept to his revenge in Act 5, crying 'Ho!' as he lustily rammed his rapier into the treacherous bosom of his uncle. Nothing wrong either with how he communicated the hallmark depth of Shakespeare's exemplary Nordic 'soul-drama'.[14] But there were grumblings too: Gründgens's acting style, the very antithesis of the 'full-blooded', 'earthy' ideal of the day, struck some as excessively mannered (Figure 7.1).[15]

This criticism was given a dangerous edge in Rosenberg's *Völkischer Beobachter*, although the article in which it appeared was ostensibly not about Gründgens's performance at all and never even mentioned his name. Its declared purpose, taking a by now familiar line, was to clear Hamlet of any suspicion of weakness. 'Uniting hero and thinker', 'Hamlet's Political Heroism' made him the paragon of a 'Nordic sense of responsibility' for his country and people.[16] In order to see this, the author declared, one had to discard 'once and for all the totally wrong idea—prejudiced by a Jewish mentality'—that Hamlet was weak-willed, loquacious, and a hypocrite: 'the Dorian Gray of the sixteenth century'. Oddly incongruous as this may seem at the beginning of the article, the mention of Dorian Gray is by no

---

[12] Müthel is now mostly remembered for his production of *The Merchant of Venice* at Vienna's Burgtheater in 1943, in which Werner Krauss gave a notoriously anti-Semitic performance of Shylock. See Hortmann, *Shakespeare on the German Stage*, vol. 2, 134–6; Andrew G. Bonnell, *Shylock in Germany: Antisemitism and the German Theatre from the Enlightenment to the Nazis* (London and New York: I. B. Tauris, 2008), 161–4.

[13] Klaus Mann, *Mephisto: Roman einer Karriere* (Amsterdam: Querido Verlag, 1936); Engl. trans. Robin Smyth (New York: Random House, 1977).

[14] Papsdorf, 'Theaterschau', 248. See Thilo von Trotha, 'Shakepeare und wir', discussed in Chapter 6, section II.

[15] Hortmann, *Shakespeare in Germany*, 160, cites the actor Will Quadflieg (later a famous Faust to Gründgens's even more famous Mephisto), who 'found the court scene "ingenious, clever, but too clever by half"'. Quadflieg 'was irritated by Gründgens's "mannered melodiousness of delivery" and deplored the coolness and formality of the Gründgens style which he felt "revealed . . . a lack of spontaneous power of feeling"'.

[16] Waldemar Hartmann, 'Hamlets politisches Heldentum: Gedanken zum "Hamlet", als der Tragödie nordischen Verantwortungsgefühls', *Völkischer Beobachter*, 3 May 1936, 5. Hartmann was the deputy cultural editor of the paper. For a detailed account of the Gründgens-Hamlet affair see Peter Jammerthal, *Ein zuchtvolles Theater: Bühnenästhetik des 'Dritten Reiches'. Das Berliner Staatstheater von der 'Machtergreifung' bis zur Ära Gründgens* (PhD dissertation: Free University Berlin, 2007), 217, <http://www.diss.fu-berlin.de/diss/servlets/MCRFileNodeServlet/FUDISS_derivate_000000002953/06_kap3b.pdf?hosts=>, accessed 20 June 2015.

Figure 7.1. Gustaf Gründgens as Hamlet, 1936. Photo by permission of ullstein bild—René Fosshag.

means gratuitous. In fact, it recurs, after much preaching on Hamlet's tragic struggle for the national cause, in the climactic final paragraph:

> Who could fail to recognize in this [Hamlet's predicament] a parable of our people's experience? Has National Socialism not suffered hundreds of casualties for the sake of preventing a civil war, fought for the liberty of the German people with naked shield? The representation of Hamlet therefore requires a heroic *Weltanschauung* at its base. Only an actor who finds this in himself will be up to the part. But never will an actor do justice to Hamlet if he merely indulges his sickly, decadent vanity in the vein of Oscar Wilde and his gentleman-criminal Dorian Gray by playing Hamlet's witticisms as the substance, not the mask of the character, playing him without the ability to show the naked blade of readiness under the cloak of deceptive words: for 'the readiness is all'.

The threat, none too subtly encoded in the Wilde reference, was not lost on Gründgens, whose homosexuality was an open secret. Panicked, he fled to Switzerland, but returned a couple of days later, his nerves calmed by Göring's assurances of protection and by his appointment as Prussian state councillor. *Völkischer Beobachter* duly noted the bestowal of this honour, using the occasion, only five days after its attack on Gründgens, to celebrate his Hamlet as 'a breakthrough for the new view of a purposeful, responsible, and combative Hamlet'.[17]

<hr />

[17] *Völkischer Beobachter*, 8 May 1936.

An echo of the Dorian Gray allegation lingers in an otherwise laudatory entry on Gründgens's Hamlet in Goebbels's diary:

A magnificent evening at the theatre. Wonderfully coordinated ensemble play. Gründgens only occasionally somewhat decadent. But on the whole a high point of German theatre. The audience is enthusiastic. A very great success. Genius Shakespeare! How small everything else is by comparison. (14 June 1938)[18]

The majority of contemporary responses chimed in with the praise. The performance at Vienna's famous *Burgtheater* could otherwise hardly have taken place. Three months after Hitler's annexation of Austria, the guest appearance of Gründgens's Berlin ensemble served as a showpiece of the Reich's highest achievement in the art of theatre.

Audiences adored Gründgens's Hamlet. By 1941, when the production was chosen as the opener for the State Theatre's third 'War Season', he had appeared in the part about 140 times.[19] Most reviewers either did not, or chose not to, see anything politically untoward in his performance. One writer celebrated the production as a landmark in theatre history, a restoration of the play's 'Renaissance character' by which 'the Romanticization of the part' was definitively 'invalidated': 'Each new staging of the work will have to look back to this first *Hamlet* born from the conscience of the present.'[20] Together with the 'soldierly' Mannheim Hamlet of Willy Birgel, Gründgens's performance was perceived as an exemplary realization of a heroically energetic Hamlet who was in tune with the heroic ethos of the new Germany. These commentators did not overlook the despair and world-weariness Gründgens showed in the early stages of the play. But the production made it possible to integrate these initial displays of a sensitive, even narcissistically self-centred disposition into an overall development from dejection to action. It was just such a trajectory that propelled Goebbels's Michael from aimlessly brooding to embarking on a crusade for national regeneration. The same 'dramaturgy of conversion' (*Wandlungsdramaturgie*) became a standard pattern of Nazi dramas.[21]

What complicates this straightforward conformist reading was 'the uncanny degree of consciousness with which Gründgens endowed the part. His Hamlet was not only a superb analyst of his own impulses and the moral state of the world, he was also fully aware that he was acting a part. His knowledge extended [...]

---

[18] *Die Tagebücher von Joseph Goebbels*, pt. 1, vol. 5, ed. Fröhlich (2000), 344.

[19] While some authors speak of over 200 performances, statistical evidence supports a lower figure. See Jammerthal, *Ein zuchtvolles Theater*, 217.

[20] Richard Biedrzynski, *Schauspieler, Regisseure, Intendanten* (Heidelberg, Berlin, and Leipzig: Hüthig, 1944), 40.

[21] Markus Moninger, *Shakespeare inszeniert: Das westdeutsche Regietheater und die Theatertradition des 'dritten deutschen Klassikers'* (Tübingen: Niemeyer, 1996), 69. Hanns Johst's *Schlageter* is a case in point. This play about one of the Nazis' martyr-heroes (see Chapter 6, n. 21) was praised by *Völkischer Beobachter* as 'the first drama of the German revolution'. While the historical Schlageter had long been involved in militant free corps activities, Johst's play has him undergo a dramatic conversion from harmless student to resistance fighter.

to the dramaturgy of his own fate.'[22] In a vividly detailed description of his performance, Paul Fechter extolled Gründgens's precision, calling him 'the most calculated Hamlet since Kainz'.[23] In contrast to the melancholy dreamer of the Romantics, Gründgens 'everywhere stresses the active elements but he also makes visible the self-control through consciousness' (128).[24] This Hamlet is incapable of 'the naïve unscrupulousness' required for action (123) not only because of his 'constant awareness' (or 'conscience') but also, more specifically, because Gründgens renders his character as essentially that of an actor: a man always conscious of acting and to whom acting is the only available mode of existence:

> This is a very modern Hamlet, [...] nervous, obsessed with himself as he is with his task, a very aesthetic Hamlet [...] [,] very aware of himself and the impression he makes [...]; he very deliberately brings his hands and face into pictorial contrast with the black costume he always, and the black cap he sometimes wears. [He] lives in total isolation from the world surrounding him. He has no real relationship with anyone, neither with Ophelia, nor his mother, nor even Horatio. He lives entirely through himself, through the world of his words and his feeling for the pictorial effect of his actions, and out of the obligation to grandly stage his task. He does not permit himself the right to an immediate, unmoulded life [...]. (123)

Fechter leaves us in no doubt of his high regard for Gründgens's achievement, but his insistence on the self-conscious artistry of his performance, which strikes a similar note—albeit in a less insidious key—as *Völkischer Beobachter*, stung the actor to write a reply in his own defence. Agreeing with Fechter's main point, Gründgens confirmed that his rendering of the character was indeed centred on Hamlet as an actor. But this was not due to superficial aestheticism or straining for effect: 'When the curtain opens', he wrote, 'I do not want to play Hamlet, I want to go back to Wittenberg' (132).

> What saddens me is that you write that I use 'the contrast between the light areas of the face and hands and the black of the costume for impressive effect', that the gestures are carefully chosen, effectively executed. I object to your remark about 'the elegant, calculated crowning of it all'. And when you write that my Hamlet is just as obsessed with himself as with his task and that he is acutely aware of the impression he makes, I only accept this if you concede that Hamlet is in a situation that requires him to do all these things in self-defence. (132)

Gründgens's reply, especially when he speaks about acting as a self-defence strategy, has been read as an encrypted account of his position in the Third Reich. This

---

[22] Hortmann, *Shakespeare on the German Stage*, 159.

[23] Paul Fechter, 'Deutsche Shakespeare-Darsteller; I: Gustaf Gründgens als Hamlet', *Shakespeare-Jahrbuch* 77 (1941), 123–32 at 123. Page references are given in brackets in the text. Josef Kainz (1858–1910): as a member of the Munich National Theatre he became the Bavarian King Ludwig II's favourite actor and repeatedly performed his stage roles in private exclusively for the monarch. In 1883 he joined the newly established Deutsches Theater in Berlin, where he gave celebrated performances of Hamlet, Richard II, and other classical parts. For his Shakespearean roles see Williams, *Shakespeare on the German Stage*, 197–204.

[24] Quoted in Hortmann, *Shakespeare on the German Stage*, 160.

Hamlet, who is totally isolated, acting, as it were, for dear life—was he not the perfect doppelganger of Gründgens himself, the homosexual star actor and the State Theatre's director general by the grace of Hermann Göring, the pampered darling of a regime from which he inwardly recoiled, the observed of all observers, always keeping up appearances, while secretly putting himself at risk for at least some fellow actors who were under direct threat from the Gestapo? In this reading Gründgens's Hamlet offers 'a cryptic analogy of the dangerous game of double bluff he was playing with and against the Nazis'.[25]

At least one contemporary theatre-goer lends credibility to this view. This is the critic and Holocaust survivor Marcel Reich-Ranicki, who saw Gründgens's Hamlet as a sixteen-year-old grammar school boy in Berlin:

> I too recognized features of my existence in Nazi Germany in Hamlet—thanks to Gründgens. He played a young, lonely intellectual [...] He gave special emphasis—or so it seemed to me—to Hamlet's words 'The time is out of joint' and 'Denmark is a prison'. In this kingdom of Denmark, a police state, everyone is spied upon by everyone [...]
>
> After I had seen Gründgens, I read every scene of *Hamlet* differently from before— most of all the tragedy of the intellectual amid a cruel society and a murderous state. Did theatregoers perceive this production as I did? Probably only a small minority. But could it escape the Nazis, notably their cultural politicians and journalists, that this Hamlet could be understood as a political manifesto, a protest against the tyranny prevailing in Germany?[26]

III THOMAS MANN AND 'THE GREAT CONTROVERSY'

Gründgens's Hamlet, who had much to hide from the rotten state of Denmark, but more from the vigilant state of Nazi Germany, presents a case of questionable exemplarity. Outwardly conforming, but inwardly detached from, or even hostile to, the regime: after the collapse of the Third Reich, this is how many Germans who had adjusted less conspicuously than Gründgens to the powers that be construed their behaviour under Nazi rule. The term for this Hamletian split between seeming and being was 'inner emigration' (*innere Emigration*). It gained high public profile in a controversy arising from Thomas Mann's radio message on

---

[25] Hortmann, *Shakespeare on the German Stage*, 161.

[26] Marcel Reich-Ranicki, *The Author of Himself: The Life of Marcel Reich-Ranicki* (1999), trans. Ewald Osers (Princeton, NJ: Princeton University Press, 2001), 84. Gründgens played Hamlet again after the war, at Düsseldorf in 1949. At fifty somewhat overage for the part, he apparently gave a more accessible, less mannered performance. He returned to *Hamlet* once more in 1963, when he directed his farewell production at the *Deutsches Schauspielhaus* in Hamburg. Passing the baton on to a new, more modern generation, he cast Maximilian Schell in the title part. But Schell returned to an older model, the tender soul as described by Wilhelm Meister. Hamlet, Schell explained in an interview, 'is an actor *manqué*, in the double meaning of the English word "actor": a stage actor who tries to express his inner, unrealizable world in his gestures and speeches—and someone who tries to perform an action but never achieves his goal' (*Der Spiegel*, 18 [1963]). I am grateful to Werner Habicht for directing my attention to this.

German guilt (8 May 1945)[27] and his explanation of why he would not follow the call of Walter von Molo, head of the poetry section of the Prussian Academy before 1933, for Mann to return from exile and help restore his devastated homeland. Ostensibly seconding Molo's plea for Mann's return from his Santa Monica exile, but clearly motivated by his annoyance at Mann's unsparing exposure of German guilt, the writer Frank Thiess contested Mann's right to judge the suffering German people and especially those of his German colleagues who had chosen to stay in the country and suffered the hardships of what he calls 'inner emigration'.[28]

Thiess's argument reverses the moral onus: while the exiles had 'watched the German tragedy from their theatre seats in foreign countries' (24), those who had stayed had borne the brunt of the disaster and grown through the experience:

> It does make a difference, after all, whether I actually suffer the burning of my house or watch it in a newsreel, whether I am actually hungry or read about hunger in the papers, whether I live through the hail of bombs on German cities or have it reported to me, whether I can see the unparalleled fall of a people in a hundred individual instances or register it as a historical fact. (24)

Exile is made to appear as the soft option. The nobler course, according to Thiess, was to 'hold out at our post' (24) and suffer the slings and arrows of a regime that made, as Molo put it, the whole of Germany a concentration camp where the population was divided into wardens and inmates (19) and where writers, according to Thiess, were either followers or suspects (23). 'I think,' Thiess wrote, 'it was more difficult to preserve one's personality here than to send messages to the German people from over there' (25). Sitting in the comfort of his Californian villa, Mann had not only forfeited the right to lecture his compatriots,[29] he was simply out of touch with German realities. His messages from 'over there' were lost on those who were deaf anyway, 'while we, the knowing, always felt lengths ahead of them' (25).

Thiess's main claim, the claim on which the whole idea of 'inner emigration' hinges, is that it was possible for those who stayed to maintain 'an inner space which Hitler, despite all his efforts, could never conquer' (23). Mann's counter-claim reads like an elaboration on the famous dictum by his Californian co-exile and collaborator on *Doctor Faustus*, Theodor Adorno: 'Wrong life cannot be lived rightly.'[30] 'It was not permissible,' Mann declares, 'it was impossible to produce

---

[27] It was first printed under the title 'Thomas Mann über die deutsche Schuld', *Bayerische Landeszeitung*, Munich, 18 May 1945, and features under the title 'Die Lager' ('The Camps') in Mann, *Gesammelte Werke*, vol. 12: *Reden und Aufsätze* (Frankfurt: S. Fischer, 1974), 951–3.

[28] Von Molo's letter first appeared in *Hessische Post*, 4 August 1945, and was reprinted in *Münchner Zeitung*, which also published Thiess's supporting statement 'Die innere Emigration' (18 August 1945). Contributions to the debate triggered by Molo's open letter are gathered in J. F. G. Grosser, ed., *Die große Kontroverse. Ein Briefwechsel um Deutschland. Walter von Molo, Thomas Mann* (Hamburg: Nagel, 1963). References to this edition are given in brackets in the text.

[29] Or rather former compatriots; Mann had become an American citizen in 1944, an act that was also, more or less openly, held against him.

[30] 'Es gibt kein richtiges Leben im falschen.' Theodor W. Adorno, *Minima Moralia: Reflections from Damaged Life* (1951), trans. E. F. N. Jephcott (London and New York: Verso, 2005), 39. Cf. Thomas Mann and Theodor W. Adorno, *Correspondence 1943–1955*, trans. Nicholas Walker (Cambridge: Polity Press, 2006). For discussion of Adorno's role in the making of Mann's *Doctor Faustus* see Evelyn

"culture" in Germany while all around one were happening the things that we know were happening; one would be glossing over the depravity, adorning the crimes' (25).

Art, Mann argued, could not escape its exploitation as a fig leaf covering the inhuman atrocity of the regime, not only art which overtly supported the regime but also, and even more insidiously, that which presented itself as above political bias. 'A *Kapellmeister*' (and it is clear that Mann refers to Wilhelm Furtwängler) 'sent out by Hitler to conduct Beethoven in Zurich, Paris or Budapest was guilty of an obscene lie under the pretext that all he did was play music' (25). Such pretence was even more obscene at home: 'How could Beethoven's *Fidelio*, this celebration dedicated to the day of German self-liberation, not be banned in the Germany of these last twelve years? It was a scandal that it was not banned, but performed in highly cultivated productions, that there were singers to sing it, musicians to play it, audiences to listen to it' (25–6).

Mann's verdict is most rigorous when it comes to his fellow writers. The books they had published during his absence and now sent to him as proof of their secret opposition to the regime, he writes, were not welcome to him:

> It may be superstition, but in my eyes all books that made it into print in Germany between 1933 and 1945 are less than worthless and do not sit comfortably in the hand. A smell of blood and shame clings to them. They should all be pulped. (25)

The rebuke was bitterly resented. Its opening qualification ('it may be superstition') did little to soften the blow. In the increasingly heated debate, Mann was accused of repeating the book-burnings of 1933, of hating not just the Nazis but the German people as a whole. His moral authority was questioned, his right to judge denied.[31]

Mann was not entirely blameless in this. His critique of the figureheads of artistic excellence, people like Furtwängler or Richard Strauss, who had served to bolster the regime's pretended allegiance to humanist values, is compelling. But his summary rejection of all writing published under Nazi rule, although it was a logical extension of that critique, was unjust to those who could rightly claim to have been persecuted by the regime, their literary output a tightrope act under constant threat of censorship and reprisals.

This does not, however, invalidate Mann's argument that much of what his attackers brought against him was 'written for the purpose of self-recommendation and the glorification of their own heroism' (76). 'Inner emigration', precisely

---

Cobley, 'Avant-Garde Aesthetics and Fascist Politics: Thomas Mann's *Doctor Faustus* and Theodor W. Adorno's *Philosophy of Modern Music*', *New German Critique* 86 (2002), 43–70.

[31] Mann speaks of 'pulping'; this becomes 'burning' in a response to Mann by the art historian Edwin Redslob, one of the founders of the Free University, Berlin, in 1948. Grosser, ed., *Die große Kontroverse*, 38. In his retrospective résumé of 'the great controversy', the editor, J. F. G. Grosser, goes even further: after the collapse of the Third Reich, he writes, 'the crazy book-burnings of the National Socialists were followed by the book-burnings of their victorious adversaries, both German and foreign' (142). Affecting a semblance of impartiality, Grosser is clearly on the side of the conservative 'inner emigrants' throughout. This is hardly surprising, seeing that he claims credit for the idea of asking Mann to return to Germany, which led to von Molo's initial letter.

because of being 'inner', was difficult to prove, but even more difficult to disprove. It became a highly attractive bandwagon, one for almost anyone to jump on. 'Innocence is spreading like the plague', wrote the once best-selling Erich Kästner, whose books had been publicly burned in 1933 and who eked out a living by pseudonymously writing for Goebbels's film industry.[32]

At the core of the dispute over 'inner emigration' lay the issue of German guilt. It was this that made the debate so bitterly resentful. Mann's initial radio statement was motivated by the newly revealed horrors of the death camps. For a German, any German, there was no escaping the shame of belonging to the people that had perpetrated these unprecedented crimes against humanity:

> Our disgrace lies before the world, in front of the foreign commissions before whom these incredible pictures are presented and who report home about this surpassing of all hideousness that men can imagine. 'Our disgrace' German readers and listeners! For everything German, everyone that speaks German, writes German, has lived in Germany, has been implicated by this dishonorable unmasking.[33]

Although the Germans were not all equally guilty, they could not escape, as Mann insisted, being collectively responsible. Only one of Mann's respondents was prepared to admit this.[34] All the others, notably Molo and Thiess, spoke not of guilt but of suffering—*German* suffering. That this suffering had been caused in reaction to the immeasurable suffering Germany had inflicted on the world went unmentioned. It is characteristic not only for this particular debate but of the prevalent state of mind among Germans at the time that the editor of *The Great Controversy* fills the whole opening page of his preface with a graphic description of the (only too real) sufferings of the defeated German people, but has not a single word to say about the Holocaust or the devastations wrought by Germany on the Soviet Union, Poland, or any other country. Molo's letter to Mann intones with characteristic pathos:

> Your people, who have been starving and suffering now for a third of a century, have, in their innermost core, nothing in common with the misdeeds and crimes, the shameful atrocities and lies [...]. (20)

Blanking out the glory years of the Third Reich when no one was starving and the vast majority of Germans applauding, rather than suffering under, their new rulers, Molo short-circuits the misery of the early Weimar years with the misery of the 1945 present. In his claim that the German people had ultimately nothing to do

---

[32] Under the pseudonym Berthold Bürger, Erich Kästner wrote the script for the prestigious film *Münchhausen*, which came out in 1943 on the occasion of the twenty-fifth anniversary of the UFA film studios. Kästner is best known as a writer for young readers, in particular for *Emil and the Detectives* (*Emil und die Detektive*, 1929), a German children's favourite. The screenplay for the first of several film versions, released in 1931, was written by Billy Wilder.

[33] Mann, 'Die Lager', trans. Andrei S. Markovits and Beth Simone Noveck, 'West Germany', in *The World Reacts to the Holocaust*, ed. David S. Wyman and Charles H. Rosenzveig (Baltimore, MD and London: Johns Hopkins University Press, 1996), 391–446 at 413.

[34] This was the stage designer Emil Preetorius, whom Mann satirizes as Sextus Kridwiss in *Doctor Faustus*, chap. 34. Thomas Mann, *Doctor Faustus: The Life of the German Composer Adrian Leverkühn, as Told by a Friend* (1947), trans. John E. Woods (New York: Vintage, 1999), 362–70.

with 'the misdeeds and crimes' of the Nazis, the reader will recognize a by now familiar dualism, a new variation of the idea we have encountered in previous chapters of this book that there was not one, but two Germanies: a bad one and a good one; Germany as it appeared and Germany as it really was. As in all previous versions of this dualism, the 'real' Germany was one that could not be found in actual realities; it was a Germany that transcended them. It was 'that within which passes show' (*Ham.* 1.2.85): an ideal essence or telos of the nation's 'soul'. George's 'secret' Germany shaped and sharpened its identity against the 'official' Germany. In 1945, one way of dealing with national disaster and disgrace was to exempt the 'real' Germany from what Nazi Germany had done. In their responses to Mann, Molo and Thiess cling to this widespread strategy of denial. The Nazis are always 'them', not 'us'. There were 'countless Germans', Thiess writes, 'who were filled with the deepest hatred of National Socialism' (81). Only in their hostility to the regime do Thiess's 'countless' Germans figure as agents; in every other respect they are victims: 'Guilt and suffering, these two great iron ploughshares of world history, have gone over our people and left us torn up' (85).[35]

The edgy defensiveness of Mann's opponents stems from his rejection of the German dualism, his refusal to accept 'the theory of the two Germanies, a good one and a bad one' (34). 'The bad Germany', he insisted, 'is the good Germany gone astray, the good Germany in disaster, in guilt and perdition' (34). No one was more aware of this than Mann, whose *Doctor Faustus* (1947) was nearing completion at the time of the controversy. Reflecting the fate of Germany in the life of its Nietzschean protagonist, the composer Adrian Leverkühn, the novel explores precisely this entanglement of good and bad in the intellectual tradition that helped precipitate the political catastrophe.

The personal appearance of the devil and other forays into the supernatural did not prevent Mann's novel from displaying an acute realism in its portrayal of the political mentalities which furnished the breeding ground for Hitler's success.[36] By contrast, commentators who purported to be unsparingly realistic in their assessment of the situation in 1945 often tended to bypass political specificities, heading straight for the vast and vague domain of the metaphysical. German 'interiority' (*Innerlichkeit*), with its entrenched aversion to the sphere of public discourse and political praxis, could draw its ultimate justification from the abhorrent experience of the tyranny. This, it was thought, proved once and for all that politics was corrupt beyond redemption, not only the politics of the Nazis but all politics—which, in turn, gave force to the belief that the horror of the Third Reich could not be explained from merely political causes. It was a *Verhängnis*, a catastrophe inflicted by the transcendent powers of fate. 'Demonic' became a favourite adjective in arguments that depoliticized the political disaster. The anti-rationalism of Nazism survived into the anti-rationalist explanations of its rise to power.

---

[35] For a searching account of German mentalities in 1945, see Werner Sollors, *The Temptation of Despair: Tales of the 1940s* (Cambridge, MA and London: Harvard University Press, 2014).

[36] See, for example, Mann's devastatingly apt satire of Munich's grandiloquent right-wing bourgeois intellectuals. In Sextus Kridwiss's salon they outdo each other in propounding a 'rebarbarization' of modern civilization. *Doctor Faustus*, 370.

IV HAMLET RE-CHRISTIANIZED

It is this frame of mind, the attempt to come to terms with Germany's disgrace by removing its causes from political agency onto a 'higher', more universal plane, that gave *Hamlet* its special appeal in the immediate aftermath of the Third Reich, making it the most frequently performed Shakespeare play on West German stages between 1945 and 1950. As Jane Rice observes, '[a]t a time when the morality of different responses to National Socialism was a smouldering issue in West German society, the Hamlet figure provided a positive model for withdrawal from political involvement and served indirectly to support the position of "inner emigration".'[37] The heroically active Hamlet had breathed his last in the now bombed-out theatres of the Reich. Reborn in the ruins was a new version of the older type: a descendant of Wilhelm Meister's 'pure, noble and most moral nature', a Hamlet who thought instead of taking action, but not because he was too weak for his task, but because *he knew*. His inactivity was not a flaw, but a badge of his superior insight into the nature of things. This Hamlet was stronger than Wilhelm Meister's. He resembled the Hamlet celebrated by Nietzsche, not the one upbraided by Freiligrath, although his semblance to the *Rebirth of Tragedy* was softened by the rebirth of Christian humanism. This rebirth followed rather hard on the heels of the demise of Nordic paganism and was frequently touted by the selfsame flexible pens. The Germanic Shakespeare was reclaimed for Christianity.

The first issue of a newly founded journal for the teaching profession ran an article entitled 'Shakespeare Today' in which the author poses the question: 'What is the ultimate meaning of all of Shakespeare's plays?'[38] Her confident answer: 'Shakespeare's dramas are the artistic distillation of the Christian message of sin and judgment, but also of forgiveness and reconciliation' (93). A Shakespeare who endorsed the Christian message 'that the world has fallen under the rule of evil and must therefore end in judgment and redemption' (92) clearly could not be properly understood in merely political terms. His plays, much like Calderon's *Great Theatre of the World*, are acted out on a cosmic stage.

An essay by Otto Knapp, 'Hamlet—Our Contemporary', in the Catholic journal *Hochland*, argued in the same direction, if in a more nuanced manner. Unlike 'Shakespeare Today' (which, despite its title, never referred to the specific evils of today), 'Hamlet—Our Contemporary' did make reference to these evils, albeit in a way that diminished their exceptionality. The world is evil. The things that happen in it, however horrendous they may be, bear out the general sinfulness of fallen humanity, 'the fundamentally evil condition of the world'.[39] Thus Hamlet, when he enumerates the slings and arrows of life, 'does not speak from his own innermost being, not as a specific individual with his own subjective concerns, but as the representative of tormented, suffering humanity [...] inflicting misery on one

---

[37] C. Jane Rice, '*Handeln oder Nichthandeln*: Hamlet in Inner Emigration', *Monatshefte* 84 (1992), 8–22 at 8.
[38] Ilse Märtens, 'Shakespeare heute', *Pädagogische Rundschau* 1.1/2 (April/May 1947), 89–93 at 92.
[39] Otto Knapp, 'Hamlet—unser Zeitgenosse', *Hochland* 39 (1946/7), 532–45 at 539.

another' (539–40). The reciprocity of the inflicting is typical. It deflects the focus from contemporary Germany to mankind and its timeless predicament. However, the timeliness of Hamlet is not ignored either: 'One can easily discover similarities', Knapp writes,

> between his [Hamlet's] situation and ours in the recent past: a criminally usurped regiment whose wild goings-on[40] harm the country's repute; cowardly subservience, an atmosphere of falsehood and lies, ever new crimes committed in order to nip resistance in the bud. (538)

Just as the situation was comparable, so was the response to it:

> Faced with a similar world, did we not come to instinctively adopt a similar style of communication and of expressing our views? (540)

Knapp has a whole nation cloaking its real feelings in Hamlet's antic disposition and, like Hamlet, refraining from taking action. But is Hamlet (and are they) to blame for this? Knapp's answer is no:

> His sense of responsibility, not weakness or timidity, is the reason for Hamlet's hesitation; in this his character becomes his fate. He is a man of thought, of reflection, and as such a man of high culture. He does not act straight away, and hence for a long time has no success in fulfilling his task. But he is eventually carried to his goal by prevailing justice. (543)

Note the passivity: Hamlet does not carry out justice; he is carried by it. In the last analysis, the rarer action is inaction. It is the Christian way, as Knapp affirms in his conclusion. Hamlet's tragedy, he writes, is that of Shakespeare himself, who had to experience, along with the rest of humanity, 'the disappointment of existence' (545). There is no escaping this disappointment: it is the 'outcome of every observant human life' (545). Political activity may be recommendable but will ultimately not make a difference. Liberation from the inevitable existential disappointment

> is not to be sought in outward reforms only, even though these should always be aimed for, but first and foremost in an inner attitude: the insight, without any illusion, into the true condition of this world. Here Christianity bravely declares: Thy will be done! Here begins the succession of Him who carried His cross of tremendous heaviness up to His last word: It is finished! (545)

In decisively turning away from the external constitution of the world and the political task of setting it right, this post-war version of Hamlet continued the nineteenth-century German tradition of interiority which had cherished him as an identificatory icon. In this tradition, Manfred Pfister explains, 'the public or political sphere is presented as something alien and hostile, as something too sordid or messy for the poet-philosopher-prince, while the fact that he shies away from his task is viewed with considerable sympathy. [...] This reading proposed

---

[40] An odd euphemism, '*ausgelassenes Treiben*' would more usually refer to a noisy party or the abandon of children's play.

nothing less than the justification, or even glorification, of political inactivity or failure.'[41] The parallels, as Jane Rice points out, are unmistakable:

> For the post-war Hamlet too, the primacy of intellectual and spiritual concerns and his distaste for the realm of political praxis reflected his superior moral stature and a noble nature that was inwardly at odds with the world in which he lived. The return to the Romantic reading of the play could serve not only to justify but even to ennoble political withdrawal before and after 1945.[42]

V 'FORTINBRAS IS AMERICA'

At first sight, the twenty-odd pages devoted to Hamlet in the over 1000-page disquisition *Of Truth* (1947) by Karl Jaspers, the once famous, now somewhat neglected philosopher,[43] seem to fall into the same apologetic mould, relieving Hamlet of any blame for his inactivity. What makes him hesitate is not a weakness of character but 'the situation of knowing and not knowing—with the sovereign power of seeing to the bottom of things'.[44] 'The whole play', Jaspers maintains, 'is Hamlet's search for truth', and this is more than the question of who committed the one particular crime, it is a question of 'the whole state of the world' (937). From the concrete and particular to the universal and metaphysical—the move is typical of *Hamlet* readings of the time. And so, it would seem, is the favouring of thought over 'mere' action: Fortinbras, 'this not-knowing realist, unaware of not knowing' may be 'able to live' (941), but even though Hamlet acknowledges, even admires, his activeness, Fortinbras is the lesser figure of the two, caught up in a way of living that is not just more 'limited', but 'false' (941).

This looks very much like the familiar condoning of passivity. What sets Jaspers's Hamlet off from the quietist slant of other contemporary readings, however, is his commitment to a search for knowledge, a commitment at the heart of Jaspers's mission as a public intellectual after 1945. The most prominent advocate of facing up to *The Question of German Guilt*,[45] Jaspers argued that only by facing the truth and acknowledging their share of responsibility could the German people come to terms with their complicity in the Nazi horrors. This was their only chance of an honest new start. Differentiating degrees and various kinds of guilt, Jaspers held that not all Germans were guilty in the criminal sense, but that none, no matter

---

[41] Pfister, 'Germany is Hamlet: The History of a Political Interpretation', 112 and 110.

[42] Rice, '*Handeln oder Nichthandeln*', 18–19.

[43] Work on a new critical edition of Jaspers's writings has been in progress at the Heidelberg and Göttingen Academies of Arts and Sciences since 2013. See <https://heidelberger-forum-edition.de/jaspers>.

[44] Karl Jaspers, *Von der Wahrheit* (Munich: Piper, 1947), 939. References are given in brackets in the text.

[45] Karl Jaspers, *Die Schuldfrage* (Heidelberg: Schneider, 1946); Engl. trans. E. B. Ashton: *The Question of German Guilt* (New York: Dial Press, 1948).

how 'apolitical' and uninvolved in the regime, could claim exemption from the collective *political* guilt. Facing this was a continuing obligation:

> That which has happened is a warning. To forget it is guilt. It must be continually remembered. It was possible for this to happen, and it remains possible for it to happen again at any minute. Only in knowledge can it be prevented. (14)

In this view, Hamlet's pursuit of truth, which Jaspers regards primarily as a thought process, is indeed superior to the unreflective course of action pursued by Fortinbras. It is Fortinbras who comes to represent an attitude that evades rather than fulfils the obligation imposed on him, an attitude recognizable in the post-war reconstruction era, the years of (West) Germany's 'economic miracle': 'The horizon has shrunk. People do not like to hear of guilt, of the past; [...] they want to get out of this misery, to live but not to think' (21).

Was Fortinbras entirely wrong in choosing life over thought? Thomas Mann for one did not think so. In the last of his addresses at the Library of Congress, delivered on 2 May 1949, he spoke about 'Goethe and Democracy', a topic that once again enabled him, as befitted his role as authoritative 'consultant' on all things German,[46] to combine historical illumination with comment on issues of relevance in the present. Goethe was, of course, very topical in 1949, the two-hundredth anniversary of his birth, and Mann very much in demand as a speaker.[47]

'Goethe and Democracy' is a hymn to all that is life-affirming, open to the future, dynamically pragmatic in Goethe's personality and writings. He is set up as a singularly exceptional figure, the antagonist of the much more typically German glorification of noble failure, doom, and death. Mann cites Georges Clémenceau: 'The Germans love death [...] Just look at their literature!' but adds that 'the psychologizing statesman cannot have had Goethe in mind, for Goethe resisted the German-Romantic cult of death [...]'.[48] Goethe also defended—again atypically—what Mann, quoting another Frenchman, Maurice Barrès, calls the 'rights of society against the arrogance of the spirit' (110):

> Goethe's praise of 'common sense' is equivalent to an admonition to the spirit and the intellect not to hover in the clouds but to unite with life and to assume responsibility toward it. It points in the direction of *democratic pragmatism*, which has always been lacking in Germany, even when life was dionysiacally extolled as the greatest good, and the leading German poet took its side against the arrogance of the spirit in more than one instance. (110)[49]

---

[46] Mann was appointed 'Consultant in Germanic Literature' to the Library of Congress in 1941. Don Heinrich Tolzmann, 'Editor's Introduction', in *Thomas Mann's Addresses Delivered at the Library of Congress*, ix–xiii at ix.

[47] It was the Goethe anniversary that occasioned Mann's first visit back to his old country, which despite considerable advance hostility turned out to be a success. He delivered his 'Address in the Goethe Year' in Frankfurt's St Paul's Church, the seat of the short-lived national parliament of 1848, and received the city's Goethe Prize. Moving on from Goethe's birthplace to the place where he had lived, Mann proceeded, much to the chagrin of the West German public, to East German Weimar, where he gave the same address and collected the East German Goethe Prize.

[48] Mann, 'Goethe and Democracy', in *Thomas Mann's Addresses*, 105–32 at 112. Page references are given in brackets in the text.

[49] '[W]hen life was dionysiacally extolled' refers, of course, to Nietzsche, and 'the leading German poet' is Stefan George.

Goethe, as Mann describes him, is the best guide to lead his compatriots away from the wrong turns of German history, the German cure to the German malaise, that 'discrepancy between spirit and power, between ideas and deeds' (109) which prevented the formation of a civil society and spawned a rampant nationalism. There is much in Goethe that actually contradicts his recruitment to the cause of democracy. But Mann uses all his powers of persuasion to wrest Germany's greatest literary figure from the clutches of reactionary parochialism and win him for the democratic rebuilding of the country.

A final clinching point in Mann's argument—and one that had scandalized German nationalists in the past[50]—is Goethe's cosmopolitanism. Mann introduces it in his discussion of *Wilhelm Meister*, the work whose growth and mutation spanned many decades of its author's long life and many of his ideas and concerns. Mann singles out from the sprawling riches of the novel an element that resonated strongly with his own experience: 'the new world, America, [...] and [...] the idea of emigration to the new continent, upon which most of the characters decide in the end' (128). 'Goethe and America', Mann exclaims, 'Goethe as an American— an amazing combination and idea, for he is the arch-European; nothing more "continental" can be imagined than his person' (128). But America, '[e]scape to America' (128), became something of a favourite fantasy of the older Goethe, a way out from the old continent, whose future, Mann suggests, Goethe saw with increasing pessimism. He was increasingly drawn to a land where he could 'stand on free soil with a free people' (130). This quotation from *Faust*, Mann says, 'sounds extraordinarily American' (130), and he continues:

> The future belongs to the man of the day, whose mind and 'common sense' are directed toward the nearest, most useful matters; it belongs to him whose energy is not tainted by the pallor of thought. Not only Germany, all of Europe is Hamlet, and Fortinbras is America. (130)

Preaching the gospel of American democracy, Mann the complicated 'arch-European' embraced the uncomplicated Fortinbras with the zeal of a convert. His writing, however, continued much in the mould of an older Europe. His attitude is encapsulated in his remarks on his late novel *The Holy Sinner* (*Der Erwählte*, 1951), a pastiche on the medieval epic *Gregorius* by the German Minnesinger Hartmann von Aue:

> *The Holy Sinner* is a late work in every sense, not only with regard to the age of its author, but the product of a late period. It plays on time-honoured venerabilities, an old tradition. There is much—not unaffectionate—travesty in this, [...] signs of a lateness in which culture and parody are closely related concepts. [...] It seems to me that nothing will come after this. Our contemporary literature [...] often seems to me like a leave-taking, a quick remembering, evoking and recapitulating the occidental myth one last time before night falls, a long night and a deep forgetting. A little work like this [*The Holy Sinner*] is a late blossoming of culture before barbarism comes

---

[50] Goethe's cosmopolitanism had also won him special praise from, for example, Nietzsche (*Twilight of the Idols*, 553) and Kantorowicz: '[T]he perfect German always has to be more than German' ('Das Geheime Deutschland', 87).

[...] But if its parody smiles at the old and pious legends, this smile is melancholy rather than frivolous [...].[51]

Faced with the choice between Jaspers's truth-seeking Hamlet with his stubborn refusal to forget, and Mann's plea for the pragmatism of Fortinbras, German society mostly opted for the latter course. The analogy is, however, somewhat misleading. By no stretch of wishful oblivion could Germans attain to the unburdened fresh start of a Fortinbras. The more fitting analogy is with the pragmatism of Claudius. They set about the business of rebuilding the country in 'remembrance of ourselves' (Ham. 1.2.7) rather than in remembering their guilty past, and couched their evasion in Claudius-like speechifying. Whatever else it was, the Germany of the economic miracle years was certainly not Hamlet.

VI RE-EDUCATION, OR, THE ROAD TO FORGIVENESS

Perhaps another Shakespeare play provided an altogether more fitting template. The title page of the May 1947 issue of *Prisma*, one of the literary magazines founded soon after the war, featured a drawing of Caliban by the Austrian symbolist Alfred Kubin, to illustrate the lead article, Hans Eberhard Friedrich's 'Caliban and the Drama of the Twentieth Century' (Figure 7.2).[52]

According to Friedrich, *The Tempest*, 'Shakespeare's arguably most political play' (1), offered a perfect mirror of the contemporary world: 'Prospero: he is everything that culture, custom, religion, wisdom and insight have given to the human race. But Caliban is the human race of our enlightened century' (2), a Caliban 'who hates, rebels, cringes, bootlicks, who is dull, brutish and dumb, nasty, foul and full of devilry' (1). All of humanity may be slavish like Caliban, but 'let us not speak of the Calibanism of the rest of the world; it does not justify our own. [...] In order for us to regain the right to liberty we must recognize the mote that is in our own eye' (2). The world, Friedrich concludes, is at a crossroads between the Caliban way of 'cursing, slavishness, revenge and hate [...], egoism, nationalism, chauvinism, unforgivingness and malice', and Prospero's way: 'forgiving, upholding justice, practising virtue, being free and granting freedom. [...] We are standing at the beginning of the fifth act [...]: this last act will show whether humankind will opt for atonement and for regaining its humanity or whether Caliban will determine our fate' (3).

The fifth act of *The Tempest*, in which Prospero pardons his undeserving enemies, offered a timely lesson in magnanimity for the Allied occupying powers, a lesson which the British were quick to recognize. One of their earliest contributions to the attempt to 're-educate' the German people was a radio programme

---

[51] Thomas Mann, 'Bemerkungen zu dem Roman *Der Erwählte*', in Mann, *Gesammelte Werke*, vol. 11, 687–91 at 690–1.

[52] Hans Eberhard Friedrich, 'Caliban und das Drama des 20. Jahrhunderts', *Prisma* 1.7 (May 1947), 1–3. Another image of Caliban, a lithograph by Rudolf Großmann (1921) illustrated the essay. Also relevant to its theme was 'The Delinquent', by Alfred Kubin as well, which was featured in the same issue.

Figure 7.2. 'Caliban' by Alfred Kubin on the cover of *Prisma* (1947). Reproduced by permission of VG-Bildkunst.

entitled '*England—die unbekannte Insel*' (England the Unknown Island) broadcast by the BBC's German Language Service on 7 June 1945, barely four weeks after Germany's capitulation. The programme, which was referred to within the BBC as the 'Shakespeare Feature', was written and presented by the German Service's Productions Director, the well-known Shakespearean and West End actor Marius Goring (1912–98), whose post-war screen appearances included so many Nazi villains 'that he claimed to have played every rank in the German Army from private to field marshal'.[53] To his German listeners he chose to be Charles Richardson—presumably because his real second name was distinguished by a mere umlaut

[53] According to the *Daily Telegraph* obituary (10 October 1998), Goring 'briefly attended the universities of Frankfurt, Vienna, Paris and Munich before studying at the Old Vic dramatic school from 1929 to 1932'. These periods must have been brief indeed—spanning, all in all, no more than a year—and Goring, aged 16, must have been at least two, if not three years younger than the youngest of his continental fellow students. After playing Romeo to Peggy Ashcroft's Juliet at the Old Vic in 1932, he toured France and the Low Countries with Jacques Copeau's *Compagnie des Quinze*, playing Hamlet and other roles in French. After the war he and his wife, Lucie Mannheim, toured the British zone of Germany, performing in German. Mannheim, a former principal actress of the Berlin Theatre who had escaped from the Nazis and continued her career in Britain, heads the cast list of the BBC 'Shakespeare Feature'.

from that of Hitler's *Reichsmarschall*. Tactfully acknowledging Germany's great Shakespeare tradition, while at the same time firmly maintaining Shakespeare's essential Englishness, Goring/Richardson introduces Shakespeare as the poet of the English countryside. This theme is introduced with a song from *Love's Labour's Lost*, 'When Daisies Pied'. It does not matter, Richardson tells his listeners, if you do not understand the English lyrics: they are only about cowslips and violets and girls washing their summer dresses. All that matters is the feeling of spring that this simple song conveys; of English spring, to be sure, because only if you know and have suffered English weather will you be able to appreciate the brief joy of English spring which the song celebrates. The escapist appeal that such a pastoral Shakespeare would have had in 1945, a Shakespeare deeply rooted in the sentimentalized simplicity of rural England, is not difficult to appreciate.

The rustic harmony conjured up in the name of Shakespeare, the poet-magician for whom 'all things in nature are one' (6), soon gives way to the existential dilemma of Hamlet. 'If we are all one', the narrator continues,

> we should live in peace; but instead one nation fights against another, one individual against another [...] What can the poet do in his desperation? In the end he longs for death, for only in death will he be able to find complete peace and harmony. But is this longing for death a good thing? That is the question [...] (6)

Hamlet's monologue, which the BBC Shakespeare Feature recites in full, constitutes the innermost sanctum of Germany's Shakespeare adoration, the site where English Bard and German *Geist* consummate their mystical union. Quoting the passage is just as inevitable as it is fraught with potentially undesirable associations: associations with a German tradition of speculative philosophizing, a tradition that not only proved incapable of stemming the tide of Germany's recent disastrous history but was, as Thomas Mann insisted, actually conducive to it.

Richardson extricates Hamlet from this tradition with an aside of no more than four words. Both Shakespeare and Hamlet answer the temptation of suicide with a clear no—'*anders als Goethes Werther*' ('unlike Goethe's Werther') (7). In highly suggestive shorthand, Werther, Goethe's sensitive ersatz Hamlet, comes to stand both for a persistent German misreading of Shakespeare's true English message and for the wrong turn the history of a whole nation had taken. But to a German radio audience on 7 June 1945, the mention of Werther's suicide could hardly fail to evoke the suicides of Hitler and Goebbels, less than six weeks earlier, and that of Heinrich Himmler, head of the SS, who killed himself just over a fortnight before the Shakespeare Feature went on the air.

The extremes of German culture and German barbarism thus blend into one another, as if to confirm Walter Benjamin's dictum that every cultural monument conceals within itself a document of barbarism—a dictum visibly perpetuated to this day by the close proximity of Weimar and the site of the Buchenwald concentration camp. Rejecting the drive towards self-destruction, the 1945 BBC Hamlet finally makes up his mind that life, 'in spite of everything, must be lived to its natural conclusion' (7). This is the message that Richardson extracts (with a bit of arm-twisting) from the prince's dying words to Horatio: 'Absent thee from felicity awhile' (*Ham.* 5.2.325). Again Hamlet and Shakespeare become one and the same person. The poet, we learn, must live on 'to tell his story', and the purpose of his living on is 'to castigate injustice wherever he finds it' (7).

The Shakespearean code-word for the most horrendous injustice, the one most painfully relevant to Goring's German audience is, of course, Shylock, whose speech—'Has not a Jew eyes'—the programme renders in full. Goring's presentation of that speech is highly instructive. He could have used it as a devastating indictment of German collective guilt, collective moral failure. He could, in other words, have impressed on his listeners the gravity of their failing. The speech itself, one may of course argue, says it all. But the commentary before and after it is clearly designed to soften, not to increase the speech's shock value. Rather than seeking to confront German listeners with their shame, it cushions them from that shame. In his lead-in, Goring again uses the conciliatory 'we' very effectively, and he heightens the effect by embedding it in a rhetorical question which creates a rapport between speaker and addressee in its assumption of a shared view: 'Can there be a more uncompromising condemnation of that racial prejudice which we all know so well than these sentences from *The Merchant of Venice*?' (7). The comment after Shylock's speech is even more remarkable. Shakespeare demands justice, the text says, but justice is not all. 'Justice must not be cruel: cruelty must be overcome by mercy' (8). Shylock is put in his place, his demand for justice overruled by Portia's 'The quality of mercy is not strained', which is also quoted in full.

A radio broadcast cannot be stopped and repeated by the listener at will. The implication of Goring's argument—the glib transition from a Jew demanding equal rights to a Christian extolling mercy—may thus have escaped the programme's first audience. Within a matter of seconds, the programme puts Jews back where, in Germany, they had been for the last twelve years: in the dock. But what could not have failed to come across—and no doubt constituted the programme's intended 'official' message—was the comforting promise of forgiveness: forgiveness rather than retaliation, a sense of being let off the hook, and of having, like the narrowly escaped Antonio, Portia-England on one's side. The encouraging rather than punitive tenor of the passage, and indeed of the Shakespeare Feature as a whole, is fully in keeping with the principles of re-education. And so is the projection of Britain[54] which dominates the next passage. In extolling mercy and justice, Richardson says, Shakespeare is celebrating the two essential norms of English civilization. This, rather predictably, leads up to Gaunt's 'sceptred isle' speech from *Richard II*, which is, however, accompanied by the democratic caveat that blind patriotism is wrong.

Having started with *The Tempest*, the programme finally returns to it and, by way of introduction to Prospero's 'We are such stuff / As dreams are made on' (*Tmp.* 4.1.156–7), has this to say:

[54] 'The projection of Britain' had been the official term for British propaganda policy since the end of the First World War. It was assimilated into the re-education effort. Philip M. Taylor, *The Projection of Britain: British Overseas Publicity and Propaganda 1919–1939* (Cambridge: Cambridge University Press, 1981).

In a cruel and unjust world he [Shakespeare] had found his peace in the certain knowledge that, in this life, there is only one weapon against injustice: justice and mercy; and that after this life everything—his own country as well as other countries, human cruelty and kindness, fame and vanity, love, hate, human beings themselves and all things in nature pass into the unalterable will of God and dissolve into peaceful forgetting. Thus speaks Prospero, the great magician, the great poet, Shakespeare in his own person. (9)

It is easy to dismiss this—and much else in the 45-minute feature—as platitudinous. But the passage is also revealing. Quick-stepping from Shylock's demand for justice to Portia's decree of mercy to Prospero's peaceful forgetting, the programme manages, as it were, to face and efface the Holocaust, or, more precisely, to not quite face and not quite efface it. In doing so, it offers German listeners the terms of a contract: a toning down of the all-too-insistent voice of memory in return for a willingness to cooperate. It offers Germans a not-too-uncomfortable starting point for a new future on condition that this future be governed by an acceptance of the rules of Western democracy.

In Goring's version of the contract, the Christian element, pulled out of the hat just before the arrival at peaceful forgetting, adds a comforting note of cosmic quietism. Human agency, which the programme had earlier enlisted for the good fight against injustice, is ultimately rendered futile by 'the unalterable will of God'. If the Almighty is responsible, politics becomes fate and Hitler something like a natural disaster beyond human control. Goring does not spell this out, but his text indicates the kind of premise from which such exoneration became possible, and indeed, as we have seen, widespread, in German writing of the time. One cannot but marvel at the degree of psychological intuition which allowed him to register and cater to the sensibilities of his audience with such precision. Setting out to demonstrate the Englishness of Shakespeare, Goring makes him a composite portrait of topical German issues; and in retrospect, the treatment of these issues looks like a blueprint of the attitudes and mentalities which were to become typical of the Adenauer era. *Forgiveness and Mercy in Shakespeare* (*Vergebung und Gnade bei Shakespeare*), the title of one of the few German Shakespeare monographs of the early post-war period, may serve to illustrate this point. Published in 1952, the book established its author, the Göttingen professor of English Ernst Theodor Sehrt, as one of the country's leading Shakespeareans. 'Forgiveness', Sehrt sums up his findings, 'is the point in Shakespeare which opens up a passage leading from the tragic to the Christian.' Of all his Elizabethan contemporaries, it is Shakespeare who 'has most clearly shown the access to a spiritual world where human weakness finds its answer in forgiving love'.[55]

---

[55] Ernst Theodor Sehrt, *Vergebung und Gnade bei Shakespeare* (Stuttgart: Koehler, 1952), 256.

8

Hamlet in Plettenberg
Carl Schmitt and the Intrusion of the Time

I THE KING LEAR OF PUBLIC LAW

There is a typewritten note among Carl Schmitt's papers in the North Rhine Westphalian state archives in Düsseldorf:

> I make a bet that the Democratic candidate in the upcoming presidential election in the USA, Adlai Stevenson, will *not* be elected. I base my prognosis solely on the fact that Adlai Stevenson is called 'Hamlet', the 'Hamlet of Illinois'.
>
> Plettenberg, 28 October 1956
> Prof. Carl Schmitt[1]

There is also a list of correspondents (among them the writer Ernst Jünger) to whom Schmitt intended to—or actually did—communicate his thought, along with Schmitt's handwritten remark: 'Agree entirely: Americans don't deserve an intellectual president. Joseph H. Kaiser 29/10'.[2] The note, coming about six months after the publication of *Hamlet or Hecuba*,[3] is one of several records indicating Schmitt's abiding interest in Shakespeare's most famous play and character (Figure 8.1). Slight as his little witticism about the doomed Democrat from Illinois may seem, Schmitt liked it enough to use it in a public lecture on Hamlet in January 1957; and he returned to it again and again at what he saw as decisive historical junctures, adding further scribbled glosses: 'Bet overrun by the wheel of world history (Hungary—Egypt—Suez October 1956)'; 'But meanwhile (end of 1960) Kennedy elected (with minimal majority)'; 'Meanwhile August 1968 (occupation of Prague)'; 'Meanwhile Jimmy Carter November 1976'.

In Shakespeare's melancholy prince Schmitt saw not only 'a primal image of the human condition' (*HH* 7) but also a usable persona for newly emerging actors on the contemporary political stage. 'Hamlet-spotting' apparently became a kind of hobby with him. A slip of paper headed '*Hamlet-Galerie*' lists the Italian Socialist

---

[1] Landesarchiv NRW, Abteilung Rheinland, Standort Düsseldorf (Nachlass Carl Schmitt) RW 265–21086. I would like to thank Prof. Dr Jürgen Becker, trustee of the Schmitt estate, for kindly granting me permission to quote from the unpublished materials in the Düsseldorf archive.

[2] Joseph H. Kaiser (1921–98), a constitutional law professor, was a student of Schmitt's in Berlin and later trustee of his estate.

[3] Carl Schmitt, *Hamlet oder Hecuba. Der Einbruch der Zeit in das Spiel* (Düsseldorf and Cologne: Eugen Diederichs, 1956). Published in English as *Hamlet or Hecuba: The Intrusion of the Time into the Play*, trans. Pan and Rust. References are identified as *HH* and given in brackets.

Figure 8.1. Carl Schmitt in the mid-1950s. Photo by permission of the Carl Schmitt Estate.

Giuseppe Saragat, 'Pope Montini (Paul VI)', Paul Sheffer,[4] and once more Adlai Stevenson and Kennedy, the latter with a question mark and the explanatory term '*Ko-Existenz*'.[5] An article Schmitt—by then aged 91—found in *Der Spiegel* (26 November 1979) and kept in his stack of Hamlet-related press-cuttings adds another candidate to the file: Enrico Berlinguer, the leader of Italy's Communist Party, whom the *Spiegel* article styles 'Red Hamlet'.[6] Trivial though this pursuit of latter-day Hamlets may seem, it is grounded in serious existential concerns. For Schmitt, Hamlet becomes a primal image of the condition of the post-war world and of his own place, or rather displacement, in it.

---

[4] Paul Sheffer, originally Scheffer (1883–1963), was a journalist whom Schmitt had known since the 1920s. Why he is on this list remains obscure.

[5] RW 265–20313.

[6] RW 265–21086, vol. 1. Other press-cuttings in the Schmitt archive refer to J. Robert Oppenheimer as the 'Hamlet of modern physics' (obituary in *Die Zeit*, 3 March 1967, 9) and to Pope Paul VI, the 'Hamlet of Milan' (*Deutsches Allgemeines Sonntagsblatt*, 25 September 1977, 12) on the occasion of his eightieth birthday. A piece from *Rheinischer Merkur*, 29 November 1957, quotes Marcel Brion as calling Hamlet 'a prototypical European'. All in RW 265–20311.

This chapter looks at Schmitt's engagement with *Hamlet* from a perspective that takes full account of its personal and political contexts. Since its rediscovery in the early 2000s, *Hamlet or Hecuba* has come to be perceived as a major statement of Schmitt's thought and has been discussed in connection with the work of other major twentieth-century thinkers such as Benjamin and Adorno.[7] My attempt here is to obtain a fuller view of what Schmitt is doing and why by giving more attention than has hitherto been done to his situation in post-war Germany. One way to illuminate this context is to relate *Hamlet or Hecuba* to the theatre discourse of its time; another, to collate it with Schmitt's other Shakespearean writings of this period. These consist of his 1952 preface to Lilian Winstanley's book on *Hamlet*,[8] the brief 'defence' of *Hamlet or Hecuba* that Schmitt delivered in June 1956, and the *Hamlet* lecture he gave in January 1957. The defence, entitled 'Was habe ich getan?' (What have I done?), has been published;[9] the unpublished lecture—part typescript, part notes—is among the Schmitt papers in the Düsseldorf archive.[10] Regarding these writings as a coherent though by no means homogeneous ensemble will cast a somewhat different light on *Hamlet or Hecuba*, making it less easy to ignore what has been politely described as Schmitt's 'sometimes blunt allegorical reading of Hamlet'[11] and less politely as 'crass'.[12] It means that the more dubious features of the essay will not be quite so hastily cleared away as they usually are when critics draw a bead on what they regard as the genuinely valuable core of Schmitt's 'remarkable', 'crucial', or even 'key' text. Most recent articles on *Hamlet or Hecuba* are at pains to separate the wheat, as it were, from the chaff; to pass over, in other words, the cranky literary detective, Lilian Winstanley, to whom Schmitt is massively indebted, in order to reach the loftier plane on which Schmitt 'corresponds' with Walter Benjamin.[13]

I want to linger on the chaff here, not least because this seems in keeping with Schmitt's own approach. A crucial argument in *Hamlet or Hecuba* is Schmitt's insistence that Shakespeare's art cannot be cordoned off from the public sphere of the Elizabethan popular theatre, from the 'filthy reality' he mockingly cites as the

---

[7] For the latter, see Pan, 'Afterword: Historical Event and Mythic Meaning in Carl Schmitt's *Hamlet or Hecuba*', in Schmitt, *Hamlet or Hecuba*, 69–119 at 73–86.

[8] This is available in an English translation: Schmitt, 'Foreword to the German Edition of Lilian Winstanley's *Hamlet and the Scottish Succession*', trans. Kurt R. Buhanan, *Telos* 153 (2010) (Special Issue: Carl Schmitt's *Hamlet or Hecuba*), 164–77. References to this translation, cited as FW, are given in brackets.

[9] Schmitt, 'Was habe ich getan?', *Schmittiana* 5 (1996), 13–19. This text is cited in brackets as WH.

[10] Schmitt, 'Hamlet als mythische Figur der Gegenwart' (Hamlet as a mythical figure of the present), RW 265–20311. This text is cited in brackets as HM.

[11] Jennifer Rust and Julia Reinhard Lupton, 'Introduction: Schmitt and Shakespeare', in Schmitt, *Hamlet or Hecuba*, xv–li at xix.

[12] Michael Dobson, 'Short Cuts' (=review of Schmitt, *Hamlet or Hecuba*), *London Review of Books* 31.15 (6 August 2009), 22.

[13] Rust and Lupton, 'Introduction: Schmitt and Shakespeare', xv–xvi, speak of 'Schmitt's correspondence with Walter Benjamin'. We know that Benjamin wrote an adulatory letter to 'Esteemed Professor Schmitt' in December 1930. But we do not know what Schmitt wrote back or whether he wrote back at all, though it is perhaps unlikely that he did not acknowledge Benjamin's praise. To speak of a correspondence is misleading. For an English translation of Benjamin's letter and a discussion of his debt to Schmitt, see Samuel Weber, 'Taking Exception to Decision: Walter Benjamin and Carl Schmitt', *Diacritics* 22 (1992), 5–18.

bugbear of idealist aesthetics.[14] It is a misconception, he wrote in a letter to the Shakespeare scholar Wolfgang Clemen, to conceive of Shakespeare 'after the model of our great classics: Goethe, Schiller, Grillparzer, Hebbel' as 'a writer working in his study, a literary homeworker who submits his finished literary work to a literary publisher'.[15] The *im*purity of Shakespearean drama, its non-exclusiveness, provides a strong argument for Schmitt's fundamental critique of the liberal-bourgeois notion of a tidily separable autonomous sphere of the aesthetic. Shakespeare's art, its very greatness, Schmitt argues, is inseparable from its 'seat in life', from the rough, 'barbaric' time in which Shakespeare and his audience lived, and whose 'intrusion into the play' elevates *Hamlet* to the status of authentic myth and effects its quantum leap from *Trauerspiel* to tragedy.

It seems only appropriate then to approach Schmitt's *Hamlet* with the same openness to the intrusion of the time that Schmitt himself deemed indispensable for a proper understanding of Shakespeare. Schmitt represents his *Hamlet* essay as an attack on a 'purity taboo deeply rooted in the tradition of German *Bildung*, a taboo which does not permit one to speak of intrusions of the time into the play' (WH 17). It would hardly be consistent, then, to swaddle Schmitt's attack in a similar purity taboo and dissociate *Hamlet or Hecuba* from the ghosts of its author's past and from the ghost he himself raised from one of the weirder cold case files in the annals of Shakespeare scholarship.

Carl Schmitt's career, which I have briefly sketched in Chapter 5, has been the subject of endless debate.[16] Reinhard Mehring's painstakingly fair, if somewhat laborious biography offers an extremely detailed account, but no conclusive assessment. *Carl Schmitt at Close Quarters*, a slim collection of excerpts from the personal memoirs of some forty contemporary observers, vividly illustrates why it is so difficult to reach a conclusive judgement on the 'Proteus' Schmitt, this 'political chameleon'.[17]

Schmitt's eminence as the most brilliant right-wing legal and political thinker of the Weimar Republic carried him seamlessly into the Third Reich.[18] Though he eventually failed to secure the position of 'Hitler's crown jurist'[19]—a label that has

---

[14] *HH* 47. The English translation has 'miserable reality', which does not quite capture the German '*dreckichte Wirklichkeit*'.

[15] Copy of an excerpt from a letter to Prof. Wolfgang Clemen in Munich, 14 July 1954. RW 265–21087. The thought, including the term 'literary homeworker', recurs almost verbatim in *HH* 34.

[16] For a lucid exposition of the controversial issues, see Peter C. Caldwell, 'Controversies over Carl Schmitt: A Review of Recent Literature', *The Journal of Modern History* 77 (2005), 357–87.

[17] 'Proteus': Gerhard Nebel; 'political chameleon': Edgar Salin, both quoted in *Carl Schmitt aus der Nähe betrachtet. Zeugnisse von Weggenossen*, ed. Gerd Giesler and Ernst Hüsmert (Plettenberg: Carl-Schmitt-Gesellschaft, 2013), 12 and 24.

[18] As mentioned in Chapter 5, section VII, Schmitt did not actively support Hitler's takeover in 1933 but served as legal adviser to General von Schleicher who sought to prevent that takeover. But his views needed no major adjustments in order to be compatible with, indeed emphatically supportive of, the new regime. See, e.g. Dirk Blasius, *Carl Schmitt: Preussischer Staatsrat in Hitlers Reich* (Göttingen: Vandenhoeck & Ruprecht, 2001).

[19] The term '*Kronjurist*' was apparently first used with reference to Schmitt in a 1932 article by Hellmut von Gerlach in *Die Weltbühne* ('Schleicher und sein Stahlhelm', 28.2, 343) which castigates the anti-republican militarism of General von Schleicher, minister for the *Reichswehr*, and Schmitt as

nonetheless stuck to his name—this was not for want of trying. Deploying his legal expertise to justify the dismantling of constitutional and civil rights by the Nazis between 1933 and 1936, Schmitt applauded both the 'night of the long knives'[20] and the Nuremberg race laws.[21] The pre-eminent jurist of the Third Reich, he fell victim nevertheless to an intrigue hatched by Nazi rivals within the legal profession.[22] Their attack, ironically, was abetted by some articles published in a Swiss émigré journal in which Schmitt's former student Waldemar Gurian—one of those emigrants whose expulsion from Germany Schmitt had warmly welcomed[23]— exposed inconsistencies between Schmitt's Weimar opinions and his Nazi zealotry.[24] Gurian's points were avidly taken up by Schmitt's Nazi enemies. In an attempt to clear himself from charges of opportunism, Schmitt organized a conference on *Das Judentum in der Rechtswissenschaft* in October 1936 which he addressed with a rabidly anti-Semitic keynote lecture on the perniciousness of the Jewish element in German jurisprudence.[25] Fighting the Jews, Schmitt declaimed, was an 'exorcism'

a legal apologist of anti-parliamentarian measures. Prussia, von Gerlach said, had a history of jurists like Schmitt who would legally justify any breach of international or constitutional law committed by the crown.

[20] Schmitt celebrated Hitler's liquidation of the SA leader Röhm on trumped-up charges of high treason as the epochal transition from the obsolete liberal *Rechtsstaat* to the '*unmittelbar gerechte Staat*' (immediately just state) in which the (merely formal) principle of legality is superseded by the '*Lebensrecht des Volkes*' (a people's right to live). Carl Schmitt, 'Der Führer schützt das Recht' (The Führer protects the law) (1934), in Schmitt, *Positionen und Begriffe im Kampf mit Weimar—Genf—Versailles 1923–1939*, 3rd edn (Berlin: Duncker & Humblot, 1994), 227–32.

[21] Schmitt, 'Die Verfassung der Freiheit' (The Constitution of Liberty).

[22] See Blasius, *Carl Schmitt*, 153–80; Mehring, *Carl Schmitt*, 309–10 and 325–48.

[23] Following the introduction of the law excluding non-Aryans from public service (7 April 1933), Schmitt wrote in a celebratory article in the Nazi paper *Westdeutscher Beobachter*: 'The new regulations [...] cleanse public life from non-Aryan, alien elements [...] We are learning again how to distinguish. But principally we are learning to distinguish correctly between friend and enemy' ('Das gute Recht der deutschen Revolution', 2 May 1933). Among those who fled Germany because of the new law was Schmitt's famous colleague Hans Kelsen: 'Schmitt helped in ousting Kelsen, the Jewish liberal enemy, from the Law Faculty at Cologne (shortly after personally securing Kelsen's help to get himself appointed there).' David Dyzenhaus, *Legality and Legitimacy: Carl Schmitt, Hans Kelsen, and Herman Heller in Weimar* (Oxford: Oxford University Press, 1997), 84. In another article for *Westdeutscher Beobachter* ('Die deutschen Intellektuellen' [The German Intellectuals], 31 May 1933) Schmitt reviled emigrants as scum: 'may they be spit out for all times!'

[24] Between October 1934 and December 1936 Gurian published ten articles about Schmitt's role in the Third Reich in *Deutsche Briefe*. *Deutsche Briefe 1934–1938. Ein Blatt der katholischen Emigration*, 2 vols, ed. Heinz Hürten (Mainz: Matthias-Grünewald-Verlag, 1969). Gurian emigrated to the US in 1937, where he became a professor of political science at Notre Dame. In her tribute to Gurian, Hannah Arendt emphasizes 'his enormous capacity for loyalty'. Schmitt made use of this capacity when he commissioned Gurian to publish a hostile review of Hugo Ball's *Die Folgen der Reformation* (1924) and then let Gurian bear the brunt of Ball's indignation while denying his own part in the affair (cf. Mehring, *Carl Schmitt*, 153–6). Hannah Arendt, 'Waldemar Gurian, 1903–1954', in *Men in Dark Times* (New York: Harcourt, Brace & World, 1968), 251–62, quotation at 254. The essay first appeared in the Gurian Memorial Issue of *The Review of Politics* 1955.

[25] Gopal Balakrishnan, *The Enemy: An Intellectual Portrait of Carl Schmitt* (London: Verso, 2000), 207, calls this event 'a well-organized intellectual pogrom' but then goes on to speculate that 'perhaps Schmitt thought that if the role and presence of Jews in German legal culture could be precisely delimited, libelous, indirect insinuations of Jewish influence could be curtailed'. There is not a shred of evidence for such an apologetic assessment. What the publication of Schmitt's diaries reveals with ever more irrefutable clarity is, on the contrary, his deeply ingrained anti-Semitism. See *Carl Schmitt. Tagebücher 1930 bis 1934*, ed. Schuller. Raphael Gross, *Carl Schmitt und die Juden: Eine deutsche*

accomplishing, now quoting Hitler, 'the work of the Lord'.[26] But the public campaign his enemies had launched against him in the SS-journal *The Black Corps* had already gone too far. Schmitt lost all his positions in the Nazi hierarchy.[27] Only personal intervention by Hans Frank and Hermann Göring prevented further reprisals and saved Schmitt the title of Prussian state councillor as well as his chair at Berlin University. 'Henceforth his life "in the belly of the beast" was, while not comfortable, not exactly dangerous, either, and after 1941 it included once again trips abroad: it was, essentially, the life of a privileged scholar.'[28]

But despite his reversal of fortune in 1936, Schmitt's glory years under the Nazis were not forgotten in 1945. While many an active supporter of National Socialism was quietly absorbed into the new system, with the legal profession in particular notoriously prone to turning a blind eye to its members' pasts, Schmitt was never readmitted into the fold. He had simply been too visible. Thwarted in his ambition to become the Third Reich's authoritative legal spokesman, he was now also thwarted in the hope to earn some credit for the hardships he had undergone at the hands of his SS adversaries. He thus felt doubly punished, the victim of both Hitler and Allied victors' justice. Never regaining a university professorship, he retreated to his provincial Westphalian hometown of Plettenberg, where he spent the remaining forty years of his long life, at first in the cramped family home of his childhood, then in a modest abode he christened 'San Casciano' after Machiavelli's refuge in exile. Unreconciled to post-war West German democracy, he cultivated the role of the outcast, the victim of history, more sinned against than sinning, 'the King Lear of public law' as he styled himself in a letter to a former student in 1950.[29] Banished from the public arena, the dethroned king of jurists turned to literature. Ever '*unzeitgemäss*' (untimely, but not so much premature as belated), the 'last conscious representative of the *ius publicum Europaeum*', he also became the last in a long line of German writers, poets and intellectuals to find in *Hamlet*

Rechtslehre (Carl Schmitt and the Jews: A German Legal Doctrine) (Frankfurt: Suhrkamp, 2000) makes anti-Semitism the very core of Schmitt's thinking. Although this overstates the case, George Schwab much more seriously *under*states it when he claims that anti-Semitism was 'a trait Schmitt [...] acquired overnight' (as late as 1936) and that this 'lip service to the Nazi vogue' constituted the whole extent of Schmitt's post-1933 opportunism. George D. Schwab, 'Carl Schmitt: Political Opportunist?', *Intellect* 103 (1975), 334–7 at 336–7.

[26] Schmitt, 'Die deutsche Rechtswissenschaft im Kampf gegen den jüdischen Geist. Schlusswort auf der Tagung der Reichsgruppe Hochschullehrer des NSRB vom 3. und 4. Oktober 1936', *Deutsche Juristen-Zeitung* 41 (1936), cols 1193–9 at 1197.

[27] 'From one day to the next, he was removed from all his party offices. From that day [...] one could at last talk sensibly with him again.' Joseph Pieper (1942), quoted in Giesler and Hüsmert, eds, *Carl Schmitt aus der Nähe betrachtet*, 18.

[28] Michael Stolleis, *A History of Public Law in Germany 1918–1945*, trans. Thomas Dunlap (Oxford: Oxford University Press, 2004), 264.

[29] Letter to Karl Lohmann, 21 July 1950. RW 569–490. One of the issues Caldwell seeks to clarify in his review essay is 'whether Schmitt served in the Federal Republic as an enemy of democracy or as a mentor to some of the most important political thinkers of the post-war democratic order' ('Controversies over Carl Schmitt', 358). The answer must be that he did both. The complexities of Schmitt's post-war affiliations and influence are aptly traced in Jan-Werner Müller, *A Dangerous Mind: Carl Schmitt in Post-War European Thought* (New Haven, CT and London: Yale University Press, 2003).

'the form and pressure' (3.2.22) of their own life and times. Schmitt, it is true, sought to distance himself from this tradition, which he dismissed as romantic and subjectivist. But in this, as in much else, he doth protest too much. If Hamlet, as Schmitt says in his 1957 lecture, 'has become the mythical figure of the European intellectual' (HM 1) then the nineteenth-century Romantic legacy is the enabling condition of the myth's continuing discursive presence. And it is this legacy that enables Schmitt to use Hamlet as a mirror of his own present.

II WHAT'S JAMES TO US?

In its 5 November 1952 issue, *Der Spiegel*, Germany's investigative weekly news-magazine, ran an article titled 'Hamlet war Jakob' (Hamlet was James). 'Carl Schmitt', the article begins, 'the ostracised Nestor of German constitutional law, has written the preface to a book that his daughter, the stage designer Anima Schmitt, has translated for the first time into German'.[30] Schmitt's notoriety apparently made for a good opening. The rest of the article, which summarizes Winstanley's main propositions and the critical responses her book elicited from English reviewers in the 1920s, mentions neither Schmitt nor his preface again.[31]

How and when exactly Schmitt chanced upon Lilian Winstanley's *Hamlet and the Scottish Succession*[32] has to my knowledge not been ascertained. By 1952 the book had clearly outlived its moment of critical attention and was gathering dust as one of the more eccentric fruits of Shakespeare philology. For Schmitt's daughter Anima, who subsequently translated several of her father's works into Spanish, the rendering of Winstanley's book into German was the first step into a career as a translator. The preface by her famous father certainly helped to promote the book, as did the more in-your-face title *Hamlet, Sohn der Maria Stuart* (Hamlet, Son of Mary Stuart),[33] which cleverly flags not just one but two icons of German literary culture.

Winstanley's study was first published in 1921 to mixed and in some cases unsparingly vitriolic reviews. Given its medley of speculative ingenuity and sheer Fluellenism, this is hardly surprising. At the heart of her argument is the hypothesis that Shakespeare's play owes more to contemporary history than to the 'Nordic saga' from which its protagonist derives his name, more to the turbulent life of

---

[30] Unsigned review, 'Hamlet war Jakob', *Der Spiegel*, Wednesday, 5 November 1952, 26–7.

[31] Four years later, *Der Spiegel* also ran an article on *Hamlet or Hecuba* ('Die Mutter ist tabu', *Der Spiegel*, 29 August 1956, 41–2). Rudolf Augstein (1923–2002), founder and part-owner of *Der Spiegel*, was another influential public intellectual of the post-war period who maintained contact with Schmitt. Apropos of *Hamlet or Hecuba* he wrote to Schmitt: 'I almost like it better than your previous discussion of the same theme.' Quoted in Mehring, *Carl Schmitt*, 461 (trans. modified).

[32] Lilian Winstanley, *Hamlet and the Scottish Succession: Being an Examination of the Relations of the Play of 'Hamlet' to the Scottish Succession and the Essex Conspiracy* (Cambridge: Cambridge University Press, 1921). Page references to this edition are given in brackets in the text.

[33] Lilian Winstanley, *Hamlet, Sohn der Maria Stuart*, trans. Anima Schmitt (Pfullingen: Günther Neske, 1952).

Mary Queen of Scots as chronicled by George Buchanan[34] than to the Amleth of Saxo Grammaticus. Hamlet, she claims, is a covert portrait of James I, whose father, Lord Darnley, was murdered in February 1567 and whose mother Mary Queen of Scots married the murderer, the Earl of Bothwell, in 'most wicked speed' (*Ham.* 1.2.156) just over three months later. In addition, Hamlet's character also contains features borrowed from the Earl of Essex. A veritable forest of resemblances proliferates round this central cluster of identifications. The circumstances and manners depicted in Shakespeare's Denmark, Winstanley writes, 'are, in the highest degree, distinctive and strange; but they can *every one* be paralleled in the case of sixteenth-century Scotland' (7). A mix of barbarism and erudition, of Protestantism and Catholicism, with notorious drinking habits, Shakespeare's fictitious Denmark is the spit and image of historical Scotland. In the play, 'a councillor is murdered in the presence of a queen' (9); the same fate befell Mary's secretary, Rizzio. At the Danish court we find a Guildenstern, a Rosencrantz, and a Francisco; at the Scottish court, a (Danish!) Guildenstern and 'a Francesco, a friend of Rizzio's' (10), with an Eric Rosencrantz figuring marginally in the later life of Bothwell. No doubt, then, Horatio must be the faithful Earl of Mar, the only loyal friend of James's troubled youth; and Hamlet's self-accusations must echo the many letters in which Elizabeth I enjoined her hesitant successor-to-be not to bear the whips and scorns of his proud enemies, but to take arms against them. Exasperated by James's lack of resolution, Elizabeth writes: 'And since it so likes you to demand my counsel, I find so many ways your state so unjoynted, that it needs a skilfuller bone-setter than I to joyne each part in its right place' (81). 'One may compare this,' Winstanley says, 'with Hamlet's bitter cry: The time is out of joint: O cursed spite / That ever I was born to set it right.' And she continues: 'In exactly the same way as Elizabeth piles up the indignities James has suffered, so Hamlet piles up those he endures himself' (81).

'So the thirty-year-old Shakespeare', a Swiss reviewer scoffed in 1924, 'had cognizance of Elizabeth's letter in 1592, or the words "unjointed" and "joined" were passing from mouth to mouth between London and Edinburgh ten years later! The whole book is built on such *salti mortali*.'[35]

Horatio says of Old Hamlet that he 'was a goodly king' (*Ham.* 1.2.186); Darnley's dead body was eulogized by Buchanan as 'the goodliest corpse of any gentleman' (61). The Ghost wears full armour; Darnley was noted for often doing the same. Hamlet's father is killed in an orchard; so was Darnley. Hamlet's father has poison poured in his ear; so had—at least according to Mary's detractors—her first husband, François II. Darnley, too, was said to have been poisoned. He survived the attack, but the 'black Pimples breaking out all over his body' (53) parallel

---

[34] George Buchanan, *Ane detectioun of the duinges of Marie Quene of Scottes, touchand the murder of hir husband, and hir conspiracie, adulterie, and pretensed mariage with the Erle Bothwell. And ane defence of the trew Lordis, mainteineris of the Kingis graces actioun and authoritie. Translatit out of the Latine quhilke was written by G.B.* (London: John Day, 1571).

[35] Bernhard Fehr, untitled review of Winstanley, *Hamlet and the Scottish Succession*, in *Beiblatt zur Anglia* 35 (1924), 1–16 at 6. Fehr, featuring anonymously as 'a well-known Anglicist in Zurich' who sought to 'destroy' Winstanley's 'disruptive book', in turn receives a sound dressing-down in Schmitt's foreword (FW 176).

the 'vile and loathsome crust' that covers '[a]ll [the] smooth body' (*Ham.* 1.5.72–3) of Hamlet's dying father. Once this kind of paper-chase is set in motion, there is no stopping it. It generates evidence with the same snowball momentum that immunizes anti-Stratfordians from doubt. 'Today the author is firmly convinced of the reality of her discoveries,' the same Swiss reviewer concludes, 'but when, in years to come, she will calmly reread her book, she will recognize that she went flying to *Neverland* with Peter Pan.'[36]

Schmitt must have read a different book altogether. Winstanley's great achievement, he declares, the achievement that 'real critics' have recognized all along, is a turning away from the vagaries of subjectivism towards 'the objective' (FW 176). 'The mists of fanciful interpretation dissipate, the flickering [*Geflimmer*] of psychological possibilities ends. One sees the granite rock of a singular historical truth emerge, and the figure of a real king with a concrete fate appears' (FW 170, translation modified). Thinly disguised as the 'old Scandinavian Hamlet saga' (FW 164), the true core of Shakespeare's *Hamlet* drama is to be found in its 'most immediate actualization of the directly lived event, the directly experienced fate' (FW 169). Shakespeare has not invented the dramatic plot but found it in contemporary historical reality.

Schmitt's 1952 preface is even more emphatic about the immediacy and presence of the dramatized events than *Hamlet or Hecuba* would be four years later. Shakespeare's play is 'the most amazing instance of immediate proximity to its time that the history of great drama has ever seen' (FW 165, translation modified). The events it stages are as much 'topical present' for Shakespeare and his audience as 'the death in 1889 of Crown Prince Rudolf von Habsburg and the "tragedy of Mayerling" would have been for a Viennese audience or the Röhm affair for a Berlin audience in 1934' (FW 168, translation modified).

Such hammering home of real-life immediacy is yoked up with an equally forceful thrust towards a time-transcending essence or 'core'. As a key passage in the preface argues, it is 'the timely core of its presence' (FW 169) that 'holds the mysterious power to carry the drama from the present of its time and place of origin into posterity and to make possible the thousand interpretations and symbolizations of later centuries, without the drama losing its hero or its countenance [*Gesicht*]' (FW 169, translation modified).[37] The more closely Shakespeare's play is linked to its historical present, the more it can transcend that present. The logic of Schmitt's argument is encapsulated in an oxymoron: 'infinite singularity' (*unendliche Einmaligkeit*) (FW 169, translation modified).[38] It is in this coincidence of opposites—time-bound *versus* time-transcending, but also time-bound *ergo* time-transcending—that the mythical force of *Hamlet* has its origin.

Schmitt's argument is based on a linking of two oppositions: the opposition of historical truth and poetic invention, in which *Hamlet* is firmly located on the side of history; and the opposition of accidentals and essentials, surface and core.

---

[36] Fehr, *Beiblatt zur Anglia*, 6.
[37] The translator, Kurt Buhanan, renders *Gesicht* as 'vision'. This makes sense, but is not what Schmitt wrote.
[38] Buhanan drops the adjective *unendlich*.

The latter proves somewhat harder to maintain. Shakespeare's *Hamlet*, Schmitt says, 'is a mirror, but not a mere copy [*Abbild*] of this historical reality. It is not a *pièce à clef*, nor an old-fashioned form of what we would now call a newsreel' (FW 165, translation modified). But a *pièce-à-clef* (*Schlüsselstück*), whose every detail can be traced to a current event or living person, is precisely what Winstanley's relentless hunting for historical parallels makes of *Hamlet*. A *pièce-à-clef* is also what Schmitt suggests when he speaks of the 'transparent *incognito*' that 'heightens the tension and the participation of the knowing spectators' in *Hamlet* (HH 37). And how if not as a *pièce-à-clef* are we to imagine Schmitt's hypothetical play about the killing of Röhm and his associates in the so-called night of the long knives? '[H]unting for resemblances,' Drew Daniel cautions, 'is to miss Schmitt's point.'[39] But then, it seems, Schmitt sometimes missed his own point, too. His praise for Winstanley—boosted, no doubt, by a feeling of affinity with a fellow outsider—insists that her 'astounding findings' prove the factual basis of Shakespeare's dramatic plot 'down to the finest detail' (FW 164); 'her evidence', he maintains, 'is clear and simple' (FW 170). Topical allusions confirm 'the most intense historical presence and the most immediate contemporary reality' (FW 167). This makes *Hamlet* the essential modern drama. And yet, he says, 'my claim here is not that sheer topicality makes great art' (FW 168).[40]

In order to reconcile these somewhat contradictory assertions, Schmitt introduces a three-tiered distinction in *Hamlet or Hecuba*. History enters either in the form of 'simple allusions' which are of limited scope and hence little interest or in the form of 'true mirrorings'—reflections of a major contemporary event such as the Essex rebellion. But only the third and most important type, the 'genuine intrusion' of a truly epochal event or figure, has the capacity to unsettle the stage play in a way that raises it to the level of tragedy and generates myth. The fate of James I constitutes such an intrusion. The taboo of his mother's alleged complicity in the murder of his father accounts for the major blind spot in *Hamlet*: the irresolvable question of Gertrude's guilt. And what Schmitt calls the 'Hamletization of the avenger' is directly due to the figure of James himself, the overly thoughtful, hesitant prince entangled in 'the fate of the European religious schism' that killed his mother and his son Charles and would eventually shatter the whole royal line of 'the unhappy Stuarts' (HH 52).

The distinction goes some way towards separating the Schmittian wheat from the Winstanleyan chaff, towards untangling 'one of the leading political thinkers of the 20th century' from the embrace of his dubious British muse.

Some way, but not all the way. The real stumbling block for Schmitt's reading is not that he swallows Winstanley's 'findings [...] down to the finest detail' (FW 164); the details, after all, are of little consequence compared to the myth-generating historical 'core'. The problem, rather, has to do with the core itself. It results from the inclusion of what Schmitt professes to categorically exclude: psychological

---

[39] Drew Daniel, '"Neither Simple Allusions Nor True Mirrorings": Seeing Double with Carl Schmitt', *Telos* 153 (2010), 51–69 at 58–9.

[40] See also FW 175 (translation modified): 'I have not said that every writer who puts the events of his own time on the stage is therefore a greater dramatist than Schiller.'

interpretation. Psychology intrudes not so much as a 'flickering of [...] possibilities' but as a floodlit psychodrama of revelatory veracity. Schmitt prefaces his reading of Hamlet with T. S. Eliot's *bon mot* that, although 'it is probable that we can never be right' about Shakespeare, 'it is better that we should from time to time change our way of being wrong' (*HH* 6). But Schmitt leaves the reader in no doubt that his own effort is invested with a truth claim far beyond such relativist modesty. This claim is inseparable from what could best be described as an empathetic psychogram of the troubled Stuart monarch. In this, too, Schmitt takes his cue from Winstanley.

Viewing Shakespeare through the lens of nineteenth-century psychology, she argues, can only produce anachronistic distortion. What needs to be explored instead is '[t]he point of view of an Elizabethan audience'. This 'can only be understood by means of a careful study of the history of the time' (31). Careful study reveals not only that James and Hamlet are of the same age (thirty), build (fat) and dressing habits (sloppy) but also (94–6), more importantly, that they are plagued with the same incapacity for resolute action. Time and again, in her letters, Elizabeth chiding James for his lethargy sounds like Hamlet chiding himself for the same weakness. 'Does it not look', Winstanley asks, 'as if the mental malady in the two were identical?' (83). Of course it does, and the reason is not hard to find: 'Elizabeth and Shakespeare were both people of genius and they were analysing one and the same case' (83).

The operation that leads to this breathtaking conclusion is not, as Winstanley would have us believe—and no doubt believed herself—a replacement of fallacious psychology by reliable history; it is, in fact, quite the opposite: a takeover of history by psychology, indeed the very kind of psychology—not sixteenth- but nineteenth-century—that has produced the myriad-faceted modern image of Hamlet, the Mona Lisa of literature. This image, the cumulative result of a century of character criticism, is by no means discarded; rather, it is the lens through which Winstanley looks at James, the template from which she constructs her image of the Scottish successor. What Winstanley finds in Elizabeth's letters, what directs her choice of quotations from the letters, is determined by this image. And so is her neglect of all those of James's personality traits that were anything but Hamlet-like. Dramatic fiction, in other words, precedes, and determines, historical 'fact'. Her James thus becomes a doppelganger of Hamlet, the historical king an offshoot of the fictional prince, not, as she claims, vice versa.

Schmitt, too, could not be more categorical in his rejection of psychological interpretation. Psychology has nothing to offer but sundry ways of being wrong about Shakespeare. Echoing Winstanley, Schmitt maintains that the only way to be right about Hamlet is to turn to history: 'it is clear that the distortion [*Abbiegung*] of the avenger figure *can only be explained* by the historical presence of King James' (*HH* 30, my italics). But in order to explain Hamlet, Schmitt, like Winstanley, must first Hamletize James. In his account, James becomes a tragic character, laden not only with his own troubles, past and present, but also with those that would befall his doomed progeny in the course of the seventeenth century (*HH* 52).

The two-and-a-half pages Schmitt spends on his portrayal of James draw a picture of unrelieved doom and gloom. The cataclysmic rifts of the age are ingrained unmediated in the existential angst of a 'philosophizing and theologizing' intellectual (*HH* 25) who 'conducted [...] great—although, of course, quite fruitless' learned debates (*HH* 29, translation modified), whose 'being was torn' (*HH* 29, translation modified) and whose 'ideological position was simply hopeless' (*HH* 29). This last attribute connects the Hamletized James to another of Schmitt's favourite figures: the fighter for a lost cause, defeated by history, as exemplified by the Spanish Catholic anti-liberal Donoso Cortés and, of course, Schmitt himself.[41] The emphatic claim to objectivity and 'the granite rock' of historical truth thus loops back to the undeniably subjective.

Schmitt's highly dramatic version of history clenches the fate of a whole era not just in a single man but in a single moment. If James personifies the conflicts of the age, 1603 becomes the *catastrophe*, the turning point, not just for England but for the whole of European history. To 'Shakespeare and his friends', the new king 'was their hope and their dream in a desperate moment of crisis and catastrophe' (*HH* 30–1).[42] James disappointed these hopes. 'But hope and dream had by then found their way into the brilliant play. The figure of Hamlet had entered into the world and its history, and the myth began its journey' (*HH* 31).

But, one may well ask, what's James to us? To Shakespeare's contemporaries, Schmitt avers, the fate of this tragic hero was a matter of life and death. 'The spectators', he maintains in characteristic hyperbole, 'were not mere spectators; rather, their lives were [...] at stake in the drama as it played out before their eyes' (FW 167). They felt the brute force of history burst (*einbrechen*) into the play. But what is at stake for 'us'? How are 'we' supposed to respond? If we weep for Hamlet, Hamlet becomes a mere Hecuba to us, Shakespeare no more than a superior Schikaneder, supplier of second-rate librettos for enlightened *Kunstgenuss*, for pure, self-indulgent aesthetic pleasure.[43] Should we, instead, weep for James, the tragic victim of history? One answer the text suggests is that we definitely should not—for how could we weep for anyone we aren't even supposed to think of? 'I do not expect anyone to think of James I when they see Hamlet on stage. I would also not want to measure Shakespeare's Hamlet against the historical James I or vice versa' (*HH* 38, translation modified). 'It would be foolish to play Hamlet in the mask of James. This would be either a historical panopticon [...] or [...] the attempt to pump blood into a spectre, a kind of vampirism' (*HH* 51).

In the conclusion of the essay, however, the spectre comes very much alive and another, rather different answer as to whether Shakespeare's Hamlet should make

[41] See, for example, Carl Schmitt, 'Historiographia in Nuce: Alexis de Tocqueville' in his *Ex Captivitate Salus. Erfahrungen der Zeit 1945/47*, 2nd edn (Berlin: Duncker & Humblot, 2002), 25–33. For Schmitt on Cortés, see Schmitt, *Political Theology*, 51–66.

[42] According to most historical accounts, there actually was no crisis. The Scottish succession, well prepared and shrewdly managed, went as smoothly as anyone could have hoped. James's 'peaceful accession was welcomed with practical unanimity and, we are told, "the like joy, both in London and all parts of England, was never known"'. Godfrey Davies, *The Oxford History of England*, vol. 9: *The Early Stuarts 1603–1660* (Oxford: Oxford University Press 1959), 1, quoting *Hist. MSS. Com., Salisbury MSS.* (1930), xv, 26.

[43] Cf. Schmitt's scathing critique of Mozart's *Magic Flute* (libretto by Emanuel Schikaneder), *HH* 30 n. 21, translator's comment.

us weep for James seems to emerge. Schmitt retracts his rebuttal of historicism or, rather, extracts the historical figures of James and Mary Stuart from the historical past, transplanting them into what one might call a continuing historical present. What matters here is not, to quote Eliot, 'the pastness of the past, but [...] its presence'.[44] 'Mary Stuart is still *for us* something other and more than Hecuba. Even the fate of the Atreidae does not affect us as deeply as that of the unhappy Stuarts' (*HH* 52, my italics). To Schmitt, the historical moment that gave birth to the tragic myth of *Hamlet* is not over. It is clearly *his* moment. Flanked by the Catholic Spanish Don Quixote and the Protestant German Faustus, Hamlet occupies the centre panel of a symbolic triptych: he 'stands between them in the middle of the schism that has determined the fate of Europe' (*HH* 52), a schism that in Schmitt's view continued to determine it. This continuity explains the seamless transition from Shakespeare's Elizabethan audience to 'us' in the central section of the essay. Shakespeare would not intend 'us' 'to weep for Hamlet as the actor wept for the Trojan queen' (*HH* 43) because in doing so 'we would divorce our present existence from the play on the stage', '[w]e would no longer have any purpose or cause', indulging in merely 'aesthetic enjoyment' (*HH* 43) and that 'would be bad, because it would prove that we have different gods in the theatre than in the forum and the pulpit' (*HH* 43, translation modified).

But in the autonomous sphere of post-Enlightenment art, we do of course have 'different gods', or, more precisely, 'gods' of different valency, in the theatre than in the other social domains.[45] To Schmitt this division is precisely what is wrong with liberal modernity. His vision is a regressive utopia. What he seeks to recuperate is a pre-modern unity of art, religion, and the political in a theatre that offers more than just play. In a sense that Schmitt would probably not be willing to accept, this unity is the myth, the sustaining historical fantasy,[46] to which *Hamlet or Hecuba* pays tribute.

III EINBRUCH

In hankering after this mythical unity—and especially in singling out the theatre as the site of its consummation—Schmitt's *Hamlet* essay is more typical of its historical moment than hitherto recognized.

---

[44] Eliot, 'Tradition and the Individual Talent', 38.

[45] An increasing differentiation of society into systems and subsystems is the hallmark of the modern world according to 'modernity's most meticulous theorist', Niklas Luhmann. William Rasch, *Niklas Luhmann's Modernity: The Paradoxes of Differentiation* (Stanford, CA: Stanford University Press, 2000), 10.

[46] More specifically than he ever does in *Hamlet or Hecuba*, Schmitt defines myth in his 1923 essay 'Die politische Theorie des Mythus' as a belief that empowers a people, a nation or a mass movement with a collective vision, a vital sense of historical mission. It is symptomatic of the degeneracy of parliamentary democracy, Schmitt argues, that it lacks a myth. It is equally symptomatic and a sign of genuine vitality that fascism has one. Schmitt cites Mussolini's famous rallying speech before the 'March to Rome' approvingly: '"We have created a myth, this myth is a belief, a noble enthusiasm; it does not need to be a reality, it is a striving and a hope, belief and courage. Our myth is the nation, the great nation which we want to make into a concrete reality for ourselves."' Schmitt, *The Crisis of Parliamentary Democracy*, 76. See Chapter 3, n. 41.

Schmitt's approach, so the standard view has it, is the great exception at a time when (West) German professors of literature sought to distance themselves as far as possible from the *völkisch* brand of *Geistesgeschichte* (history of ideas) and their own involvement in it by embracing a safely apolitical formalism. By launching his intrusion of the political into this reserve of literary autonomy, Schmitt trespassed against the 'purity taboo' (WH 17) observed by the professional guardians of literary study. This view conforms with Schmitt's own assessment of his role, except that he also saw himself as challenging 'the monopoly' of another critical orthodoxy—that which prevailed east of the Iron Curtain:

> He who endangers the monopoly is a reactionary and a class enemy. Between *Diamat*[47] and *schöner Schein* (beautiful appearance),[48] a German is caught between the horns of a dilemma. My way of seeing Hamlet historically endangers the monopoly of the dialectical-materialist history of art. I have learnt to my own cost what that means in practical terms. (WH 18)

Engaged in a fight on two fronts, Schmitt fashions himself as the embattled outsider (though a stand against Communism hardly qualified as a dissident stance in Cold War West Germany). Letting history 'intrude' into the rarefied confines of pure art, he himself becomes the intruder, 'the troublemaker, the taboo-violator, the anti-monopolist' (WH 18).

'Intrusion', however, the trope under which Schmitt stages his trespass has a familiar ring in cultural criticism of the post-war era. 'Irruption' would be closer in meaning to the German word Schmitt uses, *Einbruch*, which conveys a violent breaking or bursting into. In its most common use the word denotes the offence of breaking and entering. Compounds with the verb *brechen* (break, rupture) and its concomitant noun *Bruch* abound in writings of the late 1940s and 1950s. This is, of course, because the *Zusammenbruch* (breakdown) of the Third Reich constituted a radical *Bruch* (rupture) in German history, the rupture from which the post-war situation derived, most obviously the rupture of the country itself. An article by Wilhelm Backhaus (a journalist, not the pianist) published in the 1946/7 *Theatre Almanach* speaks of '*Einbruchstellen*' (break-in points) at which 'political and social mass hysteria' had engendered 'devastations of the world':

> But salvation from all of these spiritual and material troubles can only come from a new cultural wholeness [...] Only from a renovation or rather re-creation of the religious

---

[47] *Diamat* is an abbreviation of 'dialectical materialism'. The version of 'What have I done?' that was printed on the initiative of Piet Tommissen in the Flemish nationalist journal *Dietsland-Europa* (1957) has '*Diamant*' (diamond) instead of '*Diamat*'. In a handwritten note in the typescript of 'What have I done?' (RW 265–21087), Schmitt comments on the grotesque typo: 'Note for the Schiller year 1959: Most educated Germans of 1959 are no longer able to read this last sentence; they will not know where the "dilemma" comes from and be inclined to read "Diamant" rather than "Diamat". The Schiller speeches and Schiller celebrations of 1959 will be held on the basis of such diluted education.' Oddly enough, the typo survives into Tommissen's 1996 re-edition of the text in *Schmittiana*, 18.

[48] '*Schöner Schein*', a key concept of Schiller's aesthetics, is used here metonymically for the doctrine of artistic autonomy.

of the technical-scientific age', and the twentieth century the 'beginnings of film' and 'epiphany-less theatre'.[62] At this point only a catastrophe can bring salvation and guide us 'home'. 'Theatre', Vietta declares, 'is Janus-faced; it shows the struggle over departing gods and the advent of new ones. If theatre is living poetry, it gives us world-historical intrusions [*Einbrüche*] which only much later are converted into political currency.'[63]

The quality of Vietta's writing may be several rungs below Schmitt's, but his conservative cultural critique and theology of history give a good idea of the intellectual environment in which Schmitt's Hamlet essay originated. The severance of aesthetics from politics—the 'purity taboo' which Schmitt infringes upon—was the norm in literary studies, a norm which was by no means maintained only by those who had a Nazi past to cover up.[64] Theatre, however, was seen as the one domain where 'play' failed in its responsibility if it 'led away from life',[65] if it did not contribute to the regeneration of society in 'the struggle for a new order of values'.[66] 'The tragic', said the Catholic writer Reinhold Schneider in 1955, 'is that which is inherited from the past and at the same time absolutely new'; it is 'the harrowing challenge of history to us. [...] Again and again peoples have found themselves [...] on the tragic stage, rising—in utmost danger—[...] to the stature of history.'[67]

The overblown pathos of these post-war pronouncements—even those coming from individuals who, like Schneider, had resisted the Nazis[68]—is often virtually indistinguishable from the rhetorical tone of just a few years before. In the *Berlin Theatre Almanach* of 1942, the actor Mathias Wieman enthused about how he felt playing Faust, the epitome of the 'Faustian German fighting man' whom other nations would never fully comprehend, during the 'tremendous process of

---

[62] Vietta, *Katastrophe*, 229.   [63] Vietta, *Katastrophe*, 113.

[64] This is the misleading impression given by David Pan in his 'Afterword' in *HH*, 71–2. Pan is right in speaking of an 'institutionalized cover-up of *Germanistik*'s Nazi past' (*HH* 72). But his next assertion does not hold up: 'To insist on the separation of art from politics is to argue that the Nazi movement was simply a political movement with no cultural underpinnings.' It is precisely their awareness of how much Nazism had in fact permeated German culture, German universities, and especially *Germanistik* that made post-war literary scholars (not just ex-Nazis and fellow-travellers) want to steer clear of politicizing literature. That this was in itself a highly political evasion was the standard reproach of the student generation of 1968 against their professors. Pan's attempt to make Schmitt the only man honestly facing realities when everyone else (except Theodor W. Adorno) was not gives too much credit to Schmitt's own version of himself. On the role of *Germanistik* and *Anglistik* in the Third Reich, see Gerhard Kaiser, *Grenzverwirrungen: Literaturwissenschaft im Nationalsozialismus* (Berlin: Akademie-Verlag, 2008); Frank-Rutger Hausmann, *Anglistik und Amerikanistik im 'Dritten Reich'* (Frankfurt: Klostermann, 2003).

[65] Oskar Wälterlin, *Die Verantwortung des Theaters* (The Responsibility of the Theatre) (Berlin: Pontes-Verlag, 1947), 78.

[66] Backhaus, 'Bretter', 176.

[67] Egon Vietta, ed., *Darmstädter Gespräch: Theater* (Darmstadt: Neue Darmstädter Verlagsanstalt, 1955), 216. Reinhold Schneider (1903–58) was a prominent public intellectual in the 1950s. The 'Darmstadt Dialogues' (1950–75) were a series of symposia on such 'big' themes as 'Man and his Future' (1960) or 'Fear and Hope in our Time' (1963). Among the 1951 panellists ('Man and Space') were the philosophers Heidegger and Ortega y Gasset; guests at the 1955 meeting on 'Theatre' (which was co-organized by Vietta) included Adorno and the dramatist Friedrich Dürrenmatt.

[68] Schneider's 1938 play *Las Casas vor Karl V* (Las Casas before Charles V), contained a critique of political oppression, racism, and religious fanaticism. In 1941 he was prohibited from publishing, and in April 1945 was charged with high treason, narrowly escaping execution at the end of the war.

transformation'[69] in which 'the decision over our continent is being decided on the battlefield'[70]—at the very moment, in fact, when the Wehrmacht was invading Norway. Faust under these circumstances 'was no escape from reality, no lapsing into an oasis of peace or circled-off spiritual enclosure [...]. The hot breath of our time also courses through our theatre.'[71] That Wieman (1902–69) was a friend and 'welcome guest' of the Schmitt family,[72] that his was the sonorous voice reading the Nativity story from the Bible on German radio on Christmas Eve during the 1950s and 1960s is of merely incidental interest. More relevant here is the continuity of a discourse in which the 'play' of theatre is construed as serious, socially important and fatefully implicated in the process of history.

In view of this, the question why *Hamlet or Hecuba* had so little impact at the time needs to be reconsidered.[73] Schmitt's own claim that this was because he had broken 'the taboo that does not permit [one] to speak of intrusions of the time into the play' (WH 17) can hardly be credited, given that German theatre discourse had been speaking of little else for the last ten years. And given also that Theodor W. Adorno, who broke the same 'taboo', could be heard on German radio so often that some listeners complained of an 'Adorno inflation'.[74] But Adorno, despite a leftism that jarred with the conservative climate of the Adenauer era, was politically correct; Schmitt wasn't.

But the problem was not just Schmitt's association with Nazism; it was also his association with Lilian Winstanley. That his book left not a trace in the review sections of scholarly journals[75] has at least as much to do with Winstanley as with politics. The one important professional reader who deemed *Hamlet or Hecuba* worthy of attention took issue not with Schmitt's politics but with his literary views. This was Hans-Georg Gadamer whose *opus magnum* of 1959, *Truth and Method*, devotes a two-page appendix to refuting Schmitt's critical method.[76] The appendix takes up Gadamer's discussion of 'occasionality', the integral function that the imprint of historical realities has in the work of art.[77] Gadamer agrees with Schmitt that

> it is right, in principle, to exclude the prejudices of a pure aesthetics of experience [*Erlebnis*] and to situate the play of art within its historical and political context, [but]

---

[69] Mathias Wieman, '"Faust" im Kriege', *Berliner Theater-Almanach 1942* (Berlin: Paul Neff, 1942), 253–6 at 253.

[70] Wieman, '"Faust" im Kriege', 255.   [71] Wieman, '"Faust" im Kriege', 256.

[72] See Armin Mohler's note in *Carl Schmitt—Briefwechsel mit einem seiner Schüler*, 100.

[73] Tommissen's claim that Schmitt's *Hamlet* book found greater resonance than Schmitt suggests in WH has little evidence to support it. WH 14 n. 5.

[74] Michael Schwarz, '"Er redet leicht, schreibt schwer": Theodor W. Adorno am Mikrophon', *Zeithistorische Forschungen/Studies in Contemporary History* 8.2 (2011), 286–94 at 286, estimates that Adorno recorded no fewer than 300 radio broadcasts in the 1950s and 1960s with some 300 public appearances in the same period. Thus, Schwarz concludes, 'one could hear Adorno speak somewhere almost every week.'

[75] *Shakespeare-Jahrbuch*, for example, reviewed the 1952 Winstanley translation but ignored *Hamlet or Hecuba*.

[76] Hans-Georg Gadamer, *Truth and Method*, 2nd edn, trans. Joel Weinsheimer and Donald G. Marshall (London and New York: Continuum, 2004), 498–500.

[77] Gadamer, *Truth and Method*, 141.

it seems to me wrong to expect one to read *Hamlet* like a roman à clef. [...] Thus, in my opinion, Schmitt falls victim to a false historicism when, for example, he interprets politically the fact that Shakespeare leaves the question of the Queen's guilt open, and sees this as a taboo. In fact it is part of the reality of a play that it leaves an indefinite space around its real theme. [...] The more that remains open, the more freely does the process of understanding succeed—i.e., the process of transposing what is shown in the play to one's own world and, of course, also to the world of one's own political experience.[78]

The last statement could not be better illustrated than by the way in which Schmitt's reading of *Hamlet* reflects, and is inflected by, his own view of the contemporary world.

IV THE HIEROGLYPH OF THE WESTERN WORLD

Hamlet is James: this is the proposition on which Schmitt's whole argument depends. Without it, no tragedy, and without tragedy, no myth. What this makes of *Macbeth*, *King Lear*, or *Othello*, not to mention *Romeo and Juliet*, we can only guess. Are these plays just tragedies so-called, but in fact mere *Trauerspiele*? Or would at least *Macbeth* and *King Lear* qualify as genuine tragedies, though perhaps to a lesser degree than *Hamlet* and only on the condition that they be unlocked with a *clef* provided by Lilian Winstanley?[79] The question obviously never occurred to Schmitt. In this, he is typical of the German Shakespeare tradition, which has tended to treat *Hamlet* as not just the pinnacle but virtually the sum total of Shakespeare's work.

Schmitt is, of course, very much aware of this tradition, especially of its political dimension. He quotes the catch-phrase, 'Germany is Hamlet', together with parts of Ferdinand Freiligrath's poem from which it comes in the introductory section of *Hamlet or Hecuba*, where he cursorily surveys the history of Hamlet interpretation. From Goethe, who turned Hamlet into a Werther, to Freud, for whom 'every neurotic is either an Oedipus or a Hamlet', 'an excess of psychological interpretation' (*HH* 7) has clouded rather than clarified Hamlet. A particularly blatant instance of such distortion, Gerhart Hauptmann's 1935 play *Hamlet in Wittenberg*, 'remains trapped in psychologizing and contains painfully embarrassing digressions in which a subjectivist of the first half of the twentieth century seeks to foist his own erotic complexes onto Hamlet' (*HH* 8). Though spared such scathing censure, Freiligrath's 'Germany is Hamlet' is cited as another instance of such projection. Only in this case, the psychology of Shakespeare's melancholy procrastinator is not

---

[78] Gadamer, *Truth and Method*, 498–9.

[79] Cf. her two later monographs: *'Macbeth', 'King Lear' and Contemporary History: Being a Study of the Relations of the Play of 'Macbeth' to the Personal History of James I, the Darnley Murder and the St. Bartholomew Massacre and also of 'King Lear' as Symbolic Mythology* (Cambridge: Cambridge University Press, 1922); *'Othello' as the Tragedy of Italy: Showing that Shakespeare's Italian Contemporaries Interpreted the Story of the Moor and the Lady of Venice as Symbolizing the Tragedy of Their Country in the Grip of Spain* (London: Terrace, 1924).

foisted on an individual, but a whole 'tattered and fractured' people (*HH* 9). 'In this way', Schmitt concludes, 'the labyrinth becomes ever more impenetrable' (*HH* 9). After this, it comes as something of a surprise that Freiligrath's poem receives honourable mention in the climactic final paragraph of *Hamlet or Hecuba*. The poem's allusion to Wittenberg, Schmitt says, shows 'an inkling' of 'the final and greatest aspect of the Hamlet issue', the religious 'schism that has determined the fate of Europe' (*HH* 52). No longer exemplifying misguided psychologism, 'Germany is Hamlet' now bears witness to the procreative power of the Hamlet myth.

In *Hamlet or Hecuba*, Schmitt is clearly more interested in the 'birth' of this myth than in its later 'journey';[80] more, in other words, in the proposition that Hamlet is James than in the proposition that Germany is Hamlet. But the fact that he uses the same adjective, *zerrissen* (torn, tattered), to characterize both 'the unhappy Stuart' and the Germany of 1848 can be taken as a hint that Schmitt saw the predicament of the 'torn' king and that of the 'torn' nation as in some way connected; that he saw them both as being part of the same tragic history, a history that was far from over.

No sooner was *Hamlet or Hecuba* published in April 1956 than Schmitt redirected his priorities from James to Germany, from the historical origin of the Hamlet myth to its continuing historical momentum. On the back of a letter to Ernst Jünger, dated 1 August 1956, we find this 'hieroglyph of the Western world' (Figure 8.2):

> 1848: Germany is Hamlet
> 1918: Europe is Hamlet
> 1958: the whole Western world is Hamlet
> II/7 56
> Written down for Ernst Jünger by
> Carl Schmitt
> (The Hamlet-Curve)[81]

Jünger responded by drily observing that 'this would give us another two years' (1956–8), adding: 'Hamlet seems to have come much into fashion—whether this is a good sign is another question.'[82]

The present significance of *Hamlet* was also the main theme of 'What have I done?' ('Was habe ich getan?'), the statement Schmitt prepared as an introduction

---

[80] Both terms are Schmitt's; see 'Preface', 170: 'The Birth of a Myth out of a Play of Contemporary Historical Presence'; and *HH* 31: 'The figure of Hamlet had entered into the world and its history, and the myth began its journey.'

[81] *Ernst Jünger/Carl Schmitt: Briefe*, 310. The 'hieroglyph' also appears elsewhere in Schmitt's correspondence, for example in a letter to Armin Mohler, 15 July 1956. *Carl Schmitt—Briefwechsel mit einem seiner Schüler*, 220.

[82] Ernst Jünger to Carl Schmitt, 5 August 1956. *Ernst Jünger/Carl Schmitt: Briefe*, 310. In 1958, Schmitt took up the idea of the Hamlet-Curve again and varied it: 'Aubrey Beardsley seems to be proved right: Protestantism ends as Hamlet. The sons of Puritans are becoming Jesuits. The whole Western world is Hamlet and will give its *dying voice* [English in the original] to a Fortinbras' (25 May 1958). Carl Schmitt, *Glossarium. Aufzeichnungen der Jahre 1947–1951. Erweiterte, berichtigte und kommentierte Neuausgabe*, ed. Gerd Giesler and Martin Tielke (Berlin: Duncker & Humblot, 2015), 368.

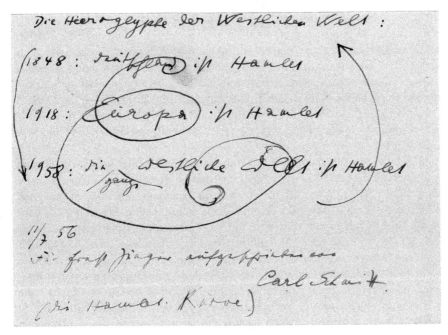

Figure 8.2. Carl Schmitt's Hamlet-Curve. Photo by permission of the Carl Schmitt Estate.

for a discussion of *Hamlet or Hecuba* at the home of the publisher Eugen Diederichs on 12 June 1956.[83] 'Hamlet is a very popular theme', Schmitt says, citing recent offshoots of Shakespeare's play, a novel by Alfred Döblin and a play by Stefan Andres with a 'Hamlet Europe' character:[84]

> I have not seen the play, but I remember that Paul Valéry said in 1919, after the First World War: Europe is Hamlet. In the previous century, before 1848, the German liberal revolutionaries used to say: Germany is Hamlet. A curious progression from Germany to Europe that should give us pause as Germans and make us apprehensive as Europeans. (WH 15)[85]

[83] Schmitt also circulated 'What have I done?' among his friends. On the initiative of one of them, Piet Tommissen, the text was first published in the Flemish nationalist journal *Dietsland-Europa* (1957) and then once more in Tommissen's own periodical, *Schmittiana* (1996).

[84] *Hamlet oder Die lange Nacht nimmt ein Ende* (1956) is the last novel by Alfred Döblin (1878–1956), author of *Berlin Alexanderplatz* (1929), one of the major works of German modernism. A Social Democrat and a Jew, who converted to Catholicism, Döblin escaped the Nazis and returned to occupied Germany in 1945 as a member of the French cultural administration. Neglect of his work and the hostility he experienced—as did many other returned émigrés—induced him to move to Paris in 1951. *Hamlet Europa* is a character in Stefan Andres's (1906–70) play *Tanz durchs Labyrinth. Dramatische Dichtung in fünf Bildern* (1948).

[85] One of the typescript copies of the text in the Düsseldorf archive (RW 265–21087) has a handwritten footnote appended to this paragraph, which gives the same Hamlet-'curve of the West' (1848–1918–1958) as the two letters.

The term 'presentism' denoting a way of 'reading the literature of the past in terms of what most "ringingly chimes" with "the modern world"'[86] did not exist in 1956 but serves to capture the embattled urgency of Schmitt's engagement with Shakespeare, an urgency not lost on his early reviewers. They responded to this urgency, and he in turn seems to have responded to them by moving more determinedly in a 'presentist' direction. This would not be the first time that Schmitt, as it were, became the student of his students,[87] and it would help explain the shifting of his interest from the Jacobean Hamlet to his nineteenth-century and Cold War descendants.

'Was habe ich getan?' opens with Schmitt's declaration that it took the reviews by Walter Warnach and Rüdiger Altmann to make him realize what 'I have actually done' (WH 15). From the defensiveness of his statement—the tone of maligned innocence is vintage post-1945 Schmitt—one would assume the reviews to have been hostile.[88] But in fact they were nothing of the kind. Given that they were both written by card-carrying Schmittians, this is hardly surprising. Warnach leaves the reader in no doubt that he is on Schmitt's side in a very contemporary culture war. Applauding Schmitt for taking the same stand against the 'bad subjectivity' of Romantic occasionalism as in his *Political Romanticism* of 1919, he calls *Hamlet or Hecuba* a 'most impressive example of intellectual continuity'.[89] But Romantic subjectivism which regards the world in general—and Hamlet in particular—as just a 'grandiose occasion for self-reflexion' is only, as it were, one side of a bad coin. The other, more pernicious, is Marxism. Schmitt's reading of *Hamlet*, Warnach writes, defies both the false autonomy of Romantic art and the Marxist subjection of art to the 'hollow sham' of 'economic realities'.

Altmann, too, is duly respectful of the master's 'magnificent' interpretation, and he castigates the usual Schmittian suspects, liberal and leftist, with George Lukács

---

[86] Ewan Fernie, 'Shakespeare and the Prospect of Presentism', *Shakespeare Survey* 58 (2005), 169–84 at 169, quoting Terence Hawkes, *Shakespeare in the Present* (London and New York: Routledge, 2002), 22. Schmitt has also been claimed as a New Historicist *avant la lettre*, but this goes to show that the antithesis between 'Presentism' and New Historicism is more rhetorical than real. The 'history' explored by the New Historicism is shaped by very present, late twentieth-century, concerns and attitudes. Greenblatt's desire 'to speak with the dead' leads, after all, to his realization that 'the dead' are accessible only 'under the terms of our own interests and pleasures and in the light of historical developments that cannot simply be stripped away'. Stephen Greenblatt, *Shakespearean Negotiations: The Circulation of Social Energy in Renaissance England* (Oxford: Oxford University Press, 1988), 20.

[87] Willy Haas, 'Eine neue politische Lehre' (review of Carl Schmitt, *Der Begriff des Politischen*, 2nd edn, 1932), *Die literarische Welt* 21 (20 May 1932), notes sardonically that 'Carl Schmitt has become the disciple of his disciples' (*der Jünger seiner Jünger*).

[88] A particularly blatant instance of Schmitt's self-pity occurs in his letter to his colleague Ernst Forsthoff (1 December 1949). Apropos a critical review of a recently published essay of his he complains: 'Never in the twelve years of Hitler's rule has a Jewish colleague been exposed to such infamous malice.' *Briefwechsel Ernst Forsthoff/Carl Schmitt (1926–1974)*, ed. Dorothee Mußgnug, Reinhard Mußgnug, and Angela Reinthal (Berlin: Akademie-Verlag, 2007), 59. Like Schmitt, Forsthoff had supported the Nazi cause with his legal expertise in the 1930s. But he regained his chair at Heidelberg in 1952 and wrote important commentaries on the Federal Republic's constitution.

[89] Walter Warnach, 'Hamlet-Mythos und Geschichte' (review of Schmitt, *Hamlet or Hecuba*), *Frankfurter Allgemeine Zeitung*, 2 June 1956, 'Literaturblatt'.

being held responsible for a 'Marxist descent into the hell of rationalism'.[90] At the same time Altmann insists that the consideration of what Hamlet meant to an Elizabethan audience should lead on to the more important question of what Hamlet means to us now. 'But if a myth can be begotten and attested to [*gezeugt und bezeugt*], not produced, then it does not only hit the core of a *historical* reality—it must in some way also concern the *present* fate of the European intellectual' (italics original). It is not entirely clear whether Altmann thinks that Schmitt has actually addressed this issue or not, or has addressed it but not rigorously enough. In one place, Altmann seems to be saying that Schmitt's whole point is 'to elevate [Hamlet] to the status of a modern myth, the myth of the intellectual'; in another, that Schmitt only hints in this direction while being more interested in delving into the foundations of modern thought. '[D]oes Don Capisco[91] intend to leave the antagonism of the present aside in order to [...] explore the bedrock of thought [*das Urgestein des Denkens*]?'[92] The word 'intellectual' appears in *Hamlet or Hecuba* only once, near the end, where Schmitt notes that 'all three great symbolic figures' of European literature, Don Quixote, Hamlet, and Faust, 'are oddly enough readers of books and thus intellectuals, so to speak' (52). Still, the final climax of the essay is not devoted to the modern intellectual but to the tragic fate of the Stuarts.

The 'antagonism of the present' (Altmann) takes centre stage in 'What have I done?' and in the *Hamlet* lecture which Schmitt was invited to deliver at Aachen Technical University in January 1957 and for which he chose 'Hamlet as mythical figure of the present' as his topic.[93] He begins by asking 'what image comes to mind when we hear the name Hamlet':

> We see a distinct figure, a prince dressed in black, who is given and takes on a great task and who for thinking and philosophizing cannot get down to action; who suffers from his own nature and the people around him; who behaves towards others with

[90] Rüdiger Altmann, 'Hamlet als mythische Situation', *Civis. Zeitschrift für christlich-demokratische Politik* 18 (June 1956), 39.

[91] Don Capisco was the sobriquet Schmitt was given by Ernst Jünger. It became a password among his devotees.

[92] Another disciple of Schmitt's, the young historian Reinhard Koselleck, had drawn similar front lines as Warnach and Altmann in a brief unpublished review of *Hamlet, Sohn der Maria Stuart* (1952). Jean-Paul Sartre's call for a *littérature engagée*, Koselleck declared, had produced nothing but 'laboured artifice' (*künstlichen Krampf*); a 'four-year-plan for productive literature' would never engender 'the inner bond between historical presence and genuine poetry'. Winstanley, by contrast, showed that truly great literature was rooted in history. She—and, of course, Schmitt—were to be thanked, Koselleck wrote, for 'opening our eyes to the fundamental precondition of all poetry, the historical roots from which any work of art must spring if it is not to be a product of pure ideology'. Reinhard Koselleck, 'Hamlet, Sohn der Maria Stuart', unpublished typescript, 2 pp., RW 265–226, no. 9. Koselleck (1923–2006), a doctoral student whose 1954 dissertation *Kritik und Krise* was strongly influenced by Schmitt, became one of the most influential German historians of the post-war era and the leading theorist of 'conceptual history' (*Begriffsgeschichte*). Cf. his *Practice of Conceptual History: Timing, History, Spacing Concepts*, trans. Todd Presner, Kerstin Behnke, and Jobst Welge (Palo Alto, CA: Stanford University Press, 2002).

[93] The role of the intellectual was a widely debated topic at the time, as is borne out by the international resonance of Raymond Aron, *L'opium des intellectuels* (Paris: Calman-Lévy, 1955); Engl. trans. Terence Kilmartin: *The Opium of the Intellectuals* (New York: Doubleday, 1957). Schmitt knew the book, whose first part is titled 'Political Myths', and consulted it for his lecture.

condescending irony and torments himself with self-reproach in his soliloquies until he is finally overrun by the course of events. In other words: we see what we could call a typical intellectual. What is typical here is the discrepancy between thinking and doing, the immobilization caused by reflection and self-observation, superior intelligence and irony but a failure to act in reality. Thus Shakespeare's Hamlet has become the mythical figure of the European intellectual.[94]

From the typed introduction and the handwritten notes for the rest of the paper, it is clear that the lecture expanded Schmitt's three-stage 'hieroglyph' of the Western world into a history of the Hamlet myth from Voltaire, 'the greatest Church father of the European intelligentsia', to the present. From the philosophers of the French Enlightenment to the Romantics and the German liberals of the *Vormärz* to the turn of the twentieth century and the Dreyfus affair, Schmitt traces the transformations of the role of the intellectual and of Hamlet in a continuous parallel. After the First World War the myth undergoes an identity crisis with Paul Valéry, and there is 'a sharp division between bourgeois and Marxist intellectuals'. Lenin becomes the archetype of the Marxist intellectual as 'the bearer of progress', whereas Hamlet becomes simply 'uninteresting', the slightly ridiculous figure of Brecht's Hamlet sonnet ('Here is the body, puffy and inert').[95] Schmitt draws a predictably gloomy picture of the present state of affairs: 'the intellectual has been made to fit in [*eingepaßt*] [...] the old myth is at an end. The Hamlet myth will no longer do for what is left of the intellectual. Should we then bury Prince Hamlet?'

The lecture notes, partly in longhand, partly in Schmitt's notoriously cryptic shorthand, are not easily decipherable. In conclusion, Schmitt protests that he did not intend to spoil his audience's enjoyment of 'one of the greatest plays of world history'. 'On the contrary', he says, 'I wanted to clear the way for a view unclouded by self-deception.' In the cultural cold war of the 1950s this is a political, not just an aesthetic imperative: 'Perceiving works of art without illusions must not remain the monopoly of dialectical materialism.'

V RESTRAINING HISTORY: THE *KATÉCHON*

Schmitt's Aachen lecture helps us to put his Hamlet-spotting in perspective. Five latter-day Hamlets, including Adlai Stevenson and the British prime minister Anthony Eden, are mentioned to demonstrate the continuing presence of Shakespeare's melancholy prince in the collective imagination. These examples may be trivial, yet even the most blatant trivialization may have a non-trivial

---

[94] Carl Schmitt, 'Hamlet as a mythical figure of the present'. The lecture was held on 21 January 1957. The untitled typescript (RW 265–20311) breaks off into handwritten notes after two pages. In a letter to Ernst Jünger (26 January 1957) Schmitt refers to it as 'Hamlet als mythische Figur der Gegenwart'. *Ernst Jünger/Carl Schmitt: Briefe*, 320. A summary of the argument is given by Mehring, *Carl Schmitt*, 498.

[95] Bertolt Brecht, 'On Shakespeare's Play Hamlet', trans. John Willett, in *Poems, 1913–1956*, ed. John Willett and Ralph Manheim with the cooperation of Erich Fried (London: Eyre Methuen, 1981), 311.

significance. The sobriquet 'Hamlet' applied to a politician, Schmitt says, 'need not be more than a journalistic tag' for indecisiveness:

> But there are also deeper uses of the name, explicable by the fact that, in the age of mass democracy, simplified and reduced symbolic figures are unavoidable ersatz-myths for the millions of viewers, listeners and readers of cinema, radio and the press. The newspapers need them and convert genuine myths into slogans, just as they convert whole primeval forests into newsprint. (HM 2)

The dividing line between genuine and ersatz is a thin one here. The ersatz, so the passage suggests, becomes indispensable for the sustenance and perpetuation of the real thing, just as being convertible to slogan is the best proof of the vitality of the myth thus converted.

Not only does this tally with Schmitt's contention that Shakespeare's art was only properly understood in its popular, even vulgar setting, it also reveals the connection between Schmitt's Hamlet-spotting and another far from trivial pursuit of his. Alongside his search for latter-day Hamlets, Schmitt scanned the modern world for embodiments of the *katéchon*, the holder-up, delayer, or restrainer. This concealed, but all-important figure took on a pivotal role in Schmitt's theology of history starting around 1942.[96] According to a single biblical mention (2 Thessalonians 2:7), the *katéchon* is one who holds up or slows down the Antichrist's seizure of power before the Second Coming. 'The whole Christian aeon', Schmitt explains, 'is not a long march but a single long waiting, a long interim between [...] the appearance of the Lord in the time of the Roman Caesar Augustus and the Lord's return at the end of time.'[97] Within this all-embracing interim 'numerous larger or smaller earthly interims constantly emerge'[98] and for each the question as to the Antichrist and the *katéchon* must be asked and answered anew.[99] 'For each epoch of the last 1948 years', Schmitt noted in December 1947, 'one must be able to name the *katéchon*. His place was never vacant, or we would not exist.'[100] However, as Heinrich Meier points out, from the obligation that we must be able to name the *katéchon* it does not automatically follow that we actually are able to do so. 'Schmitt "knows" that the restrainer exists but he does not know who the restrainer is. [...] From the *Imperium Romanum* down to the Jesuit order, Schmitt can offer a number of quite different candidates.'[101] These include, in the twentieth century, Emperor Franz Joseph of Austro-Hungary, the Czech president Masaryk, and Marshal Pilsudski of Poland.

The analogy to Schmitt's search for Hamlets is more than just an analogy. If the 'Hamlet-curve' can serve as a 'hieroglyph' for the downward trajectory of the entire

---

[96] Schmitt himself dates his 'theory of the *katéchon*' back to 1932: Schmitt, *Glossarium*, 80; but see Heinrich Meier, *The Lesson of Carl Schmitt: Four Chapters on the Distinction between Political Theology and Political Philosophy*, trans. Marcus Brainard (Chicago, IL and London: University of Chicago Press, 1998), 161 n. 106. I follow Meier's exposition of Schmitt's concept of the *katéchon* here.

[97] Carl Schmitt, *Political Theology II: The Myth of the Closure of Any Political Theology*, translated and edited by Michael Hoelzl and Graham Ward (Cambridge and Malden, MA: Polity Press, 2008), 86.

[98] Schmitt, *Political Theology II*, 86.   [99] Meier, *The Lesson of Carl Schmitt*, 163.

[100] Schmitt, *Glossarium*, 63.   [101] Meier, *The Lesson of Carl Schmitt*, 161.

Western world, then it is part and parcel of the larger eschatological scheme of Schmittian history. Both the historical figure 'behind' Shakespeare's dramatic character and that character's later doubles have a role to play in the great Manichean struggle between the forces of the Antichrist pushing the world headlong towards doom and the forces that oppose this push by 'standing in the way', 'withholding', 'restraining' it (2 Thess. 2:7).

Schmitt's portrayal of James I makes 'the unhappy Stuart' a *katéchon*, but a *katéchon manqué* whose insights into what a king should rightly be and do are woefully at odds with what he actually was and did. In holding up a tragic mirror to this royal procrastinator, Shakespeare assumes the part of what we might call a second-order *katéchon*. 'Shakespeare's *Hamlet*', Schmitt writes in his 1952 preface, 'is but an urgent entreaty addressed to James I not to expend the divine right of kings in reflections and discussions' (FW 171, translation modified). Seeking 'access to the power-holder',[102] the author of *Hamlet* is the double of the author of *Hamlet or Hecuba*, who had offered his advice to the ill-fated General von Schleicher, the last chancellor of the Weimar Republic, but to no avail.[103] It is here that the author's personal investment in the Hamlet myth emerges. Shakespeare's tragic hero serves as a 'transparent incognito' (*HH* 37) for Schmitt's own role in Germany's recent past, wishing to 'hold up' but failing. Schmitt's efforts towards saving the presidial system of Weimar in the last throes of the Papen and Schleicher administrations lend some credence to this version of himself. His career after Hitler's seizure of power clearly does not, though some of Schmitt's apologists would insist that even at the height of his pro-Nazi campaigning he was 'trying to prevent worse'—the standard excuse of many active supporters of the regime.

In his own eyes, Schmitt was 'the white raven who is missing from no black list'.[104] His sense that, no matter what he did, he was inevitably in the position of the accused seeps from every sentence of the explanatory statement on *Hamlet or Hecuba* which he delivered in June 1956. Its very title, 'What have I done?', suggests—no doubt deliberately—the situation not of someone explaining what he has tried to do in a piece of literary interpretation but of someone standing trial on much graver charges, the charges faced before a de-Nazification tribunal. Flaunting his outcast image, Schmitt plays up this association by harping on the word unobjectionable (*einwandfrei*)—not unlike Mark Antony harping on 'honourable' in the forum speech (*JC* 3.2):

> So what have I actually done? At first sight, something good or at least unobjection-able. I have written a book about Hamlet. Hamlet is a very popular subject. Tens of thousands of unobjectionable people have written about Hamlet. I thus find myself in unobjectionable company. (WH 15)

---

[102] Access to the power holder (*Zugang zum Machthaber*) is a key notion in Schmitt. Cf. Carl Schmitt, *Gespräch über die Macht und den Zugang zum Machthaber* (Pfullingen: Günther Neske, 1954).

[103] Gabriel Seiberth, *Anwalt des Reiches. Carl Schmitt und der Prozess 'Preußen contra Reich' vor dem Staatsgerichtshof* (Berlin: Duncker & Humblot, 2001).

[104] Schmitt in a letter to Armin Mohler, 6 January 1955. *Carl Schmitt—Briefwechsel mit einem seiner Schüler*, 186.

The defence of a little book about *Hamlet* is staged as a defence of its author in the court of history—a self-styled martyr, a retrospective Cassandra or Walter Benjamin's angel-of-history *manqué*: 'His face is turned toward the past. Where we perceive a chain of events, he sees one single catastrophe which keeps piling wreckage upon wreckage and hurls it in front of his feet.'[105]

Schmitt has been called 'the great unmasker'.[106] The mask of Hamlet enables him to enshroud the moral and political shortcomings of his life with the sombre radiance of tragedy.

---

[105] Walter Benjamin: 'Theses on the Philosophy of History', in *Illuminations*, 253–64 at 257. But if we see the connection between Schmitt and Benjamin we cannot but also see the *Einbruch*, the intrusion of the time that divides the professor of law who, in 1939–40, was regaining lost credit with the regime for his timely new *Großraum* theory of international law, and the refugee who, at about the same time, took his own life despairing of his chances of escaping from the *Großraum* of Hitler's Reich. Schmitt first introduced his concept of *Großraum* (large sphere of influence) at a conference in early April 1939, 'only days after the German invasion of Prague'. See Alexandra Kemmerer, 'Dark Legator: Where the State Transcends its Boundaries, Carl Schmitt Awaits Us', *German Law Journal* 7 (2006), Special Issue: *European Integration in the Shadow of Europe's Darker Pasts: The 'Darker Legacies of Law in Europe' revisited*, 149–54 at 150. Although Schmitt's concept of *Großraum* is to be distinguished from the more *völkisch*-oriented *Lebensraum*, it went well with Nazi expansionism. Writing in the Nazi weekly *Das Reich* (1940, no. 19), Schmitt celebrated the invasion of Poland as a '*Raumrevolution*'.

[106] Müller, *A Dangerous Mind*, 195.

9

Epilogue
Welcome to the Machine. Berlin 1989

I 'HERE'S FINE REVOLUTION'

History defied Schmitt's augury. The 'Hamlet-Curve' took an unexpected turn. It had spelt certain doom for the weak-willed, vacillating West. What broke instead was the impenetrable-seeming fortress of the East. At the time of Schmitt's death at almost 97 in 1985, no one could have foreseen this—except perhaps a few secretive GDR functionaries in charge of shoring up the tottering socialist economy with infusions of borrowed Western capital.

Even as late as the summer of 1989 it would have been difficult to imagine the scene that took place on 4 November of that year. On East Berlin's Alexanderplatz, a space hitherto reserved for the choreographed mass rallies of party and state, a crowd of at least half a million people gathered for the largest demonstration organized 'from below' in GDR history. It originated from a meeting of theatre people from all over the republic which had been held three weeks earlier at the *Deutsches Theater*, where rehearsals for *Hamlet* were underway.[1] Among the two dozen speakers addressing the crowd on Alexanderplatz were both the actor Ulrich Mühe (Figure 9.1), who played Hamlet, and the director of the production, the dramatist Heiner Müller.

Amidst the epochal upheaval of 1989/90, Hamlet once again made his entrance on the political stage, enacting, perhaps for the last time, his symbolic identification with the condition of Germany. Politics and theatre converged in a rare moment of reciprocity. The event on Alexanderplatz had grown out of discussions during the rehearsal process, and that process was driven by what was happening in the streets.[2] The resulting abstract and—by no means brief—chronicle of the

---

[1] A verbatim transcript based on an audio recording of the meeting is available in Hans Rübesame, ed., *Antrag auf Demonstration: Die Protestversammlung im Deutschen Theater am 15. Oktober 1989* (Berlin: Ch. Links, 2010). The meeting resolved to apply for official permission to demonstrate. Permission was granted.

[2] The situation makes for interesting comparison with Bertolt Brecht's rehearsals of *Coriolanus* in the summer of 1953. As Brecht and the Berliner Ensemble were preparing the successful rising of Shakespeare's Roman plebeians for the stage, mass protests against the East German Communist Party were taking place in the streets. The popular uprising of 17 June was violently quelled by Soviet tanks and *Volkspolizei*. Günter Grass made the parallel the subject of his play *The Plebeians Rehearse the Uprising* (*Die Plebejer proben den Aufstand*, 1966). Brecht commented on the uprising in a poem that understandably remained unpublished in the GDR:

> The Solution
> After the uprising of the 17th of June

Figure 9.1. Ulrich Mühe addressing the demonstrators at Alexanderplatz, 4 November 1989. Reproduced by permission of Deutsches Rundfunkarchiv DRA/MDR.

time, Müller's eight-hour production, offered a gigantic post-mortem on both Shakespeare's play and the German Democratic Republic. Rehearsed as the old Communist order was disintegrating, it was presented to the public after that order had ceased to exist. Its title, *Hamlet/Machine*, indicated that the production combined two texts: Shakespeare's *Hamlet* and Müller's *Hamletmachine* (1977), a densely packed nine-page intertextual collage that itself could be described as an obituary for Shakespeare's play.

Stripping the most famous of tragedies 'to [its] skeleton, [...] rid[ding] it of [its] flesh and surface',[3] *Hamletmachine* not only denies the possibility of tragic heroes but discards the very idea of subjective identity, an idea iconically embodied in Hamlet. A score made up of floating, dislocated monologues, it is 'post-' in just about every conceivable respect. Post-dramatic, post-representational, and post-historic, it tolls not only the death of the author, whose (i.e. Müller's) photograph

> The Secretary of the Writers' Union
> Had leaflets distributed in the Stalinallee
> Stating that the people
> Had forfeited the confidence of the government
> And could win it back only
> By redoubled efforts. Would it not be easier
> In that case for the government
> To dissolve the people
> And elect another?

'The Solution' (*Die Lösung*), trans. Derek Bowman, in Brecht, *Poems*, ed. Willett and Manheim, 440.

[3] In an interview Müller spoke of his obsession with *Hamlet*: '[S]o I tried to destroy him by writing a short text, *Hamletmachine*. [...] I think the main impulse is to strip things to their skeleton, to rid them of their flesh and surface. Then you are finished with them.' Heiner Müller, *Rotwelsch* (Berlin: Merve, 1982), 43.

is solemnly torn, but the death of tragedy as well, which can only be a remembrance of things past. What remains of tragedy in this ventriloquizing of the undead is the sheer, irreducible pathos of suffering located in the voice of Ophelia:

> I am Ophelia. The one the river didn't keep. The woman dangling from the rope. The woman with her arteries cut open. The woman with the overdose.[4]

At various points in Müller's eight-hour production, Hamlet utters the first lines of *Hamletmachine*: 'I was Hamlet. I stood at the shore and talked with the surf BLABLA, the ruins of Europe in back of me.'[5] More deeply pessimistic even than Valéry's 1919 Hamlet of Europe, Müller's Hamlet also 'looks upon millions of ghosts',[6] equally aware as his predecessor of the mortality of civilizations.

When rehearsals began on 29 August 1989, 'the country seemed firmly in the grip of an old clan of Stalinist politicians'[7] who were as averse to Gorbachev's pere-stroika as to Western notions of democracy. The show opened on 24 March 1990, just a week after the first free parliamentary elections in the GDR had resulted in a landslide victory for the East-CDU, the East German wing of Chancellor Helmut Kohl's Christian Democrats. 'In the interim', Maik Hamburger writes,

> the country had seen in succession the downfall of the old state leaders, then the downfall of the 'new' state leaders that had replaced them, then of the Government, then of the Communist Party, then of the transitional Government and finally of the Civic Movements that had initiated the whole process. Six months later, Germany was united.[8]

The rush of events could not fail to affect the production. Fundamental readjustments had to be made by director and cast as their work in progress was ripped from its moorings in a calculably stagnant political environment. For example, Müller's *Hamletmachine* was inserted in full between Acts 4 and 5. Twelve years after its publication in the West German journal *Theater heute* (*Theatre Today*) it had never been performed in the GDR. Including this bleakly unoptimistic text in the production was thus something of a challenge. But with so many greater challenges rocking and rapidly breaking up the East German state, what would have been a bold gesture of defiance became just laborious dramaturgy. By the time the show opened, *Hamletmachine* 'had [...] lost its subversive function'.[9] Müller himself admitted that there really was no need for it any more: 'When we planned this,

---

[4] Heiner Müller, *Hamletmachine and Other Texts for the Stage*, trans. and ed. Carl Weber (New York: Performing Arts Publications, 1984), 53–4.

[5] Müller, *Hamletmachine*, 53.

[6] Valéry, 'Letters from France', 184. See Chapter 5.

[7] Maik Hamburger, 'Theatre under Socialism: Shakespeare in East Germany', in Hortmann, *Shakespeare on the German Stage*, vol. 2, 350–434 at 429.

[8] Hamburger, 'Theatre under Socialism', 429. Hamburger's is the most substantial account in English of *Hamlet/Machine*. A dramaturge at Deutsches Theater at the time, he also took an active political part. A protest resolution drawn up by him against the police violence against demonstrators during the fortieth anniversary celebrations of the GDR was adopted by the actors and workers at Deutsches Theater on 15 October and submitted to the authorities.

[9] Martin Linzer, 'Trilogie des Umbruchs', in *Regie: Heiner Müller. Material zu 'Der Lohndrücker' 1988, 'Hamlet/Maschine' 1990, 'Mauser' 1991 am Deutschen Theater*, ed. Martin Linzer and Peter Ulrich (Berlin: Zentrum für Theaterdokumentation und -information, 1993), 9–12 at 11.

Hamletmachine was still a forbidden play in the GDR [but] the nearer we got to the end, the more historical the text became.'[10] If Carl Schmitt's Hamletian 'hieroglyph of the Western world' turned out to be off the mark, the key idea of his *Hamlet* essay proved all the more timely. With *Umbruch* (reversal, upheaval) and *Aufbruch* (new departure, new beginning) on everybody's lips and mind in 1990, *Einbruch*, 'the intrusion of the time into the play', described in shorthand what Müller and his actors were experiencing in the course of their work on *Hamlet/Machine* and what emerged as the production's central idea. In his interview-autobiography *War Without Battle: Life in Two Dictatorships*, Müller cites Schmitt's formula in recounting the experience:

> The rehearsals for *Hamlet/Machine* took place before, during and after the so-called Turning [*die Wende*]. This naturally affected the work. The actors were politically very active, outside the theatre too, and I had no answer to their question: Who is Fortinbras? He could not be the blond light-bringer from the North as in Gründgens's production [...]; nor the herald of socialism as in Mäde's production in Karl-Marx-Stadt. [...] I knew Carl Schmitt's thesis of 'The Intrusion of the Time into the Play' which turns the revenge drama into tragedy. Whereby the time takes on the function of the myth which is the precondition of tragedy. When Shakespeare was writing Hamlet the dynasty of the Tudors was replaced by the dynasty of the Stuarts, Elizabeth by James, the son of Mary Stuart, who was rumoured to have married her husband's murderer. This resulted in what Malraux said about Faulkner's *Sanctuary*: 'the intrusion of ancient tragedy into the crime novel'. Carl Schmitt: when the hesitant James = Hamlet turns into Fortinbras a mystical union of drama, dream and history is achieved. We too were given a boost by the time. Stalin's ghost, who appeared in the first hour, turned into Deutsche Bank in the last hour of the performance.[11]

That Müller, the GDR National Prize laureate,[12] should have known about *Hamlet or Hecuba* long before anyone in the West took notice of it is remarkable in itself. His modification of Schmitt's thesis is equally noteworthy. For it is Müller, not Schmitt, who has 'the hesitant James = Hamlet turn [...] into Fortinbras'. Müller also moves 'the mystical union of drama, dream and history' from one historical watershed to another: from 1603, when according to Schmitt Shakespeare and his aristocratic friends set their hopes on a new king, who signally failed to turn into Fortinbras, to those few giddy weeks in the autumn of 1989 when Müller and his friends set their hopes on a Fortinbras of democratic socialism, who did not

---

[10] Heiner Müller, 'Kopftheater', in *Regie: Heiner Müller*, ed. Linzer and Ulrich, 108–9 at 108.

[11] Heiner Müller, *Krieg ohne Schlacht: Leben in zwei Diktaturen. Eine Autobiographie*, 2nd edn (Cologne: Kiepenheuer & Witsch, 1994), 353. Gründgens acted in but did not direct the famous 1936 *Hamlet* production which Müller refers to (see Chapter 7, section II); he directed a post-war Hamlet in Düsseldorf. For Hans-Dieter Mäde's officially praised 1964 *Hamlet* production in Karl-Marx-Stadt (Chemnitz) see J. Lawrence Guntner and Andrew M. McLean, eds, *Redefining Shakespeare: Literary Theory and Theater Practice in the German Democratic Republic* (Cranbury, NJ: Associated University Presses, 1998) 37.

[12] Müller was awarded the National Prize of the GDR in 1986. The year before, he had been given the Büchner Prize, the highest literary award in West Germany. Müller was elected to the GDR Academy of the Arts in 1984, but not until 1988 was he re-admitted to the GDR Writers' Association. He had been expelled in 1961 when his play *The Resettler Woman* (*Die Umsiedlerin*) was censored after only one performance.

materialize either. Those hopes were buried in the election of 18 March 1990 which overwhelmingly endorsed German reunification. The aim was no longer to reform but to abolish the socialist state. And Müller's Hamlet, who had begun as a dissident in a rotten dictatorship, ended as a casualty of capitalist liberation.

II POST-DRAMATIC SHAKESPEARE

The time, 1989, intruded into the play, but Müller's production reduced the break-neck speed of historical change to slow motion. 'The show begins at four in the afternoon and dies at midnight', wrote Benjamin Henrichs, critic for *Die Zeit*.[13] What happened during those eight long hours brought Shakespeare's tragic action to terminal standstill. A whole country in motion, but the players paralysed, stunned by the impact of history, frozen in melancholy amazement. History was shown not to be happening but to have happened—and with shattering result. A mirror, yes, but more of a counterfoil to the dramatic overturn of the state, Müller's production was an instance of what came to be known as 'postdramatic theatre'.[14]

While history was being made, *Hamlet/Machine* proclaimed the end of history in a monumental spectacle of stagnation. *Posthistoire*, a buzzword of the 1980s, found its consummation in Heiner Müller's 'theatre of heavy heads, drooping eyelids, choked throats, tied tongues, bent shoulders. An authoritarian state in the final, undramatic gasps of its agony.'[15] This was, the *Zeit* reviewer thought, not a production but 'a demonstration': 'It tells us roadside rubberneckers that in the face of death, of the rottenness of the state and the wretchedness of love it would be ludicrous to mount any kind of "theatre".' And he adds acerbically: 'Naturally it is a very good idea not to stage the played-out, emptied-out tragedy of Hamlet for a while. But should one do the non-staging on stage?'

Müller had never had much time for the philosophical optimism of the doctrine of historical materialism. His troubles with the GDR authorities came from his refusal to trumpet the march of history towards its predestined socialist telos. What jeopardized and for years prevented the publication of most of his work in East Germany made it all the more welcome in the West.[16] The very bleakness of his vision of history, forcibly prominent in *Hamletmachine*, matched the mood of the disappointed Left in the aftermath of 1968. It was in this climate that the idea

---

[13] Benjamin Henrichs, 'Acht Stunden sind kein Theater. Keine Inszenierung, eine Demonstration: Heiner Müller, Erich Wonder und Ulrich Mühe zeigen *Hamlet/Maschine*', *Die Zeit*, 30 March 1990, <http://www.zeit.de/1990/14/acht-stunden-sind-kein-theater>, accessed 26 July 2015.

[14] The term was introduced in 1999 by Hans-Thies Lehmann, *Postdramatic Theatre*, trans. and ed. Karen Jürs-Munby (London and New York: Routledge, 2006).

[15] Henrichs, 'Acht Stunden sind kein Theater'.

[16] The East German authorities prevented the première of *Der Bau* (*Construction Site*) in 1965 and censored his *Mauser* in the early 1970s. Among his plays that premièred in the West were *Germania Death in Berlin*, first performed in 1978 at the Munich *Kammerspiele*, and *The Mission*, which Heiner Müller himself directed in Bochum in 1982. The world première of *Hamletmachine* took place in Paris in 1979.

of *posthistoire* took root among those who had set their sights on a cultural and political revolution and seen their hopes crushed and annulled by the unshaken capitalist system. Jean Baudrillard's mesmerizingly fatalistic thought clearly grew from the experience of the failed revolution. His diagnosis of a cultural impasse embraced the whole of contemporary reality, a reality that had liquidated itself through the universal workings of '*simulation*', a post-utopian state of '*hypertélie*'.[17] 'The future', Baudrillard said,

> has arrived already, everything has arrived already [....]. There's no point dreaming or entertaining any utopia of overthrow or revolution. Everything has been overthrown already. [...] Everything has lost its meaning and order. It is no exaggeration when we say that everything has happened already.[18]

With all their manifestations of belatedness and the foundering of utopian hope, Müller's texts align themselves naturally with this scenario. His breakthrough in the West coincided with a pervasively post-utopian mood which found a fertile habitat in the theatre. Images of stagnation, deadness, and decay proliferated on the (West) German stage in the 1980s. With the reheated US–Soviet arms race renewing fears of a nuclear holocaust and acid rain and global warming threatening ecological apocalypse, the belief in technological progress or any progress for that matter was dwindling fast.[19] 'No future' arrived on stage. Posthistoric resignation became *de rigueur*.[20] Shakespeare's action-packed dramas might seem to have an in-built resistance to the *posthistoire* treatment. But it was precisely the resistance that made Shakespeare a favourite patient. Presented as mere reminiscences of active conflict and strife, their violent clashes subsided into numbed indifference beyond conflict or reconciliation. Sicklied o'er with the pale cast of posthistoric fatalism, they lost the name of action.

Hamlet/Machine reflects but also exceeds this trend. It stands out not only for its sheer size but also as a memorial to the actual history that went into its making. The performance opens with Horatio's portentous lines 'A little ere the mightiest Julius fell, / The graves stood tenantless and the sheeted dead / Did squeak and gibber in the Roman streets' (Ham. 1.1.113–15), leading up to a resounding conclusion with 'This bodes some strange eruption to our state' (1.1.68). As the ghost of the dead father moves stealthily about the stage, naked but for a visored helmet and a loincloth, a muted loudspeaker murmurs the original Russian radio obituary for Stalin over Chopin's Funeral March. Claudius and his court are also on stage at this point, mute and immobile like switched-off robots. Throughout the production Müller tends to group his actors in statuesque symmetrical arrangements. Slow, stylized movements and monotonously emphatic, deliberately de-psychologized diction prevail.

---

[17] Jean Baudrillard, *Simulacra and Simulation* (1981), trans. Sheila Faria Glaser (Ann Arbor, MI: University of Michigan Press, 1994).

[18] Jean Baudrillard in *Tod der Moderne. Eine Diskussion* (Tübingen: Konkursbuchverlag, 1983), 103.

[19] These threats also generated a renewal of grassroots political activism in the peace and anti-nuclear power movements from which the Green Party emerged.

[20] See my 'A Theater of Exhaustion? "Posthistoire" in Recent German Shakespeare Productions', *Shakespeare Quarterly* 43 (1992), 80–6; also Moninger, *Shakespeare inszeniert*, 210–15.

After the 'prologue' of 1.1, the robots awaken and Claudius delivers his speech. A king who frequently prefers to play the fool, he suggests that all behaviour is just arbitrary role-playing. When Hamlet speaks for the first time, we hear the words that are usually his last: 'I die, Horatio. The rest is silence.' How the play ends is a foregone conclusion; it has, in fact, ended already. The inmates imprisoned in the gloom of the Danish court are humanoids; the actors, speaking automatons, 'hostages to a ritual they do not comprehend'.[21] The eight hours of performance time are not used in the interest of characterization. With relentless insistence the production makes the point that there can be no 'character', no real people where there is no action. With true Hegelian logic, Müller concludes that humanity must dissolve when history comes to a standstill.

In the light of the events outside the theatre, the posthistoric scenario acquires a glaring relevance. Power is crumbling, the rulers are consumed by their own plots. 'There is something rotten in the state', Hamlet says, pauses, and then adds with a sarcastic shrug: 'of Denmark.' TV monitors remind the audience that, like Hamlet's Denmark, East Germany was a state where no one was safe from vigilant eyes and ears. Erich Wonder's stage—the last and also the most expensive set in GDR theatre history—depicted this rotting nightmare world as a vast decaying bunker. With Müller's direction never allowing the cast to stray from his slow, ritualistic choreography, Wonder's monumental design develops a life of its own. In Act 3 the bunker opens up into the manneristic *trompe l'oeil* perspective of Tintoretto's 'Translation of the Body of St. Mark' (1562–6) spanning the whole height and width of the cyclorama, while the downstage area changes into a huge subway tunnel. Impressive as it is, the scenography tends to smother the play under the weight of its overwhelming splendour.

Time is much on Müller's mind, and no doubt on the spectators' too as they experience its slow passage. Meditations on the subject by St Augustine, John Donne, and Stephen Hawking can be studied in the programme during the intervals. Time is also an overarching theme in Wonder's stage design, which enmeshes the archive of human history with the larger time scheme of the natural history of the earth.[22] The cold interior of the bunker suggests a political 'ice age' in which the death of Stalin has initiated a melting process. Water keeps dripping onto the stage, the puddles spreading as the show proceeds. During the first act a milkily transparent curtain seals off the whole stage, the actors seeming enclosed in a block of ice (Figure 9.2). The lighting is confined to cold shades of grey, blue, and green. After Hamlet's departure for England a climate change occurs. The ice has melted. The stage, now covered in sand, turns into a red desert, floodlit with ever more glaring yellows and whites. The earth is nearing its final stage: heat death, terminal entropy.

'The time is out of joint', Müller's leitmotif, fixes *Hamlet/Machine* to the present moment in which the production is a play within the play inserted into the reality

[21] Matthias Matussek, 'Requiem für einen Staat', *Der Spiegel*, 26 March 1990, 290.
[22] For a perceptive reading of the production's stage design: Katharina Keim, *Theatralität in den späten Dramen Heiner Müllers* (Tübingen: Niemeyer, 1998), 241–5.

Figure 9.2. Ulrich Mühe as Hamlet. Photo: Wolfhard Theile. Reproduced by permission of DRAMA. Agentur für Theaterfotografie.

drama of history unravelling outside the theatre. This drama, in turn, is set within the even larger frame of cosmological process: from archaic beginnings to the very end of earth time. One might think that this extreme widening of the time frame would divert from the present. But it does not. On the contrary, it puts the present more sharply into focus. The vaster the temporal extension, the more acute the sense of the uniqueness of the present moment, the fragile intensity of a Now blocked in by huge stretches of past and future. '[T]he interim's mine' (*Ham.* 5.2.67.6), says Hamlet when his last scene has already begun. Hamlet's pathos lies in the brevity of the interim that is his, or rather the illusion that there *is* such an interim.

III HERO OF THE INTERIM

Ulrich Mühe's Hamlet is the hero of the interim. His performance breaks the paralysis of *Hamlet/Machine* and interrupts its monumental stagnancy while, by his very resistance to it, making it even more oppressively felt. Amidst the ruins of history he is mercurially, tragically alive. In itself an intrusion, his performance is the seismograph of the intrusion of the time, the tremors of change just beyond the black box of the stage. Benjamin Henrichs, otherwise so critical of the production, captures the impact of Mühe's performance:

> Then at last Hamlet is there, the actor Ulrich Mühe. He quietly shuts his book and King Claudius (Jörg Gudzuhn), as if scared to death, puts his hand over his heart. This

is, almost nothing having happened so far, a tremendously dramatic moment. Hamlet is there. With him there, everything will be different.

Ulrich Mühe's Hamlet is a rather small, fragile man; inordinately clever and bitter beyond measure. He speaks his sentences even more slowly, more haltingly than the others—but he also sets lucid black against their mouse-grey gloom. Every word a verdict, final. If the others move like robots just overcome by depression, Hamlet seems a sleepwalker. Graceful and yet numb with horror and disgust.

If Heiner Müller's *Hamlet* were a production [rather than a 'demonstration'], Ulrich Mühe's Hamlet would be the Hamlet of our time. Darkly he shines over the pale decay around him. His loneliness seems unbounded, indescribable—the forlornness of the thinking man in a dully dozing world.[23]

Mühe's Hamlet not just 'would be' but indeed *was* the German Hamlet of 'our time'. Just as Müller's end-of-the-world version of the play proved the definitive *Hamlet* production of its time—despite, or perhaps precisely because of, its longueurs. In search of a play that was suitably topical, Müller explained, 'we found there was practically nothing but *Hamlet*. A rift between two epochs…from state crisis to state crisis, a young man in between, an intellectual' (08:20).[24] When the show premièred after six months of rehearsals, the rift had closed up again. The die was cast, the interim was over. But while it lasted there had seemed to be a chance for Hamlet 'to set it right'. As the time intruded into the play, it even seemed possible that the play might intrude into the time. *Hamlet*, said Ulrich Mühe,

> is a play that can contain a whole world. And so it is great to do such a play at such a time. And […] from September to the beginning of November we seemed to ourselves so terribly important with this play and this project that we knew, or hoped, that we could thrust into the time with this play, and that what had upset, driven us to despair and frustrated us for all these years…well, that we could put a huge boulder into this landscape against which those who for years had forced these conditions on us could bash their heads. (16:30)

But there were also days, Mühe recalls, when rehearsals seemed to lead nowhere, when the shouting in the streets became 'so loud that the theatre had to fall silent' (30:40), days when it seemed schizophrenic to concern oneself 'with a man who had problems three hundred years ago while people were running past in the streets who had different—or similar—problems' (31:17). Occasionally it seemed best 'to abandon the whole thing' because 'one had to accept that making theatre was a privilege and that in times like these privileges disappear.' Sometimes it seemed 'ludicrous' and simply 'absurd' to occupy oneself with 'the beautiful thoughts which *Hamlet* contains' (32:00). (Figure 9.3)

---

[23] Henrichs, 'Acht Stunden sind kein Theater'.

[24] This and most of the quotations that follow are taken from interviews recorded in Christoph Rüter's hauntingly intense TV documentary on the making of *Hamlet/Machine* in the context of the events of 1989/90, first broadcast by Westdeutscher Rundfunk WDR on 20 August 1991: Christoph Rüter, *Die Zeit ist aus den Fugen. Ein Film über die Arbeit von Heiner Müller an HAMLET/MASCHINE am Deutschen Theater Berlin in der Zeit vom 29. August 1989 bis zum 24. März 1990 mit Ulrich Mühe als Hamlet*, 100 minutes, DVD with accompanying booklet, filmedition suhrkamp (Frankfurt: Suhrkamp, 2009), time-code in brackets.

Figure 9.3. Heiner Müller and Ulrich Mühe during rehearsals. Photo: Wolfhard Theile. Reproduced by permission of DRAMA. Agentur für Theaterfotografie.

On 4 November the actor Ulrich Mühe traded the rehearsal room for a make-shift stage on the back of a lorry. The speech he delivered to the gathering in the huge open-air auditorium on Alexanderplatz was not from *Hamlet* but from the constitution of the GDR. 'We are demonstrating here', he began, 'for what it says in the following paragraphs of the constitution': paragraph 27 guaranteeing freedom of speech and paragraph 28 guaranteeing the right of free assembly. The laws restricting these rights should be struck from the books. Mühe ended by proposing to change the first article of the constitution: 'We hold', he said, 'that the leadership claim of one party must not be decreed by law. Such a claim must be earned.' The applause was huge.[25]

Heiner Müller, who spoke much later during the Alexanderplatz rally, met with less enthusiasm. He had intended to read something from Brecht, but when two young workers who had not been given speaking time asked him to read their plea for independent trade unions, he consented to do so. Nervous with stage fright, he rushed to the microphone before the moderator had time to introduce him. So 'most people did not know who was speaking. They took me for something really dubious, a mafioso from some trade union basement.'[26] The text sharply attacked the official GDR trade union, the Free German Union Association (FDGB), and correctly predicted economic hardships to come. But 'on that day,

---

[25] Mühe shared the platform with his colleague, the actress Johanna Schall. Live TV coverage of the Alexanderplatz addresses is available on YouTube.

[26] Heiner Müller quoted in Rübesame, *Antrag auf Demonstration*, 24.

no one wanted to hear warnings about the collapse of the factories and the threat of unemployment.'[27] There were hisses and catcalls, with people shouting 'demagogue' and 'stop, stop'. Only with his exit line did he redeem himself somewhat. It was typical Müller: 'If the government decides to abdicate next week, it will be permissible to dance at demonstrations.'

The government did not abdicate. Something much more momentous happened. On 9 November, Günter Schabowski, a member of the central committee of the Socialist Unity Party (SED), who had also spoken on Alexanderplatz (and been deafeningly booed), read the government's bulletin at the daily press conference for international journalists. The bulletin was routinely dull. But a passage on the suspension of travel restrictions caught the reader as much by surprise as it did his listeners. Asked when this would go into effect, Schabowski stumblingly uttered: As of now. That same night, thousands of jubilant East Berliners streamed through the opened checkpoints of the no longer impenetrable Wall.

The interim was over. The fourth of November, Ulrich Mühe said, was the happiest day in his 36-year history as a citizen of the GDR. But the happiness of that day was eclipsed by the happiness of 3 October 1990, the date of reunification, which several of the speakers at the official festivities celebrated as 'the happiest day of the Germans'.[28] The demonstration on Alexanderplatz was a landmark event in the peaceful revolution that ended the division of Germany. But the end the theatre people had hoped for was quite a different one: not reunification but democratic reform of the socialist state: a third way between the Scylla and Charybdis marked out in Müller's *Hamlet* question: 'Who is the ghost? On the one hand, it is Stalin, on the other, it is Deutsche Bank: the spectre of Communism—the phantom of the antisocial market economy.'[29] What happened on 9 November, Mühe felt, was 'comparable to the last scene of *Hamlet* when, more or less by accident, the catastrophe is triggered'.[30]

The peaceful revolution of 1989 was a triumphant success—or it was a revolution that failed, its promise unfulfilled. There are two opposing versions of the story and any number of variations on both. Müller's view was unequivocal: 'The road now taken by the majority leads from one servitude to the next.' And, quoting Ernst Jünger: 'There is a degree of oppression that is perceived as freedom', he added: 'This is western freedom.' In the downward spiral of Müller's 'Hamlet-Curve', the end-point is just as fatally clear as it is in Schmitt's, though in Müller's version doom engulfs not the West but the socialist world. Or indeed the whole world after Hamlet has turned into Fortinbras, the no-man with the briefcase and the gold-painted no-face who steps primly from the carnage at the end of *Hamlet/Machine*.

[27] Rübesame, *Antrag auf Demonstration*, 25.
[28] Sabine Bergmann-Pohl, the last president of the GDR People's Chamber, 3 October 1990. Walter Momper, the mayor of West Berlin, said after the fall of the Wall on 9 November 1989: 'Tonight the German people are the happiest people in the world.'
[29] Müller in Rüter, *Die Zeit ist aus den Fugen*, 08:48.
[30] Mühe in Rüter, *Die Zeit ist aus den Fugen*, 1:20:13.

Hamlet's dying voice proves right every time. The people of the GDR voted for this capitalist Fortinbras, first 'with their feet' by leaving their sinking socialist state for the promised land of the D-Mark, then in the elections of 18 March 1990 by massively endorsing the Christian Democrats, the party that had set the course for the GDR's incorporation into that promised land. Müller's response was 'We are one stupid people', the variation of 'We are one people' which he saw written on a wall and liked best.[31] Less flippantly, he recorded his sense of being uprooted in the poem 'Television 3: Self-Criticism':

> My editors are rummaging in old texts
> Sometimes I shiver when I read them THIS
> I wrote IN POSSESSION OF THE TRUTH
> Sixty years before my likely death
> On the screen I watch my countrymen
> Voting with their hands and feet against the truth
> That was my possession forty years ago.
> What grave will now protect me from my youth?[32]

IV THE TRIUMPH OF FORTINBRAS

Hamlet cannot change history. He perishes in the rift. When he finally takes up arms against the rotten state, it is too late and he ends buried under the ruins. What remains is a figure of unfulfilled potential, one who did not actually do great things, but might have:

> For he was likely, had he been put on,
> To have proved most royally. (*Ham.* 5.2.3375–6)

On the evening of election day, 18 March 1990, an hour before the polls closed, the actor Ulrich Mühe conducted an interview with Hans Modrow.[33] The former first party secretary of Dresden, Modrow was currently a leader of the Party of Democratic Socialism (PDS), the successor to the former SED and acting head of the GDR government. He was regarded as one of the few members of the former politburo who might have implemented the reforms demanded on Alexanderplatz.[34]

The interview was staged as a conversation between two Hamlets. Even before the first results were in, it was clear that Modrow would be the loser. Mühe's questions cast him as the tragic hero of the 'Turning'. Mühe began by presenting

---

[31] Quoted in Helmut Schödel, 'Wir sind ein blödes Volk. Ein Heiner-Müller-Tagebuch zur Frankfurter Experimenta 6', *Die Zeit*, 8 June 1990, <http://www.zeit.de/1990/24/wir-sind-ein-bloedes-volk>, accessed 14 August 2015.

[32] Heiner Müller, *Gedichte* (Berlin: Alexander-Verlag, 1992), 94–5; English translation (modified) taken from Ann Stamp Miller, *The Cultural Politics of the German Democratic Republic: The Voices of Wolf Biermann, Christa Wolf, and Heiner Müller* (Boca Raton, FL: Universal Publishers, 1999), 148.

[33] The interview was arranged and filmed by Christoph Rüter. It is in his *Die Zeit ist aus den Fugen*, 1:14:05–1:21:54.

[34] Subsequent inquiry into Modrow's role during the 'Turning' produced a more ambivalent picture.

Modrow with a gift from Heiner Müller, a book with the author's dedication '[t]o Hans Modrow with admiration for [...] his integrity in the quagmire of corruption, old and new'. Had Modrow hesitated too long? Mühe asks. Does he feel that he should have acted three to five years sooner towards 'breaking up the [old] political structure'? A legitimate question, Modrow concedes, 'I should have been more resolute.' As things had turned out, he says, he now stood 'in between', 'as Heiner Müller writes in his kind of dialectic'. The question with Hamlet, Mühe continues, is whether 'one says he was simply incapable of accomplishing anything at all in this kingdom or—that is, it is in his personality or it is in the political circumstances somehow which would never have allowed him to do anything. And this Hamlet says of himself that he suffers from weakness and melancholy. If you just look at your biography up until October, would you say that you might be something like a Hamlet-figure?'

In the end Modrow polled a respectable 16 per cent, much better than the citizens' movement which had started the process that made free elections possible in the first place.

'The time of art', says Heiner Müller, 'is a different time from that of politics. They touch only sometimes, and if you are lucky, there will be sparks' (47:05). *Hamlet/Machine* was sparked by such a rare conjunction. At first, its critique of the faltering regime shared in the popular movement for political change. Then, for one brief moment on Alexanderplatz, the theatre was not just in step with but actually at the head of this movement. But when the masses turned to the West, the theatre was left stranded, thrown back on itself, suddenly no longer needed. One moment at the leading edge; the next, hopelessly belated. Back in the confines of its insularity, the theatre found itself in the quintessential Hamlet situation: railing against fate, unable to change it.

Horatio (Jörg Michael Koerbl) is Müller's representative on stage in *Hamlet/Machine*. Bespectacled and dressed in a shabby overcoat, he is a melancholy, stoic observer. His part is extended in Christoph Rüter's documentary on *Hamlet/Machine* where he recounts the collision of art and politics with wistful irony:

> So I was Horatio. There is more Roman in me than Dane. In Denmark another revolution has just failed. The Danes just don't cut it. Luckily we began rehearsing before the failed revolution so everything could be paid for. [...] *Hamlet/Machine* will take eight hours. As always, but this time especially, Heiner Müller will try to take the theatre off its hinges. Naturally he won't succeed. But it will look as if he did. At the moment we are all somewhat shaken because something that began rather well has ended. Now we have a Fortinbras with a pear-shaped head.[35] We still have to get used to this. He is not the shining hero who was expected. [...] (*A woman screams offscreen.*) I just heard Ophelia scream. I have to go back and go on again for a moment. Because I have a letter for Hamlet from England. I know its content naturally but theatre is when you still walk across the stage and read it out loud.[36]

---

[35] At this point in his chancellorship, Helmut Kohl was frequently caricatured as pear-shaped, even acquiring Pear (*Birne*) as a less than respectful nickname.
[36] This and his other comments were supplied by Jörg-Michael Koerbl, who is also a writer. The director, Christoph Rüter, suggested themes which Koerbl improvised on. (My thanks to Christoph

Rüter's film also shows Heiner Müller watching the news on the evening of 18 March 1990. When the election results are announced, he comments with a quotation from Marx: 'The Germans always experience freedom only on the day of its funeral.' Unlike most East Germans, Müller had been able to travel to the West since the 1970s. But this did not make him any more sympathetic to the new unified Germany. Somewhat like Schmitt in the post-war years, he nursed a sense of exile in this changed environment. Unlike Schmitt, he was showered with public honours and media attention. The last president of the East Berlin Academy of the Arts (1990–3) and a director of the Berliner Ensemble (1992–5), he was awarded the Kleist Prize in 1990 and the European Theatre Award in 1991. He was constantly in the public eye, wanted on every panel, and a tireless public reader from his own work and the works of others.[37] But the new political environment was not conducive to his work: he knew, he said, how to deal with dictatorships but was inept when it came to democracy and that, along with the burden of other commitments, stalled his production. The interview became his characteristic form of expression during his final years. In 1994, two years before his death from cancer, the past caught up with him and revelations of contacts with the GDR state security service, the Stasi, caused a scandal. The extent of his collaboration was probably exaggerated and it seems certain that Müller never wrote reports for the Stasi or harmed anyone, but the scandal overshadowed the final two years of his life.[38]

Müller's Hamlet, Ulrich Mühe, continued his career with great success in united Germany. Popular on television, he gave his most memorable performances in films like *Lives of Others*, the 2007 winner of the Oscar for best foreign film, where he played a Stasi officer who defects to the side of his victims. Mühe also discovered that the past was not over. In the media coverage of *Lives of Others* he unwisely mentioned that his ex-wife, GDR actress Jenny Gröllmann, had been an 'unofficial employee' of the Stasi and might well have informed on him. Gröllmann, suffering from terminal cancer, denied the allegation. A bitter legal struggle ensued, and former East German colleagues accused him of having slandered his dying ex-wife in order to hype his film. As in Müller's case, the evidence is ultimately inconclusive, with Stasi files often mingling fact with fiction.[39]

The two cases spotlight a grey area of moral compromise, a fuzzy divide between resistance and conformity that runs deep in Müller's work. It is both the object of his critique and a source of his inspiration, the political habitat in which his creativity thrived. What repelled him about people in the West and induced him to

Rüter for this information.) Among Koerbl's writings for the stage is *Gorbatschow/Fragment* (1988) which anticipates the end of the USSR. It premièred at the Volksbühne in East Berlin on 19 January 1990 under Koerbl's direction while *Hamlet/Machine* was in rehearsals.

[37] Jan-Christoph Hauschild, *Heiner Müller oder Das Prinzip Zweifel. Eine Biographie* (Berlin: Aufbau, 2001), 458–9.

[38] Hauschild, *Heiner Müller*, 476–83. The second edition of Müller's interview-autobiography *Krieg ohne Schlacht* (1994) contains an appendix with the relevant Stasi documents in facsimile, 427–69.·

[39] Mühe died a year later at only fifty-four, also of cancer. The actor is portrayed in a documentary by Christoph Rüter, *Jetzt bin ich allein. Der Schauspieler Ulrich Mühe*, 60 min., Germany 2008.

remain in the GDR, he told an interviewer in February 1989, was their innocence. 'They are all innocent and I don't like innocent people. It is almost nauseating to me, this innocence. They are not guilty of anything and never have been [...] and, subjectively, they really are innocent. That I am not.'[40] There is a blindness in such innocence, Müller seems to say, and if there was one thing which life in the GDR protected one from it was this blindness.

One of the strongest moments in *Hamlet/Machine* occurs in the scene when Claudius attempts to pray. Claudius is not kneeling in prayer but sitting on a low step, weighing the pros and cons of his case. Hamlet, instead of hovering over the king, threatening and unseen, keeps him company, attentively listening and even nodding his understanding once or twice. Then Claudius taps his knee invitingly and Hamlet sits down, letting himself be gently rocked like an infant, wide-eyed and smiling, immured from the world as Claudius speaks on. Nothing could convey better the specific nature of the rottenness of the state that is carried to its grave in this production: a prison, certainly, but one that offers protection too, a corrupt, clingy kind of comfort, *Gemütlichkeit* of sorts.

The intellectual is repressed but pampered, the artist stifled but snugly in the embrace of power. Müller's end-of-the-world vision is most clear-sighted when it probes into the musty greys of the old corruption which new corruption will blow away and replace. And Hamlet turns into the Fortinbras of the new world order.

V SPECTRES

If Müller's Fortinbras carries a book in his briefcase, it must be Francis Fukuyama's *The End of History*, the affirmative counter-version of *posthistoire*. 'What we may be witnessing', Fukuyama wrote in 1989, 'is not just the end of the Cold War [...] but the end of history as such: that is, the end point of mankind's ideological development and the universalization of Western liberal democracy as the final form of human government.'[41] Müller would agree with the finality, but reverse the judgement. In his view, too, capitalism had scored a victory that was lasting if not final. But for Müller this was no cause for rejoicing. He commented with a quotation from Brecht: 'From now on for a long time there will be no victors in this world, only vanquished.' In Fukuyama's *End of History* the victory of liberal democracy and the capitalist economy is a triumph for humanity. And this triumph is irreversible. To critics' objection that the end of the Cold War had not reduced but actually increased violent conflict in the world, he replied that they had missed the point. '[W]hat I suggested had come to an end was not the occurrence of events, even large and grave events, but History: that is, history understood as a single, coherent, evolutionary process [...].'[42]

---

[40] The interview is included in a TV documentary by Jürgen Miermeister, *Gesichter hinter Masken: Heiner Müller*, 36 min., Germany, ZDF/3Sat, 1996.

[41] Francis Fukuyama, 'The End of History?', *The National Interest* (Summer 1989), 3–18 at 3.

[42] Francis Fukuyama, *The End of History and the Last Man* (New York: Free Press, 1992), xii.

The end of the Cold War, like the First World War that was thought to be 'the war to end all wars', did not prevent sequels. The quarter century since its first publication has forced Fukuyama to adapt and qualify his hypothesis. Almost like the Elizabethan martyrologist John Foxe, who after 1564 had to postpone the Second Coming in every new edition of his *Acts and Monuments*, Fukuyama has had to bring the end that has already happened up to date against a spring tide of new developments which proclaim that it has nowhere near yet come.[43]

A counterblast to Fukuyama was delivered by Jacques Derrida, whose grim view of the contemporary world is close to Heiner Müller's:

> For it must be cried out, at a time when some have the audacity to neo-evangelize in the name of the ideal of a liberal democracy that has finally realized itself as the ideal of human history: never have violence, inequality, exclusion, famine, and thus economic oppression affected as many human beings in the history of the earth and of humanity. Instead of singing the advent of the ideal of liberal democracy and of the capitalist market in the euphoria of the end of history, instead of celebrating the 'end of ideologies' and the end of the great emancipatory discourses, let us never neglect this obvious macroscopic fact, made up of innumerable singular sites of suffering: no degree of progress allows one to ignore that never before, in absolute figures, have so many men, women and children been subjugated, starved or exterminated on the earth.[44]

Derrida's *Specters of Marx*, from which this quotation is taken, deploys *Hamlet* to turn the alleged end of history into perpetual imminence.[45] Rather than being over, history continues into a future that will arrive from the past. The perfect image of this forward return is the spectre: the spectre at the beginning of Marx's *Communist Manifesto* ('A spectre is haunting Europe—the spectre of Communism') which Derrida complects with the spectre at the beginning of *Hamlet* whose imminence is announced with 'Who's there?' (*Ham.* 1.1.1):

> [E]verything begins by the apparition of a specter. More precisely by the *waiting* for this apparition. The anticipation is at once impatient, anxious, and fascinated: this, the thing ('this thing') will end up coming. The *revenant* is going to come. It won't be long. But how long it is taking.[46]

The Shakespeare-haunted culture of Derrida's political agenda, grounded in his ethics of radical openness to the other, clearly aligns itself with what he calls, in the passage just quoted, 'the great emancipatory discourses'. It is thus diametrically opposed to the rightist intellectual tradition which has been our subject here. Yet

---

[43] See Francis Fukuyama, 'At the "End of History" Still Stands Democracy', *The Wall Street Journal*, 6 June 2014.

[44] Jacques Derrida, *Specters of Marx: The State of the Debt, the Work of Mourning and the New International* (1993), trans. Peggy Kamuf (New York and London: Routledge Classics, 2006), 106.

[45] *Specters of Marx* has attracted many Shakespeare critics. See particularly Richard Wilson, 'When the Cock Crows: The Imminence of *Hamlet*', in his *Shakespeare in French Theory: King of Shadows* (London and New York: Routledge, 2007), 227–41, and Ewan Fernie, 'The Last Act: Presentism, Spirituality and the Politics of *Hamlet*', in *Spiritual Shakespeares*, ed. Ewan Fernie (London and New York: Routledge, 2005), 186–211.

[46] Derrida, *Specters of Marx*, 2.

the 'hauntology' developed in *Specters of Marx*, Derrida's attempt to carve out a future for the future by raising spectres from the past, is not so removed from much that has been discussed here. The dream of a future which lies in the past, most keenly pursued by George and his circle, is a persistent spectre of the political imagination. And Shakespeare's Hamlet is a revenant forever waiting to meet us at the next turning, both a figure in and an emblem of that dream.

With Müller's Hamlet it looks as if we have come full circle. Blackly sulking at the feast of German reunification, he ends up in much the same position where we found him at the start of this inquiry when the triumphant unification of 1871 proved 'once for all' that Germany was not Hamlet. Ousted from the new order, he lingered on, a voice from the shadows, 'this fellow in the cellarage' (*Ham.* 1.5.153): dead and buried, yet still 'here and everywhere' ('*hic et ubique*', 1.5.159). Will another collision of the time of art with the time of politics cast him back onto the stage?

History never stops ending. Hamlet never stops starting.

Bibliography

Abrams, M. H. *The Mirror and the Lamp: Romantic Theory and the Critical Tradition* (New York: Oxford University Press, 1953).

Adorno, Theodor W. *Notes on Literature*, 2 vols, trans. Shierry Weber Nicholsen (New York: Columbia University Press, 1991–2).

Adorno, Theodor W. *Minima Moralia: Reflections from Damaged Life*, trans. Edmund Jephcott (London and New York: Verso, 2010).

Alekseev, Mikhail P., ed. *Shekspir i russkaya kultura* (Leningrad: Nauka, 1965).

Allen, Julie. 'Tea with Goebbels and Hitler: Asta Nielsen in Nazi Germany'. *Journal of Scandinavian Cinema* 2.3 (2012), 333–41.

Altmann, Rüdiger. 'Hamlet als mythische Situation'. *Civis. Zeitschrift für christlich-demokratische Politik* 18 (1956), 39.

Ammon, Frieder von. *Ungastliche Gaben: Die 'Xenien' Goethes und Schillers und ihre literarische Rezeption von 1796 bis in die Gegenwart* (Tübingen: Niemeyer, 2005).

Andermann, W. Th. (= Werner Thomas). *Bis der Vorhang fiel* (Dortmund: Schwalvenberg, 1947).

Ankum, Katharina von, ed. *Women in the Metropolis: Gender and Modernity in Weimar Culture* (Berkeley, Los Angeles, and London: University of California Press, 1997).

Anon. 'Shakespeare 1940'. *Wille und Macht*, 1 February 1940, 1.

Anon. 'Hamlet war Jakob'. *Der Spiegel*, 5 November 1952, 26–7.

Anon. 'Die Mutter ist tabu'. *Der Spiegel*, 29 August 1956, 41–2.

Anon. 'Rothes Irrungen'. *Der Spiegel*, 26 October 1960, 84–5.

Ansell-Pearson, Keith. 'Introduction: On Nietzsche's Critique of Morality'. In Friedrich Nietzsche, *On the Genealogy of Morality*, revised edn, trans. Carol Diethe, ed. Keith Ansell-Pearson (Cambridge and New York: Cambridge University Press, 2006), xiii–xxix.

Appel, Frederick. *Nietzsche Contra Democracy* (Ithaca, NY and London: Cornell University Press, 1999).

Arendt, Hannah. *Men in Dark Times* (New York: Harcourt, Brace & World, 1968).

Aron, Raymond. *The Opium of the Intellectuals* (1955), trans. Terence Kilmartin (New York: Doubleday, 1957).

Aschheim, Steven E. *The Nietzsche Legacy in Germany, 1890–1990* (Berkeley and Los Angeles: University of California Press, 1992).

Aspetsberger, Friedbert. *Arnolt Bronnen. Biographie* (Vienna, Cologne, and Weimar: Böhlau, 1995).

Auden, W. H. 'Musée des Beaux Arts'. In *Another Time* (London: Faber and Faber, 1940), 34.

Backhaus, Wilhelm. 'Bretter, die die Welt nicht mehr bedeuten?' *Der Theater-Almanach 1946/47* (Munich: Kurt Desch, 1946), 168–81.

Baehr, Peter, and Melvin Richter, eds. *Dictatorship in History and Theory: Bonapartism, Caesarism, and Totalitarianism* (Cambridge and New York: Cambridge University Press, 2004).

Balakrishnan, Gopal. *The Enemy: An Intellectual Portrait of Carl Schmitt* (London: Verso, 2000).

Balke, Friedrich. 'Die Figur des Fremden bei Carl Schmitt und Georg Simmel'. *Sociologia Internationalis* 1 (1992), 35–59.

Barnett, David. 'Joseph Goebbels: Expressionist Dramatist as Nazi Minister of Culture'. *New Theatre Quarterly* 17.2 (2001), 161–9.

Bates, Jennifer Ann, and Richard Wilson, eds. *Shakespeare and Continental Philosophy* (Edinburgh: Edinburgh University Press, 2014).

Baudelaire, Charles. *The Flowers of Evil* (1857–68), trans. William Aggeler (Fresno, CA: Academy Library Guild, 1954).

Baudelaire, Charles. 'Les phares'. In *Les fleurs du mal*, ed. Jacques Dupont (Paris: Flammarion, 2012).

Baudrillard, Jean. *Tod der Moderne. Eine Diskussion* (Tübingen: Konkursbuchverlag, 1983).

Baudrillard, Jean. *Simulacra and Simulation* (1981), trans. Sheila Faria Glaser (Ann Arbor, MI: University of Michigan Press, 1994).

Becker, Howard Paul. *German Youth: Bound or Free* (New York: Oxford University Press, 1964; reprinted London: Routledge, 1998).

Beebee, Thomas O. 'Carl Schmitt's Myth of Benito Cereno'. *Seminar: A Journal of Germanic Studies* 42.2 (2006), 114–34.

Behrens, Franz Richard. *Blutblüte* (Berlin: Verlag Der Sturm, 1917).

Behrens, Franz Richard. *Werkausgabe*, vol. 1: *Blutblüte. Die gesammelten Gedichte*, 2nd edn, ed. Gerhard Rühm (Munich: edition text+kritik, 1995).

Behrens, Franz Richard. *Werkausgabe*, vol. 4: *Mein bester Freund—Hamlet. Drehbücher, Kinotexte, Filmkritiken*, ed. Gerhard Rühm and Monika Lichtenfels (Munich: edition text+kritik, 2012).

Belsey, Catherine. *A Future for Criticism* (Chichester: Wiley-Blackwell, 2011).

Benders, Raymond J., and Stephan Oettermann, eds. *Friedrich Nietzsche. Chronik in Bildern und Texten* (Munich and Vienna: Hanser, 2000).

Benedix, Roderich. *Die Shakespearomanie. Zur Abwehr* (Stuttgart: Cotta, 1873).

Benjamin, Walter. 'Über Stefan George'. *Die Literarische Welt* 28, 13 July 1928.

Benjamin, Walter. 'The Work of Art in the Age of Mechanical Reproduction'. In *Illuminations*, trans. Harry Zorn, ed. Hannah Arendt (New York: Schocken Books, 1969), 217–51.

Benjamin, Walter. *Gesammelte Schriften*, vol. II, pt. 2: *Aufsätze, Essays, Voträge*, ed. Rolf Tiedemann and Hermann Schweppenhäuser (Frankfurt: Suhrkamp, 1977).

Benjamin, Walter. 'Against a Masterpiece'. In Benjamin, *Selected Writings*, vol. 2, part 1: *1927–1939*, ed. Michael W. Jennings (Cambridge, MA and London: Harvard University Press, 2005), 378–85.

Benne, Christian. 'Ecce Hanswurst—Ecce Hamlet: Rollenspiele in *Ecce Homo*'. *Nietzscheforschung. Jahrbuch der Nietzsche-Gesellschaft* 12 (2005), 219–28.

Berend, Alice. *Der Glückspilz* (Munich: Albert Langen, 1919).

Bertram, Ernst. *Deutsche Gestalten. Fest- und Gedenkreden*, 2nd edn (Leipzig: Insel, 1935).

Bertram, Ernst. *Nietzsche: Attempt at a Mythology*, trans. Robert E. Norton (Urbana, IL: University of Illinois Press, 2009).

Biedrzynski, Richard. 'Tragödie—mathematisch gelöst'. *Völkischer Beobachter*, 25 November 1940.

Biedrzynski, Richard. *Schauspieler, Regisseure, Intendanten* (Heidelberg, Berlin, and Leipzig: Hüthig, 1944).

Blank, Claudia. 'Der "andere" Hamlet: Ulrich Wildgruber und Fritz Kortner'. In *Sein oder Nichtsein: Hamlet auf dem deutschen Theater*, ed. Winrich Meiszies and Claudia Blank (Leipzig: Henschel, 2014), 53–66.

Blasius, Dirk. *Carl Schmitt: Preussischer Staatsrat in Hitlers Reich* (Göttingen: Vandenhoeck & Ruprecht, 2001).

Bloom, Harold. *The Anxiety of Influence* (Oxford: Oxford University Press, 1973).

Blumenberg, Hans. *The Legitimacy of the Modern Age* (1966), trans. Robert Wallace (Cambridge, MA: MIT Press, 1983).

Bochum, City of, ed. *Saladin Schmitt. Blätter der Erinnerung* (Bochum: Kamp, 1964).

Boehringer, Robert. *Mein Bild von Stefan George*, 2 vols (Düsseldorf and Munich: Küpper, 1951).

Boehringer, Robert. *Ewiger Augenblick* (Düsseldorf and Munich: Helmut Küpper, 1965).

Bollums, Reinhard. *Das Amt Rosenberg und seine Gegner. Studien zum Machtkampf im nationalsozialistischen Herrschaftssystem* (Stuttgart: Deutsche Verlags-Anstalt, 1970).

Bonnell, Andrew G. *Shylock in Germany: Antisemitism and the German Theatre from the Enlightenment to the Nazis* (London and New York: I. B. Tauris, 2008).

Bonwit, Marianne. '*Michael*, ein Roman von Joseph Goebbels, im Licht der deutschen literarischen Tradition'. *Monatshefte* 49.4 (1957), 193–200.

Borchardt, Rudolf. *Aufzeichnung Stefan George betreffend*, ed. Ernst Osterkamp (Munich: Rudolf Borchardt-Gesellschaft, 1998).

Borchardt, Rudolf. *Gesammelte Werke in Einzelbänden*, vol. 6: *Prosa I*, ed. Gerhard Schuster (Stuttgart: Klett-Cotta, 2002).

Börne, Ludwig. 'Hamlet. Von Shakespeare' (1828). In Börne, *Sämtliche Schriften*, 3 vols, ed. Inge Rippmann and Peter Rippmann (Düsseldorf: Melzer, 1964), vol. 1, 482–98.

Böschenstein, Bernhard, Jürgen Egyptien, Bertram Schefold, and Wolfgang Vitzthum, eds. *Wissenschaftler im George-Kreis* (Berlin and New York: De Gruyter, 2005).

Boureau, Alain. *Kantorowicz: Stories of a Historian* (1990), trans. Stephen G. Nichols and Gabrielle M. Spiegel (Baltimore, MD and London: Johns Hopkins University Press, 2001).

Bowra, C. M. *The Heritage of Symbolism* (London: Macmillan, 1943).

Bowra, C. M. *Memories 1899–1939* (Cambridge, MA: Harvard University Press, 1967).

Brackmann, Albert. 'Kaiser Friedrich II in "mythischer Schau"'. *Historische Zeitschrift* 140 (1929), 534–49.

Brand, Matthias. *Fritz Kortner in der Weimarer Republik* (Rheinfelden: Schäuble, 1981).

Brandes, Georg. 'An Essay on Aristocratic Radicalism'. In *Friedrich Nietzsche* (1909), trans. A. G. Chater (London: Heinemann, 1914), 1–56.

Braumüller, Wolf. '"Der Kampf um Shakespeare": Eine Entgegnung auf Hans Rothes Bericht'. *Bausteine zum deutschen Nationaltheater* 4 (1936), 51–62.

Braumüller, Wolf. 'Schlagt die Rezensenten tot! Kritik, Kunstbetrachtung und Kulturpolitik'. *Niedersächsische Hochschul-Zeitung*, December 1936, 41–2.

Braungart, Wolfgang. *Ästhetischer Katholizismus. Stefan Georges Rituale der Literatur* (Tübingen: Niemeyer, 1997).

Brecht, Bertolt. 'A Short Organum for the Theatre'. In *Brecht on Theatre: The Development of an Aesthetic*, trans. and ed. John Willett (London: Methuen, 1964), 179–205.

Brecht, Bertolt. *Poems, 1913–1956*, ed. John Willett and Ralph Manheim with the cooperation of Erich Fried (London: Eyre Methuen, 1981).

Breuer, Stefan. *Anatomie der Konservativen Revolution* (Darmstadt: Wissenschaftliche Buchgesellschaft, 1993).

Breuer, Stefan. *Ästhetischer Fundamentalismus: Stefan George und der deutsche Antimodernismus* (Darmstadt: Primus, 1996).

Breysig, Kurt. *Stefan George. Gespräche, Dokumente* (Amsterdam: Castrum Peregrini, 1960).

Brooks, Van Wyck. 'On Creating a Usable Past'. *The Dial* 64.7 (1918), 337–41.

Buchanan, George. *Ane detectioun of the duinges of Marie Quene of Scottes, touchand the murder of hir husband, and hir conspiracie, adulterie, and pretensed mariage with the Erle*

Bothwell. And ane defence of the trew Lordis, mainteineris of the Kingis graces actioun and authoritie. Translatit out of the Latine quhilke was written by G.B. (London: John Day, 1571).

Buchanan, Judith. *Shakespeare on Silent Film: An Excellent Dumb Discourse* (Cambridge and New York: Cambridge University Press, 2009).

Burckhardt, Jacob. *Die Kultur der Renaissance in Italien. Ein Versuch* (1860), ed. Walther Rehm (Herrsching: Pawlak, 1981).

Burckhardt, Jacob. *Briefe*, vol. 10, ed. Max Burckhardt (Basle and Stuttgart: Schwabe, 1986).

Burckhardt, Jacob. *The Civilization of the Renaissance in Italy* (1860), trans. S. G. C. Middlemore, ed. Peter Murray, with an introduction by Peter Burke (London: Penguin, 2004).

Burgdorf, Wolfgang. *Ein Weltbild verliert seine Welt: Der Untergang des Alten Reiches und die Generation 1806*, 2nd edn (Munich: Oldenbourg, 2009).

Burte, Hermann. 'Der englische und der deutsche Tag'. *Wille und Macht* 8 (1 February 1940), 3–9.

Burte, Hermann. *Sieben Reden* (Strasbourg: Hünenburg, 1943).

Byron, Lord, George Gordon. *The Poetical Works of Lord Byron* (London, New York, and Toronto: Oxford University Press, 1966).

Cacciari, Massimo. *The Unpolitical: On the Radical Critique of Political Reason*, trans. Massimo Verdicchio (New York: Fordham University Press, 2009).

Caldwell, Peter C. 'Controversies over Carl Schmitt: A Review of Recent Literature'. *The Journal of Modern History* 77 (2005), 357–87.

Cantor, Norman F. 'The Nazi Twins: Percy Ernst Schramm and Ernst Hartwig Kantorowicz'. In Cantor, *Inventing the Middle Ages: The Lives, Works, and Ideas of the Great Medievalists of the Twentieth Century* (New York: William Morrow, 1991), 79–117.

Celan, Paul. 'Todesfuge/Death Fugue'. In *Poems of Paul Celan*, trans. Michael Hamburger (London: Anvil Press Poetry, 1995), 62–5.

Chambers, E. K. 'The Disintegration of Shakespeare'. In *Aspects of Shakespeare: Being British Academy Lectures (1923–1931)*, ed. J. W. Mackail (Oxford: Clarendon Press, 1933), 23–48.

Clauß, Ludwig Ferdinand. *Die nordische Seele. Eine Einführung in die Rassenseelenkunde* (Munich: J. F. Lehmann, 1932).

Cobley, Evelyn. 'Avant-Garde Aesthetics and Fascist Politics: Thomas Mann's *Doctor Faustus* and Theodor W. Adorno's *Philosophy of Modern Music*'. *New German Critique* 86 (2002), 43–70.

Coleridge, Samuel Taylor. 'Hamlet' (1818). In Coleridge, *Lectures and Notes on Shakspere and Other English Poets* (London: Bell, 1904), 342–68.

Coleridge, Samuel Taylor. 'Kubla Khan'. In *The Major Works*, ed. H. J. Jackson (Oxford and New York: Oxford University Press, 1985), 102–4.

Coy, Jason Phillip, Benjamin Marschke, and David Warren Sabean, eds. *The Holy Roman Empire, Reconsidered* (Oxford: Berghahn Books, 2010).

Critchfield, Richard D. *From Shakespeare to Frisch: The Provocative Fritz Kortner* (Heidelberg: Synchron, 2008).

Curtius, Ernst Robert. *European Literature and the Latin Middle Ages* (Princeton, NJ: Princeton University Press, 1953).

Daniel, Drew. '"Neither Simple Allusions Nor True Mirrorings": Seeing Double with Carl Schmitt'. *Telos* 153 (2010), 51–69.

Danson, Lawrence. 'Gazing at Hamlet, or the Danish Cabaret'. *Shakespeare Survey* 45 (1992), 37–51.

Dante Alighieri. *Commedia*, vol. 2: *Purgatorio*, ed. Anna Maria Chiavacci Leonardi (Milan: Mondadori, 1994).

David, Claude. 'Gundolf und George'. *Euphorion. Zeitschrift für Literaturgeschichte* 75 (1981), 159–77.

Davies, Godfrey. *The Oxford History of England*, vol. 9: *The Early Stuarts 1603–1660* (Oxford: Oxford University Press, 1959).

Deetjen, Werner. 'Die Zweite Deutsche Shakespeare-Woche'. In *Festschrift zur Zweiten Deutschen Shakespeare-Woche*, ed. the City of Bochum and the German Shakespeare Society (Leipzig: Max Beck, 1937), 6–10.

Delano, Amasa. *Narrative of Voyages and Travels in the Northern and Southern Hemispheres: Comprising Three Voyages Round the World; Together with a Voyage of Survey and Discovery, in the Pacific Ocean and Oriental Islands* (Boston: House, 1817).

Derrida, Jacques. *Specters of Marx: The State of the Debt, the Work of Mourning and the New International* (1993), trans. Peggy Kamuf (New York and London: Routledge Classics, 2006).

Detering, Nicolas. 'Shakespeare im Ersten Weltkrieg'. In *Shakespeare unter den Deutschen*, ed. Christa Jansohn (Stuttgart: Franz Steiner, 2015), 175–96.

Detwiler, Bruce. *Nietzsche and the Politics of Aristocratic Radicalism* (Chicago, IL: University of Chicago Press, 1990).

Deubel, Werner. *Kulturrevolution, Weltbild einer Jugend* (Berlin: Verlag für Zeitkritik, 1931).

Deubel, Werner. *Der deutsche Weg zur Tragödie* (Leipzig: Wolfgang Jessen, [1935]).

Devecchio, Alexandre. 'Onfray, Sapir: le retour en force de la gauche du non'. *Le Figaro*, 21 September 2015. <http://www.lefigaro.fr/vox/politique/2015/09/21/31001-20150921ARTFIG00338-onfray-sapir-le-retour-en-force-de-la-gauche-du-non.php>, accessed 24 September 2015.

Diethe, Carol. *Nietzsche's Sister and the Will to Power: A Biography of Elisabeth Förster-Nietzsche* (Urbana, IL: University of Illinois Press, 2003).

Dilthey, Wilhelm. *Selected Works*, vol. 1: *Introduction to the Human Sciences*, ed. Rudolf A. Makkreel and Frithjof Rodi (Princeton, NJ: Princeton University Press, 1991).

Dingelstedt, Franz von. *Studien und Copien nach Shakespeare* (Pest, Vienna, and Leipzig: Hartleben, 1858).

DiPietro, Cary. 'The Shakespeare Edition in Industrial Capitalism'. *Shakespeare Survey* 59 (2006), 147–56.

Dobson, Michael. 'Short Cuts', review of Carl Schmitt, *Hamlet or Hecuba*. *London Review of Books* 31.15 (6 August 2009), 22.

Domeier, Norman. *Der Eulenburg-Skandal. Eine politische Kulturgeschichte des Kaiserreichs* (Frankfurt and New York: Campus, 2010).

Donald, David Herbert. *Lincoln* (New York: Simon & Schuster, 1995).

Döring, Tobias, and Ewan Fernie, eds. *Thomas Mann and Shakespeare: Something Rich and Strange* (New York and London: Bloomsbury, 2015).

Drewaniak, Boguslaw. *Das Theater im NS-Staat* (Düsseldorf: Droste, 1983).

Dyzenhaus, David. *Legality and Legitimacy: Carl Schmitt, Hans Kelsen and Herman Heller in Weimar* (Oxford: Oxford University Press, 1997).

Eckhardt, Eduard. *Shakespeares Anschauungen über Religion und Sittlichkeit, Staat und Volk. Ein Versuch* (Weimar: Hermann Böhlaus Nachf., 1940).

Eicher, Thomas. 'Teil II: Spielplanstrukturen 1929–1944'. In *Theater im 'Dritten Reich'*, ed. Henning Rischbieter (Seelze-Velber: Kallmeyer, 2000), 279–486.

Eichner, Barbara. *History in Mighty Sounds: Musical Constructions of German National Identity, 1848–1914* (Martlesham: Boydell & Brewer, 2012).

Eliot, T. S. 'A Romantic Patrician', review of George Wyndham, *Essays in Romantic Literature*, ed. Charles Whibley. *The Athenaeum*, 2 May 1919, 265–7.

Eliot, T. S. 'Criticism in England', review of Robert Lynd, *Old and New Masters*. *The Athenaeum*, 13 June 1919, 456–7.

Eliot, T. S. 'Hamlet and His Problems'. *The Athenaeum*, 26 September 1919, 940–1.

Eliot, T. S. *The Sacred Wood: Essays on Poetry and Criticism* (London: Faber and Faber, 1920).

Eliot, T. S. *On Poetry and Poets* (New York: Farrar, Straus and Cudahy, 1957).

Eliot, T. S. *Collected Poems 1909–1962* (London: Faber and Faber, 1963).

Eliot, T. S. 'Tradition and the Individual Talent' (1921). In *Selected Prose of T. S. Eliot*, ed. Frank Kermode (London: Faber and Faber, 1973), 37–44.

Emerson, Ralph Waldo. 'Shakespeare; or, the Poet'. In Emerson, *Representative Men*, in *Essays and Lectures*, ed. Joel Porte (New York: Library of America, 1983), 710–26.

Engel, Ingrid. *Werther und die Wertheriaden. Ein Beitrag zur Wirkungsgeschichte* (St. Ingbert: Röhrig 1986).

Engler, Balz. *Rudolf Alexander Schröders Übersetzungen von Shakespeares Dramen* (Berne: Francke, 1974).

Engler, Balz. 'Shakespeare in the Trenches'. *Shakespeare Survey* 44 (1991), 105–11.

Ernst, Paul. *Der Weg zur Form. Ästhetische Abhandlungen vornehmlich zur Tragödie und Novelle* (Berlin: Julius Bard, 1906).

Ernst, Paul. 'Zur Shakespearefrage'. In Ernst, *Zusammenbruch des deutschen Idealismus. An die Jugend* (Munich: Georg Müller, 1918), 173–231.

Eschenbach, Gunilla. *Imitatio im George-Kreis* (Berlin and New York: De Gruyter, 2011).

Espinosa, Ruben. *Masculinity and Marian Efficacy in Shakespeare's England* (Farnham and Burlington, VT: Ashgate, 2011).

Faber, M. D. 'The Suicide of Young Werther'. *Psychoanalytical Review* 60 (1973), 239–76.

Fechter, Paul. 'Deutsche Shakespeare-Darsteller; I: Gustaf Gründgens als Hamlet'. *Shakespeare-Jahrbuch* 77 (1941), 123–32.

Fechter, Paul. 'Gründgens as Hamlet'. *Shakespeare-Jahrbuch* 77 (1941), 123.

Fehr, Bernhard. Untitled review of Lilian Winstanley, *Hamlet and the Scottish Succession* (1921). *Beiblatt zur Anglia* 35 (1924), 1–16.

Feinberg, Anat. 'Leopold Jessner: German Theatre and Jewish Identity'. *Leo Baeck Institute Year Book* 48 (2003), 111–33.

Feise, Ernst. Review: 'Stefan George: Poems by Carol North Valhope, Ernst Morwitz'. *Modern Language Notes* 58.7 (1943), 568–9.

Fennell, Stephen. 'Johann Wolfgang Goethe'. In *Great Shakespeareans*, ed. Adrian Poole and Peter Holland, vol. 3: *Voltaire, Goethe, Schlegel, Coleridge*, ed. Roger Paulin (London and New York: Continuum, 2011), 44–91.

Fernie, Ewan. 'The Last Act: Presentism, Spirituality and the Politics of Hamlet'. In *Spiritual Shakespeares*, ed. Ewan Fernie (London and New York: Routledge, 2005), 186–211.

Fernie, Ewan. 'Shakespeare and the Prospect of Presentism'. *Shakespeare Survey* 58 (2005), 169–84.

Fernie, Ewan. *The Demonic: Literature and Experience* (London and New York: Routledge, 2013).

Ferry, Luc, and Alain Renaut, eds. *Why We Are Not Nietzscheans* (1991), trans. Robert de Loaiza (Chicago, IL: University of Chicago Press, 1997).

Fischer, Jens Malte. 'Hans Pfitzner und die Zeitgeschichte. Ein Künstler zwischen Verbitterung und Antisemitismus'. *Neue Zürcher Zeitung*, 5 January 2002.

Fischer-Lamberg, Hanna, ed. *Der junge Goethe*, 5 vols (Berlin and New York: De Gruyter, 1999).

Förster-Nietzsche, Elisabeth. *The Young Nietzsche*, trans. Anthony M. Ludovici (London: Heinemann, 1912).

Förster-Nietzsche, Elisabeth, ed. *The Nietzsche–Wagner Correspondence*, trans. Caroline V. Kerr (London: Duckworth & Co., 1922).

Forsthoff, Ernst, and Carl Schmitt. *Briefwechsel Ernst Forsthoff/Carl Schmitt (1926–1974)*, ed. Dorothee Mußgnug, Reinhard Mußgnug, and Angela Reinthal (Berlin: Akademie-Verlag, 2007).

Foucault, Michel. *The History of Sexuality*, vol. 1: *The Will to Knowledge* (1976), trans. Robert Hurley (London: Penguin, 1998).

Franke, Manfred. *Albert Leo Schlageter. Der erste Soldat des Dritten Reiches. Die Entmythologisierung eines Helden* (Cologne: Prometheus-Verlag, 1980).

Frecot, Janos, Johann Friedrich Geist, and Diethart Krebs. *Fidus, 1868–1948* (Munich: Rogner & Bernhard, 1972).

Freiligrath, Ferdinand. *Ein Glaubensbekenntniß* (Mainz: Zabern, 1844).

Freiligrath, Ferdinand. 'Hamlet', trans. William Howitt. In *Poems from the German of Ferdinand Freiligrath* (Leipzig: Tauchnitz, 1871).

Freiligrath, Ferdinand. *Freiligraths Werke*, 2 vols, ed. Paul Zaunert (Leipzig and Vienna: Bibliographisches Institut, 1912).

Frenzel, Herbert A. 'Ist Shakespeare ein Problem?' *Wille und Macht* 8 (1 February 1940), 2–3.

Freud, Sigmund. 'Mourning and Melancholia'. In *The Standard Edition of the Complete Psychological Works of Sigmund Freud*, 24 vols, ed. James Strachey, vol. 14: *On the History of the Psycho-Analytic Movement, Papers on Metapsychology and Other Works* (London: Hogarth Press, 1953), 243–58.

Friedländer, Saul. *The Years of Extermination: Nazi Germany and the Jews 1939–1945* (London: Weidenfeld & Nicolson, 2007).

Friedrich, Hans Eberhard. 'Caliban und das Drama des 20. Jahrhunderts'. *Prisma* 1.7 (1947), 1–3.

Fukuyama, Francis. 'The End of History?' *The National Interest* (Summer 1989), 3–18.

Fukuyama, Francis. *The End of History and the Last Man* (New York: Free Press, 1992).

Fukuyama, Francis. 'At the "End of History" Still Stands Democracy'. *The Wall Street Journal*, 6 June 2014.

Fulbrook, Mary. *A Concise History of Germany*, 2nd edn (Cambridge: Cambridge University Press, 2004).

Gadamer, Hans-Georg. *Truth and Method*, 2nd edn, trans. Joel Weinsheimer and Donald G. Marshall (London and New York: Continuum, 2004).

Gajek, Ludwika. *Das Breslauer Schauspiel im Spiegel der Tagespresse: das Lobetheater im ersten Jahrfünft der Weimarer Republik (1918–1923)* (Wiesbaden: Harrassowitz, 2008).

Gall, Lothar. *Bismarck. Der weiße Revolutionär* (Frankfurt am Main: Propyläen, 1980).

Gay, Peter. *Weimar Culture: The Outsider as Insider* (1968) (New York and London: Norton, 2001).

Genée, Rudolph. *Geschichte der Shakespeareschen Dramen in Deutschland* (Leipzig: Engelmann, 1870).

George, Stefan. *Maximin. Ein Gedenkbuch* (Berlin: Blätter für die Kunst, 1907).

George, Stefan. *Shakespeare Sonnette. Umdichtung von Stefan George* (Berlin: Georg Bondi, 1909).

George, Stefan. *Das neue Reich* (Berlin: Georg Bondi, 1928).

George, Stefan. *The Works of Stefan George. Rendered into English by Olga Marx and Ernst Morwitz*, trans. Olga Marx and Ernst Morwitz (Chapel Hill, NC: University of North Carolina Press, 1949; reprinted New York: AMS Press, 1966).

George, Stefan. *Sämtliche Werke*, 18 vols, ed. the Stefan George Society (Stuttgart: Klett-Cotta, 1982–2013).

George, Stefan, and Friedrich Gundolf. *Stefan George/Friedrich Gundolf. Briefwechsel*, ed. Robert Boehringer and Georg Peter Landmann (Düsseldorf and Munich: Küpper, 1962).

Gerhart, Walter (= Waldemar Gurian). *Um des Reiches Zukunft. Nationale Wiedergeburt oder politische Reaktion?* (Freiburg: Herder, 1932).

Gerlach, Hellmut von. 'Schleicher und sein Stahlhelm'. *Die Weltbühne* 28.2 (1932), 343.

Gerlach, Kurt. 'Das deutsche Drama zwischen Antike und Shakespeare'. *Der Türmer. Deutsche Monatshefte* 43 (1940), 1–6.

Gervinus, Georg Gottfried. *Shakespeare Commentaries*, 2 vols, trans. Fanny E. Bunnett (London: Smith, Elder, 1863).

Gibson, James M. *The Philadelphia Shakespeare Story: Horace Howard Furness and the New Variorum Shakespeare* (New York: AMS Press, 1990).

Giesler, Gerd, and Ernst Hüsmert, eds. *Carl Schmitt aus der Nähe betrachtet. Zeugnisse von Weggenossen* (Plettenberg: Carl-Schmitt-Gesellschaft, 2013).

Gilman, Sander L. *Nietzschean Parody: An Introduction to Reading Nietzsche* (Bonn: Bouvier, 1976).

Glöckner, Ernst. *Begegnung mit Stefan George. Auszüge aus Briefen und Tagebüchern 1913–1934* (Heidelberg: Lothar Stiehm, 1972).

Goebbels, Joseph. '*Heinrich Kämpfert. Ein Drama in drei Aufzügen*' (1919), handwritten MS (Bundesarchiv Koblenz NL 1118/114), fol. 1.

Goebbels, Joseph. '*Michael Voormann. Ein Menschenschicksal in Tagebuchblättern*' (1923), unpublished typescript (Bundesarchiv Koblenz NL 118/127, fols. 1–256).

Goebbels, Joseph. 'Rede des Reichspropagandaministers Dr. Joseph Goebbels vor den deutschen Theaterleitern am 8. Mai 1933'. *Das deutsche Drama* 5 (1933), 28–40.

Goebbels, Joseph. *Vom Kaiserhof zur Reichskanzlei: eine historische Darstellung in Tagebuchblättern (Vom 1. Januar 1932 bis zum 1. Mai 1933)* (Munich: Eher, 1934).

Goebbels, Joseph. *Michael, ein deutsches Schicksal in Tagebuchblättern*, 17th edn (Munich: Franz Eher Nachfolger, 1942).

[Goebbels, Joseph.] *Wie konnte es geschehen? Auszüge aus den Tagebüchern und Bekenntnissen eines Kriegsverbrechers*, ed. Max Fechner (Berlin: Dietz, 1945).

Goebbels, Joseph. *Michael*, trans. Joachim Neugroschel (New York: Amok Press, 1987).

Goebbels, Joseph. *Die Tagebücher von Joseph Goebbels*, 27 vols, ed. Elke Fröhlich et al. (Munich: K. G. Saur, 1993–2008).

Goethe, Johann Wolfgang von. 'Zum Schäkespears Tag'. *Allgemeine Monatsschrift für Wissenschaft und Literatur*, April 1854.

Goethe, Johann Wolfgang von. 'Zahme Xenien I'. In *Sämtliche Werke. Briefe, Tagebücher und Gespräche*, vol. I, 2: *Gedichte 1800–1832*, ed. Karl Eibl (Frankfurt: Deutscher Klassiker-Verlag, 1988), 623.

Goethe, Johann Wolfgang von. 'Zwischen beyden Welten'. In *West-östlicher Divan*, ed. Hendrik Birus (Frankfurt: Deutscher Klassiker-Verlag, 1994), 84.

Goethe, Johann Wolfgang von. *The Collected Works*, vol. 9: *Wilhelm Meister's Apprenticeship* (1795/6), trans. and ed. Eric A. Blackall (Princeton, NJ: Princeton University Press, 1995).

Goldsmith, Ulrich K. Review: 'The Works of Stefan George by Stefan George, Olga Marx, Ernst Morwitz'. *Books Abroad* 24.3 (1950), 302.

Golomb, Jacob, and Robert S.Wistrich, eds. *Nietzsche, Godfather of Fascism? On the Uses and Abuses of a Philosophy* (Princeton, NJ: Princeton University Press, 2002).

Goodrich, Thomas. *The Darkest Dawn* (Bloomington, IN: Indiana University Press, 2005).

Grabbe, Christian Dietrich. 'Über die Shakspearo-Manie' (1827). In Grabbe, *Werke und Briefe. Historisch-kritische Gesamtausgabe*, vol. 6, ed. Alfred Bergmann (Emsdetten: Lechte, 1966), 27–55.

Grady, Hugh. *Shakespeare's Universal Wolf: Studies in Early Modern Reification* (Oxford: Clarendon Press, 1996).

Grady, Hugh. *Shakespeare and Impure Aesthetics* (Cambridge and New York: Cambridge University Press, 2009).

Grange, William. 'Ordained Hands on the Altar of Art: Gründgens, Hilpert, and Fehling in Berlin'. In *Theatre in the Third Reich, the Prewar Years*, ed. Glen W. Gadberry(Westport, CT and London: Greenwood Press, 1995), 75–89.

Grant, Madison. *The Passing of the Great Race; or, The Racial Basis of European History* (New York: Charles Scribner's Sons, 1916).

Greenblatt, Stephen. *Shakespearean Negotiations: The Circulation of Social Energy in Renaissance England* (Oxford: Oxford University Press, 1988).

Greis, Friedhelm, and Stefanie Oswalt, eds. *Aus Teutschland Deutschland machen: Ein politisches Lesebuch zur 'Weltbühne'* (Berlin: Lukas, 2008).

Groh, Ruth. *Arbeit an der Heillosigkeit der Welt: Zur politisch-theologischen Mythologie und Anthropologie Carl Schmitts* (Frankfurt: Suhrkamp, 1998).

Groppe, Carola. *Die Macht der Bildung. Das deutsche Bürgertum und der George-Kreis 1890–1933* (Cologne, Weimar, and Vienna: Böhlau, 1997).

Gross, Raphael. *Carl Schmitt und die Juden: Eine deutsche Rechtslehre* (Frankfurt: Suhrkamp, 2000).

Grosser, J. F. G., ed. *Die große Kontroverse. Ein Briefwechsel um Deutschland. Walter von Molo, Thomas Mann* (Hamburg: Nagel, 1963).

Grünewald, Eckhart. *Ernst Kantorowicz und Stefan George. Beiträge zur Biographie des Historikers bis zum Jahre 1938 und zu seinem Jugendwerk 'Kaiser Friedrich der Zweite'* (Wiesbaden: Steiner, 1982).

Gundolf, Ernst. 'Zur Beurteilung der Darmstädter Shakespeare-Maske'. *Shakespeare-Jahrbuch* 64 (1928), 132–40.

Gundolf, Friedrich. *Shakespeare in deutscher Sprache. Herausgegeben und zum Teil neu übersetzt von Friedrich Gundolf* (Berlin: Georg Bondi, 1908).

Gundolf, Friedrich. *Shakespeare und der deutsche Geist* (Berlin: Georg Bondi, 1911).

Gundolf, Friedrich. 'Vorbilder' [Models, or, Exemplary Men]. *Jahrbuch für die geistige Bewegung* 3 (1912), 1–19.

Gundolf, Friedrich. 'Tat und Wort im Krieg'. *Frankfurter Zeitung*, 11 October 1914.

Gundolf, Friedrich. *Stefan George in unserer Zeit* (Heidelberg: Weiss, 1918).

Gundolf, Friedrich. *George* (Berlin: Georg Bondi, 1920).

Gundolf, Friedrich. *Dichter und Helden* (Heidelberg: Weiss'sche Universitätsbuchhandlung, 1921).

Gundolf, Friedrich. *Caesar im neunzehnten Jahrhundert* (Berlin: Georg Bondi, 1926).

Gundolf, Friedrich. *Shakespeare. Sein Wesen und Werk*, 2 vols (Berlin: Georg Bondi, 1928).

Gundolf, Friedrich. *The Mantle of Caesar* (1924), trans. Jacob Wittmer Hartmann (London: Cayme Press, 1929).

Gundolf, Friedrich. 'Caesar und Brutus'. In *Gedichte von Friedrich Gundolf* (Berlin: Georg Bondi, 1930), 41–5.

Gundolf, Friedrich. *Shakespeare. Sein Wesen und Werk*, 2 vols, 2nd edn (Düsseldorf: Küpper, 1949).

Gundolf, Friedrich. *Briefwechsel mit Herbert Steiner und Ernst Robert Curtius*, ed. Lothar Helbing and Claus Victor Bock (Amsterdam: Castrum Peregrini, 1963).

Gundolf, Friedrich. *Friedrich Gundolfs Shakespeare-Sonetten-Fragmente*, ed. Jürgen Gutsch (Dozwil: EDITION SIGNAThUR, 2011).

Gundolf, Friedrich, and Friedrich Wolters, eds. *Jahrbuch für die geistige Bewegung*, vol. 3 (Berlin: Verlag der Blätter für die Kunst, 1912).

Günther, Hans F. K. *The Racial Elements of European History*, trans. G. C. Wheeler (London: Methuen, 1927).

Günther, Hans F. K. 'Shakespeares Mädchen und Frauen'. *Shakespeare-Jahrbuch* 73 (1937), 85–106.

Guntner, J. Lawrence, and Andrew M. McLean, eds. *Redefining Shakespeare: Literary Theory and Theater Practice in the German Democratic Republic* (Cranbury, NJ: Associated University Presses, 1998).

Gurian, Waldemar. 'Ein Traum vom Dritten Reich'. *Hochland* 22 (1924/5), 237–42.

Haas, Willy. 'Hamlet'. *Film-Kurier* 31.5 (5 February 1921).

Haas, Willy. 'Eine neue politische Lehre', review of Carl Schmitt, *Der Begriff des Politischen*, 2nd edn. *Die literarische Welt* 21 (20 May 1932).

Habicht, Werner. 'Shakespeare and Theatre Politics in the Third Reich'. In *The Play out of Context: Transferring Plays from Culture to Culture*, ed. Hanna Scolnicov and Peter Holland (Cambridge: Cambridge University Press, 1989), 110–20.

Habicht, Werner. *Shakespeare and the German Imagination* (Hertford: International Shakespeare Association, 1994).

Habicht, Werner. 'Shakespeare Celebrations in Times of War'. *Shakespeare Quarterly* 52.4 (2001), 441–55.

Habicht, Werner. 'Shakespeare und der deutsche Shakespeare-Mythus im Dritten Reich'. In *Anglistik: Research Paradigms and Institutional Policies, 1930–2000*, ed. Stephan Kohl (Trier: Wissenschaftlicher Verlag Trier, 2005), 79–111.

Habicht, Werner. 'German Shakespeare, the Third Reich, and the War'. In *Shakespeare and the Second World War: Memory, Culture, Identity*, ed. Irena R. Makaryk and Marissa McHugh (Toronto, Buffalo, and London: University of Toronto Press, 2012), 22–34.

Halpern, Richard. 'The King's Two Buckets: Kantorowicz, *Richard II*, and Fiscal *Trauerspiel*'. *Representations* 106 (2009), 67–76.

Hamburger, Maik. 'Theatre under Socialism: Shakespeare in East Germany'. In Wilhelm Hortmann, *Shakespeare on the German Stage*, vol. 2: *The Twentieth Century* (Cambridge: Cambridge University Press, 1998), 350–434.

Hamecher, Peter. 'Der männliche Eros im Werke Stefan Georges'. *Jahrbuch für sexuelle Zwischenstufen* 14 (1914), 10–23.

Hartmann, Waldemar. 'Hamlets politisches Heldentum: Gedanken zum *Hamlet*, als der Tragödie nordischen Verantwortungsgefühls'. *Völkischer Beobachter*, 3 May 1936, 5.

Hauptmann, Gerhart. 'Deutschland und Shakespeare'. *Shakespeare-Jahrbuch* 51 (1915), vii–xii.

Hauptmann, Gerhart. *Diarium 1917–1933*, ed. Martin Machatzke (Frankfurt and Berlin: Propyläen, 1980).

Hauptmann, Gerhart. 'Hamlet. Einige Worte zu meinem Ergänzungsversuch'. In Hauptmann, *Sämtliche Werke*, vol. 4: *Erzählungen, theoretische Prosa*, ed. Hans-Egon Hass (Frankfurt and Berlin: Propyläen, 1996), 934–61.

Hauschild, Jan-Christoph. *Heiner Müller oder Das Prinzip Zweifel. Eine Biographie* (Berlin: Aufbau, 2001).

Hausmann, Frank-Rutger. *Anglistik und Amerikanistik im 'Dritten Reich'* (Frankfurt: Klostermann, 2003).

Haverkamp, Anselm. 'Stranger Than Paradise. Dantes irdisches Paradies als Antidot politischer Theologie'. In *Geschichtskörper. Zur Aktualität von Ernst H. Kantorowicz*, ed. Wolfgang Ernst and Cornelia Vismann (Munich: Fink, 1998), 93–103.

Hawkes, Terence. *Shakespeare in the Present* (London and New York: Routledge, 2002).

Heaney, Seamus. *North* (London: Faber and Faber, 1975).

Heftrich, Eckhard. *Zauberbergmusik: Über Thomas Mann* (Frankfurt: Klostermann, 1975).

Hegel, Georg Wilhelm Friedrich. *Werke*, 18 vols, ed. Ph. Marheineke et al. (Berlin: Duncker & Humblot, 1832–40).

Hegel, Georg Wilhelm Friedrich. *Hegel's Aesthetics: Lectures on Fine Art*, 2 vols, trans. and ed. T. M. Knox (Oxford: Clarendon Press, 1975).

Hegel, Georg Wilhelm Friedrich. *The Phenomenology of Spirit*, trans. A. V. Miller, ed. J. N. Findlay (Oxford: Clarendon Press, 1977).

Heiber, Helmut, ed. *Goebbels-Reden*, vol. 1: *1932–1939* (Düsseldorf: Droste, 1971).

Heilmann, Matthias. *Leopold Jessner—Intendant der Republik. Der Weg eines deutsch-jüdischen Regisseurs aus Ostpreußen* (Tübingen: Niemeyer, 2005).

Heine, Heinrich. *Shakespeares Mädchen und Frauen* (Paris and Leipzig: Brockhaus & Avenarius, 1839).

Heinrich, Anselm. '"It Is Germany Where He Truly Lives": Nazi Claims on Shakespearean Drama'. *New Theatre Quarterly* 28.3 (2012), 230–42.

Helbing, Lothar (= Wolfgang Frommel). 'Gundolf und Elli. Vorwort'. In Elisabeth Gundolf. *Stefan George. Zwei Vorträge mit einem Vorwort von Lothar Helbing* (Amsterdam: Castrum Peregrini, 1965), 5–33.

Henrichs, Benjamin. 'Acht Stunden sind kein Theater. Keine Inszenierung, eine Demonstration: Heiner Müller, Erich Wonder und Ulrich Mühe zeigen *Hamlet/Maschine*'. *Die Zeit*, 30 March 1990. <http://www.zeit.de/1990/14/acht-stunden-sind-kein-theater>, accessed 26 July 2015.

Herder, Johann Gottfried. *Shakespeare* (1773), trans. and ed. Gregory Moore (Princeton, NJ and Oxford: Princeton University Press, 2008).

Hermand, Jost. *Old Dreams of a New Reich: Volkish Utopias and National Socialism* (1988), trans. Paul Levesque (Bloomington and Indianapolis: Indiana University Press, 1992).

Heywood, John. *The Proverbs of John Heywood* (1546), ed. Julian Sharman (London: George Bell & Sons, 1874).

Hirschfeld, Magnus. *Berlins Drittes Geschlecht* (Berlin and Leipzig: Seemann, 1904).

Hirschfeld, Magnus. 'Vor fünfundzwanzig Jahren'. *Die Freundschaft* 15.2 (1933), 2.

Hitler, Adolf. *Mein Kampf*, trans. James Murphy (London: Hurst and Blackett, 1939).

Hoenselaars, Ton. 'Great War Shakespeare: Somewhere in France, 1914–1919'. *Actes des congrès de la Société française Shakespeare* 32 (2015). <http://shakespeare.revues.org/2960>, accessed 26 August 2015.

Höfele, Andreas. 'Leopold Jessner's Shakespeare Productions 1920–1930'. *Theatre History Studies* 12 (1992), 139–55.

Höfele, Andreas. 'A Theater of Exhaustion? "Posthistoire" in Recent German Shakespeare Productions'. *Shakespeare Quarterly* 43 (1992), 80–6.

Höfele, Andreas. 'Oscar Wilde, or, The Prehistory of Postmodern Parody'. *European Journal of English Studies (EJES)*, Special Issue: *Postmodern Parody* (1999), 138–66.

Höfele, Andreas. 'From Reeducation to Alternative Theater: German–American Theater Relations'. In *The United States and Germany in the Era of Cold War*, ed. Detlef Junker, vol. 1: *1945–1968* (Cambridge: Cambridge University Press, 2004), 464–71.

Höfele, Andreas. 'Reeducating Germany: BBC Shakespeare 1945'. In *Shakespeare and European Politics*, ed. Dirk Delabastita, Jozef De Vos, and Paul Franssen (Newark, DE: University of Delaware Press, 2008), 255–77.

Höfele, Andreas. 'The Rebirth of Tragedy, or No Time for Shakespeare (Germany, 1940)'. *Renaissance Drama* 38 (2010), 251–68.

Höfele, Andreas. *Stage, Stake, and Scaffold: Human and Animals in Shakespeare's Theatre* (Oxford and New York: Oxford University Press, 2011).

Höfele, Andreas. 'Beware the Ides of March: Shakespeare and the 19th-Century Caesar Myth'. *Cahiers Elisabéthains* 89, Special Issue: *Shakespeare and Myth*, ed. Florence March, Jean-Christophe Mayer, and Nathalie Vienne-Guerin (Autumn 2016, forthcoming).

Hoffmann, Paul Th. *Theater und Drama im deutschen Geistesschicksal* (Hamburg: J. P. Toth, 1948).

Hoffmann, Peter. *Claus Schenk Graf von Stauffenberg und seine Brüder* (Stuttgart: Deutsche Verlags-Anstalt, 1992).

Hoffmann, Peter. *Stauffenberg: A Family History, 1905–1944*, 3rd edn (Montreal: McGill-Queen's University Press, 2008).

Holbrook, Peter. 'Nietzsche's *Hamlet*'. *Shakespeare Survey* 50 (1997), 171–86.

Holbrook, Peter. 'Nietzsche's Shakespeare'. In *Shakespeare and Continental Philosophy*, ed. Jennifer Ann Bates and Richard Wilson (Edinburgh: Edinburgh University Press, 2014), 76–93.

Hollaender, Felix. Review of Leopold Jessner's *Hamlet*. *8-Uhr-Abendblatt*, 4 December 1926; reprinted in *Theater für die Republik*, ed. Günther Rühle (Frankfurt: S. Fischer, 1967), 764–7.

Holthusen, Hans Egon. *Das Schöne und das Wahre. Neue Studien zur modernen Literatur* (Munich: Piper, 1958).

Hopkins, Lisa. '"Black but beautiful": Othello and the Cult of the Black Madonna'. In *Marian Moments in Early Modern British Drama*, ed. Regina Buccola and Lisa Hopkins (Farnham and Burlington, VT: Ashgate, 2013), 75–86.

Hortmann, Wilhelm. *Shakespeare on the German Stage*, vol. 2: *The Twentieth Century* (Cambridge: Cambridge University Press, 1998).

Höver, Ulrich. *Joseph Goebbels: ein nationaler Sozialist* (Bonn and Berlin: Bouvier, 1992).

Howard, Tony. *Women as Hamlet: Performance and Interpretation in Theatre, Film and Fiction* (Cambridge: Cambridge University Press, 2007).

Hudson, Henry N. *Shakespeare: His Life, Art, and Characters* (Boston: Ginn, 1872).

Hugo, Victor. *William Shakespeare*, trans. Melville B. Anderson (Chicago, IL: McClurg, 1887).

Hunt, Marvin W. *Looking for Hamlet* (New York and London: Palgrave Macmillan, 2007).

Hürten, Heinz, ed. *Deutsche Briefe. Deutsche Briefe 1934–1938. Ein Blatt der katholischen Emigration*, 2 vols (Mainz: Matthias-Grünewald-Verlag, 1969).

Hutson, Lorna. 'Imagining Justice: Kantorowicz and Shakespeare'. *Representations* 106 (2009), 118–42.

Jaeger, Hans. 'Review: The Works of Stefan George by Olga Marx, Ernst Morwitz'. *Monatshefte* 45.6 (1953), 391–3.

Jäger, Georg. 'Goethes Werther im gesellschaftlichen Kontext'. *Goethezeitportal*. <http://www. goethezeitportal.de/digitale-bibliothek/forschungsbeitraege/autoren-kuenstler-denker/ goethe-johann-wolfgang-von/georg-jaeger-goethes-werther-im-gesellschaftlichen-kontext. html>, accessed 28 October 2014.

Jammerthal, Peter. *Ein zuchtvolles Theater: Bühnenästhetik des 'Dritten Reiches'. Das Berliner Staatstheater von der 'Machtergreifung' bis zur Ära Gründgens* (PhD dissertation: Free University Berlin, 2007). <http://www.diss.fu-berlin.de/diss/servlets/MCRFileNodeServlet/ FUDISS_derivate_000000002953/06_kap3b.pdf?hosts=>, accessed 20 June 2015.

Jaspers, Karl. *Von der Wahrheit* (Munich: Piper, 1947).

Jaspers, Karl. *The Question of German Guilt* (1946), trans. E. B. Ashton (New York: Dial Press, 1948).

Jeffreys, Mark. 'The Rhetoric of Authority in T. S. Eliot's *Athenaeum* Reviews'. *South Atlantic Review* 57.4 (1992), 93–108.

Jessner, Leopold. 'Das Theater. Ein Vortrag'. *Die Scene* 18.3 (1928), 66–74; reprinted in Jessner, *Schriften: Theater der zwanziger Jahre*, ed. Hugo Fetting (Berlin: Henschel, 1979), 97–110.

Jones, Henry Arthur. *Shakespeare and Germany* (London: Wittingham, 1916).

Joyce, James. *Ulysses*, ed. Jeri Johnson (Oxford: Oxford University Press, 1993).

Jungblut, Peter. *Famose Kerle. Eulenburg—Eine wilhelminische Affäre* (Hamburg: Männerschwarm Skript, 2003).

Jünger, Ernst, and Carl Schmitt. *Briefwechsel. Briefe 1930–1983*, ed. Helmuth Kiesel (Stuttgart: Klett-Cotta, 1999).

Kaempfer, Wolfgang. 'Das Ich und der Tod in Goethes *Werther*'. *Recherches Germaniques* 9 (1979), 55–79.

Kahler, Erich von. *Der Beruf der Wissenschaft* (Berlin: Georg Bondi, 1920).

Kahn, Victoria. 'Hamlet or Hecuba: Carl Schmitt's Decision'. *Representations* 83 (2003), 67–96.

Kahn, Victoria. 'Political Theology and Fiction in *The King's Two Bodies*'. *Representations* 106 (2009), 77–101.

Kahn, Victoria. *The Future of Illusion: Political Theology and Early Modern Texts* (Chicago, IL and London: University of Chicago Press, 2014).

Kaiser, Gerhard. *Grenzverwirrungen: Literaturwissenschaft im Nationalsozialismus* (Berlin: Akademie-Verlag, 2008).

Kalkmann, Ulrich. *Die Technische Hochschule Aachen im Dritten Reich (1933–1945)* (Aachen: Wissenschaftsverlag Mainz, 2003).

Kantorowicz, Ernst. 'Das Geheime Deutschland. Vorlesung, gehalten bei Wiederaufnahme der Lehrtätigkeit am 14. November 1933', ed. Eckhart Grünewald. In *Ernst Kantorowicz. Erträge der Doppeltagung Institute for Advanced Study, Princeton, Johann Wolfgang Goethe-Universität, Frankfurt*, ed. Robert L. Benson and Johannes Fried (Stuttgart: Steiner, 1997), 77–93.

Kantorowicz, Ernst H. *Frederick the Second 1194–1250*, trans. E. O. Lorimer (London: Constable, 1931).

Kantorowicz, Ernst H. *Kaiser Friedrich der Zweite. Ergänzungsband* (Berlin: Georg Bondi, 1931).

Kantorowicz, Ernst H. *Laudes Regiae: A Study in Liturgical Acclamations and Medieval Ruler Worship* (Berkeley, CA: University of California Press, 1946).

Kantorowicz, Ernst H. *The Fundamental Issue. Documents and Marginal Notes on the University of California Loyalty Oath* (Berkeley, CA: privately printed, 1950). <http://sunsite.berkeley.edu/uchistory/archives_exhibits/loyaltyoath/symposium/kantorowicz.html>.

Kantorowicz, Ernst H. *The King's Two Bodies: A Study in Medieval Political Theology* (Princeton, NJ: Princeton University Press, 1957).

Kantorowicz, Ernst H. 'Die Wiederkehr gelehrter Anachorese im Mittelalter'. In *Selected Studies* (Locust Valley, NY: J. J. Augustin, 1965), 339–51.

Kantorowicz, Ernst H. 'The Sovereignty of the Artist: A Note on Legal Maxims and Renaissance Theories of Art'. In *Selected Studies* (Locust Valley, NY: J. J. Augustin, 1965), 352–65.

Karlauf, Thomas. *Stefan George. Die Entdeckung des Charisma* (Munich: Blessing, 2007).

Karlauf, Thomas. 'Meister mit eigenem Kreis. Wolfgang Frommels George-Nachfolge'. *Sinn und Form* 2 (2011), 211–19.

Kästner, Erich. *Notabene 45. Ein Tagebuch* (Berlin: Dressler, 1961).

Kauffman, Michael W. *American Brutus: John Wilkes Booth and the Lincoln Conspiracies* (New York: Random House, 2004).

Kaufmann, Walter A. *Nietzsche: Philosopher, Psychologist, Antichrist* (Princeton, NJ: Princeton University Press, 1950).

Keats, John. 'On First Looking into Chapman's *Homer*'. In *Major Works*, ed. Elizabeth Cook (Oxford: Oxford University Press, 2001), 32.

Keilson-Lauritz, Marita, and Friedemann Pfäfflin, eds. *100 Jahre Schwulenbewegung an der Isar I: Die Sitzungsberichte des Wissenschaftlich-humanitären Komitees München 1902–1908* (Munich: forum homosexualität und geschichte münchen e.v., 2003).

Keim, Katharina. *Theatralität in den späten Dramen Heiner Müllers* (Tübingen: Niemeyer, 1998).

Keller, Wolfgang. 'Shakespeares Römerdramen'. In *Festschrift zur Zweiten Deutschen Shakespeare-Woche*, ed. the City of Bochum and the German Shakespeare Society (Leipzig: Max Beck, 1937), 11–14.

Keller, Wolfgang. 'Ansprache und Jahresbericht des Präsidenten Professor Wolfgang Keller'. *Shakespeare-Jahrbuch* 76 (1940), 1–10.

Kemmerer, Alexandra. 'Dark Legator: Where the State Transcends its Boundaries, Carl Schmitt Awaits Us'. *German Law Journal* 7 (2006), Special Issue: *European Integration in the Shadow of Europe's Darker Pasts: The 'Darker Legacies of Law in Europe' Revisited*, 149–54.

Klemperer, Klemens von. *German Resistance Against Hitler: The Search for Allies 1938–1945* (Oxford: Oxford University Press, 1994).

Kilian, Eugen. Review: 'Shakespeare. *Macbeth. König Lear. Troilus und Cressida. Wie es euch gefällt. König Richard II. Was ihr wollt.* Übersetzt von Hans Rothe. Meyer & Jessen, Verlag, München. 6 Bändchen. [1922–24]'. *Shakespeare-Jahrbuch* 59/60 (1924), 205–17.

Kindermann, Heinz. 'Shakespeare und das deutsche Volkstheater'. *Shakespeare-Jahrbuch* 72 (1936), 9–41.

Knapp, Otto. 'Hamlet—unser Zeitgenosse'. *Hochland* 39 (1946/7), 532–45.

Kniesche, Thomas W. *Dancing on the Volcano: Essays on the Culture of the Weimar Republic* (Rochester, NY: Camden House, 1994).

Knight, George Wilson. *The Wheel of Fire: Interpretations of Shakespearean Tragedy* (London: Methuen, 1930).

Koebner, Thomas, Rolf-Peter Janz, and Frank Trommler, eds. *'Mit uns zieht die neue Zeit': Der Mythos Jugend* (Frankfurt: Suhrkamp, 1985).

Körber, Thomas. *Nietzsche nach 1945: zu Werk und Biographie Friedrich Nietzsches in derdeutschsprachigen Nachkriegsliteratur* (Würzburg: Königshausen & Neumann, 2006).

Kortner, Fritz. *Aller Tage Abend* (1959), 3rd edn (Munich: dtv, 1971).

Koselleck, Reinhard. *Practice of Conceptual History: Timing, History, Spacing Concepts*, trans. Todd Presner, Kerstin Behnke, and Jobst Welge (Palo Alto, CA: Stanford University Press, 2002).

Kott, Jan. *Shakespeare Our Contemporary*, trans. Boleslaw Taborski (London: Methuen, 1964).

Kristeva, Julia. 'Approaching Abjection'. In Kristeva, *Powers of Horror* (New York: Columbia University Press, 1982), 1–31.

Kühl, Stefan. *The Nazi Connection: Eugenics, American Racism, and German National Socialism* (New York: Oxford University Press, 1994).

Kuhn, Annette, ed. *Alien Zone* (London: Verso, 1990).

Kunhardt, Philip, Jr. *A New Birth of Freedom* (Boston: Little, Brown, 1983).

Künkler, Karl. 'Hans Rothe und das Theater'. *Bausteine zum deutschen Nationaltheater* 4 (1936), 43–7.

Kurz, Werner. 'Verbrechen an Shakespeare'. *Bausteine zum deutschen Nationaltheater* 4 (1936), 33–42.

Kurzke, Hermann. *Thomas Mann: Epoche—Werk—Wirkung* (Munich: Beck, 2010).

L., H. Review: 'Hamlet'. *Deutsche Lichtspiel-Zeitung*, 26 February1921.

Landauer, Carl. 'Ernst Kantorowicz and the Sacralization of the Past'. *Central European History* 27 (1994), 1–25.

Landauer, Gustav. *Shakespeare in zwei Bänden. Dargestellt in Vorträgen*, 2 vols (Frankfurt: Rütten & Loening1922).

Landesarchiv NRW, Abteilung Rheinland, Standort Düsseldorf (Nachlass Carl Schmitt), RW265–20311.

Landesarchiv NRW, Abteilung Rheinland, Standort Düsseldorf (Nachlass Carl Schmitt), RW265–20313.

Landesarchiv NRW, Abteilung Rheinland, Standort Düsseldorf (Nachlass Carl Schmitt), RW265–21086.

Landesarchiv NRW, Abteilung Rheinland, Standort Düsseldorf (Nachlass Carl Schmitt), RW265–226.

Landesarchiv NRW, Abteilung Rheinland, Standort Düsseldorf (Nachlass Carl Schmitt), RW569–490.

Landmann, Edith. *Gespräche mit Stefan George* (Düsseldorf and Munich: Küpper, 1963).

Landmann, Georg Peter, ed. *Der George-Kreis. Eine Auswahl aus seinen Schriften* (Stuttgart: Klett-Cotta, 1980).

Lane, Melissa S., and Martin A. Ruehl, eds. *A Poet's Reich: Politics and Culture in the George Circle* (Rochester, NY: Camden House, 2011).

Langenbeck, Curt. 'Christentum und Tragödie'. *Münchner Neueste Nachrichten*, 24 February 1940.

Langenbeck, Curt. 'Shakespeare—ein Problem für unsere Zeit'. *Münchner Neueste Nachrichten*, 2/3 March 1940.

Langenbeck, Curt. *Treue* (Munich: Albert Langen and Georg Müller, 1940).

Langenbeck, Curt. *Die Wiedergeburt des Dramas aus dem Geist der Zeit* (Munich: Albert Langen and Georg Müller, 1941).

Laqueur, Walter. *Young Germany: A History of the German Youth Movement* (New York: Basic Books, 1962).

Laqueur, Walter. *Young Germany: A History of the German Youth Movement* (Piscataway, NJ: Transaction, 1984).

Ledebur, Ruth von. *Der Mythos vom deutschen Shakespeare. Die Deutsche Shakespeare-Gesellschaft zwischen Politik und Wissenschaft 1918–1945* (Cologne: Böhlau, 2002).

Lehmann, Hans-Thies. *Postdramatic Theatre*, trans. and ed. Karen Jürs-Munby (London and New York: Routledge, 2006).

Leiter, Brian. 'Nietzsche's Moral and Political Philosophy'. In *The Stanford Encyclopedia of Philosophy* [Summer 2011 edn], ed. Edward N. Zalta. <http://plato.stanford.edu/archives/sum2011/entries/nietzsche-moral-political/>, accessed 25 November 2012.

Lepsius, Sabine. *Stefan George: Geschichte einer Freundschaft* (Berlin: Die Runde, 1935).

Lerner, Robert E. 'Ernst Kantorowicz and Theodor E. Mommsen'. In *An Interrupted Past: German-Speaking Refugee Historians in the United States after 1933*, ed. Hartmut Lehmann and James Sheehan (Cambridge: Cambridge University Press, 1991), 188–205.

Lerner, Robert E. 'Ernst H. Kantorowicz (1895–1963)'. In *Medieval Scholarship: Biographical Studies on the Formation of a Discipline*, vol. 1: *History*, ed. Helen Damico and Joseph B. Zavadil (New York and London: Garland Publishing, 1995), 263–76.

Lerner, Robert E. 'Letters by Ernst Kantorowicz concerning Woldemar Uxkull and Stefan George'. *George-Jahrbuch* 8 (2010), 157–74.

Lessing, Gotthold Ephraim. '17. Literaturbrief'. In *Werke und Briefe in zwölf Bänden*, ed. Wilfried Barner, vol. 4: *Werke, 1758–1759*, ed. Gunter E. Grimm (Frankfurt: Deutscher Klassiker-Verlag, 1997), 499–501.

Lichtenberg, Christoph Georg. *Aphorisms*, trans. and ed. R. J. Hollingdale (London: Penguin, 1990).

Linzer, Martin, and Peter Ulrich, eds. *Regie: Heiner Müller: Material zu Der Lohndrücker' 1988, 'Hamlet/Maschine' 1990, 'Mauser' 1991 am Deutschen Theater* (Berlin: Zentrum für Theaterdokumentation und -information, 1993).

London, John. 'Non-German Drama in the Third Reich'. In *Theatre under the Nazis*, ed. John London (Manchester and New York: Manchester University Press, 2000), 222–61.

Longerich, Peter. *Joseph Goebbels. Biographie* (Munich: Siedler, 2010).

Losurdo, Domenico. *Nietzsche, il ribelle aristocratico: Biografia intellettuale e bilancio critico* (Turin: Bollati Boringhieri, 2002).

Lukács, Georg. 'The Sorrows of Young Werther' (1936). In Lukács, *Goethe and His Age*, trans. Robert Anchor (London: Merlin Press, 1968), 35–49.

Lukács, Georg. 'The Metaphysics of Tragedy' (1910). In Lukács, *Soul and Form*, trans. Anna Bostock (Cambridge, MA: MIT Press, 1974), 152–74.

Lupton, Julia Reinhard. *Citizen-Saints: Shakespeare and Political Theology* (Chicago, IL and London: University of Chicago Press, 2005).

Lupton, Julia Reinhard. *Thinking with Shakespeare: Essays on Politics and Life* (Chicago, IL and London: University of Chicago Press, 2011).

McGregor, Neil. *Germany: Memories of a Nation* (London: Allen Lane, 2014).

Maiatsky, M. A. *Spor o Platone. Krug Stefana George i nemetskiy universitet* (Moscow: Izdatel'skiĭ dom Vyssheĭ shkoly ėkonomiki, 2012).

Mailand, Arnulf von. *Liber gestorum recentium*, ed. Claudia Zey (Hannover: Hahn, 1994); trans W. North, <http://www.acad.carleton.edu/curricular/MARS/Arnulf.pdf>, accessed 9 March 2015.

Maillet, Greg. 'Desdemona and the Mariological Theology of the Will in Othello'. In *Marian Moments in Early Modern British Drama*, ed. Regina Buccola and Lisa Hopkins (Farnham and Burlington, VT: Ashgate, 2013), 87–110.

Maltarich, Bill. *Samurai and Supermen: National Socialist Views of Japan* (Oxford, Berne, and Berlin: Peter Lang, 2005).

Mann, Klaus. 'Das Schweigen Stefan Georges'. *Die Sammlung* 1.2 (October 1933), 98–103.

Mann, Klaus. *Mephisto* (1936), trans. Robin Smyth (New York: Random House, 1977).

Mann, Thomas. 'Thomas Mann über die deutsche Schuld'. *Bayerische Landeszeitung*, 18 May 1915.

Mann, Thomas. *Thomas Mann an Ernst Bertram—Briefe aus den Jahren 1910–1955*, ed. Inge Jens (Pfullingen: Günther Neske, 1960).

Mann, Thomas. *Gesammelte Werke*, 18 vols (Frankfurt: S. Fischer, 1974).

Mann, Thomas. 'Die Lager', trans. Andrei S. Markovits and Beth Simone Noveck, 'West Germany', in *The World Reacts to the Holocaust*, ed. David S. Wyman and Charles H. Rosenzveig (Baltimore, MD and London: Johns Hopkins University Press, 1996), 391–446.

Mann, Thomas. *Doctor Faustus: The Life of the German Composer Adrian Leverkühn, as Told by a Friend* (1947), trans. John E. Woods (New York: Vintage, 1999).

Mann, Thomas. *Thomas Mann's Addresses Delivered at the Library of Congress*, ed. Don Heinrich Tolzmann (Berne: Peter Lang, 2003).

Mann, Thomas, and Theodor W. Adorno. *Correspondence 1943–1955*, trans. Nicholas Walker (Cambridge: Polity Press, 2006).

Marlowe, Christopher. *Edward II*. In *Doctor Faustus and Other Plays*, ed. David Bevington and Eric Rasmussen (Oxford and New York: Oxford University Press, 1995), 323–402.

Märtens, Ilse. 'Shakespeare heute'. *Pädagogische Rundschau* 1.1/2 (1947), 89–93.

Marx, Peter W. 'Stufen der Abstraktion: Leopold Jessners Shakespeare-Inszenierungen 1919–1932'. *Shakespeare-Jahrbuch* 146 (2010), 60–77.

Mason, Eudo C. 'Gundolf und Shakespeare'. *Shakespeare-Jahrbuch* 98 (1962), 110–77.

Mattenklott, Gert. 'Benjamin und Adorno über George'. In *Wissenschaftler im George-Kreis. Die Welt des Dichters und der Beruf der Wissenschaft*, ed. Bernhard Böschenstein et al. (Berlin and New York: De Gruyter, 2005), 277–90.

Matussek, Matthias. 'Requiem für einen Staat'. *Der Spiegel*, 26 March 1990, 290.

Mehring, Reinhard. *Carl Schmitt: A Biography* (2009), trans. Daniel Steuer (Cambridge and Malden, MA: Polity Press, 2014).

Meier, Heinrich. *The Lesson of Carl Schmitt: Four Chapters on the Distinction between Political Theology and Political Philosophy*, trans. Marcus Brainard (Chicago, IL and London: University of Chicago Press, 1998).

Meinecke, Friedrich. *Die deutsche Katastrophe: Betrachtungen und Erinnerungen* (Wiesbaden: Brockhaus, 1946).

Meißner, Paul. *Shakespeare* (Berlin: De Gruyter, 1940).

Melville, Herman. 'Benito Cereno'. In *The Writings of Herman Melville*, vol. 9: *The Piazza Tales and Other Prose Pieces 1839–1860*, ed. Harrison Hayford et al. (Evanston, IL: Northwestern University Press, 1987).

Menzel, Wolfgang. *Die deutsche Literatur* (Stuttgart: Franckh, 1836).

Meyer-Kalkus, Reinhart. 'Werthers Krankheit zum Tode. Pathologie und Familie in der Empfindsamkeit'. In *Urszenen. Literaturwissenschaft als Diskursanalyse und Diskurskritik*, ed. Friedrich A. Kittler and Horst Turk (Frankfurt: Suhrkamp, 1977), 76–138.

Michel, Kai. *Vom Poeten zum Demagogen: Die schriftstellerischen Versuche Joseph Goebbels* (Cologne, Weimar, and Vienna: Böhlau, 1999).

Mikhailovsky, Alexander. *Three Principles of 'Political Theology' in the Stefan George Circle* (Moscow: National Research University, Higher School of Economics, Basic Research Program, Working Papers, Series: Humanities WP BRP 26/HUM/2013). <http://www.hse.ru/data/2013/05/08/1299213257/26HUM2013.pdf>, accessed 3 September 2014.

Miller, Ann Stamp. *The Cultural Politics of the German Democratic Republic: The Voices of Wolf Biermann, Christa Wolf, and Heiner Müller* (Boca Raton, FL: Universal Publishers, 1999).

Milton, Sybil H. '"Gypsies" as Social Outsiders in Nazi Germany'. In *Social Outsiders in Nazi Germany*, ed. Robert Gellately and Nathan Stoltzfus (Princeton, NJ: Princeton University Press, 2001), 212–32.

Minetti, Bernhard. *Erinnerungen eines Schauspielers*, ed. Günther Rühle (Stuttgart: Deutsche Verlags-Anstalt, 1985).

Moeller, Felix. *The Film Minister: Goebbels and the Cinema in the 'Third Reich'* (Stuttgart and London: Edition Axel Menges, 2000).

Moeller van den Bruck, Arthur. *Germany's Third Empire*, trans. E. O. Lorimer (London: George Allen & Unwin, 1934).

Mohler, Armin. *Die konservative Revolution in Deutschland 1918–1932. Grundriss ihrer Weltanschauungen* (Stuttgart: Friedrich Vorwerk, 1950).

Mohler, Armin, ed. *Carl Schmitt—Briefwechsel mit einem seiner Schüler* (Berlin: Akademie-Verlag, 1995).

Moninger, Markus. *Shakespeare inszeniert: Das westdeutsche Regietheater und die Theatertradition des 'dritten deutschen Klassikers'* (Tübingen: Niemeyer, 1996).

Moran, Dermot, and Joseph Cohen. *The Husserl Dictionary* (London and New York: Continuum, 2012).

Morris, Gary. 'Asta Nielsen'. *Bright Lights* 16 (1996). <http://brightlightsfilm.com/16/asta.php>, accessed 23 March 2014.

Morris, William. *The Collected Letters of William Morris*, ed. Normal Kelvin, vol. 2, part B: *1885–1888* (Princeton, NJ: Princeton University Press, 1987).

Mouffe, Chantal. *The Return of the Political* (London and New York: Verso, 1993).

Mouffe, Chantal. *On the Political* (London and New York: Routledge, 2005).

Mühlhausen, Walter. 'Die Weimarer Republik enblößt: Das Badehosen-Foto von Friedrich Ebert und Gustav Noske'. In *Das Jahrhundert der Bilder, 1900–1949*, ed. Gerhard Paul (Göttingen: Vandenhoeck & Ruprecht, 2009), 236–43.

Müller, Heiner. *Rotwelsch* (Berlin: Merve, 1982).

Müller, Heiner. *Hamletmachine and Other Texts for the Stage*, trans. and ed. Carl Weber (New York: Performing Arts Publications, 1984).

Müller, Heiner. *Shakespeare Factory 2* (Berlin: Rotbuch, 1989).

Müller, Heiner. *Gedichte* (Berlin: Alexander-Verlag, 1992).

Müller, Heiner. *Krieg ohne Schlacht: Leben in zwei Diktaturen. Eine Autobiographie*, 2nd edn (Cologne: Kiepenheuer & Witsch, 1994).

Müller, Jan-Werner. *A Dangerous Mind: Carl Schmitt in Post-War European Thought* (New Haven, CT and London: Yale University Press, 2003).

Murray, Kathleen. *Taine und die englische Romantik* (Munich and Leipzig: Duncker & Humblot, 1924).

Muschg, Walter. 'Deutschland ist Hamlet'. *Die Zeit* 17, 24 April 1964, and 18, 1 May 1964. <http://www.zeit.de/1964/17/deutschland-ist-heimat> and <http://www.zeit.de/1964/18/deutschland-ist-hamlet-ii>.

Nabokov, Vladimir. *The Real Life of Sebastian Knight* (Norfolk, CT: New Directions, 1959).

Nabokov, Vladimir. 'An Interview with Vladimir Nabokov, conducted by Alfred Appel, Jr.'. In *Nabokov: The Man and his Work*, ed. L. S. Dembo (Madison, WI: University of Wisconsin Press, 1967), 19–44.

Neuhaus, Helmut. 'Der Gemanist Dr. phil. Joseph Goebbels. Bemerkungen zur Sprache des Joseph Goebbels in seiner Dissertation aus dem Jahre 1922'. *Zeitschrift für deutsche Philologie* 93 (1974), 398–416.

Neuhof, Hans. 'Moderne Shakespearekritik: Paul Ernst'. *Shakespeare-Jahrbuch* 70 (1934), 65–88.

Neumann, Helga, and Manfred Neumann. *Maximilian Harden (1861–1927): ein unerschrockener deutsch-jüdischer Kritiker und Publizist* (Würzburg: Königshausen & Neumann, 2003).

Newman, Lea Bertani Vozar. *A Reader's Guide to the Short Stories of Herman Melville. A Reference Publication in Literature* (Boston, MA: G. K. Hall, 1986).

Niemeyer, Christian. '"die Schwester! die Schwester! 's klingt so fürchterlich!" Elisabeth Förster-Nietzsche als Verfälscherin der Briefe und Werke ihres Bruders—eine offenbar notwendige Rückerinnerung'. *Nietzscheforschung* 16 (2009), 335–55.

Niemeyer, Christian. *Nietzsche-Lexikon* (Darmstadt: Wissenschaftliche Buchgesellschaft, 2009).

Nietzsche, Friedrich. *Selected Letters of Friedrich Nietzsche*, trans. Anthony M. Ludovici, ed. Oscar Levy (Garden City, NY and Toronto: Doubleday Page, 1921).

Nietzsche, Friedrich. *Werke. Kritische Gesamtausgabe*, 47 vols, ed. Giorgio Colli and Mazzino Montinari (Berlin and New York: De Gruyter, 1967).

Nietzsche, Friedrich. *The Gay Science. With a Prelude in Rhymes and an Appendix of Songs*, trans. and ed. Walter A. Kaufmann (New York: Vintage, 1974).

Nietzsche, Friedrich. *The Portable Nietzsche* (1954), trans. and ed. Walter A. Kaufmann (London: Penguin, 1976).

Nietzsche, Friedrich. *Thus Spoke Zarathustra*, in *The Portable Nietzsche* (1954), trans. and ed. Walter Kaufmann (London: Penguin, 1976), 103–439.

Nietzsche, Friedrich. *Sämtliche Werke. Kritische Studienausgabe*, 15 vols, ed. Giorgio Colli and Mazzino Montinari (Munich: dtv; Berlin and New York: De Gruyter, 1980).

Nietzsche, Friedrich. *Sämtliche Briefe. Kritische Studienausgabe*, 8 vols, ed. Giorgio Colli and Mazzino Montinari (Munich: dtv, 1986).

Nietzsche, Friedrich. *Jugendschriften, 1854–1861*, ed. Hans Joachim Mette (Munich: dtv, 1994).

Nietzsche, Friedrich. *Jugendschriften, 1861–64*, ed. Hans Joachim Mette (Munich: dtv, 1994).

Nietzsche, Friedrich. *Schriften der Studenten- und Militärzeit, 1864–1868*, ed. Hans Joachim Mette and Karl Schlechta (Munich: dtv, 1994).

Nietzsche, Friedrich. *Selected Letters of Friedrich Nietzsche*, trans. and ed. Christopher Middleton (Indianapolis: Hackett, 1996).

Nietzsche, Friedrich. *Daybreak: Thoughts on the Prejudices of Morality* (1881), trans. R. J. Hollingdale, ed. Maudemarie Clark and Brian Leiter (Cambridge: Cambridge University Press, 1997).

Nietzsche, Friedrich. *On the Uses and Disadvantages of History for Life* (1874). In Nietzsche, *Untimely Meditations*, 2nd edn, trans. R. J. Hollingdale, ed. Daniel Breazeale (Cambridge: Cambridge University Press, 1997), 57–123.

Nietzsche, Friedrich. *Basic Writings* (1967), trans. and ed. Walter A. Kaufmann (New York: Modern Library, 2000).

Nietzsche, Friedrich. *Ecce Homo. How One Becomes What One Is*, trans. and ed. R. J. Hollingdale (London: Penguin, 2004).

Nietzsche, Friedrich. *Human, All Too Human*, trans. Marion Faber and Stephen Lehmann, ed. Marion Faber (London: Penguin, 2004).

Nietzsche, Friedrich. *On the Genealogy of Morality*, trans. Carol Diethe, ed. Keith Ansell-Pearson, revised edn (Cambridge and New York: Cambridge University Press, 2006).

Nietzsche, Friedrich. *Das griechische Musikdrama/The Greek Music Drama* (1870), trans. Paul Bishop (New York: Contra Mundum Press, 2013).

Nipperdey, Thomas. *Deutsche Geschichte 1866–1918*, vol. 1: *Arbeitswelt und Bürgergeist* (Munich: Beck, 2013).

Nippold, Erich. *Theater und Drama* (Gotha: Engelhard-Reyher-Verlag, 1949).

Niven, William. 'The Birth of Nazi Drama? *Thing* Plays'. In *Theatre under the Nazis*, ed. John London (Manchester and New York: Manchester University Press, 2000), 45–95.

Norbrook, David. 'The Emperor's New Body? *Richard II*, Ernst Kantorowicz, and the Politics of Shakespeare Criticism'. *Textual Practice* 10.2 (1996), 329–57.

Norton, Robert E. *Secret Germany: Stefan George and His Circle* (Ithaca, NY and London: Cornell University Press, 2002).

Norton, Robert E. 'Lyrik und Moral'. *Die Zeit*, 20 July 2009. <http://www.zeit.de/2009/30/Dichter-George>, accessed 21 June 2015.

Oberlin, Gerhard. *Goethe, Schiller und das Unbewusste. Eine literaturpsychologische Studie* (Giessen: Psychosozial-Verlag, 2007).

Oelmann, Ute. 'The George Circle: From *Künstlergesellschaft* to *Lebensgemeinschaft*'. In *A Poet's Reich: Politics and Culture in the George Circle*, ed. Melissa S. Lane and Martin A. Ruehl (Rochester, NY: Camden House, 2011), 25–36.

Oelmann, Ute. 'Shakespeare Sonnette. Umdichtung'. In *Stefan George und sein Kreis. Ein Handbuch*, ed. Achim Aurnhammer, Wolfgang Braungart, Stefan Breuer, and Ute Oelmann (Berlin and New York: De Gruyter, 2012), 238–54.

Oelmann, Ute, and Ulrich Raulff, eds. *Frauen um Stefan George* (Göttingen: Wallstein, 2010).

Osterkamp, Ernst. 'Friedrich Gundolf zwischen Kunst und Wissenschaft. Zur Problematik eines Germanisten aus dem George-Kreis'. In *Literaturwissenschaft und Geistesgeschichte 1910–1925*, ed. Christoph König and Eberhard Lämmert (Frankfurt: Fischer, 1993), 177–98.

Osterkamp, Ernst. *Poesie der leeren Mitte: Stefan Georges Neues Reich* (Munich: Carl Hanser, 2010).

Osterkamp, Ernst. 'Shakespeare und der Georgekreis'. In *Shakespeare unter den Deutschen*, ed. Christa Jansohn (Stuttgart: Franz Steiner, 2015), 131–42.

Ottmann, Henning. *Philosophie und Politik bei Nietzsche*, 2nd edn (Berlin and New York: De Gruyter, 1999).

Owen, David. *Nietzsche, Politics, and Modernity* (London: Sage, 1995).

Pan, David. 'Afterword: Historical Event and Mythic Meaning in Carl Schmitt's *Hamlet or Hecuba*'. In Carl Schmitt, *Hamlet or Hecuba: The Intrusion of the Time Into the Play* (1956), trans. and ed. David Pan and Jennifer R. Rust (New York: Telos Press, 2009), 69–119.

Papsdorf, Werner. 'Theaterschau'. *Shakespeare-Jahrbuch* 72 (1936), 248.

Pater, Walter. *The Renaissance* (1893) (Berkeley and Los Angeles: University of California Press, 1980).

Paulin, Roger. *The Critical Reception of Shakespeare in Germany 1682–1914* (Hildesheim, Zurich, and New York: Olms, 2003).

Persky, Stan. 'Letter from Berlin: Secret Germany'. <http://stanpersky.de/index.php/articles/letter-from-berlin-secret-germany>, accessed 4 September 2013.

Petro, Patrice. *Joyless Streets: Women and Melodramatic Representation in Weimar Germany* (Princeton, NJ: Princeton University Press, 1989).

Pfister, Manfred. 'Germany is Hamlet: The History of a Political Interpretation'. *New Comparison* 2 (1986), 106–26.

Pfitzner, Hans. 'Shakespeare-Dämmerung?' *Shakespeare-Jahrbuch* 77 (1941), 74–92.

Plessner, Helmut. *Das Schicksal deutschen Geistes im Ausgang seiner bürgerlichen Epoche* (Zurich: Niehans, 1935).

Plessner, Helmut. *Die verspätete Nation: Über die politische Verführbarkeit bürgerlichen Geistes* (Stuttgart: Kohlhammer, 1959).

Plessow, Gustav L. *Um Shakespeares Nordentum* (Aachen: J. A. Mayer'sche Verlagsbuchhandlung, 1937).

Pol, Heinz. 'Goebbels als Dichter'. *Die Weltbühne* 27.1 (1931), 129–33.

Pope, Alexander. *An Essay on Man. In Epistles to a Friend. Epistle IV* (London: J. Wilford, 1734).

Praz, Mario. *The Romantic Agony*, trans. Angus Davidson (London: Oxford University Press, 1933).

Pye, Christopher. 'Against Schmitt: Law, Aesthetics, and Absolutism in Shakespeare's *Winter's Tale*'. *South Atlantic Quarterly* 108.1 (2009), 197–217.

Pyta, Wolfram. *Hitler. Der Künstler als Politiker und Feldherr. Eine Herrschaftsanalyse* (Munich: Siedler, 2015).

Radkau, Joachim. *Max Weber. A Biography*, trans. Patrick Camiller (Cambridge: Polity Press, 2009).

Ranke, Leopold von. *Geschichte der romanischen und germanischen Völker von 1494 bis 1535* (Leipzig: Reimer, 1824).

Ranke, Leopold von, ed. *Aus dem Briefwechsel Friedrich Wilhelms IV. mit Bunsen* (Leipzig: Duncker & Humblot, 1873).

Rasch, William. *Niklas Luhmann's Modernity: The Paradoxes of Differentiation* (Stanford, CA: Stanford University Press, 2000).

Raschel, Heinz. *Das Nietzsche-Bild im George-Kreis, ein Beitrag zur Geschichte der deutschen Mythologeme* (Berlin and New York: De Gruyter, 1984).

Raulff, Ulrich. 'Ihr wisst nicht, wer ich bin'. *Süddeutsche Zeitung*, 11 June 2002.

Raulff, Ulrich. *Kreis ohne Meister: Stefan Georges Nachleben* (Munich: Beck, 2010).

Regenbogen, Otto. 'Friedrich Gundolf zum Gedächtnis'. In Regenbogen, *Kleine Schriften*, ed. Franz Dirlmeier (Munich: Beck, 1961), 555–70.

Rehberg, Karl-Siegbert. 'Das Bild des Judentums in der frühen deutschen Soziologe. "Fremdheit" und "Rationalität" als Typusmerkmale bei Werner Sombart, Max Weber und Georg Simmel'. In *Rassenmythos und Sozialwissenschaften in Deutschland*, ed. C. Klingemann (Opladen: Westdeutscher Verlag, 1987), 80–127.

Reich-Ranicki, Marcel. *The Author of Himself: The Life of Marcel-Reich-Ranicki*, trans. Ewald Osers (Princeton, NJ: Princeton University Press, 1999).

Reuth, Ralf Georg. *Goebbels*, trans. Krishna Winston (San Diego, CA: Harvest, 1994).

Rice, Jane C. '*Handeln oder Nichthandeln*: Hamlet in Inner Emigration'. *Monatshefte* 84 (1992), 8–22.

Richter, F. K. Review: '*Poems* by Stefan George'. *The German Quarterly* 17.1 (1944), 52–3.

Ricoeur, Paul. *Freud and Philosophy: An Essay on Interpretation*, trans. Denis Savage (New Haven, CT: Yale University Press, 1970).

Ried, Matthias. *Joachim von Fiore—Denker der vollendeten Menschheit* (Würzburg: Königshausen & Neumann, 2004).

Robertson, J. M. *The Shakespeare Canon*, 5 vols (London: Routledge; New York: E. P. Dutton, 1922–30).

Rosenberg, Alfred. *The Myth of the Twentieth Century*, trans. James Whisker. <https://archive. org/details/TheMythOfThe20thCentury>, accessed 19 August 2015.

Rößner, Hans. *Georgekreis und Literaturwissenschaft* (Frankfurt: Diesterweg, 1938).

Rothe, Hans. *Gründe, die gegen eine Neuübersetzung Shakespeares sprechen* (Leipzig: Paul List, 1927).

Rothe, Hans. *Kampf um Shakespeare. Ein Bericht* (Leipzig: Paul List, 1935/6).

Rothe, Hans, trans. *Der Elisabethanische Shakespeare*, 9 vols (Baden-Baden and Geneva: Holle, 1957).

Rowe, Eleanor. *Hamlet: A Window on Russia* (New York: New York University Press, 1976).

Rübesame, Hans, ed. *Antrag auf Demonstration: Die Protestversammlung im Deutschen Theater am 15. Oktober 1989* (Berlin: Ch. Links, 2010).

Rühle, Günter. *Theater in Deutschland, 1887–1945. Seine Ereignisse—seine Menschen* (Frankfurt: S. Fischer, 2007).

Rust, Jennifer R., and Julia Reinhard Lupton. 'Introduction: Schmitt and Shakespeare'. In Carl Schmitt, *Hamlet or Hecuba: The Intrusion of the Time into the Play*, trans. and ed. David Pan and Jennifer R. Rust (New York: Telos Press, 2009), xv–li.

Ryle, Simon. *Shakespeare, Cinema and Desire: Adaptation and Other Futures of Shakespeare's Language* (Basingstoke: Palgrave Macmillan, 2010).

Salin, Edgar. *Um Stefan George*, 2nd edn (Düsseldorf and Munich: Küpper, 1954).

S[alin], E[dgar]. *Ernst Kantorowicz, 1895–1963* (n.p.: privately printed, 1963).

Salz, Arthur. 'Für die Wissenschaft gegen die Gebildeten unter ihren Verächtern'. *Jahrbuch für Gesetzgebung, Verwaltung und Volkswirtschaft im Deutschen Reich* (*Schmollers Jahrbuch*) 45 (1921), 65–94.

Sauder, Gerhard. 'Positivismus und Empfindsamkeit: Erinnerung an Max von Waldberg'. *Euphorion* 65 (1971), 368–408.

Schaeffer, Albrecht. *Elli oder Sieben Treppen. Beschreibung eines weiblichen Lebens* (Leipzig: Insel, 1919).

Scharfschwerdt, Jürgen. 'Werther in der DDR. Bürgerliches Erbe zwischen sozialistischer Kulturpolitik und gesellschaftlicher Realität'. *Jahrbuch der Deutschen Schillergesellschaft* 22 (1978), 235–76.

Scheier, Claus-Artur. 'Maximins Lichtung: Philosophische Bemerkungen zu Georges Gott'. *George-Jahrbuch* 1 (1996/7), 80–106.

Schelp, Hanspeter. 'Friedrich Gundolf als Shakespeare-Übersetzer'. *Shakespeare-Jahrbuch West* (1971), 97–117.

Scherpe, Klaus R. *Werther und Wertherwirkung: Zum Syndrom bürgerlicher Gesellschaftsordnung im 18. Jahrhundert* (Bad Homburg: Gehlen, 1970).

Scheuermann, William E. *Carl Schmitt: The End of Law* (Lanham, MD: Rowman & Littlefield, 1999).

Schieder, Theodor. 'Nietzsche and Bismarck', trans. Alexandra Hendee. *The Historian* 29.4 (1967), 584–604.

Schiller, Friedrich. *Sämtliche Werke*, 5 vols, ed. Peter-André Alt et al., vol. 1: *Gedichte/ Dramen 1*, ed. Jörg Robert and Albert Meier (Munich and Vienna: Carl Hanser, 2004).

Schlayer, Clotilde. *Minusio: Chronik aus den letzten Lebensjahren Stefan Georges*, ed. Maik Bozza and Ute Oelmann (Göttingen: Wallstein, 2010).

Schlegel, August Wilhelm. 'Etwas über William Shakespeare bei Gelegenheit Wilhelm Meisters', *Die Horen* 4 (1796), 57–112.

Schlieben, Barbara, Olaf Schneider, and Kerstin Schulmeyer, eds. *Geschichtsbilder im George-Kreis. Wege zur Wissenschaft* (Göttingen: Wallstein, 2004).

Schlösser, Rainer. 'Die Jugend als Erbe der deutschen Bühnenkunst'. *Frankfurter Theater Almanach* 20 (1936/7), 21.

Schlösser, Rainer. 'Das unsterbliche Gespräch über das Tragische. Dramaturgie als Gesetzeswerk nordischer Kultur'. *Wille und Macht*, 1 June 1937, 5–14.

Schlösser, Rainer. 'Der deutsche Shakespeare'. *Shakespeare-Jahrbuch* 74 (1938), 20–30.

Schmidt, Jochen. *Die Geschichte des Genie-Gedankens in der deutschen Literatur, Philosophie und Politik 1750–1945*, 2 vols (Darmstadt: Wissenschaftliche Buchgesellschaft, 1988).

Schmitt, Carl. 'Illyrien—Notizen von einer dalmatinischen Reise'. *Hochland* 23.3 (1925), 293–8.

Schmitt, Carl. 'Das gute Recht der deutschen Revolution'. *Westdeutscher Beobachter*, 2 May 1933.

Schmitt, Carl. 'Die deutschen Intellektuellen'. *Westdeutscher Beobachter*, 31 May 1933.

Schmitt, Carl. 'Der Führer schützt das Recht'. *Deutsche Juristen-Zeitung* 39 (1934), cols 945–50.

Schmitt, Carl. 'Die Verfassung der Freiheit'. *Deutsche Juristen-Zeitung* 40 (1935), cols 1133–5.

Schmitt, Carl. 'Rechtsstaat'. In *Nationalsozialistisches Handbuch für Recht und Gesetzgebung*, ed. Hans Frank (Munich: Zentralverlag der NSDAP, 1935).

Schmitt, Carl. 'Die deutsche Rechtswissenschaft im Kampf gegen den jüdischen Geist. Schlusswort auf der Tagung der Reichsgruppe Hochschullehrer des NSRB vom 3. und 4. Oktober 1936'. *Deutsche Juristen-Zeitung* 41 (1936), cols 1193–9.

Schmitt, Carl. *Ex Captivitate Salus: Erfahrungen der Zeit 1945–47* (Cologne: Greven, 1950).

Schmitt, Carl. *Gespräch über die Macht und den Zugang zum Machthaber* (Pfullingen: Günther Neske, 1954).

Schmitt, Carl. *The Crisis of Parliamentary Democracy*, trans. Ellen Kennedy (Cambridge, MA: MIT Press, 1988).

Schmitt, Carl. *Glossarium. Aufzeichnungen der Jahre 1947–1951*, ed. Eberhard Freiherr von Medem (Berlin: Duncker & Humblot, 1991).

Schmitt, Carl. *Positionen und Begriffe im Kampf mit Weimar—Genf—Versailles 1923–1939* (Berlin: Duncker & Humblot, 1994).

Schmitt, Carl. *Staat, Großraum, Nomos: Arbeiten aus den Jahren 1916–1969*, ed. Günter Maschke (Berlin: Duncker & Humblot, 1995).

Schmitt, Carl. *The Leviathan in the State Theory of Thomas Hobbes*, trans. George D. Schwab and Erna Hilfstein (Santa Barbara, CA: Greenwood Press, 1996).

Schmitt, Carl. *Roman Catholicism and Political Form* (1923), trans. and ed. G. L. Ulmen (Westport, CT: Greenwood Press, 1996).

Schmitt, Carl. 'Was habe ich getan?' (1957). *Schmittiana* 5 (1996), 13–19.

Schmitt, Carl. 'The Constitution of Freedom', trans. Belinda Cooper. In *Weimar: A Jurisprudence of Crisis*, ed. Arthur J. Jacobson and Bernhard Schlink (Berkeley, Los Angeles, and London: University of California Press, 2000).

Schmitt, Carl. *Ex Captivitate Salus. Erfahrungen der Zeit 1945–47*, 2nd edn (Berlin: Duncker & Humblot, 2002).

Schmitt, Carl. *Legality und Legitimacy* (1932), trans. Jeffrey Seitzer (Durham, NC: Duke University Press, 2004).

Schmitt, Carl. *Die Militärzeit 1915–1919. Tagebuch Februar bis Dezember 1916. Aufsätze und Materialien*, ed. Ernst Hüsmert and Gerd Giesler (Berlin: Akademie-Verlag, 2005).

Schmitt, Carl. *Political Theology: Four Chapters on the Concept of Sovereignty* (1922), trans. George D. Schwab (Chicago, IL and London: University of Chicago Press, 2005).

Schmitt, Carl. *Tagebücher Oktober 1912 bis Februar 1915*, 2nd edn, ed. Ernst Hüsmert (Berlin: Akademie-Verlag, 2005).

Schmitt, Carl. *The Concept of the Political* (1932), trans. George D. Schwab (Chicago, IL and London: University of Chicago Press, 2007).

Schmitt, Carl. *Political Theology II: The Myth of the Closure of Any Political Theology*, trans. and ed. Michael Hoelzl and Graham Ward (Cambridge and Malden, MA: Polity Press, 2008).

Schmitt, Carl. *Hamlet or Hecuba: The Intrusion of the Time into the Play* (1956), trans. and ed. David Pan and Jennifer R. Rust (New York: Telos Press, 2009).

Schmitt, Carl. 'Foreword to the German Edition of Lilian Winstanley's *Hamlet and the Scottish Succession*', trans. Kurt R. Buhanan. *Telos* 153 (2010) (Special Issue: Carl Schmitt's *Hamlet or Hecuba*), 164–77.

Schmitt, Carl. *Tagebücher 1930 bis 1934*, ed. Wolfgang Schuller and Gerd Giesler (Berlin: Akademie-Verlag, 2010).

Schmitt, Carl. *Political Romanticism*, trans. Guy Oakes, with a new introduction by Graham McAleer (New Brunswick, NJ and London: Transaction, 2011).

Schmitt, Carl. *Der Schatten Gottes. Introspektionen, Tagebücher und Briefe 1921–1924*, ed. Gerd Giesler, Ernst Hüsmert, and Wolfgang H. Spindler (Berlin: Duncker & Humblot, 2014).

Schmitt, Carl. *Glossarium. Aufzeichnungen aus den Jahren 1947 bis 1948. Erweiterete, berichtigte und kommentierte Neuausgabe*, ed. Gerd Giesler and Martin Tielke (Berlin: Duncker & Humblot, 2015).

Schock, Peter A. *Romantic Satanism: Myth and the Historical Moment in Blake, Shelley, and Byron* (Basingstoke and New York: Palgrave Macmillan, 2003).

Schödel, Helmut. 'Wir sind ein blödes Volk. Ein Heiner-Müller-Tagebuch zur Frankfurter Experimenta 6'. *Die Zeit*, 8 June1990. <http://www.zeit.de/1990/24/wir-sind-ein-bloedes-volk>, accessed 14 August 2015.

Scholz, Anne-Marie. '*The Bridge on the River Kwai* (1957) Revisited: Combat Cinema, American Culture and the German Past'. *German History* 26 (2008), 219–50.

Schroeder, Friedrich Ludwig. *Hamlet, Prinz von Dänemark. Ein Trauerspiel in sechs Aufzügen. Zum Behufe des Hamburgischen Theaters* (Hamburg: Heroldsche Buchhandlung, 1778).

Schulze, Hagen. *Germany: A New History* (1996), trans. Deborah Lucas Schneider (Cambridge, MA and London: Harvard University Press, 1998).

Schumann, F. L. *Hitler and the Nazi Dictatorship: A Study in Social Pathology and the Politics of Fascism* (London: Hale, 1936).

Schümmer, Karl. 'Shakespeare. Nordischer Mythus und christliche Metaphysik'. *Hochland* 9 (1938/9), 191–205.

Schwab, George D. 'Carl Schmitt: Political Opportunist?' *Intellect* 103 (1975), 334–7.

Schwarz, Michael. '"Er redet leicht, schreibt schwer": Theodor W. Adorno am Mikrophon'. *Zeithistorische Forschungen/Studies in Contemporary History* 8.2 (2011), 286–94.

Scott, Cyril. *Die Tragödie Stefan Georges: ein Erinnerungsbild und ein Gang durch sein Werk* (Eltville: Hempe, 1952).

Sehrt, Ernst Theodor. *Vergebung und Gnade bei Shakespeare* (Stuttgart: Koehler, 1952).

Seiberth, Gabriel. *Anwalt des Reiches. Carl Schmitt und der Prozess 'Preußen contra Reich' vor dem Staatsgerichtshof* (Berlin: Duncker & Humblot, 2001).

Seydel, Renate, and Allan Hagedorff. *Asta Nielsen. Ihr Leben in Fotodokumenten, Selbstzeugnissen und zeitgenössischen Betrachtungen* (Munich: Universitas, 1981).

Shakespeare, William. *Dietragische Geschichte von Hamlet Prinzen von Dænemark in deutscher Sprache*. Neu übersetzt und eingerichtet von Gerhart Hauptmann (Weimar: Cranach-Presse, 1929).

Shakespeare, William. *The Norton Shakespeare*, 3rd edn, ed. Stephen Greenblatt et al. (New York and London: Norton, 2016).

Shapiro, Stephen A. 'Othello's Desdemona'. *Literature and Psychology* 14 (1964), 56–61.

Sidney, Philip. *An Apology for Poetry (or The Defence of Poesy)*, 3rd edn, ed. Geoffrey Shepherd and R. W. Maslen (Manchester and New York: Manchester University Press, 2002).

Siemens, Daniel. *The Making of a Nazi Hero: The Murder and Myth of Horst Wessel* (London and New York: I. B. Tauris, 2013).

Silk, M. S., and J. P. Stern. *Nietzsche on Tragedy* (Cambridge: Cambridge University Press, 1981).

Simmel, Georg. *Soziologie: Untersuchungen über die Formen der Vergesellschaftung* (Leipzig: Duncker & Humblot, 1908).

Simmel, Georg. *On Individuality and Social Forms*, ed. Donald Levine (Chicago, IL: University of Chicago Press, 1971).

Singer, Hans-Jürgen. 'Michael oder der leere Glaube'. *1999. Zeitschrift für Sozialgeschichte des 20. und 21. Jahrhunderts* 2.4 (1987), 68–79.

Sokel, Walter H. *The Writer in Extremis: Expressionism in Twentieth-Century German Literature* (Stanford, CA: Stanford University Press, 1959).

Sokolova, Boika. 'Between Religion and Ideology: Some Russian Hamlets of the Twentieth Century'. *Shakespeare Survey* 54 (2001), 140–51.

Sollors, Werner. *The Temptation of Despair: Tales of the 1940s* (Cambridge, MA and London: Harvard University Press, 2014).

Sontag, Susan. 'Fascinating Fascism'. *The New York Review of Books*, 6 February 1975. <http://www.nybooks.com/articles/archives/1975/feb/06/fascinating-fascism>, accessed 14 May 2015.

Spender, Stephen. *European Witness* (New York: Reynal & Hitchcock, 1946).

Spengler, Oswald. *Reden und Aufsätze* (Munich: Beck, 1937).

Sprengel, Peter. *Der Dichter stand auf hoher Küste: Gerhart Hauptmann im Dritten Reich* (Berlin: Ullstein, 2009).

Stachura, Peter D. *The German Youth Movement, 1900–1945: An Interpretative and Documentary History* (London: Macmillan, 1981).

Staël, Anne Louise Germaine de. *Germany, by Madame the Baroness de Staël-Holstein*, ed. O. W. Wight (Boston, MA: Houghton Mifflin, 1859).

Steakley, James D. 'Iconography of a Scandal: Political Cartoons and the Eulenburg Affair'. In *History of Homosexuality in Europe and America*, ed. Wayne R. Dynes and Stephen Donaldson (New York: Garland, 1992), 323–85.

Steinbömer, Gustav. *Staat und Drama* (Berlin: Junker und Dünnhaupt, 1932).

Stern, Fritz. *The Politics of Cultural Despair: A Study in the Rise of the Germanic Ideology* (Berkeley and Los Angeles: University of California Press, 1961).

Stern, Fritz. *The Varieties of History from Voltaire to the Present* (New York: Vintage, 1973).

Stevenson, Robert Louis. *Strange Case of Dr Jekyll and Mr Hyde*, ed. Richard Dury (Edinburgh: Edinburgh University Press, 2006).

Stolleis, Michael. *A History of Public Law in Germany 1918–1945*, trans. Thomas Dunlap (Oxford: Oxford University Press, 2004).

Strobl, Gerwin. *The Swastika and the Stage: German Theatre and Society, 1933–1945* (Cambridge and New York: Cambridge University Press, 2007).

Stroedel, Wolfgang. *Shakespeare auf der deutschen Bühne vom Ende des Weltkriegs bis zu Gegenwart* (Weimar: Hermann Böhlaus Nachf., 1938).

Stroux, Johannes. *Nietzsches Professur in Basle* (Jena: Frommannsche Buchhandlung, 1925).

Stürmer, Michael. '1848 in der deutschen Geschichte'. In *Sozialgeschichte heute: Festschrift für Hans Rosenberg zum 70. Geburtstag*, ed. Hans-Ulrich Wehler (Göttingen: Vandenhoeck & Ruprecht, 1974), 228–42.

Sühnel, Rudolf. 'Gundolfs Shakespeare: Rezeption—Übertragung—Deutung'. *Euphorion. Zeitschrift für Literaturgeschichte* 75 (1981), 245–74.

Sukhanova, Ekaterina. *Voicing the Distant: Shakespeare and Russian Modernist Poetry* (Cranbury, NJ: Associated University Presses, 2004).

Symington, Rodney. *The Nazi Appropriation of Shakespeare: Cutural Politics in the Third Reich* (Lewiston, NY: Edwin Mellen Press, 2005).

Taylor, A. J. P. *The Course of German History: A Survey of the Development of German History since 1815* (London: Hamish Hamilton, 1945).

Taylor, Philip M. *The Projection of Britain: British Overseas Publicity and Propaganda 1919–1939* (Cambridge: Cambridge University Press, 1981).

Taylor, Seth. *Left-Wing Nietzscheans: The Politics of German Expressionism 1910–1920* (Berlin: De Gruyter, 1990).

Thacker, Toby. *Joseph Goebbels: Life and Death* (Basingstoke: Palgrave Macmillan, 2009).

Thompson, Ann. 'Asta Nielsen and the Mystery of Hamlet'. In *Shakespeare the Movie: Popularizing the Plays on Film, TV and Video*, ed. Lynda E. Boose and Richard Burt (London: Routledge, 1997), 215–24.

Troeltsch, Ernst. 'Die Revolution in der Wissenschaft'. In *Kritische Gesamtausgabe*, 19 vols, ed. Friedrich Wilhelm Graf et al., vol. 13: *Rezensionen und Kritiken (1915–1923)*, ed. Friedrich Wilhelm Graf (Berlin and New York: De Gruyter, 2010), 519–63.

Trotha, Thilo von. 'Shakespeare und wir'. *Nationalsozialistische Monatshefte* 5 (1934), 74–5.

Ullrich, Volker. *Otto von Bismarck* (Reinbek: Rowohlt, 1998).

Valéry, Paul. 'Letters from France. I. The Spiritual Crisis'. *The Athenaeum*, 11 April 1919, 182–4.

Vallentin, Berthold. *Gespräche mit Stefan George* (Amsterdam: Castrum Peregrini, 1960).

Venturelli, Aldo. 'Nietzsches Renaissance-Bild zwischen Erasmus und Cesare Borgia'. In *Kunst, Wissenschaft und Geschichte bei Nietzsche. Quellenkritische Untersuchungen*, ed. Aldo Venturelli (Berlin and New York: De Gruyter, 2003), 127–35.

Verhandlungen des Reichstags. *Stenographische Berichte*, 1914/16, vol. 306.

Vietta, Egon, ed. *Darmstädter Gespräch: Theater* (Darmstadt: Neue Darmstädter Verlagsanstalt, 1955).

Vietta, Egon. *Katastrophe oder Wende des deutschen Theaters* (Düsseldorf: Droste, 1955).

Vining, Edward P. *The Mystery of Hamlet: An Attempt to Solve an Old Problem* (Philadelphia: J. P. Lippincott & Co., 1881).

Vollhardt, Friedrich. 'Hochland-Konstellationen: Programme, Konturen und Aporien des Kulturkatholizismus am Beginn des 20. Jahrhunderts'. In *Moderne und Antimoderne. Renouveau Catholique und die deutsche Literatur des 20. Jahrhunderts*, ed. Wilhelm Kühlmann and Roman Luckscheiter (Freiburg: Rombach, 2008), 67–100.

Voltaire. *Complete Works*, vols 23–26C: *Essai sur les mœurs et l'esprit des nations* (1756), ed. Bruno Bernard et al. (Oxford: Voltaire Foundation, 2009–15).

Vondung, Klaus. 'Apokalyptische Erwartung. Zur Jugendrevolte zwischen 1910 und 1930'. In *'Mit uns zieht die neue Zeit': der Mythos Jugend*, ed. Thomas Koebner, Rolf-Peter Janz, and Frank Trommler (Frankfurt: Suhrkamp, 1985), 519–45.

Walser Smith, Helmut. 'When the *Sonderweg* Debate Left Us'. *German Studies Review* 31.2 (2008), 225–40.

Wälterlin, Oskar. *Die Verantwortung des Theaters* (Berlin: Pontes-Verlag, 1947).

Walther, Peter Th., and Wolfgang Ernst. 'Ernst H. Kantorowicz. Eine archäo-biographische Skizze'. In *Geschichtskörper. Zur Aktualität von Ernst H. Kantorowicz*, ed. Wolfgang Ernst and Cornelia Vismann (Munich: Fink, 1998), 207–31.

Walzel, Oskar. Review of Friedrich Gundolf, *Shakespeare und der deutsche Geist. Shakespeare-Jahrbuch* 48 (1912), 259–74.

Wambach, Lovis Maxim. *'Es ist gleichgültig, woran wir glauben, nur dass wir glauben':* *Bemerkungen zu Joseph Goebbels' Drama 'Judas Iscariot' und zu seinen 'Michael-Romanen'* (Bremen: Schriftenreihe des Raphael-Lemkin-Institutes für Xenophobie- und Antisemitismusforschung, 1996).

Warnach, Walter. 'Hamlet-Mythos und Geschichte', review of Carl Schmitt, *Hamlet or Hecuba*. *Frankfurter Allgemeine Zeitung,* 2 June 1956, 'Literaturblatt'.

Weber, Marianne. *Max Weber. Ein Lebensbild* (Tübingen: Mohr and Siebeck, 1926).

Weber, Max. *Der Nationalstaat und die Volkswirtschaftspolitik: akademische Antrittsrede* (Freiburg: Mohr, 1895).

Weber, Max. *Economy and Society : An Outline of Interpretive Sociology*, trans. Ephraim Fischoff et al., ed. Günther Roth and Claus Wittich (Berkeley, Los Angeles, and London: University of California Press, 1978).

Weber, Samuel. 'Taking Exception to Decision: Walter Benjamin and Carl Schmitt'. *Diacritics* 22 (1992), 5–18.

Wehner, Josef Magnus. 'Der Dichter und der Hades'. *Münchner Neueste Nachrichten,* 16 February 1940.

Wehner, Josef Magnus. 'Curt Langenbeck und Shakespeare'. *Münchner Neueste Nachrichten,* 18 February 1940.

Wehner, Josef Magnus. 'Die Wiedergeburt des Dramas'. *Münchner Neueste Nachrichten,* 21 February 1940.

Wehner, Josef Magnus. 'Der Streit um den Hades'. *Münchner Neueste Nachrichten,* 6 March 1940.

Wehner, Josef Magnus. 'Götter, Sowohl-als-auch-Leute und Shakespeare'. *Münchner Neueste Nachrichten,* 9/10 March 1940.

Wehner, Josef Magnus. *Vom Glanz und Leben deutscher Bühne: Eine Münchner Dramaturgie. Aufsätze und Kritiken 1933–1941* (Hamburg: Hanseatische Verlagsanstalt, 1944).

Weigand, Hermann J. Review: 'Stefan George *Poems* by Carol North Valhope, Ernst Morwitz'. *The Journal of English and Germanic Philology* 43.1 (1944), 141–9.

Weisstein, Ulrich. *Comparative Literature and Literary Theory: Survey and Introduction* (1968), trans. William Riggan (Bloomington, IN: Indiana University Press, 1973).

Wellbery, David E. '1774, January–March: Pathologies of Literature'. In *A New History of German Literature*, ed. David E. Wellbery, Judith Ryan, and Hans Ulrich Gumbrecht (Cambridge, MA: Harvard University Press, 2004), 386–92.

Whaley, Joachim. *Germany and the Holy Roman Empire*, 2 vols (Oxford and New York: Oxford University Press, 2012).

Wiemann, Mathias. '"Faust" im Kriege'. *Berliner Theater-Almanach 1942* (Berlin: Paul Neff, 1942), 253–6.

Wigger, Iris. '"Die schwarze Schmach". Afrikaner in der Propaganda der 1920er Jahre'. In *Das Jahrhundert der Bilder 1900–1949*, ed. Gerhard Paul (Göttingen: Vandenhoeck & Ruprecht, 2009), 268–75.

Williams, Simon. *Shakespeare on the German Stage*, vol. 1: *1586–1914* (Cambridge: Cambridge University Press, 1990).

Wilson, John Dover. 'Introduction'. In William Shakespeare, *King Richard II* (Cambridge: Cambridge University Press, 1939), ix–lxxxvi.

Wilson, John Dover. 'The Political Background of Shakespeare's Richard II and Henry IV'. *Shakespeare-Jahrbuch* 75 (1939), 36–51.

Wilson, John Dover. *Milestones on the Dover Road* (London: Faber and Faber, 1969).

Wilson, Peter H. *The Holy Roman Empire 1495–1806* (Oxford and New York: Oxford University Press, 2011).

Wilson, Richard. *Shakespeare in French Theory: King of Shadows* (London and New York: Routledge, 2007).

Wilson, Richard. 'Hamlet in Weimar: Gordon Craig and the Nietzsche Archive'. *Shakespeare-Jahrbuch* 146 (2010), 26–48.

Wilson, Richard. 'The Exception: Force of Argument in Terry Eagleton's *William Shakespeare*'. *Shakespeare* 8.1 (2012), 1–12.

Wilson, Scott. 'Reading Shakespeare with Intensity: A Commentary on Some Lines from Nietzsche's *Ecco Homo*'. In *Philosophical Shakespeares*, ed. John J. Joughin (London: Routledge, 2000), 86–104.

Winstanley, Lilian. *Hamlet and the Scottish Succession: Being an Examination of the Relations of the Play of 'Hamlet' to the Scottish Succession and the Essex Conspiracy* (Cambridge: Cambridge University Press, 1921).

Winstanley, Lilian. *'Macbeth', 'King Lear' and Contemporary History: Being a Study of the Relations of the Play of 'Macbeth' to the Personal History of James I, the Darnley Murder and the St Bartholomew Massacre and also of 'King Lear' as Symbolic Mythology* (Cambridge: Cambridge University Press, 1922).

Winstanley, Lilian. *'Othello' as the Tragedy of Italy: Showing that Shakespeare's Italian Contemporaries Interpreted the Story of the Moor and the Lady of Venice as Symbolizing the Tragedy of Their Country in the Grip of Spain* (London: Terrace, 1924).

Winstanley, Lilian. *Hamlet, Sohn der Maria Stuart*, trans. Anima Schmitt (Pfullingen: Günther Neske, 1952).

Wolf, Werner. 'Metareference across Media: The Concept, its Transmedial Potentials and Problems, Main Forms and Functions'. In *Metareference across Media: Theory and Case Studies. Dedicated to Walter Bernhart on the Occasion of his Retirement*, ed. Werner Wolf (Amsterdam and New York: Rodopi, 2009), 1–85.

Wolfskehl, Karl. 'Künder der Größe. Friedrich Gundolf zu seinem heutigen fünfzigsten Geburtstag'. *Münchner Neuste Nachrichten*, 20 June 1930.

Wolfskehl, Karl, and Hanna Wolfskehl. *Briefwechsel mit Friedrich Gundolf 1899–1931*, ed. Karlhans Kluncker (Amsterdam: Castrum Peregrini, 1977).

Wolters, Friedrich. *Stefan George und die Blätter für die Kunst. Deutsche Geistesgeschichte seit 1890* (Berlin: Georg Bondi, 1930).

Woods, Roger. *The Conservative Revolution in the Weimar Republic* (New York: St. Martin's Press, 1996).

Yarrow, Andrew L. 'Humanism and Deutschtum: The Origins, Development, and Consequences of the Politics of Poetry in the George-Kreis'. *The Germanic Review* 58 (2001), 1–11.

Young, H. F. *Maximilian Harden, Censor Germaniae: The Critic in Opposition from Bismarck to the Rise of Nazism* (The Hague: Nijhoff, 1959).

Zeydel, Edwin H. Review: '*Poems* by Stefan George, Carol North Valhope, Ernst Morwitz'. *The Modern Language Journal* 27.4 (1943), 294–5.

Zeydel, Edwin H. Review: 'The Works of Stefan George by Stefan George, Olga Marx, Ernst Morwitz'. *The German Quarterly* 24.3 (1951), 205.

Zickel von Jan, Reinhold. 'Wir brauchen Shakespeare!' *Bausteine zum deutschen Nationaltheater* 4 (1936), 47–51.

Zimmermann, Heiner O. 'Is Hamlet Germany? On the Political Reception of *Hamlet*'. In *New Essays on Hamlet*, ed. Mark ThorntonBurnett and JohnManning (New York: AMS Press, 1994), 293–318.

Index